LUCKY ASTROLOGY

The Definitive Volume

Harnessing Your Cosmic Power

LANI SHARP

We were born at a given moment, in a given place, and like vintage years of wine, we have the qualities of the year and of the season in which we are born.
Carl G. Jung

There was a star danced, and under that I was born.
William Shakespeare

DEDICATION
INSPIRED BY ALL THE SIGNS

Aries imparted youth and courage,
And helped me dance away the pain.
Taurus gave me unwavering loyalty,
And shelter from the rain.
Gemini provided me with laughter,
And reawakened my sense of fun.
Cancer protected and nurtured me,
By reflecting back my Sun.
Leo reminded me of my power,
When I thought I'd had enough.
Virgo illuminated my inner glow,
By giving unconditional love.
Libra brought me back to life,
By judging not a single thing.
Scorpio imparted strong, silent power,
To take away the sting.
Sagittarius's generous nature,
Offered deep wisdom and truth.
And Capricorn showed the Way up the mountain
And through her strength, I grew.
Aquarius gave me the gift of friendship,
By treating me as his brother.
And Pisces swam with me to the depths,
With a compassion like no other.

SPECIAL NOTE

Throughout this text, all zodiac signs are referred to as 'he', 'she', 'his' or 'her', according to whether the sign concerned is known as a masculine or a feminine sign. This is solely for the purpose of consistency and clarity, and not because one pronoun is favoured over another. I regard all star signs as gender-neutral, but in keeping with traditional astrology, the masculine and feminine terms are used for each sign accordingly. The masculine signs are Aries, Gemini, Leo, Libra, Sagittarius and Aquarius. The feminine signs are Taurus, Cancer, Virgo, Scorpio, Capricorn and Pisces.

CONTENTS

Introduction
Astrology | 1
Astrology & The Individual | 5
How Astrology Works | 7
Know Thyself | 9
The Zodiac & Your Place In The Sun | 10
The Sun | 11
The Sun ✦ The Ultimate Source Of Life On Earth | 12
The Sun ✦ What It Represents In The Human Psyche & Natal Chart | 13
The 12 Signs Of The Zodiac ✦ Their Basic Essence & Characteristics | 15
The Constellations | 59
The Zodiac Symbols | 65
Personal, Interpersonal & Transpersonal Signs | 75
The Three Decans Of Each Sign | 76

The Four Elements ✦ Fire, Earth, Air, Water | 83
The Fire Element ✦ Aries, Leo, Sagittarius | 84
The Earth Element ✦ Taurus, Virgo, Capricorn | 99
The Air Element ✦ Gemini, Aquarius, Libra | 112
The Water Element ✦ Cancer, Scorpio, Pisces | 126

The Modes ✦ Cardinal, Fixed, Mutable | 140
Cardinal | 140
Fixed | 141
Mutable | 142

The Ruling Planets | 145
Mars ✦ Ruling Planet Of Aries & Scorpio | 146
Venus ✦ Ruling Planet Of Taurus & Libra | 150
Mercury ✦ Ruling Planet Of Gemini & Virgo | 156
Moon ✦ Ruling Planet Of Cancer | 164
Sun ✦ Ruling Planet Of Leo | 171
Pluto ✦ Ruling Planet Of Scorpio | 179
Jupiter ✦ Ruling Planet Of Sagittarius & Pisces | 185
Saturn ✦ Ruling Planet Of Capricorn & Aquarius | 192
Uranus ✦ Ruling Planet Of Aquarius | 198
Neptune ✦ Ruling Planet Of Pisces | 205
The Ten Human Life Stages ✦ What Each Ruling Planet Represents | 212

The Houses In The Horoscope | 218

Powerful Life Lessons From Opposite Signs | 243
Aries & Libra | 245
Taurus & Scorpio | 245
Gemini & Sagittarius | 246
Cancer & Capricorn | 247
Leo & Aquarius | 248
Virgo & Pisces | 248

Astrology & Magic | 249

Your Natal Moon | 254

Moon Signs ✦ Harnessing Sun & Moon Magic Combined | 256
Aries ✦ Sun & Moon Combinations | 256
Taurus ✦ Sun & Moon Combinations | 262
Gemini ✦ Sun & Moon Combinations | 267
Cancer ✦ Sun & Moon Combinations | 272
Leo ✦ Sun & Moon Combinations | 277
Virgo ✦ Sun & Moon Combinations | 282
Libra ✦ Sun & Moon Combinations | 287
Scorpio ✦ Sun & Moon Combinations | 293
Sagittarius ✦ Sun & Moon Combinations | 299
Capricorn ✦ Sun & Moon Combinations | 305
Aquarius ✦ Sun & Moon Combinations | 311
Pisces ✦ Sun & Moon Combinations | 316

Body & Health ✦ Bach Flower Essences, Oriental Physiology, Vitamins & Minerals, Tissue Salts, Humors | 322

Money Attributes & Business Partners | 366
Aries ✦ Money Style & Doing Business | 367
Taurus ✦ Money Style & Doing Business | 368
Gemini ✦ Money Style & Doing Business | 370
Cancer ✦ Money Style & Doing Business | 371
Leo ✦ Money Style & Doing Business | 373
Virgo ✦ Money Style & Doing Business | 375
Libra ✦ Money Style & Doing Business | 376

Scorpio ✦ Money Style & Doing Business | 377
Sagittarius ✦ Money Style & Doing Business | 379
Capricorn ✦ Money Style & Doing Business | 380
Aquarius ✦ Money Style & Doing Business | 382
Pisces ✦ Money Style & Doing Business | 384

Colour Luck & Magic ✦ Lucky Colours For Each Sign | 386

Chakra Correspondences For Each Sign | 394
Aries & Leo ✦ Solar Plexus Chakra | 396
Taurus & Libra ✦ Heart Chakra | 397
Gemini & Virgo ✦ Throat Chakra | 399
Cancer & Scorpio ✦ Sacral Chakra | 400
Sagittarius & Pisces ✦ Third Eye Chakra | 401
Capricorn ✦ Root Chakra | 403
Aquarius ✦ Crown Chakra | 404

Lucky Career Tips | 406

Lucky Places | 427

Crystal Magic ✦ Lucky Crystals, Stones & Gems | 436

Lucky Sun Sign Numbers | 445

Lucky Days For Each Sign | 448
Sunday ✦ Lucky Day For Leo & All Zodiac Signs | 449
Monday ✦ Lucky Day For Cancer | 450
Tuesday ✦ Lucky Day For Aries & Scorpio | 451
Wednesday ✦ Lucky Day For Gemini & Virgo | 452
Thursday ✦ Lucky Day For Sagittarius & Pisces | 453
Friday ✦ Lucky Day For Taurus & Libra | 454
Saturday ✦ Lucky Day For Capricorn & Aquarius | 455

Lucky Charms & Talismans | 456

Gods, Goddesses, Animal Totems & Other Guides | 457

Power Metals | 488

Power Foods | 504

Plants & Magic: Power Flowers & Flower Remedies | 510

Trees & Lucky Woods | 519

Sacred Celtic Calendar Trees | 528

The Power Of Love | 535
General Lucky-In-Love Tips | 536
Gemstones: Zodiac Love Stones | 539
How To Attract Each Sign | 541
Zodiac Love Styles | 542

Tarot Cards ✦ For Luck, Magic, Energy, Abundance, Questing & Meaning | 560

Lucky 13 Tips For Increased Magic, Luck & Magnetism | 577

Have You Packed Your Magical Bag For The Journey? | 597

Final Words ✦ Tapping Into The Magic Of Each Sign | 602

INTRODUCTION

Astrology is a language. If you understand this language,
the sky speaks to you.
Dane Rudhyar

This book is a condensed version of my super popular *Lucky Astrology* book series. Until recently, I had assumed most people are really only interested in their own zodiac sign. So, I was surprised to learn via feedback from my readers and social media followers, that many people are also intensely interested in finding out more about their loved ones' star signs also. I wasn't so surprised to learn that because we are social beings by nature, we tend to have an avid interest in the dynamics of those around us who enrich our lives: our friends, lovers, parents, children, teachers, mentors, work colleagues, business partners, even celebrities and other famous people we admire. Bing! Cue lightbulb moment: I decided, based on these invaluable comments, to create this one-volume, all-inclusive, condensed, information-rich version that you are now reading; in essence *The Definitive Volume* of my entire Lucky Astrology 12-book series.

I sincerely hope it is enriching, enchanting and deeply informative for not only yourself, but for anyone else you wish to know more about. Don't keep it under lock and key, or in your mind's expanse; share it around, spread the love, impart the advice, reveal the tips herein, so that others may also benefit from the magical tips within these pages. Share the wisdom of the ages that I have painstakingly researched, studied and practised, with everyone you know, so that they too may move through life with greater self-awareness, knowledge and confidence about the unique and special qualities that were bestowed on them as their birth-given gifts.

As the Oracle at Delphi so sagely and succinctly stated: "Know Thyself". All personal wisdom, empowerment and growth centre upon this. At the time of writing, I have been a practising astrologer for over 40 years (yes, I began when I was seven years old!) so I consider myself divinely qualified and experienced enough to testify that astrology really is the perfect tool to truly *know thyself*.

Within these pages, you will discover a whole world of special tips to enhance the power and luck of your zodiac sign, thereby attracting more luck, happiness, health, abundance, potential, love and expansion into your life experience!

ASTROLOGY

Man, as the greatest minds have ever perceived, is a microcosm of the universal Macrocosm - 'As Above so below'.
Christmas Humphries

To the extent that the ruling heavens favour your beginnings and further life, you will pursue the promise of your birth; especially if Plato is correct, and antiquity with him, in saying that when anyone is born, they are given a certain daemon, a life guardian - destined by one's very own star.
Marsilio Ficino

Man... carries the stars hidden in himself. He is a microcosm, or a little world, because he is an extract from all the stars and planets of the whole firmament, from the Earth and the elements; and so he is their quintessence.
Paracelsus

Astrology can be defined as the calculation and meaningful interpretation of the positions and motions of the heavenly bodies, and their correlation with human and earthly experiences. Its central concept is based upon this interconnectedness between the cosmos and ourselves.

The word astrology is derived from the Greek word *astron*, meaning 'star' and *logos*, meaning 'word'. Thus, astrology quite literally translates as *words (language) of the stars*. It is based on the ancient phrase many of us are familiar with: *'As Above, So Below'*, otherwise known as the Law of the Macrocosm and Microcosm. The Macrocosm is the Universe, symbolised by the sky, the starry dome that we can see from our planet Earth; the Microcosm is us - humans, animals, plants, elements, minerals, and all other life on Earth.

'As Above, So Below' is a well-known and deeply impressing maxim of Hermetic origin, inscribed upon the famed Emerald Tablet among cryptic wording by the enigmatic figure Hermes Trismegistus around 5,000 years ago. These four powerful words are adopted by astrologers and believers in magic to explain, in very succinct wording, the meaning behind the art and science of celestial influences upon our earthly affairs.

Astrology and many other esoteric and occult studies, propose that we are not separate from the Universe, but are an intricate part of it. The Sun, Moon and planets all follow exact patterns of movement and their motions can be observed and/or measured precisely by astronomers and astrophysicists. The basic idea of astrology is that all individual parts of the Universe, from plants and minerals to animals, cooperate with each other and work together in synchronistic harmony.

Anyone can apply astrological knowledge in their daily lives, but it hasn't always been like that. At one time, astrology was reserved only for Kings and nations, and only the court astrologer/astronomer could cast and interpret horoscopes. Ancient astrology and astronomy used to be one and the same. To be an astrologer, one first had to be able to interpret the stars in some systematic way, and then track the movement of the Moon and the planets against the background of the constellations.

Astrology, the knowledge and language of the cosmos, goes back to the ancient kingdom of Babylonia and was adapted by the Mesopotamians, Greeks, Egyptians and Romans to incorporate their own deities (as indicated in mythology). It is upon a combination of Greek and Egyptian interpretations of astrology that our present knowledge is based.

In the ancient Mesopotamian world, as far back as 800 BC, people lived precariously beneath the open skies. Today we are aware that the Sun and Moon exert a profound influence upon our Earthly affairs, but for our primitive ancestors, the heavens, stars and planets must have been a matter of great and mysterious significance. Early humankind, its senses influenced by natural processes of ebbs, flows, growth, decay and cycles, tended naturally towards a physical explanation of the Universe. At first, the movements of the planets - and all celestial occurrences - were observed as omens affecting the Ruler and his nation; it was only in fifth century AD Egypt that the calculation of the planetary positions at the time of one's birth, and the casting of horoscopes for individual people, became widespread.

The first astrologers, the Chaldeans, mapped the stars and later passed this knowledge and wisdom on to the ancient Greeks, who, during the third century BC, developed astrology into a science with the use of mathematical aids and instruments to measure planetary movements. The Greeks were the first to cast individual horoscopes. And it was the Greeks who associated the four elements with the signs of the zodiac.

The word "zodiac" can be translated from Greek to mean the "circle or path of the animals." The Greeks not only had names for the twelve Solar phases but had symbols for each, and many correspond with the ones we use today.

The Greeks passed on much of their knowledge to the Romans. During the second century BC, Roman astrologers were primarily forecasters who were consulted frequently by rulers of the church and state. By the early third century AD, astrology co-existed with early Christianity. This harmonious co-existence was possible because it was considered that celestial bodies could foretell events, but did not determine the future - indeed, the stars seen by the shepherds at the time of Christ's birth were only predictors of his arrival. After the fourth century AD, Christianity strengthened and the popularity of astrology declined as Christian reluctance to support 'pagan' or 'superstitious' beliefs became more prominent. The Middle Ages saw a revival in astrology, with courses being taught in universities and other educational establishments, and connections were made between the zodiac, alchemy, herbs, and medicine. Astrology was once again able to exist alongside the Church, although many remained suspicious of astrologers.

Around the beginning of the fifteenth century, academics of the Renaissance movement examined the past for knowledge, and ancient philosophies, including astrology, flourished; this coincided with arts and science movements developing. The famed prophet and astrologer Nostradamus lived during this period. Leonardo da Vinci depicted aspects of astrology combined with geometry in his art. Writers and poets of the time, including Shakespeare, alluded to celestial influences in their work.

During this period, astrology had numerous practical applications. Agricultural calendars were introduced, indicating favourable planting times according to the phases of the Moon; health and illness were linked with movements of celestial bodies; and emotional states and mental health afflictions correlated with the planetary positions.

Eventually, new ways of thinking led to a split between astronomy and astrology, and by the seventeenth century, the realm of science had developed to such a degree that astrology was no longer taken seriously.

The study of the sky above us has been charted for more than 5,000 years. This fact is known because ancient 'horoscopes' imprinted on clay tablets have been unearthed, dating back almost 5,400 years ago. However, no one knows for certain just how, when and where astrology first began, although it is apparent that it flourished in ancient Chaldea, Mesopotamia, Babylon and Egypt.

Astrology is a science which has spanned many centuries and still remains extraordinarily popular, its truths having the potential to speak to and *through* all of us. Long before today's interest in it, great visionaries like Ptolemy, Hippocrates, Plato, Galileo, Jefferson, Franklin, Newton, Columbus and Jung respected its inherent truths, mythology and timeless knowledge. Furthermore, astrology predates many other 'sciences' - for out of it grew religion, medicine and astronomy, not the other way around.

The discipline of astrology is ultimately a study of the interlocking and interrelated forces of the twelve zodiacal forces, or constellations, which grace the skies, as they radiate their energies onto the earthly kingdoms below. As these various energies circulate throughout the etheric realm of our Solar system, these zodiacal entities and archetypes imprint their vibrational frequencies and harmonic resonances upon our bodies, minds, souls and spirits. And although to a large degree this cannot be 'proven' by science, our very existences in their constant unravelling, are testament to this incredibly powerful, if intangible, influence.

ASTROLOGY & THE INDIVIDUAL

There's a flame of magic in every stone and every flower, every bird that sings and every frog that croaks. There's magic in the trees and the hills and the river and the rocks, in the sea and the stars and the wind, a deep, wild magic... It's in you too, my darling, and in me, and in every living creature... Even the dirt I'm sweeping up now is star dust. In fact, all of us made from the stuff of stars.

Kate Fortsyth

Since the earliest periods of human history, people studied the starry vaults of the heavens and conceived that their presence, movements and positions endowed planet Earth's inhabitants with divine influences. There is much evidence that positions and movements of the planets as seen from Earth at the time of one's birth, are linked to the personality characteristics of that individual.

Human energy and emotional cycles are governed by the forces and networks of magnetic impulses from all the planets. Of all the heavenly bodies, the Moon's effects and power are the most marked due to its visibility and close proximity to Earth. But the Sun, Venus, Mars, Mercury, Jupiter, Saturn, Uranus, Neptune and Pluto exercise their influences just as surely. In fact, scientists are aware that plants and animals are affected by natural cycles which are governed by forces such as fluctuations in barometric pressures, the gravitational field, and electricity in the air. These Earthly dynamics were originally triggered by atmospheric magnetic vibrations, or outer space, from where the planets send forth their unseen waves. No living organism or mineral on Earth escapes these immense influences.

The geomagnetic field seems to affect life on Earth in certain observed ways, and these influences appear to correlate with planetary positions. The Earth is itself a living planet, constantly surrounded by these electrical fields. The two polar regions are like giant magnets which drive unseen currents around the globe. Indeed, our upper atmosphere is bombarded by charged particles from the Solar system and even beyond. Most of us are only dimly aware of this electrical power that is swirling around us consistently, because it is largely invisible. It is not only the biosphere of the Earth that contains these charged fields; they circulate within human beings and we all have a certain amount of body electricity and can even store static charge like a capacitor.

It has been suggested that the fluctuations of the Earth's magnetic field are picked up by the in-utero infants nervous system, which acts like an antenna, and these synchronise the internal biological clocks of the foetus that then control the moment of birth. This foetal magnetic antenna, therefore, is sensitive enough to sense these planetary vibrations and fields, and through a combination of inherited genetics and the positions of the planets at birth, each individual is imprinted with the certain basic inherited personality characteristics that are absorbed and incorporated throughout the perinatal period.

Carl Jung, the Swiss psychiatrist and psychological theorist, suggested that the inherent disposition of the individual is present at birth, and is reflected in the patterns of his or her natal chart. Further, he theorised that there is a 'priori factor' in all human activities, namely the inborn, preconscious, and unconscious individual structure of the psyche. The preconscious psyche, for example that of a newborn baby, is not simply an empty vessel into which practically anything can be poured, but rather it is this preconscious psyche that gives us the free will to become what we are instead of what others or our environment impels us to become. The child is not merely a receptacle for the psychic life of those around him or her, albeit still sensitive and susceptible to these surrounding influences, because each individual brings something of his/her own experience of them.

Further, Dr Harold S. Burr, author of *The Nature of Man and the Meaning of Existence* (1962), asserted that there is order in the Universe and unity in the organism, and that man is endowed with a soul. He stated that a complex magnetic field not only establishes the pattern of the human brain at birth, but continues to regulate and control it through life, and that the human central nervous system is a superb receptor of electro-magnetic energies, indeed the finest in nature. He contended that the electro-dynamic fields of all living things, which may be measured and mapped with standard voltmeters, mould and control each organism's development, health and mood, and named these the 'fields of life'.

It can therefore be suggested that astrological and planetary influences endow us with the majority of our characteristics at birth, traits bestowed upon us according to our Sun sign and other planetary forces as seen in the birth chart.

The ancients taught that astrology was one of the keys to the many enigmas that plague humans in their ceaseless quest to determine what the meaning of life is, and what their role and place in the Universe is - and this quest still persists today. Astrology, which dates back over 5,000 years, is indeed one such key to unlocking the vast many secrets of the Universe - and ultimately, the power and potential of the individual Self.

HOW ASTROLOGY WORKS

If the unique magnetic waves that all stars and planets in the heavens release are separate secret codes, every individual shall be bestowed with his own combination on the day of his birth.
Master Tan Khoon Yong

Nothing exists nor happens in the visible sky that is not sensed in some hidden moment by the faculties of Earth and Nature.
Johannes Kepler

Astrology is an oracular divinatory tool, which allows us to interpret our character, 'read' our past, uncover clues about our present experiences, and predict with oft startling accuracy the possibilities of the future.

Author Dan Millman sums it up well in his book *Everyday Enlightenment*: "Such holistic and intuitive systems (like astrology) are, almost by definition, non-rational and have been mistakenly associated with occult practices and shunned by both science and religion. Yet these systems have lasted, and will continue to last, throughout time - not because they can (or should) unerringly guide your life, but because they remind us of the mystery and interconnectedness of the Universe".

Whether you personally view astrology as a symbolic art, a whimsical tool, or a tangible reflection of cosmic influences upon our lives, it's nice to keep an open mind to the myriad ways it can enhance any and all areas of life, and perhaps most importantly, your self-awareness and knowledge.

Many people believe that astrology works to a greater or lesser degree, and use it to great advantage, capitalising on the personal strengths of their zodiac sign, and downplaying their weaknesses. However it is used, astrology always offers the supreme opportunity for you to strengthen your best points so that you may ultimately be the best you can be!

KNOW THYSELF

Man, know thyself. All wisdom centres on this.
Carl Jung

Before the temple of the Oracle at Delphi, the ancient Greeks imparted a special piece of advice that was carved onto one of the portals: "Know Thyself." These two powerful words are easy enough to understand, but much more difficult to apply.

Despite this, throughout life's inner and outer journey, astrology can provide us with an inner navigational system by which we can be guided towards our highest potential, and ever closer towards the eternal quest of 'knowing thyself'. It provides the hope that this higher spiritual plane exists and that if we can 'read' and therefore be guided by the unique inner blueprint that our individual birth chart has stamped upon us at the moment we take our very first breath, indeed we can reach this higher spiritual plane and realise our innate potential.

Always remember that astrology is not fatalistic; the stars may incline, but they do not compel. Astrology simply provides us with an inner guide for our journey through life and the finding of our true selves - and what we do with the resulting knowledge is entirely up to us.

THE ZODIAC & YOUR PLACE IN THE SUN

I will follow the Sun through the zodiac, and as each sign is illuminated, I will seek to discover its inner meanings and its message. At each new station, a new adventure and a cosmic truth, revealed.

Patricia Crowther

The zodiac is a circle of 360 degrees, consisting of equal segments of 30 degrees each. These represent the twelve houses of the twelve astrological signs. This zodiac is how the early astrologers imagined the Solar system to be, a perfect circle with the Earth at its centre, around which the Sun, Moon and the planets revolved.

Each sign of the zodiac corresponds to one of the twelve segments, following a chronological order and established according to the rhythm of the seasons and cycles of the Sun and the Moon. But the zodiac itself, or the band of constellations that comprise it, has shifted over the millennia, creating division between astronomical and astrological schools of thought. It has been said that due to this shift over time, one who once considered themselves as an Aquarian, is actually a Capricorn, the sign before it, and a Leo is actually a Cancerian, its preceding sign. This is the result of misunderstandings and differences in perspectives, and explanations around it are beyond the scope of this book, but can be researched further should you wish to delve a little deeper.

From the astronomical point of view, it is true that the zodiac to which we refer today is not situated where it 'should' be, but indeed, nothing is fixed under the celestial vault. And so, the starting point of the ancient zodiac does not correspond exactly to the one we can observe today.

But for the purposes of increasing your power and luck, let's keep things simple and enjoy the ride; after all, astrology - while based upon many scientific theories, mysteries, scepticism, superstitions, facts, patterns, ambiguities, correlations, paradoxes, contradictions, stigmatisms and observations that seek to support, refute, prove and disprove this ancient art time and again - is ultimately meant to be fun too!

THE SUN

Earth's Luminary ✦ Our Brightest Shining Star

Our Centre, Core Self, Identity & Inner Guiding Light

Perfect is what I have said of the work of the Sun.
Hermes Trismegistus, The Emerald Tablet

The Sun is our essence, centre, source, ego strength, power, life force, will, vitality, creative expression, purpose, life's direction, our sense of identity, and who we really *are*.

Our brightest star is the core of our individuality, our inner guiding light.

The Sun is externalising, and represents totality, infinity, eternity, the striving toward and ultimate reaching of one's personal destiny and *completion* in all areas. It is the creative energising giver of life and the 'father' of the zodiac. It endows us with our inherent creative potential and personal identity - our urge to *create* and to be.

The Sun is our core self, conscious purpose, our sense of creating something out of our own being. It is the integrated personality and represents the *present*, the present moment being the only constant that really exists.

The Sun rules the heart and is thus symbolically the centre of Self. Indeed, the Sun is the heart and the most commanding presence in our birth chart; the luminary Ruler which governs our essential being and wants to be noticed and appreciated, and above all, *to shine*.

KEY WORDS

Core Self, Spirit, Life Force, Power, Essence, Inner Authority, Will, Expression, Identity, Creativity, Higher Self, the Father, Ego, Vitality, Pride, Individuality, Leadership, Majesty, Willpower, Purpose.

The Journey, the Path & the Destiny.

THE SUN ✦ THE ULTIMATE SOURCE OF LIFE ON EARTH

You are the unconditioned spirit that is trapped in conditions, the boundless spirit that is trapped in boundaries, like the Sun and an eclipse.
Rumi

Throughout the ages, and indeed since life forms began emerging, the electromagnetic waves generated by the Sun have kept planet Earth habitable for humans, animals, plants and minerals. The Sun is, in fact, the only true source of energy on planet Earth. It provides the perfect amount of energy for plants to synthesise all of the products required for growth and reproduction, which is then stored by plants and ingested by humans and animals who, through many complex processes, utilise these various forms of encapsulated Solar energy - and so the cycle continues. Wood, fuel and minerals (crystals included) too, are merely various forms of this encased Sun energy. In fact, all matter is essentially 'frozen' light. Human body cells are bundles of Sun energy; we couldn't conceive or process a single thought without the molecules of Solar-energised oxygen and glucose.

In essence, the Sun supports the growth of all species, including human beings and microscopic life forms, and without it life on Earth would simply not be possible. The mathematical and metaphysical complexity that stands behind a system of organisation and order so infinitely diverse and intricate as planetary life cannot be truly fathomed, but unerringly and miraculously, the Sun instinctively knows what each species, from a tree to a human, intrinsically needs in order to fulfil its evolutionary purpose and cycles.

Ultimately, the electromagnetic waves generated by the Sun come in a variety of lengths, which determine their specific course of action and responsibility. There are gamma rays, x-rays, cosmic rays, various kinds of ultraviolet rays, infrared, short-wave infrared, radio waves, electric waves, and of course the visible light spectrum, consisting of the seven colour rays.

Most of these energy waves are absorbed and used for various processes in the atmospheric layers that encircle the Earth, and only a small portion of them - the electromagnetic spectrum - reach the surface of our planet. Although the human eye is only able to perceive about one percent of this spectrum, the waves exert a significant influence upon us. These waves and rays allow all life forms to undergo constant cycles of change necessary for growth and renewal. Physically, we can observe this, but on a deeper, more spiritual level, we can even feel it and allow its radiance to permeate our very souls. Such is the might, force and power of that astonishing ball of fire in our sky: the brilliant, ever-shining Sun.

THE SUN ✦ WHAT IT REPRESENTS IN THE HUMAN PSYCHE & NATAL CHART

The Sun is the most powerful of all the stellar bodies. It colours the personality so strongly that an amazingly accurate picture can be given of the individual who was born when it was exercising its power through the known and predicable influences of a certain astrological sign; these electromagnetic vibrations will continue to stamp that person with the characteristics of their Sun sign as they go through life.

Linda Goodman

There is a reason your Sun sign is otherwise known as your Star Sign - it's because, quite simply, the Sun is a star; in fact, it's the largest, brightest, most luminous one in Earth's known visible Universe.

The Sun is our essence, our core self, conscious purpose and sense of identity, our creative potential, our spirit, the integrated personality that shines outward from within us. It is concerned with the present. It is our centre, source, power, life force, will, vitality, purpose, life's direction, what and who we *really* are.

The Sun represents our basic urge for self-expression. It is the 'Solar energy cell' in a person's character, the Lord and giver of life, and symbolises the way in which an individual will shine out to the world. Our Sun is our personal identity and aspects to it from other components in the chart show the ease or otherwise of assuredness and confidence with which one will project and express one's individuality. The Sun sign will also show how an individual bounces back from setbacks and disappointments, their resilience.

The Sun is the archetype of the Father and represents the primary masculine principle in the natal chart. It indicates how we express and experience our masculine side, or animus, our conscious self, how we express ourselves creatively, our personal potential, individuality, self-expression and personal power. It has to do with courage, power, generosity, vitality, self-confidence, nobility, self-worth, dignity and strength of will. It symbolises authority and purpose, the *ruler*, and its potential is the peak of constructive maturity. It signifies self-sufficiency and abundance, containing enough energy to radiate warmth and give life to everything around it.

The sign and placement in which one's Sun is posited in the birth chart, strongly indicates the level and type of vitality available to the personality (the sign), and in which area of life this may be most strongly directed (the house).

The Sun in a natal chart is a powerful symbol because everything is filtered, at a conscious level, through it. It tells us what we need to do to feel fully alive, the type of engine 'driving' us, what we need to do to be authentic and to be fully functioning. Listening to the special message of one's Sun sign can provide one with greater direction, and a more dynamic energy and life purpose.

The symbol for the Sun ☉ depicts a circle with a dot or 'seed' at its centre, from which the core self, power, creativity and the first sparks of life spring. The circle around this 'seed' represents spirit, symbolising wholeness, eternity, infinite energy.

While the Moon, the night sky's luminary, represents the *soul*, the Sun, the day sky's luminary, represents our *spirit*.

This book is about your Sun sign and how you can become much larger, glow with far more brilliance, and shine brighter than you ever dreamed possible!

I wish you all the magic in the galaxy for your dreams to come true and your deepest wishes to become reality, through tapping into the amazing power and inherent potential of your Sun sign. So get set for a galactical ride through the lucky stars of your constellation - and may a shooting star cross the path in front of you as you go!

THE 12 SIGNS OF THE ZODIAC
THEIR BASIC ESSENCE & CHARACTERISTICS

Before we bound through the lush pastures of the Bull, scuttle across the glistening sands of the Crab's ocean home, charm our way through Gemini's party, or dive into the bottomless depths of the Piscean soul, bear in mind that not all people of the same sign share the same traits, or indeed to the same degree. In fact, sometimes we relate to very few of our sign's qualities and characteristics. This is because, quite simply, we are coloured by our entire astrological horoscope, and as such, carry a little of all twelve signs within us.

Despite being a combination of all signs to varying degrees, the Sun in the chart is arguably regarded as the strongest influence that most readily endows us with our basic personality, temperament, character, and overall essence.

Should you wish to explore your whole character in greater depth, having your birth chart drawn up is a fantastic place to start, and may explain some discrepancies. However, bear in mind that most astrologers will examine the placement and sign of the Sun first and foremost, hence its well-earned and deserved prominence in the beautiful and timeless cosmic art that is astrology.

ARIES THE RAM

Cardinal Fire, Masculine, Positive, Intuitive
The Golden Child
21 March - 19 April
Ruled by Mars

KEY PHRASE ✦ "I Am"
GEMSTONES ✦ Bloodstone, Diamond, Aquamarine
BODY & HEALTH ✦ Head, Brain, Face, Blood Pressure
ASTROLOGICAL HOUSE ✦ First

How Aries Emanates its Life Force / Energy
Enthusiastically, Impulsively, Assertively, Courageously, with Initiative

Is Concerned With

- Leadership
- Self
- Coming First
- Self-assertion
- Leadership
- Initiation, New Beginnings
- Ego
- Action
- Daring
- Challenge, Adventure
- Exploration, Pioneering, Discovery
- Pursuits

- Aggression
- Conquest
- Ambition
- Personal Control
- Originality
- Competition, Winning
- Bravery
- Courage
- Nobility
- Honesty
- Openness
- Loyalty
- Directness

Main Characteristics

- Adventurous
- Initiating
- Dynamic
- Impulsive
- Headstrong
- Urgent
- Energetic
- Selfish
- Pioneering
- Courageous
- Impatient
- Strong
- Enthusiastic
- Confident
- Egocentric,
- Foolhardy
- Tactless
- Direct
- Self-assured
- Zealous
- Fearless
- Eager
- Naïve
- Cheerful
- Trusting
- Wilful
- Brash
- Arduous
- Innocent
- Affable
- Brave
- Driven
- Bossy
- Curious
- Ambitious
- Enterprising
- Carefree
- Leader
- Autonomous
- Bold
- Temperamental
- Rash
- Hearty
- Interested
- Passionate
- Optimistic

The Ram having passed the Sea serenely shines
And leads the Year, the Prince of all the Signs.
Manilius

A realist, yet a decided idealist, Aries often defies emotional description.
No one can show such tough, forceful behaviour.
Yet, few others are capable of such sentimentality,
wistful innocence, and belief in miracles.
Linda Goodman

Aries is the sign of the Ram, a hard-horned sheep who leads the pack and keeps the rest of the herd in line. Bold, direct, fearless, spontaneous, courageous, enthusiastic, impetuous, self-centred and active are Aries's most notable traits. Being a fabulous Fire sign, this sign burns brightly but can burn itself out just as quickly if he loses interest in someone or something, being quick as a flash to move on to the next challenge if a new one presents itself. This is a sign that thrives on adventure and pursues excitement. Impatient and confident, Aries loves to be first at everything and is flattered and easily won over by loads of attention, recognition and compliments. The Ram believes his own hype, but in a most childlike and non-malicious way. Novelty is a big thing for the driven Ram's spirit, and he needs plenty of new and novel stimulation to keep his passion alive and his flames burning. Aries is impulsive, adventurous and initiating, without thought nor care for tomorrow, and never pausing long enough to reflect upon yesterday; today is his day! A dynamic lover, fun-loving, if a little selfish, friend and an independent go-getter, Aries is the first sign and the energetic leader of the zodiac, blazing through life at a speed that can be dizzying but breathtakingly refreshing to all those who are lucky enough to encounter one!

Spiritual Aries
Archetypal Universal Qualities
The Initiator, Pioneer, Warrior, Leader, Adventurer, Winner, Voyager

What Aries Refuses
To accept failure or defeat, to be ignored, to be second best in anything.

What Aries is an Authority On
Self-confidence, Taking Initiative, Courage, Pioneering, Winning, Leadership, Battle, Conquest, Victory

The Main Realms Through Which Aries Experiences Reality
Action, Freedom, Adventure, Directness, Being, Self, Movement

How Aries Loves
Passionately, Enthusiastically, Arduously, Trustingly, Wholeheartedly

Most Compatible With
Leo, Sagittarius, Libra

To Bring Out Personal Best of Character
Undertake regular physical exercise. Eat the odd helping of humble pie. Go on activity-oriented holidays. Take on a long-term commitment. Write an autobiography. Teach others self-confidence. Take on a leadership role. Lead by example. Inspire!

Spiritual Goals
To learn the meaning of selfless love. To be more reflective, more aware of shortcomings. To tap into emotions more often. To become more enduring and persistent. To develop a greater awareness of the needs of others.

TAURUS THE BULL

Fixed Earth, Negative, Feminine, Sensate
The Earth Child
20 April - 20 May
Ruled by Venus

KEY PHRASE ✦ "Possess"
GEMSTONES ✦ Emerald, Sapphire, Diamond
BODY & HEALTH ✦ Throat, Tonsils, Neck, Thyroid, Thymus, Vocal Cords
ASTROLOGICAL HOUSE ✦ Second

How Taurus Emanates its Life Force / Energy

Steadily, Thoroughly, Affectionately, Sensually, Productively, Patiently, Gently, Gracefully

Is Concerned With

- Beauty
- Romance
- Sentimentality
- Sensuality
- The Good Life
- Food, Wine, Sensual Pleasures
- Affection
- Materialism, Money, Possessions
- Prosperity, Abundance, Wealth
- Material Comforts
- Aesthetics
- Nature
- Harmony
- Dependability
- Fixation of Purpose
- Security
- Productivity
- Habit
- Tenacity
- Kindness
- Calmness
- Persistence
- Routine
- Peace
- Gentleness
- Sameness
- Security

Main Characteristics

- Patient
- Loving
- Strong
- Loyal
- Practical
- Determined
- Sensual
- Down-to-Earth
- Passive
- Obstinate
- Stubborn
- Possessive
- Reliable
- Warm
- Stable
- Gentle
- Affectionate
- Security-seeking
- Self-indulgent
- Measured
- Steady
- Solid
- Persistent
- Consistent
- Materialistic
- Placid
- Nature-loving
- Arduous
- Industrious
- Smouldering
- Gluttonous
- Complacent
- Domestic
- Laidback
- Dependable
- Rooted
- Conservative
- Enduring
- Slow
- Resourceful
- Composed
- Productive
- Trustworthy
- Physical
- Calm
- Easygoing
- Careful
- Graceful

The far-off Venus showers him with the love of luxury, he pays dearly for his possessions and treasures them for a lifetime. His home is his castle - and let no man disturb the peace of the Bull. Taurus is as patient as time itself, as deep as the forest, with a dependable strength that can move mountains.

Linda Goodman

Taurus is the sign of the Bull, a steady, placid animal who is hard to budge but when angered can dig those heels into the dust and charge with great, determined force. Stubborn, easygoing, sensual, indulgent, materialistic, obstinate, possessive, productive, patient, loyal and affectionate are Taurus's most notable traits. Being a solid Earth sign, this sign is practical, persistent and pragmatic, but can lack imagination, passion and spontaneity. Warm-hearted and loving, Taurus loves to give and receive affection and is romantic and consistent in her approach to love. The Bull is materialistic and loves to be surrounded by beauty and the simple pleasures in life, such as good food, quality wine and of course Earthy and non-pretentious décor. Loyalty is a big thing for the sure and steady Bull's spirit, and she is said to be the most loyal of the zodiac, sometimes to a fault, such is her tenacity and endurance in friendship and romance. Taurus is cautious and takes slow steps towards her goals, being ever careful to lay a solid foundation before building slowly upwards. A warm and demonstrative lover, dependable friend and industrious worker, Taurus is the second sign and assuring 'rock' of the zodiac, never letting her emotions get in the way, possessing amazing common sense - the Bull never loses her head when all around are losing theirs, making Taurus reassuring and comforting to have around in the midst of life's chaos.

Spiritual Taurus
Archetypal Universal Qualities
The Earth Dweller, Manifester, Builder

What Taurus Refuses
To change, live in poverty, be denied the luxuries of life, or surrender.

What Taurus is an Authority On
Sensuality, Affection, Resourcefulness, Romance, Consistency, Endurance, Loyalty, Beauty, Investments

The Main Realms Through Which Taurus Experiences Reality
Touch, Substance, Ownership, Worth, Value, Form, the Material

How Taurus Loves
Sensually, Warmly, Steadfastly, Enduringly, Romantically

Most Compatible With
Virgo, Capricorn, Scorpio

To Bring Out Personal Best of Character
Give and receive cuddles and massages. Share love further and wider. Clear out clutter regularly. Do some gardening. Enjoy luxury weekends away. Consume good quality food and wine. Get out in nature as often as possible.

Spiritual Goals
To learn the value of insight. To delve deeper and explore emotions. To overcome obstinacy and truly see others' points of view on things. To steer clear of ruts. To focus more on spiritual wealth. To engage in more adventure and spontaneity. To take leaps of faith even when afraid. To take regular chances, risks and make more decisions on a whim.

GEMINI THE TWINS

Mutable Air, Masculine, Positive, Thinking
The Eternal Youth
21 May - 20 June
Ruled by Mercury

KEY PHRASE ✦ "I Think"

GEMSTONES ✦ Alexandrite, Agate, Citrine

BODY & HEALTH ✦ Hands, Shoulders, Arms, Lungs, Body Tubing, Nervous System

ASTROLOGICAL HOUSE ✦ Third

How Gemini Emanates its Life Force / Energy
Swiftly, Skilfully, Youthfully, with Versatility and Wit

Is Concerned With

- Communication
- Speech
- Articulation
- Social Interaction
- Dexterity
- Nimbleness
- Light-footedness
- Change
- Variety
- Wit
- Persuasion
- Charm
- Knowledge
- Freedom
- Youth
- Agility
- Movement
- Mobility
- Curiosity
- Short Journeys
- Education
- Learning
- Trivia
- Gathering Facts
- Adaptability
- Intellect
- The Mind

Main Characteristics

- Curious
- Witty
- Youthful
- Adaptable
- Fun
- Sociable
- Clever
- Restless
- Agile
- Flirtatious
- Changeable
- Alert
- Fickle
- Nervous
- Eloquent
- Friendly
- Flighty
- Open-minded
- Scattered
- Superficial
- Versatile
- Talkative
- Cunning
- Busy
- Candid
- Cheeky
- Inquisitive
- Lively
- Spontaneous
- Charming
- Inconstant
- Indecisive
- Intelligent
- Glib
- Insincere
- Dexterous
- Impatient
- Communicative
- Inquiring
- Mischievous
- Clear
- Shifty
- Excitable

One way or another, Gemini will triumph with words... he can sell ice cubes to an Eskimo or dreams to a pessimist.
Linda Goodman

In Gemini, the soul craves variety and attention and is forever on the move, searching, always searching, for the new or unusual. Geminians love to talk and chatter on aimlessly to anyone who cares to listen. Literature holds them in thrall, and the mind, seizing upon the written word, is almost intoxicated with the journey of discovery.
Patricia Crowther

There is much to be learned about the strength of Two when we examine the symbol of twins. Throughout the world since ancient times, twins have been thought to be endowed with supernatural powers. In some cultures, there is an entire discipline devoted to the balancing of the nature of twins, for they are thought to be two entities which share one soul.
Clarissa Pinkola Estes

What makes Geminis' moods and evasions tolerable is that they are really, really interesting... To those who have had quite enough of dull people leading dull lives, where imagination never takes wing & humour never sparkles, Gemini is like a draught of elixir. He reminds you that life is new and fun and fascinating. Spend some time around one, and you might even discover you've grown wings yourself.

Linda Goodman

Gemini is the sign of the Twins, two childlike figures who represent the dual nature of this sign. Versatile, two-faced, sociable, childish, talkative, cunning, flirtatious, curious, superficial and inquisitive are Gemini's most notable traits. Being an intellectual air sign, this sign is the flightiest of the air signs, being mutable and therefore changeable and easily bored by sameness and distracted and influenced by anything new or interesting presenting itself. Constantly on the move, restless and possessing a nervous energy, Geminis need to be occupied at all times. If they are not feeling stimulated by activity, this energy can become destructive, making the Gemini spirit prone to tantrums, arguments and meltdowns, before quickly recovering and bounding jubilantly into their next adventure. The Twins never stay mad for long, given their short attention span, flitting instead from one situation to the next, with little reflection or brooding over past upsets. Cunning and witty, Gemini is the quintessential class clown and revels in the resulting attention. Charming in an almost childlike way, Gemini is the life of the party and is easily recognised as the one who is moving from person to person engaging in refreshing, albeit superficial, exchanges around the punch bowl. A fun and flirty lover, light-hearted friend and a clever jack-of-all-trades, Gemini is the third sign and the cheeky Peter Pan of the zodiac, never quite growing up but always managing to pull it off with a refreshingly breezy pizzazz!

Spiritual Gemini

Archetypal Universal Qualities
The Youth, Trickster, Charmer, Communicator, Networker, Student

What Gemini Refuses
To stay still, remain stuck, stop learning, or be pinned down.

What Gemini is an Authority On
Mental and Communicative Abilities, Fun, Assimilation of Information, Social Charm, Flirting

The Main Realms Through Which Gemini Experiences Reality
Thought, Perception, Exploration, Speech, Communication, Social Interaction, Learning

How Gemini Loves
Youthfully, Dazzlingly, with Charm

Most Compatible With
Libra, Aquarius, Sagittarius

To Bring Out Personal Best of Character
Travel to offbeat intellectually awakening places. Be an influencer on social media. Attend parties and other social events regularly. Stay occupied and mentally stimulated. Undertake short courses. Make new friends.

Spiritual Goals
To learn how to explore things in greater depth. To endure and face things head on. To be more consistent and reliable by keeping promises. To fight rather than take flight. To take time out for grounding. To learn the value of commitment and endurance. To set long-term goals and achieve them.

CANCER THE CRAB

Cardinal Water, Negative, Feminine, Feeling
The Moon Child
21 June - 22 July
Ruled by the Moon

KEY PHRASE ✦ "I Feel"

GEMSTONES ✦ Moonstone, Pearl, Ruby

BODY & HEALTH ✦ Stomach, Breasts, Fluids, Membranes, Womb, Chest, Elbows

ASTROLOGICAL HOUSE ✦ Fourth

How Cancer Emanates its Life Force / Energy
Emotionally, Intuitively, Protectively, Tenaciously, with Feeling

Is Concerned With

- Receptivity
- Defence
- Care
- Protection
- Security
- Loyalty
- Childhood
- Family
- Emotions, Feelings
- Sympathy
- Sensitivity
- Home
- Comfort
- Domesticity
- Food
- Nurturing
- Maternal Instincts
- Experience of the Mother
- Sentiments
- Roots, Origins, Family History
- Antiques
- The Psychic Realm
- Intuition
- History, Nostalgia, Memory

Main Characteristics

- Emotional
- Sensitive
- Tenacious
- Changeable
- Imaginative
- Receptive
- Feeling
- Clingy
- Tender
- Psychic
- Kind
- Private
- Sympathetic
- Security-seeking
- Moody
- Loving
- Persistent
- Intuitive
- Maternal
- Possessive
- Cautious
- Retentive
- Protective
- Loyal
- Unable to Let Go
- Dependent
- Reflective
- Home-loving
- Touchy
- Snappy
- Crabby
- Shrewd
- Despondent
- Irritable
- Nostalgic
- Nurturing
- Insightful

> Children born under the sign (of Cancer) are extremely sensitive, and will only thrive if given plenty of fresh air and sunshine.
> The sea calls them...
> **Linda Goodman**

Cancer is the sign of the Crab, a hard-shelled, soft-centred crustacean who retreats into her shell when feeling threatened or hurt. Protective, nurturing, emotional, intuitive, changeable, tenacious, moody and private are Cancer's most notable traits. Being a sensitive and feeling Water sign, this sign feels her way through life guided by her instincts and inner knowing, being either engulfed or empowered by her emotions in all situations. Tenacious and shrewd in both business and matters of the heart, Cancerians tend to both lead and protect, and show an almost blind loyalty to their loved ones and those in their charge. The Crab is home-loving, domestic and security-seeking, needing her family and home life to be running smoothly in order to function at her highest level. Moods are a strong feature of the imaginative Crab's spirit, and she needs plenty of love and understanding to keep her Watery nature in check. Cancer is sympathetic and clingy, often holding on with tight pincers; she finds it hard to let go. The Crab lives in the past, being the most reminiscent, sentimental and nostalgic of all the signs, possessing an excellent memory but often remembering past hurts long after everyone else has moved on. A nurturing lover, loyal friend and at times deeply private and hidden soul,

Cancer is the fourth sign and the caring 'mother' of the zodiac, providing warmth, love, comfort and nourishment to anyone lucky enough to be in close orbit.

Spiritual Cancer
Archetypal Universal Qualities
The Moon Child, Water Baby, Mother, Nurturer, Sustainer, Homekeeper

What Cancer Refuses
To forget, deny her feelings, or to let go

What Cancer is an Authority On
Sustaining, Protecting, Nurturing, Preserving, Domesticity, Sympathy, Feelings, Tenacity

The Main Realms Through Which Cancer Experiences Reality
Security, Containment, Home, Belonging, Memory, Intuition, Emotions, Holding On

How Cancer Loves
Protectively, Lovingly, Loyally, with Tenacity

Most Compatible With
Scorpio, Pisces, Capricorn

To Bring Out Personal Best of Character
Cook a meal. Build up a large savings account. Spend quality time with family. Own a home. Live near the sea. Frolic in an ocean rock pool. Nurture, care for and sustain others.

Spiritual Goals
To learn how to feel secure in oneself instead of seeking it externally outside of the self. To curb clinginess and possessiveness. To regulate moods. To share more of the self with others and emerge from shell. To allow others 'in'. To overcome shyness and over-sensitivity. To discern when and how to let go. To use emotions constructively to help others.

LEO THE LION

Fixed Fire, Masculine, Positive, Intuitive
The Zodiac King
23 July - 22 August
Ruled by the Sun

KEY PHRASE ✦ "I Will"

GEMSTONES ✦ Citrine, Ruby, Peridot

BODY & HEALTH ✦ Heart, Back, Spine, Upper Back, Forearms, Wrists

ASTROLOGICAL HOUSE ✦ Fifth

How Leo Emanates its Life Force / Energy
Extravagantly, Confidently, Brightly, Naturally, Dramatically, with Style and Flair

Is Concerned With

- Pleasure
- Power
- Winning Others Over
- Pride
- Expansion
- Being the Boss, Authority, Command
- Ambition
- Organisation
- Loyalty
- Fun
- Play, Leisure
- Entertainment
- Open Displays of Affection and Love
- Attention, Applause, Recognition, Compliments
- Talent, Flair
- Romances, Love Affairs, Sex
- Charm
- Children
- Appreciation
- Gambling, Sports, Games, Taking Risks
- Arts
- Drama
- Performance
- Creativity, Arts
- Limelight
- Rulership, Leadership
- Luxury, Opulence

Main Characteristics

- Generous
- Warm-hearted
- Strong
- Dynamic
- Open
- Ambitious
- Loyal
- Charming
- Loving
- Courageous
- Creative
- Regal
- Confident
- Driven
- Bold
- Patronising
- Bossy
- Leader
- Expansive
- Enthusiastic
- Passionate
- Arrogant
- Extravagant
- Pompous
- Direct
- Affectionate
- Honest
- Dignified
- Powerful
- Noble
- Playful
- Attention-seeking
- Demanding
- Vain
- Dramatic
- Protective
- Dominating
- Proud
- Overbearing
- Magnanimous
- Conceited
- Fun
- Chivalrous
- Wholehearted
- Ostentatious
- Stubborn
- Organised
- Strong-willed
- Naïve
- Affected
- Pushy
- Daring
- Brave
- Imperious
- Determined
- Fearless

With pride the Lion lifts his mane
And takes a look at his wide domain
He knows that he must rule with might
Yet ever so gently with Love and Light

Alan Oken

To subdue him, simply flatter him. His vanity is his Achilles' heel... Leo is a fiercely loyal friend, a just but powerful enemy, creative and original, strong and vital - whether he's a quiet or a flamboyant lion, for there are both kinds. We overlook his arrogance, his sometimes-insufferable ego, his rather ridiculous spells of vanity and laziness, because his heart, like his metal, is pure gold.

Linda Goodman

> The lion is beyond dispute
> Allowed the most majestic brute;
> His valour and his generous mind
> Prove him superior of his kind.

John Gay

Leo is the sign of the Lion, the (often self-declared) 'King of the Jungle', a regal and magnificent animal who rules over the pride and expects it in turn to cater to his every whim and demand. Vain, bossy, arrogant, warm, playful, good-humoured, driven, dynamic, attention-seeking, dramatic, confident, dignified and noble are Leo's most notable traits. Being of the fabulous Fire element, this sign burns brightly and warmly, but can become overbearing and pushy in his constant need for attention and centre stage position. Confident and dominating, Leo loves to lead and is easily seduced by flattery and compliments, which he just as readily gives to others. The Lion is enthusiastic and generous to a fault, always willing to give someone the shirt off their backs or their last dollar, but only if it doesn't compromise their own comforts, indulgences and extravagances. The larger-than-life Leo craves attention and adoration, but his pride is easily hurt and he will retreat temporarily to lick his wounds if he loses a battle or feels slighted. Being a fixed sign, loyalty is a big thing for the big-hearted Lion's spirit - he gives it and expects it in equal measure. A hearty, enthusiastic and affectionate lover, fun-loving friend and playful performer on life's stage, Leo is the all-powerful King of the zodiac, winning people over and lighting the way with his commanding presence, powerful personality, warm nature, and ever-luminous spirit.

Spiritual Leo
Archetypal Universal Qualities
The Leader, Boss, Golden Child, Performer, Dramatist, Lover

What Leo Refuses
To accept no for an answer, to submit, to be ignored, to look drab or be a wallflower, to be a subordinate, to take a backseat in life

What Leo is an Authority On
Generosity, Chivalry, Spirit, Creativity, Play, Charm, Romance, Vanity

The Main Realms Through Which Leo Experiences Reality
Command of Self and Others, Warmth, Love, Attention, Playfulness, Creative Expression

How Leo Loves
Heartily, Romantically, Generously, Proudly, Passionately, Creatively, Expressively, Affectionately

Most Compatible With
Aries, Sagittarius, Aquarius

To Bring Out Personal Best of Character
Throw lavish parties. Host events. Get involved with children. Make plenty of time for play and leisure. Buy and wear expensive gold jewellery. Attend or teach acting or drama classes. Write and star in own play. Indulge in luxury.

Spiritual Goals
To learn to share the stage and attract more genuine appreciation and respect. To be more authentic. To lower expectations of others. To use natural flair for leadership to encourage others to shine too. Sit backstage occasionally. To be more modest and endearing by toning down dominating and attention-seeking behaviours. To be less self-focused and more humble.

VIRGO THE VIRGIN

Mutable Water, Negative, Feminine, Sensate
The Polished Gem
23 August - 22 September
Ruled by Mercury

KEY PHRASE ✦ "I Analyse"

GEMSTONES ✦ Sapphire, Carnelian, Peridot, Sardonyx

BODY & HEALTH ✦ Intestines, Digestive System, Lymphatic System, Pancreas, Spleen, Nervous System, Abdomen, Colon, Hands, Fingernails, Toenails

ASTROLOGICAL HOUSE ✦ Sixth

How Virgo Emanates its Life Force / Energy
Prudently, Shrewdly, Humbly, Intelligently, Reliably, Diligently, Rationally

Is Concerned With

- Self-perfection
- Detail, Logic, Order
- Self-improvement
- Organisation
- Responsibility
- Altruism
- Wholesomeness
- Service and Duty
- Virtue
- Self-discipline
- Hygiene, Cleanliness
- Health
- Efficiency
- Routine
- Reliability
- Strength of Characte
- Veiled Sensuality
- Hard Work
- Modesty
- Passivity
- Perfection
- Analysis
- Communication
- Shrewd Logical Thought
- Practicality
- Healing
- Purity

Main Characteristics

- Devoted
- Modest
- Precise
- Diligent
- Sensual
- Discerning
- Fussy
- Reserved
- Worrier
- Critical
- Observant
- Smart
- Gentle
- Reliable
- Meticulous
- Practical
- Measured
- Lucid
- Serious
- Cool
- Conservative
- Efficient
- Perfectionist
- Choosy
- Analytical
- Shrewd
- Tidy
- Nit-picky
- Intelligent
- Helpful
- Snobbish
- Conscientious
- Aloof
- Discriminating
- Thrifty
- Logical
- Rational
- Courteous
- Serving
- Sacrificing
- Painstaking
- Virtuous
- Tense
- Inhibited
- Dependable
- Differentiating
- Apprehensive
- Calculating
- Introspective
- Withdrawn
- Prudent
- Outwardly Calm

All too often, Virgo will knit the patches but neglect to put them together to form the quilt.
Alan Oken

You'll seldom see them blowing bubbles in the air or building castles in the sand. Virgos are too busy to daydream, and they're usually too tired at night to wish on stars.
Linda Goodman

This sign is the alchemist of the zodiac, differentiating spirit and matter and refining them in the crucible of life. Virgo is the sign of purity, so that which is sought is the end product produced by sifting the wheat from the chaff, so to speak. Nothing less than that tiny nugget of gold is acceptable to the soul in Virgo.
Patricia Crowther

Virgo is the sign of the Virgin, a beautiful maiden holding sheaves of wheat in her hand and often sitting in a field of fertile crops. Shy, modest, conscientious, pure, hard-working, self-sacrificing, practical, sensual, serious, discriminating, analytical, considerate and nit-picky are Virgo's most notable traits. Being a solid Earth sign, she is practical, persistent and pragmatic, but can lack imagination, warmth and passion at times. Cool, calm and reliable, Virgo loves to serve others and is therefore often the first person others will go to for advice. The Virgin is incredibly shrewd and intelligent in her undertakings, and her discriminating and perfectionist nature help her climb to the top in her steady, consistent manner; she is the quintessential quiet achiever. Helping others is a big thing for the Virgin's helpful spirit, and she will be unfalteringly there for anyone who may need her for anything, always putting others first - a trait which comes naturally to this modest sign. Virgo is meticulous, no-nonsense, conscientious and fussy, making her great to have onside, however she has a tendency towards being critical, over-analysing and worrying, characteristics that can cause trouble in both her inner and outer worlds. Virgo is more often her own worst enemy, being nagged by her inner critic and perfectionist, and falling into pessimistic and gloomy attitudes at times. A sensual and dependable lover, deeply caring friend and possessing a sensible approach to life and love, Virgo is the most practical and helpful of all the signs, making her a pure delight to have around!

Spiritual Virgo
Archetypal Universal Qualities
The Server, Healer, Worker, Quiet Achiever, Humble One

What Virgo Refuses
To overlook detail, be idle or shirk responsibility

What Virgo is an Authority On
Providing Efficient Service, Analysis, Detail, Organising, Helping Others, Sacrifice, Self-improvement, Perfection

The Main Realms Through Which Virgo Experiences Reality
Order, Duty, Discipline, Purity, Devotion, Correctness

How Virgo Loves
Discerningly, Devotedly, Sensuously, Cautiously, Seriously

Most Compatible With
Taurus, Capricorn, Pisces

To Bring Out Personal Best of Character
Undertake self-improvement courses and disciplines. Let the self go occasionally - be less inhibited. Undertake a regular fasting or cleansing regime. Power-walk. Go to a health retreat. Volunteer in an underprivileged community. Share and apply health knowledge. Serve others. Stop worrying!

Spiritual Goals
To learn to discriminate between destructive criticism and humble wisdom. To blow own trumpet once in a while. To learn to be bolder and more spontaneous. To replace worrying with trust. To stop taking life too seriously. To learn to be less self-critical. To compromise more often, meet others halfway, and be less choosy and nit-picky.

LIBRA THE SCALES

♎

Cardinal Air, Masculine, Positive, Thinking
The Great Harmoniser
22 September - 22 October
Ruled by Venus

KEY PHRASE ✦ "I Balance"

GEMSTONES ✦ Opal, Tourmaline, Sapphire

BODY & HEALTH ✦ Kidneys, Skin, Glands, Adrenals, Lumbar Area of Spine, Acid/Alkaline, Sugar & Temperature Balance, Lower Back

ASTROLOGICAL HOUSE ✦ Seventh

How Libra Emanates its Life Force / Energy
Elegantly, Fairly, Sociably, Gracefully, with Charm

Is Concerned With

- Partnerships, Marriage, Relationships, Other People
- Ideas, Opinions
- Diplomacy
- Balance, Harmony, Equilibrium
- Romance, Love, Sharing, Relating
- Aesthetics, Beauty
- Tact
- Self-control
- Debate, Argument
- Good Manners
- Personal Appearance
- Refinement
- Good Taste
- Sophistication
- Rational Thought
- Sociability
- Grace, Charm
- Luxury, Culture, Arts

Main Characteristics

- Diplomatic
- Agreeable
- Sociable
- Charming
- Easygoing
- Indecisive
- Elegant
- Romantic
- Articulate
- Cultured
- Impressionable
- Artful
- Refined
- Flirtatious
- Considerate
- Pleasant
- Gullible
- Lazy
- Manipulative
- Impartial
- Procrastinating
- Fair
- Trusting
- Graceful
- Gentile
- Aesthetic
- Popular
- Tactful
- Peaceable
- Likeable
- Idealistic
- Compromising
- Extravagant
- Hedonistic
- Tasteful
- Self-indulgent

A sense of harmony surrounds this person that never quite disappears. He rarely loses his charm. Social graces come naturally to him. No matter what the circumstances of his birth, he possesses a quality of refinement, an appearance of culture, and a gentleness of manner.

Jeanne Avery

Libra is the sign of the Scales, an instrument that keeps its harmony, symmetry and equilibrium only when in balance. Elegant, refined, artful, well-versed, aesthetic, pleasant, polite, sociable, graceful and indecisive are Libra's most notable traits. Being a socially and mentally oriented air sign, Librans are in love with love, and enjoy being engaged in conversation and social interaction. He is at his best when around other people; partnerships, whether they be in the form of marriage, business, or a close friendship, are where he excels. Fair and tactful, Librans are masters at diplomacy and impartiality, making them great mediators and peacemakers. The Scales are also known to be fence-sitters when it comes to debate, conflict, argument and crossroads in life, finding it difficult to determine or assert his opinions. Relationships are a big thing for the romantic Scales's spirit, and he constantly needs love, union, connection, marriage and an 'other' to make him feel complete. Libra is charming, eloquent and tasteful, with a great appreciation for art, beauty and the finer things life has to offer. A considerate and well-versed lover, easygoing friend and idealistic charmer, Libra is usually the most pleasant and popular guest at any social event, who enchants all in his presence with his gentle, agreeable and graceful nature.

Spiritual Libra

Archetypal Universal Qualities
The Harmoniser, Diplomat, Relator, Lover, Peacemaker

What Libra Refuses
Relationships, Art, Style, Diplomacy, Social Graces, Etiquette

What Libra is an Authority On
Providing Efficient Service, Analysis, Detail, Organising, Helping Others, Sacrifice, Self-improvement, Perfection

The Main Realms Through Which Libra Experiences Reality
Love, Balance, Harmony, Justice, Beauty, Cooperation

How Libra Loves
Romantically, Gracefully, Courteously

Most Compatible With
Gemini, Aquarius, Aries

To Bring Out Personal Best of Character
Host stylish dinner parties. Act as a mediator between warring parties. Nurture relationships. Live in beautiful surroundings. Visit museums and art galleries. Attend parties and social gatherings regularly. Learn how to balance work with lifestyle.

Spiritual Goals
To learn the meaning of sincere charm. Stop being a people-pleaser. To be more reflective and less dependent on others for personal happiness. To be more personal in interactions and come across as more genuine. To cultivate a greater sense of self and ego strength. To learn the value and virtues of solitude and independence. To focus more on self-improvement and self-love.

SCORPIO THE SCORPION

Fixed Water, Negative, Feminine, Feeling
The Strong & Silent One
23 October - 21 November
Ruled by Pluto

KEY PHRASE ✦ "I Desire"

GEMSTONES ✦ Topaz, Malachite, Peridot

BODY & HEALTH ✦ Reproductive Systems, Pelvis, Excretory & Immune Systems, Bladder, Prostate, Rectum

ASTROLOGICAL HOUSE ✦ Eighth

How Scorpio Emanates its Life Force / Energy
Secretively, Passionately, Intensely, Complexly

Is Concerned With

- Birth, Life, Death
- Sexuality, Sensuality
- Passion
- Power, Control
- Defence
- Willpower
- Extremes
- Pushing Boundaries
- Regeneration, Metamorphosis, Transformation
- Finance, Investments, Inheritances, Wills
- Depths
- Secrets, Occult, Taboos, Magic, Hidden Matters
- Defence Systems
- Investigation
- Personal Power
- Renewal, Resilience
- Reformation
- Emotions
- Dark Nights of the Soul
- Self-mastery

Main Characteristics

- Passionate
- Intense
- Secretive
- Magnetic
- Loyal
- Perceptive
- Strong-willed
- Enduring
- Persistent
- Powerful
- Complex
- Enigmatic
- Intuitive
- Penetrative
- Jealous
- Vindictive
- Vengeful
- Mysterious
- Investigative
- Psychic
- Suspicious
- Probing
- Sarcastic
- Sceptical
- Insightful
- Extreme
- Deep
- Self-mastering
- Pitiless
- Malicious
- Twisted
- Controlling
- Unforgiving
- Destructive
- Resilient
- Defensive
- Merciless
- Manipulative
- Resolute
- Discerning
- Steadfast
- All-or-nothing Oriented
- Tenacious
- Unflinching
- Power-seeking
- Cathartic
- Hypnotic
- Aware
- Ruthless
- Unapologetic
- Obsessive

Scorpio can do just about anything he wants to do. If he really wants it, it's most definitely no longer a dream. The dark, magical and mysterious power of Pluto turns desire into reality with cool, careful, fixed intent.
Linda Goodman

The art of keeping secrets comes naturally to the soul in Scorpio. This sign speaks of fixed, or still, water which shows a calm, unruffled exterior. But what cauldron of emotions seethe beneath the smooth surface?
Patricia Crowther

Scorpio is the sign of the Scorpion, the all-powerful stinging arachnid whose menacing presence strikes fear in the hearts of all she encounters. Intense, loyal, jealous, vengeful, penetrative, extreme, destructive, perceptive and enigmatic are Scorpio's most notable traits. Being a sensitive and highly emotional Water sign, her feelings brew under the surface and although she may intuit others' feelings and even probe her loved ones relentlessly, the Scorpio character is very secretive about her *own* inner self. Charismatic and magnetic, Scorpio loves to have control and power over others, sometimes in a tyrannical way, but mostly in a benignly, albeit fiercely protective way. The Scorpion is complex and secretive, with an inner turbulence that rarely reaches the surface; once it does, however, the Scorpion can become vindictive and merciless, plotting and exacting revenge like no other sign. Loyalty is a big thing for the passionate Scorpion's spirit, and if she senses any hint of disloyalty or infidelity, she will not hesitate to punish the offender with her powerful sting and send them on their way. Scorpio is transformative and regenerative, symbolically 'dying' or shedding her skin in order to rebirth herself, rising above the ashes like the powerful Phoenix, another symbol of this sign. Scorpio is mysterious, perceptive and insightful, with an amazingly investigative and probing nature, helping her to uncover what no one else can see; however, she's also suspicious and sceptical; everyone in the Scorpio's experience is guilty until proven innocent. A passionate lover, intense friend, and all-or-nothing superpower, Scorpio is the mysterious detective of the zodiac, helping the rest of us reveal our own hidden truths.

Spiritual Scorpio
Archetypal Universal Qualities
The Transformer, Seeker, Hypnotist, Investigator, Prober, Uncoverer of Secrets

What Scorpio Refuses
To be shallow, weak, or to surrender

What Scorpio is an Authority On
Death and Rebirth, Self-mastery, Resilience, Emotions, Fortitude, Depths, the Dark Side of Human Nature

The Main Realms Through Which Scorpio Experiences Reality
Willpower, Passion, Desire, Extremes, Possession, Death, Transformation

How Scorpio Loves
Possessively, Intensely, Passionately, Obsessively, Smoulderingly

Most Compatible With
Cancer, Pisces, Taurus

To Bring Out Personal Best of Character
Read detective and crime novels. Do a course in psychology. Make passionate love. Explore the spiritual nature of the Self. Share secrets rather than keeping them hidden. Help others to transform and renew themselves. Master the Self at all costs.

Spiritual Goals
To learn that true deep love involves freedom, surrendering, trusting, and letting go. To learn the beauty of forgiveness and how to sincerely accept an apology. To not misuse or abuse personal power or control. To reveal more secrets and to better understand effect on others. To distinguish between proper use and abuse of personal influence. To use powers of magnetism to attract only positive things and people.

SAGITTARIUS THE ARCHER

Mutable Fire, Masculine, Positive, Intuitive
The Great Philosopher
22 November - 21 December
Ruled by Jupiter

KEY PHRASE ✦ "I Aim"

GEMSTONES ✦ Topaz, Zircon, Turquoise

BODY & HEALTH ✦ Hips, Thighs, Liver, Sciatic Nerve, Blood, Sacral Region, Gluteous Muscles

ASTROLOGICAL HOUSE ✦ Ninth

How Sagittarius Emanates its Life Force / Energy
Idealistically, Meaningfully, Truthfully, Eloquently, with Charm

Is Concerned With

- Philosophy
- Truth
- Freedom
- Idealism
- Travel
- Adventure
- Quests
- Expansion
- Honesty
- Religion
- Spiritual Growth
- Vision
- Optimism
- The Future
- Positive Outlook
- The Great Outdoors
- Generosity
- Charm
- Justice
- Morality
- Ethics
- Aspirations
- Higher Learning
- Open-mindedness
- Flirting
- The Intellect
- Wit
- Social Interactions
- Sharing Ideas
- Conversation

Main Characteristics

- Outgoing
- Idealistic
- Generous
- Confident
- Optimistic
- Risk-taker
- Jovial
- Independent
- Traveller
- Freedom-loving
- Broad-minded
- Blunt
- Impulsive
- Fearless
- Outdoorsy
- Higher Learner
- Fun
- Sociable
- Bold
- Gregarious
- Open-minded
- Honourable
- Reckless
- Impractical
- Sincere
- Direct
- Frank
- Reasonable
- Impatient
- Outspoken,
- Flirtatious
- Honest
- Flighty
- Philosophical
- Non-committal
- Cheerful
- Enthusiastic
- Endearing
- Friendly
- Clumsy
- Exaggerated
- Untidy
- Tactless
- Adventurous
- Charming

Ah, but the Sagittarius-influenced man or woman isn't just any horse: he's Silver and the Lone Ranger combined... Sagittarian types always know what's best for everybody, and they're not shy about saying so. They are the sheriff; we are the posse. (We should) gallop after our dauntless leader, who is absolutely certain where he's going even if it happens to be exactly opposite to where he thinks he's going to get. The beautiful self-assurance of the misaimed Sagittarian is a phenomenon which has to be experienced to be believed.

Charlotte MacLeod

To the Sagittarian, life is secretly a circus, and he's the clown, rolling and tumbling through purple hoops in a sky-blue suit... He curves his bow towards the sky. When he aims straight, he shoots higher than man can see - past the stars - to the place where all dreams are really born.

Linda Goodman

The eloquent Sagittarian finds the arrow of light illuminating the man or woman within. And then, under the fortunate rays of Jupiter, the lawgiver of the stars, the enlightened soul becomes a source of wisdom and inspiration to all, often holding a high office.

Patricia Crowther

The Centaur and Archer are both symbols of this gregarious, big-natured sign. Generous, reckless, adventurous, charming, honest, independent, optimistic and sociable are Sagittarius's most notable traits. The Archer is the quintessential freedom-seeker. Generous to a fault but reckless in equal measure, the Archer, like his opposite counterpart Gemini, is frivolous and careless when it comes to what he *should* do; he seeks always to do what he *wants* to do. The Sagittarian spirit is one of deep, unwavering optimism; even if he has been crushed by life's tragedies, this ever-philosophical sign will always invariably see the best in a person or a situation. The most likely to be a charming philanderer, he is also the most likely to have your back when the rest of the world has turned theirs, because he genuinely believes in you. Warm, open-minded, frank and tolerant, Sagittarius is one of the best dinner party guests of the zodiac. With his wit and sense of humour, he is flamboyant and larger than life in almost any situation, even those in which he doesn't feel he belongs; his mutable nature means he can wear any mask. With an innate way of making others feel welcome and included, he can be a formidable ally. Just don't try and pin him down, because if you try to tether an Archer's spirit, he will break free and you won't see this Centaur for dust as he rides off into the horizon.

Spiritual Sagittarius
Archetypal Universal Qualities
The Philosopher, Explorer, Wise Teacher, Traveller, Adventurer

What Sagittarius Refuses
To be dishonest or immoral, to be cynical, to commit, to be tied down, or to stop believing

What Sagittarius is an Authority On
Faith, Optimism, Honesty, Frankness, Ideals and Philosophy

The Main Realms Through Which Sagittarius Experiences Reality
Hope, Optimism, Abundance, Clarity, Expansion, Righteousness, Vision, The Higher Mind

How Sagittarius Loves
Adventurously, Playfully, Charmingly, Generously

Most Compatible With
Aries, Leo, Gemini

To Bring Out Personal Best of Character
Travel, especially to foreign places. Study a subject of interest in depth. Undertake adventure sports and activities. Enjoy the good life in moderation. Delve into different cultures and customs. Share philosophical ideas with like-minded others. Throw dinner parties and enjoy stimulating intellectual exchanges.

Spiritual Goals
To learn to stop fearing the loss of freedom. To take more responsibility. To use talents to guide and be an example to others. To be more tactful and sensitive towards others. To exercise more caution, consideration, and care in everything. To be more committed and less flighty.

CAPRICORN THE GOAT

Cardinal Earth, Negative, Feminine, Sensate
The Quiet Achiever
22 December - 19 January
Ruled by Saturn

KEY PHRASE ✦ "I Utilise"
GEMSTONES ✦ Garnet, Turquoise, Smoky Quartz, Jet
BODY & HEALTH ✦ Knees, Joints, Bones, Skin, Hair, Teeth, Gall Bladder
ASTROLOGICAL HOUSE ✦ Tenth

How Capricorn Emanates its Life Force / Energy

Methodically, Purposefully, Ambitiously, Dutifully

Is Concerned With

- Practicality
- Reality
- Accomplishment
- Hard Work
- Planning
- Order, Organisation
- Persistence
- Success
- Determination, Perseverance
- Status, Reputation
- Responsibility
- Achievement
- Overcoming Difficulties and Hardships
- Discipline
- Authority
- Dedication to Long-term Projects
- Austerity
- Wisdom
- Loyalty
- Sensitivity to Beauty
- Frugality
- Money
- Material Realm
- Duty
- Morals

Main Characteristics

- Responsible
- Dependable
- Steady
- Wise
- Ambitious
- Reliable
- Efficient
- Stern
- Loyal
- Traditional
- Authoritarian
- Persevering
- Cynical
- Rigid
- Constant
- Persistent
- Melancholic
- Brooding
- Cautious,
- Self-controlled
- Realistic
- Hard-working
- Conservative
- Uncompromising
- Assiduous
- Industrious
- Respectful
- Cool
- Solid
- Inhibited
- Serious
- Shrewd
- Strict
- Self-disciplined
- Measured
- Consistent
- Devoted
- Dedicated
- Gloomy
- Avaricious
- Dignified
- Composed
- Sensual
- Conscientious

He seldom stumbles. His eyes aren't fastened on the stars. He keeps his gaze fastened ahead, and his feet firmly planted on the ground. Jealousy, passion, impulse, anger, frivolity, waste, laziness, carelessness - all are obstacles. Let others trip and fall over them. Not Capricorn.

Linda Goodman

The (Capricornian) soul moves on through life, knowing, with an inner certainty, that the best is yet to come; that Saturn will bring all the rewards in the years of maturity. And, hidden within the deep wells of the spirit, the light, which has long been guarded, will finally be displayed for all to see. The Priest-Initiate comes into his own and becomes the focus of power, love and wisdom. (For) this sign is known as the Gate of the Gods and Capricornus symbolises consolidation.

Patricia Crowther

Capricorn is the sign of the Goat, a lone, sturdy, sure-footed climber of mountains that strives to - and almost always does ~ reach the highest peaks. Ambitious, serious, wise, industrious, materialistic, responsible, reserved and conservative are Capricorn's most notable traits. Being a solid earth sign, this sign is practical, determined and pragmatic, but can lack spontaneity, passion and warmth at times, and can be ruthless in her striving to reach the top in any area of life. Hard-working and disciplined, Capricorn loves to be in control of all her endeavours and is easily seduced and tempted by lofty career ideals. The Goat is shrewd and intelligent, making her a great partner in business, although she ultimately prefers to work alone and to her own far-reaching but rigid personal and professional standards. Responsibility is a big thing for the traditional and authoritarian Goat's spirit, and she takes her roles seriously, rarely shunning her duties. Capricorn is cautious, calm and collected in even the most turbulent of situations, and is strong and dependable in all manner of crisis. A cool but sensuous lover, steadfast and trustworthy friend, and unerring steady climber to the top of life's mountaintops, Capricorn is the zodiac's solid 'rock', never faltering in her obligations or deviating from her true path, forever maintaining her focus on the end result - which, without hesitation nor fail, she reaches every single time.

Spiritual Capricorn
Archetypal Universal Qualities
The Purposeful One, Taskmaster, Mountain Climber, Father, Wise Sage

What Capricorn Refuses
To be frivolous or undisciplined, to do things the easy way, or to neglect duty

What Capricorn is an Authority On
Organisation, Order, Duty, Devotion, Perseverance, Ambition, Achievement, Success

The Main Realms Through Which Capricorn Experiences Reality
Status, Structure, Ascension, Discipline, Boundaries, Purpose, Measurement

How Capricorn Loves
Cautiously, Devotedly, Dutifully, Lovingly, Sensually

Most Compatible With
Taurus, Virgo, Cancer

To Bring Out Personal Best of Character
Eat out in expensive, classy restaurants. Collect antiques. Release and share feelings. Regularly spend time in nature. Live in as natural surroundings as possible. Help others to realise their ambitions. Use your innate wisdom to guide and encourage others. Climb life's highest mountains and help others up.

Spiritual Goals
To learn to understand the feelings and needs of others better. To stop stepping on toes to reach the top. To sacrifice more discriminately. To not put money and material ambitions ahead of personal relationships. To develop more warmth and less cynicism. To fear less and live more. To develop natural ability to lead, mentor and help others achieve their goals.

AQUARIUS THE WATER BEARER

Fixed Air, Masculine, Positive, Thinking
The Eccentric Genius
20 January - 18 February
Ruled by Uranus

KEY PHRASE ✦ "I Know"

GEMSTONES ✦ Amethyst, Garnet, Aquamarine

BODY & HEALTH ✦ Calves, Ankles, Circulation, Spinal Cord, Nervous System

ASTROLOGICAL HOUSE ✦ Eleventh

How Aquarius Emanates its Life Force / Energy
Originally, Objectively, Unconventionally, Gregariously

Is Concerned With

- Experimentation
- Scientific Thinking
- Objectivity
- Friendship
- Brotherhood
- Humanity
- Kindness
- Humaneness
- Originality
- Mystery, Intrigues, Enigmas
- Magic
- Genius
- Eccentricity
- Independence
- Freedom
- Politics
- Creative Arts
- Detachment
- Electricity
- Magnetism
- Idealism
- Logic
- Telecommunications
- Intellect
- Rationality
- Electricity
- Metaphysics

Main Characteristics

- Original
- Unpredictable
- Unusual
- Visionary
- Objective
- Bohemian
- Idealistic
- Friendly
- Inventive
- Futuristic
- Progressive
- Detached
- Independent
- Tolerant
- Innovative
- Sociable
- People-oriented
- Honest
- Impersonal
- Eccentric
- Rebellious
- Reforming
- Liberal
- Democratic
- Altruistic
- Unconventional
- Unstable
- Erratic
- Distant
- Paradoxical
- Perverse
- Intellectual
- Contrary
- Quick
- Aloof
- Experimental
- New Age
- Mental
- Unorthodox
- Intuitive
- Brilliant
- Electric
- Scientific
- Different
- Quirky
- Egalitarian
- Self-willed
- Cool-headed
- Rational
- Unique

Lots of people like rainbows. Children makes wishes on them, artists paint them, dreamers chase them, but the Aquarian is ahead of everybody. He lives on one...

Linda Goodman

Aquarius is a Fixed Air sign, notorious for its quality of detachment from personal feelings, although emotionally involved with ideas, usually dedicated to perfecting something, or bringing intuitions of a cosmic plan or Divine order far removed from the stuff of human life.

Melanie Reinhart

Aquarius is the water carrier, and the astrological motif is of a man pouring water into a stream from a flask. The 'typical' Aquarian is quiet, shy, patient, intuitive, and confident that truth will prevail.

Nevill Drury

Aquarius is the sign of the Water Bearer, a man who pours the water of knowledge from his urn to benefit all of humankind. Friendly, inventive, detached, future-oriented, unconventional, rebellious, eccentric, aloof, idealistic and humanitarian are Aquarius's most notable traits. Being an intellectual air sign, this is a thinking rather than feeling character, and he possesses a scientific and forward-thinking mind which he often puts to use for the advantage of all to great effect. Group-oriented but impersonal, Aquarius is often hard to pin down due to his aloof, cool and contrary nature. The Water Bearer is a paradoxical sign, with a great love of humankind but an aversion to close personal relationships; he is also broad-minded and far-sighted but tends to hide his intuitive truths and prophecies (which almost always come true) under a veil of contradiction, and frequently and perversely rebels for its own sake. Humanitarian and social causes are a big thing for the progressive Water Bearer's spirit, and he will always fight for the underdog and those he feels are treated unfairly. Aquarius is futuristic, unorthodox, honest and truth-seeking, with a refreshing lack of ego but much conviction invested in his many ideals. An independent lover, loyal friend and freedom-seeker at all costs, Aquarius is the offbeat and wayward social crusader of the zodiac, whose lack of personal warmth is more than made up for by his gregarious, affable nature and charitable and original contributions to all his fellow terrestrial inhabitants.

Spiritual Aquarius

Archetypal Universal Qualities
The Humanitarian, Rebel, Reformer, Innovator, Crusader, Defender of the Underdog, Global One

What Aquarius Refuses
To be a follower, ordinary or conventional

What Aquarius is an Authority On
Truth, Innovation, Originality, Genius, Humanity, Futuristic Thinking, Challenging the Status Quo

The Main Realms Through Which Aquarius Experiences Reality
Freedom, Independence, Truth, Invention, Social Reform, the Intellect

How Aquarius Loves
Good-naturedly, Loyally, Detachedly, Idealistically, with Friendship

Most Compatible With
Gemini, Libra, Leo

To Bring Out Personal Best of Character
Travel to offbeat places and immerse the self in different cultures. Study foreign languages and diverse subjects. Share scientific, genius, insightful thinking with others. Discover a cure for an incurable disease. Buy and use high-tech gadgets. Express true individuality and shine!

Spiritual Goals
To shine brighter by unleashing talents. To learn to commit and see that it ultimately leads to freedom. To be more discriminate in social crusades. To develop greater self-confidence. To be more consistent and less contrary. To rein in rebellion for the sake of it.

PISCES THE FISH

Mutable Water, Negative, Feminine, Feeling
The Whimsical Daydreamer
19 February - 20 March
Ruled by Neptune

KEY PHRASE ✦ "I Believe"

GEMSTONES ✦ Amethyst, Turquoise, Aquamarine, Bloodstone

BODY & HEALTH ✦ Feet, Lymphatic System, Nervous Digestion, Immune System, Liver, Gastro-abdominal System

ASTROLOGICAL HOUSE ✦ Twelfth

How Pisces Emanates its Life Force / Energy
Dreamily, Passively, Kindly, Softly, Sensitively

Is Concerned With

- Compassion
- Sympathy
- Altruism
- Love, Romance
- Whims, Fairytales, Dreams
- Psychic Realm
- Otherworlds, Mysteries
- Precognition, Sixth Sense, the Unseen
- Illusions, Magic, Fantasy
- Make-believe
- Art, Film, Drama, Music, Poetry, Dance, Prose
- Memory
- Intuition, Impressions
- Unusual Talent
- Sensitivity
- Humour
- Satire
- Secrets
- Retreat, Withdrawal
- Rose-coloured Perspectives

Main Characteristics

- Whimsical
- Endearing
- Sensitive
- Imaginative
- Romantic
- Sacrificing
- Mystical
- Trusting
- Emotional
- Poetic
- Understanding
- Sympathetic
- Impressionable
- Selfless
- Weak-willed
- Artistic
- Withdrawing
- Escapist
- Delusional
- Timid
- Introverted
- Vague
- Prone to Addictions
- Deceptive
- Spiritual
- Gullible
- Indecisive
- Perceptive
- Compassionate
- Daydreamer
- Unassuming
- Unreliable
- Helpless
- Vulnerable
- Impractical
- Idealistic
- Confused
- Disorganised
- Retiring
- Charitable
- Saviour
- Psychic
- Insightful

> He is stronger than he thinks and wiser than he knows, but Neptune guards this secret until he discovers it for himself.
> **Linda Goodman**

> The evolved soul in Pisces has inwardly turned away from the material world … More and more, it perceives the land of youth from whence it came, and the experiences hitherto gained are refined in this sign, so that only the essence remains.
> **Patricia Crowther**

Pisces is the sign of the Fish, two fish swimming in opposite directions but still connected by a cord. Sympathetic, compassionate, caring, spiritual, gullible, escapist, psychic, kind, dreamy and artistic are Pisces's most notable traits. Being a sensitive and feeling water sign, this sign feels her way through life guided by her instincts and well-developed intuition, but being the chameleon of the zodiac, she will often merge into whatever situation she finds herself in, regardless of reason. Gentle and impressionable, Pisces is easily swayed and her trusting and weak-willed nature can make her easy prey to undesirable circumstances, elements, or people. The Fish is a self-sacrificing sign who will always put others before herself, ever offering a shoulder to cry on, and others frequently call upon her sympathetic and insightful nature. Escapism is a big thing for the Piscean spirit; she will swiftly retreat into a world of inner fantasy and delusion if the real world becomes too much to bear, making her prone to addictions which can - and do - often bring about her self-undoing. Pisces is poetic, mystical and spiritual, with a love of peaceful surroundings and pleasant company. A selfless and romantic lover, understanding friend and imaginative artist, Pisces is the empathetic healer of the zodiac, jumping in feet first, swimming in whichever direction life takes her and forever acting on whims.

Spiritual Pisces
Archetypal Universal Qualities
The Compassionate One, Mystic, Dreamer, Psychic

What Pisces Refuses
To stop dreaming, to be hemmed in, to shatter an illusion, or to face reality

What Pisces is an Authority On
Dreams, Fantasy, Empathy, Escapism, Spirituality, Mysteries, Psychic Insights, Imagination

The Main Realms Through Which Pisces Experiences Reality
Dreamworlds, Imagination, Intuition, Collectivity, Forgiveness, Spirit

How Pisces Loves
Romantically, Dreamily, Idealistically, Spiritually, Imaginatively

Most Compatible With
Cancer, Scorpio, Virgo

To Bring Out Personal Best of Character
Meditate. Tap into creative potential; create works of art. Go on a spiritual retreat. Take a ghost tour. Learn to read the Tarot and other spiritual disciplines. Capitalise upon psychic and intuitive abilities. Develop greater self-confidence. Regularly spend time or live near the ocean.

Spiritual Goals
To learn the meaning of sacrifice without loss of self. To learn boundaries and tap into more authentic inner self. To avoid the tendency to 'drift' and miss opportunities through aimlessness. Find a creative purpose and live it.

THE CONSTELLATIONS

The signs of the zodiac are the twelve symbolic features that ancient people imagined while observing the skies. They saw shapes, patterns, faces, and natural and supernatural beings in the stars, from which they established, over centuries, a kind of celestial hierarchy and system based upon these observations. Groupings of stars became constellations, and twelve of these constellations make up the zodiac, a Greek word meaning 'circle of animals', that we know today.

Star constellations are not really self-contained groups but are particularly bright stars that give the appearance of being close together, forming distinctive patterns. These are the patterns that over the ages have been identified as animals, deities, heroes, and mythological figures. But the zodiac didn't necessarily come into being because certain constellations *looked* like animals or figures; most were designed to show the kind of cosmic energy operating at various times of the year. Aries's symbol the ram, for example, was chosen in order to depict the Divine mind actually pushing life into manifestation, which is a principle of Aries, the powerful, initiating, driving force of the zodiac. The Bull was chosen for Taurus and the second period of the astrological year, when the Ram's initial impetus manifests on the material plane, Bulls being representative of strength, fertility, tangibility, and steady charge. The sign of Gemini, the Twins, brings male and female energies together to demonstrate their intellectual life-giving capacities (the Twins were usually shown as two males but most modern astrologers depict them as male and female, to accentuate the inherent dual-natured essence of the sign).

Essentially, the stars are the living past. We receive their light long after it has left the star itself and so they are a good focus for escaping from the parameters of time. Their stellar influence is analogous with the aura, the biopsychical energy field surrounding humans, animals, plants, crystals and even places. These individual energy systems interact with the energy waves emanated by other people, and even the cosmic rays emitted by planetary bodies, for psychic energies are not limited by time or distance.

ARIES CONSTELLATION

The Aries constellation is situated in the northern celestial hemisphere near the Pleiades, between the constellations of Pisces and Taurus. This cluster of stars we know as Aries the Ram, is a small and unremarkable constellation, comprising three primary stars which form the Ram's horns. To the naked eye, it is little more than these three prominent stars; the triangle of stars forming its horns and nose, and its hindquarters, appear to merge with the rear portion of its neighbour Taurus.

It is found in the autumn (fall) sky, nearby the great square of Pegasus, the winged horse. The brightest of these three very bright stars is known as Hamal, or the sheep, more poetically described in the Akkadian language as 'Dilkur', the 'dawn proclaimer'.

The Chinese have a tradition giving the greatest prominence to Aries from the fact that it was believed to have occupied the centre of the heavens at the Creation of the World, a belief that was also held by the Babylonians.

TAURUS CONSTELLATION

The Taurus constellation is quite clearly marked, with a V-shape of stars known as Hyades representing the Bull's face. The most noticeable feature of this V is a large reddish star which is clearly visible to the naked eye and is often referred to as the 'Eye of the Bull'.

This is a large and significant constellation, containing two spectacular star clusters. Although the starry Bull's head component only has his frontal segments, the constellation of Taurus is rich in stellar components: a group of hot, bright stars surrounded by an ethereal blue glow of light, can be found in this cluster. The Seven Sisters (the Pleides) and Hyades, seven mythological maiden daughters, lie within this constellation also.

The Bull's horns are long and extend quite far from its head; near the southern horn is the lovely Crab Nebula, a wondrous cloud of stardust and fragments that are remnants of a star which exploded hundreds of years ago.

GEMINI CONSTELLATION

The cluster of stars we know as Gemini the Twins are associated with the mythological pair Castor and Pollux, one of which has its root meaning 'pure', the other 'polluted'. Gemmation, linked with the name of this sign, refers to propagation by budding, emphasising the connection of Gemini with all young life.

The Twins are usually depicted as holding hands or bound together by each other's arms, and are most easily seen in the April sky. They are easy to recognise due to their position behind the constellation of Orion.

The Gemini constellation has a pair of bright stars, both of magnitude 1, which are very close together in the sky. These two stars mark the Twins' heads, with one more orange and the other more northerly. The two great stars which bear the names of Castor and Pollux, are situated not more than five degrees from each other and were long known as the sole representatives of the entire constellation. But over time many more stars were added and the brothers 'grew'. Castor is really two very closely placed white stars which revolve around each other, resulting in a 'binary system' effect, the name given by astronomers to the phenomenon of two stars revolving together around a common centre of gravity.

CANCER CONSTELLATION

The cluster of stars we know as Cancer the Crab is a small, faint constellation, but both its shape and its glyph contain a representation of the crab's claws. It contains Sirius, one of the brightest stars in the zodiac, in its constellation. It also contains a cluster of stars known as the 'Praesaepe', the manger or crib. Aside from Praesaepe, the Crab is composed of only five or six stars.

It is best seen during the evenings of early (northern hemisphere) spring when it is almost directly overhead.

LEO CONSTELLATION

The cluster of stars we know as Leo the Lion, are bright and form a shape vaguely resembling an animal like a lion, for Northern Hemisphere viewers - in the Southern Hemisphere it is seen upside down. The Lion's mane is said to be featured in the pattern of stars, and in Leo's glyph.

Leo contains a very bright star called Regulus (Latin for 'little king'), so named by Copernicus, also known as the Heart of the Lion, which sits right on the ecliptic, and which is very significant astrologically. Because it is so bright and luminous, Regulus is often mistaken for a planet.

An extremely bright and easily identifiable constellation, the most recognisable feature of the constellation is his 'mane', which looks like a large question mark or huge sickle, at which the base is Regulus, the lion's heart. Often depicted in a crouching position, as if preparing to leap, the body of the Lion forms a rectangle of less prominent but still noticeable stars, and culminates in the triangle of the Lion's hindquarters. The constellation's 'tail' is long and curved, the tip of which is a blue star known as Denebola.

The Leo constellation can be spotted in the sky by first locating the Big Dipper, for Leo's head is found just under its giant ladle.

VIRGO CONSTELLATION

The cluster of stars we know as Virgo is the second largest constellation, after Hydra the Water Snake. It is a disappointing naked eye constellation, but of great interest to modern astronomers because it contains a large number of relatively close galaxies, extending into a neighbouring star cluster.

The Virgo constellation has one bright star, Spica, which is often mistaken for a planet; Spica is the shaft of wheat the Virgin holds in her hand, and actually one of the brightest stars in the sky. Within the boundary of her vast (46 degrees long) body, reside over 500 nebulas. As the goddess of the harvest, she symbolises this by being situated in a very bountiful area of the heavens.

Usually depicted in an angelic form with her two wings extending out into space, the Virgo constellation encapsulates the fecundity and fruitfulness of the female principle.

LIBRA CONSTELLATION

The cluster of stars we know as Libra the Scales, the only constellation not named after a living thing, has no truly bright stars, and in ancient times was not distinguished as a separate constellation, its two brightest stars belonging to the neighbouring constellation of Scorpius, as the claws of the Scorpion*.

Libra is the smallest of the constellations, and is an unremarkable grouping, but is easily found by its relative position to its more noteworthy neighbours: the luminous Scorpio and extensive, ethereal Virgo.

Libra contains the northern and southern claws, two bright stars that were once part of Scorpius.

SCORPIO CONSTELLATION

One of the most easily distinguishable constellations, composed of notably bright and large stars, Scorpio is among the largest of the twelve constellations. The cluster of stars we know as Scorpius, or Scorpio to astrologers, is aptly named, for its brightest stars resemble a Scorpion poised to inflict its sting.

Scorpius is most easily seen in the Southern Hemisphere, being directly overhead Sydney at around 10 p.m. in July. In the more northerly latitudes only some of its body can be seen, for it is best observed in southern United States, the Caribbean Islands and Mexico.

At its heart, Scorpius contains a bright red star called Antares, which lies at the approximate centre of the enormous Cloud Nebula in Scorpio. Although Scorpius contains many bright stars, this brightest one, Antares, also called the Heart of the Scorpion, is distinctly reddish. The beauty of this constellation is increased by virtue of the fact that it lies in a part of the Milky Way which is thick with fainter stars.

Scorpio is known for its secrecy, and this characteristic seems to correspond with only the tip of its fore claws emerging above the ecliptic, the circle which defines the boundaries of the zodiac. The rest of the Scorpion's body and long, arched tail is 'hidden' (although visible) against the backdrop of the Milky Way's multitude of stars.

SAGITTARIUS CONSTELLATION

The Sagittarius constellation is composed of eight bright but otherwise unremarkable stars, divided into two groups: the Milk Dipper, representing the Centaur's body and the bow, and an additional star, Al-Nasl, which is the head of the arrow. The Centaur-Archer's arrow is aimed at Antares, the red heart of the Scorpion, his neighbour.

This cluster of stars is best seen in the Southern Hemisphere, because here the Milky Way is at its most impressive. Rising in the east after Scorpius, Sagittarius the Archer, a Centaur with his bow drawn, has his arrow pointing towards Scorpio's constellation. When we look at Sagittarius, we are looking towards the centre of our galaxy, so the sky here is thick with nebulae, stars, and star clusters.

Sagittarius lies in the centre of the Milky Way, and although the actual constellation is not outstanding from an astronomical point of view, its region in space is. Within the Archer's range is the huge Sagittarius stellar cloud, which is composed of millions of 'suns' and is easily seen with the naked eye for it is the Milky Way's brightest 'cloud'.

Enormous nebulas and dark masses of cosmic dust that are so dense they obscure the space beyond them, can also be found here. Sagittarius also contains a globular star cluster which contains at least 50,000 stars (but to the naked eye appears as one large bright star) that are each probably greater in size than our own Sun.

CAPRICORN CONSTELLATION

The cluster of stars we know as Capricornus, the Sea-Goat, is dim, its only discernible pattern that of a rough, faint triangle. After its polar opposite, Cancer, Capricorn is the most inconspicuous constellation of the zodiac. However, it contains two objects of astronomical interest. The first is a global cluster, which can be viewed through a good pair of binoculars; the second, a phenomenon called the Capricornids, consists of a shower of long, bright, slow-moving meteors which occurs each year in late July.

Plato's followers called this constellation the Gate of the Gods, through which the soul ascended to heaven. In oriental philosophy it was known as the Southern Gate of the Sun, while the Latin poets named it the Rain-bringing One.

AQUARIUS CONSTELLATION

The cluster of stars we know as Aquarius the Water Bearer, is, like Capricorn, a large, faint and unremarkable constellation, and its shape is hard to relate to its name, although it has been said to vaguely resemble the shape of a water urn.

It is likely that its name was derived from ancient times when heavy rains and floods tended to occur in the Northern Hemisphere when the Sun was located in this sign.

PISCES CONSTELLATION

The cluster of stars we know as Pisces can only be seen in a very dark sky, and is another unremarkable and faint constellation. Two fish are supposedly represented in this group of stars, joined by a thick line of dim stars, reminiscent of the cord connecting the two creatures.

The ecliptic and the celestial equator intersect within this constellation and in Virgo (Pisces' opposite sign).

THE ZODIAC SYMBOLS

Astrology uses symbols or 'glyphs' to represent the planets and signs. The glyph is made up of shapes representing the energy and physical matter of which the Universe is composed, and how these shapes are used in each symbol provide hints as to the properties of the sign or planet that reigns over it.

The ancient view was that there were five elements: Fire, Water, Air, Earth and Ether* (or Spirit). Ether is invisible energy, while the four tangible elements are known as 'matter'.

Ether, as pure energy, cannot be influenced by any of the physical/matter elements, although it surrounds them and indeed fuels them. The Greek philosopher and scientist Aristotle regarded this idea as a circle (Ether/Spirit) with a cross (matter) in the centre. This glyph is used in astrology as a symbol for Earth, and the cycle of life. All the symbols used in astrology represent the relationship between energy and the more material elements.

'All of the elements of Creation, Fire, Earth, Air and Water, originated from the Etheric Principle, or the element of Spirit. Spirit is often called the fifth power, but in actuality it is the first power. The element of Spirit is supreme, ultimate and inconceivable. Spirit is spaceless and timeless. Many occultists refer to it as the 'unmanifest Universe'.

ARIES SYMBOL ♈

In its most simplistic interpretation, the symbol of Aries resembles a Ram's horns, but it could be interpreted in other ways as well. From a physical standpoint, it could represent the eyebrows and nose, two parts of the body under the governance of Aries.

The glyph consists of a vertical line, indicating a directed, upward and outward gushing forth of energy, which so epitomises the nature of this sign. Two curved lines sprout outwards from the top; all curved lines, whether half or complete circles, are considered emotionally driven and responsive.

The Aries glyph suggests a fountain gushing up from some hidden spring (as indeed the entry of the Sun into Aries heralds the beginning of spring in the northern hemisphere, when nature 'springs' to life). It also represents the shooting forth of plant life and, by extension, the appearance of new forms on every level in response to some hidden Creative Force.

Aries's animal the Ram unquestioningly assumes leadership of his flock and dashes in head down (Aries rules the head) when danger threatens. The lamb is traditionally the animal of sacrifice but the entry of the Sun into the first degree of Aries, when the sign is still young, symbolises the sacrifice of Spirit as it transforms into incarnation (from its preceding sign Pisces), into the form of matter.

TAURUS SYMBOL ♉

The glyph of Taurus depicts the face and horns of the Bull, in essence the Bull's head. It clearly shows the circle of Ether with curved 'horns'. This symbol represents the unlimited potentiality (always signified by an empty circle) of the feminine principle in the Universe (shown by the crescent, here lying on its back and exalted over the circle to denote the predominance of receptivity and instinct). The symbol of the Bull, an animal which can either plough the earth or goaded into more rigorous activity, represents the fertility of nature and the power of natural resources.

This symbol also illustrates the fecundity of Taurus, for it is representative of the fertile Full Moon with a crescent Moon attached, the Moon having celestial maternal associations and representing the principles of new growth and fertility. The semi-circle on top of the circle of Spirit may also symbolise Taurus being a receptacle for material wealth and abundance; the upturned 'cup' is open, awaiting gold in all its forms to be poured in and received.

'Taurus' is a Roman word that derived from the Greek *tau*. *Tau* (a prototype of our T) was a pictogram for sexual intercourse, the short bar on top representing the female vulva, and the longer bar, the male phallus, together suggestive of life's roots and continuity.

GEMINI SYMBOL ♊

Gemini's glyph looks like the Roman numeral two (II).. It represents two pillars of wisdom, dual lines of intellect or mentality. There are no curves, meaning it is detached and cerebral. The horizontal line is considered concrete or physical when at the bottom of the glyph, abstract or metaphysical when at the top, therefore Gemini combines these two principles.

The vertical lines symbolise destiny or intellect, and represent detachment, objectivity and the unemotional realm; in fact, because this glyph consists entirely of straight lines, it contains no emotional elements, which are essentially indicated by rounded and circular strokes.

Consisting of these two horizontal and two parallel lines linked together by two narrower vertical and parallel lines, they also represent the Twins of the zodiac, corresponding to the stars in Gemini's constellation, Castor and Pollux.

Although essentially implicit of objectivity, Gemini's glyph represents the duality of existence and the possibility of making a choice between good and evil through knowledge arising from the union of spirit and matter. The symbol of the Twins also conveys this same idea of duality. In its highest form, Gemini embodies the principle of the joining together of the rational mind and greater creativity through wise, discerning application.

CANCER SYMBOL ♋

The glyph for Cancer, which consists of two circles and two curved lines, is a typical Ether-themed glyph. The half-circle, or crescent, depicts the soul force or consciousness. This is a combination of the Solar circle and the Lunar crescent. All curved lines, whether half or complete circles, are considered emotional and responsive. These two inverted and intertwined loops resemble the breasts, the spiral of shells, or the Crab's claws. This glyph also brings to mind the symbol of the Chinese yin and yang.

Cancer's glyph shows the same duality as its preceding sign, Gemini, in its passive form, shown by the horizontal lines, but imbued with a new potentiality, shown by the small added circles, giving the idea of two seeds, from the combination of which a mature organism can grow.

The symbol of the Crab, whose hard shell protects its soft interior and whose tenacious grip is like the hold of the emotional life upon humans, aptly sums up the characteristics of this sign.

LEO SYMBOL ♋

The glyph of Leo is a little more obscure than those of the previous four signs before it. It represents the serpent power (creative force) of the body in its coiled (latent) form. The lion is the undisputed king in his own sphere and is noted for his great strength and ferocity when roused, as difficult to cope with as the human passions when unrestrained. The full heat of the Sun˚ in Leo ripens the corn for harvest in Virgo, encapsulating this symbol's associations with latency.

Leo's symbol is also represented by a kind of distorted hook, but in many interpretations is said to be a Lion's tail or a Lion's mane.

˚In the Northern Hemisphere's summer.

VIRGO SYMBOL ♍

The glyph of Virgo is based upon the Hebrew letter 'Mem' signifying the female principle with an added hook apparently based on the Phoenician symbol for a fish, the symbol used by the early Christians for Jesus, hinting at the inexplicable mystery of the 'virgin' birth of Jesus. Through purity and dedication, Virgo's energy provides the necessary conditions for the birth of the 'Messiah' that becomes embodied in the human form.

The symbol of this sign, a Virgin, is often depicted holding a sheaf of corn, a staple food produced from the Earth, the harvest gathered at summer's end. It is indeed the symbol of the end of the harvest and is reminiscent of the architecture of ancient grain stores.

The three straight lines can be interpreted in a couple of ways. Firstly, they are symbolic of the coils of energy latent in Virgo's essence. They seem held back from release into their full expression by the closed circle, which could represent a wall or a closed door. The three lines also represent three levels of consciousness. The third line of the super-conscious curves slightly upward, in an outpouring motion, but is held back by the last line that turns completely inwards and ends below the horizon, signifying Virgo's links with introversion, materialism and Earthly matters.

In astrological symbology, the vertical line is designated as the line of destiny or intellect. It is detached, objective and unemotional, traits that Virgo is often purported to possess. A further interpretation could be the pure, untouched female genitalia, the coils being the loops of the ovaries and uterus, the circle the intact hymen of the Virgin. And lastly, given that Virgo rules the intestines, these twisting and twirling lines could be a symbol of the tubes that make up the intestines.

LIBRA SYMBOL ♎

The glyph of Libra represents the setting Sun, showing that the essence of being is projected into the world of the 'not-self' (or other). It's also symbolic of a pair of scales; Libra is Latin for a pound, suggesting that the self is to be weighed against the not-self and some kind of balance and equilibrium is struck between the objective and subjective consciousnesses. In this symbol, we see a 'sun' about to sink below the horizon, symbolising the in-drawing of the life forces after the activity of spring and high summer. Evocative of the declining Sun on the horizon, this links in with Libra's coinciding with the autumn Equinox and the beginning of shorter days.

Libra's glyph also hints at the sign's dualism. There are three recognised dual signs: Gemini, Sagittarius and Pisces. But Libra is also endowed with a certain duality and indeed its symbol illustrates its two polarising extremes, as described previously. The symbol's upper line illustrates the higher nature of Libra, which is primarily influenced by the elevated powers of intellect: the objective state of mind, which is the impartial aspect of the Libran character that is not attached to form or matter but is solely interested in the flow of ideas. But the lower part of the glyph represents matter, and so it reveals this struggle with the dualism inherent in our very human natures; the essence of Libra, therefore, is to teach others as well as himself, and how to balance the two opposing urges or forces within himself, with the condition of his Earthly affairs.

It has also been said that Libra's glyph could depict a bird, its outstretched wings parallel with the horizontal plane of the Earth but never quite touching it.

The symbol of Libra, represented by these two parallel and horizontal lines, the top one being slightly curved upwards in its centre, is usually interpreted to be the two pans and central arm of a pair of scales. The lower line symbolises the physical, while the upper represents the metaphysical, revealing again, the inherent dual nature of the Libran spirit.

SCORPIO SYMBOL ♏

Scorpio is symbolised by the tail of the Scorpion. Its three lines represent three levels of consciousness: the first representing the lower mind, the second the higher mind, and the third the superconscious mind. The three lines could also be interpreted to symbolise the coils of the serpent, a creature closely associated with Scorpio.

The end stroke ends with a barb and arrow, which seem to hold it back and imbue it with Earthly desire.

Scorpio's glyph depicts the sting in the tail, but can also be seen as phallic. This symbol is very similar to that of Virgo, being based on the same Hebrew letter, Mem, to which is added a barb, reminding us of the sting in the Scorpion's tail. This barb may be regarded as Cupid's dart, emphasising the lure of the senses; the barb-arrow also prominently features in Mars's symbol, Scorpio's planetary ruler.

SAGITTARIUS SYMBOL ♐

The glyph of Sagittarius is essentially the arrow propelled from the bow of the centaur that symbolises Sagittarius, a mythical being, half man, half horse.

The Arrow symbolises upward and outward motion, a fire sign quality, and aspiration, which when correctly directed, can lead one to his ultimate goal.

The lower part of the shaft connotes the animal nature of this symbol, likened to the Centaur; the intersecting line dividing the shaft may indicate a certain duality or indecisiveness as to how or where to aim one's greatest physical and mental powers.

CAPRICORN SYMBOL ♑

Capricorn is the only zodiac glyph to incorporate the straight line, crescent *and* circle, endowing it with the significance of all three principles. This glyph suggests the curve of the goat's horns and is said to represent the serpent power of the body aroused.

The name 'Capricorn' comes from the Latin *caper* ('goat') and *cornu* ('horn'). In times past, horns were symbols of royalty, power and strength, as well as fertility and abundance (the cornucopia, which is likewise linked with Capricorn, the 'copious horn' or horn of plenty, also symbolises prosperity, plenitude and growth).

The symbol of the Mountain Goat with the dolphin's tail shown in many images of this sign, illustrates that the destiny of Capricorn is to rise to perfection through experience on all levels, from the lowest depths of the sea to the heights of the mountain, where the sure-footed goat comes into his own, carrying himself with sturdy independence and living off very little.

The stylised curve of the mythical Sea-Goat, combined with the line of intellect symbolises the realm of realism and matter which has the potential to rise, and at its highest level, when it reaches self-actualisation, forms the circle of spirit.

The symbol of Capricorn could also be interpreted as a waterfall, which cascades down from the top of the mountain. But ultimately it is represented by two variations of the same animal: the Mountain-Goat and the Sea-Goat˚, its glyph being more symbolic of the Sea-Goat as it implies a curving fishtail.

˚*The source of the Sea-Goat is the Babylonian God Ea, a prominent god of the Assyro-Babylonian pantheon. Ea was the ruler of the waters and his name means 'House of the Water', but this divinity is not to be confused with the sea, as his sphere of influence covered the springs and great rivers, and expanses of fresh water. In Sumer, Ea was known as Enki, Lord of the Earth, and held in awe as a deity of supreme wisdom. His was the gift of prophesy and magical incantations, and he was thus invoked as an oracle, manifesting through a shaman or priest. In ancient Babylon, this god of water was known as the 'Lord of Wisdom', the patron of magic, arts and crafts, and the creator of people. Another of his titles was that of Lord of the Sacred Eye, most likely referring to the Third Eye, which gives clear sight. Overall, Ea had the gifts of prophecy and divination, and was often represented as having the body and head of a goat and the tail of a fish.*

AQUARIUS SYMBOL ♒

The image of Aquarius is that of a Water Bearer pouring forth the waters of knowledge and consciousness onto humanity. However, these flowing waters are often mistakenly linked with the Water element, leading many to consider Aquarius a Water sign, when it is in fact an Air sign and indeed aligns much more closely with Air's vast intellectual undercurrents. Furthermore, the glyph for Aquarius is two waves, one on top of the other, and this was the Egyptian hieroglyphic for water. With all the obvious references to liquid ('Aquarius' itself was derived from the Latin aqua = water), it is little wonder that Aquarius is often mistaken for a Water sign.

The meaning of Aquarius is intertwined with the concept of a divine substance which nourishes all life, this substance being variously described as the waters of life, or a life-giving liquid. The esoteric significance of its meaning and symbol relates to the fluids that the Man in the image distributes from his urn, in that they are actually the waters of consciousness, or knowledge, which are related to the mind (the Air element) that he is pouring from his vessel, and not related to 'gushing forth' of feelings and emotions (the Water element). This consciousness embraces the concept that all humans are brothers (and sisters), a concept which can only be felt intuitively, and it is this powerfully intuitive aspect of mind that is embodied by the intellectually based Air sign of Aquarius. The water from his urn is flowing, swarming with ideas that can be beneficially useful for humanity, brother- and sisterhood.

One modern interpretation is that because Aquarius rules electricity, then its glyph should be interpreted as electrical waves rather than as liquid.

The glyph does not represent a still pool, it depicts waves rippling over water, and it is the winds, or air, which cause the waves to ripple; the Aquarian symbol is therefore suggestive of air currents creating the motion, indicating that Aquarius is indeed a sign of Air and movement, the 'mover' and disseminator of knowledge, the teacher, the inspirational visionary. Being strongly connected with communication, electrical charges, and the transmission of information through the activity of brain waves, for example, it seems valid that the Aquarian symbol represents all communication functioning through air currents and electrical impulses - again, symbolised by the two waves.

PISCES SYMBOL ♓

Pisces is often regarded as the most misunderstood sign of the zodiac, and it certainly merits this appellation, for this sign embodies unique and complex esoteric principles.

The glyph, or symbol, for Pisces is composed of two semicircles, resembling crescent Moons, with a straight line dissecting them horizontally through the centre. One of these arcs represents the finite consciousness of Man, while the other stands for the infinite consciousness of the Universe, or cosmic consciousness. The centre line is our Earth - said to be that point in the Grand Plan where the spiritual and the material realms unite. The two semi-circles could also be interpreted as representing the two fish˚, one facing down towards deep waters and the other facing up towards the water's surface.

This symbolism reflects the inherent dualism of the Fish: the urge to connect itself with the invisible forces of the Soul struggling with the desire to merge with and manipulate the material sphere that humans reside within. On a personal level, these diverging currents reflect one of Pisces's greatest internal conflicts: the need to completely sacrifice her own desires for the sake of others, and the need to fulfil her own wishes. It represents that there is always a choice between two apparent opposites: whether to follow the high road or the low road, to go with the current or swim against it, or to express the negative charge or the more positive, Divine charge.

The simplistic symbol is drawn like a pair of parentheses, their backs to each other, with a line across the middle. This simplified glyph can be likened to the image of two fish, back to back, swimming in opposite directions to each other, but still essentially connected (by the cord in the imagery of Pisces, or by the line running through the centre in the symbol). This 'line of force' between the halves can symbolise a burdensome 'chain', as we are split between our spiritual nature and our physical selves, both from which we can never fully swim away from. Pisces herself seeks eternally to reconcile these contradictory aspects, but rarely succeeds as the cord is often too strong and ultimately inseverable.

As the part of the body under the influence of Pisces is the feet, this glyph is also believed to represent the two heels tied together, signifying both limitation of movements, and of paying one's dues, or Karma, to the Earth. The feet, being always in some kind of physical contact with the Earth, therefore absorb the vibrations of our Mother planet.

PERSONAL, INTERPERSONAL & TRANSPERSONAL SIGNS

PERSONAL ✦ Aries, Taurus, Gemini, Cancer

INTERPERSONAL ✦ Leo, Virgo, Libra, Scorpio

TRANSPERSONAL ✦ Sagittarius, Capricorn, Aquarius, Pisces

Three spheres of human development and experience are represented in the zodiacal mandala: personal, interpersonal and transpersonal.

The first group, which comprises the first four signs Aries, Taurus, Gemini and Cancer, are the personal signs, which represent the earliest psychological foundations of the personality. In a developmental sense, these signs symbolise early development beginning at birth, followed by the childhood experience, and ending with the feeling of secure attachment within the familial structure.

The second group, which comprises the next four signs, Leo, Virgo, Libra and Scorpio, are the interpersonal signs, and describe the maturation process beyond the personal sphere of self and external to the family of origin. These signs represent psychological development in the context of interpersonal relationships and the forging of the self beyond the primary phases of childhood; they also symbolise the evolution of personal autonomy and the seeking and formation of intimate relationships outside the family-of-origin 'container'. Here, there is a movement away from the familial matrix into the world beyond family roots and one's 'tribe'.

The third and final group, which comprises the final four signs of the astrological mandala, Sagittarius, Capricorn, Aquarius and Pisces, are the transpersonal signs. These signs represent an individual's more collective development, describing the unfoldment of the self in relation to the wider world of social contact, spiritual development, the self in the context of society and the global community, as well as one's quest for purposeful meaning, soul, destiny, and self-actualisation. These signs represent our participation in the collective and ancestral realms, and the search for the *whole* self in the context of All-That-Is, which, once understood and fulfilled, can signify a kind of enlightenment and thereafter may release the self back into a new cycle once again - that is, returning to the birth (or re-birth) of the personal being that begins its journey in the personal sign of Aries.

THE THREE DECANS OF EACH SIGN

Decans are thirty-six groups of stars that rise in a particular order on the horizon throughout each Earth rotation. These decans were developed in Egypt thousands of years ago. The rising of each decan marked the beginning of a new 'decanal hour' of the night for these ancient people, and eventually three decans were assigned to each zodiac sign. Each decan covers ten degrees of the zodiac wheel, and is ruled by different planetary rulers that rule over the other two signs of the same element (and a traditional ruler, when only seven of the planetary bodies were known). Decans continued to be used throughout the Ages, in astrology and in divination, but many modern astrologers, for whatever reasons, tend to disregard them.

*The decan's traditional ruler based on the Chaldean order of the planets.

THE THREE DECANS OF ARIES

FIRST DECAN ✦ March 21 - 30
RULER(S) ✦ Mars* / Mars (modern)
Keywords ✦ Dynamic, adventurous, outspoken
3 Tarot Cards ✦ The Emperor, Queen of Wands & Two of Wands

SECOND DECAN ✦ March 31 - April 9
RULER(S) ✦ Sun* / Sun (modern)
Keywords ✦ Charismatic, ambitious, powerful
3 Tarot Cards ✦ The Emperor, Queen of Wands & Three of Wands

THIRD DECAN ✦ April 10 - 19
RULER(S) ✦ Venus* / Jupiter (modern)
Keywords ✦ Idealistic, generous, intuitive
3 Tarot Cards ✦ The Emperor, King of Pentacles & Four of Wands

THE THREE DECANS OF TAURUS

FIRST DECAN ✦ April 20 - 30
RULER(S) ✦ Mercury* / Venus (modern)
Keywords ✦ Sensible, stable, determined
3 Tarot Cards ✦ The Hierophant, King of Pentacles & Five of Pentacles

SECOND DECAN ✦ May 1 - 11
RULER(S) ✦ Moon* / Mercury (modern)
Keywords ✦ Pleasant, productive, sensual
3 Tarot Cards ✦ The Hierophant, King of Pentacles & Six of Pentacles

THIRD DECAN ✦ May 12 - 20
RULER(S) ✦ Saturn* / Saturn (modern)
Keywords ✦ Tenacious, loyal, disciplined
3 Tarot Cards ✦ The Hierophant, Knight of Swords & Seven of Pentacles

THE THREE DECANS OF GEMINI

FIRST DECAN ✦ May 21 - 31
RULER(S) ✦ Jupiter* / Mercury (modern)
Keywords ✦ Intuitive, articulate, adventurous
3 Tarot Cards ✦ The Lovers, Knight of Swords & Eight of Swords

SECOND DECAN ✦ June 1 - 10
RULER(S) ✦ Mars* / Venus (modern)
Keywords ✦ Idealistic, creative, charismatic
3 Tarot Cards ✦ The Lovers, Knight of Swords & Nine of Swords

THIRD DECAN ✦ June 11 - 20
RULER(S) ✦ Sun* / Saturn (modern)
Keywords ✦ Versatile, perceptive, brilliant
3 Tarot Cards ✦ The Lovers, Queen of Cups & Ten of Swords

THE THREE DECANS OF CANCER

FIRST DECAN ✦ June 21 - July 1
RULER(S) ✦ Venus* / Moon (modern
Keywords ✦ Creative, generous, sensitive
3 Tarot Cards ✦ The Chariot, Queen of Cups & Two of Cups

SECOND DECAN ✦ July 2 - 12
RULER(S) ✦ Mercury* / Mars (modern)
Keywords ✦ Empathetic, resourceful, imaginative
3 Tarot Cards ✦ The Chariot, Queen of Cups & Three of Cups

THIRD DECAN ✦ July 13 - 22
RULER(S) ✦ Moon* / Jupiter (modern)
Keywords ✦ Sensitive, intelligent, spiritual
3 Tarot Cards ✦ The Chariot, King of Wands & Four of Cups

THE THREE DECANS OF LEO

FIRST DECAN ✦ July 23 - August 2 (This decan has its beginning from the Royal Star of Leo)
RULER(S) ✦ Saturn* / Sun (modern)
Keywords ✦ Extreme, gregarious, proud
3 Tarot Cards ✦ Strength, King of Wands & Five of Wands

SECOND DECAN ✦ August 3 - 12
RULER(S) ✦ Jupiter* / Jupiter (modern)
Keywords ✦ Confident, optimistic, inspirational
3 Tarot Cards ✦ Strength, King of Wands & Six of Wands

THIRD DECAN ✦ August 13 - 22
RULER(S) ✦ Mars* / Mars (modern)
Keywords ✦ Powerful, bold, passionate
3 Tarot Cards ✦ Strength, Knight of Pentacles & Seven of Wands

THE THREE DECANS OF VIRGO

FIRST DECAN ✦ August 23 - September 1
RULER(S) ✦ Sun* / Mercury (modern)
Keywords ✦ Clever, refined, disciplined
3 Tarot Cards ✦ The Hermit, Knight of Pentacles & Eight of Pentacles

SECOND DECAN ✦ September 2 - 13
RULER(S) ✦ Mercury* / Saturn (modern)
Keywords ✦ Tactful, practical, patient
3 Tarot Cards ✦ The Hermit, Knight of Pentacles & Nine of Pentacles

THIRD DECAN ✦ September 14 - 22
RULER(S) ✦ Venus* / Venus (modern)
Keywords ✦ Altruistic, creative, sensitive
3 Tarot Cards ✦ The Hermit, Queen of Swords & Ten of Pentacles

THE THREE DECANS OF LIBRA

FIRST DECAN ✦ September 23 - October 2
RULER(S) ✦ Moon* / Venus (modern)
Keywords ✦ Sociable, artistic, affectionate
3 Tarot Cards ✦ Justice, Queen of Swords & Two of Swords

SECOND DECAN ✦ October 3 - 13
RULER(S) ✦ Saturn* / Saturn (modern)
Keywords ✦ Thoughtful, decisive, shrewd
3 Tarot Cards ✦ Justice, Queen of Swords & Three of Swords

THIRD DECAN ✦ October 14 - 22
RULER(S) ✦ Jupiter* / Mercury (modern)
Keywords ✦ Fair, eloquent, charming
3 Tarot Cards ✦ Justice, King of Cups & Four of Swords

THE THREE DECANS OF SCORPIO

FIRST DECAN ✦ October 23 - November 2
RULER(S) ✦ Mars* / Mars (modern)
Keywords ✦ Vital, strong-willed, loyal
3 Tarot Cards ✦ Death, King of Cups & Five of Cups

SECOND DECAN ✦ November 3 - 11
RULER(S) ✦ Sun* / Jupiter (modern)
Keywords ✦ Soulful, resilient, passionate
3 Tarot Cards ✦ Death, King of Cups & Six of Cups

THIRD DECAN ✦ November 12 - 21
RULER(S) ✦ Venus* / Moon (modern)
Keywords ✦ Intuitive, seductive, powerful
3 Tarot Cards ✦ Death, Knight of Wands & Seven of Cups

THE THREE DECANS OF SAGITTARIUS

FIRST DECAN ✦ November 22 - December 1
RULER(S) ✦ Mercury* / Jupiter (modern)
Keywords ✦ Wise, idealistic, generous
3 Tarot Cards ✦ Justice, Queen of Swords & Two of Swords

SECOND DECAN ✦ December 2 - 12
RULER(S) ✦ Moon* / Mars (modern
Keywords ✦ Adventurous, impulsive, kind
3 Tarot Cards ✦ Temperance, Knight of Wands & Nine of Wands

THIRD DECAN ✦ December 13 - 21
RULER(S) ✦ Saturn* / Sun (modern)
Keywords ✦ Knowledgeable, bold, charismatic
3 Tarot Cards ✦ Temperance, Queen of Pentacles & Ten of Wands

THE THREE DECANS OF CAPRICORN

FIRST DECAN ✦ December 22 - 31
RULER(S) ✦ Jupiter* / Saturn (modern)
Keywords ✦ Organised, intellectual, vital
3 Tarot Cards ✦ Death, King of Cups & Five of Cups

SECOND DECAN ✦ January 1 - 10
RULER(S) ✦ Mars* / Venus (modern)
Keywords ✦ Ambitious, tenacious, witty
3 Tarot Cards ✦ The Devil, Queen of Pentacles & Three of Pentacles

THIRD DECAN ✦ January 11 - 19
RULER(S) ✦ Sun* / Mercury (modern)
Keywords ✦ Courageous, clever, resolute
3 Tarot Cards ✦ The Devil, King of Swords & Four of Pentacles

THE THREE DECANS OF AQUARIUS

FIRST DECAN ✦ January 21 - 30
RULER(S) ✦ Venus* / Uranus (modern)
Keywords ✦ Original, progressive, eccentric
3 Tarot Cards ✦ The Star, King of Swords & Five of Swords

SECOND DECAN ✦ January 31 - February 9
RULER(S) ✦ Mercury* / Mercury (modern)
Keywords ✦ Inspirational, open, imaginative
3 Tarot Cards ✦ The Star, King of Swords & Six of Swords

THIRD DECAN ✦ February 10 - 19
RULER(S) ✦ Moon* / Venus (modern)
Keywords ✦ Idealistic, mysterious, charismatic
3 Tarot Cards ✦ The Star, Knight of Cups & Seven of Swords

THE THREE DECANS OF CAPRICORN

FIRST DECAN ✦ February 19 - 29
RULER(S) ✦ Saturn* / Neptune (modern)
Keywords ✦ Perceptive, visionary, romantic
3 Tarot Cards ✦ The Moon, Knight of Cups & Eight of Cups

SECOND DECAN ✦ March 1 - 10
RULER(S) ✦ Jupiter* / Moon (modern)
Keywords ✦ Open-minded, intuitive, generous
3 Tarot Cards ✦ The Moon, Knight of Cups & Nine of Cups

THIRD DECAN ✦ March 11 - 20
RULER(S) ✦ Mars* / Pluto (modern)
Keywords ✦ Receptive, charming, dreamy
3 Tarot Cards ✦ The Moon, Queen of Wands & Ten of Cups

THE FOUR ELEMENTS - FIRE, EARTH, AIR, WATER

This grand show is eternal. It is always sunrise somewhere; a shower is forever falling; vapour is ever rising. Eternal sunrise, eternal sunset, eternal dawn... on sea and continents and islands, each in its turn, as the round Earth rolls.

John Muir

- Earth my body -

- Water my blood -

- Air my breath -

- Fire my spirit -

According to the *Oxford English Dictionary*, the word *element* has a mysterious origin, and was first found in Greek texts meaning 'complex whole' or 'a single unit made up of many parts'. From the ancient up to medieval times, there were only four elements - Earth, Air, Fire and Water - and the occult-oriented also believed in a fifth: Spirit, or ether. (Cornelius Agrippa called Spirit the 'quintessence'.). The pentacle or pentagram, with its five points, embodies the four elements as well as the fifth element of *Spirit*, which in white magic, is always at the highest point of the symbol.

Alchemy is a tradition of visions, transformation and dreams, and images can combine on different levels of reality. Alchemists have long used images in their illustrations to express the enigma and mystery of their art, and to include all dimensions of our experience. The traditional worlds of Earth, Water, Fire and Air symbolise these dimensions very well. Broadly speaking, and in human terms, Earth corresponds to the level of the body and the senses, Water to the flow of emotions and feelings, Fire to inspiration and energy, and Air to the plane of the intellect and higher mind. Each of these worlds has its own realm of concepts and imagery.

MAKING A WISH BY INVOKING THE ELEMENTS

Magic is a journey of discovery for the brave individual... The path of the magical initiation calls for the journeying of the spirit to be armed with the stability and practicality of the elements of Earth (gnomes); the loyalty, ardour and creativity of the elements of Fire (salamanders); the mental speed, communication and inventiveness of the elements of Air (sylphs), and the receptivity, understanding and adaptability of the Water elements (undines)... Man needs his fourfold nature fully verified and readily available.

Murry Hope

Wish magic is associated particularly with the Air elementals, as wishes made through them are carried along with the winds and released into the cosmos, though you can also burn wishes with candles or pass them through fire to activate the Fire spirits (and send your wish into the Universe in the form of smoke), 'plant' wishes in the ground or etch a symbol onto a stone to activate the Earth essences, or sprinkle blessed water over a wish or release flower petals as offerings into a fast-flowing stream to carry your desires far and wide using the Water elementals' powers.

When the four elementals are combined, they can magically create the fifth, powerful energy known as *Ether, Aether* or *Akasha*, in which the centre of the circle forms a swirling vortex, allowing desires, wishes, hopes and dreams to be transformed into material reality.

THE FIRE ELEMENT - ARIES, LEO, SAGITTARIUS

✦ **The Passionate Group** ✦
The path to INSPIRATION
Focused on Identity & Action
King ✦ Djin
Rulers ✦ Salamanders, Firedrakes, the consciousness of flames
Colour & Direction ✦ White or Red; South
Wind ✦ Notus
Lucky Star ✦ Regulus

Symbols & Associations ✦ Sun, stars, lightning, volcanoes, change, vision, illumination, will, passion, destruction, purification

Magical Tools ✦ Athames, wands, lamps, candles, incense, censers, burned herbs or requests on paper

Alchemical Associations ✦ Transformation, Sulphur, the Colour Red

Alchemical Stage ✦ Calcinatio

Key Attributes ✦ Vitality, passion, decisiveness, illumination, expansion

Symbolism ✦ Energy, inspiration, leadership, light, life spark

Governed by ✦ The Spirit & intuition

Fire Characteristics ✦ Passionate, energetic, courageous, wild, vibrant, transformational

✦ The Magic of Fire ✦

Love in its essence is spiritual fire.
Emanuel Swedenborg

The element of Fire governs the southern quarter (in magic). Its ruler is Djin (dee-yin) who oversees the Salamanders, Firedrakes, and the little ones of the sunbeams. Its colour is pure red; it is considered warm and dry. The positive associations of Fire are noon, summer, the dagger and sword, candles, any kind of helpful fire, the Sun, the stars, the blood, enthusiasm, activity, courage, daring, willpower, leadership.

D.J. Conway

Fire was the first element that sprang from the Akashic principle; therefore, it is the closest in quality to spirit. Fire's power is electric and expansive, radiating outward, affecting everything it touches. Fire is the fuel that drives willpower and gives you the energy you need to turn your dreams into reality. In its constructive sense, Fire is warming, empowering and enlightening. It has the freedom of Spirit and is the activating principle behind everything in existence. No other element initiates action on its own without the direct influence of this element. Beware, however, as Fire can easily flare out of control. In its destructive sense, Fire is consuming, burning and sometimes deadly. Powerful, dynamic and constantly changing, it is difficult to contain and control, but when used wisely it brings light, warmth and hope to your experience. Without the action Fire drives, you would stay grounded and uninspired - rooted to the spot. Fire brings your desires into fruition by bringing determination and bravery - a natural, inspired call to action.

Fire is associated with the intuitive function and its motivating force is inspiration. Characterised by movement, force and energy, it offers new possibilities, regeneration, and a buoyant, spontaneous expression. Fire's essential characteristic is the energetic exploration of life: to conquer, to lead and to travel - both mentally and physically. Fire signs are creative and perceptive, experiencing life through intuition and spirit. Fire is a conceptual and visionary element, ever searching for meaning. Its energy can light up the world, or scorch it out of existence. Stimulating and spontaneous, it has a warm, passionate, enthusiastic and active approach to life. Fire initiates and motivates, and it is optimistic and explorative. Fire is also connected with heroism, a sense of beginning, regrowth, and the future. Aries represents personal development, Leo represents interpersonal development, and Sagittarius represents transpersonal development. They are masculine polarity, extroverted in action.

Fire is fundamentally different to the other three elements, but it is the essential fourth. The other elements are eternal - only Fire has a birth and a death. Fire is ephemeral; even the blazing, glowing ball in the sky, our Sun, will burn out in time. Remember also that you need to nurture and replenish this primal force of expression, as Fire is not self-sustaining and it needs fuel to maintain its heat, light, movement and momentum.

"To be alive is to be burning," asserted psychoanalyst Norman O. Brown. Too much burning, however, can lead to burnout. And too much unrestrained Fire can burn the self *and* others. When Fire people are out of control, fire extinguishers (water) and stamping it out with a heavy material (Earth) can work wonders.

Fire generated by a spark can spread as a forest fire spreads, creating excessive heat and smoke, which can sear and smother. But after the fire, comes the regeneration, another potent symbol of this element. From the blackened stumps, sprout new green leaves, in a sense symbolising the natural law that sometimes something needs to be burned away, reduced to ashes, before it can be given a chance at new, fresh life, a concept symbolised by the magnificent mythological Phoenix rising anew from the ashes. The salamander living in the flames is another such fire symbol. Many symbols for this element are birds, like the legendary Phoenix, the Firebird from Russian folklore, the Simurgh - bird of Divine Light in Asian mythology - and the Sunbird of ancient Lycia, which takes souls and flies them up to the sky after death.

Fire is, quite simply, the element of creation, identity, and the life force made manifest. The most active and consuming astrological energy, it is the element of spirit, roaming far and wide in search of inspiration and meaning. Ultimately, it has the power to animate, transmute and energise all that it touches. And when we are carriers of such a flame, we can go forth into the world as a beacon of warmth and light.

Keywords
Adventurous, energetic, ardent, independent, passionate, enthusiastic^, optimistic, impulsive, honest, exuberant, self-motivated, physical, individualistic, assertive, inspirational, courageous, has faith, spirited, warm, takes initiative, confident, extroverted, spontaneous, impatient, restless, simple and direct in approach, creative, idealistic, freedom-seeking, dramatic, forceful, Joi de Vivre!*

^*The word enthusiasm derives from a Greek word, translating to "a God within."*

**All these words don't necessarily describe all three Fire signs. Leo, for example, is not necessarily restless or freedom-seeking.*

Aries ✦ is the Fire of personality, the spark of life, the impulse to incarnate, the enthusiasm to act, the strength of spirit to be individualistic, the courage to take bold, bounding, initial leaps of faith.

Leo ✦ is the Fire of warmth and affection, of generosity, the Fires of enduring loyalty, romance, and the search for an ideal other.

Sagittarius ✦ is the Fire of wisdom and understanding, the impulse to soar, the urge to travel and explore, the quest for meaning, and the search for the answers to the questions of the soul. This third and final Fire sign fuses the meanings of Aries and Leo. The great spur of Sagittarius is one of aspiration and quite literally, the starry sky is the only limit. With agility and grace the arrow is aimed, then set loose upon infinity in the quest for truth. Indeed, Sagittarius is referred to as the 'traveller to the stars'.

AN EXCESS OR LACK OF THE FIRE ELEMENT

Sometimes, upon examining a birth chart, an astrologer may find that the subject has too much or too little of a certain element (e.g. a high concentration of planets in the Earth element and little or no planets in Air signs). Even if your Sun is in a certain element, you may still have a lack of that element overall in your chart. So, what do you do if you have an excess or a lack of your particular element, Fire?

Excess Fire can make one hot-tempered, impulsive, impetuous, irate, risk-taking, impatient, aggressive, angry, and even violent. To balance an over-abundance of Fire, try cooling foods, swimming and bathing, wearing cooling colours such as blues and greens, using blue and green gemstones, taking flower remedies such as Impatiens, and using calming herbs such as chamomile, lemon balm and passionflower.

For those lacking Fire, strengthening and empowering activities like doing aerobics-type exercises, hiking and mountain-climbing might help. Increasing your self-confidence and courage, using warming spices such as cayenne, cinnamon, curry, chilli and cardamom, drinking peppermint and ginger teas, wearing the colours red and orange, using the gemstones ruby, carnelian, bloodstone and topaz, taking flower remedies such as Scarlet Monkeyflower and Indian Paintbrush, and using essential oils of basil, cinnamon and black pepper may also ignite your inner flame.

THE ARCHANGEL OF FIRE ✦ MICHAEL
The Fire element vibrates to the essence of Michael.

An archangel is an angel of greater than ordinary rank. They possess a stronger, more powerful essence than the guardian angels, through overseeing and guiding the other angels who are said to be with us here on Earth.

The word 'angel' derives from the Greek word *angelos* meaning 'messenger'. To humans, angels are often seen as bringers as all sorts of messages. Angels in all their forms are believed to bring the message of 'spirit' into matter, carrying the blueprints of creation and the Source from the Divine into the manifest world.

Angels are not and never have been human; they, like fairies and nature spirits, are part of a different evolutionary pattern – but they do appear to us in human form (usually with wings) because that is what we understand.

An angel can be in many different places at once, and with the same intensity and concentration, and wish for us to be aware of them and benefit from them.

Four of the multitude of archangelic beings work intimately with the Earth. These are Raphael (Air), Michael (Fire), Gabriel (Water) and Uriel (Earth). Associated with each of these archangels are one of the four elements, specific colours, one of the four directions or quarters of the Earth, three signs of the zodiac, and a variety of other energies and powers. Understanding these associations and considering them in relation to our own paths, can help us determine with which of them we are more likely to resonate.

ARCHANGEL MICHAEL'S ASSOCIATIONS

Element of Fire
The southern quarter of the Earth
The autumn (fall) season
The colour red
The astrological signs of Aries, Leo and Sagittarius

Michael, meaning "Who is like God or the Divine," is the leader of all the archangels and is in charge of courage, truth, strength and integrity. He protects us physically, emotionally and psychically. Michael helps us to follow our truth without compromising our integrity, and helps us find our true natures so we can be faithful to who we really are. Michael encourages us to fight for just and noble causes; he gives us the courage and strength to stand up for what is right, especially when persecuted. Overall, Michael is the archangel of protection, peace, safety, clarity, balance, and moving forward. This being works to bring patience and a safeguard against any psychic imbalances or dangers, and if your problem is a very powerful adversary, you can invoke his help. Michael helps us to tear down the old and build the new.

INDIVIDUAL ZODIAC ARCHANGELS OF THE FIRE ELEMENT SIGNS

Angels are our link to the Divine, helping us in our soul's journey and gently highlighting wisdom, beauty, benevolence and trust in our world. Everyone has a guardian angel aligned to their soul and their life's pathway.

Alicen & Neil Geddes-Ward

Additionally, each sign is associated with a particular archangel. Such knowledge can help you to build up a relationship with these beings, based upon your needs. However, no link is rigid, and as you work with angels you will come to develop your own affinities. When invoking a specific archangel, a useful ritual to draw them closer is to light a candle in that angel's colour, burn some oil or incense of its scent, and hold the appropriate crystal while focusing on what you are needing guidance on.

ARIES'S ZODIAC ARCHANGEL ✦ JOPHIEL

Jophiel's name means 'beauty of God'. He is the bringer of sunshine, wisdom and joy. He carries the flame of intuition, and his blessings include creativity and inspiration. Believed to have guarded the Tree of Knowledge in the Garden of Eden, Jophiel is one of the princes of Divine Presence and is said to be a close friend of Metatron. He has a strong interest in beauty and can be called upon by anyone involved in creating beauty in any form. Jophiel helps people who are using their creativity and can be invoked by those who need help with a creative project. He is also the dispeller of clouds of doubt and thereby increases courage, vitality, strength and self-esteem.

SCENT/OIL ✦ Cinnamon
CANDLE COLOUR ✦ Gold
CRYSTAL ✦ Citrine
OTHER SPECIAL ANGELS FOR ARIES ✦ Malahidae, Machidiel & Camael

LEO'S ZODIAC ARCHANGELS ✦ MICHAEL* & RAZIEL

*See previous information under the heading 'Archangel Michael's Associations'.

Raziel means 'secret of God' and he is the keeper of secrets and lord of the mysteries of life. He awakens the spirit so that it can comprehend things which cannot be understood by the intellect. The insights of Raziel run deep and can be life-changing and difficult to express or explain to others, but ultimately these insights can bring about profound transformation. Raziel's gifts include self-awareness, release of obsessions, inner peace and harmony, and the clearing away of mental chatter to make way for true knowing.

SCENT/OIL ✦ Frankincense
CANDLE COLOUR ✦ Bright yellow, sapphire blue
CRYSTALS ✦ Amber, topaz, sapphire
OTHER SPECIAL ANGEL FOR LEO ✦ Verchiel

SAGITTARIUS'S ZODIAC ARCHANGEL ✦ ZADKIEL

Zadkiel is the ruler of Jupiter, regent of Sagittarius, and the angel of Divine justice. Because of his association with Jupiter, Zadkiel bestows abundance, benevolence, mercy, tolerance, prosperity, happiness, and good fortune. He can be invoked for help with legal or financial problems. Zadkiel teaches us to trust in the Universe. Labelled 'the holy one', he brings mercy and kindness and aids meditation, brings psychic protection, and boosts the immune system. He advocates teaching, the learning of new ideas, compassion and forgiveness. Zadkiel removes emotions and obstacles that are holding you back, so that you are able to see the bigger picture.

SCENT/OIL ✦ Cedarwood
CANDLE COLOUR ✦ Violet
CRYSTAL ✦ Amethyst
OTHER SPECIAL ANGELS FOR SAGITTARIUS ✦ Advachiel or Adnachiel

THE DEVIC REALMS & FIRE ✦
SOUTH: REALM OF THE SALAMANDERS

Deva is a Sanskrit word that means 'shining one'. Devas are the life force within nature, and there are four devic realms - Fire, Earth, Air and Water - which contain ethereal elemental spirits or sprites. Elementals are the building blocks of nature, and close to being true energy and consciousness. The four elements correspond to four different states of matter: energy/transmutation (Fire), gas (Air), liquid (Water) and solid (Earth), which are linked to the four human states of consciousness: inspiration, thought, feeling and practicality. There are four spirits, or elementals, which reside in the devic realms, associated with each element. In the sixteenth century, the famous Swiss physician, alchemist, and mystic Paracelsus* defined these beings as 'Elementals', classifying them according to the element of nature they inhabit.

There are four main levels of elemental beings: Gnomes (Earth), Undines (Water), Sylphs (Air), and Salamanders (Fire). The fifth element of Ether is the element from which came forth the other four, and Ether, or Spirit, has never been defined in any particular category, and encompasses the aspects and beings of all the other elements.

Elementals are usually benevolent guardian beings or spirits that look after nature's secrets and treasures in whatever part of the natural realm they occupy. If you wish to re-connect and re-harmonise yourself by working with nature and its messages and lessons, you could begin by learning a little about your element's realm: The element of Fire is connected with the South direction and the realm of the Salamanders. Salamander comes from the Greek word *salambe*, meaning 'fireplace'.

Philippis Aureolus Paracelsus is considered the most original medical thinker of the sixteenth century. A Swiss chemist, physician, astrologer, botanist and philosopher who lived from 1493 - 1541, he is credited with the Doctrine of the Four Elements, from which early nineteenth-century occult practitioners drew the belief that an element (Fire, Earth, Air and Water) is not only physical, but also contains a spiritual essence. His belief in supernatural beings, intuition and the invisible causes of illness helped him discover hydrogen and nitrogen. His hermetical views were that the health status of the body relied on harmony between the macrocosm (nature) and the microcosm (the individual). Paracelsus believed that "Elementals are unlike pure spirits for they are mortal, but they are not like man for they have no soul."

SALAMANDERS

Fire spirits are described as thick, red, and dry-skinned beings called salamanders, which look similar to the common scaleless lizard-like amphibians that share their name (the two are distinct entities however, despite having the same name).

Elemental salamanders are sometimes visible as small balls of fire and have also been seen in the shape of tongues of flame that can run over fields and peer into dwellings. It's said that no fire is lit without their help. In fact, the salamander comes from the Greek word *salambe*, meaning 'fireplace'.

These spirits rule over all manner of flame, lightning, explosions, volcanoes and combustion. Mostly they are active underground and internally within the body and mind. Salamanders evoke powerful emotional currents in humans, and stimulate sparks of spiritual idealism and perception.

Their energy is much like that of the Tarot Card The Tower, assisting in the tearing down of the old and the building of the new - as fire can be both constructive and destructive in its creative expression. Fire provides us with warmth, fuel and heating, and voraciously destroys the old so new life can spring forth out of the ashes - it is the essence from which the legendary Phoenix arises, and indeed the Star that heralds the new dawn after the collapse of The Tower in the Tarot.

Salamanders are the guardians of summer and Fire, and reside in the realm of passion, change, prophetic visions, personal power, inspiration, and the inner child. They function in the physical body by aiding circulation and in maintaining proper body temperature, and working with the body's metabolism for greater health.

Fire elementals work with humans via heat, fire and flame. This includes everything from the flame of a candle to the ethereal flames and daily light of the Sun. They can be powerfully effective in healing work, but must be used carefully for such applications, as their energies are dynamic and sometimes difficult to control.

They are almost always present when there is any healing about to occur.

Fire represents the inner child, that place of innocence from which we all stem. As it gives rise to sexual fervour it is also the root of our creative spirits. The fire elementals can indeed awaken in us higher spiritual visions and aspirations. They strengthen and stimulate the entire auric field to enable easier attunement to and recognition of Divine forces within our lives.

Despite their luminosity and warmth, Fire spirits are the most unpredictable and volatile of the elementals. They are elusive, fierce and untameable, and because they are made of balls of energy or light, they tend to be far shorter-lived than other elemental nature forms. In fact, the smaller ones may literally burn themselves out.

They vary in size and intensity, from mighty dragons to tiny but potent fire fairies. They may also manifest as glow worms or fireflies, dancing over sacred sites or within caves.

The salamanders can be seen in the heart of fires, frolicking like dragons in the flames, and this dragon symbology is used in many Eastern religions to pay homage to them.

Salamanders love the Fire for they are nourished by it - yet they are so cold within themselves, that they cannot be harmed by the flames.

Fire spirits are of immense value as light-bringers; as mighty and tenacious defenders of Fire, they inspire us to reach up and out to fulfill our loftiest dreams and ambitions. They help blacksmiths in their task of forging mighty swords and armour, feeding strength into the flames to have it then yield into the blacksmith's intention or purpose.

The King of Fire is Belenos or Djinn*, its archangel is Michael, its magickal tool is the wand (which calls down the spirits into form), and its sacred ceremonial stones are Yellow Topaz, Amber and Citrine.

*Djinn is a fiery elemental spirit who, being made of pure fire, is a glorious flamelike creature with flashing luminous ruby eyes. He is never still and lives in the mystical Emerald Mountains of Kaf, ruling over all other fire beings. Djinn is called the 'wish-granter', and is an efficient shapeshifter and magician who travels with the speed of light. Although his natural *home is in the Emerald Mountains, he can appear almost anywhere, especially in bottles or lamps as a genie. As well as granting wishes, Djinn can endow the powers of creativity, inspiration, small miracles, travel, change and courage.*

INVOKING THE FIRE DEVAS

If you wish to increase your sexual prowess, inspiration, creativity, or overall success, need some career or goal luck, are fearful of an imminent but necessary change or move, or you need courage or energy to meet a challenge, ask the fire devas for their help. Suitable offerings you can use to attract their energy, are fires (obviously), candles, anything gold or glittery, certain crystals*, some essential oils*, sparkling stones, fibre-optic lamps, mirrors, jack o' lanterns, sun catchers, clear crystal spheres, golden fruits, and golden flowers.

You can encounter salamanders most easily in a bonfire or open hearth. Some see them as sparks or flashes of colour. Dragon-like beings that live within flames, you can see them coiling within the swirling and lapping heat of the flames, and watch others dance and crackle in the sparks. They also reside in every beam of sunlight and flow of electricity. If you do not have access to a proper fire, a candle can serve the same purpose: call upon their help by meditating upon a lit candle. Lighting several at once, particularly in the colours of red, gold or orange, may heighten the power.

Some crystals you can use to attract salamander activity and illumination in your experience, are hematite, obsidian, amber, ruby, bloodstone, carnelian, pyrite, lava, dragon's eggs, garnet, Boji stone and topaz.

Some essential oils you can use to invoke the Fire elementals are basil, frankincense, chamomile, allspice, orange, clove, nutmeg, cinnamon, dragon's blood, cedarwood, angelica, rosemary and tangerine.

THE SOUTH DIRECTION'S CORRESPONDENCES

If you wish to work more with your particular element and direction, the following may help propel your wishes and magical journey:

Time of Day ✦ Noon
Polarity ✦ Male, negative
Exhortation ✦ To dare
Musical Instruments ✦ Brass instruments
Colours ✦ Scarlet red
Season ✦ Summer
Magical Instrument ✦ Sword, dagger, athame
Altar Symbol ✦ Lamp
Communion Symbol ✦ Heat
Archangel ✦ Michael
Human Sense ✦ Sight
Art Forms ✦ Dance, drama
Animals ✦ Salamanders, lizards
Mythical Beast ✦ Dragon
Magical Arts ✦ Ritual
Guide Forms ✦ Sun, protector god
Meditation ✦ Bonfires
Images & Themes ✦ Flames, volcanoes, midday Sun, walking through fire

HOW TO GET IN TOUCH WITH FIRE ENERGY

"To be alive is to be burning"

A woman must be willing to burn hot, burn with passion, burn with words, with ideas, with desire for whatever it is that she truly loves... Too often we turn away from the pot, from the oven. We forget to watch, forget to add fuel, forget to stir... The fire requires watching, for it is easy to let the flame go out. The (Wild Woman) must be fed. There's hell to pay if she goes hungry.

Clarissa Pinkola Estes

- Use Fire energy when making wishes around the following: Banishing bad habits, enthusiasm, initiative, inspiration, playfulness, leadership, bringing out the inner child, courage, confidence, dynamic energy, psychic protection, passion and desire
- In magical practices, Fire can be represented by a candle (red or yellow will strengthen its fiery association), a fireplace, smudge sticks, bonfires or, symbolically, a wand. The candle wax of a burning candle represents Fire's powers of change and transformation - melting as it burns, changing its shape and substance
- The best days on which to employ Fire magic are Tuesday, ruled by the fiery Red Planet Mars, or a Sunday, ruled by the blazing Sun. If possible, choose midday when the Sun is at its zenith
- Fire can be activated and refuelled by being outdoors and soaking up the Sun; engaging in physically active and demanding activities; engaging in sports, adventure, and creative pursuits; and being involved in promotional and inspirational endeavours
- Eat spicy, hot foods, such as chilli and cayenne, and use fiery spices and sauces
- Burn a bridge, clean a slate
- Write your wish/es down on a piece of red paper, then burn it to release the smoke along with its message into the Universe to be fulfilled
- Spend time in the Sun every day if possible, and around fires of all kinds - stoves, candles, fireplaces, campfires
- Yellow and orange-coloured crystals will activate your connection with the element of Fire and enhance your creativity.
- Practice candle magic
- Drink green tea
- Indulge in forms of caffeine such as coffee and chocolate, but do so moderately or you may become jittery, scattered and jumpy, thereby rendering your inner Fire ineffective
- Use supplements which are designed to support and believed to enhance your Fire energy, such as ginger, spirulina and ginseng. Some energy bars may also prove beneficial
- Practice deep breathing and meditation exercises and disciplines, which help to increase and circulate energy and blood throughout your body
- Meditate using the Fire mantra "Ram"

- Indulge in sexual release regularly
- Schedule and maintain an ongoing physical exercise routine
- Learn and practice yoga
- Create a 'fire ritual', during which you regularly 'burn' away something which needs releasing or banishing
- Take an acting, drama, or theatrics class - or better still, become an actor on camera or on stage!
- Learn about Fire gods and goddesses, and how they can benefit you. The Hawaiian Fire goddess Pele, is a great place to start
- Meditate on the Wands suit in the Tarot (the Wands suit represents the Fire element)
- Express yourself regularly and freely, either through the expressive arts, social events, or even a journal
- Be bold, brave and courageous, even when you are not feeling like it
- Choose a challenge and rise to it
- Build your confidence daily by listing three achievements or goals you have reached, no matter how seemingly small or large
- Wear and surround yourself with the colours red and orange
- Commit yourself to a bright future by creating a vision or dream, and maintain it by keeping track of your steps along the way
- Think and act big. As Marianne Williamson said: "Our deepest fear is not that we are inadequate. Our deepest fear is that we are powerful beyond measure. It is our light, not our darkness, that most frightens us. Your playing small does not serve the world... We are all meant to shine as children do... And as we let our own lights shine, we unconsciously give other people permission to do the same." So be bold and shine!
- When working with the Fire element in magical practice, stand at the South quarter of your magical space, as the South is its domain, and invite its living essence into your circle or space
- Fire spirits are known by metaphysicians as salamanders, and they inspire passion, blessings, new life, creativity, and spiritual healing. With all this in mind, Fire signs would be wise to adopt one as their very own spirit guide!

THE EARTH ELEMENT - TAURUS, VIRGO, CAPRICORN

✦ The Practical Group ✦
The path to SERVICE & DUTY
Focused on Materiality & Security

King ✦ Ghob (Gob or Ghom)

Rulers ✦ Gnomes, Dwarfs and Trolls who inhabit the interior of the Earth and are the guardians of treasures, precious gems, minerals and of the Earth herself

Colour & Direction ✦ Black or Green; North

Wind ✦ Boreas

Lucky Star ✦ Fomalhaut

Symbols & Associations ✦ Fields, rocks, mountains, plains, caves, mines, midnight, winter, riches, treasures, prosperity, success, money, business, stability, fertility

Magical Tools ✦ Pentagram and pentacle, salt, stones, minerals, gems, trees, herbs, soil

Alchemical Associations ✦ The Physical, the Mineral Salt, the Colour Black

Alchemical Stage ✦ Coagulatio

Key Attributes ✦ Stability, balance, patience, practicality, realism

Symbolism ✦ Groundedness, stability, structure, protection, solidity, common sense, connection to the material and physical planes, and the five senses

Governed by ✦ The physical body, the tangible & sensations

Earth Characteristics ✦ Grounded, practical, balanced, realistic, materialistic, solid

✦ The Magic of Earth ✦

The element of Earth rules the northern quarter (in magic). Its ruler is Ghob who oversees the gnomes and dwarfs and the little ones of the moonbeams. Its colour is clear dark green; it is cold and dry. The positive associations of Earth are midnight, winter, the pentacles, ritual salt, gemstones, mountains, caves, soil, respect, endurance, responsibility, stability, thoroughness, purpose in life.

D.J. Conway

Earth is the solid rock on which everything else is grounded. It provides the soil for the roots you need to lay down at some point in your life, and yields the minerals and food needed to survive and thrive. Earth is the provider, the protector, the material aspect of the world and of the human form. If you have forgotten to keep both your feet on the ground, your dreams will carry you away - Earth is needed to provide grounding for them. Earth is supportive and reminds you that everything in life needs to be built on solid, sound, dependable foundations. The element of Earth is indeed life's great anchor.

Keywords
Cautious, methodical, organised, predictable, substantial, stable, reliable, practical, pragmatic, sensual, patient, enduring, productive, grounded, persevering, dependable, useful, sensible

Earth is both of this world and the Otherworld, for she is host to all the other Elements besides: Air doth blow upon her face, Fire doth ignite within her belly and spew forth from her mountains, Water flows through her deep valleys, and Spirit marketh upon her skin the sacred pathways of our quest.

Nevill Drury

Taurus ✦ is the Earth of the foundation, our first roots, of coming into being, the soil that contains the sprouting seed, the persistent builder, the steadiness when we stumble, the enduring solidity that sustains our footing, the loyalty, love and affection that expands us, the ground itself.

Virgo ✦ is the Earth of the budding flower coming into bloom, of potential and proficiency, of methodology and diligence, of practical organisation, of humble service and thorough analysis, the professional problem-solver, that which grows from the ground with effortless efficiency.

Capricorn ✦ is the Earth of productive authority, persistence and responsibility; of mastery and ascension, of the mountains, the peaks, our sure-footedness as we climb, and the solidity of the very ground beneath our feet.

Earth is the material substance principle. It gives form and substance to manifest what Fire has inspired and initiated. Earth is associated with the sensation function and its motivating force is material gain and security. Characterised by function, practicality and solidity, Earth seeks straightforward engagement with the physical world, mastery of it through efficient organisation and structure, and attainment of physical and economical comforts, respect and status.

Taurus represents personal development and the soil, Virgo represents interpersonal development and what is planted and grown, and Capricorn represents transpersonal development and the high mountainous backdrop. These signs are feminine in polarity and introverted in expression.

Earth symbols include tortoises, caves, underground tunnels, mines, grottos, soil, rocks, minerals, farms, fields and mountains.

In ancient legends, the Earth was regarded as maternal and protective, symbolising abundance and fertility. In mythology, Gaia or 'Mother Earth' was one of the first beings to emerge, along with Ouranos 'Father Sky'. They were bound by the ocean which whirled in an endless circle, keeping them together.

Symbolising the inexhaustible spirit of material creation, Earth is associated with abundance. When we work with this element, not only are we calling upon the powers of the mountains, caves, minerals and deserts that comprise its wondrous expanse, we are also invoking its support and monumental strength, for from it emerges hidden treasures from the deep and the dark. Such treasures include gold, silver, other precious minerals, crystals, resources, and other materials.

From the esoteric standpoint, Earth has the lowest vibration of the four elements because it is so solidly manifest in our world. Rooted in practical concerns, it governs the primal facets of life and of physical regeneration. It provides all we need for life, in the form of nourishment and shelter, and also provides tangible comforts and wealth.

As the element suggests, Earth signs are down-to-earth and self-sufficient. Pragmatic and conservative, they need structure and routine to feel safe and secure. Whether a practical Taurus, analytical Virgo or determined Capricorn, Earth signs approach life with caution and careful, methodical planning. They are inherently sensory-orientated, experiencing the world through a physical body. Concerned with moulding matter into form, Earth is productive, sensual, tactile and fertile.

In Earth we see the great cycles of nature and the effects it has on all the other elements. Though the cycles of the seasons rely upon the Sun, these seasons would become stagnant and motionless if it weren't for the movement of the Earth. For that reason, the mysteries of life, death and rebirth can be associated with this element - and although it is the Water element's inherent nature to explore these things on a deeper, more spiritual plane, Earth is the starting point for this exploration.

Overall, Earth supports, embodies, incarnates, contains, protects, and provides a sense of groundedness, an incredible, breathing, pulsating, living, vibrating entity, majestically supporting all life on our planet with Her steady hand and solid ground.

AN EXCESS OR LACK OF THE EARTH ELEMENT

Excess Earth can make one dense, heavy, sluggish, lethargic, insensitive, depressed, slow to perceive new ideas, rigid, and overly concerned with material values. To balance an over-abundance of Earth, try exercise of all kinds to get things moving, eat spicy foods such as cayenne and ginger to create more vitality and movement in the body, wear colours such as bright yellows and oranges to energise your aura, use the crystals hematite, rhodochrosite, fire agate and carnelian, taking flower remedies such as Chestnut Bud and Chicory to break old patterns and crystallised thoughts, and Oak and Mustard to alleviate deep-set depression.

For those lacking Earth, grounding techniques and outdoor exercise to strengthen and empower your soul might help, as well as walking barefoot on the Earth to soak up her energies and power, eating an abundance of grains and Earth-based root vegetables, wearing and using the colour green and gemstones such as malachite, chrysoprase, aventurine and emerald, and taking flower remedies such as Clematis and Manzanita for grounding.

THE ARCHANGEL OF EARTH ✦ URIEL

The Earth element vibrates to the essence of Uriel.
(For further information on archangels, see under 'The Archangel of Fire').

✦ Archangel Uriel's Associations ✦

Element of Earth
The northern quarter of the Earth
The summer season
The colours white, burnished gold, all earth tones
The crystals tiger's eye and rutilated quartz
The astrological signs of Taurus, Virgo and Capricorn

Uriel, whose name means 'Fire of God', is the archangel who brought alchemy* to humankind. He is said to be the brightest archangel, a pure pillar of Fire, he can bring warmth to the winter and melt the snows with his flaming sword. Uriel is the archangel of alchemy and vision, overseeing healing, magic, nature, and manifestation. This being is known as the tallest of the archangels with eyes that can see into and across eternity. Uriel is often depicted with one bare foot and the other with a shoe, and he carries an olive bough, signifying peace. He is also frequently shown with a thick book of wisdom in his left hand. Uriel oversees the work of all nature spirits - working with Uriel will open you to the fairy kingdoms - and works to assist humanity by awakening to them and working in harmony with them. Inspiring us to work with angels, devas and higher spiritual essences, to perfect our vision of Divine realms, and to refine our mystical nature by burning away our deep-seated desire for comfort and blind ignorance, Uriel is the gatekeeper to the Garden of Eden, the gates of which we can only pass through once we have mastered the wisdom we are given to find our own path to enlightenment. In essence, Uriel is considered the guardian of the emotions, of love and of the heart. Uriel is served by Ghob, King of the Gnomes, seen traditionally as a gnome or goblin who is squat, heavy and dense.

*Alchemy is the sacred art of transmuting base metal into gold by reducing it to the primal black matter and then, by chemico-magical processes, striving to extract and refine spiritual as well as actual gold, the key to finding the way back to Paradise or Source.

INDIVIDUAL ZODIAC ARCHANGELS OF THE EARTH ELEMENT SIGNS

Additionally, each sign is associated with a particular archangel. Such knowledge can help you to build up a relationship with these beings, based upon your needs. However, no link is rigid, and as you work with angels you will come to develop your own affinities. When invoking a specific archangel, a useful ritual to draw them closer is to light a candle in that angel's colour, burn some oil or incense of its scent, and hold the appropriate crystal while focusing on what you are needing guidance on.

TAURUS'S ZODIAC ARCHANGEL ✦ SANDALPHON

Sandalphon is an androgynous angel, depicted as a beautiful young man. He is guardian of the Earth, concerned with the spirit behind Earthly manifestations. Sandalphon stimulates awareness of the Earth's needs, blessings and gifts. Bringing a sense of grounding, practicality and responsibility, Sandalphon can help you be more aware of your bodily power and assist in treating your physical body as a temple.

SCENT/OIL ✦ Patchouli
CANDLE COLOUR ✦ Deep green or brown
CRYSTAL ✦ Jade or brown jasper
OTHER SPECIAL ANGELS FOR TAURUS ✦ Asmodel & Anael

VIRGO'S ZODIAC ARCHANGEL ✦ RAPHAEL

Raphael is the Divine healer, bringing healing in all its forms to those who need it. He leads the guardian angels, takes care of travellers, supports those in the healing professions, and bestows knowledge, wisdom, and therapeutic skill. Soothing and calming, he can help you to heal yourself and to feel a connection and oneness with nature. Raphael can be invoked using a caduceus.

SCENT/OIL ✦ Chamomile
CANDLE COLOUR ✦ Vibrant green
CRYSTAL ✦ Emerald or green tourmaline
OTHER SPECIAL ANGELS FOR TAURUS ✦ Hamaliel

CAPRICORN'S ZODIAC ARCHANGEL ✦ HANIEL

Haniel is a protective angel, bringing determination and the energy to understand your life's mission and true purpose. In the female form, this archangel has a loving, nurturing, motherly presence and helps us to honour our natural cycles. Archangel Haniel can assist you with communication, soothes panic, and helps you to overcome deeply ingrained negativity and to receive communication from the higher planes. Haniel's gift is the development of pure individuality, independent of the expectations and pressures of others.

SCENT/OIL ✦ Pine
CANDLE COLOUR ✦ Turquoise
CRYSTAL ✦ Turquoise
OTHER SPECIAL ANGELS FOR TAURUS ✦ Cassiel

THE DEVIC REALMS & EARTH ✦ NORTH: REALM OF THE GNOMES

Deva is a Sanskrit word that means 'shining one'. Devas are the life force within nature, and there are four devic realms - Fire, Earth, Air and Water - which contain ethereal elemental spirits or sprites. Elementals are the building blocks of nature, and close to being true energy and consciousness. The four elements correspond to four different states of matter: energy/transmutation (Fire), gas (Air), liquid (Water) and solid (Earth), which are linked to the four human states of consciousness: inspiration, thought, feeling and practicality. There are four spirits, or elementals, which reside in the devic realms, associated with each element.

The four main levels of elemental beings are: Gnomes (Earth), Undines (Water), Sylphs (Air), and Salamanders (Fire). The fifth element of Ether is the element from which came forth the other four, and Ether, or Spirit, has never been defined in any particular category, and encompasses the aspects and beings of all the other elements.

Elementals are usually benevolent guardian beings or spirits that look after nature's secrets and treasures in whatever part of the natural realm they occupy. If you wish to re-connect and re-harmonise yourself by working with nature and its messages and lessons, you could begin by learning a little about your element's realm: The element of Earth is connected with the North direction and the realm of the Gnomes. The gnomes are the 'knowing ones', from the Greek gnoma, meaning 'knowledge'.

✦ Gnomes ✦

All things within the cosmos are interrelated and it is only natural for kindred souls to come to the aid of their own kind, especially when threatened from alien or non-harmonious frequencies. The secret lies in being able to become one of that 'kind', whatever it may be, so that you attract its help in time of need. It is said... that he who relates to the gnome kingdoms never wants for a penny.

Murry Hope

Gnome: *noun* - A legendary dwarfish creature, supposed to guard the Earth's treasures; diminutive spirits or small fey 'humanoids' in Renaissance magic and alchemy, first introduced by Paracelsus in the 16th century, known for their eccentric sense of humour, inquisitiveness, and engineering prowess; are typically said to be small, humanoid creatures who live underground.

Gnomes are a race of small, misshapen, dwarf-like creatures that dwell in the Earth and often protect secret treasures in vast caverns. Their actions are reflected in the presence of mineral deposits and other geological formations. Ultimately, these devas work with humans through nature.

As beings of supreme craftsmanship, they are needed to build the plants, flowers and trees. As guardians of the treasures of the Earth, they are attuned to helping humans find the treasures within it; this can be in the form of hidden riches, the energy found in crystals and stones, or the finding of 'gold' within one's own life.

According to Paracelsus, gnomes cannot stand the light of the Sun, and even one ray would turn them to stone. If you wish to retrieve any treasures that are buried underground or associated with the Earth, it is said you must first appease the gnomes or they will cause you mischief.

The gnomes are the 'knowing ones', from the Greek *gnoma*, meaning 'wisdom and knowledge'. Indeed, they are extremely wise and knowledgeable about how all things of the Earth work. Another theory regarding their naming relates to Paracelsus, who was the first to use 'gnome' as a collective term for the spirits of the Earth. It is believed that he probably based this usage on the Greek term ge-nomos, meaning 'Earth-dweller'.

As knowing ones, the gnomes teach us respect and reverence for the collective wisdom and traditions of old age. They wish us to learn the knowledge garnered over many lifetimes of experiences, and the wisdom of our elders, crones and sages. Gnomes stand for respect for old and advanced age, and they ensure that the two stages of life represented by the crone and the sage are upheld, embraced, respected and honoured.

The gnomes are the guardians of winter, the physical-material world, fertility, abundance, and the north direction. The north is traditionally known as the gateway to inner wisdom.

The gnomes are caretakers of everything that grows, from tiny flowers, to the food that we consume, to towering trees. Their role is to protect the soil, mountains, trees, sacred sites, plants, minerals and land.

Their Goddess is Cerridwen, and the King of Earth is Cernunnos, Ghob or Geb*, its archangel Uriel, its magickal tool the pentacle or disc (which calls down the spirits into form), and its sacred ceremonial stone is the garnet in its four colours.

Perhaps Merlin sums up the gnome realm best: "From time to time, no doubt, these gnomes do make merry with the lives of humanfolk, having their ways in mischief and making jokes. And yet, for all their pranks and mischief, are these gnomes good and virtuous within their natures, and offer gifts of kindness when hard times come upon our lives".

*Geb was the Egyptian god of the Earth and a member of the Ennead of Heliopolis. An elemental fey king whose throne is covered in silver and gold crystals, Geb is the guardian of miners and others who work within the Earth. He can endow those who invoke him with the powers of prosperity, skill in all practical crafts, moneymaking by steady means, success in property matters, older people, animals, and finding and restoring what is lost.

INVOKING THE EARTH DEVAS

Gnomes are said to be the easiest of the devas to sense since their energy is almost tangible. Earth spirits can be very helpful since they embody practicality and common sense, and have an innate knowledgebase around money, the material, and how to grow things. They relate to food, nourishment, health, healing, tree magic, treasures, fertility, gardening, protection, wealth, craft skills, and all Earth magic.

Although they can be connected with at all times, they are easier to contact at midnight and throughout winter. They tend to prefer to emerge after dark. Their colours are black, dark green, browns, and all hues of the Earth. They associate strongly with ancient trees, particularly the hawthorn, the oak, the Moreton Bay fig, and ancient eucalypt forests, in whose roots they dwell. Other places they live are anywhere close to the Earth, caves, gardens, mines, old stone and crop circles, near ley and psychic power lines, and in mounds or hillocks. Suitable offerings to attract the Earth guardians are flowers, herbs, salt, corn and wheat, crystals*, stones, coins, certain essential oils*, nuts, berries, sand, small wooden items, and petals.

As keepers of Earth's riches, they are able to awaken us to our planet's treasures. Therefore, salt, crystals, quality soil, minerals, ores, and all solid landforms come under their domain. Many of those who work in mining, or with gemstones and metals, are also working with the gnomes.

Gnomes can also assist with the security of your home and are excellent guardians, so it is no accident that many gardens around the world are filled with representations of these powerful beings, as they are said to protect the home to which they are attached. Gnomes can also be called upon to bring financial stability to your household, attracting the funds needed to pay a bill or meet an urgent expense.

If you have a laborious task ahead, have employment or financial worries, need to ground your ideals, or are in need of developing a special hands-on skill, ask the earth devas for their help. The easiest way to contact them is to spend some time outdoors around the Earth element and natural features, particularly rocks and thick-trunked trees. It is best to invoke the gnomes using a wand made of crystal, linking to the Earth kingdom, or an athame, as things of the Earth such as steel and iron are also directly in tune with the gnomes.

*Some crystals to attract the Earth spirits are most agates (especially moss and tree agate), boulder opal, malachite, emerald, red or gold tiger's eye, aventurine, jet, petrified or fossilised wood, smoky quartz, and all stones with holes in the centre.

*Some essential oils to attract the Earth spirits are geranium, tea tree, cypress, vervain, oakmoss, honeysuckle, vetiver, patchouli and magnolia.

THE NORTH DIRECTION'S CORRESPONDENCES

If you wish to work more with your particular element and direction, the following may help propel your wishes and magical journey:

Time of Day ✦ Midnight

Polarity ✦ Female, positive

Exhortation ✦ To keep silent

Musical Instruments ✦ Drums, percussion

Colours ✦ Black, deep green, all Earthy hues

Season ✦ Winter

Magical Instrument ✦ Pentacle, stone

Altar Symbol ✦ Platter

Communion Symbol ✦ Bread, salt

Archangel ✦ Uriel

Human Sense ✦ Touch

Art Forms ✦ Sculpture, embroidery

Animals ✦ All domestic

Mythical Beast ✦ Unicorn

Magical Arts ✦ Talismans

Guide Forms ✦ Earth, underworld goddess

Meditation ✦ Fertile landscapes

Images & Themes ✦ Caves, rocks, organic produce, Moon, night, growth, life

HOW TO GET IN TOUCH WITH EARTH ENERGY

The mountain's position is strong only when it rises out of the Earth broad and great, not proud and steep.

I Ching, hexagram 23, ken/k'un

The old people came literally to love the soil and they sat or reclined on the ground with a feeling of being close to a mothering power ... (They) liked to remove their moccasins and walk with bare feet on the sacred Earth. Their tepees were built upon the Earth and their altars were made of it. The soil was soothing, strengthening, cleansing and healing.

Chief Luther Standing Bear

- Use Earth energy when making wishes around the following: Financial security and stability, material possessions, practical areas of your life, solidity, endurance and stamina, fertility and fertile opportunities, abundance, work and career, home and garden, children, manifesting anything on the physical plane
- In magical practices, Earth can be represented by soil, salt, crystals and minerals. Earth spells are most powerful when performed outside. A forest, cave or mountain make naturally sacred spaces in which you can attune to the Earth's energy, infusing your work with the forces of nature. Use tools made with materials grown in the ground, such as clay or stone, salt, herbs, sand, rocks and crystals - and try using a pentagram disc as a base to strengthen the links with your element
- The best days on which to employ Earth magic are on a Saturday, ruled by the Earthy planet Saturn, or a Friday, ruled by the Norse Earth Goddess Frigg. If possible, choose dawn or dusk when the magical half-light is neither day nor night, a truly mystical time
- Hike in the mountains
- Indulge in some hot-stone massage therapy
- Go camping
- Spend time outdoors, connecting yourself to the Earth itself - in the form of trees, rocks, mountains and fields
- Smell a flower, appreciate its fragrance
- Heal your emotional body with flower essences

- Red, brown and black-coloured crystals will activate your connection with the element of Earth and will nurture you and enhance healing
- Exercise regularly, focusing your full attention on your body and its movements
- Undertake physical activities that enhance your mind/body integration, such as t'ai chi or yoga
- Learn to love your body
- Eat Earthy foods and heavy foods which will help ground you, including breads, and rooted fruits or vegetables that grow in soil
- Aim for greater order and organisation in your life, with regard to time, resources, and possessions
- Cook. Consciously attune yourself to the meals and food you prepare
- Climb trees
- Hug trees
- Lie down in a field of flowers
- Meditate on the Pentacles suit in the Tarot (the Pentacles suit represents the Earth element)
- Collect and carry stones, shells, gems and wood, and any other products of the Earth that you find meaningful
- Study the Earth sciences, such as geology, crystallography, or environmental studies
- Plant, grow and tend your own garden. Flowers, cacti, fruits and root vegetables are ideal
- Help others learn how to be more realistic, hands-on and practical; as an Earth sign, you are an excellent role model
- Learn how to make pottery or sculpt using your hands
- Wear and surround yourself with the colours green, brown, and other Earthy tones
- Cultivate a whole-body sensuality, by giving and receiving massages regularly. You're a natural!
- Attune yourself to the Earth goddess Gaia
- Formulate and maintain a regular schedule and routine to help stabilise your energies

- Devote yourself to finding a home, space, or plot of land to call your own, helping to provide you with a foundation and a sense of rootedness in the one place
- Invest your money in something secure and long-term
- Surround yourself with friends who are also bodily-oriented and practical; they will help to reinforce and strengthen these facets of yourself
- When working with the Earth element in magical practice, stand at the North quarter of your magical space, as the North is its domain, and invite its living essence into your 'circle'
- Earth spirits are also known as fairies, gnomes, tree devas or elves. They provide grounding and attend to emotional healing, so Earth signs would be wise to adopt one (or all) as their very own spirit guide!

THE AIR ELEMENT - GEMINI, AQUARIUS, LIBRA

✦ **The Intellectual Group** ✦
The path to BROTHERHOOD
Focused on Mental & Social Interactions

King ✦ Paralda

Rulers ✦ Sylphs, Zephyrs and Fairies who inhabit the world of flowers, winds, breezes, mountains

Colour & Direction ✦ Red or Yellow; East

Wind ✦ Eurus

Lucky Star ✦ Aldebaran

Symbols & Associations ✦ Sky, wind, breezes, spring, knowledge, intellect, thoughts, ideas, breath, vibration, truth, freedom, sunrise

Magical Tools ✦ Incense, wands, dreamcatchers, creative visualisation

Alchemical Associations ✦ The Intellect, Gold, the Colour Yellow

Alchemical Stage ✦ Solutio

Key Attributes ✦ Communication, intelligence, reason, perspective, renewal, thought, logic

Symbolism ✦ Clear thought, communication, study, connection to the Universals

Governed by ✦ The mind & the psyche

Air Characteristics ✦ Intelligent, wise, thoughtful, analytical, detached, objective

✦ The Magic of Air ✦

The element of Air governs the eastern quarter (in magic). Its ruler is Paralda who oversees the Sylphs, Zephyrs, and Nature spirits or fairies. Its colour is pure yellow; it is considered warm and moist. The positive associations of Air are sunrise, spring, incense, the wand, clouds, breezes, breath, optimism, joy, intelligence, mental quickness, any kind of helpful air.

D.J. Conway

Many Eastern philosophies believe that the vital force that energises both humans and the cosmos is carried in the Air, entering our bodies when we breathe. This fundamental energy is called prana in India, chi in China and ki in Japan. Spiritual prayers from Buddhist prayer flags are believed to be carried in the wind. In Witchcraft and alchemy, the East corresponds to the mind, dawn, spring, to pale, airy colours, white and violet, to the eagle and high-flying birds, and the power to know. Its tools are the athame and the sword, which are used interchangeably.

Air is invisible and intangible, but it drives life continuance and is necessary to animate all living things. Air gives us life, but its absence also denotes death; therefore, it is connected with both living and dying, being urgently necessary for survival and yet inherently ambiguous, being everywhere and nowhere at once. In astrology, the exact moment the newborn inhales its first breath is when we choose to establish the birth chart. But this rhythm of life is also a rhythm of death. In fact, the breath which enables a child to live independently and freed from its cord, depends on a continuous movement. At the other end of life, withholding your breath signifies drawing your last and expiring, or dying.

Represented by sky, wind, flight and breath, Air can be a cool breeze, fanning the flames of desire, or a strong wind, creating a hurricane. Taking deep breaths can calm and soothe the spirits.

According to Shiva, the knowledge of the breath 'is a jewel in the crown of the wise'. To the swara yogi, who is attuned to the subtle currents of energy, the secret of his mastery of himself and the Universe lies in his attention to these currents and in learning how to blend with them through conscious breathing. 'In the flow of the breath is the wisdom of the Scriptures', is beautiful wisdom attributed to Shiva.

Air is the mental principle. The most intellectual and innovative of the four elements, it is unconcerned with the material side of life, but rather it seeks to share with and communicate ideas to others. It is a connective energy, driven to share thought and mental rapport. Air is associated with the thinking function and its motivating force is mind-thought stimulation. Characterised by intellect and aspiration over passion, Airy types are ideas people, using rational and logical thought processes, seeking mental understanding, and experiencing life through the mind. They are also objective and 'head-orientated', sometimes to the detriment of their emotions and intuition.

The Air signs are masculine in polarity, extroverted in expression, and are aligned with the realms of relationships and connections of all kinds. These signs, relating to communication and the intellect, express themselves in differing ways: Gemini, through its quickness to see both sides of any issue and to generate thoughts and ideas from what has been learned; Libra, through its ability to balance many different viewpoints and find a harmonious consensus to maintain the status quo; and Aquarius, through its foresight and vision to understand how Universal principles can be used for the betterment of humankind.

Air is perhaps the most misunderstood of the elements, because of its intangible nature and lack of visible manifestation. However, without Air there can be no Fire; Water devoid of oxygen is merely hydrogen gas; and in the absence of Air there is simply no conscious, breathing life. Air is usually invisible and one only notices its effects when it is directed through another element. Indeed, its magical powers can be activated through Fire (smoke), Earth (dust storms, moving through windchimes), and Water (inhalation, steam, vaporisation, cyclones).

The soul and breath have always been closely linked. But breath is not the soul; it is its vehicle. Both are unseen and impalpable. Breath is also the vehicle for thought, sound, spirit, speech and language.

Air is the same for everyone, yet our breath is unique to us alone. Perhaps that is why those born of the Air element often have a delicate albeit superficial sensitivity to the Air around them, its nuances and temperature, its feel, its nature, its fragrance, and its moisture.

Air is also associated with inspiration, ideas and exchange, representing the Divine energies and messages from the gods. Inspired by birds, shamans use spirit flight in their healing ceremonies and rituals. Air can open your mind to new possibilities and allow your imagination to take flight. All cultures have legends of wise 'messengers' descending from the air, such as angels, birds, winged dragons and science fiction aliens, all of whom, it is supposed, have access to higher sources of information. Witches are often depicted flying through the Air on their broomsticks, a symbol of their wisdom and magic. And the sky gods of ancient times were all guardians of arcane studies and were thought to pass on these gifts to the humans who believed in as well as called upon them. Hermes, the Greek messenger god, and his Roman counterpart Mercury, are both associated with the Air element.

When we work with Air, we think of the Divine breath of spirit, the ability to move through space and time, and the wisdom derived from experience, breathwork and study.

As the element suggests, Airy spirits are constantly on the move, shifting, changing and evolving. Air signs are generally unnerved by states of flux, as movement is a chance for growth and exploration to these inquisitive souls. Independent, open-minded and spontaneous, Air signs loathe restrictions and anything which curtails their freedom, especially of thought, and love to broaden their horizons through circulating amongst people, places and experiences.

Keywords
Broad-minded, fair, objective, refined, ideas-oriented, communicative, observant, versatile, rational, theoretical, social, learning-oriented, impersonal, logical, innovative, connective, detached, active-minded, clever, curious, impartial, cooperative, abstract, integrating, networking, analytical, relationship-oriented, intellectual

✦ On Gemini & the Air Element ✦

"In spite of all the people around him, he shares his deepest emotions only with his one constant companion - his other twin self. The Air is his element and his real home. He's a stranger to Earth."

Linda Goodman

Gemini ✦ is the Air of knowledge, of learning and intelligence, the flow of thoughts and the flight of fancies, the changeable breeze that adapts to the environment, and twists and turns at its direction.

Libra ✦ is the Air of balanced wisdom, the winds of relatedness, the whispers of love, harmonious expression, the fair dissemination of thought and knowledge.

Aquarius ✦ is the Air of imagination, of innovation, original thought, and change for the better; is Fixed Air, the Air of opinion and inspiration, the cold turning winds and electrically charged ions that fuel thoughts and whims, the Air that changes the direction of the world.

AN EXCESS OR LACK OF THE AIR ELEMENT

Excess Air can make one impersonal, restless, overly idealistic, nervous, detached, anxious and jittery. To balance an over-abundance of Air, increase your intake of water and beneficial fluids, do outdoor exercise such as swimming and walking, supplement your diet with B complex vitamins, magnesium and manganese, wear deep blue and violet colours to calm your spirit, use the crystals lapis lazuli, blue tourmaline, green calcite, chrysocolla, sapphire and aquamarine to settle the nervous system, drink nerve tonic herbal teas such as chamomile, skullcap, vervain, catnip, valerian and hops, and take flower remedies such as Morning Glory, White Chestnut, Mimulus and Lavender.

For those lacking Air, deep breathing exercises can help, as can developing one's communication and expression skills, and dancing and being more aware of movement through space, drinking herbal teas such as gotu kola and fo ti (a Chinese herb known as the 'elixir of life') to stimulate brain activity, wearing and using the colours yellow and blue for communication and expression, and taking flower remedies such as Sweet Pea, Quaking Grass, Scelranthus, Penstemon to help one relate more effectively to people and groups.

THE ARCHANGEL OF AIR ✦ RAPHAEL

The Air element vibrates to the essence of Raphael.
(For further information on archangels, see under 'The Archangel of Fire').

✦ Archangel Raphael's Associations ✦

Element of Air
The eastern quarter of the Earth
The spring season
The colour blue (or blue and gold)
The astrological signs of Gemini, Libra and Aquarius

Raphael, meaning 'Healing power of God' or 'The Divine has healed', is the archangel of healing and safe travels. Raphael is the Divine healer, bringing healing in all its forms to those who need it. He leads the guardian angels, takes care of travellers, supports those in the health professions, and bestows knowledge, wisdom, and therapeutic skill. Soothing and calming, he can help you to heal yourself and to feel a connection and oneness with nature. This being works to stimulate energies for overall life and success. Raphael awakens a sense of beauty, wonder and creativity which stimulates higher mental faculties. As the supreme healer in the angelic realm, his chief role is to support, heal and guide in all matters of health, working to soothe people's minds, bodies and spirits so they can enjoy overall peace and wellbeing. He also helps animals and guides Earthly healers and light-workers in their education and practice. Overall, he is in charge of physical health and wellness. Raphael has as his servant Paralda, King of the Sylphs, who appears to clairvoyant vision as a tenuous form made of blue mist always moving and changing shape. Raphael can be invoked using a caduceus, and is regarded as the Keeper of the Holy Grail.

INDIVIDUAL ZODIAC ARCHANGELS OF THE AIR ELEMENT SIGNS

Additionally, each sign is associated with a particular archangel. Such knowledge can help you to build up a relationship with these beings, based upon your needs. However, no link is rigid, and as you work with angels you will come to develop your own affinities. When invoking a specific archangel, a useful ritual to draw them closer is to light a candle in that angel's colour, burn some oil or incense of its scent, and hold the appropriate crystal while focusing on what you are needing guidance on.

GEMINI'S ZODIAC ARCHANGEL ✦ METATRON

Metatron is the king of the angelic host and angel of the covenant. Once the prophet Enoch, he is the knower of secrets and the transmitter of mysteries between angels and humanity, overseer and keeper of the Akashic records, the books of life of all beings.

Paul Hougham

Metatron has been called the bright twin to Sandalphon's (preceding sign Taurus's archangel) darkness. His is the light of revelation. He is the supernal teacher of Divine intelligence. Versatile and bestowing the gift of spiritual illumination to those who are receptive, Metatron may blind those who are not ready to receive this blessing, so he must be approached with an open mind and heart. He enables you to de-clutter your life so you are able to move forward and be freer to develop.

SCENT/OIL ✦ Lavender
CANDLE COLOUR ✦ White
CRYSTAL ✦ Herkimer diamond
OTHER SPECIAL ANGELS FOR GEMINI ✦ Ambriel & Raphael

LIBRA'S ZODIAC ARCHANGELS ✦ CHAMUEL & JOPHIEL

Chamuel ✦ Chamuel is the relationship balancer and healer, enabling the heart to open and encouraging you to value yourself and realise what you have to offer. Chamuel brings comfort if a relationship is in distress, giving you the gift of insight that you still have much to offer and that your love has not been wasted. He can also connect you with your soulmate.

SCENT/OIL ✦ Ylang Ylang
CANDLE COLOUR ✦ Soft pink
CRYSTAL ✦ Rose quartz

Jophiel ✦ Jophiel's name means 'beauty of God'. He is the bringer of sunshine, wisdom and joy. He carries the flame of intuition, and his blessings include creativity and inspiration. He is the dispeller of clouds of doubt and thereby increases self-esteem, courage, vitality and strength.

SCENT/OIL ✦ Cinnamon
CANDLE COLOUR ✦ Gold
CRYSTAL ✦ Citrine
OTHER SPECIAL ANGELS FOR LIBRA ✦ Uriel, Zuriel & Anael

AQUARIUS'S ZODIAC ARCHANGEL ✦ URIEL

Uriel means 'fire of God' and he is linked with lightning, thunder, and sudden happenings. He may be depicted carrying a scroll that contains revelations about your true path in life. Uriel is dynamic, and his gifts are stamina, action, dynamism, and dispelling fears. Stimulating physical desires, call on Uriel if you are feeling desperate, depleted, or rejected and he will help to restore your vitality and get you back on your feet.

SCENT/OIL ✦ Clove
CANDLE COLOUR ✦ Ruby red
CRYSTAL ✦ Carnelian or red jasper
OTHER SPECIAL ANGELS FOR AQUARIUS ✦ Cambiel & Gabriel

THE DEVIC REALMS & AIR ✦
EAST: REALM OF THE SYLPHS

Deva is a Sanskrit word that means 'shining one'. Devas are the life force within nature, and there are four devic realms - Fire, Earth, Air and Water - which contain ethereal elemental spirits or sprites. Elementals are the building blocks of nature, and close to being true energy and consciousness. The four elements correspond to four different states of matter: energy/transmutation (Fire), gas (Air), liquid (Water) and solid (Earth), which are linked to the four human states of consciousness: inspiration, thought, feeling and practicality. There are four spirits, or elementals, which reside in the devic realms, associated with each element.

The four main levels of elemental beings are: Gnomes (Earth), Undines (Water), Sylphs (Air), and Salamanders (Fire). The fifth element of Ether is the element from which came forth the other four, and Ether, or Spirit, has never been defined in any particular category, and encompasses the aspects and beings of all the other elements.

Elementals are usually benevolent guardian beings or spirits that look after nature's secrets and treasures in whatever part of the natural realm they occupy. If you wish to re-connect and re-harmonise yourself by working with nature and its messages and lessons, you could begin by learning a little about your element's realm: The element of Air is connected with the East direction and the realm of the Sylphs. Slyph is from the Greek *silphe*, meaning 'butterfly'.

✦ Sylphs ✦

Sylphs are fairy-like spirits that inhabit the air, winds and atmosphere as well as high mountain tops (not all sylphs are restricted to living in the air, however). They are probably more closely in line with our concept of fairies and angels than the other elemental beings; and indeed, they work alongside the angels.

Always active and extremely quick of movement and sound, Air Elementals are also known to be highly intelligent as they can gather vast amounts of information in a short period of time. They are aloof and detached and usually very subtle in their persuasiveness. People with strong sylph influence or activity often find that sexuality is not high on their list of priorities, and may not understand how it can be so with others. But the sylphs stimulate the expression of the creative 'sexual' drive into other avenues of one's life, such as work, interests, or hobbies.

The sylphs are guardians of spring, the east direction, and the wind; indeed, they control all winds. Therefore, they are chiefly concerned with communication, the mind, the intellect, and the kingdom of the feathered and winged creatures.

As the east is the doorway to new beginnings and the direction through which the sacred circle is always entered, air has a uniquely ethereal, otherworldly, wispy quality to it. It makes its presence felt through its four winds: the north brings cold and withering; the east brings new life and freshness; the south brings vitality and warmth; and the west brings fertility and gentle abundance.

Air, and its various components, is our vital life force, enabling us to exist. It also supports that which flies - from birds to human-made technology. It allows fire to burn and for communication to flow with ease, and stimulates our intellect so we can exercise good reason, judgment and rational thought to enhance our lives.

Air makes its home in the heavens and yet it flows freely as an all-pervasive, omnipresent gift for all to share.

The King of Air is Lugh or Paralda*, its archangel is Raphael, its magickal tool is the athame (which calls down the spirits into form), and its sacred ceremonial stones are Lapis Lazuli, Sapphire, Blue Topaz and Azurite.

Perhaps Merlin sums up the sylph realm best: "For these beings are like unto jewels of light, their wings glistening as crystal butterflies in the first Dawn. We may see them in a dance of light upon a leaf or petal, perchance amidst the forest dells or in the hidden glades where few have ventured."

Paralda, King of the Air elementals, is a mysterious, misty being who lives on the highest mountain on Earth, who shimmers in the early morning sunlight and breaks through the mist in an occasional flash of radiance. He has appeared both as a quick and youthful being, and as a wise and elderly scholar.

INVOKING THE AIR DEVAS

Sylphs are best contacted in high, open spaces where the wind blows freely, such as hillsides, mountains, grasslands, meadows, and open planes. They can be found in wind, clouds, rain, storms and snowflakes. They can travel in the form of butterflies, ribbons, birds, feathers, dream catchers, thistledown, or dandelion seeds.

Air spirits are the fastest moving in nature and form, changeable in action and mood, and unpredictable. They are movers of energy, carrying seeds for new life, stripping dead leaves from trees, and assisting birds on their migratory paths.

To attract sylph energies, use wind chimes, trailing scarves, fragrances, feathers, mobiles, mist, bubbles*, and bird-call music. Make a wish on each butterfly you see, or blow dandelion seeds softly into the air while stating your desires out loud or in your mind.

If you are in need of clearer thought and memory, greater freedom, or better communication skills, ask the Air devas for their help. They can help guide you if you have an important exam or journey to undertake, if you have to give a speech, or if you are doing anything that requires clear, swift thought and efficient self-expression.

To make contact with a sylph, make or acquire a dream catcher. A Native American craft, usually hoop-shaped with dangling beads and feathers, these are designed to 'catch' bad dreams and protect you while you sleep. Dream catchers can be adapted to attract sylphs, because they can never really be caught, since they embody the essence of liberty and unencumbered flight. Perhaps you could get a new dream catcher for this very purpose, and imbue it with your positive intentions through a special affirmation. When you become aware of your sylph stirring your dream catcher, ask for the specific help you are requiring, thank the sylph for his or her help, then set them free back into their realm of flight and free-flow, knowing that their help has been given, your wish granted, and their work done.

Sylphs also respond well to the burning of incense, conscious breathing, and music. Suitable offerings are the crystals amethyst, diamond, sapphire, blue lace agate, sodalite, citrine, lapis lazuli, clear quartz and turquoise, and essential oils and fragrances of lemongrass, bergamot, lavender, fennel, dill, almond, peppermint, sage, anise, and lemon verbena.

*You can send your wishes into the Air in the form of bubbles. Bubbles rise high and can carry them to the Air spirits who can transform your dreams and desires into reality. Wednesday and Thursday are particularly good days for Air elemental wish magic. Dawn is a good time to undertake your wish, especially when the wind is blowing noticeably but gently enough to carry your desire into the unseen ether.

THE EAST DIRECTION'S CORRESPONDENCES

If you wish to work more with your particular element and direction, the following may help propel your wishes and magical journey:

Time of Day ✦ Dawn

Polarity ✦ Male, positive

Exhortation ✦ To will

Musical Instruments ✦ Wind instruments, harp

Colours ✦ Gold, white

Season ✦ Spring

Magical Instrument ✦ Wand

Altar Symbol ✦ Incense

Communion Symbol ✦ Scent

Archangel ✦ Raphael

Human Senses ✦ Hearing, smell

Art Forms ✦ Poetry Painting

Animals ✦ Birds, bats

Mythical Beast ✦ Winged horse

Magical Arts ✦ Divinations

Guide Forms ✦ Sky/weather gods

Meditation ✦ Sky, clouds

Images & Themes ✦ Mountain tops, flying, sunrise, wisdom, knowledge

HOW TO GET IN TOUCH WITH AIR ENERGY

"When we are present with and summon the magic of Air, we gain wings"

Stand still and fill your lungs with air. With every breath you inhale a thousand billion billion atoms. A few million billion of them are long-living argon atoms that are exhaled within the second and dispersed with the winds. Time mixes them and has been mixing them for a long time. Some of them may have visited Buddha or Caesar, or even earlier paid a call on the man from Makapan.

A. Rolf Edberg

- Use Air energy when making wishes around the following: Travel, exam success and study, job interviews, meditation, relaxation, more effective communication with others, improved expression and articulation of needs, mental stability, increasing knowledgebase, nervous stress relief
- In magical practices, Air can be represented by smoke, which can be created by burning a joss stick or incense. The following tools and methods can also be used to carry your dreams to the skies and ether: Feathers, hanging mobiles in the breeze with your wishes attached, paper darts, autumn leaves, and airborne seeds
- The best days on which to employ Air magic are Wednesdays, ruled by the planet of communication Mercury, or Thursdays, ruled by Thor, the Norse god of thunder. If possible, choosing a windy day with gales or thunderstorms will make your work more powerful. Air spells are also most effective when performed beneath an open sky; a high mountain would be an ideal location. Writing a wish on a kite or a balloon and guiding it through the air, as high as possible, by a piece of string can harness the magic of the Air spirits, who will help you clarify and manifest your desires, through quite literally releasing your wish into the wind
- Spend time in open, fresh, clean air regularly
- Spend time in wide open spaces and engage in outdoor activities that make use of the air around you, such as flying a kite or ballooning
- Learn Prana-, Chi- or Ki-related disciplines, martial arts, meditation and yoga that focus on breathing, focus, mental-detachment and concentration
- Read as much as you can; be an eternal student

- Blue-coloured crystals will activate your connection with the element of Air and enhance your dreams, soothe your fears, calm your nervous system, help you communicate, bring about inner peace, and assist in self-transformation
- Develop your networking skills
- Throw intellectual dinner parties
- Join a discussion group or an online Internet chat room
- Practice deep breathing
- Learn about meteorology, cloud formations, the atmosphere, and the weather
- Use a negative ion machine, humidifier, or air purifier in your home
- Don't smoke, or if you do, quit (being associated with the lungs, Geminis should particularly take note of this)
- Sleep on an air mattress
- Meditate on the Swords suit in the Tarot (the Swords suit represents the Air element)
- Take a course - in anything and everything!
- Know a little bit about everything; trivia is more powerful than it's given credit for!
- Write; keep a journal
- Visit the library on a regular basis; join a book discussion group
- Look after your lungs, other components of your respiratory system, and your nervous system
- Take a course, learn a language, or otherwise make a commitment to a learning activity which requires discipline, focus and mental energy
- Take a course on improving your relationships
- Hire a jumping castle and invite your friends over!
- Jump on a trampoline
- Practice public speaking often, even solo in front of a mirror
- Forget your mind chatter and allow your heart to lead occasionally; it always knows where to go
- When working with the Air element in magical practice, stand at the East quarter of your magical space, as the East is its domain, and invite its living essence into your 'circle'

- Air spirits are also known as air devas, zephyrs, builders or sylphs, and can be called upon to calm our nerves, cleanse our thoughts, clear anxiety and fear, and to help us focus with greater mental clarity, so Air signs would be wise to adopt one (or all) as their very own spirit guide!

THE WATER ELEMENT - CANCER, SCORPIO, PISCES

✦ **The Emotional Group** ✦
The path to SPIRITUALITY
Focused on Emotion & Feelings

King ✦ Niksa or Necksa

Rulers ✦ Undines, Nymphs, Mermaids and Mermen who live in the sea, streams, springs and lakes, and Fairies of the rivers, ponds, and ocean

Colour & Direction ✦ Grey or Blue; West

Wind ✦ Zephyrus

Lucky Star ✦ Antares

Symbols & Associations ✦ Oceans, lakes, wells, springs, rivers, pools, rain, fog, mist, sunset, emotions, healing, absorbing, communion with the spiritual, the subconscious, sleep, fertility, love, pleasure, the psychic

Magical Tools ✦ Goblets, wishing wells, cauldrons, mirrors, chalices

Alchemical Associations ✦ The Subconscious, Quicksilver, the Colour White

Alchemical Stage ✦ Sublimatio

Key Attributes ✦ Sensitivity, flexibility, intuition, creativity, feeling

Symbolism ✦ Healing, reflection, cleansing

Governed by ✦ The Soul & the feelings

Water Characteristics ✦ Subjective, emotional, intuitive, sensitive, imaginative, receptive

✦ The Magic of Water ✦

The element of Water governs the western quarter (in magic). Its ruler is Niksa who oversees the Nymphs, Undines, Mer-people, and the little ones of the springs, lakes, ponds, and rivers. Its colour is pure blue; it is cold and moist. The positive associations of Water are sunset, fall (autumn), the chalice and cauldron, any form of helpful water, compassion, peacefulness, forgiveness, love, intuition.

D.J. Conway

Water is the flow of emotions, the tide that carries you out to sea and will bring you back to a safe shore after a whimsical adventure. It can be placid or tempestuous, and without it life cannot flourish. It can cause your dreams to carry you away on the waves, without anchoring your aspirations. You can sink or swim in Water, having nothing to cling to for support, as it has no form, shaping itself into its surroundings. It needs a container to prevent your dreams being swept away; cups, goblets and bowls are often associated with water, and the term 'Holy Grail' describes one's greatest desires.

The sage is like water.
Water is good, nourishes all things,
and does not compete with them.
It dwells in humble places that others disdain;
hence it is close to the Tao.
In his dwelling, the sage loves the earth.
In his mind, he loves what is profound.
In his associations, he is kind and gentle.
In his speech, he is sincere.
In his ruling, he is just.
In business, he is proficient.
In his action, he is timely.
Because he does not compete,
he does not find fault in others.

Lao Tzu (604-517 BC), Tao Te Ching, VIII

Keywords

Impressionable, compassionate, reflective, insightful, merging, fertile, receptive, absorbing, responsive, habitual, perceptive, secretive, submissive, possessive, nurturing, sensitive, dependent, instinctive, emotional, sympathetic, intriguing, protective, empathetic, psychic, mysterious*

*All these words don't necessarily describe all three Water signs. Pisces, for example, is not possessive, and Scorpio is not submissive.

Cancer ✦ is the Water of the ocean's gentle ebbs and flows, of the Moon, the emotions and memories, the babbling brook, the feelings of family, home, ancestry, heritage, nostalgia, roots, childhood, and motherly love.

Scorpio ✦ is the Water of transformation, the clear pond, or the stagnant puddle about to spring forth back into life, the feeling of intimate love and the powerful invisible feelings that dwell beneath the surface.

Pisces ✦ is the Water of the meandering stream of the imagination, the vast ocean, the ripples on a river when a stone is thrown in it, the sense of All Is One, the feeling for all of humanity, and of Universal love.

Thales of Miletus, the first philosopher, commented that the world is made of one element and that element is Water. Water is a fundamental principle; quite simply – and not unlike the other three elements – we need it to survive. Associated with wisdom, intuition, knowledge, prophecy, fluidity, formlessness, power, beauty, and a paradoxical tremendous but subtle force, Water is bound up with the Divine, as a source and renewer of Life.

Water is the most important element of all, for without it there would be no life on planet Earth. Without Water the land would not be fruitful or fertile, but dry and sterile. It has long been revered as the wellspring of life, enabling human civilisations to grow and flourish across the planet. The ancients understood the generative energy inherent in Water, and it has given rise to many myths, stories, superstitions and symbols. For example, the chalice, a vessel for holding this element, is a legendary symbol of abundance and spiritual power. The Moon and its compelling influence on the seas and female reproductive cycles, is strongly linked with the Water element and its deeply feminine nature.

As the ultimate source of life and growth, Water is the most significant element in terms of regeneration and metamorphosis. Water follows a relatively unchanging cycle, going from a liquid state to a solid state, and according to scientific observations, changes form around thirty-four times in the course of the terrestrial year.

Under the combined influence of the movement of the Earth's rotation upon itself and of gravity, water shapes the Earth's surface. The perpetual motions and meandering courses of all the bodies of water on the surface of the globe, as well as the numerous currents, are caused by this terrestrial rotation, and also by the movements of the Moon around our planet.

Water is the Universal Solvent and Coagulant in nature's alchemical laboratory. The Sun of Life, the Ego, passes through the waters of parturition in three definite stages symbolised by the Watery signs. They are the most primitive of all the animals depicted in the zodiac: the scorpion, the fish, and the crab. The different astrological animal and human symbols, are said to represent the hierarchical instincts (e.g. aquatic, deep, dark) and the temperament of each creature or human type - our primal, instinctive, and unconscious sides. Two of the Water signs - Scorpio and Cancer - are symbolised by half land-half water creatures, amphibious and flexible, but the Fish that represents the sign of Pisces can't breathe air and must live eternally in the cool water, sometimes muddy, sometimes clear, but always flowing.

In Greek mythology, Poseidon (Neptune to the Romans) rules the oceanic and water domains. Symbols and images most associated with the Water element include mermaids, wells, reservoirs, swimming, fish, crabs, lakes, rivers, dolphins, whales, diving, water-skiing and boating.

Water has long been associated with the powers of birth and regeneration, representing the feelings and healing energy. Ancient people built their settlements close to the life-giving rivers, streams and springs that became the source of several magical traditions and beliefs. In most cultures, wells, lakes and ponds were worshipped and venerated. Offerings were dropped into the watery depths in return for blessings - a ritual that survives today in the form of a wishing well.

Pulled by the Moon, the tides of Water can help you attune to change. The unpredictable nature of the waves and tides can be overwhelming however, and it's for this reason that Water brings powerful emotions to the surface, where they can be purged. Working with Water in your daily magic rituals can restore and cleanse your spirit, increase your sensitivity, awareness and receptivity, and gently renew your faith in the flow of the Universe.

Astrologically, Water is associated with the feeling principle and function, representing the emotional realm, integration, transformation, purification, dependence, merging, blending and union. The Water signs, living in the fluid world of emotion and feeling, express themselves in these differing ways: Cancer, through a great nurturing compassion, especially in home and family affairs; Scorpio, through its enormous sexual intensity and capacity, and its fascination for, and immersion in, the ultimate forces of life and death; and Pisces, through its acute sensitivity to the environment and its strongly developed sense of subconscious Universal undercurrents.

As the element suggests, Water is sometimes turbulent, sometimes flowing, sometimes deep and murky, merges with its surroundings, and almost always fluid. Psychic, penetrative and intuitive, Water signs rely on instincts rather than logic.

Overall, Water is the cleansing, purifying element, necessary for all life. It is the major component of the human body and is associated with our lymphatic systems. In the form of rain, it nourishes the Earth, promoting and enabling fertility, unfurling and growth. Formless and meandering, it connects and merges, while still retaining its own essence.

AN EXCESS OR LACK OF THE WATER ELEMENT

Be soft in your practice. Think of the method as a fine silvery stream, not a raging waterfall. Follow the stream, have faith in its course. It will go its own way, meandering here, trickling there. It will find the grooves, the cracks, the crevices. Just follow it. Never let it out of your sight. It will take you.

Sheng-yen

Excess Water can make one overly sensitive, too emotional, dreamy, self-indulgent, over-reactive, drowsy, overweight, dependent, clingy and insecure. To balance an over-abundance of Water, eat mostly cooked foods and increase your intake of spicy, warming foods and drinks, drink diuretic herbal teas such as nettles, celery seed, dandelion leaf and alfalfa, use the crystals kunzite, rose quartz, pink tourmaline, amethyst, fluorite, sugilite and green aventurine to heal and soothe the emotions, and take flower remedies such as Red Chestnut, Honeysuckle, Chamomile, Pink Yarrow and Clematis for psychic protection and emotional security.

For those lacking Water, drink more fluids like vegetable juices and herbal teas, live near the water, indulge in artistic and expressive endeavours to foster your creative spirit, take flower remedies such as Black-Eyed Susan, Holly, Sticky Monkeyflower, Garlic and Fuchsia to express and release feelings, and use the crystals tourmaline, pearl and opal to inspire creativity, and smoky quartz and black obsidian to help release unhelpful emotions.

THE ARCHANGEL OF WATER ✦ GABRIEL

The Water element vibrates to the essence of Gabriel.
(For further information on archangels, see under 'The Archangel of Fire').

✦ Archangel Gabriel's Associations ✦
Element of Water
The Western quarter of the Earth
The winter season
The colours emerald, silver, sea green
The crystals opal, fluorite, moonstone
The astrological signs of Cancer, Scorpio and Pisces

Gabriel, meaning "Strength of God" or "The Divine is my strength," is known as the messenger and can help us to find our true soul's purpose. As archangel of the Moon and ruler of dreams, Gabriel is chief archangel of the night and the alter ego of Michael, the Sun archangel. Some consider Gabriel a feminine energy. The archangel of life, hope, truth, astral travel, unconscious wisdom, illumination and love, he inspires and motivates artists and communicators, and delivers important prophetic messages to people. He guards the sacred places of the world and the sacred waters of life. Gabriel provides intuitive teaching, guidance, mystical experiences, inspiration, and enlightenment of spiritual duties, including awakening within us a greater understanding of dreams. He can be called upon when you are feeling alone, afraid, or vulnerable. Gabriel is said to be the angel who chooses the souls to be born and cares for them in the womb. He is also an angel of death, but a gentle one, bringing release from sorrow and pain. Gabriel's servant is Nixa, King of the Undines, who is seen as an ever-changing shape, fluid with a greenish blue aura splashed with silver and grey.

INDIVIDUAL ZODIAC ARCHANGELS OF THE WATER ELEMENT SIGNS

Additionally, each sign is associated with a particular archangel. Such knowledge can help you to build up a relationship with these beings, based upon your needs. However, no link is rigid, and as you work with angels you will come to develop your own affinities. When invoking a specific archangel, a useful ritual to draw them closer is to light a candle in that angel's colour, burn some oil or incense of its scent, and hold the appropriate crystal while focusing on what you are needing guidance on.

CANCER'S ZODIAC ARCHANGEL ✦ GABRIEL*

*See previous information under the heading 'Archangel Gabriel's Associations'.

SCENT/OIL ✦ Jasmine
CANDLE COLOUR ✦ Orange-gold
CRYSTAL ✦ Moonstone or beryl
OTHER SPECIAL ANGELS FOR CANCER ✦ Muriel

SCORPIO'S ZODIAC ARCHANGEL ✦ RAZIEL

Raziel means 'secret of God' and he is lord of the mysteries of life. He awakens the spirit so that it can comprehend things which cannot be understood by the intellect. The insights of Raziel run deep and can be life-changing and difficult to express or explain to others, but ultimately these insights can bring about profound transformation. Raziel's gifts include self-awareness, release of obsessions, inner peace and harmony, and the clearing away of mental chatter to make way for true knowing.

SCENT/OIL ✦ Neroli
CANDLE COLOUR ✦ Indigo
CRYSTAL ✦ Garnet or electric blue obsidian
OTHER SPECIAL ANGELS FOR SCORPIO ✦ Barbiel & Azrael

PISCES'S ZODIAC ARCHANGEL ✦ TZAPHKIEL

Tzaphkiel is understood as a feminine presence and is close to Sophia, the 'mind of God'. Tzaphkiel is a capable nurturer and encourages mystical states, altered consciousness and the blessings of an open heart. She reveals other realities and the mysteries of the Universe and Source. Tzaphkiel can help you release the thoughts, feelings or pressures that emanate from others, as well as releasing tension and bringing deep emotional healing.

SCENT/OIL ✦ Clary sage
CANDLE COLOUR ✦ Lilac
CRYSTAL ✦ Labradorite or purple fluorite
OTHER SPECIAL ANGELS FOR PISCES ✦ Barchiel & Asariel

THE DEVIC REALMS & WATER ✦ WEST: REALM OF THE UNDINES

Deva is a Sanskrit word that means 'shining one'. Devas are the life force within nature, and there are four devic realms - Fire, Earth, Air and Water - which contain ethereal elemental spirits or sprites. Elementals are the building blocks of nature, and close to being true energy and consciousness. The four elements correspond to four different states of matter: energy/transmutation (Fire), gas (Air), liquid (Water) and solid (Earth), which are linked to the four human states of consciousness: inspiration, thought, feeling and practicality. There are four spirits, or elementals, which reside in the devic realms, associated with each element.

The four main levels of elemental beings are: Gnomes (Earth), Undines (Water), Sylphs (Air), and Salamanders (Fire). The fifth element of Ether is the element from which came forth the other four, and Ether, or Spirit, has never been defined in any particular category, and encompasses the aspects and beings of all the other elements.

Elementals are usually benevolent guardian beings or spirits that look after nature's secrets and treasures in whatever part of the natural realm they occupy. If you wish to re-connect and re-harmonise yourself by working with nature and its messages and lessons, you could begin by learning a little about your element's realm: The element of Water is connected with the West direction and the realm of the Undines. Undine is from the Latin unda, meaning 'wave'.

✦ Undines ✦

Originating from the Latin unda, meaning 'wave', these spirits are said to control the waters of the Earth. Undines are perhaps the best known of the four elementals as they appear frequently in stories and legends. Usually female nymph-like beings, they are beautiful, eager to tempt, and enjoy associating with humans. They lure with their musical enchantments, creating sweet, intoxicating melodies with their harps, or singing pure, uplifting songs for those who are still and near enough to listen. Undines guard and carry the secrets of the Dreamtime, inner visions, emotions, feelings and journeys.

Found wherever there is a natural source of water, the undines are responsible for the vitality within liquids and they also work with aquatic plants.

The undines govern the realm of autumn and Water, the west, and the Tarot's Cups. In many religions, water symbolises the initiation through baptism in the 'waters of life'. In ancient times all great rivers were considered holy and sacred, without which nothing could prosper; springs, wells, ponds, pools and fountains were regarded as holy places where great healing properties and energies could be found and prophecies foretold.

All water upon our planet - rain, rivers, oceans, lakes, steam, etc. - has immense undine activity. Undines, like the gnomes, are subject to mortality, but they are more enduring.

One of the most famous of the Water elementals is the Lady of the Lake who features in the legends of King Arthur. This undine beauty rose from the depths to present Arthur with the sword Excalibur, and captured the hearts of many of the Knights of the Round Table.

The Undines work to maintain the astral body of humans and to stimulate our feeling nature. This is associated with heightened psychic functions as well as emotional ones. Theirs is an energy of intuition, creation and birth.

Water is the springwell of life, and these beings are essential to our finding that springwell within. Essential to the gifts of healing, purification and empathy, they work with humans to help us discover both our inner and outer beauty.

Human beings are made of around 75 per cent water, which acts as a channel, stream, or reservoir for all physiochemical processes to occur; and the same percentage again is echoed by our planet's water composition - three quarters of the Earth's surface is covered by seas, rivers and oceans, and governed by the Moon, which provides a natural rhythmical rulership over planetary phenomena.

The King of Water is Llyr or Nixa (or Necksa*), its archangel is Gabriel, its magickal tool is the Cup (a Divine receptacle), and its sacred ceremonial stones are Amethyst, Moonstone and Pearl. Folklore suggests that water gives to us what we give to it. The undines, who dwell in the Watery realms, will indeed do the same.

*Necksa (or Nixa or Nicksa) is the Queen of the deep oceans who rides a chariot of pearl. Necksa is pulled by pure-white seahorses dressed in all the colours of the sea and has shells braiding her hair. She can endow the powers of good luck, granting wishes, fertility, love, marriage, reconciliation, peaceful endings and new beginnings, and psychic powers.

INVOKING THE WATER DEVAS

Water represents flow and change – in many myths crossing a stream signifies a shift in consciousness, all cultures regard water as the biggest life-giving source, and baptism is a rite of passage in some religions.

Water is mysterious, moody and changeable, but is almost the easiest elemental to connect with as it is linked so inherently with human emotions. The Undines are associated with compassion, inner harmony, gradual growth, natural cycles, unconscious wisdom, purity, peacemaking, and blessings for babies, children and families. Water devas embody all of these attributes, and help us achieve harmony in these areas.

Water can be a tricky medium to work with, but overall, these devas help to connect you with the wellsprings of your feelings, bringing sympathy, empathy, and the bonds of human love, endowing their gifts of purification, healing and cleansing. If you are feeling raw, lonely, sad, uncared for or buffeted by life, ask the water devas for their help. You'll find them in any body of water, the tides, and the rains, in mists and in fogs, estuaries, springs, aquariums, flood plains, streams, oceans, pools and ponds, rivers and tidal rivers, whirlpools, marshlands, sacred wells, and waterfalls.

To attract undines into your experience, you can use silver, copper, kelp, scrying bowls, crystal spheres, some essential oils˚, certain crystals˚, wine offerings, steam, water features, misty mirrors, fish in tanks, and silver bells on cords. Undines will indeed endow you with blessings when you are going into any situation that requires deep emotional strength.

˚Some essential oils you can use to attract water spirits are coconut, jasmine, lemon, lilac, orchid, lily, heather, sweet pea, orchid, violet, peach, passionflower, vanilla, strawberry, myrrh, eucalyptus, hyacinth and apple blossom.

˚Some crystals that can help to bring undines into your experience are calcite, fluorite, aquamarine, mother of pearl, jade, opal, coral, moonstone, selenite and pearl.

THE WEST DIRECTION'S CORRESPONDENCES

If you wish to work more with your particular element and direction, the following may help propel your wishes and magical journey:

Time of Day ✦ Sunset
Polarity ✦ Female, negative
Exhortation ✦ To know
Musical Instruments ✦ Strings, bells
Colours ✦ Blue, green
Season ✦ Autumn (fall)
Magical Instrument ✦ Cup
Altar Symbol ✦ Chalice
Communion Symbol ✦ Wine, Water
Archangel ✦ Gabriel
Human Sense ✦ Taste
Art Forms ✦ Music, song
Animals ✦ Fish, whales
Mythical Beast ✦ Sea serpent
Magical Arts ✦ Healing
Guide Forms ✦ Moon, Water goddess
Meditation ✦ The ocean, rivers
Images & Themes ✦ Lakes, pools, living underwater, healing, calm, the setting Sun

HOW TO GET IN TOUCH WITH WATER ENERGY

Water flows on and on... It does not shrink from any dangerous spot nor from any plunge, and nothing can make it lose its own essential nature. It remains true to itself under all conditions.

I Ching, hexagram 29, k'an/k'an

> The highest motive is to be like water.
> Water is essential to all living things,
> Yet, it demands no pay or recognition
> Rather, it flows humbly to the lowest levels
> Nothing is weaker than water
> Yet for overcoming what is hard and strong,
> Nothing surpasses it.
>
> **Lao Tzu**

- Use Water energy when making wishes around the following: Healing, spiritual and psychic development, relationship harmony, emotional issues, psychosomatic illnesses, dreams, trust and faith
- Spend time in and around water - oceans, rivers, streams, lakes, waterfalls
- Carry a small spray bottle of water with you and spritz yourself with it throughout the day
- Float in the water - surrender to its unerring support and let it keep you afloat
- Research, make and use gem (crystal) essences
- Try to take a bath rather than a shower; you can linger for longer, and even meditate more effectively, in a still bath
- Engage in water sports (not too extreme though, unless Scorpio is strong in your chart!), such as water skiing, swimming, kayaking, surfing, yachting, scuba diving, canoeing, sailing, or water volleyball
- Drink lots of H_2O
- Meditate on the Cups suit in the Tarot (the Cups suit represents the Water element)
- Eat watery, water-based foods, such as brothy soups, watermelon, and other juicy fruits
- Purify and cleanse your body occasionally, by undertaking a day-long fast / liquid diet
- Sleep on a waterbed
- Green-coloured crystals will activate your connection with the element of Water and enhance hope, healing, love and creativity
- Join an emotional support group - or facilitate one
- Install a water fountain in your home, garden, or office - water features, placed strategically, are believed in Feng Shui tradition to attract certain desired things into your environment and experience

- Wear and surround yourself with the colours blue, silver and green
- Decorate your home or office with soothing watery images, such as scenic lakes, panoramic beach photographs, ocean-side postcards, and themed paintings
- Listen and meditate to ocean waves and bubbling brook sounds on an audio system
- Walk in the rain, jump in puddles
- Visit a spa regularly, and indulge in saunas and jacuzzis - better still, install one in your home!
- Learn and practice graceful, flowing forms of movement, such as t'ai chi
- Express your emotions fearlessly; try to use them as your ally
- Nurture others and inspire them to nurture themselves
- Express your feelings through art, poetry and drama
- Cultivate a spiritual practice
- Develop your counselling and listening skills so you can help others - and yourself!
- Meditate regularly. Embrace your inner silence, peace, and spiritual essence
- When working with the Water element in magical rituals, stand at the West quarter of your special space, as the West is its domain, and invite its living essence into your 'circle'
- Use chalices, bowls, crystals, blue or silver items, and cauldrons to represent your element. If you are fortunate enough to live near the ocean, its tides can be a great energising force that evokes dramatic magical transformations. When the tide goes out, visualise your worries being drawn away. High tide is an optimum time to focus on wish magic, and as the waves move in closer, imagine your dreams coming towards you. Spells cast on a riverbank or near a spring will also be empowered by the moving energy of Water
- The best days on which to employ Water magic are Monday, ruled by the Moon, and Friday, ruled by the planet of love Venus
- Water spirits are also known as sea nymphs, naiads, undines, or sprites. They are responsible for the cleansing, refreshing, and clearing of our spirits, so Water signs would be wise to adopt one (or all) of these as their very own spirit guide!

THE MODES ✦ CARDINAL, MUTABLE, FIXED

Each sign belongs to one of the three quadruplicities, Cardinal, Fixed and Mutable. If we closely examine the Earth's yearly cycle, a very accurate picture of the nature of these quadruplicities is formed, for they correspond directly with the manifestation of the seasons.

Each season has three months: the first month brings the new phase of the cycle, the second month brings a concentration of the season's energy to its fullest expression, and the third month represents the transition from the current season into the next one.

The astrological quadruplicities represent the three basic circular qualities in all life: creation (Cardinal), preservation (Fixed) and destruction (Mutable). Every thing that is born, from a period of time to a human being, experiences an existence and then dies – or transmutes – in some way or another. In this context, death can be taken to mean that the form of the energy changes; but the energy itself can never be annihilated, for form may be mortal, but its essence is immortal, in that it merely changes form. This may be understood from Einstein's concept that energy cannot be created or destroyed, it can only be changed from one form to another.

CARDINAL ✦ ARIES, CANCER, LIBRA, CAPRICORN

The Cardinal mode covers the signs Aries, Cancer, Libra and Capricorn, and is the most initiating and self-motivated group of the three modes, able to instigate and inspire beginnings; in other words, to "get the ball rolling".

The Cardinal signs represent the four points of the compass and govern the changes of the seasons. They represent the equinoxes (Aries/Libra) when the day and night forces are equally balanced, and the solstices (Cancer/Capricorn) when the Sun is at its maximum distance north or south of the Equator. The solstices mark the longest and shortest days of the year.

The Cardinal mode has an initiating action and quality, operating with ambition, enthusiasm, independence and enterprise. Forceful, opportunistic, and at times aggressive, they have the will to accomplish and creatively project themselves onto the world.

They charge right in to get the job done - but can fail just as spectacularly.

Although they possess great start-up ability, tenacity and endurance are not their forte, and they often don't follow things through to the end.

If there is no crisis for them to tackle, they may even create one just to generate a challenge for themselves.

They find it hard to be held under anyone's thumb and will always find a way to wriggle free from any restrictions, so they can set off on their next quest.

Their energies may be directed towards themselves, their homes and families, or the wider world of career or society, but in any case, it is difficult to divert their attention away from their chosen course.

Ultimately, Cardinal signs have great drive, are self-motivated and would rather lead than follow. It is hard to influence them because they make their own firm decisions and believe that they know best.

Overall, the Cardinal mode signifies beginnings, decision-making, boldness, courage, will, fresh starts, and initiations of all kinds.

FIXED ✦ TAURUS, LEO, SCORPIO, AQUARIUS

The Fixed mode covers the signs Taurus, Leo, Scorpio and Aquarius, and is the most determined and unshakable of the three qualities. The positive side of the Fixed signs is stability. These are the builders, whether of Earthly creations (Taurus), artistic endeavours (Leo), occult powers (Scorpio), or world-changing visions and ideas (Aquarius).

The Fixed mode signifies the manifestation of purpose and its subjects are concerned with ownership, concentration, stability, fixation, and working with a cool head and calm demeanour under pressure.

The Fixed quality is associated with stabilisation, depth, preservation, persistence, loyalty, and enduring strength of will, operating with purpose, dedication, self-reliance and determination, forging ahead with a steadfast fixity, until goals are achieved and peaks reached.

Fixed signs are a fearsome, formidable and quietly forceful group, but often possess a stubborn, win-at-all-costs, and wilful attitude.

Rarely are they distracted in their quests, for they have the ability to stay on firm course and track until a project's end. Enduring, deliberate, single-minded and steady-footed, they can be rigid with a strong sense of routine, ritual and control.

Fixed subjects work hard to consolidate and preserve the things that matter to them, but they can be inflexible and resistant to change, often persisting with situations or relationships even when they are outworn. Loyal and dependable, they do not yield and may lack spontaneity.

Their energy and natures are powerful, robust, concrete, limited, set in its ways, purposeful, conscientious, slow, consistent, innately cautious, unimpulsive, opinionated, unchanging, and are generally strong in opinions, habits, likes and dislikes. Not easily distracted, they always keep their eyes on the prize, but tend to brood or become stuck in ruts.

They may project an image of strength as an effective shield against their considerable, albeit unseen, vulnerability.

The Fixed mode indicates the midpoints of the seasons, which are very strong ritualistic times and 'fixed points', signifying points of power in the zodiac. Because Fixed signs fall in the middle of the season, this term signifies that the season is firmly established - fixed - by the time the Sun enters these signs.

MUTABLE ✦ GEMINI, VIRGO, SAGITTARIUS, PISCES

The Mutable mode covers the signs Gemini, Virgo, Sagittarius and Pisces, and is the most flexible group of the three modes, able to shift and change to facilitate action.

They instinctively know how to 'go with the flow' and adapt most easily to new situations. These signs usually have diverse interests, but can lack perseverance and are prone to restlessness. Operating with flexibility and mobility, they are adaptable to change and have a circulating quality.

Cooperative, accommodating and friendly, they can fit in almost anywhere, put up with nearly anything, and turn most situations to their advantage. They can steer projects through periods of transition and can also bring them to a conclusion, but are conspicuously absent when hard work, long hours or persistent effort is necessary (with the exception of Virgo).

Although gentle, generally easy-going and likeable, they can be childish, sulky and ruthless when threatened. And although they have a natural benevolent streak and love to help others, they can also be paradoxically selfish.

The natural versatility of the Mutable quadruplicity can develop into a willingness to change and compromise, which gives an enormous sense of resourcefulness to these signs. Being so versatile, they constantly seek ways they can make improvements to themselves and their lot in life; indeed, Mutable signs can always be relied upon to think of new and ingenious ways of dealing with changing circumstances. However, without proper focus, stable footing, firm direction or sturdy persistence, their energy can become easily scattered and disoriented - and thus ultimately ineffective. They often lack a fixity and determination of purpose, which are needed to concretise goals, but their zest for 'enjoying the journey, not the destination', is enviable and more than makes up for their lack of perseverance.

Their essential energy is one of movement, fluidity, adaptability, adjustability, harmony, flow and versatility, although their feelings can switch and shift easily, making them often moody, flighty, indecisive, unreliable, inconsistent and unpredictable. And although resourceful and ingenious, they frequently project nervousness and worry.

Mutable signs may act as the intermediate between the Cardinal and Fixed signs, and indicate the ending of seasons, which are times of change and transition, shifting conditions, and merging into new territories.

THE RULING PLANETS

Planetary Meditation

I am my Earth (my body), and my Sky (my transcendence)
I am my Sun (my spirit), and my Moon (my soul)
I am my Venus (my pleasure), and my Jupiter (my faith)
I am my Mars (my courage), and my Saturn (my lessons)
I am my Mercury (my thoughts), and my Uranus (my truth)
I am my Neptune (my dreams), and my Pluto (my transformation)

Each planet has its own distinctive and original meaning which, according to its position in the zodiac, combines with the qualities that are inherent in each of the twelve astrological signs. If a planet is your sign's ruler, however, it exerts a significant influence upon your life, regardless of its birth chart or zodiacal position.

The birth chart is a symbolic map of one's contract with life. The planets represent different kinds of intelligence, various parts of the psyche. When we feed each part of ourselves, as represented by the planets, we bloom and expand as individuals.

The planets move against the backdrop of the zodiac wheel, which is the outer circle of the chart. The zodiac signs give the planets their flavouring, their myriad permutations of expression, and tells us how they will express themselves in our lives.

A NOTE ON THE THREE OUTER OR DISTANT PLANETS ✦ URANUS, NEPTUNE & PLUTO

It has been said that the distant planets are actually more powerful than the others as they take longer to orbit the Sun; they therefore affect whole generations of people rather than individuals. But as a result of their longer-spanning orbits, these slower moving planets (Uranus, Neptune and Pluto) dwell in the zodiac constellations for longer periods of time, allowing them to leave a deeper and more indelible imprint on both the collective and the personal psyches and human experience, than the swifter moving planets. In other words, their effect is thought to be more lingering and embedded.

MARS ✦ RULING PLANET OF ARIES & SCORPIO

The Great Warrior & Brave Crusader

Malefic ✦ Associated with Drive, Passion, Aggression & Confidence
687 Day Cycle

Keywords

Action, Drive, Will, Competition, Desire, Courage, Force, Prowess, Vitality, Impulse, Bravery, Passion, Initiative, Anger, Power, Ego, Achievement, Ambition, Wilfulness, Vigour, Assertiveness, Confidence, Territoriality, Conquering and Overcoming, Energy, Motivation, Aggression, Masculinity: 'the Animus', Confrontation, Battle, Enthusiasm, Virility, Heat, Dynamism

✦ Key Concepts ✦

The Inner Warrior
Ego in Action
Passion, Desire, Drive
Warfare, Weapons, Tools of Destruction
Fearlessness, Courage
Vitality, Vigour
Desire
The Fighting Spirit
The Slayer of Inner Demons
Primal & Survival Instincts

Day ✦ Tuesday
Number ✦ 9
Basic Energy & Magic ✦ Action, Motivation
Principles ✦ Energy, Force
Alchemy ✦ Separation
Intelligence ✦ Graphiel
Spirit ✦ Bartzabel

Colours ✦ Strong Reds, Scarlet, Magenta, Autumnal Shades

Gods/Goddesses/Angel ✦ Ares, Mars, Samael

Metals ✦ Iron, Steel, Brass

Gems/Minerals ✦ Ruby, Amethyst, Diamond, Red Jasper, Pyrite, Bloodstone, Malachite, Lodestone, Garnet, Flint, Carnelian, Hematite, Red Coral

Trees/Shrubs ✦ Monkey-puzzle, Heather, Holly, Pine, Hawthorn

Flowers/Herbs ✦ Nasturtium, Nettle, Cayenne, Allspice, Burdock Root, Tobacco, Garlic, Geranium, Honeysuckle

Essential Oils ✦ Basil, Ginger, Black Pepper

Wood ✦ Mahogany

Fabric ✦ Tweed

Animals ✦ Tiger, Falcon, Wolf, Snake

Element ✦ Fire

Zodiacal Signs ✦ Aries, Scorpio

Zodiacal Influences ✦ Rules Aries (co-rules Scorpio); Exalted in Capricorn; Detriment Libra; Fall Cancer

Mars is nicknamed the Red Planet* due to its red-orange colour and its brilliant appearance in the night sky. Forceful, fearless and daring, Mars governs the whole spectrum of traditionally 'masculine' concepts from sexual prowess to combat, strenuous activities, domination, leadership, and nerves-of-steel risk-taking. It is also known as the warrior planet, due to its ability to outlast and outdistance its adversaries.

Bringing endurance, ambition, thrills and determination, when strongly placed in a natal chart it can add a touch of boldness and dynamism to one's character, and brings movement, 'noise' and plenty of activity to the area of life that its house placement in the horoscope indicates.

Mars rules sharp instruments, fire, and anything combustible; its sheer force can destroy matter, and hot-headed outbursts are likely when it is free to run rampant in one's life or psyche. Yet in its more positive expression, Mars brings zest, spirit, passion, and energy to everything it touches.

It is easy to see why astrologers of medieval times observed the Red Planet with trepidation, for often it foretold war, plague, and fever.

Named after the Roman god of war and spring, Mars is the planet most concerned with the way we assert ourselves and what it is that drives us. The god Mars is always shown powerfully built and dressed for combat-style activities, and was known for his courage and impetuosity both on the battlefield and in the bedroom; indeed, its natives also frequently leap impetuously into love and battle. He is a strong leader in times of crisis, and a staunch defender of the weak.

Mars has earned a bad reputation for being an 'aggressor', but the Romans highly esteemed Mars and attributed many positive qualities to him. He was a giver of fertility, a god of nature, a protector of herds and fields, and a great inspiration to all new ideas and projects. They even dedicated the first month, the period of the vernal equinox signifying the coming of spring, and named it in his honour - hence the word, 'March'.

Flying on the wings of passion, Martians can learn much from disasters and collapse, and heed their planet's message: Act now, for life is far too short to waste time on regrets.

The glyph (or symbol) for Mars is pure masculinity, a circle with an arrow pointing upward, suggesting that Mars works on an entirely material plane. There are no crescent circles indicating spirit, as Mars deals with the here, now and immediate. The arrow is phallic, symbolising sexuality and direct action. It represents the masculine in biology and iron in physics. Mars also has an impressive history with all things warlike, which is reflected in its traditional glyph - a heavy metal helmet.

Mars is the secondary masculine principle in our natal chart, the 'male within'. It represents our directive energy the way we direct it and the targets we direct it towards, the urge for activity, masculinity, our survival impulse, the sexual instinct and drive, personal power, confidence, ego, achievement, progress, conquering fear, and overcoming obstacles.

The last of the personal planets, its position and condition shows how the principles of both action and desire are expressed, revealing the kinds of projects and battles we choose and how they are tackled.

The adrenaline of the horoscope, Mars denotes the urge towards 'fight or flight' tendencies and indeed our mode of attack when threatened. Therefore, it is also connected with our basic energy, territoriality, personal power through wilful expression, impulsiveness, self-mastery, motivation, drive, aspiration, assertiveness, power, courage, and unchecked emotion and anger.

The position of Mars in one's birth chart also indicates one's energy levels, the way one uses his energy, his level of assertiveness or bravery. Mars shows the nature of the challenges one is likely to face and his ability to confront them.

One's sexual desires also come under the rule of Mars and in a female's birth chart it often shows the kind of men she is attracted to, and in a male's birth chart it shows his attitude towards other men and his masculinity.

Mars's element tells us how we replenish our stores of energy; its sign tells us what turns us on in laughter, play and sex. People with a strong Mars in their chart are go-getters, assertive, courageous, need to win, need to come first, love a challenge and are unafraid of confrontation. Too much Mars influence can make one contentious, quarrelsome, overly competitive, prone to accidents, aggressive and even violent.

However, giving us strength of will and direction, he can also be used constructively, even when seemingly uncontrolled, as he signifies the ultimate power and purpose we need to slay our demons. But because Mars excels at achieving immediate aims, he is not capable of long-term or strategic planning and generally relies on force and aggression rather than negotiation, finesse, or diplomacy. So, whether we are working on ourselves, or battling with others, the fight will be won quickly or not at all, as Mars's confrontations simply fizzle out over long periods of time, and may result in undesirable manifestations like exhaustion, burnout, or depression.

Mars is a planet which operates strongly when we are young, as it is a basic energy used in the search for our identity. While its aggression and feeling comes from a primitive part of ourselves, in maturity it is more likely to be either controlled or sublimated so the function of Mars is bound to change during one's lifetime.

The Gauquelins, who undertook the most highly acclaimed and recognised statistical research in the field of astrology, found that a prominent Mars in the horoscope, produced individuals who excelled in the fields of military, medicine, business and science; conversely and not surprisingly, Mars was least prominent for musicians, artists, and writers.

Mars is the polar opposite and husband of Venus. Just as Venus, daughter of the Moon, represents the feminine archetype, Mars, son of the Sun, is the active male archetype. Interestingly, Taurus and Libra, the signs ruled by Venus, are directly opposite Scorpio and Aries, the domains of Mars.

Mars is the great achiever. He can and will perform any task you set for him. In order to attain your goals, you must let him know exactly what you desire - the more details you give him, the less he will be led astray. His force will forge ahead to bring your wishes to manifestation for as long as you hold the image firmly in mind, maintain your focus, and continue to work at it. And work is the operative word here, as Mars is no dreamer and will smash through any obstacles to get the job done.

Red, as well as being the colour of lust and passion, has strong links with Mars by virtue of red being the colour that appears when tempers rise to boiling point, as well as being the colour of blood (spilt by battle).

VENUS ✦ RULING PLANET OF TAURUS & LIBRA

The Great Love & Harmony Principle

Benefic ✦ Love, Beauty, Harmony, Unison, Pleasure
225 Day Cycle

Keywords
Love, Beauty, Art, Harmony, Affection, Sensual Desire, Relating, Relationships, Pleasure, Acceptance, Social Graces, Vanity, Sociability, Persuasion, Luxury, Unison, Aesthetics, Outward Style, Indulgence, Refinement, Values, Comfort, Resources, Enjoyment, Agreeableness, Good Humour, Symmetry, Proportion, Mutuality, Sympathy

✦ Key Concepts ✦

Love, Relating, Harmony
Beauty in Form
Social Orientation
Refinement of Artistic Tastes
Values & Priorities
Leisure, Pleasure, Music, Art
Sentiments in Love & Sharing
Sensual Enjoyment
Ostentation & Luxury
Emotions Connected to Love & Possessions
Justice & Fair Play

Day ✦ Friday
Number ✦ 6
Basic Energy & Magic ✦ Love, Sociability
Principles ✦ Beauty, Art
Alchemy ✦ Fermentation
Intelligence ✦ Hagiel, Beni Seraphim
Spirit ✦ Kedemel
Colours ✦ Light Blue, Green, Pink, Soft Yellow, Pastels
Gods/Goddesses/Angel ✦ Aphrodite, Venus, Raphael
Metals ✦ Copper, Bronze, Brass

Gems/Minerals ✦ Jade, Lapis Lazuli, Rose Quartz, Emerald, Kunzite, Peridot, Malachite (Copper Ore), Sapphire, Green Aventurine, Carnelian, Chrysolite, Green Jasper, Tourmaline, Opal, Pink Coral

Trees/Shrubs ✦ Peach, Pear, Alder, Ash, Birch, Cypress, Fig, Almond, Apple, Cherry, Linden, Chestnut

Flowers/Herbs ✦ Rose, Carnation, Lilac, Pomegranate, Anise, Dandelion Leaf, Alfalfa, Liquorice, Apple, Uva Ursi, Orchid, Primrose, Violet, Columbine

Essential Oils ✦ Geranium, Jasmine, Bergamot, Ylang Ylang, Rose

Wood ✦ Sycamore

Fabric ✦ Satin

Animals ✦ Cat, Deer, Butterfly, Dove, Sparrow, Rabbit, Swallow

Element ✦ Air

Zodiacal Signs ✦ Taurus, Libra

Zodiacal Influences ✦ Rules Libra and Taurus; Exalted in Pisces; Detriment Aries; Fall Virgo

Venus is a woman. At her best, she is what every mortal female might aspire to become and every male to have as his mate. She is capable of any depth of understanding, every height of love. She is the ultimate in beauty of spirit as well as of body. She can show any tenderness, any strength in expressing her love.

Charlotte MacLeod

Discovered by the Babylonians in about 3000 B.C., Venus was one of the five planets known in ancient times, appearing in the astronomical records of several old civilisations. Venus or Aphrodite as she is sometimes referred to, was said to have sprung from the seed of Uranus and to have risen naked from the foaming sea water, as infamously depicted in Botticelli's painting The Birth of Venus.

The glyph for Venus is a circle with a cross underneath it, connoting spirit (the circle) over matter (the cross). Without the crescent of soul of consciousness, Venus is objective, a quality seen in its native subjects Libra and Taurus.

This glyph is related to the Egyptian life-giving symbol, the Ankh, representing the 'mirror' of Venus reflecting our attitudes and values, and is also the biological symbol for female.

Pythagoras, as well as the Mayans, revered the planet Venus, since it is the only planet which is bright enough to lighten the shadows. It can be seen immediately before Sunrise as the Morning Star, and after Sunset as the Evening Star, and due to these properties, the ancients ascribed many names to it, such as Vesper, the 'false light' and 'Lucifer' (meaning bringer of light, since it rises before the Sun). Its solar connections earned it other names, like Astarta, Venera, Isis and the Mother of the Gods.

Venus, named in honour of the goddess of love Aphrodite (her Greek counterpart), is concerned with one's relationships and the choices one makes in life on both the personal and the material levels. It also shows one's experiences and expression of grace, sensual desire, luxury, femininity, self-esteem, personal values, aesthetics, pleasures, adornment, love, beauty and harmony. It can enhance self-confidence, not only encouraging the giving of love, but the receiving of it too. One can analyse what makes people fall in love by observing their Venus position, and also what kind of validation or assurance they need from others to bring about their own inner love.

Venus is the secondary feminine principle in one's natal chart, after the Moon, signifying the 'female within'.

Ultimately, Venus is concerned with two principal human desires: love and money.

The signs in which Venus falls in one's horoscope will determine how one expresses affection and appreciates beauty, and shows the sort of relationships and people one attracts, as well as one's behaviour in love. In a male's birth chart, the position of Venus, a feminine archetype, reveals what he typically projects onto the women he encounters, what he is attracted to in a partner, the qualities he seeks, and what he desires and is turned on by. Venus is his idealised picture of the feminine, his anima, his ideal woman. Venus in a female's birth chart describes a woman's femininity, her image of herself (the hand-mirror), how she presents herself to the world, her desire to look good, what she values in herself and how comfortable she feels with her feminine side.

It has been said that while women are more likely to project Mars in relationships, men are more likely to project Venus in relationships. Because Venus so strongly represents our urge for relationships, in both sexes she reveals how we give and receive, appreciate, and merge with others.

While Venus and Mars are the feminine and masculine elements of a chart respectively, this is an oversimplification: desire is the province of Mars, attraction of Venus. Where desire seeks to acquire its object, love seeks to attract it. Venus does not need to exert much effort to attract the things she loves and values; she simply magnetises them to her. However, she invariably always operates in concert with Mars when she sets her heart on something or someone. What Venus wishes for, Mars sets off to attain and conquer for her.

Venus is never more than 48 degrees from the Sun, so it either occupies the same sign in a birth chart as the Sun, or falls within two signs either side of it. When it is possible to see Venus, only during the three hours before sunrise or three hours after sunset, it is the most brilliant object in the sky other than the Sun and the Moon. Living up to its reputation for beauty and symmetry, Venus is a perfect sphere, unlike the other planets which are flattened somewhat at their poles. Through telescopes her surface appears serenely smooth, and she has the least eccentric orbit of all the cosmic bodies.

This beautiful planet is also about appreciation, equality and fairness, our sense of values, aesthetics, our likes and dislikes, and our tastes. She plays a role in our creativity, as she is closely linked with what repels or attracts us, and motivates us to 'create' and artistically express accordingly.

Finances, resources, money and gifts are also ruled by Venus, as well as sensuous indulgences, such as fine wines, jewellery, gourmet foods, fancy adornments, imported chocolates, perfumes, music and other arts. There is indeed a decorative quality about Venus, as well as a feeling of abundance, opulence and luxury.

Coupled with the Moon, Venus is also associated with fertility, creation, fruitfulness and reproduction. Hence the purpose of Venus is to bestow creativity, fecundity, and new life. Venus is known as the 'lesser benefic' after Jupiter, the 'higher benefic', with Venus being more material and sensual than her moralistic, loftier counterpart.

Our inner Venus is the part of us that moves to bridge the gap again after a conflict, and has to do with mediating, negotiating and resolution.

Because Venus rules over two zodiac signs, Taurus and Libra, and both are essentially different (Taurus being Fixed, Libra being Cardinal for one thing), it manifests itself in different ways in each sign: in Taurus pleasure can be found in the Earthly pleasures of material comforts, while in Libra it comes out as a more intellectual approach to beauty and aesthetic appreciation.

Venus's influence in the Libran realm is also more concerned with the interplay of opposites that exist in relationships, and bringing these polarities into harmony. Many astrologers and psychoanalysts believe that we are often magnetised by precisely those qualities that we lack in ourselves, and that we subconsciously choose to incorporate those absent characteristics into ourselves by becoming immersed in them through the medium of a partner who embodies them. However, many people forget why they 'attracted' such a partner in the first place, and then attempt to transform that person into a clone of themselves, or perhaps into a projected idealised image.

Marriage falls under the dominion of Libra, while the more mundane, practical aspects of Earth life such as food, nourishment, shelter and home, are attributed to Taurus. In Taurus, she shows us our ability to prosper in the material sense, describing how we acquire, use and conserve our resources. In Libra, she lends an energy of social grace, physical attractiveness, and the apparently effortless ability to enjoy good relationships with the opposite sex. However, the downside of Venus in both signs is that one may inherit her less desirable characteristics: self-indulgence, vanity, hedonism, insincerity, low self-worth, gluttony, promiscuity (the word 'venereal', pertaining to sexually transmitted infections, is derived from Venus), or being emotionally demanding in one's relationships.

Associated with the things one holds dear, Venus is intrinsically linked with sensuality and in short, anything that appeals to the senses, which could include anything from music, art, dancing and movies, to food, sex, exercise, and anything else that feels good or enlivens one's senses somehow. Because one can be very attached to the things one possesses or enjoys, Venus reveals what we will fight to keep.

MERCURY ✦ RULING PLANET OF GEMINI & VIRGO
The Great Communicator & Eternal Student

Errant ✦ **Associated with the Mind, Communication, Intellect, Learning, Transport, Information Transmission**
88 Day Cycle

Visualise the guardian of Mercury in swirls of coloured smoke surrounded by herbs and potions, crystals and gleaming phials of jewel-coloured healing liquids, writing in huge books in strange writing. He is ageless, in some lights an earnest young scientist, in others one of the ancient alchemists who have spent a lifetime in study.

Cassandra Eason

Keywords

Information, Communication, Movement, Mobility, Intellect, Change, Adaptability, Rational Thinking, Learning, Analysis, Dissemination, Synchronicity, Perception, Inventiveness, Correspondence, Short Trips, Transportation, Eloquence, Knowledge, Assimilation, Cunning, Coordination, Logic, Expression, Interpretation, Thought Deduction

Deep inside his searching, impatient nature, the Gemini seeks an ideal, and his chief problem is in recognising what it is... Money, fame, wealth, love and career are never quite enough. Mercury calls Gemini higher and higher.

Linda Goodman

✦ Key Concepts ✦
Mental Processes
Active Intelligence
Communication & Expression
The Neighbourhood Experience
Mind, Logic & Reason
Short Trips & Travel
The Movement of Goods & Ideas
Theft, Trickery & Cunning

Early Education
Transmitter of the Spiritual to the Material
Negotiations
Sales & Marketing
outhful Vitality

Day ✦ Wednesday
Number ✦ 5
Basic Energy & Magic ✦ Speed, Communication
Principles ✦ Intelligence, Thought
Alchemy ✦ Distillation, Circulation
Intelligence ✦ Tiriel
Spirit ✦ Taphthartharath
Colours ✦ Yellow, Silver, Blue, Metallics, Mixed Hues, Checks, Plaids
Gods/Goddesses/Angel ✦ Hermes, Mercury, Raphael
Metals ✦ Quicksilver, Zinc
Gems/Minerals ✦ Citrine, Agate, Carnelian, Opal, Emerald, Tiger's Eye, Topaz, Sardonyx, Chalcedony
Trees/Shrubs ✦ Hazel, Forsythia, Filbert, Acacia, Myrtle, Mulberry
Flowers/Herbs ✦ Bittersweet, Fern, Lavender, Catnip, Skullcap, Lily of the Valley, Elecampane, Azalea
Essential Oils ✦ Fennel, Cardamom, Lavender, Rosemary, Peppermint, Thyme
Wood ✦ Beech
Fabric ✦ Linen
Animals ✦ Monkey, Magpie, Hare, Coyote, Raven, Ibis, Fly
Element ✦ Air
Zodiacal Signs ✦ Rules Gemini; Exalted in Virgo; Detriment Sagittarius; Fall Pisces
Zodiacal Influences ✦ Gemini, Virgo

On Thoth (the Egyptian Mercury) ◆ Thoth is the guardian of Chokmah, the speaker of the secrets of the Universe whose words, both spoken and written, are the invisible codex of creation. Divine scribe and herald, it is his wisdom that holds the infrastructure of the vast and complex design of All That Is. He holds the keys of sound and sigil that are the perpetual ways of creation and its continued invitation to the people to join the quest.

Paul Hougham

Mercury is the smallest planet and as one of the closest to the Sun is the fastest in its orbit. Mercury was named after the Roman winged messenger of the gods, and known as Hermes to the Greeks. He traversed the land as a messenger between the heavens, Earth, and the Underworld, carrying a caduceus˘, a rod entwined with two serpents that could induce sleep and bring about healing. Mercury was said to be the son of Jupiter in mythology, and through his dexterity, communication skills and quicksilver intellect, Mercury came to rule over medicine, commerce, and then later science and technology.

Mercury was discovered around 5,000 years ago, and was one of the five known ancient planets.

This versatile and variable planet has a duality which shows in the signs it rules. It governs Gemini and Virgo; the extrovert Gemini and introvert Virgo are two sides of the same essential function - the way we communicate and move, and the way we think and discern.

Ancient people rarely saw Mercury in their skies, and when they did it was for a brief period of time, explaining the reasoning behind its association with speed and haste. Since Mercury can never be more than 28 degrees from the Sun, it is only when it is farthest from the Sun that it can be seen for scant amounts of time just before or after sunset - and due to its close proximity to the Sun, it can never be seen in the night sky, being swallowed by the Earth alongside its Solar neighbour.

Analytical, methodical, determined and deliberate is the way Earthy Virgo will express her Mercurial nature. In Virgo, Mercury denotes the reality principle. It expresses thoughtfully and with consideration for the facts, is stable-minded, not easily swayed by emotion or passion, and has an essentially practical, sensible and focused thinking style.

Connected to writing, speech, journalism and information-gathering, Mercury represents the power of communication, interpretation and self-expression, intelligence, reason, the ability to perceive relationships and connections, gathering facts, mobility, adaptability to environment, siblings, young people, writers, travellers, speakers, students, teachers, editors, and transport workers.

It reveals one's intellect and the way in which one express ideas, and also how one deals with siblings, neighbours, neighbourhood, and the immediate environment.

The Egyptians saw Mercury as Thoth^^, transporter of souls, the conductor of sleepers to dreamland and souls of the dead to Hades, while the Greeks and Romans saw him as Hermes and Mercury, the messenger of the gods. Always pictured with wings on his feet, to represent the speed of thought and the ceaseless activity of the mind, Mercury symbolises all things cerebral and linked with communication. In some mythology, he is a direct descendent of Hermes, the messenger of Zeus, and the god of travels. The deity of roads, protector of travellers, god of doorways, commerce and thievery, of good and bad luck, of treasure troves, of honest and dishonest gain, Mercury is widely known as a thief and a cunning trickster. Using the nimble wit for which Mercury was noted, he was an immortal go-getter, a lightning flash whose mental frequency was always switched to 'high', a god who got things done.

However, Mercury's charm, quick wit, speed, fluidity and cleverness requires positive direction, for he can just as easily turn into a prankster and cheat as into a brilliant genius. Pure Mercurial intellect needs to be humanised, to connect with something worthwhile and significant, to discover greater purpose, otherwise it can lose itself in the frivolity of its own emotionally detached efficiency. Despite this, Mercury is an eternal and willing student.

Mercury relates to one's education (particularly early education), early learning experiences, and the foundations of learning rather than abstract thinking, and how one uses that knowledge to function and articulate effectively.

The planet in closest aspect to Mercury is the most important as Mercury is very much coloured by its contacts with other planets and by the sign it resides in. Mercury is the bridge between our inner selves (Sun) and the people we wish to share with (Venus). People with a strong Mercury in their chart are quick thinkers and fast talkers, often intelligent and learned, but can occasionally 'burn out' those around them with incessant talking that outpaces their thinking. In short, the strongly Mercurial soul can be exhausting, albeit exhilarating and captivating, company.

Astronomically, Mercury is the swiftest moving of the independent planets and makes rapid changes of declination in the sky. At inferior conjunction (when Mercury lies between the Sun and the Earth), its magnetic field deviates the stream of electrified particles emitted by the Sun; these particles have an influence on the nervous systems of living organisms on Earth, hence astrological tradition linking Mercury's with this body system in medical astrology. Mercurial types, such as those with a strong Mercury placement, or those born under its rule, i.e. Geminians and Virgoans, are prone to restless energy and tend to be nervous, neurotic, flighty and restless, frequently suffering from all manner of nervous disorders and disturbances.

In medieval astrology works Mercury was a significator of youth and young people, and those with a strong Mercury, Gemini, or Third House in their birth chart, often appear to be 'Peter Pans', possessing a glittering, lively charm and never quite growing up. This youthful quality may mark a highly creative, inquisitive person, or a completely undeveloped naïve individual – very often both. Such is the trickery of Mercury. Jungian analysts call this personality type the puer aeternus, the 'eternal boy', and indeed having all the innocence of children, these characters float effortlessly through life with no noticeable purpose or direction.

Like its namesake, those quicksilver globules that are ever moving and never still, Mercury is a hard energy to pin down. Three of its main keywords - communication, intelligence and knowledge - are equally difficult to define. The actual process of communication is a complex series of skills, emotions, experiences, and other human capacities that defy simple or universally accepted description.

Mercury is not knowledge itself, but the means and nature by which it is collected, codified, deciphered, and dispersed. So, although these three words are associated with Mercury, the planet's energy itself is really more nebulous than any of them, much like the uncontainable quicksilver, as it is merely the facilitator, the channel, the conductor, the fuel that brings the mind's vast mechanisms to life.

Associated with quickness, astrologers have always examined the speed of Mercury to determine the speed or agility of a person's mind or thought patterns. The slow-moving, stationary, or retrograde * Mercury describes a slower intellect, people who take longer to come up with answers and solutions, working things out slowly and carefully, while those with a faster-moving Mercury are quick to answer and possess minds which move at great speeds and are one mind-step ahead of everyone else.

The glyph (or symbol) for Mercury is a complex symbol, open to various interpretations. It appears as the cross of matter sitting below the circle of spirit, surmounted by the crescent of soul. This stands for the triumph of mind over matter, as in an intellect that can channel energies from above and below. In essence, this emblem stands for active intelligence. The combination of the crescent, the circle and the cross, shows receptivity resulting from the exaltation of spirit over matter, which one is destined, if one hasn't already, to master. This icon suggests manifested (crescent) spirit (circle) over matter (cross), and indeed, Mercury's function is to link the spirit to everyday matters to facilitate this process.

Another well-known symbol for this planet is the caduceus of Mercury, which depicts two serpents coiled around a magic wand or herald's staff whose heads are facing each other. On top of the wand or staff is often a pair of wings and a circle, again symbolising spirit. This symbol attests to Mercury being a giver of the healing arts, and it is still used today as the logo of modern chemists and the medical profession. It also protects messengers, who traditionally carried it.

In medieval times, Mercury was also known as Mercurius, the god of the alchemists. Mercurius is 'the alchemical androgyne', lending the astrological Mercury an androgynous quality, which is neither male or female. As Mercury has neither a feminine or masculine energy to it - it is neutral and objective - it works in accordance with its aspects to other planets, its brothers and sisters, effectively plugging itself into their forces and being driven by the resulting power. (According to a Greek myth, the union of Hermes and Aphrodite produced the being known as hermaphrodite, who was both male and female).

In some Tarot decks, the Magician card is depicted as Thoth or Hermes, standing before the four elemental symbols representing the four functions of the human psyche - thinking, feeling, intuition and sensation. Mercury, the true alchemist of times past, possesses the ability to unite these elements into a single, unified whole.

The Sun and Mercury's relationship describes the intellect's link with a sense of direction, purpose and will. If these factors marry up harmoniously, the individual's expression will come forth accordingly. It is believed, however, that when Mercury forms too close a conjunction to the Sun, it can metaphorically 'combust', and burn out. The two can also produce too intense an energy, so it is arguably more desirable for them to occupy different signs, or at least be as far away from each other as possible so that the energies of both signs can more easily complement each other by virtue of their distance and consequent objectivity.

However, a close conjunction (i.e. Sun and Mercury occupying the same sign) may just as easily signify a powerful focus of that sign's qualities. Further, one's intellect may be somewhat detached from one's central purpose if Mercury is at its maximum distance from the Sun, but in the case of a close conjunction it can symbolise that the mind and will are united in harmony.

There seems to be a strong link between Mercury and Uranus. Esoteric astrologers consider Uranus to be the 'higher octave' of Mercury; Uranus, denotes the archetype of rebelliousness, the inventor, the bohemian, and any relationship between it and Mercury will reveal a person's attitudes towards traditional thought. The well-aspected Mercury-Uranus type is stimulated and spurred on by progressive technology, especially that which advances the speed and style of communication, and seeks to forge new pathways of thought, after shattering any boundaries to mental growth. When teaming up with Uranus, Mercury's powers are intensified, for Mercury likes also to improve things, to add to Universal knowledge through inventions. A planet of progress through experimentation, Mercury is never satisfied by established, ingrained thought and rather is ever seeking new avenues for his agile mind to explore.

Unlike its higher-minded planetary companion, the planet Jupiter**, which represents one's faith and beliefs systems, Mercury has no in-built bias, nor is it concerned with principles or ethics. Mercury is completely amoral and deals solely in rationale and concepts. It can be likened to the postal officer who delivers your letters; he or she is not responsible for the writing of the letters, nor the contents or the reactions they engender; Mercury, like the postal officer, simply operates as a neutral medium for the interchange of information.

A caduceus is a wand entwined by two snakes and topped by wings or a winged helmet. It is associated with magic, spiritual enlightenment, wisdom, immortality, and healing. The caduceus is most strongly connected with Hermes, the Greek messenger god of magic who flies as fleet as thought. Hermes carries his magical wand when escorting souls to the underworld, and his is made of olive wood, symbolic of peace and the continuity of life. The wand's shaft represents power; the serpents represent wisdom or prudence; the wings represent diligence; and the helmet represents high thoughts. The caduceus appears in Mesopotamian cultures in about 2600 B.C.E. where its serpents signified a god who cured illness. Its association with healing and medicine survives today.

**Thoth is an Egyptian God who created the Universe and all mystical wisdom, healing, learning, knowledge, writing, arithmetic, astrology, and magic. Called the Lord of the Divine Books and Scribe of the Company of Gods, Thoth is usually portrayed as an ibis-headed man with a pen and ink holder. As a healer and magician, Thoth restored the Eye of Horus after it was torn to pieces in battle, and it then became a funerary amulet and magical, all-seeing eye. The Greeks associated their god Hermes so closely with Thoth that the two blended together. Thoth/Hermes became identified with Hermes Trismegistus, the mythical figure and alleged author of the Hermetic texts on occult, philosophical, and religious topics. Nobody is a better supplier of books than Thoth. A request to him, or an invocation for help to the keeper of the Divine library, will produce the necessary volumes in a phenomenal swiftness. As Murry Hope says in his book The Ancient Wisdom of Egypt, "If your thirst for knowledge is genuine, have no hesitation in asking the favour of this God. But remember, as keeper of the Akashic records he knows more about you than you probably know yourself, so he will see in your mind whether your intentions are wise, foolish, egotistical, or humble and dispense his favours accordingly".

*Retrograde means that these planets appeared to be travelling backwards at the time of birth. Despite the fact that this is only an apparent phenomenon, a planet in retrograde motion tends to internalise its effect and direct its energies inward. This internalised energy may be somewhat suppressed, rather than expressed externally. Retrograde planets indicate energies that function in an indirect, ineffective, compulsive, or other unconscious manner. Even though all the planets except the Moon and Sun will go retrograde for a period of time, it is Mercury's retrogradation (three times a year for approximately three weeks at a time) that has earned the reputation as a time when everything gets a little chaotic, especially around communication, travel plans, and correspondence. While Mercury is not responsible for the breakdown of its associated correspondences, such as computers, phones, air travel, fax machines, commerce and information services, there is a widespread notion that these breakdowns most often happen when Mercury is retrograde.

**The relationship between the mind and will is imaged mythically by the relationship between Mercury and Jupiter. Jupiter serves to focus one's consciousness. It could be said that Mercury is the servant of Jupiter, i.e. the intellect must be directed towards a higher purpose.

MOON ✦ RULING PLANET OF CANCER

The Subconscious Soul

Luminary ✦ Associated with the Subconscious, Instincts, Intuition, Habits, Fluctuations, Emotions, Feelings
27.3 Day Cycle

Keywords
Childhood, the Past, Memory, Emotions, Feelings, Reflection, the Subconscious, Instincts, Habits, Habitual and Instinctive Responses, Mothering, the Mother, Fluctuations, Nurturing, Empathy, Soul, the Inner Personality, Receptivity, Moods, Security

✦ **Key Concepts** ✦
Attachments to the Past
Memory & Subconscious
Emotions & Feelings
Ancestral Inheritance
The Soul
Impressionability
Domesticity
The Childhood Experience
The Mother or Mother Figure
Receptivity & Magnetism

Day ✦ Monday

Number ✦ 2

Basic Energy & Magic ✦ Emotions, Intuitiony

Principles ✦ The Feminine Principle, Feeling

Alchemy ✦ Conjunction, Coagulation

Intelligence ✦ Chashmodai, Tarshism, Malcah Betarshisim Ve-Ad Ruachoth Ha-Schechalim

Spirit ✦ Chashmodai, Shad Barschemoth Haschartathan

Colours ✦ Silver, Pastel Shades, White, Blue, Cream, Silvery Grey, Opalescent & Iridescent Hues

Gods/Goddesses/Angel ✦ Artemis, Luna, Gabriel, Selene, Diana, Hecare, Isis

Metals ✦ Silver, Aluminium

Gems/Minerals ✦ Moonstone, Opal, Pearl, Selenite, Emerald, Angelite, Celestite, Diamond, Beryl, Clear Quartz, Aquamarine

Trees/Shrubs ✦ Willow, Hawthorn, Silver Birch, Lemon, Eucalyptus, Sycamore, Tamarind, Maple, Alder, Magnolia

Flowers/Herbs ✦ Convolvulus, Watercress, Myrrh, Poppy, Jasmine, Lotus, Clary Sage, Rosewood, Wintergreen, Ylang Ylang, Mimosa, Freesia, Chamomile, Gardenia, Lemon Balm, Lily, Mugwort, Hops

Essential Oils ✦ Chamomile, Juniper, Cypress
Wood ✦ Birch
Fabric ✦ Silk
Animals ✦ Crab, Owl, Shellfish, Wolf, Nightingale, Moth, Spider
Element ✦ Water
Zodiacal Signs ✦ Cancer
Zodiacal Influences ✦ Rules Cancer; Exalted in Taurus; Detriment Capricorn; Fall Scorpio

Soon as the evening shades prevail,
The Moon takes up the wondrous tale.
And nightly to the listening Earth
Repeats the story of her birth.

Addison

The Moon rules Cancer much the way it governs the ocean tides, pulling in and letting go, sensing what needs nourishment and what needs release.

Caroline W. Casey

Although not essentially a planet, the Moon is our nearest celestial neighbour and exerts a great influence upon the Earth and all life that dwells upon it. The gravitational pull of the Moon affects our bodily fluids, which contribute to about ninety per cent of our biological make-up. Taking an average of 27.3 days to pass through the twelve zodiac signs, it stays in each for around 2.5 days.

People with a strong Moon placement in their natal chart, and those ruled by this powerful sphere – Cancerians – are especially under Lunar influences, and are prone to be moody, irrational, changeable, over-reactive, insecure, emotional and clingy.

The Moon is essentially receptive and passive; it reflects the life experience rather than initiating it. Fluctuating and cyclical, the Moon is the planet (although technically a satellite) of feelings, emotions, habits, the subconscious, and instinctual reactions.

The symbol for the Moon ☽ is a representation of its crescent in its waxing phase from New to Full, but it can also be seen as two half circles - these form a bowl shape, a receptacle, a feminine container that 'receives' and 'holds' anything put into it. The half circle, unlike the full circle of the Sun, is finite and incomplete, almost as if striving for wholeness, and symbolising in a way the fluidity and changeability of the human psyche's fluctuating emotions it represents. The crescent symbol for the Moon was chosen by the ancient astrologers to represent a person's soul, complementing the Sun's symbolism of one's spirit or outer manifestation of character; indeed, the Moon reveals one's innermost self.

The Moon and one's emotional nature go hand in hand. It influences the type of nurturing we need from our mothers or mother-female figures to make one a complete, well-rounded, secure person. It describes one's symbolic womb, where and how one seeks comfort and feels safe. It also influences how one relates to others on an intimate emotional level, one's emotional responses, moods, and instinctual 'knowing'.

The Moon, Earth's satellite, is about a quarter of the size of our planet, and its light is merely a reflection of sunlight, giving the Moon a reflective quality in astrological symbolism.

Around five billion years old, as estimated by the study of Lunar dust, the Moon has four basic phases in its cycle: new Moon, first quarter, full Moon, and last quarter. It is known by scientists that plant growth is affected by the Moon, that the tidal rhythms depend upon her movements, and that the female menstrual cycle corresponds to the sidereal Lunar month.

In mythology, the Moon is personified as the goddess Luna, Selene, Artemis, or Diana. The Moon has long been worshipped under a multiplicity of names, and there is hardly a goddess in the entire pantheon of the Greeks or Celts who does not possess a Lunar aspect or manifestation of some kind. In the Tarot deck, The Moon - card number 18 of the Major Arcana - is a reminder that, like the Moon, some things can be hidden from view and we may not always be able to see the full picture.

Astrologically, the Moon's influence is cold, fruitful and feminine, and because its visual image alters constantly, it characterises changeability.

Consequently, its influence is often unsettling, and those with a prominent Moon in their horoscope, such as someone with a Cancer Sun, Moon or Ascendant, will likely be emotionally sensitive.

The Moon has two major cycles: the sidereal period (its relation to the stars) - the 27 days, 7 hours, and 43 minutes it takes to make a complete revolution through the constellations of the zodiac - and the synodic period, the 29 days, 12 hours and 44 minutes of time between one new Moon and the next one, completing one Lunar cycle in a slightly longer period than the first. The synodic period is commonly called the Lunar month (the words 'Moon' and 'month' share the same roots).

The earliest calendars were in fact Lunar, and had these stayed in effect, we would have thirteen months of 28.5 days each. Indeed, a standard year is composed of thirteen Lunar months. As the complete sequence of Moon phases from new to full takes a little over 29 days, some years will have twelve full Moons, while others will have thirteen, meaning that one month will occasionally have two Moons; this second full Moon in a calendar month is known as the legendary 'Blue Moon' and happens roughly once every two-and-a-half years. It is believed that any magic performed under a Blue Moon is more powerful than normal.

The Lunar calendar gave us knowledge of natural cycles, for many creatures and plants follow the ebb and flow of the Lunar sphere. Tides, animal behaviour, plant growth and human cognitive functions are all affected by the phases of the Moon. Knowledge of this cycle was a momentous first step to understanding the structure of time, helping humankind take steps towards some mastery of their environment and its often-challenging conditions.

It was patriarchal culture that deleted the thirteenth month, contrived the Solar calendar we use today, and put an aura of bad luck around the number thirteen.

After knowledge of the Lunar cycle came knowledge of the Solar cycle, with the Sun-Moon relationship being able to be measured by noting the changing proportions of day and night. This knowledge is what marks out the equinoxes and solstices. Observing the Solar cycles enclosed the Lunar cycle into a longer, 365-day calendar. The calendar we use today, the Gregorian calendar, is based on the Solar cycle, but is disconnected from the year's natural 'cross' formed by the solstices and equinoxes. Further, the Gregorian calendar indicates no resonance with the Lunar cycle. The natural world, however, continues to be influenced and moved by the Moon's cycles.

The Moon in the birth chart is very important, second only or arguably even equal to the Sun in its cosmic influence, because it is thought to reflect the true character of one's soul and thus forms an integral part of the personality. In fact, throughout most of human history, the Moon has been of more symbolic importance than the Sun, but in many cultures still, it is this Lunar influence that plays a larger role in chart interpretation.

The Moon governs that inner part of ourselves that can only be seen when someone knows us well. In many ways it is hidden for the most part, and must be drawn out. Your Lunar side reveals how you deal with feelings, how you handle relationships, how you respond emotionally to experiences with others, and how you react to other people unconsciously. Often the Moon reflects a great deal more about a person than any other planet, particularly in regard to their interpersonal relationships. It could even be regarded as the archetypal mirror, reflecting back to us our true self. But it has an outer expression also, and not only reveals our own inner motivations and security needs, but the style in which we seek to comfort and nurture others.

Some esoteric astrologers label the Moon the 'planet of past karma', another way of describing it as a limitless well of feeling patterns which, for the most part, subconsciously directs our behaviours and actions in the present. And while the Sun symbol represents the infinite and unmanifested potential, the Moon symbol reveals the finite and manifested, or that which already exists, and that we carry on our journey as a genetically gifted ancestral imprint or memory. As the Moon signifies the past and rules all life-giving and life-sustaining liquids*, it follows that in the fluids of brain and body, it accumulates and carries forward our personal evolutionary history.

While the Sun signifies our individuality, the Moon describes our personality. In one's horoscope, it is favourable if the Sun and Moon are in harmonious aspect, so that the will of the individuality and the feelings of the personality can be integrated and expressed in a sound, balanced manner. A disharmonious relationship between these two luminaries does not mean that an individual will not be successful, but it will usually indicate challenges and conflicts when learning to balance the will and the emotions.

The Moon is the innermost core of one's being, private feelings, and subconscious habits. It is the caring, nurturing sustainer of life, the 'mother' of the zodiac. Representing the infancy stage of the lifespan, as well as the mother and any other matriarchal influences that leave a deep impression on the psyche, it informs one of their earliest, unconscious memories.

As the Moon is oriented to survival and security, its pull in a person's horoscope can be stronger than that of the Sun. And where the Sun acts, the Moon reacts. Because it carries the energy of ingrained habits and the instinctual behaviours one expresses without conscious thought, it seems to flow more naturally than any of the other planetary forces. But the Moon also has a dark side as well, for one may continue to dwell within the frame of reference they set for themselves in childhood, repeating the same behaviours and thoughts until they form deep habitual patterns and entrapping ruts which one may find difficult to climb out from.

Contrary to popular belief, and the fact that the word 'lunatic' has its origins in the Latin luna meaning 'Moon' (arising from the belief that changes in the Lunar cycles caused intermittent insanity), the Moon does not always signify madness - far from it - but it can show one's darker side and any psychological blocks that are stubbornly difficult to shift.

With a strong feminine energy emanating from it, the Moon is about one's birth experience, fertility, containment, development of empathy, responses to received impressions (differing from Mercury's perceptions of received impressions), unconditional love, bonding mechanisms, intuitive functions, dependency style, attachment behaviours, and how one responds if their security is threatened. The Moon is, in many ways, one's vulnerable Inner Child.

Because one's consciousness does not fully develop until later in life, the traits of the Moon sign one was born under seems to be more apparent in their younger years. The Moon, influencing one's childhood so much, also plays an indirect role in adult relationships. It reveals whether or not and how one's emotional needs were met during this crucial stage of life development, and how this will be replayed and carried into one's adult relations. For many, 'grown-up' relationships are driven by an unconscious quest to get those earlier, unfulfilled needs met, or one may put up a barrier to resist being overwhelmed by another person's needs.

Overall, the strength or weakness of the Moon's natal position is said to determine in many ways one's personal magnetism, general sympathies, imagination, and sometimes unknowable inner landscape: the Soul Mystery.

In fact, the Apollo astronauts who landed on the Moon in 1969 collected samples which, scientists later concluded, posed more questions about Lunar origins than they answered. Those who returned from that iconic mission spoke of a profoundly moving spiritual experience which ultimately changed many of their life directions. And so, the Moon remains shrouded in mystery, a keeper of sacred enigmas that it may or may not reveal. She may guard her secrets closely, but if you listen closely enough through the Sun's shouting and Mercury's chatter, she may very well reveal your Soul's Truths to you.

The Moon rules the digestive juices, the glandular secretions of the lymphatic system, the stomach, breasts, ovaries, and the sympathetic nervous system. The last is intimately associated with reactive behavioural patterns, emotions, affections and desires. Hence the origin of the term lunacy to describe severe emotional disturbances.

SUN ✦ RULING PLANET OF LEO
The Core Essential Self

Luminary ✦ Associated with the Authentic Self, Essence, Identity, Ego, Creativity, Life Force, Will, Spirit, Purpose
365 Day Cycle

Were I to choose a religion, I would probably become a worshipper of the Sun. It gives life and fertility to all things. It is the true God of the earth.
Napoleon Bonaparte, Leo

> Some people say there is a new Sun every day, that it begins its life at dawn and lives for one day only. They say you have to welcome it. You have to make the Sun happy. You have to make a good day for it.
>
> **Byrd Baylor**

Keywords

Self-Expression, Vitality, Creativity, Identity, Centre, Core Self, Majesty, Inner Guiding Light, Source, Essence, Authentic Self, Pride, Life Force, Power, Purpose, Will, Potential, Talents, Assertiveness, Honour, Self-Confidence, the Masculine Self, Leadership, Determination, Authority, the Father, Consciousness, Awareness, Ambition, the Present, Spirit

> An actual vibrational or energy exchange happens when we're in sunlight as opposed to when we're away from sunlight. When we're outdoors, it's not just that we feel warm in the Sun - a vibrational field actually merges with our own and enhances the quality or the flow of energy through our body. To put it in plain terms, the effect of sunlight on our energy system is similar to that of a battery being charged.
>
> **Caroline Myss**

✦ Key Concepts ✦

The Individual
Outlook on Life
The Indestructible Self
The Father
Success and Achievement
The Masculine Expression
Consciousness
Glamour and Glitter
Self-integration
The Creative Principle
The Animating Force of All Life
Electricity
Nucleus of the Atom
Vitality of the Organism

Day ✦ Sunday

Number ✦ 1

Basic Energy & Magic ✦ Will, Success

Principles ✦ Consciousness, Vitality

Alchemy ✦ Coagulation, Conjunction, Digestion

Intelligence ✦ Nakhiel

Spirit ✦ Sorath

Colours ✦ Gold, Orange, Deep Yellow

Gods/Goddesses/Angel ✦ Helios, Sol, Michael

Metals ✦ Gold, Brass

Gems/Minerals ✦ Diamond, Amber, Citrine, Topaz, Chrysoprase, Ruby, Hyacinth, Chrysolite, Jasper, Tiger's Eye

Trees/Shrubs ✦ Juniper, Laurel, Palm, Walnut, Ash, Citrus

Flowers/Herbs ✦ Marigold, Saffron, Sunflowers, Hawthorn, Cinnamon, Peony, Musk, Frankincense, Yellow Poppy, Chamomile, Mistletoe, Almond, Heliotrope, Lavender

Essential Oils ✦ Benzoin, Melissa, Neroli, Patchouli

Wood ✦ Walnut

Animals ✦ Lion, Hawk, all Cats, Blackbird

Element ✦ Fire

Zodiacal Influences ✦ Rules Leo; Exalted in Aries; Detriment Aquarius; Fall Libra

The Way To Start a Day
The way to start a day is this -
Go outside and face the east and greet the Sun
with some kind of blessing or chant or song
that you made yourself and keep for early morning.
The way to make the song is this -
Don't try to think what words to use
until you're standing there alone.
When you feel the Sun
you'll feel the song, too.
Just sing it.
Byrd Baylor

The Sun occupies a unique position in astrology. Unrivalled by any other planetary body, it stands out, towering above the rest by virtue of the fact that all the planets revolve around it. The Sun proudly takes centre stage position; it is the main attraction, the leader of the pack. This spectacular luminary is the giver and sustainer of all life, a vast, unrivalled, and unconquerable life-force.

The Sun is, quite simply, one's true essential conscious self. It is the authentic, pure be-ing, as it is not veiled by superficialities, shrouded emotions, or hidden agendas. Indeed, tear these down and one is left with his Sun, outshining all around him.

The Sun is not a planet but a star, a superstar if you like. In astrology, it is referred to as a planet for clarity purposes. But considering that the origin of the word 'planet' is a Greek term that translates as 'wandering star', perhaps its classification is not too far off the mark.

The Sun is the generator of life, the channel through which one's self-expression is propelled outward, and the motivating force behind all activities. Like the physical heart, its energy operates and emanates from one's centre, or core.

This luminary rules the heart and is therefore symbolically the centre of self. Indeed, the Sun is the heart and the most commanding presence in our birth chart; the mighty Ruler who governs, guards and maintains our core essence.

The Sun is an energising, enlightening giver of life and vitality, revealing one's creative abilities as well as general overall health, energy, strength, recuperative powers, and fervour. It is the Sun's inexhaustible light which vitalises all the other planetary bodies, for without its electromagnetic radiation there could be no life anywhere, either in the Solar system or in the human organism.

The Sun is found in the outer edges of the Milky Way galaxy and is the Earth's primary source of energy, warmth, sustenance and light. All nine known planets and their Moons in our Solar system revolve around the Sun (although when astrology first began, the prevailing worldview was that the planets revolved around the Earth). All the personal planets - that is the Moon, Mercury, Venus and Mars - as well as the two social planets Jupiter and Saturn, are the means through which the Sun works in developing one's true, authentic, core identity.

Historically, the Sun was the chief and central deity of all cultures. Over time, it became representative of the Solar system's God-principle. To the Hindus the Sun was known as Brahma; it was Mithra to the Persians, Lugh to the Celtics, Bel to the Chaldeans, Hu to the Druids, Amun-Ra and Aton to the Egyptians, Apollo˚ to the Romans and Greeks, Helios to the Greeks, and Sol to the Latins. The Hebrew word for Sun is Ashahed, meaning 'all-bountiful fire'.

Since we live in a Solar ecology, we already know a great deal about how the Sun works and its power in our lives. Essentially a star, this mass is 1,300,000 times the size of Earth and about 750 times the combined mass of all other bodies in its system. What we see when we look at the Sun through a photographic filter, is not a solid object but a sphere of gas burning at about 6,000 degrees Celsius on the surface and reaching temperatures of 20,000,000 at the centre. The Solar centre, or 'nucleus', though in a gaseous state, is extremely dense, nine times the density of iron. With all this in mind, it is easy to imagine why the Sun is the unrivalled mighty ruler of our collective existence, and indeed, of our individual natal birth charts.

However, it is well to keep in mind that the Sun is only such a phenomenal concept because of our perspective of it from Earth. In reality, it is probably one of the feeblest and tiniest stars in the entire Universe. This star, from which we receive our energy vibrations, is certainly not stable. Astronomers tell us it is nothing but a ball of gases, constantly devouring and rekindling itself, held together solely by the regenerative force of its own combustion. Additionally, photographs show that it fluctuates in size, emitting sudden flashes out into the void, and then folding back upon itself - in essence, experiencing constant deaths and subsequent rebirths.

Even if it is tiny in the context of the entire Universe, the Sun is still the brightest in our very small world. The Sun sign is the focal point of any astrological birth chart in the same way that it is the focal point of our physical existence, wellbeing, and survival. Indeed, most astrologers will invariably check one's Sun placement in a birth chart first and foremost, for it reveals convincing and compelling clues as to where an individual will shine at their optimum fullest in life.

In ancient times, the alchemical Sun frequently stood as a metaphor for sulphur, a fiery, burning substance. In psychological terms, 'sun' or 'sulphur' or the 'Solar lion' signified the vital commanding life-force, that same force which manifests itself in our daily lives as the ego. The Sun or inner king is for most of us what it was to those old cultures - the vital force and masculine directive principle. According to the alchemists, the Self can only appear when the king unites with the queen in a mystical or sacred union, of Sol and Luna, the Sun and Moon. They asserted that the true emergence of the Self is dependent upon this marriage of masculine and feminine qualities within the human psyche.

Traditionally, the Sun is in fall in Libra, which is the symbolic 'sunset point' in the astrological mandala. Here the individual's will and purpose is suppressed somewhat by the desire to compromise or harmonise with others. And though the Sun is considered weak in its expression when in Libra, its symbolism reveals one thing that the Solar ego is not good at: relating. The Sun is essentially a self-centred, egocentric power, driven by an individual's own self-satisfying desires. Strongly Solar people are therefore considered to be self-absorbed, their sense of direction and achieving goals meaning everything to them. After all, they don't really have the inclination to relate to others and see others' viewpoints, as they are too busily involved in the business of leading and conquering their world. There is certainly an arrogance and self-interest in excessively Solar types, but bearing in mind the physical mechanics of our Solar system, it is also important to recognise that the planets do revolve around the Sun.

The glyph (or symbol) for the Sun ☉ depicts a circle with a dot or 'seed' at its centre, from which the core self, power, creativity and the first sparks of life can spring, and represents the spirit's unlimited potential brought into clear focus. The circle around this 'seed', is a symbol for infinity, a perfect shape that is without beginning or end, symbolising spirit, wholeness, eternity, and the never-ending flow of energy.

The Sun is commonly known as the great 'Father' of the zodiac, represents the father or father figure (an individual's experience and expectations of fatherly and male figures), how one expresses and experiences their masculine side, and the male principle, indicating how strongly these manifest in an individual, whether female or male. The Sun describes how well the active, masculine component of the personality can flow. Symbolising the father, either as a parent, authority figure or other significant male influences, the Sun reveals one's expectations and attitudes around their own father, as well as fathering itself.

The placement of the Sun also indicates leadership qualities, the degree of desire for power and authority, willpower, strength, determination, resilience, the ability to conquer goals, and one's sense of pride and honour, as well as honours bestowed upon one. The Sun also shows us our playful, experimental and creative urges, our capacity for pleasure, joy and happiness.

The Sun's function is to illuminate, vitalise, improve, individualise, stabilise, integrate, and elevate. It is the primary expression of the instinctive inner self, individuality, the unfolding of our personality, the core around which are structured all the elements of one's character, nature and essence.

The Sun represents our individuality, our ability to stand apart from the rest, our inner shining light that can never be dulled or snuffed out, for its essence and energy are eternal and pure, and energy can never be created or destroyed.

Something that is often overlooked is that the Sun is also associated with successful business ventures, and it is the creative aspect of such enterprises which comes under the providence of the Sun. A business, especially a small one, is often the manifestation of someone's personal creative vision. It can be confidently asserted that if the Sun shines upon a business venture, it will be successful and blessed.

The Sun also rules anything which glistens, therefore jewellery, ornaments and adornments, especially those made from gold, comes under its auspice. Into this category also falls show business, glamorous clothes, flamboyant people, entertainment and dazzling, star-studded events.

The Sun is externalising, and represents totality, infinity, and the striving towards and ultimate attainment of your optimal personal potential. Endowing us with our inherent creative potential and personal identity, it describes our urge to create and to be.

Our greatest luminary represents the present, which is arguably our greatest gift, because the present moment is all we ever truly have. The same could be said for the Sun - for stripped bare of our pretensions, masks, façades and bravado, the Sun is all that remains and – being the spirit - all that ever will.

It could be said that most people do not live up to the potential of their Sun, for most of us are only dimly aware of our pure, undiluted essence. If you were to be in complete harmony with your Sun (self), then you would be able to achieve a high level of authenticity and self-mastery. By consciously developing the potentialities of our Sun sign, we emit a bright illumination to light the way ahead.

The Sun of the Tarot deck - card 19 of the Major Arcana - contains an extremely positive image and meaning, heralding health, joy, exuberance, success, vitality, and good fortune.

The Sun is what calls you to your greatness. It is your potential, the truth of who you are and the truth of who you can be. If you are courageous enough to answer its calling, it will show you the Way.

Ultimately, the Sun represents the search for - and indeed the need to be - one's true self, the becoming of which signifies the ultimate pinnacle of the human experience.

Apollo is most renowned today as the classical Greek deity of music and the Sun. A very complex god with many functions and associations,

Apollo came to Greece from the North bearing shamanic skills and oracles. Apollo is known as a god of the Sun, fertility, purity and truth, and is also associated with healing, poetry and music. He was the son of Zeus and one of the Twelve Great Olympians. Among his other names are Helios, Hyperion and Phoebus. Apollo had numerous shrines dedicated to him and was the chief deity of the oracles at Delphi, Delos and Tenedos. Delphi, the most prominent oracle of its time, was originally an Earth oracle, guarded by a serpent of wisdom. His Colossus at Rhodes was one of the Seven Wonders of the ancient world. According to mythology, Apollo slew the sacred guardian and violently settled himself in charge, where he consistently displayed his amazingly accurate prophetic ability. Because he epitomises light and therefore mystical illumination, Apollo's influence in esoteric literature, as well as in the arts generally, has been substantial.

PLUTO ✦ RULING PLANET OF SCORPIO

The Powerful Undercover Agent of Change, Transformation & Regeneration

Errant ✦ Associated with Death, Rebirth, Transformation, Elimination, Eruptive Change

248 Year Cycle

Keywords
Regeneration, Transformation, Power, Death, Rebirth, Renewal, Wealth, Riches, Yearning, Elimination, Control, Metamorphism, Eruption, Compulsion, Passion, Penetration, Insight, Self-mastery, Occult, Hidden Secrets, Obsession, Transmutation, Charisma, Magnetism, Subversion, Depth, Darkness, Psychoanalysis, Research, Sex

✦ Key Concepts ✦
Elimination
The Reformer, the Purger by Fire
The Passage to the Other Side
Changing from One State to Another
Mining, Excavation & Archaeology

Wills, Legacies & Taxes
The Redeemer, the Master Builder
The Beginning & the End
Transmutation of Energy
Psychiatry, Unlocking the Unconscious
Investigation, Research, Espionage
Regenerative Principles of Death
The Annihilator, the Eliminator, the Transformer
Renewal of the Life-Force, Redemption

Deities ✦ Hades, Persephone, Demeter

Basic Energy & Magic ✦ Destruction, Transformation, Personal Power

Colours ✦ Dark Reds, Black, Dark Purple, Magenta, Violet, Ultraviolet (beyond sight)

Metals ✦ Plutonium

Gems/Minerals ✦ Jade, Pearl, Beryl, Smoky Quartz, Black Obsidian, Jet, Kunzite

Trees/Shrubs ✦ Cypress

Flowers ✦ Narcissus, Daffodil

Herbs/Essential Oils ✦ Ginseng, Damiana, Squawvine, Dong Quai, Pennyroyal, Sage, Cedarwood, Sandalwood, Ylang Ylang, Jasmine

Tree ✦ Cypress

Zodiacal Influences ✦ Rules Scorpio; Exalted in Aquarius; Detriment Taurus; Fall Leo

As far as we know, Pluto is the planet furthest from the Sun and could be described as our galaxy's sentinel to the mysteries of the Universe - like the sign of Scorpio, itself.

Patricia Crowther

Discovered in 1930, Pluto is the most distant known planet, and hence the most mysterious. A small, solid body, it may once have been a satellite of its neighbour Neptune. Pluto is so far from the Earth and its cycle so long - 248 years - that its influence is seen as largely impersonal and having more of a mass, or generational, effect *, unless it is prominently placed in a birth chart. Accordingly, because it generally influences larger groups of people by staying in one sign for many years, only Pluto's house placing can help decipher the individual psyche.

For eighteen years before it was discovered, Pluto was called planet X, a factor which was known to exist but could not be found. The name Pluto was apparently proposed by an 11-year-old girl who was thinking of the Disney dog.

A commonly used glyph (or symbol) for Pluto is monogram P with a horizontal line extending out at its foot, parallel with the P's semi-circle. This is simply a combination of the first two initials of Percival Lowell, the astronomer whose calculations led to Pluto's discovery.

Another glyph of more recent origin for Pluto is three-fold: the circle of spirit sits inside the crescent of soul atop the cross of matter. The circle is detached from the semi-circle and hovering above it, appearing to rise up. Its esoteric meanings have very ancient roots, as it encapsulates the whole process and concept of involution and evolution. It symbolises that the energy of the spirit descends through the soul in order that continuously changing finite forms of concretised energy may manifest on the Earthly plane (signifying involution).

Pluto, or Hades as he was known to the Greeks, was the ruler of the dead and the underworld; nobody was ever known to have escaped transportation to his land of death beyond the river Styx. He was the son of Saturn and brother of Jupiter and Neptune. Jupiter came to rule the skies and Neptune inherited power over the oceans, leaving Pluto to rule the underworld. The ancients associated Pluto with wealth and riches because underground gold and other precious stones and minerals were said to dwell in his domain and therefore to be in his custody. Greek mythology thus depicted Pluto as the god of wealth and buried treasure, and the word 'plutocracy' - referring to governments ruled by a group of rich men - derives its title from Pluto.

As lord of the underworld, Pluto invariably shows up on everyone's doorstep at some stage in life, and his visit will alter the course of your life forever. The underworld or inner world of your psyche often contains areas of unhealed grief, loss, pain, or brokenness. By our very natures, and as a kind of self-protective survival mechanism, we tend to repress trauma, grief, loss, unresolved painful feelings or potentially damaging hidden secrets. All that is repressed is the domain of Pluto. Chaos, drama and betrayal can all ensue as a result of stored emotions. Though Pluto often puts us through this process of initiation by imposing loss, pain, grief and darkness, he also symbolises the rising up again through resurrection. And herein lies his greatest power: rebirth. The Plutonian descent is inevitably linked with a subsequent resurfacing and re-emergence.

Although it is small and far-away, Pluto has a symbolically potent effect in one's birth chart. Pluto rules intense energy and describes the areas in which one consciously or unconsciously seeks to exercise power or control, revealing the areas in which one must gain the deepest level of understanding. But it can also reveal contradictions in oneself, presenting us with maddening paradoxes: it is both an annihilator and transformer, constructive and destructive, a psychiatric healer and brainwashing propagandist, self-destructive and self-empowering, user and misuser of power. It embodies mass communication and mass hysteria, gives rise to intense hatred and consuming love, and evokes both toxic build-ups and swift disposal. Its contradictory nature can be best illustrated by the concept that its era of discovery coincided with giving us the blessings of nuclear power but the curse of the atomic bomb.

Pluto reveals one's urge for transformation, penetration, power, self-mastery and how we access deep insights. Associated with renewal and rebirth, Pluto represents endings and new beginnings, as well as spiritual growth and regenerative powers. It rules the inevitable changes that take place in the cycles of life, from birth to death.

Indeed, Pluto's energy can be linked to many analogies and metaphors: a snake shedding its skin to allow its new self to emerge, the caterpillar morphing into a butterfly, autumn leaves decomposing so that a tree may grow from the resultant nutrients generated in the soil. In its role as the transformer, it brings about the end of one form so that another form may be brought to life. This sometimes requires total disintegration in order to rebuild from scratch. Pluto represents the change brewing within - the earthquake, the volcano, the all-powerful seed. But first we must understand the nature of crisis, in that it is not always the disaster it may seem and often offers opportunity for upward growth. In fact, the Chinese character is the same for both words: crisis = opportunity.

Ruling the psychological and subconscious aspects of life, especially obsessions and compulsions, cold, icy, dark Pluto is distant and enigmatic. He embodies the drive to confront all that is darkest and deepest in the psyche. He rules anything that is toxic, contaminating and polluting - both inner and outer - and is the repository of all things that are deemed unacceptable or 'evil'. One of Pluto's primary functions is to transform our egos through facing ourselves, for when we do confront the secrets and complexities of our deepest recesses, we can free ourselves from the ball and chains we did not even realise we were bound by.

As master eliminator and purger, Pluto rattles the skeletons in our closets, and challenges the inner demons to do battle so that we are forced to examine ourselves. And so, it is Pluto's job to ensure that we confront our darker aspects so that new, fresh life may spring forth when the war is over.

The sign and house that Pluto occupies in one's birth chart reveals the intuitive nature and power, how these are utilised, and in which area of life they are exerted. It describes where and in what form a compulsion, obsession, self-destructive streak may exist. And scary as this may be, it has much to offer those who are prepared to explore places where angels fear to tread. Used wisely, Pluto can transmute dark experiences into a potent, overcoming force.

The house Pluto resides in shows in what areas Plutonian qualities manifest themselves, the way in which one uses his personal power, and the activities that can offer avenues for personal growth.

The formidable Pluto will be forceful if necessary, and it is important to remember that he is involved in life, death, and decay, so his lessons will not always be easy to bear. A necessary evil at times, if you like.

Pluto is the higher octave of Mars. While Mars brings the energy, Pluto directs this energy where it is needed for spiritual growth, metamorphosis and enlightenment. Mars is the aggressive force, while Pluto is the destructive Fire whose power is far mightier than the comparatively small sword Mars wields. Mars manifests itself in short, intense bursts of energy and often exhausts itself, burning out quickly. Pluto, however, explodes like a bomb but his planning is done in secret and its effects more enduring.

Pluto reveals not only our purpose and powers of regeneration, but our style of evolutionary growth, destruction and renewal, and our interest or otherwise in the occult, black magic, release, purging, catharsis, resurrection, metamorphism, the underworld, and corruption. People with a strong Pluto in their chart are often attracted to mysteries and probe to get to the bottom of things, being commonly found in police work, scientific and medical research, paranormal studies, and psychoanalytical work where an essential quality is the courage to confront painful, disturbing or difficult truths. Plutonian types make excellent psychiatrists, transcendental guides, and psychic healers. Indeed, Pluto's associations with matters of the darker aspects of the human psyche can be illustrated by the fact that after Pluto's discovery, all kinds of 'obscure' mental illnesses began to be seriously studied. As a result of these studies and findings, psychiatric and psychological phenomena were approached in a manner totally unknown previously.

If you are able to accept your suffering, to give yourself permission to mourn or grieve losses, to bring pain to the surface rather than sending it to the hidden recesses of the mind, if you can admit those darker aspects of your character, you give yourself a much better chance to find redemption amid the chaos and ruins that scatter the landscape after Pluto has swept through. Surrender is the key. Because Pluto wisely knows that many deaths constitute any life well-lived, and for there to be a rebirth, first there has to be a death of sorts.

Pluto often unleashes the underground turbulence of years of repressed feelings that have been left to simmer far too long. But Pluto serves in a dual capacity as both eliminator and renewer. His Fire may destroy all in its path, but it is all made worthwhile by the new life that springs up once the embers have turned to ash.

It has been said that the distant planets are actually more powerful than the others as they take longer to orbit the Sun. As a result, these slower moving planets (Uranus, Neptune and Pluto) dwell in the zodiac constellations for longer periods of time, allowing them to leave a deeper and more indelible experience on the human psyche and experience than the swifter moving planets. In other words, their effect is thought to be more lingering.

JUPITER ✦ RULING PLANET OF SAGITTARIUS & PISCES
The Great Benefic, Expander & Bringer of Joy

Benefic ✦ Associated with Expansion, Religion, Faith, Philosophy, Higher Education, Travel
11.9 Year Cycle

See where my planet, great Jupiter, is positioned (in the horoscope), for there lies your Crock of Gold in this life. The house he inhabits will reveal the type of fortune he brings. It will come to you of its own accord.

Patricia Crowther

Jupiter's navigational pole star is always enthusiasm, which is neither subtle nor ambiguous. Its magnetism carries its own plucky confidence. When the right path opens there is no hesitation. You are enthused and experience an absolute abundance of YES!

Caroline W. Casey

Keywords
Expansion, Wisdom, Travel, Abundance, Faith, Ethics, Morals, Ideals, Distant Horizons, Inflation, Culture, Philosophy, Beliefs, Knowledge, Enthusiasm, Religion, Luck, Fortune, Trust, Hope, Vision, Justice, Opportunities, Joy, Benevolence, Optimism, Exploration, Education, Success, Wellbeing, Confidence, Indulgence, Creative Visualisation, Opulence, Conscience, Betterment, Extravagance, Generosity

Jupiter expresses the outer quest in its rulership of Sagittarius, and inner question in its affinity for Pisces, which is also ruled by Neptune, representing dreams, vision, and imagination.

Caroline W. Casey

✦ Key Concepts ✦

Exploration of New & Foreign Places
Belief, Philosophy, Theology & Religion
Morals, Ethics, Truth, Laws & Justice
Higher Education
Understanding of Universal Laws Governing Humanity
Expansion on the Spiritual, Mental & Physical Levels
Luck, Expansion & Opportunities
Publishing & Legal Matters
Large Animals & the Great Outdoors
Gambling, Risk & Speculation

Day ✦ Thursday

Number ✦ 3

Basic Energy & Magic ✦ Expansion, Faith, Philosophy

Principles ✦ Truth, Justice

Alchemy ✦ The colour grey, Dissolution

Intelligence ✦ Cophiel

Spirit ✦ Hismael

Colours ✦ Purple, Deep Blue, Mauve, Indigo

Gods/Goddesses/Angel ✦ Zeus, Jupiter, Zadkiel, Sachiel*

Metals ✦ Tin, antimony

Gems/Minerals ✦ Amethyst, Lapis Lazuli, Blue Diamond, Turquoise, Emerald, Jacinth, Green Jasper, Sapphire, Topaz, Aquamarine, Chrysocolla, Tanzanite

Trees/Shrubs ✦ Oak, Cedar, Maple, Ash, Birch, Linden, Chestnut

Flowers/Herbs ✦ Sweet William, Sage, Hyssop, Nutmeg, Dandelion Root, Chicory, Lilac, Hyancinth

Essential Oils ✦ Cedarwood, Sandalwood

Wood ✦ Oak, Cedar

Fabric ✦ Velvet

Animals ✦ Horse, Eagle, Dolphin, Elephant, Bee, Whale

Element ✦ Fire

Zodiacal Signs ✦ Sagittarius, Pisces

Zodiacal Influences ✦ Rules Sagittarius (co-rules Pisces); Exalted in Cancer; Detriment Gemini; Fall Capricorn

*The angel Sachiel is considered the lord of Jupiter and is a member of the choir of cherubim. He has an interest in legal matters, good fortune, expansion and beneficence. He can be invoked for financial matters.

All the verdant growth and luxuriance of nature, including the majestic beauty of the great trees, comes under the providence of Jupiter. With such an embarras de richesses there is no wonder that the (Sagittarian) soul is intoxicated with life and has an inner certainty that it was born with more than its share of luck.

Patricia Crowther

A giant planet shrouded in swirling cloud, Jupiter was considered the beneficent father of the gods by many ancient cultures. This mighty sphere is the largest orbiting the Sun, bigger than all the other planets in our Solar system combined. The wonder of its size can be imagined when we consider that it is approximately 800 million kilometres away from the Sun, and can still be viewed in the sky as our second brightest planet (after Venus).

The vast 'empty' space between its nearest neighbour Mars, and Jupiter, is almost as inconceivable - 550 million kilometres - and is littered with cosmic rubble, a space otherwise known as the 'asteroid belt'.

In mythology, the Roman god Jupiter, Zeus to the Greeks, the Nordic Thor, and parallel deities in other cultures, sometimes appears more powerful than even the Sun gods, suggestive of Jupiter's mighty influence. Wisdom, learning and justice were their attributes, thunder and lightning their visible power; Jupiter was called the Thunderer and his chief weapon was the thunderbolt. Zeus, who sat upon his throne atop his holy mountain with a thunderbolt in one hand and the staff of wisdom and life in the other, was seen as a combined Divine package of creator (the staff), preserver (the mountain), and destroyer (the lightning bolt).

Known as a 'cloud gatherer', and sky and weather god in more ancient incarnations, Zeus was the omnipotent ruler of the ancient Greek gods who lived on the summit of Mount Olympus, and was regarded as the father of men and master of fate. He controlled thunderbolts, which were said to be carried by eagles, monarchs of the bird kingdom. The Romans considered him the guardian of the law, protector of justice and virtue, and defender of the truth, hence Jupiter's long-held associations with principles concerning these.

In astrology, Jupiter is the first of the transpersonal planets, which is less associated with the self and more concerned with interactions with others - in other words, it can be classified as a 'social planet'. Regarded as the most benevolent and wise of the planets, Jupiter is the joy-bringer and is related to expansion in every form, the acquisition of knowledge, and the desire to be free and unrestrained.

In its purest sense, Jupiter encompasses morals, altruism, good fortune, prosperity, higher values, ethics, beliefs, exploration, spiritual leanings, aspirations, ideals, faith, hope and trust.

Buoyantly optimistic, Jupiter's main function is to grow and magnify everything he touches. However, he inflates and expands indiscriminately, often making bad points worse and good points better, for Jupiter's blind enthusiasm can just as easily lead to fanaticism and perilous excesses. Being a planet that influences lifestyle - namely, excess and indulgence – under his powerful influence, one may become extremist, careless, or make poor decisions; similarly, losses are likely through ill-judged investments, gambling and extravagance.

He not only brings material benefits, but also philosophical wisdom. He imparts this knowledge frequently by coming to the rescue at the last minute, when all hope seems lost. Saturn is also a wise teacher, but teaches through restriction, limitations and adversity, without any immediately apparent saving graces. Jupiter's very nature is to fulfil - he delivers the rewards at the end of the lesson. At his best, he can be the happy ending, the strength that allows us to endure trials.

Jupiter's symbol shows a Moon-like half circle of soul that rises slightly above the cross of matter, suggesting a higher wisdom and mastery over material things.

Broad-visioned and future-oriented, Jupiter brings hope, spirituality and fortuity to the birth chart, expanding and creating opportunities in whichever area of the chart it is found. Where he exists in your chart, you will find special opportunities for progress. Finding one's higher purpose, or inner riches, is an important theme of Jupiter. You will observe clues to furthering your career, for broadening your relationships with the material world, and ways to heighten your spirituality. You will see ways to make money or to acquire skills to help you get what you want. But always bear in mind that the flip side of Jupiter's coin is that he simultaneously reveals those areas of life in which we may be drawn to adverse excesses or blind adherences. In itself however, Jupiter's expansive influence is neither beneficial nor harmful, for what it does for us depends on how we channel it.

Jupiter has much to reveal about our urge for expansion, and the types of physical and mental travel, opportunities, justice, religious viewpoints, and philosophical wisdom we undertake and express. His energy is philosophising, and as such is deeply connected with our search for meaning in life. Largely to do with morals, ethics, beliefs and ideals, it describes the means by which we grow and ultimately find that meaning.

Jupiter is also linked with prosperity, wealth, luck and good fortune, as well as our faith, hope, trust and optimism in a bright future. As Jupiter expands everything with which it comes into contact, it is frequently the giver of gifts and blessings. By knowing which sign and which area of life this abundance is likely to manifest, you will be equipped with a higher understanding and knowledge of how to go about opening up to and receiving it more fully into your experience.

Jupiter spends approximately one year in each zodiac sign, completing a full cycle every twelve years. Its oppositions and returns are the most significant milestones of its cycle, and one of these will occur every six years of our lives, beginning at the age of six. If transiting Jupiter conjuncts, or aligns with, your natal Jupiter (every 12 years), you have an increased chance of having a lucky break, receiving a windfall, or experiencing something that advances and expands you in mind, body, or spirit.

Revealing much about our urge for higher learning and long-distance travel, particularly of the varieties that expose us to other people and new ideas, it signifies the modes by which we both physically and mentally travel. Jupiter's influence enhances our creative visualisation skills, holding them in the vortex of creation and manifestation. Its essence is what lies at the heart of making one's own luck: if you can visualise something with enough passion, intensity and faith, you can seize the chance when it arises to make what you want to happen. In this sense, Jupiter is all about seizing the day!

In our birth chart, the Sun and Jupiter both exercise the kingly function of harnessing vital energies for the purpose of conscious achievement and personal growth. And indeed, both planets participate in the expressions of the male archetype in all of us. The Sun and Jupiter are quite different planets, however. Jupiter has often been described as a social planet, whereas the Sun is termed a personal planet and, along with the Moon, the most personal of planets. Furthermore, the Sun is considered a spiritual influence, while Jupiter a more temporal force. Despite this, Jupiter has been integrally linked to the Sun in mythology, religion - and astrology, and in ancient Greece and Rome, Jupiter was assigned an even higher position than its Solar counterpart.

With Jupiter, our directed will is focused on opportunities and general expansion in whatever area of life we wish to grow. The important questions to ask our chart's Jupiter is what kind of attitudes do we bring to our goals? And what kind of spirit do we embody during our quest for success? Our wise inner kings, the Sun and Jupiter, organise and focus the entire range of our psycho-spiritual energy and directs it to a specific purpose, while the Warrior (Mars) lends the motivation and drive to do the actual work.

Especially in esoteric astrology, Jupiter has been described as the protector or 'inner guide' of the natal chart. For example, a Sixth House Jupiter may protect our health, while a Twelfth House Jupiter may offer spiritual protection. Its place in our horoscope is where it bestows upon us gifts; and it also represents our own capacity for generosity, particularly if placed in a warm or giving sign or house.

Indeed, this kingly planet impels us to be benevolent and generous. However, it does have its drawbacks, and there is such a thing as excess and too much abundance. These excesses of lifestyle or thinking, may manifest as a weight problem, extreme or overbearing behaviour, or an inflated sense of self-confidence or entitlement. It may lead to a certain arrogance or smugness, and in combination with a strongly placed Venus and/or Neptune, may increase one's tendencies towards hedonism, or indulgence in sex, alcohol, drugs, or food.

Jupiter has always been the significator of good fortune, spiritual faith, good fellowship, and joy; another name for the God in Latin was 'Jove', from which where the word 'jovial' derives.

Knowing all this about Jupiter, it is perhaps not so coincidental that Sagittarius, ruled by Jupiter, falls in the part of the year between Thanksgiving and Christmas, a time of year that is associated with Jupiterian-themed activities of exchanging gifts and offerings, indulging in large spreads of food and drinks, engaging in social merriment, and the gathering together of family and friends from far and wide to celebrate the season's spirit.

Overall, Jupiter's most noble gift is to guide you to your highest happiness and fulfilment, its birth chart placement offering clues about where and how to take leaps of faith.

Mercury is concerned with mentality in a pure and simple sense, while Jupiter gives the ability to think ahead, to understand the ramifications of your thought processes, to appreciate long-term significance and purpose; in other words, Jupiter will assist you to find meaning and direction. Also, Jupiter in your birth chart will show the nature of your belief systems - what you find meaningful - and the measure of your faith (this of course, does not relate necessarily to organised religion, but rather our adherence to personal creeds, moral standards and sets of principles). Jupiter goes beyond the rational faculties embodied by Mercury, and gives the gift of prophecy, while Mercury chooses the mode of expression and words in which these Divine revelations are to be imparted.

Jupiter is strongly associated with principles and matters on a higher plane, its expansive nature allowing one to see the bigger picture by broadening and opening the mind. The combination of this vision with thought, leads to the attainment of Jupiter's loftiest aim: wisdom.

SATURN ✦ RULING PLANET OF CAPRICORN & AQUARIUS
The Wise Teacher

Malefic ✦ Associated with Boundaries, Structure, Control, Limits, Restrictions
29.4 Year Cycle

There's always a faint melancholy and seriousness surrounding the Saturn personality. None of them completely escape the Saturnine influence of stern discipline and self-denial. (And) respect for the wisdom of age and experience is ingrained in the Saturnine nature.

Linda Goodman

Keywords
The Teacher, Practicality, Boundaries, Restrictions, Limitation, Ambition, Control, the Father, Duty, Authority, Obstacles, Reality Checks, Contraction, Rigidity, Solitude, Wisdom, Caution, Discipline, Perseverance, Austerity, Inhibition, Frustration, Thrift, Consolidation, Direction, Denial, Responsibility, the Shadow, Karma, Endurance, Patience

✦ Key Concepts ✦
Time and the Wisdom Gained Through Experience
Karmic Lessons
Lord of Time
Maturity & Old Age
Self-imposed Limits & Fears
Lessons to be Learned
Tradition & Conservatism
The Father, The Boss, The Authority Figure
Solidification, Structure, Foundation & Stability
Ambition, Endurance & Self-Discipline
Crystallisation & Concretisation
Satan & the Reality Check

Day ✦ Saturday

Number ✦ 4 & 8

Basic Energy & Magic ✦ Authority, Boundaries, Banishing, Stabilising

Principles ✦ Concentration, Limitation, Inhibition

Alchemy ✦ The black stage, Calcination

Intelligence ✦ Agiel

Spirit ✦ Zazel

Colours ✦ Black, Midnight Blue, Green, Grey, Dark Brown

Gods/Goddesses/Angel ✦ Cronos (sometimes spelt 'Kronos'), Ceridwen, Cassiel

Metals ✦ Lead, Iron, Steel

Gems/Minerals ✦ Onyx, Jet, Diamond, Green Calcite, Obsidian, Garnet, Coal, Black Coral, deep-hued Sapphires

Trees/Shrubs ✦ Cypress, Elm, Buckthorn, Willow, Aspen, Pine, Beech, Holly, Poplar, Yew

Flowers/Herbs ✦ Patchouli, Myrrh, Wintergreen, Iris, Maize, Cornflower, Comfrey Root & Leaf

Essential Oils ✦ Camphor, Pine, Eucalyptus

Wood ✦ Birch, Ebony, Alder

Animals ✦ Crow, Wren, Tortoise, Ant, Beaver

Element ✦ Earth

Zodiacal Influences ✦ Rules Capricorn*; Exalted in Libra; Detriment Cancer; Fall Aries

Traditional ruler of Aquarius.

Saturn, whose unique and distinctive rings make it one of the most spectacular bodies in our Solar system, is second only to Jupiter in size. It is the farthest planet from the Sun that we can see with the naked eye. Before the discovery of the outer planets Uranus, Neptune and Pluto in more recent times, Saturn was considered to mark the outer edge of the Solar system. The most visually beautiful of all the planets, Saturn's array of colours are astonishing: its equatorial zones appear brilliantly white, its subtropical and temperate zones darker yellow, and the polar caps often look green. The system of rings that surround the planet and its lustrous, contrasting colours can be clearly seen with a telescope, through which is(it?) appears as a blue sphere encircled with three yellow rings against the velvety blackness of deep outer space.

Saturn has ten known satellites, the largest, Titan, being bigger than Mercury. To guess at Saturn's astrological functions by virtue of its known physical attributes, one conclusion drawn is that its influence must be enormous; aside from being massive in size, it is capable of exerting huge pressures, capturing and holding weaker bodies and even using them to create what are apparently impenetrable barriers around itself. On closer inspection, Saturn actually behaves very eccentrically and its highly unusual orbit makes it remarkably oblate in shape.

If our assumptions are correct, we can see why Saturn has acquired such a fearsome and arguably unlikeable reputation. Perceived and described as dull and malevolent, it has given us the term 'saturnine', which quite literally means sluggish, cold and gloomy in temperament. Relating to lead, its medical connotation, 'afflicted by lead poisoning', derives from medieval alchemy, whose work attributed the force of Saturn with the element lead, or plumbum. But Saturn is also one of the least understood energies in the astrological matrix. Although its principles are partly perceived as difficulties, obstacles and limitations, Saturn is also a teacher, and it has often been said that "when the student is ready the teacher will appear". And appear Saturn does, always in a timely manner (although this may not be welcomed or even apparent to the uninitiated). The position of Saturn in a chart will reveal the lessons to be learned - the negative karma - which, according to house and position, must be purged.

The astrological glyph of Saturn combines the crescent of consciousness with the cross of the Earth, or matter, in other words, the mastery of the conscious mind in relation to its position and experience of the physical environment. It also implies that the cross of matter is imposed upon the crescent soul, symbolising the responsibilities and challenges that mortality imposes. Worked with constructively, one's natal Saturn can temper the soul with structure, order and discipline.

Associated with boundaries, restrictions, limitations and concretisation, and the urge to build structure and stability, Saturn in one's birth chart shows where in life there are lessons to be learned, or the burdens of duty or responsibility.

It could be said that each individual has a Soul which has chosen to wrestle with the challenge of expressing spirit through the base material of a human body; Saturn represents that battlefield. But Saturn often takes with one hand and gives with the other, for if one enlists his help, the apparent difficulties experienced on this harsh plane can be transmuted into qualities which can enhance one's Soul Journey. As the way-pointer, Saturn shows one where the Soul must dwell in order to fulfil one's inner purpose and destiny. Representing rules and lessons on many levels - personal, collective, societal, cosmic and karmic - if one allows it, Saturn can be a great sage-like presence in our lives.

Saturn produces its effect by causing difficulties in the expression of the qualities of its zodiac sign, in the affairs of its house, and in the relationships (or 'aspects') it has with any other planets in the birth chart. The arising discomfort and fear often cause one to shrink away or obliterate the negative feelings with overcompensating behaviours. However, the discomfort cannot be ignored or swept under the carpet; it has to be accepted, confronted, understood, and worked with so that the Saturnian energy in the birth chart can be transformed into the fortitude and enlightened understanding it so promises.

Saturn is the archetype of the judge. Many approach him with fear and trepidation as a result. Saturn limits you, says "No", punishes. He is unmoved by one's protests that life is unfair, as he sagely knows that one always has a choice: to accept responsibility for one's actions, or to resist authority and necessary restrictions to one's detriment. Indeed, Saturn has always been associated with the letter of the law rather than the spirit, and as such he does have a dark, ruthless side. However, in astrological tradition his benefits may be greater - or at least more substantial - than those of all the other planets. His lessons may be tough, but they are what we need to learn in order to grow, materialise and manifest through what is learned and applied from these tests.

As a symbol of wisdom (or folly), lessons learned (or not learned) and obstacles overcome (or not overcome), Saturn defines the outline of one's personal story, particularly as it unfolds as one ages. In this sense, he forces you to examine and analyse yourself sincerely, honestly and solemnly.

Saturn is often regarded as a significator of 'the father' in astrology, alongside the Sun, but in Saturn's context the connection to the father often symbolises problems with him. In order to break free of any restrictive fathering issues one has had, one must consciously develop one of the more positive aspects of Saturn - his role as mentor or positive role model.

Repressed instincts, the soul's recesses, disowned feelings, suppressed compulsions, the Shadow Self, may all come up for review under Saturn's scrutiny. And as long as one remains bogged down by limiting attitudes, Saturn cannot function at its best. Subjecting one to delays and restrictions on all planes, Saturn may induce a state of depression, helplessness, or melancholia - states of mind in which one feels confined to an endless dark tunnel. Medieval and Renaissance scholars associated Saturn with one of the four humors of ancient medicines and unsurprisingly linked it with the melancholic humor, which provides as good a metaphor for Saturn's depressive influence. Marcilio Ficino, an influential scholar, priest and humanist philosopher of the early Italian Renaissance, warned his fellow magi of Saturn's gloomy power over scholars and philosophers, asserting that learned men were more likely than other people to suffer from Saturnian afflictions. However, it could also be said that if scholarly gloom was associated with Saturn, so too was scholarly wisdom, for Father Time (another label for Saturn) bring serenity as well as doom and melancholy. And indeed, Saturn can impart a great sense of character and resilience when it is functioning effectively.

Many people who suffer from Saturn's impositions remain in their dark corner of isolation for years because they have not yet taken personal accountability for the predicament in the first place, but rather point the finger at parents, or blame society, authority, or outside circumstances for any continuing misfortune in their lives.

Saturn's wisdom is of the Earth itself, and it rules the 'golden years' of old age. People with a prominent Saturn will age with dignity and wisdom, returning to the Earth in proper time; Saturn is Old Father Time, the Lord of Death. Saturn is happiest in maturity, when burdens and responsibilities apparently weigh the least. As well, age confers wisdom and the profound knowledge that comes from a life thoroughly examined, other Saturnian domains. Saturn has guardianship of inner mysteries and secrets that are acquired over years rather than weeks.

To understand Saturn's functions, we have to associate him with Jupiter. In symbolic astrology, we see many of the workings of the cosmic law of polarity. Jupiter expands; Saturn contracts. All motion, all life, depends on expansion and contraction, drawing in and expelling, inhaling and exhaling, push and pull. In one's birth chart, Saturn and Jupiter can potentially complement each other to bring out each other's best qualities. It is notable that Saturn's glyph is composed of the same two symbols as Jupiter's but in Saturn, the two are inverted. Saturn's symbol is the cross imposed over the crescent semi-circle, representing the principle of contraction. Despite Saturn's reputation as the harsh disciplinarian, his common sense and practicality blend well with the extroverted optimism and enthusiasm of Jupiter, creating a breadth of vision combined with sensible caution. He is also the tester and teacher who shows us that in order to successfully operate as both a Universal and a social being (Saturn is a social planet, along with Jupiter), we must abide by certain cosmic and terrestrial laws, rules, concepts and impositions that govern our behaviour. Saturn can also serve in the role of Satan, the tempter, whose force allows us liberation if we learn our lessons wisely.

But not all teachers or fathers are wise, kind and guiding. And the more often we fail to strike a balance between contraction by expansion, the more we set ourselves up for failure and disappointment. Saturn, while providing a shelter, can just as easily turn into a prison.

Despite its reputation as a greater malefic and bringer of sorrows, Saturn does allow for personal growth to a spiritual end, but does so only through the fulfilment of one's Earthly obligations, duties and responsibilities. He does not deal in emotions and has little tolerance for feelings; his job is purely to get the job done effectively and efficiently.

Indeed, in the birth chart, Saturn reveals the area of life the Hindus call Dharma, which is the duty one has to undertake in order to build and fortify one's character. Saturn will also describe what obstacles one needs to overcome to achieve success and satisfaction. But, being the harsh teacher, he can just as easily be the one who puts those very obstacles right in one's path!

Representing the crystallisation/concretisation principle of one's birth chart, Saturn builds the foundation upon which the structure is placed, and will only put another layer of bricks on top when the ones underneath have solidified.

Saturn forces us to take stock of our assets, liabilities, limitations and shortcomings, often through 'reality checks'. And while it imposes boundaries, its purpose is to keep us safe and realistic. However, too much Saturnian influence can make one rigid, lonely, limited, isolated, emotionally repressed, fearful, over-cautious, pessimistic, cynical, austere, unfeeling, sceptical, and unwilling to accept anything that is new or pushes established boundaries. But in his positive expression, Saturn teaches the value of patience, maturity, sacrifice and prudence, bringing gifts of longevity, commitment and temperance. Serious, reserved and devoted, Saturn teaches one to take ownership of their life, a full ownership that can only be achieved by learning the deep lessons that have been assigned to one at birth, and conquering any associated battles, so that one may become a mature and wise person. A person that Saturn would be proud of.

URANUS ✦ RULING PLANET OF AQUARIUS*

The Great Awakener & Divine Rebel

Transcendental ✦ Associated with Change, Disruption and Shock
84 Year Cycle

Aquarius's esoteric ruler is Jupiter. The Air Signs Gemini, Libra & Aquarius are also said to be co-ruled by the asteroid Pallas (Pallas Athena is known for her mental creativity and resonates most strongly with Libra and Aquarius). Pallas Athena, the virgin goddess of wisdom who ruled the city of Athens, was the goddess of war and is always pictured wearing her armour. She also rules the visual arts, crafts, and as Hyegia, she was the goddess of health and healing. She portrays the independent, aggressive, and competitive woman who is astute in business and foresight, and the prominent presence of Pallas in a natal chart suggests an involvement in social causes, inspired vision, counselling, healing, and possible work in the arts. The glyph for Pallas is her spear.

Because Uranus makes a complete orbit every eighty-four years, around the age of forty-two Uranus opposes everyone's natal position. This period has been boringly labelled the 'midlife crisis'. What's really going on here is that the wild, authentic part of us has completed half of its orbit and is checking in with itself. It is a time of self-assessment … how truly are we living our unique wildness?

Caroline W. Casey

Keywords
Intuition, Electrifying Force, Innovation, Disruption, Higher or Psychic Functions, Individuality, Cosmic Consciousness, Inventions, Shock, Sudden or Unexpected Change, Originality, Electricity, Revolution

✦ **Key Concepts** ✦
The intuitive faculties, the Sixth Sense
The bohemian, the beatnik, the hippie, the nonconformist
The inventor, the 'mad scientist', the revolutionary, the anarchist
Destroyer of old ideologies, ways of life, concepts and structures
The global crusader, the social reformer
The embracer of Brotherhood, the humanitarian
The force for the awakening of the higher consciousness: individually, collectively and Universally
He who marches to the beat of his own drum

Numbers ✦ 4 & 22
Basic Energy & Magic ✦ Invention, Innovation, Change
Colours ✦ Light Blues, Electric & Glaring Hues, Stripes
Metals ✦ Uranium
Gems/Minerals ✦ Amber, Jacinth, Jargoon, Chalcedony, Aquamarine, Azurite, Sapphire, Lapis Lazuli
Herbs/ Essential Oils ✦ Valerian, Borage, Vervain, Raspberry Leaf, Hyssop, Marjoram
Zodiacal Influences ✦ Rules Aquarius; Exalted in Scorpio; Detriment Leo; Fall Taurus

Aquarius is ruled by Uranus, known as the Magician of the Zodiac, because this planet is the transformer and has a fervour for change and innovation… Before the discovery of Uranus, Aquarius was considered to be governed by Saturn, and is sometimes given the double rulership of both Saturn and Uranus. But Aquarius is so obviously connected with the revolutionary, the new and unusual, that Uranus must always have been the sign's natural ruler.

Patricia Crowther

Uranus was discovered in 1781, an era during which the American, French and Industrial revolutions took place, correlating it with the time's social themes: freedom, independence, technological advancement, culture shifts, innovation and rebellion. It is therefore fitting that Uranus, which sits beyond Saturn, should represent a break from tradition, restrictions and barriers, and a certain emancipation from the structure, authority and order that its neighbour Saturn imposes.

Discovered by musician and astronomer William Herschel, Uranus was at first believed to be a comet until further investigation confirmed its planetary nature. Its discovery was a startling revelation for the fields of astronomy and astrology, as the two disciplines believed the Solar system extended only to the limit of Saturn's orbit.

The glyph for Uranus is a cross with a circle suspended from the lower arm and a semi-circle attached to each of the side arms of the cross. The symbol is derived from H for Herschel, the surname of its discoverer, and looks uncannily like an early television aerial, hence its link with televisions and other signal-receiving or electronic gadgetry. Uranus is also said to govern astrology itself, which may be linked to the similarity of Uranus' name with that of Urania, the Greek muse of astronomy and astrology.

Uranus is the iconoclast and the divine rebel of the Solar system, and he drives the human will through his creative powers. In fact, according to mythology, he started out as a creator before he became the 'rebel of the skies'.

Uranus is the first of the 'impersonal' planets and rules less intimate relationships such as friendships and acquaintanceships. It also denotes memberships of clubs, societies, groups, and political organisations, and is associated with modern inventions such as electricity, computers, aviation, television, and the discovery of radiation.

Uranus offers a welcome chance to seize our freedom, liberate ourselves, and be progressive. An astronomical maverick, alone in rotating horizontally, on a personal level, Uranus's electrically charged energy denotes individualists, reformers, outsiders, and intellectual brilliance; people who break the norms of a cultural or political mould. People born under the sign of Aquarius are particularly sensitive to its influence, and being born with an (often) emphasised Uranus factor makes them susceptible to being extremely stimulated most of the time, living in a constant state of wired or other-worldly energy. Indeed, a powerfully aspected or placed Uranus in one's horoscope, is seen as a powerful totem by astrologers.

Uranus is an erratic planet, orbiting on its axis at a 90-degree angle, different from the way everything else in the Solar system behaves, giving a good allusion to the nature of the Uranian mind: a different way of 'spinning' to almost everything and everyone around it. The Aquarian mind seems to have adopted this quirk from its ruling planet. It also lends humanist impulses to its Earthly subjects, and is certainly closely linked with the breakthrough works and revolutionary thinking of such eminent minds as Sigmund Freud, Charles Darwin and Isaac Newton.

Uranus embodies esoteric principles which symbolise vibrations of cosmic energy that affect whole generations and collective humankind, rather than touching us on a personal level; however, Aquarians and other people whose Uranus is strongly placed or emphasised in their birth chart, can certainly be individually affected by this planet's influence.

Concerned with the realm of ideas and the intellect, it exudes an air of coolness and logic. But most of all, this planet's role is to break down the established 'order' and replace it with experimental, novel, or idealistic regimes - whether these are applied to the wider world, or in one's personal life. It acts to break up the crystallisation that Saturn has imposed, acting to electrify, galvanise, vivify, awaken and mobilise, often working in a spasmodic, unexpected fashion, but highly effective as an agent of change.

Before the discovery of the three outer planets which lay beyond the detection of the naked eye, the ruler of Aquarius was Saturn. Today, after the discovery of Uranus, Saturn is regarded as Aquarius's secondary or traditional ruler. Indeed, very old astrology texts describe

Aquarians in Saturnian terms, which seems odd to most now, given the Aquarian temperament is regarded as the polar opposite of everything traditional or Saturnian. Occasionally, however, you may still meet with an Aquarian who is cautious, conservative, even dull, slow-going, melancholy, quiet, thoughtful, deep, reticent and restrained in their passions. But more often than not, a typical Aquarian will have been endowed with all that is Uranian: unpredictable, convention-defying, unusual, occasionally shocking, different and eccentric. It is Uranus's influence that helps make the Water Bearer the prophet, social reformer, brilliant thinker, and free spirit.

Uranus, as one of the three outer or generational planets, is regarded as a 'planet of a higher octave', along with Neptune and Pluto. These higher octave forces account for those flashes of inspiration we are occasionally jolted with, when we become especially aware of our life's purpose, albeit usually only very fleetingly - unless of course you are an Aquarian!

Uranus is Mercury's higher octave, and although both function on an intellectual level, Mercury rules the everyday and logic, while Uranus rules intuition and sees far further than the immediate moment and environment. It could also be said that Mercury is the trickster, Uranus the magician. Here, the versatile is raised to the volatile. In its elevated role, Uranus allows mortals to bring the beauty of knowledge and intellect to a more original, inventive and creative level, and in the birth chart, Uranus rules the higher mind, a planetary energy that helps one deal not only with what is but also with what can be. While Mercury is connected with the gathering and learning of information on a daily, mundane basis, Uranus rules the vast amounts of information accumulated over long periods of time, and are therefore manifested as intuition and sustained intelligence. Aquarians can see how fortunate they are to have such a powerful guardian planet, and must also make it their duty to use this power advantageously. Both Aquarians and Uranus work in sudden and unexpected ways, which is why this planet is called the Great Awakener, and its offspring so rebellious.

Uranus never seeks to put up boundaries around the soul or spirit, allowing one to more easily build and create things according to their own inner visions, ideals and worldviews.

Uranus is not content with leading the way along existing roads; instead, it will carve a new channel through the mountains where nobody thought roads could ever be created. Sometimes this road takes unexpected twists and turns; such is the nature of this unpredictable sphere. But Uranus doesn't make us believe in magic, for that belief already exists within most of us, instead it reinforces our belief in it, by dropping moments of serendipity, dazzling insights, or unexpected surprises into our laps. Uranus may pull rabbits out of the cosmic hat and enchant us with its inexplicable genius, but it is also capable of pulling the magical carpet out from under us just as suddenly, leaving us shocked and a little bewildered. Life - and Uranus - has a way of doing that.

We are entering the cusp of the Age of Aquarius, and while we are not all the way into it yet, we are certainly in transition. Considering that an astrological age takes around 2,100 years to complete, the cusp can take a couple of hundred years. The reason the Age of Aquarius has been so glorified and embraced with mounting excitement, is that Uranus rules this sign. We can expect a Uranian rush of energy, thrills, adventure, progress, changes and above all, advancement. This planet has a tendency of sending us rushing off in all directions to find the gold at the end of the rainbow, which is yet to be found - but the pot of gold that the Age of Aquarius stands for is nearly upon us. In fact, Aquarians are already in firm possession of it, as they are living already in that rosy-coloured utopian future its profound influence promises us all.

Revolutionary by nature, those influenced by Uranian rays are idealistic and work towards the betterment of humanity, never satisfied with past traditions or present 'realities'. Its sign and placement signify one's level of individuality, quest (or non-quest) for freedom, extremism, radicalism, reformist side, anarchism, fanaticism, inventiveness and unpredictability.

Uranian energy, magnetism and attraction is often at work in matters of love. Romantic adventures that begin under a strong Uranian influence often end as intensely and abruptly as they began. This is especially true during natal Uranian transitions or aspects, when one may find themselves overwhelmingly drawn to another's magnetic field or 'aura', only to be brought back down to Earth and reality once the transit is complete or aspect has passed. These transit periods are often characterised by a feeling of being elevated to euphoric states and lofty heights, but Uranus has a way of delivering the unexpected with its characteristic shock value.

In fact, all significant Uranus aspects can have a profound effect upon our lives. It takes 84 years to fully return to the position it was in at the time of our birth. Therefore, approximately every 20 to 21 years, it will form a significant aspect to its natal position, with the first square aspect occurring at 21 years of age, when the spirit of rebellion and 'breaking free' is often at its height. At around the age of 42, it forms an opposition to its natal position, and this is when we start to really assess and search our souls to work out whether or not we have achieved our goals or realised our dreams. Wisdom may very well teach us that this is the time to shift the focus of our attention from purely material or worldly concerns to more spiritual, creative and individuated goals, which is much more aligned with Uranus's nature. The final square occurs at the age of approximately 63, and significantly, this is around the age of retirement, a time to break free from the restrictions of working life and paying off a traditional mortgage or other material goals. Uranus returns to its natal position when we are 84, usually the end of the life span - that's if we don't miss it altogether through death or dementia. These are the years when arguably truly magical things can happen for us. If we were to take a cue from native tribes who honour, respect and revere their elders, we may even experience the ultimate Uranian enlightenment of this phase of life, if we are destined to achieve this. Symbolically, this final Uranian infusion suggests a potential for spiritual re-birth, particularly for the Aquarian spirit, and a new adventure in detaching ourselves at last from the world altogether in order to fix our sights upon freer horizons.

NEPTUNE ✦ RULING PLANET OF PISCES
The Great Artist, Mystic & Dreamer

Transcendental ✦ Associated with Fantasies, Dreams and Spirituality
165 Year Cycle

Keywords
Inspiration, Dreams, Mystical Longings, Sensitivity, Mysticism, Imagination, Higher or Psychic Functions, Otherworldliness, Escapism, Delusions, Artistry, Enigmas, Compassion, Intrigues, Cloudiness, Unreality, Spirituality, Subtlety, Idealism, Deception, Creativity, the Subconscious, Illusions, Fantasies

✦ **Key Concepts** ✦
Dreams, ideals, illusions, fantasies
The drifter, the fantasiser, the psychic, the dreamer
The mystic, the spiritualist, the prophet
Dissolver of boundaries
The great deceiver
The artist, the musician, the dancer, the filmmaker
The self-sacrificer, the carer, the spiritualist
The embracer of Universal love and compassion
The force for the awakening of the higher spiritual consciousness
The bestower of Universal love
She who swims to the ebbs and flows of her own ocean

Number ✦ 7 & 11
Basic Energy & Magic ✦ Dreams, Fantasies, Magic
Colours ✦ Lavender, Mauve, Aquamarine, Sea Green, Etheric Colours, Indigo, Violet
Metals ✦ Neptunium, Platinum
Gems/Minerals ✦ Coral, Aquamarine, Amethyst, Fluorite, Jade, Sugilite
Herbs/Essential Oils ✦ Plantain, Frankincense, Clary Sage, Myrrh
Zodiacal Influences ✦ Rules Pisces; Exalted in Leo; Detriment Virgo; Fall Aquarius

> The negative aspects of Neptune foster an attraction for drugs and the desire to live in a world of fantasy, which can be dangerous. On the positive side, however, we find that the muse-inspired poet, par excellence, is usually a Piscean. These souls can be vague, nebulous and often irritating, but at the same time, can act as mirrors with which we view ourselves.
>
> **Patricia Crowther**

Neptune, the eighth planet of the Solar system, situated between Uranus and Pluto, was 'discovered' before it was actually seen. A sphere that lies beyond Saturn's boundaries, Neptune was in fact discovered in 1846 as a result of its gravitational effects on neighbouring Uranus. Twelve years prior, an amateur astronomer, the Rev. T. J. Hussey, had suggested that the erratic motion of Uranus might be caused by the pull of an unknown body. His theory was developed by two mathematicians: John Couch Adams in England, and Urbain Le Verrier in France, who both calculated the hypothetical position of another planet from observed discrepancies in Uranus's position. Eventually Le Verrier's ephemeris and calculations were received by an astronomer named Johan Galle at the Berlin Observatory and Neptune, recognised at first as a starlike object, was located; it was found that Neptune had been seen and thought to be a fixed star by previous observers.

The Roman sea god Neptune is named after, represents aqueous themes such as dissolution, formlessness, haziness and impressionability. Neptune, also known as Poseidon, was not always a nice presence in mythology, and indeed excelled at throwing storm clouds and nets in the way of his intended victims, making them lose their way at sea for long periods of time. Although this may be frightening, the vision ahead often comes to us more clearly when we are cut off from a purely physical sense of reality. Therefore, one of Neptune's functions may be to encouraging the opening of the third eye so that we can see the unseen, and develop trust and faith in, and reliance upon, a higher power that can only come to us when we are adrift on a vast ocean and no longer able to control our course.

Neptune's well-known associations with anaesthetics and mind-altering drugs can be explained through the use of ether in surgery for the first time in the same year of its discovery. That year also belonged to an age where gas lighting illuminated foggy streets, alcohol binges abounded in gin palaces, consumptive poets downed laudanum and yearned for transcendence, spirituality was striven for, and occult 'sciences' permeated everyday life. Beyond 1846, a renewal of interest in spiritual and psychic subjects and a proliferation of new religions occurred.

Perhaps nothing is more Neptunian in nature than the medium of photography, which appeared in 1839, a few years before Neptune's discovery and which, appropriately enough, given Neptune's strong connection with state-altering substances, was derived from chemical processes. In fact, the word 'photography' was coined by Sir John Herschel, son of the astronomer William, who discovered Uranus. Sir John was, perhaps not surprisingly, a Piscean. Photography shows real life in a way that a painting could never convey, but is still prone to ambivalence and trickery. Cinema and the world of moving pictures and films, too, are ruled by Neptune, and all are simultaneously the ultimate illusion, an act of mass escapism and enchanting glamour.

The glyph (or symbol) for Neptune is a cross with an upturned semi-circle cutting through the upper arm of the cross, giving the appearance of the three-pronged trident that the sea god Neptune carries.

Originally Neptune was just a big fish in a small pond. Starting as a god of fresh water, it became identified, in around 390 B.C. with Poseidon, a grandson of Uranus. To Neptune fell power over all the waters on Earth, and his powers could seemingly invoke storms, cause shipwrecks, or send favourable winds to blow mariners safely back to shore. It could undermine the land with hidden rivers, dry up lakes and streams, or strike barren rock with its trident, causing life-giving springs to gush forth.

The ocean has always been the symbolic keynote of Pisces, over which Neptune rules. Artists and mystics are able to reach into the deep ocean of images that this sign's symbolism evokes, connecting Pisces with psychics and dreamers, artistic types, and idealists; after all it is precisely from these watery depths that they garner their visions, poetry, and melodic symphonies. Neptune is the planet of altruism, dreams, and deep faith, and as such engenders great compassion, insight and inspiration, as well as a profound sensitivity to beauty. Its trident symbol, Poseidon's pitchfork, symbolises the threefold parts to each person: body, mind and spirit, the latter being a significant realm of the Piscean experience.

Neptune's placement in a birth chart can indicate the magician, the artist, or the drunkard – perhaps all three at once - and how one will likely express these personas. It also tells one how they relate to their own soul, and how they react to the tides, ebbs and flows of their beliefs, emotions and feelings.

Seeing the world through rose-coloured glasses much of the time, it compels its subjects to believe in magic, dreams, fairy tales and happy endings.

Before the discovery of the three outer planets which lay beyond the detection of the naked eye, the ruler of Pisces was Jupiter. Today, after Neptune's discovery, Jupiter is regarded as Pisces's secondary or traditional ruler. Indeed, the Piscean temperament seems to encompass qualities of both these planets, but Neptune is regarded as more fitting for the dreamy, nebulous and watery Fish.

Naturally, due to its distance from the Earth, few among us are capable at all of being affected by Neptune, save that it produces a chaotic state of mind when placed in difficult aspect. When placed in angles, and particularly in elevations near the Midheaven, it produces occultists and mystics of the highest stamp. It is the highest string in the Soul's lyre and is therefore the least used and the one to get most easily out of tune. Astrologers are the most affected by it, as are stringed instrument musicians. The ecstasy and heightened expression that comes about as a result, is both the gift and the fatal flaw of the Neptunian individual. In no time in history is this better illustrated than during the 1960s. Astrologers refer to this decade as a decidedly Neptunian period - and indeed, the drugs, the peace-for-all, the love-ins, the seeds of the iconic song Imagine, the long-flowing hair, the acceptance of and pervading compassion for others, the idealism, and the colourful bohemian attire, all suggest a strong Neptune influence.

One of its primary functions is to remove barriers, not by tearing them down, like Pluto does, but by gently dissolving them; in fact, Neptune would like everything rendered to a state of liquid suspension, to be formless, to be returned to the state of nebulousness that existed in the beginning.

Neptune shares the 'sub'-dimensions with Pluto; their two respective gods were relegated to the underwater and the underworld realms, and both reside in domains where it's easier to ignore or sweep undesirable elements of our lives under the magic carpet rather than to deal with them directly.

Neptune is also associated with spontaneous kindness and charity, through looking after those who cannot care for themselves, and the desire to give hope to the hopeless. Further, it rules solitary, confined and 'hidden' places such as hospitals, orphanages, institutions, mental homes, hospices, and any form of imprisonment, real or imagined.

Neptune's energy is dreamy, mystical, fantastical, delusional and magical. This planet pulls the veil of dreams over our eyes but it can just as readily pull it away. Its influence often coincides with both mystical and romantic experiences. Its adverse side can cause carelessness, impracticality, foolish decisions, needless worrying, and the tendency to live in either a fantasy world or under the influence of substances.

Denial literally means 'to look away', and denial, as played out in our lives or in society, is based upon this principle - looking away from reality. When reality (Saturn) is resisted or ignored, Neptune can take over with dreams, fantasies, addictions, anxiety and escapism - which is what seems to plague our society in the last part of the Piscean age, on both individual and collective levels. In examining an individual's astrological position of Neptune at birth, life areas most prone to denial or self-delusion, and how self-deceptions may be expressed, are highlighted.

Perhaps not surprisingly, Neptune appears strongly in the horoscopes of idealists, musicians, dancers, painters, as well as among alcoholics, drug addicts, therapists, and those who follow a metaphysical or spiritual vocation, such as healers, astrologers, mediums and psychics.

Neptune is often regarded as the higher octave of Venus, and Venus is exalted in the sign Neptune rules, Pisces, suggesting that Neptune's highest function and manifestation is a Universal, transcendental, all-encompassing love and compassion.

It can intoxicate us at times, so we connect this influence with alcohol, gases, hallucinogens, and the many experiences to which they give rise. With this Neptunian influence, there is a tendency towards addictions, drug experimentation, lymphatic issues, foot problems, and nervous disorders. Money may be made in strange ways, but there is a likelihood of trusting others too much and so being exploited or defrauded, or of just frittering money away.

Being so romantic and tender, there is also a tendency to fall in love easily, and to bring great romance and idealism into a marriage. This planet lends a raw boldness, a childlike innocence, and deep romance to love affairs, which may typically contain an element of the Knight in Shining Armour or Prince Charming ideal contained somewhere within them.

Neptune's bag of tricks is akin to being in a funhouse full of distorting mirrors. It works its magic by offering us a glimpse of ourselves in an infinitude of images, which are all essentially ourselves. Some are amusing, others disturbing, some flattering, others grotesque, some fantastical, others frightening. Should we be curious – or courageous - enough to enter Neptune's House of Mirrors, no one will stop us if we gladly and willingly pay the price of admission and accept the conditions of entry. But Neptune never reads the fine print, and inside, we usually discover nothing there but deceiving, warped reflections of ourselves, with no firm answers reflected back to us.

Upon emerging, we often come to the gradual realisation that the experience has cost us far more than the freak show was actually worth. If we insist on lingering, we learn to our detriment that the longer we remain inside, the higher the cost becomes. Even worse, we discover that what initially seemed amusing now begins to scare us and then we wind up confused by the maze, bewildered by the trickery, and unable to find our way out again.

An ice cube provides a fine metaphor for Neptune's message. What our senses perceive as solid substance is in fact a temporary arrangement of moving energy particles, and by making the right kind of effort we can alter the arrangement to turn the substance into something more useful. We take the ice cube out of its tray and it is an ice cube, but soon it loses its identity by melting. The water re-emerges, only to be used again in one form or another: we may drink it, retain it for a while in our bodily tissues, then excrete it as sweat, respiratory droplets, or urine; or we may just pour it down the sink where it ends up somewhere only to evaporate into the atmosphere and contribute to cloud formations, which then rain it back down to turn dust to mud, nourish a plant, cleanse the terrain, or contribute to a river system. Whatever happens to the water, it does not cease to exist; it may go through any number of recirculation processes and undoubtedly take on different forms, but it still exists in its essence. This example illustrates that we are working not with specific units of matter but with Universal, widespread - and sometimes intangible - forces.

Water's infinite capacity to dissolve other substances and assume new forms offers us a physical demonstration of Neptune as the Universal Solvent. We associate Neptune with clairvoyance, telepathy, behind-the-scenes activities and that which is hidden. Indeed, Neptune has the ability to see more than meets the eye, and the ability to forgive, washing the slate clean and suggesting we start anew by trying again.

Wherever we find Neptune in our natal charts, it tells us where and what we need to change, perhaps some aspect of our life experience which we are viewing from a distorted angle. The house in which Neptune resides and the sign to which it is linked will indicate where the problem lies.

It also teaches us where to look for beauty in our lives through the manifestation of those higher, creative urges of the artistic realms. Indeed, a work of art is an act of love. Neptune is both the inspiration and the expression of that love, on personal and universal levels.

Neptune's most fundamental principle can be found in the following analogy. Observing waves lapping gently to the ocean's shoreline, in rhythmic, non-resistant flows, smoothing out sand patterns and gently frothing with each lunge, it is easy to momentarily forget the power and turbulence that lies just beneath the surface. An undertow can pull the unsuspecting out of their depth without warning, an earthquake can shift the sandy plates so violently that it results in an all-engulfing tsunami, or a swirling rip can suck you under with a silent, powerful force, but unless you have the courage to float wherever the water may take you, you may never truly know what interesting new shores and depths can be discovered. Indeed, for those who stand safely back, feet planted in the practical, tangible world, Neptune may seem remote, but anyone seeking a deeper understanding of life will have to get their feet wet.

THE TEN HUMAN LIFE STAGES ✦ WHAT EACH RULING PLANET REPRESENTS

Planetary symbolism is correlated with different stages of life. The astrological scheme of the ten human life stages describes how each phase of seven years duration, is represented by a particular planet. These planetary energies and therefore the particular effect each has on one during the time span it governs, have been ascribed to the traditional planets for thousands of years.

THE MOON AGE ✦ 0 - 7 YEARS

I have always been regretting that I was not as wise as the day I was born.
Henry David Thoreau, Cancer

The Moon, the closest body to the Earth, has always signified those things most in sync with the Earth's rhythms, instincts, cycles, water, and all other life-giving liquids. It reflects the dual nature of the primally evolving human spirit, part conscious, part unconscious. The Moon represents the subconscious side of the personality, bound by habitual responses, reflexes, and emotional and nurturing needs. It is passively receptive to outside influences. Throughout the first seven years of one's life, before the ego is developed, one registers and reflects the effects of its environment and in doing so displays the characteristics of an acutely impressionable being. Beginning life in a physiologically and psychologically fluid state, suspended in the womb's amniotic fluid, and largely helpless, dependent and vulnerable, our early experiences are usually shaped by the maternal mould; this is fitting, for the Moon represents the mother or mother figure, and our early attachments to this caregiver. Although we outgrow our many formative survival needs and reflexive behaviours, some remain and indeed stay with us throughout the course of our lives. Most psychologists agree that these early years are the most crucial in the developing emotional consciousness of an individual.

THE MERCURY AGE ✦ 7 - 14 YEARS

Mercury is the intellectual force that governs intellectual style and expression, speech, learning nature, communication, writing, and the general mental functions of an individual. The early school years are when a child learns the basics and bases of communication, finds his place in social hierarchies, and forms his identity within the context of the educational construct, whatever form that may take. These years are also when a person learns to articulate, assert ideas, make connections, disseminate information, and analyse and discern any information received. Filled with a greater sense of inquisitive purpose, this age group begins to learn how to control and manipulate certain aspects of his environment through the advancing powers of his mental faculties.

THE VENUS AGE ✦ 14 - 21 YEARS

Venus influences love, art, beauty, values, aesthetics, culture, social relationships, desires for intimacy, and the need for harmony. All emotions with a sexual or sensual basis begin to develop prominently during this stage, when the first stirrings of passionate attraction may be felt. Venus aims to unify, and to make beautiful – the arts, dancing, poetry, and music all fall under her rule. This is the time when one's mental vigour and attention are turned towards love and romance, to connections, when intense feelings come and go with brief but often profound impact. This is the age of fads, phases and crazes that later develop into more mature and sophisticated tastes. The teenager usually learns to discriminate, to evaluate people and situations, to test moral boundaries, and to begin to understand the power of his social presence. Social mores, proper conduct, personal style, the value of cooperation, the advantages of belonging and popularity, and the deeper meaning of intimacy and connecting with others begin to develop as the individual prepares for adult life and wider society.

THE SUN AGE ✦ 21 - 28 YEARS

Our twenties are generally when we emerge completely into the world, as a fully-fledged adult. It is during this stage that, perhaps after many turbulent teenage years, we finally 'find ourselves' and our place in the world; our identity is largely sealed, albeit remains a work in progress for the rest of our lives. In fact, the concept of 'finding oneself' epitomises the Sun's essence. This is the age during which we may truly find what we are good at and direct our purpose, giving us the opportunity to step onto the centre stage of our life experience to truly shine.

THE MARS AGE ✦ 28 - 35 YEARS

Mars is the planet of energy, activity through enterprise, assertion, willpower, confrontation and leadership, so it is only natural that this would be a strenuous life stage, during which the individual, now more stabilised in character and having found his place within surrounding society, endeavours to make a personal imprint on his world. He may become a dynamic influence, more ambitious than ever, determined to achieve and succeed, respond with passion to challenges, or compete for leadership, recognition and acclaim. The need to accomplish at any cost is usually present, with ambition being the prime concern, money second. Those who laid solid foundations in the preceding Earth age (21 - 28 years) are now eager to build their structures with relentless energy and determination - the result is a glorious rise, or a tremendous fall. If one has started a family by now, there is the ever-present challenge of juggling the work-life balance. Pressure is usually quite high during this life stage, but with Mars onside, it is usually handled like a true warrior with skill, efficiency, and good humour.

THE JUPITER AGE ✦ 35 - 42 YEARS

Jupiter represents expansion - by growth, acquisition, understanding and meaning - and signifies philosophy, religion, morals, ethics, foreign affairs, distant journeys, intellectual questing, and reason. During this stage, the individual begins to prosper or benefit somehow from earlier efforts and experience. He is usually established in his chosen calling, or at least knows himself a bit better by now, and feels comfortable about who he is and where he is headed in life. This is arguably the 'prime of life', when a person expands financially, spiritually and mentally, and has emotionally matured enough to understand his firm place in the world. The individual has a finely developed sense of personal morals, codes, order, convictions, ethics and belief systems, and applies these in every area of his life with a more assured and humble sense of confidence than ever before. Since the direction of life is now probably pretty well fixed, the individual begins to seek ever deeper meaning to reach and experience a more dynamic level of fulfilment and self-progression.

THE SATURN AGE ✦ 42 - 49 YEARS

One aspect of Capricornus and its ruler, Saturn, is that of time and age and the knowledge that we, as humans, occupy a mere fraction of eternity from birth to death. Yet here, at the winter solstice, we have the regeneration of the Sun, which speaks most forcibly of rebirth and renewal.

Patricia Crowther

Sometimes symbolised as Father Time, an old man with the hourglass and scythe, Saturn represents the ticking clock with a firm but wise hand, rigidity, discipline and restriction. He stands for prudence, profundity, caution and organisation, and is the symbol of physical limitation, through which the human spirit, evolving as a mental being, must overcome to progress onwards. This is the period when the individual learns the lessons and values of self-discipline and applied, focused work. The 'young' years, physically, are behind him now, and he is now probably a fixed and determined entity in his own right. If errors have been made along the journey, this is the stage when they are apt to be called up to account and demand rectification. This is the time during which the habitual or regret-ridden person may find himself heading for the abyss of decline or depression. But if he has fulfilled the earlier stages with wisdom, this age marks the way up, and a new deeper path unfolds ahead as a compensation for the prospect of growing old. For many, it can be difficult to withstand the constrictive and ossifying influence of the Saturn age, as some people who have not cultivated wisdom or learned from their mistakes, are confronted with the erosive, gnawing inner voices of bitterness and rue. If a strong foundation of personal fortitude has been properly developed however, one need not despair, for in this person, his best years are yet ahead of him.

THE URANUS AGE ✦ 49 - 56 YEARS

Uranus represents independence, change, anarchy, scientific thought, brilliant genius, intuitive and often, after a lightning strike of sorts perhaps, a renewed sense of purpose. This planet also represents metaphysics, telepathy, curiosity, astrology and wonder, so it is no surprise that this is the age of a second flowering, a rebirth of the spirit, for those who can embrace the change and happily release their old selves to make way for the new, improved version. It is here that the newfound self can leap forward with a more profound sense of wisdom and into a new state of consciousness. This is the age that offers the individual the chance to break away from any previous restrictions or rigidly controlled norms. Within each individual is the power to be exceptional and outstanding, and this is the stage during which he can discover that instead of reaching out, he must reach within to unlock the spontaneous forces that will liberate him from societal or personal limitations or expectations. From this new life force springs inspiration, originality, renewal, abstract thought, inventiveness, and even a little rebellion! Indeed, it is during this stage that many produce their most valuable and original work, as only a free, born-again, unencumbered spirit can.

THE NEPTUNE AGE ✦ 56 - 63 YEARS

Neptune symbolises the evolving human spirit as the mind transcending the physical condition. Neptune dissolves boundaries, and this is where one's spirit may reach out further than ever before. As a dissolver of form, and like the sea over which it rules, Neptune is the master of subtlety with no material roots. Under this planet's influence, during this age, one can soar to new heights and the fully developed individual now begins to break loose from inordinate attachments to the surrounding world and merge with the cosmos. A spiritual rebirth, ripening and deepening will likely occur during this stage, and yearnings may make him a born-again believer in as-yet-unrealised dreams, which he may pursue with renewed vigour. If life has so far been relatively fulfilling, a serene acceptance of the past may be present. Having risen above the Earthly concerns of security and material desires, the person in this age group may indeed find that both these needs are effortlessly filled.

THE PLUTO AGE ✦ 63 - 70 YEARS

Pluto is said to be the deliverer. As the Sun represents the beginning of the individual, so Pluto symbolises the cyclic return through experience to that emergence. Many people survive well beyond seventy in modern times, but when the life stages were ascribed planetary meanings, seventy usually signalled the end of the average life. As the Sun is the unexpressed potential and central force, so Pluto, as the final stage of the human's progression through life, represents the seed - of a new crystallised beginning. The fully developed person at this stage knows himself, and in knowing himself and his true power, which he has by this stage accumulated over a lifetime of experience, acquisition and lessons, he can face the other side fearlessly and thereby come to instinctively comprehend the great mysteries of the life he has lived thus far. The road from here can lead to enlightenment, and even a sense that the highest pinnacle of the human spirit has been reached – that of self-actualisation. And this newfound self can then give rise to a profound acceptance, peace of spirit, and deep surrender to All That Is.

THE PLUTO AGE ✦ 63 - 70 YEARS

Pluto is said to be the deliverer. As the Sun represents the beginning of the individual, so Pluto symbolises the cyclic return through experience to that emergence. Many people survive well beyond seventy in modern times, but when the life stages were ascribed planetary meanings, seventy usually signalled the end of the average life. As the Sun is the unexpressed potential and central force, so Pluto, as the final stage of the human's progression through life, represents the seed - of a new crystallised beginning. The fully developed person at this stage knows himself, and in knowing himself and his true power, which he has by this stage accumulated over a lifetime of experience, acquisition and lessons, he can face the other side fearlessly and thereby come to instinctively comprehend the great mysteries of the life he has lived thus far. The road from here can lead to enlightenment, and even a sense that the highest pinnacle of the human spirit has been reached – that of self-actualisation. And this newfound self can then give rise to a profound acceptance, peace of spirit, and deep surrender to All That Is.

THE HOUSES IN THE HOROSCOPE

A house is one of the twelve sections dividing the terrestrial globe, viewed from a precise time and geographical place, into sectors from the poles to the horizon. The horoscope, or birth chart, is divided into these twelve sections, which are called houses. Each house governs a different area or 'department' of life, such as relationships, career, leisure, and even karma.

The reason for this division of the Earth into houses can be understood when we consider that the Sun's rays affect us differently in the morning, at noon and at dusk, and also in summer and winter, and if we study the cause, we will readily observe that it is the angle at which the ray strikes us or the Earth that produces that difference in effect. Similarly, with the stellar rays, astrologers have observed that a child born at or near midday, when the Sun's rays strike the birthplace from the Tenth House, appears to have an improved chance of public or career advancement in life than one born after sunset or deep in the night.

By similar observations and tabulations, it has been found that the other planetary rays affect the various departments of life when their beam is projected through the other houses, and therefore each house is said to 'rule' or govern certain compartments of the human life experience.

THE FIRST HOUSE ✦ ARIES

ASCENDANT - ASC - Cusp of the First House.

The Ascendant is the degree of the zodiac rising on the eastern horizon at the moment of birth. It signifies the point of self-awareness: "I am."

The First House is the first thing others notice about you. In a literal house, it would be the front door. It shows your outer personality and the impression you give on first meeting others.

The First House, ruled by Aries, is the house of individuality, the projected self, incarnation, self-image, basic approach to life, physical characteristics and personal appearance, one's reaction to the immediate environment, outer mannerisms, identity and persona. This house, also known as the Ascendant, is commonly known as our 'social mask', and is often the first impression others have of us. It represents how directly and immediately we express our individuality, our outer behaviour, and how we come across before others truly know our inner drives and selves.

The importance of the Ascendant/First House cannot be over-emphasised, for it is the most sensitive part of the horoscope, colouring your whole personality. It reveals the way in which you relate to those around you, and shows who you are and how you approach life. The signs and planets that reside in this area, show the aspects that are most valuable in realising your unique identity. In fact, the Ascendant is almost, if not equally, as important as your Sun sign, and offers further insights into the rich tapestry of your individuality. Any planet which is found on or near (within 8 degrees either side of) the Ascendant, will play a strongly significant role in defining your character.

As a Fire-ruled domain (Aries), this is one of the three Houses of Life, and is an all-important 'angular' House, being the Ascendant, meaning that it forms one of the four significant angles of the birth chart (the other three being the Fourth House or Imum Coeli, the Seventh House or Descendent, and the Tenth House or Midheaven). But where Leo is concerned with life on an interpersonal level and Sagittarius with life on a transpersonal, wider-reaching level, Aries and the First House are concerned with life on a close, personal level.

It has been said that if your Sun sign is the message that you have to give to the world, then your Ascendant or First House is the style in which you deliver that message. The First House is that set of characteristics that you present to the outside world, and that which other people perceive initially, before they get to know the 'authentic' core you, your Sun sign. As such, it is an 'astrological overcoat', your outer shell, and what others see first - that all-important first impression you make on other people.

The First House covers our levels of self-absorption and self-protection, our social mannerisms, self-expression, our basic 'superficial' personality and temperament, self-discovery, and what we may hide behind.

Other esoteric keywords include: the self, ego, anima, projected image, expression of inner motivations, initial approach to life, and the aura. It is connected with one's overall temperament, vitality, mannerisms, and the general course of life. Planets and signs in this house pervade the whole of one's life, describing particular expectations and the way in which interaction with the outside world takes place.

On a physical and physiological level, it shows our constitution, physical appearance and build, health, disposition, wellbeing, and the level of physical vitality or energy available to us. As a sensitive chart angle point, this is arguably one of the most important of the houses, as it is a vital link in life, showing how vital we are, correlating to the spark of life and the resultant energy that bursts forth into the world.

This house also indicates which body areas or systems are chiefly vulnerable to illness, weakness, or injury. Furthermore, it describes our physical birth and the circumstances surrounding it, and the reception our arrival engendered. Therefore, the Ascendant marks the moment you joined the world, and the nature of any planet within the first house, or within 8 degrees either side of it, describes the impact you made. As well, it describes the projection of the Self into the immediate environment into which it is born. It provides insights into the conditions of your early environment that shaped you into the person you are today and may become in the future.

Overall, as a house of beginnings, the First House is considered our birthing point, how we 'emerge' into the world (both literally and metaphorically), our social mask, outlook, idiosyncrasies, persona, image, and our powerful, unique Birth Story. Most importantly, it is what we appear to be but not who we actually are, concerning what is 'visible' externally. Through the sign on its cusp, it describes your basic nature and the manner in which you approach your goals in life, and significantly, the type of Path you'll walk towards your ultimate destiny.

THE SECOND HOUSE ✦ TAURUS

ASCENDANT - ASC - Cusp of the First House.

How you spend money is an accurate reflection of what matters most to you and therefore, is a good indication of your whole value system. The Second House deals with how you spend money, what you value, your material possessions, and your overall attitudes toward security, both on personal and financial levels.

The Second House, ruled by Taurus, is the house of possessions and assets, personal values, money, self-worth, personal resources, attachments, property and real estate, earning power and spending habits, attitudes towards money and possessions, skills, the acquisitive urge, material circumstances and security, wealth and expenditure.

It describes our ability to earn and retain money, how we earn and spend it, our profits and losses, income levels (i.e. whether they fluctuate or stay the same), the things that we buy for other people, our level of materialism, the prosperity or otherwise that we attract, how 'comfortable' we are, and our overall financial security in life.

Ruled by the realm of the Earth element, this is one of the three Houses of Substance. But where Virgo is concerned with substance on an interpersonal level and Capricorn on a transpersonal and wider-reaching level, Taurus and the Second House are concerned with substance on a personal level, which strives to acquire possessions on a personal level rather than aiming for those that benefit wider relationships or society.

The Second House could be referred to as the House of Personal Values as well as of Money and Possessions, as it reveals a lot about our self-esteem, how much or how little we value ourselves, the attachments we make (emotional and material possessiveness are both themes here), self-preservation, our sense of body awareness, personal security, what we find comfort in, emotional priorities, how and what we appreciate and desire, our affinity with the natural environment, how and what we value, our inner resources, our sensuality and how we enjoy sensual pleasures. This house shows what resources we have to draw on to experience success and fulfilment - potential to be developed – and identifies the strengths that we can call on within ourselves to reach this potential.

The sign and element on the cusp of this house in the birth chart indicate whether an individual seeks security in the tangible or intangible, with Earth and Water signs valuing material, extrinsic, worldly possessions, and Air and Fire signs valuing knowledge, ideas, and intrinsic qualities. The sign also indicates whether any financial gain or income is lucrative or otherwise, and whether money comes easily to you or not. It concerns building a foundation and generally where we make our income/money, and indicates your financial standing through life: whether you are a spendthrift, generous, a hoarder, greedy, shrewd, or downright miserly or mean.

How you actually use your possessions and financial position to your best advantage is within the realm of this House. In addition to relating to your material possessions and worldly goods, it covers items that are gifted to you, assistance and support from others, and money lent to you or by you. Overall, the Second House can tell you much about whether you will labour under misery, obligation, or joy.

THE THIRD HOUSE ✦ GEMINI

ASCENDANT - ASC - Cusp of the First House.

The domain of Mercury and its charge Gemini, the Third House indicates your logical mind, conscious thought processes, speech, articulation, and how you write and express yourself in other forms of communication. It has a strong link with early education, siblings, your immediate environment and neighbours, as well as your neighbourhood and community.

The Third House, ruled by Gemini, is the house of communication, mental activity, speech, siblings, and the immediate environment. It is also associated with neighbours, networks, how we speak and listen to others, mechanical dexterity, transport, early education, study, routine interactions, basic intellectual endeavours, correspondences, conversations, and short distance travel.

This House encompasses the early learning environment and shaping of mental patterns, and consequently, one's everyday thinking, basic communication systems, personal style of communication in speaking and writing, early schooling from pre-school through high school, immediate environment or neighbourhood, and connections with the people in those environments; and planets in this house can tell us about our early learning, learning style, how we absorb information, our level and type of intelligence, and how we express our intellect. Essentially, it concerns all forms of communication - mental and physical - such as mail, newspapers, letters, writers, magazines, advertisements, contacts, agents, your car, phone calls, public transport, errands, discussions, interviews, deliveries, debates, conferences, chatter and rumours. It tells you about the type of mind you possess, your mental interests and attitudes, habits of thought.

The Third House also governs travel over short distances or for short periods of time, like local trips and weekends away. Whatever our culture, our knowledge, the environment in which we grew up and our social background, we all have our beliefs, preferences, ideas, styles, convictions and ideals. They have an influence over the way of life we have chosen, our lifestyle, our tastes, our choices, and undeniably, our exchanges and relationships with others. Such is the greatest principle of the Third House, as it tells us about one's mentality, the way one thinks and the behaviours that emanate from this. It is within the context of our personal thinking style that we take a stand, understand, express, share, exchange, absorb and transmit the information we receive.

This House also relates to close relatives (such as aunties, cousins, uncles), and everyday affairs and minor business dealings. It symbolises our first experiences of relationships outside of our parents, and the planets within or sign on the cusp of this house explain how we experience our place in the familial sibling sub-system. It also signifies our first move away from self-absorption, or from putting our own needs first.

The Third House is associated with connections, sequencing and compartmentalising, making sense of our immediate surroundings and how we react to and interact within this environment. It enables us to gather facts and pieces of information, while the opposite Ninth House synthesises this into a whole and gives it significance and meaning. The sign and planets placed here either facilitate or restrict the flow, and the sign on the cusp indicates whether communication will be inhibited or clear, and how easy it is to learn and utilise information.

THE FOURTH HOUSE ✦ CANCER

THE NADIR - IC - Cusp of the Fourth House. The IC is the degree of the zodiac directly below us at the moment of birth. The most private and deepest part of ourselves, it is the inner self: "My roots."

The Fourth House shows your home, both during childhood and in later life. It has a particular connection with the nurturing parent, not necessarily your biological mother, but whoever played that role for you. It also indicates our roots, origins, heritage and what we need in order to feel secure.

The Fourth House, ruled by Cancer, is the house of family, home, roots, heritage, origins, and one's childhood experience. As it is an Angular House, the Fourth House is an exquisitely sensitive point; any planet touching, or within 8 degrees of an angle, has an enhanced sphere of influence in one's natal chart.

As a Water sign, this is one of the three Houses of Soul or Endings, and, being an all-important Angular House, it forms one of the four significant angles of the birth chart (the other three being the Ascendant, Descendent and Midheaven). But where Scorpio is concerned with life on an interpersonal level and Pisces with life on a transpersonal, or Universal level, Cancer and the Fourth House are concerned with life on a personal level.

Traditionally the Fourth House is known as the House of Family and the Home, but it covers a wider and deeper range of concerns, too. Through the first three houses the 'frame' is constructed; in the Fourth House, the structure is established and we put down roots.

The Fourth house tells us much about our origins, existential roots, psychological conditioning in early life, attitudes to our background, and sense of belonging, showing how we feel about the family unit and our home. It reveals the formative conditions in which our emotional growth took place, first during childhood - how and in which family, material, moral, cultural and social background one grew up - and about the way these roots unfolded in adulthood. The sign on its cusp will colour how we view our childhood home and family beginnings.

This house serves as a retreat, a haven to which you can return to restore yourself when the need arises, and provides a springboard, support, or foundation for your very existence. It is also the place to which you will come back once your 'life part' has been played and your destiny realised. In this way, it signifies both the beginning and the ending of the physical life experience. However, this return is not necessarily a pilgrimage to your childhood home, nor a regression; rather, it can be considered a return to oneself in its profound human and spiritual origins. Essentially, growth continues thereafter, but it can no longer be seen or measured with scientific instruments or methods.

Fundamentally, the Fourth House is about home and family. It rules your family circle and all matters concerning the domestic front, even including the building, block of land and everything in and around the house. This section gives indications about visitors, house guests, lodgers, intruders, and others who call at your residence, whether invited, uninvited, welcome, or unwelcome. It also rules any additional property or real estate interests you have. Other exoteric and esoteric keywords include private life, ancestry, psychological foundations, biological inheritance, place of abode, the ashram and karma.

The Fourth House usually informs about the parents (and more specifically the primary caregiver), the home environment and whether it is discordant or harmonious, as well as indicating what our conditions will be at the end of life, in old age, as life closes[**]. It tells us about the nature of our 'home base', how we feel secure, our sense of foundation, and the challenges of the home and how we deal or have dealt with them. It is connected with what we stand on, our foundations, the unconditional parent, and/or the parent who had the most influence, and significantly, from where we launch off into the more public arena when that time of life arrives.

The first level of this House deals with the basics: the physical home, emotional security, and the mother. The second level reveals the development of emotional stability and feeling connected to the family roots. And the third level describes the integration of our emotional security as a foundation for our life (which projects straight up into the Tenth house, the house of career, public status, and worldly achievements).

Overall, the Fourth House is strongly connected with the hearth, feeling at home, the parental home, the mother* or nurturing parent, our experience of the mother or mother figure, the circumstances influencing childhood, our overall childhood experience, our early domestic life and environment, traditions, heritage, background, emotional security, and inherited patterns. It represents conditions we are likely to encounter in the second half of life, after the age of forty, and tells us that maturity turns out to be much more fun than youth, for in our forties we have met most of life's challenges in the years before, survived them and established our life's principles and values.

**The concept of the home and the protective enclosing also has an analogy with the womb and the grave (coffin) - thus, the beginning and end of life are also concerns of this house.*

Many astrologers link the Tenth house with the mother and the Fourth with the father, but this rule seems variable. Some say that the parent who has the strongest influence is described in the Tenth house, others say the same sex parent is described in the Tenth house. Classically however, the Fourth house rules the mother (natural ruler Moon) and the Tenth house rules the father (natural ruler Saturn). It is also fitting that father or father figure matters are indicated in the Tenth house, as the father is usually (though not always) the conditional caregiver and Saturn carries a conditional energy-message. Although there is debate about whether the Fourth House is concerned with the mother or father - after all, the 'father' gives us our name and our 'genealogical line', or origins - there is no fixed rule, and your chart will have a way of telling you anyway.

THE FIFTH HOUSE ✦ LEO

The fun spirited Fifth House is all about leisure, holidays, romance, hobbies, recreation, sport and speculation. It is connected with creativity in the broadest sense, children as a creative act, and romance as a true, playful expression of ourselves.

The Fifth House, ruled by Leo, is the house of creativity, romance, children, love affairs, sex, games and gambling, amusements, and creative expression in all its forms. Recreation and leisure activities that are enjoyable and life-enhancing to the individual will be shown here; this house is where you play, develop a sense of wonder, and discover and express your inner child. Under these umbrellas fall things such as entertainment, holidays, vital energy, pleasures, the ability to love and procreate, and the relationship with one's offspring.

It also reveals the amount of love you are prepared to offer, including within courtship and lovemaking. If there is a strong sign or planets within this house, any or all of these will play a key role in your overall enjoyment of life.

Traditionally, the Fifth House is primarily concerned with creative self-expression. Encompassing everything that is creative and artistic, including dreams, ideas, music, art and dancing, this can include artistic and leisure pursuits that you are attracted to, sports and lovers, or it could be those procreational instincts that lead to pregnancy, the production of children and then your relationship with them.

Love, romance, your romantic life, sexual desire, dating and socialising not involving a deeper commitment, all come under the reign of the Fifth House also, but this is not the deep, serious, committed love of the Seventh House; rather it is the fun, playful kind of romantic love that is enjoyed for its pleasures and pure, uncomplicated simplicity.

The Fifth House marks the beginning of the journey of our individuality and our individual quest. At the first level, it concerns amusement, our sense of humour, how we approach play and our style of playfulness. Level two deals with recognising the power of creativity and its impact on our social relationships and connections. At the third and highest level, the Fifth House deals with our integration of self-expression and the development and acquisition of a solid, secure ego strength.

The Fifth House broadly governs two areas of life - pleasure and creation. Creation refers not only to the children we bring into the world, but artistic work also, the talent for living life to the full, and developing our optimum potential. But the single core task of this house is the development of ego strength. As it is concerned with courtship, affairs, emotional experiences, sweethearts and lovers, it can reveal how we first have our heart broken or stolen, our experience of it and our journey to recapture it.

Further, we each have our own unique style of loving. While the planet Venus in our birth chart reveals the expression and manifestations of an individual's emotions, motivations and feelings, it is the Fifth House that describes the context in which these will be shown, the appearance they will take and how the individual will experience these feelings in the reality of social and material life. But it also has the function of informing us about the love or feelings towards any children that we may have. Some astrologers claim that in examining this House in the natal chart, it is quite possible to even determine whether or not the individual will have, or desires to have, children. Realistically, other elements in the chart need to be considered, but the Fifth House is the strongest indicator in the horoscope when it comes to fertility and offspring, and the subject's attitudes around both.

Commonly known as the sector of luck, it also rules gambling, risk-taking, and all forms of speculation such as lotteries, casinos, racing, the stock market, and any other activities where there is an element of chance involved.

This house is significant for joys and happy events in life; it will give directions as to what entertains us, and gains or losses at play, when there are favourable or unfavourable planets in the house, respectively.

It relates to many of the things we think of as constituents of The Good Life, such as parties, gatherings, galas, events, pampering, treats, amusement, holidays, relaxation, luxuries, celebrations, banquets and dinner parties, movies, dancing, and artistic, creative, mystical, theatrical, dramatic, or cultural pursuits.

THE SIXTH HOUSE ✦ VIRGO

The Sixth House indicates your work, duties, obligations, service, duties, responsibilities, and the daily minutiae of your life. It is connected with your health, diet, how you feel about helping others and your attitudes towards routine.

The Sixth House, ruled by Virgo, is the house of daily work or employment, service, duty, day-to-day routines and health. It also concerns small animals and pets.

It covers everyday work, daily chores, the usual work environment, job and labour skills, competence, training, the use of time, routine tasks, basic organisational skills, efficiency, co-workers, employees, staff, hired help, workforces, the working classes, servants, place of work, and the conditions under which any duties are undertaken.

As the House of Work, it is also concerned with colleagues, obligations, responsibilities, and which type of daily work routine and environment most suits us. While the Tenth house relates to one's career, the Sixth House is primarily concerned with the everyday aspects of one's work. The Sixth House specifies the type of work we do, the workplace and working conditions, and our job as opposed to our career, as well as our level of service, servitude, and the employment of servants.

Strongly associated with health, it encompasses tendencies towards self-improvement, self-discipline, conditions of the body, our health status, and overall shows our general health, sickness, hygiene habits and dietetics. It is a truly holistic house, being linked with the integration of the mind, body, soul and spirit, and how this integration or dis-integration is expressed: a state of overall sound health reflects an inner harmony, while dis-ease indicates an inner discord of some kind. It indicates tendencies to certain illnesses, diet, nutrition, exercise, healing capacities, nutrition, diet and lifestyles fostering healthy and efficient body functioning.

The Sixth House is responsible for our own inner discipline, gives down-to-Earth advice and never shirks its duties. It is where we recognise what needs to be done and where we learn to improve ourselves, through patience, hard work, common sense and practical application.

The service and duty carried out in this house comes from the heart or from a true calling, without thought of reward or recognition. This is a dedicated and devoted energy, which also indicates the type of assistance we give others in need. It reveals activities carried out to benefit someone else - whether these are acts of pure altruism or the result of duties tied to your work or your family. As this sphere signifies where your obligations lie, it also contains a degree of self-sacrifice; how selfless or selfish you are in daily life will depend largely on planetary and sign placements in this house.

The first level of the Sixth House concerns physical wellbeing, service, daily routine and rituals. The second level regards introspection, and one's awareness of the need for personal growth, improvement and evolution. At the third and highest level, it deals with the acceptance of self through accepting our imperfections, our altruism, charity and helpfulness towards others, and the ability to deal with oneself through analytical, honest judgement. Service to ourselves and to others, stress management, analysis, personal discernment and fussiness or sloppiness, coherence, focus, discrimination, tasks, structured time, physical wellbeing, how we feel 'centred' and well, our housekeeping style, attitudes towards health, what we need to accomplish in our work to feel fulfilled, meditation and yoga as a means to grounding, and regimentation, are all Sixth House concerns.

THE SEVENTH HOUSE ✦ LIBRA

DESCENDANT - DESC - Cusp of the Seventh House. This is the degree of the zodiac rising on the western horizon at the moment of our birth. It is the point of awareness of others: "How I Relate to An Other."

The Seventh House deals with your closest and most intimate relationships, those on a personal basis and in a marriage or similar situation. Close professional partnerships and associations, as well as more hostile and competitive forces such as open enemies, are also indicated.

The Seventh House, ruled by Libra, is the house of marriage, partnerships, and close relationships with others. As an Air sign, this is one of the three houses of relationships, and is an all-important 'angular' House, being the Descendant, meaning that it forms one of the four significant angles of the birth chart (the other three being the First

House or Ascendant, the Fourth House or Imum Coeli, and the Tenth House or Midheaven). But where Gemini is concerned with relationships on a personal level (the Self) and Aquarius with relationships on a transpersonal or wider-reaching level (humanity), Libra and the Seventh House are primarily linked with relationships on an interpersonal level, that is, through relating and dealing with others.

The Seventh House is otherwise known as the House of Marriage, and is all about partnerships: in business, marriage, or committed relationships.

The Seventh House is often, and most aptly, called the House of Relationships. As such, it describes one's interactions with other people, one's awareness of and dealings with others, open enemies and adversaries, how one selects partners, and significantly, the types of relationships and partners one seeks and attracts.

It reveals the significant other in one's life, what one needs most from them, and the rapport that develops.

As the Descendant (directly opposite the projected self of the Ascendant), it indicates the qualities we unconsciously look for in others and what we magnetise, our anima or animus, our 'shadow', what is foreign to us (e.g. the opposite sex), and what is unknown, foreign territory. It also reveals our attitudes towards close relationship and our ability to get along with and cooperate with others.

Interestingly, often we are subconsciously attracted to those who carry a strong emphasis of the sign on the cusp of our own birth chart's Seventh House. Your 'shadow' self can indeed be reflected by your partner, as we tend to marry our own shadow, something we may not be conscious of or recognise in ourselves. This is usually the result of projecting ourselves onto others - personal projection is a matter of the First House, and any projections are directed outwards and onto those closest to us. The Seventh House, being the First House's direct opposite, is the recipient of this process. The process of being able to recognise our own qualities in another, things we can't always access in ourselves, encapsulates the essence of the Seventh House, and the qualities of this house desire expression in one-to-one relationships.

The Seventh House, on a more mundane level, is connected with cooperation, joint undertakings, healthy competition, everyone we approach as an equal, mutuality, and also rules any significant contractual undertaking between two people, mostly in marriage or business, as it is associated with agreements and contracts, including legal ones like divorce. Because this house encompasses dealings with others in general, it can also include hostilities and conflicts, opponents, competitors and open (known) enemies, suggesting the nature of any relationship discord or harmony you are likely to encounter.

THE EIGHTH HOUSE ✦ SCORPIO

Analogy for the Eighth House:

A caterpillar spends several weeks happily munching on leaves, occasionally shedding its skin as it grows into a bigger and stronger caterpillar. But eventually, it recognises the fact that it has reached its limits and can grow no more. If the caterpillar resists change, it will die, for life will be untenable in its present form. But, paradoxically, in order to survive, it must volunteer for death. It must spin a shroud, and willingly relinquish life for the unknown. It has no idea, as its eyes close in sleep (and) consciousness slips away... whether Nature will keep faith. It only knows what must be done. It has no idea that weeks later, it will emerge into the daylight once again, reborn, metamorphosed, into a beautiful butterfly.

Jill Davies

A The Eighth House is connected with shared resources, other people's values, sex, regeneration, inheritances, assorted other financial dealings such as tax, insurance and loans, and on a deeper level shows change, depth, transformation, renewal, death and rebirth and complexities, including spiritual values beyond the material world.

The Eighth House, ruled by Scorpio, is the house of sex, death and rebirth, shared resources, regeneration and transformation. It describes secret powers, money belonging to others, shared money, common property, investments, loss, how we deal with material loss, 'rising from the ashes', sharing, letting go, intense unions, attitudes towards growth and change, release, transcendence, elimination, our occult* tendencies, and our thoughts about the afterlife.

This house deals with the support you receive from other people, taxes, debt, gifts, insurance, legacies, joint resources (including any money you might receive from your partner), and addresses financial back-up as well as spiritual, emotional and physical support. It relates to all business transactions that involve other people's money, and anything that is hidden, such as things found within the occult realm.

Strongly linked with monetary gain and of things inherited, these inheritances may be on the physical or psychic plane, including ancestral patterns and potential. As it governs death, it also deals with money connected with death, such as wills, legacies, gifts, property and estates. The Eighth House tells us about how we share and provide our finances and resources with others, allowing others access (e.g. to bank accounts, 'what's mine is yours').

As the house of sex and sexuality, it reveals intimacy, what can be gained by fusing with another, trust, the transferring of loyalties to outside of family, sharing on its deepest level, one's powerlessness, helplessness and vulnerabilities, as well as opening oneself up through being vulnerable; in essence, where the ego dissolves and the self is surrendered.

In the Eighth House we are indeed impelled to let go of our ego and abandon our separateness in order to merge with another, and to transcend our-selves. This merging almost always involves change, and change is only possible when we accept that one cycle must end before another can begin, in a new form. This house tells us that if we don't allow these 'secrets' to come to the surface and transform us for the better, they may engulf and ultimately destroy us.

Being the house of grief, it also shows us how and where we learn to love in the face of loss, e.g. through a death; love and loss are united in this house. It shows patterns of intimacy, the uncovering of parts of ourselves, the entering into unions that change and transform us, where we most invest in a relationship, and at its highest realisation, the attainment of self-mastery.

As the house of regeneration, it covers sex, death, birth and rebirth, renewal, transmutation, intense emotions, ritual work, relinquishing of the physical form into formlessness (involving surrender, trust, flow), and metaphysics. It describes your resourcefulness and resilience, as well as your abilities to develop and use your material assets and personal skills and talents in all joint ventures.

Although there is an emphasis on shared financial resources in this sphere, it also represents your capacity to become detached from material assets, and perhaps paradoxically, what you can gain from doing so. Indeed, in the Eighth House you can become detached; you no longer need to provide, and you can release your material possessions and attachments. You can transcend those nitty gritty mundane matters and connect to your innate power again; the ultimate Source. This goes some way to explaining the concept of inheritance, something this house governs. Inheritance and legacies are the things which we acquire without any effort on our part. Still, to many astrologers, many planets, difficult angles, or afflictions in this house are not favourable to Earthly, material happiness.

The Eighth House is connected with the realm of sex and sexuality, sexual tastes and attitudes, deep interactions, secret powers and personal magnetism. It also describes your response to death, divorce, separations and endings of any kind, the capacity to rebirth and re-emerge from an ending, how easily you will surrender control or power, and how you try to manipulate others or try to avoid being controlled yourself. Planets in the Eighth House reflect the level of control and power you have over your own life.

As a house of soul or endings, it can even provide clues as to the cause or nature of one's death experience.

There is a secretive aspect about this house, which is concerned with veiled wishes, power, criminal tendencies, complexes, compulsions, obsessions, secret undertakings and, from the health standpoint, the 'secret' or hidden parts of the body such as the sex organs.

The word 'occult' comes from the Latin occultus, which literally means 'the knowledge of the hidden'.

THE NINTH HOUSE ✦ SAGITTARIUS

The Ninth House is connected with thinking and ideas, and how they are applied as organised schemes of thought in wider society. Religion, higher learning, the law, justice, philosophy, personal freedom, and travel to broaden the mind also feature here.

The Ninth House, ruled by Sagittarius, is the house of philosophy, higher education, travel and religion. The gesture of the Archer shooting suggests the meaning of this house, which astrology further describes as the realm of abstract thinking, dreams, visions, and the higher mind and spirit. This domain is where we outreach our physical and mental embrace of what we know as reality, and aspire toward that which we can sense spiritually, but may not be able to see. It is here that we formulate into creeds and philosophical systems the thoughts which the preceding sign Scorpio scooped from the hidden depths.

As a house strongly connected with ethics, philosophical thoughts, viewpoints and morals, this house allows for judgement regarding your intellectual and moral qualities, and states whether or not you have a propensity for travel, particularly extensively or to foreign lands. It can also indicate whether changes of locations are desired.

After the complex, transformative and deeply psychological influence of the Eighth House, the Ninth House is like a refreshing, uplifting breeze that blows the cobwebs away through the winds of enlightenment. If the powerful lessons from the Eighth House have been properly learned, we will emerge a little wiser and more evolved, and substantially further forward along the Path of Life. The Ninth House is where we strive for something greater, perhaps bigger than ourselves, and where Universal Truths are explored.

Overseas affairs, higher learning, conscience, freedom, large open spaces and big animals, sports, dreams, adventure, visions, ideals, dogma, culture, doctrine, spirituality, truths, faith, wisdom, moral and legal concerns, the communication of deeper ideas, the in-depth study of profound subjects, mental exploration, foreign languages, and other intellectual matters such as religion and science are also governed by the Ninth House. It is concerned with how you understand the world and how you conduct your search for deeper meaning and purpose, revealing much about the ways you seek to expand your personal horizons, your interactions and relationships with other cultures and distant relatives, and your attitudes and points of view on all topics.

The Third House, the opposite of the Ninth House in the horoscope, enables us to gather facts and pieces of information, while the Ninth House synthesises these into a whole and gives them greater significance and meaning. The Ninth House provides spiritual guidance, and shapes our principles, world views and belief systems, encouraging us to see the bigger picture, the broader plan, and our life's overall purpose, essence and direction.

It also indicates any emphasis on morals (noble or corrupt), faith and religion (both usually with strong leanings one way or another), and ethics (honest or dishonest; pure or contaminated), depending on the planets, signs and aspects of this house. Overall, planets and signs placed in the Ninth House illustrate your response to the call of your spirit to higher places.

THE TENTH HOUSE ✦ CAPRICORN

MIDHEAVEN - MC - The cusp of the Tenth House. This is the degree of the zodiac directly above us at the moment of birth. It signifies the most public and outer part of ourselves: "How I Function in the World."

The Tenth House shows your place in society, your social status, reputation, and the regard that others have for your achievements. It relates to your aims and ambitions, to your worldly aspirations and often to your career and professional path. The Tenth House also relates to the father or the conditional parent.

The Tenth House, ruled by Capricorn, is the house of career, public life, direction in life, social status, ambition and vocation, and the conditional parent. While the opposite Fourth House deals with home and family matters, the Tenth is concerned with what you can achieve in your own right. This house therefore indicates your public role and persona in the world at large, and reveals the way in which your desire for social and existential accomplishment is manifested.

Our authentic vocational purpose and direction, public reputation, social standing and status, motivation, prestige, societal recognition, achievements, worldly honour, relationship with senior and authority figures, aspirations, professional expression, desire for fame or notoriety, father or father figure*, choice of profession, true 'calling', and all matters affecting outward appearances and one's personal image, are found in this sphere of the horoscope.

Ruled by the realm of the Earth element, this is one of the three Houses of Substance, and is an all-important 'angular' House, being the Midheaven, meaning that it forms one of the four significant angles of the birth chart (the other three being the Ascendant, Imum Coeli, and Descendent). But where fellow Earth sign Taurus is concerned with substance on a personal level and Virgo with substance on an interpersonal level, Capricorn and the Tenth House are connected with substance on a transpersonal, or wider-reaching level. Essentially, it shows how you carve out your niche in the world and in a general way shows how far you will get in realising your worldly ambitions, the level of success you are likely to achieve, and how high your reputation will grow and stand.

The Sun is at its most powerful when it culminates at midday and is represented by the line of the MC. The term MC stands for Medium Coeli, or Midheaven. It marks the point of culmination of the Sun, where the Sun is at its highest position, and corresponds to noon on your day of birth. The opposite point of this axis is the IC, the Imum Coeli, meaning the 'under sky', and it marks the lower meridian of the birth chart, corresponding to midnight. The MC culmination therefore symbolically represents those parts of ourselves that are out in the public spotlight, this 'spotlight' being the very essence of the Tenth House. Indeed, this is where we enjoy our fifteen minutes of fame and are at our most visible. It is where we make public our ambitions and thus this house can be a useful and insightful pointer to your ideal career.

The Tenth House is the gateway to your particular degree of success from the lowest (bottom of the ladder) to the highest. Depending on what planetary influences are playing out on this sector at any given time, it can bring either failure, mild satisfaction, success, recognition, promotion, honour, publicity, and even fame.

The Tenth House is your own Mount Everest, and how far you climb upward will be indicated by the planets within it and sign on its cusp - but ultimately, as with anything else, how high you ascend can be influenced by other birth chart factors, and is ultimately up to you.

Many astrologers link the Tenth house with the mother and the Fourth with the father, but it seems that this rule is variable. Some astrologers say that the parent who has the strongest influence is described in the Tenth house, others say the same sex parent is described in the Tenth house. Classically however, the Fourth house rules the mother (natural ruler Moon) and the Tenth house rules the father (natural ruler Saturn). It is also fitting that father or father figure matters are indicated in the Tenth house, as the father is usually (though not always) the conditional caregiver and Saturn is a conditional planetary energy.

THE ELEVENTH HOUSE ✦ AQUARIUS

The Eleventh House relates to society, to friendship and to groups you interact with regularly. It illustrates your hopes, wishes and aspirations on a more qualitative level than the aims and ambitions of the Tenth House before it.

The Eleventh House, ruled by Aquarius, is the house of friendships, acquaintanceships, groups, group involvement, social affinities, clubs and organisations, collectives, networking, social causes and conscience, progress, ideals, global awareness, political visions, hopes, wishes and aspirations.

It shows how you are able to get along with others in a group context, and how altruistic you are in your outlook. Personal contacts on a far and wide, and more or less impersonal, scale, and the depth of one's involvement with humanitarian or social causes is also found here.

As an Air sign, this is one of the three Houses of Relationships. But where Gemini is concerned with relationships on a personal level and Libra on an interpersonal level, the Aquarius-ruled Eleventh House is concerned with relationships on a transpersonal, or wider-reaching, level.

On a personal level, the eleventh sphere of the wheel reveals how we pursue our ideals, hopes, dreams and aspirations, and gives us hints about how we can incorporate other people socially and within groups, to help us reach our highest goals and ideals, on both personal and (more often) collective levels. It also shows what we may achieve by tailoring our personal goals to the needs of society, and teaches us that the endeavours of a coordinated group can achieve more than the sum of several individual efforts. Planets in this house indicate the type of friends who attract us and where we find common interests with others.

This house is not concerned with self-gratification or personal pleasure like its opposite Leo's Fifth House is; instead, it operates in an impersonal sphere of life, dealing with cerebral spirituality and global realisation rather than self-actualisation.

In the Eleventh House we see how we integrate into the group; how we operate within the larger system. It can also be described as the realm of communal spirit, the House of Brotherhood, or the House of Friends and Idealism. The traditional name for this house was in fact the House of Hopes, Dreams and Wishes.

If the Eleventh House influence is strong in the birth chart, such as being born under an Aquarian Sun, we will be inclined to choose forms of self-expression that involve the group more so than the individual. The Eleventh House ensures that we pour out our precious waters of consciousness where they are needed most: upon communities and societies, and the world at large. The global community, after all, is a perpetually thirsty place, ever in need of a refreshing, life-giving drink.

THE TWELFTH HOUSE ✦ PISCES

The Web of Fate is the zodiac and the placing of the stars at birth. It depends on the condition of the karma you have inherited as to whether it binds you, or not. An understanding of the star pattern, or natal chart, is a necessity for all who would attempt initiation. After studying the pattern, look carefully at the twelfth house. If this is free from negative aspects, well and good. You can be sure a heavy karmic debt will not ensue.

Patricia Crowther

The Twelfth House is the realm of the subconscious, encompassing dreams, mysticism, self-sacrifice and intuition, as well as karma and hidden enemies (including yourself). Planets placed here can be both a disguised strength and a hidden weakness, depending largely on your appreciation of their effects.

The Twelfth House, ruled by Pisces, is the house of the subconscious mind, what is repressed, secrets, spirituality, the hidden self, deep-seated fears, mystical inclinations, withdrawal, transcendence, one's spiritual path, solitude, seclusion, isolation, confinement, how we 'escape', faith, institutions, karma, the Divine and inner worlds, self-undoing, the shadow self, psychic abilities, intuition, addictions, healing, faith, unconscious impulses, and secret and hidden enemies.

As the Twelfth House is connected with clandestine relationships and concealed enemies, it may also indicate those internal factors that can contribute to one's undoing.

As a Water-ruled house, this is one of the three Houses of Soul or Endings. But where Cancer is concerned with soul or endings on a personal level and Scorpio on an interpersonal level, the Pisces-ruled Twelfth House is concerned with soul or endings on a transpersonal, or wider-reaching, level, embracing all facets and intricacies of these concepts.

The Twelfth House is about endings, karma and secrets; the situations described through a study of this domicile, uncover the circumstances an individual must overcome in order to be free of firm bindings and destructive restrictions as well as negative patterns of recurring situations, relationships and behaviours. Such institutions as hospitals, jails, asylums, monasteries, libraries, the armed services, and other forms of secluded places of residence or confinement are also associated with this house. Other esoteric keywords include fears, family secrets, reconnection, mysteries, sacrifice, surrender, 'return', unredeemed karma, disintegration, deception, and selfless service to humanity.

This house reveals whether you have many or few adversaries or enemies, and under what kind of circumstances they lurk. The Twelfth House has many labels, some of which are The House of Buried Treasures, the Realm of Concealment, the House of Retreat, Solitude and Institutions, the House of Karma, the House of Self-Undoing, the House of Sustainment, and the House of Secret Enemies.

Although this house has an ominous reputation, it is very revealing of our inner secrets, and can be very empowering if we know how to deal with these properly. It usually shows us that the worst secret enemy is actually the one residing within us, and that ultimately, we are all the creators of our own misfortunes or undoings – whether by direct implication, or by attracting certain forces to ourselves.

It shows us how we 'escape' the pressures of daily life and the planets therein describe the nature of our inner strengths that we can draw upon. Herein lies the need to confront our inner demons so that we may reconnect and unite with something infinitely greater than ourselves.

The Twelfth House acknowledges that we have been on a journey through the previous eleven realms of the human experience, accepts a kind of 'pre-existence', and realises that, since life is cyclical, we must re-join it at the end of our cycle, that we must go back to where we first began. Because the karmic principle of astrology suggests that your soul chooses a time to be born, we effectively choose the planetary pattern for that moment that indicates an appropriate horoscope for us, one that has been 'earned' by the previous incarnation. Planets within, and the nature of the sign on the cusp of the Twelfth House, therefore, reveal what you are carrying in your astrological 'suitcase' that may assist or hinder you on your current journey.

This House is chiefly concerned with the private inner self, which is often difficult to understand, and the troubles which you bring upon yourself by being what you are. It governs solitude, secrecy and self-imposed restrictions, but ultimately, the acquisition of wisdom upon self-knowing and self-mastery.

It is also the House of betrayals, ambushes, ordeals, misfortune, confinement and illnesses, and not only can it warn you about opponents of all kinds, but also offer strategies around how to handle them. For example, if involved in a lawsuit, it will indicate whether or not you will win it. It indicates whether any sadness in your life is caused by yourself, or through your associations with others. Being concerned with loss, disappointments and personal sacrifice, it may also reveal where we have imposed confinement upon ourselves, or had it imposed upon us, and shows any connections we may have with institutions, prisons and hospitals, and whether indeed we are the inmate, the patient, the redeemed, the newly released, or the worker in these settings.

The Twelfth House is like a secret diary in which we have written things we don't want other people to know about us; it reveals any secrets you might prefer to keep hidden. Those secrets we're so 'guilty' about ought to be brought out into the light and dusted off so that we can benefit from what they have to teach us. Because the Twelfth House is also related to self-sacrifice and selflessness, it is a House where we give and do not count the cost or expect anything in return.

Although not directly related to one's hopes, wishes and ideals (a domain of the preceding Eleventh House), this House shows your ability to secure the fulfilment of your dreams on many levels and in many different directions.

Being the final House in the symbolic Wheel of Life, it represents your capacity for complete integration with life. To the degree in which you fail to do this, your wishes will remain pipe dreams, weaknesses not overcome will become your undoings, misfortunes may very well abound, or you might be led into antisocial or harmful behaviours. As it offers us the opportunity to connect with the whole, it can bring into the light of consciousness all that was previously obscured. It is where the task of reintegration is undertaken, the boundaries of individuality are relinquished, and the Self surrendered back into the collective, Universal whole, the last process being either voluntary or involuntary, depending on the individual.

The Twelfth House tells us much about our personal karma and our experience of the previous eleven spheres of the horoscope wheel of life. It symbolises our ultimate (symbolic) death, and subsequent return as a 'newborn' in the First House. The Twelfth House acknowledges our 'pre-existence', and represents our acceptance that, since life is cyclical, at the end of the cycle, we are called to re-join it where it all started; we must go home. Whether one believes in life after death, or the concepts of karma or reincarnation or not, is not relevant, for in this House you are still accepting that the Universe is a continually evolving cycle of formation, dissolution and re-formation. This is known on a deep, intuitive, not-always-conscious level.

If the Twelfth House influence is strong in the birth chart, we will be inclined to choose forms of self-expression that involve our karmic interests, whether conscious or unconsciously. The Twelfth House ensures that we learn and apply the lessons of all the signs that have come before us, in some way or another, most likely expressed through the energies of the sign on its cusp and any planets within it.

POWERFUL LIFE LESSONS FROM OPPOSITE SIGNS

Most of us have trouble appreciating either our shadow or our light. (But) by illuminating your shadow, you also reclaim your light… Having met and embraced your shadow, you will have less to defend in yourself or to condemn in others.

Dan Millman

Bring all the opposites inside yourself and reconcile them; understand that you are everywhere, on the land, in the sea, in the sky; realise that you haven't yet been begotten, that you are still in the womb, that you are young, that you are old, that you are dead, that you are in the world beyond the grave; hold all this in your mind, all times and places, all substances and qualities and magnitudes.

Hermetic Writings

If we look at the zodiac, we can see that it can be broadly divided into two hemispheres, this division being based on the natural division of the year by the two equinoxes. Astrologers often refer to the first six signs, the hemisphere in which the day predominates (the days being longer in the spring and summer months), as the Personal Sphere of Experience, and the second six signs, the hemisphere in which nights are longer, as the Social Sphere of Experience.

These two halves of the zodiac perfectly balance and complement each other, and each individual 'personal' zodiac sign has something to teach its directly opposite 'social' zodiac sign. To generalise, the signs of the personal sphere tend to experience life through a type of self-projection and self-interest which is often socially uncomplicated, unsophisticated, or naïve. Their objective is to learn greater social awareness and thereby integrate themselves with the larger, more Universal human collective. On the other hand, the signs of the social sphere are prone to experience life through the use of their more developed social consciousness.

In essence, the personal signs (Aries, Taurus, Gemini, Cancer, Leo, Virgo) usually provide stimulation and new energy to their environment, while the social, more Universal signs (Libra, Scorpio, Sagittarius, Capricorn, Aquarius, Pisces) provide experience, opportunities for wider expression, and give a more broad-minded approach and perspective to their surroundings.

Each sign in a pair seeks and/or is attracted to the qualities of its complementary opposing sign.

Although the word 'opposite' conjures up feelings of separateness and differences, the astrological polarities should not be seen as two signs in conflict with each other - their positive expression is to create a natural balance and equilibrium. Each sign has something to learn from its opposite, but also has a contribution to make towards the other sign's more evolved expression.

ARIES & LIBRA

The First (Aries) and the Seventh (Libra) House polarity is concerned with awareness of self versus awareness of others.

WHAT THE SCALES CAN ULTIMATELY TEACH THE RAM

Release ✦ 'Me first' mentality, aggression, combat, impatience, hot-headedness, bossiness, impetuosity, childish behaviour, impulsivity.

Embrace ✦ The peaceful warrior, the power of partnership, graceful socialising, patience, inner balance, relational harmony, impartiality, sense of justice, better judgement, reflection, agreement, union, choosing one's battles.

WHAT THE RAM CAN ULTIMATELY TEACH THE SCALES

Release ✦ Indecisiveness, co-dependency, uncertainty, easily led temperament, lack of firmness, insincere charm, agreeableness, fear of conflicts, appeasing behaviours, pleasing everyone but oneself, complete selflessness, obsessive attachments to justice and fairness, over-reliance on harmony and balance, 'tit for tat' mentality, narcissism.

Embrace ✦ Healthy degree of self-focus, finding yourself, strong identity, audacity, fighting spirit, power of action, adventure, boldness, courage, assertiveness, direction, purpose, independence, confronting conflicts, incisiveness, self-confidence, initiative, sincerity, self-awareness, trusting your impulses, moderation and discrimination in who and what you give your energy to, and a healthy ego.

TAURUS & SCORPIO

The Second (Taurus) and the Eighth (Scorpio) House polarity is concerned with personal resources versus shared resources, in other words 'mine' versus 'ours'.

WHAT THE SCORPION CAN ULTIMATELY TEACH THE BULL

Release ✦ The path of least resistance, attachments to physical and material goods, your 'comfort zone', attitudes around monetary power, obstinacy, lusty sexual unions, possessiveness, greed, refusal to change, obsessive security needs, fears, carnal desires.

Embrace ✦ The road less travelled, complexity, greater depth, transcendence, transformative emotions, leaving your 'comfort zone', intensity of expression, empowering attitudes around personal power, inner change, the development of instincts, detachment, Tantric sensual unions, self-mastery, spiritual evolution, shamanistic powers, trust, Divine aspirations.

WHAT THE BULL CAN ULTIMATELY TEACH THE SCORPION

Release ✦ Complexity, depth, darkness, intensity of expression, constant probing, tension, suspicion, power-grabbing, self-destruction, compulsive patterns, extreme behaviours.

Embrace ✦ Simplicity, trust, abundance, beauty, being rooted and grounded, luxury, enjoyment, Earthy appetites, sensuality, practicality, healthy attachments to physical and material goods, a 'comfort zone', security, indulgence for pleasure's sake, serenity, peace, a constructive life, consistency, harmony with nature.

GEMINI & SAGITTARIUS

The Third (Gemini) and Ninth (Sagittarius) House polarity is concerned with the immediate environment versus expanded horizons.

WHAT THE ARCHER CAN ULTIMATELY TEACH THE TWINS

Release ✦ Superficiality of character, restlessness, flightiness, boredom, indiscriminate information-gathering, dispersion, double-dealing, pretence, trickery, the conflict between commitment and freedom, empty gossip, superficial social interactions, lack of depth, living too much in the moment, the need for instant gratification, taking the easy path.

Embrace ✦ Broad-mindedness, philosophical outlook, vision, nobility, truth, generous feelings, authenticity, stronger convictions and belief systems, discerning information-gathering, higher education, commitment and freedom, more meaningful social interactions, considering the future, reflection, considering all options before deciding on one path.

WHAT THE TWINS CAN ULTIMATELY TEACH THE ARCHER

Release ✦ Insatiable desire for expansion, unshakable convictions, escapism, lack of direction, intransigence, agitation, impatience, over-idealism, dwelling in the future.

Embrace ✦ Curiosity, awareness of others' ideas, flexibility, reality, everyday matters, the little things that give pleasure, trivia, being in the here and now.

CANCER & CAPRICORN

The Fourth (Cancer) and Tenth (Capricorn) House polarity is concerned with the inner world or 'home' versus the outer world or 'vocation'.

WHAT THE GOAT CAN ULTIMATELY TEACH THE CRAB

Release ✦ Subjectivity, the need to be protected, being overprotective, irrational fears, sulkiness, fear of others, clinginess, possessiveness, dwelling in the past, soppiness, defeatist attitudes, negative habits, using others as a crutch, co-dependence, smothering your family, deep-rooted insecurities.

Embrace ✦ Objectivity, ownership of feelings, trust, striving toward the future, social independence, personal ambition, career success, self-control, self-discipline, responsibility, a sense of duty, self-assurance, inner strength, perseverance.

WHAT THE CRAB CAN ULTIMATELY TEACH THE GOAT

Release ✦ Rigid structures, harsh judgement, categorising others, pride, refusal to relax or acknowledge weaknesses, coldness, insensitivity.

Embrace ✦ Nurturing and nourishing others, tenderness, imagination, intuition, softness, sensitivity, expressing emotions, compassion, warmth, affection, flow, reflection, vulnerability, supporting others in a more feeling way.

LEO & AQUARIUS

The Fifth (Leo) and the Eleventh (Aquarius) House polarity is concerned with personal creativity versus group creativity and contribution.

WHAT THE WATER BEARER CAN ULTIMATELY TEACH THE LION

Release ✦ Ego, self-serving activities, individual focus, selfishness, bossiness, arrogance, narrow vision, condescendence, pride, self-centredness, vanity, the need to show off and impress.

Embrace ✦ Humility, modesty, wider focus on others, unselfish feelings, solidarity with others, tolerance, brotherhood, cooperation, equality, objectivity, broader vision, independence, the cultivation of equal friendships.

WHAT THE LION CAN ULTIMATELY TEACH THE WATER BEARER

Release ✦ Detachment, modesty, shyness, unpredictable behaviour, off-handedness, coolness, aloofness, lack of confidence, scattered thoughts, eccentricity, perversity.

Embrace ✦ Warmth, self-confidence, pride, affection, individual focus, ego-examination, willpower, courage, nobility of spirit, generosity, vitality, power, leadership, genuine leisure and pleasure, stronger ego, personal creativity, more emphasis on the heart than the head.

VIRGO & PISCES

The Sixth (Virgo) and Twelfth (Pisces) House polarity is concerned with daily 'seen' life versus spiritual 'unseen' life.

WHAT THE FISH CAN ULTIMATELY TEACH THE VIRGIN

Release ✦ Negativity, over-analysis, rigid structures, harshness, perfectionism, worry, self-criticism, judgement of others, coldness, aloofness, tension, doubts, resentment, meanness (lack of generosity), uptight-ness, control, regimentation, only believing in tangible realities or that which can be proven.

Embrace ✦ Intuition, spirituality, imagination, going with the flow, emotions and feelings, affection, compassion, sensitivity, meditative practices, inspiration, faith, trust, innocence, Divine connection, believing in the intangible.

WHAT THE VIRGIN CAN ULTIMATELY TEACH THE FISH

Release ✦ Fantasies, delusions, illusions, pipe dreams, over-idealism, drifting aimlessly, fatalism, over-reliance on emotions and feelings, despair, irrational fears, despondency, hyperemotional behaviours, fears based on the unseen.

Embrace ✦ Organisation, selective choice, practicality, a down-to-Earth approach, a sense of the tangible, realism, discernment, decisive action, a sense of purpose, stoicism, a sense of detail and measure, precision, method, analytical mind.

ASTROLOGY & MAGIC

Everyone practices magic, whether they realise it or not, for magic is the art of attracting particular influences, events and situations within human life. Magic is a natural phenomenon because the Universe is reflexive, responding to human thoughts, aspirations, and desire...
David Fidell

To know how to make the proper gesture in the correct milieu at the right cosmic moment: this is sacred magic... In this way, often unconsciously, we are magicians. Wisdom consists in knowing how to be consciously so.
R.A. Schwaller de Lubicz

Cosmic Resonance ✦ The science of invoking and communicating with Divine forces via celestial timing.

Astrology is the most sublime of the occult* sciences, while at the same time it is one of the most practical for everyday application, for it divines the human soul itself. The cosmos, particularly the patterns that formed across it at the exact moment we were born, indicates the road along which our mental and spiritual endowments are likely to impel us, therefore enabling us to prepare in advance for life's battles, pitfalls, milestones and celebrations, and of course to make the utmost of opportunities. Such is the magic of the human mind, that it can 'see' into the future and relive the past without having to be physically present in either, and when combined with astrological knowing, particularly that which springs from the understanding of one's natal chart dynamics, our inner - and outer - magic can be lifted to phenomenal heights.

In ancient times, not only was astrology the ardent study of the most learned and powerful minds, but among the masses of ordinary people its authority and guidance were accepted and followed without question. How this powerful knowledge was used was - and still is - up to the individual, but all who used it seemed to apply it to their advantage.

In the ancient worldview, nature was neither random nor obtuse, but organised and intelligent. Some schools of modern cosmology and physics may allude to this, but they fall somewhat short of representing the Universe the way people did thousands of years ago - as conscious and immanent. Many cultures practiced a kind of sacred astronomy - that is, they observed celestial events and put them in the context of their connection to and influence on terrestrial life. This stemmed from their belief that Divine forces resided in all natural phenomena - the planets, stars, Sun and Moon - and that their rhythmic and cyclical appearances marked significant and indeed correlating events for other living beings.

As primitive humans observed the skies, no doubt they gradually realised that certain stars upon which their fate depended accompanied the seasons, or certain times of the year. Certain celestial influences were believed to emanate from the thirty-six decans of the signs, and the mysterious but apparent effect that they exercised upon humans were thought to be due to a subtle ether shed by the heavenly bodies upon the Earth, which affected not only people, but also other animals, plants and minerals. For the ancient mind, linking magic with astrology may have also provided a much-needed sense of predictability and patterns.

Early astrologers named and made associations with the imaginary divisions of the twelve signs and the twelve houses, and people born under a certain sign were said to inherit to an extent, its properties and nature. They also believed that the influence of the planets and stars corresponded with the medicinal properties of certain plants and minerals. They therefore asserted that the influence of a star or planetary position would affect the type of medicine or healing they would offer a subject to attain the most beneficial outcome. Throughout the writings of early philosophers and theorists, there is constant reference to this unmistakable mystic connection between the seven known planets and Earthly affairs and afflictions.

In subsequent years, astrology became closely related to alchemical knowledge and development, and the alchemist came to be regarded as an authority not only on the transmutation of metals, but also on astrology and magic. This goes some of the way to explaining how magic and divination, which had always been inseparably bound to astrology, came to be associated with alchemy.

In all the occult sciences, the supreme power was believed to be in the stars above, and from their mysterious emanations all the metals, crystals, minerals, plants and herbs derived their special properties over time. Further, as alchemy became ever more spiritual and concerned with more abstract and philosophical concepts, it was considered that the transmutation of lead into gold was simply a metaphor for the transformation of base matter, in this case the human soul, into a much purer and higher state of wisdom and being.

The Sun and Moon were believed to have greater influence over the human body than all the other heavenly bodies, and to exert their influence in various ways whenever they entered a certain sign of the zodiac. And although the Moon was traditionally regarded as the most important factor of a horoscope, the Sun came into its own in later centuries, with the result that almost everyone knows their Sun sign but only those who delve deeper seem to be aware of their natal Moon sign. Because of this, Sun signs and their correspondences are emphasised in this book, rather than the equally meaningful Moon sign.

The following pages contain methods, energies, materials and objects which may be used to increase the magic and power of your Sun sign's influence upon you. Precious stones, flowers, colours and so on, are regarded as having a potent effect upon good fortune by attuning your mind to receive harmonious vibrations from the abounding astral forces.

Finally, a basic working knowledge of basic astronomy and astrology is an asset when working with luck, abundance, prosperity and personal power. You can attract more of these things when you align yourself with the movements of the Sun, stars, Moon and planets and the workings of the wider Universe, and become aware of the correlations between the sky's cycles and your own inner cycles.

You don't need to know about astrology's deepest complexities to understand how everything interrelates; just learning the basics will give you an edge - and hopefully the following lucky tips will provide you with at least a small glimpse into the insights gleaned from your Sun sign and its inherent power.

The word 'occult' comes from the Latin occultus, which literally means 'knowledge of the hidden'.

USING COLOURS, CRYSTALS, DEITIES, PLANTS, FOODS & MATERIAL SUBSTANCES FOR INCREASING POWER & MAGNETISING MAGIC

Alchemist, reformer and mystic Henry Cornelius Agrippa, born in 1486, in his principal work, *On Occult Philosophy*, expressed his belief in the doctrines of astrology and that the rays of the celestial bodies are conveyed into metals, stones, herbs and animals. A firm believer in the efficacy of charms, he stated that they may "be worn on the body bound to any part of it or hung around the neck, changing sickness into health or health into sickness", and recommended that these charms be worn in the form of finger rings (that have been created using the materials in agreement and harmony with your Sun Sign's magical energy).

Material substances are connected with abstract purposes by a complex but highly usable and accessible system of correspondences. Utilising these time-honoured connections in your own spells and wishes may help magnetise your desires to you. The following pages offer ideas around materials, energies and forces you can summon in order to enhance your magic and generate luck.

PLANETS

The Planetary influence of the day is important when 'asking' for something. If you are wishing for luck, for example, try working with your Sun sign's intrinsic energies combined with the ideal day of the week for it. So an Arien might try using his natural enthusiasm and eagerness, to ask for greater luck on a Thursday, which is Jupiter's Day and Jupiter is renowned for being a lucky planet, or better still, ask for luck on a Tuesday, which is Mars's day, planetary ruler of Aries, at the time of day when Jupiter's influence is at its most powerful (information about planetary hours for each day of the week can be found elsewhere, as it is beyond the scope of this book).

DAYS OF THE WEEK & THEIR POWERS

MONDAY ✦ Moon / Cancer - The Divine feminine, changes, intuition, emotions, secrets, dealing with women, unity, psychic ability, magic, spirituality, invoking a goddess's or angel's guidance, anything that fluctuates, contracts, increases or decreases.

TUESDAY ✦ Mars / Aries & Scorpio - Masculine energy, men's mysteries, enthusiasm, competition, passion, energy, courage, protection, victory, anything requiring assertiveness, standing up for yourself, or a 'fighting spirit', determination, vitality, sexuality, self-confidence, drive, ambition, achievement, triumph.

WEDNESDAY ✦ Mercury / Gemini & Virgo - Education, travel, exams, study, networking, communication, writing and speaking, making connections, thinking, dealing with siblings, knowledge, learning, adaptability, charm, youth, absorbing information.

THURSDAY ✦ Jupiter / Sagittarius & Pisces - Increase and expansion of anything (remember to be careful what you wish for), luck, growth, fulfilment, expansion, gambling, philosophy, higher education, abundance, optimism, broadening horizons.

FRIDAY ✦ Venus / Taurus & Libra - Feminine energy, women's mysteries, love, luxury, the arts, indulgence, beauty, marriage, money, prosperity, fertility, grace, charm, pleasure, social events, aesthetics, decorating, self-worth, self-esteem, personal values, business partnerships, romance, creativity, sharing, bonding.

SATURDAY ✦ Saturn / Capricorn & Aquarius - Long-term goals, career, institutions, establishments, security, investments, karma, reversal, structure, stability, protection, solitude, privacy, determination, ending, blocking, renewing, transforming, anything to do with the public.

SUNDAY ✦ Sun / Leo - All purpose! The Divine masculine, success, wishes, generosity, happiness, optimism, spirit/essence, health, vitality, material wealth, invoking a god's aid or guidance, personal empowerment, spirituality.

YOUR NATAL MOON

For many centuries, people across the world have recognised that the Moon influences the affairs of all living things on planet Earth. In most astrological interpretations the Sun is regarded as the most important, central feature of a natal chart. But to many the Moon is equally, if not more, important than the Sun sign, because it too exerts a profound influence on your character, especially your inner one, the self you show to more intimate others or when your emotions are taking charge.

The Moon passes through the twelve signs about every 2.5 days, usually covering the whole zodiac in around 27.3 days, and symbolises one's inner world, feelings, emotions, habitual responses, instincts, intuition, security needs, and the subconscious. It describes one's nurturing style, emotional response to life, mood nature, instinctive and habitual responses, the receptive feminine side, one's experience of the mother or mother figure, and how childhood is experienced.

While the Sun represents the Spirit, the Moon represents the Soul. Your Sun and Moon work together to form the foundation of your basic personality, expression and nature. If you know what your Sun and Moon signs are, find your combination below, to reveal how these two luminaries blend to form your essential mind, soul and spirit.

MOON SIGNS ✦ HARNESSING SUN & MOON MAGIC COMBINED

The Sun / Moon Polarity
Conscious & Unconscious, Night & Day, Yin & Yang
Man does, woman is.
Edward Edinger

Great is Mind. Heaven's height is immeasurable, but Mind goes beyond heaven; the Earth's depth is also unfathomable, but Mind reaches below the Earth. The light of the Sun and Moon cannot be outdistanced, yet Mind passes beyond the light of Sun and Moon.
Eisai, *Kozen gokoku ron*

ARIES SUN & MOON COMBINATIONS

♈ With the Moon in ARIES, Sun in Aries, you are likely to be ✦ Self-centred, heroic, passionate, optimistic, egocentric, courageous, quick-thinking, bold, innovatively minded, on the go, impatient, active, blunt, self-interested, progressive, alert, childish, impetuous, enthusiastic, independent, honest, adventurous, hot-tempered, assertive, insensitive, ambitious, youthful, self-reliant, energetic, bossy, emotionally reckless, restless, speak before thinking, a fast communicator, pioneering, original, blunt, forward-looking, lively, witty, frank, bright, an individualist, and possess a touchy ego and personal integrity, as well as a maverick with a crusading temperament.

Sun/Moon Harmony Rating ✦ 7.5 out of 10

♉ With the Moon in TAURUS, Sun in Aries, you are likely to be ✦ Possessive, stubborn, persistent, jealous, materialistic, conflicted between security and freedom, sexy, tenacious, physically and mentally robust, devoted, powerfully charming, pushy, loyal, reluctant to listen to others' views if convinced your own are correct, stoic, faithful, bossy, friendly, capable, determined, resourceful, enthusiastic about making money, an entrepreneur, ambitious, strong-willed, reliable, philanthropic, in possession of a bawdy sense of humour and strong sense of self, and dedicated to activating your inspired ideas in the real, material world.

Sun/Moon Harmony Rating ✦ 5 out of 10

♊ With the Moon in GEMINI, Sun in Aries, you are likely to be ✦ Sociable, persuasive, deft, charming, a free spirit, changeable, friendly, bright, breezy, emotionally versatile, quick-witted, flippant, vital, perceptive, clever, inspiring, stimulating, flexible, adaptable, curious, childlike, emotionally impulsive, vivacious, zany, inconsistent, expressive, restless, easily bored, active, inspired, a live wire, direct, humorous, funny, creative, progressive, communicative, strongly socially aware, unsentimental, emotionally naïve, gifted, a wonderful friend, unreliable, zestful, an opportunist, original, popular, funny, easily swept away by ideas and concepts, open towards and perceptive of new ideas, pioneering, idealistic, intellectual, fun-loving, squandering of your natural talents, reluctant to delve deeper into anything, on the go, inquisitive, too busy to deal with feelings, have too many irons in the fire, and in possession of the gift of the gab and a sunny, breezy and light-hearted disposition.

Sun/Moon Harmony Rating ✦ 8.5 out of 10

♋ With the Moon in CANCER, Sun in Aries, you are likely to be ✦ Temperamental, sensitive, inspiring, clannish, devoted, romantic, affectionate, demonstrative, inspired to help others, unstable, inconsistent, torn between the past and future, feeling, richly imaginative, indirectly self-assertive, initiating, volatile, uplifting to others, intuitive, emotionally expressive, socially conscious, passionate about family, compassionate, a kind-hearted rebel, generous, imaginative, creative, kind, devoted to the triumph of the human spirit through action, helpful, companionable, a sensitive individualist, self-reliant, a good leader, emotionally defensive, and occasionally moved to emotional outbursts which may undermine your greatest talents and achievements.

Sun/Moon Harmony Rating ✦ 7 out of 10

♌ With the Moon in LEO, Sun in Aries, you are likely to be ✦ Proud, independent, warm-hearted, individualistic, strong-willed, dramatic, fearless, bold, artistic, generous to a fault, original, charismatic, passionate, radiant, zestful, vital, uplifting, immediate, sulky, childish, demanding, enthusiastic, active, adventurous, vain, friendly, a good leader, enthusiastically romantic, explorative, imaginative, open, powerful, extroverted, self-interested, honest, inclined to get carried away by drama and fun, idealistic, egotistical, direct, controlling, bossy, expressive, ambitious, despotic, self-centred, creative, emotionally radiating of warmth, luxury-loving, helpful, demonstrative, creatively imaginative, optimistic, impatient, sociable, playful, larger than life, intensely devoted, heroic, honourable, a big thinker, and able to inspire others with your large appetite for life.

Sun/Moon Harmony Rating ✦ 8 out of 10**

♍ With the Moon in VIRGO, Sun in Aries, you are likely to be ✦ Intelligent, selfish yet dutiful, judgemental, clever, discriminating, perfectionist, striving, methodical, studious, an avid researcher, outspoken yet reserved, bossy yet diffident, willing to put your cards on the table and say what you think, helpful, serious, kind-hearted, caring, innovative, mentally alert, mentally dextrous, efficient, reserved, straightforward, adaptable, quietly passionate, intolerant of others' weaknesses, analytical, critical, outrageous but often conventional, willing to help and do what needs to be done, altruistic, conscientious, effective, disciplined, genuinely kind, bright, devoted to ideals, dry-witted, zestful yet uptight, and in possession of a dedicated loyalty, with a strong craftsmanship streak.

Sun/Moon Harmony Rating ✦ 6 out of 10

♎ With the Moon in LIBRA, Sun in Aries, you are likely to be ✦
Lively, intellectually precocious, gregarious, see life from endlessly new vantage points, sociable, refined, easy-going, affectionate, forthright, confident but indecisive, convivial, amorous, popular, emotionally expressive, charming, approachable, spirited, courteous, eager for life, tolerant, ingenious, chivalrous, accessible, civilised, sharing, approval-seeking, hospitable, hedonistic, interested in others, romantically idealistic, endearing, loving of people, colourfully persuasive, procrastinating, outgoing, artistic, creative, gracefully enthusiastic, self-centred but kind, flirtatious, inspiring, hopeful, vain, considerate, thoughtful, emotionally naïve, courageous but strategic, a maverick but a seeker of justice, vacillating between one's own needs and the needs of other people, and conflicted between independence and needing others.

Sun/Moon Harmony Rating ✦ 8.5 out of 10

♏ With the Moon in SCORPIO, Sun in Aries, you are likely to be ✦
Intense, magnetic, highly motivated, self-dramatising, powerful, forceful, ambitious, highly charged, extreme, active, aggressively optimistic, determined, undeterred, pushy, possessive, keenly insightful, investigative, unbending, narcissistic, insatiable, strong-willed, dominating, intensely dedicated, passionate, unyielding, purposeful, sharp, highly sexed, overbearing, difficult, resourceful, extremely resilient, controlling, persuasive, charismatic, stubborn, persevering and thorough, devoted to truth at any cost, fiercely independent, penetrative, loyal, emotional, courageously dedicated, compulsive, perceptive, self-reliant, stern, exacting, potentially ruthless and manipulative, emotionally powerful, in possession of an unshakeable belief in yourself and others' individual worth, as well as a strong sense of self and personal integrity.

Sun/Moon Harmony Rating ✦ 6.5 out of 10

♐ With the Moon in SAGITTARIUS, Sun in Aries, you are likely to be ✦ Frank, tolerant, talkative, eager, impatient, friendly, feisty, independent, idealistic, explorative, an avid traveller, big-hearted, honest, adventurous, impatient with petty details and restrictions, visionary, confident, competitive, outspoken, big-hearted, highly strung, emphatic, prone to preach or boss others around, brash, loving of a challenge, insensitive, self-absorbed, grandiose, a daredevil, rash, inquisitive, self-assured, zestful, distant from your feelings, emotionally reckless, a free spirit, in possession of a keen sense of humour, egocentric, extravagant, careless, contagiously optimistic, inspiring, outrageous, aspiring, gregarious, trusting, naïve, expansive, verbose, philosophical, freedom-seeking, morally certain, residing in the realm of limitless possibilities and guided by your inner fire rather than emotion.

Sun/Moon Harmony Rating ✦ 8.5 out of 10**

♑ With the Moon in CAPRICORN, Sun in Aries, you are likely to be ✦ Steadfast, realistic, tough-minded, forceful, authoritarian, persistent, aggressive, ardent, the boss, the winner, resourceful, enterprising, entrepreneurial, a natural leader, astute, no-nonsense, blunt, controlling, overpowering, committed, independent, driven to succeed, ambitious, critical, cool, unstoppable, unemotional, wise, shrewd, organised, efficient, serious, sensible, materialistic, understanding of practical applications and wisdom, economical, a good leader, personally honourable, strict on self, fearless, uptight, self-contained, sardonically humorous, willing to work hard, and in possession of an overall attitude of 'shoot for the stars' (while keeping your feet firmly on the ground at the same time).

Sun/Moon Harmony Rating ✦ 7 out of 10

♒ With the Moon in AQUARIUS, Sun in Aries, you are likely to be ✦ Frank, sharp, selfish yet altruistic, intriguing, a people person, incisive, full of bright ideas, congenial, torn between Self and others, friendly, tolerant, independent, extraverted, idealistic, emotionally detached, eccentric, 'different', unconventional, revolutionary, a social activist, aloof, paradoxical, imaginative, sympathetic, unconventional, honest, original, forward-moving, inventive, impersonal in relationships, clear-headed, charismatic, a social visionary, impatient with practical details, highly observant, acutely aware of the human condition, progressive, scientifically oriented, objective, living an unusual lifestyle in some way, well-meaning, dramatic, open to the unusual, emotionally naïve, over-identifying with causes, blunt and insensitive when comparing people with your ideals, freedom-loving, unorthodox, idealistic, impractical, loyal, exceptionally individual, humanitarian, globally aware, courageous and committed to your ideals, a law unto yourself, in possession of an eternal sense of hope and belief in others, and making friends right across the fascinating broad spectrum of human viewpoints.

Sun/Moon Harmony Rating ✦ 8 out of 10

♓ With the Moon in PISCES, Sun in Aries, you are likely to be ✦ Imaginative, loving, giving, intuitive, enthusiastically mystical, idealistic, trusting, a chaser of spiritual rainbows, vulnerable, open, receptive, procrastinating, uncertain, self-doubting, weak-willed, good-natured, intriguing, kindly, friendly, emotionally aware, sentimental, single-minded but dreamy, impulsive, careless, accepting, understanding, independent but vulnerable, a zestful poet, altruistic, visionary, insightful, generous, receptive, creative, reverent, forgiving, devoted, mysterious, paradoxical, empathetic, impressionable, naïve, innocent, easily swayed, gullible, impractical, evasive, perceptive, emotionally intelligent, able to adapt to any situation, romantic, emotionally expressive, dramatic, restless, a worrier, temperamental, hopeful, able to mix and work with all types of people, aware of the needs of others, and in possession of a wonderfully offbeat but original philosophy of life.

Sun/Moon Harmony Rating ✦ 7.5 out of 10

**If your Moon is in Leo or Sagittarius, your Sun and Moon will form what is known in astrology as a trine aspect. This aspect is the easiest, most flowing and harmonious astrological aspect, ensuring that your Sun and Moon, or spirit and soul, are well integrated. With both luminaries in Fire signs, this gives them the best possible degree of complementary energy - a blending of the elements suggests a balanced expression of personality. One drawback of the trine aspect lies in the fact that its easy flow can be too harmonious; if our path is too smooth and difficulties don't arise to challenge us from time to time, we can often become lazy and complacent, stunting our growth and spiritual evolution. As Fire signs, you share the art of vitality, zest, enthusiasm, broad-mindedness, affability, idealism, independence, drive, ambition, force, affection, warm-heartedness, generosity, sociability, and have extravagant tastes, but may be temperamental, dramatic, overbearing, egocentric, restless, bossy, insensitive, careless, arrogant, and self-centred.

TAURUS SUN & MOON COMBINATIONS

♈ With the Moon in ARIES, Sun in Taurus, you are likely to be ✦ Devoted, in possession of a robust ego, loyal, persistent, insensitive, greedy, materialistic, self-reliant, self-contained, emotionally strong, bossy, bold, robust, resilient, resourceful, strongly sensual, artistic, enduring, powerful, selfish, pragmatic, firm, in possession of a strong sense of self, stubborn, steadfastly ambitious, competitive, resentful, a powerful leader, controlling, demanding, forthright, direct, irritable, established, entrepreneurial, consistent, steady, possessive, jealous, infantile, a substantial and stable influence on others, irrational, domestic, romantic, generous, practically instinctive, loving, indefatigably resilient, and have an unwavering belief in yourself and your abilities.

Sun/Moon Harmony Rating ✦ 6.5 out of 10

♉ With the Moon in TAURUS, Sun in Taurus, you are likely to be ✦ Dependable, calm, deliberate, soft, consistent, level-headed, pragmatically intellectual, dedicated, easy-going, possessive, stubborn, immovable, supportive, materialistic, nature-loving, certainty-seeking, fruitful, loving, kind, affectionate, slow to anger, in possession of a good business sense, gentle, infinitely patient, slow and steady-paced, security-seeking, tenacious, emotionally placid, rooted, unflappable, devoted, dry-humoured, self-indulgent, logical, stoic, faithful, peaceful, capable, determined, resourceful, peace-loving but strong-willed, reliable, realistic, sensible, persistent, and dedicated to making a substantial and steady income and thereby gaining security.

Sun/Moon Harmony Rating ✦ 8 out of 10

♊ With the Moon in GEMINI, Sun in Taurus, you are likely to be ✦ Changeable, moody, sociable, friendly, hot and cold, dissatisfied, bright, emotionally versatile, effective, convincing, unsympathetic, perceptive, clever, inspiring, flexible yet stubborn, curious, clear-thinking, torn between freedom and security, practically intelligent, pragmatic, charming, persuasive, brooding, occasionally impulsive, opportunistic, unemotional, unfeeling, conflicted between putting down roots and your need for movement and mobility, logical, creative, progressive, communicative, socially aware, unsentimental, a wonderful friend, a good reasoner, and have a good business sense combined with the persuasive powers of your gift of the gab.

Sun/Moon Harmony Rating ✦ 9 out of 10

♋ With the Moon in CANCER, Sun in Taurus, you are likely to be ✦ Passive, sensitive, nourishing to others, obstinate, strongly security-seeking, tenacious, retiring, intuitive, emotionally expressive, kind-hearted, tender, sentimental, sympathetic, domestic, resourceful, caring, fertile, creative, shy, emotionally reticent, hidden, private, peaceful, imaginative, poetic, devoted to family, helpful, companionable, emotional, old-fashion valued, self-protective, nostalgic, determined to put down roots, easily hurt, imaginative, sensual, protective of family and loved ones, enduringly loyal, dependable, sustained in approach, supportive, reliable, and in possession of the capacity to translate emotional experiences into artistic expression.

Sun/Moon Harmony Rating ✦ 7.5 out of 10

♌ With the Moon in LEO, Sun in Taurus, you are likely to be ✦ Proud, individualistic, flamboyant, hospitable, gentle on the surface with a great strength within, dramatic, protective, loving of beauty and the arts, artistic, generous, warm-hearted, gently passionate, persistent, dependable, capable, trustworthy, robust, romantic, affectionate, demonstrative, enduring, noble, charismatic, powerful, honest, snobbish, gently passionate, vain, stubborn, controlling, a leader, wilful, patient, expressive, ambitious, self-centred, vain, creative, comfort-seeking, luxury-loving, helpful, supportive, inspiring, regal, substantial, opinionated, unerringly loyal, materialistic, masterful, ambitious, involved, playful, and in possession of a magnetic, sociable personality with fixed ideas and opinions.

Sun/Moon Harmony Rating ✦ 7 out of 10

♍ With the Moon in VIRGO, Sun in Taurus, you are likely to be ✦ Puritanical, admired, nervous, judgemental, cool, calm and collected, aloof, critical, discriminating, methodical, studious, devoted, hard-working, nature-loving, practical, modest, reserved, helpful, an epicurean, robustly healthy, thoughtful, productive, consistent, supportive, kind-hearted, unassuming, efficient, caring, rigid, conventional, Earthy, constructive, resourceful, efficient, objectively rational, cool-headed, logical, neglectful or unaware of your deeper potential, dutiful, willing to help and do what needs to be done, pragmatic, skilful, reliable, persevering, stable, an artisan, altruistic, humble, wise, lucid, genuinely kind, responsible, poised, and in possession of a good deal of common sense and easy, sensual grace.

Sun/Moon Harmony Rating ✦ 7 out of 10**

♎ With the Moon in LIBRA, Sun in Taurus, you are likely to be ✦ Harmonious, peace-loving, aesthetically aware, pleasant, devoted, sentimental, attractive, artistic, sensual, able to work with principles easily, sociable, refined, graceful, well-balanced, moderate, easy-going, charming, social acceptance-seeking, affectionate, popular, a hider of feelings, approachable, distanced from your true emotional power, sharing, gracious, hospitable, hedonistic, comfort-seeking, pleasure-loving, superficial, romantic, endearing, delightful, gentle, persuasive, artistically sensitive, a practical idealist, and conflicted between self-reliance, self-resourcefulness, and in need of others.

Sun/Moon Harmony Rating ✦ 9 out of 10

♏ With the Moon in SCORPIO, Sun in Taurus, you are likely to be ✦ Intense, bossy, powerful, substantial, robust, highly resilient, inflexible, forceful, subjectively responsive, persistent, committed, charged, resourceful, stubborn, alternating between extreme and mild, possessive, unbending, strong-willed, dominating, sensually passionate, unyielding, sustaining, controlling, magnetic, shrewd, persevering, thorough, hard-working, devoted, dedicated, protective, penetrative, secretive, intensely loyal, emotionally strong, strategic, self-aware, obsessive, courageous, perceptive, self-reliant, exacting, potentially ruthless and manipulative, emotionally powerful, temperamental with a ruthless desire for power, and unshakeable in your ideas and opinions.

Sun/Moon Harmony Rating ✦ 7 out of 10

♐ With the Moon in SAGITTARIUS, Sun in Taurus, you are likely to be ✦ Eager, generous, giving, warm, friendly, idealistic, expressively sensual, big-hearted, moralistic, grounded yet high-flying, adventurous yet conventional, honest, rational, aware of possibilities, inspirational, philosophical, conflicted between freedom and security, idealistic but realistic, prone to preach and boss, able to see the 'bigger picture', distant from your feelings, emotionally reckless, far-sighted, gently optimistic, in possession of an inner knowingness, gently exuberant, a lover of learning, inspiring, aspiring, objective, ambitious, gregarious, broad-minded but rigid, expansive, and guided by reason and logic rather than emotion.

Sun/Moon Harmony Rating ✦ 6.5 out of 10

♑ With the Moon in CAPRICORN, Sun in Taurus, you are likely to be ✦ Devoted, disciplined, unflappable, dependable, staunch, protective, conscientious, traditional, security-seeking, steadfast, self-controlled, dictatorial, resourceful, committed, driven to succeed, ambitious, reserved, withdrawn, cool, self-restrained, unemotional, wise, shrewd, organised, down-to-Earth, efficient, reliable, organised, serious, sensible, materialistic, introverted, understanding of practical applications and wisdom, economical, practical, honourable, uptight, socially rigid, self-contained, and willing to work long and hard to achieve your goals.

Sun/Moon Harmony Rating ✦ 8 out of 10**

♒ With the Moon in AQUARIUS, Sun in Taurus, you are likely to be ✦ Friendly, tolerant, objective, living an unusual lifestyle in some way, well-meaning, open to the unusual, emotionally naïve, helpful, opinionated, sensible, artistic, faithful, no-nonsense, unique, sociable, blunt and insensitive when comparing people with your ideals, realistic, committed to principles, inflexible, conflicted between freedom and security, independence and devotion to others, deeply loyal, unshakable, unchangeable, committed to your ideals and loved ones, stubborn, a law unto yourself, and in possession of an approachable, easy-going, uncomplicated manner.

Sun/Moon Harmony Rating ✦ 6.5 out of 10

♓ With the Moon in PISCES, Sun in Taurus, you are likely to be ✦ Imaginative, feeling, warm, loving, romantic, sensual, mystical, idealistic, practically idealistic, good-natured, gentle, intriguing, kind, affable, sentimental, accepting, unassuming, understanding, supportive, strong but vulnerable, a pragmatist, a poet, generous, dry-humoured, receptive, creative, mysterious, prone to drifting and wasting time in daydreams, needy, clingy, impressionable but sometimes unshakeable, quietly strong, modest, practically sympathetic, despondent, impractical, evasive, an escapist from harsh realities, sensitive, perceptive, and in possession of an innate love of beauty, nature and peace.

Sun/Moon Harmony Rating ✦ 7.5 out of 10

If your Moon is in Virgo or Capricorn, your Sun and Moon will form what is known in astrology as a trine aspect. This aspect is the easiest, most flowing and harmonious astrological aspect, ensuring that your Sun and Moon, or spirit and soul, are well integrated. With both luminaries in Earth signs, this gives them the best possible degree of complementary energy - a blending of the elements suggests a balanced expression of personality. One drawback of the trine aspect lies in the fact that its easy flow can be too harmonious; if our path is too smooth and difficulties don't arise to challenge us from time to time, we can often become lazy and complacent, stunting our growth and spiritual evolution. As Earth signs, you share the art of practical application, devotion, rational thinking, logic, a love of beauty and peace, determination, pragmatism, sensibility, conservatism, realism, sensuality, fruitfulness and a gentle, caring approach to all your relationships and endeavours, but may be staid, rigid, unimaginative, materialistic, slow, lazy, narrow-minded and lacking in enthusiasm and zest.

GEMINI SUN & MOON COMBINATIONS

♈ With the Moon in ARIES, Sun in Gemini, you are likely to be ✦ Effervescent, observant, fresh, decisive, astute, self-interested, superficial, egocentric, alert, light-hearted, emotionally detached, impatient with lesser minds, zestful, intolerant of idleness, independent, adventurous, flighty, temperamental, nimble, monopolising of conversations, inconsistent, vital, fun-loving, unreliable, on the go, busy, insensitive, self-reliant, energetic, dextrous, persuasive, emotionally bold and reckless, restless, speak before thinking, active, a fast communicator, intellectual, inventive, insensitive to feelings of others, ideas-oriented, lively, witty, frank, bright, charming, inspired, humorous, flirty, spontaneous, sociable, popular, conversational, clear-thinking, sparkling, and in possession of an enviable gift of the gab.

Sun/Moon Harmony Rating ✦ 8 out of 10

♉ With the Moon in TAURUS, Sun in Gemini, you are likely to be ✦ Pragmatically intellectual, stubborn, materialistic, sensually flirtatious, superficial, conflicted between security and freedom, entrepreneurial, able to turn ideas into realities, flexible without compromising self, able to offer practical support and generosity to others, easily tempted by pleasures, tenacious, socially engaging, logical and detached in emotional matters, able to apply your intelligence, friendly but flighty, capable, determined, resourceful, ambitious, torn between quiet and activity, persistent, resistant to spiritual matters, and dedicated to grounding your inspiration and enthusiasm so they are more workable.

Sun/Moon Harmony Rating ✦ 5.5 out of 10

♊ **With the Moon in GEMINI, Sun in Gemini, you are likely to be** ✦
A free spirit, lively, superficial, mentally agile, suave, talented, expressive, a jack-of-all-trades, changeable, frivolous, friendly, bright, breezy, adaptable, shallow, emotionally versatile, quick-witted, cerebral, flippant, perceptive, a mimic and a juggler, nervous, on the go, clever, inspiring, stimulating, sociable, detached, flexible, curious, emotionally impulsive, restless, gossipy, easily bored, objective, communicative, unsentimental, emotionally naïve, childlike, gifted, a wonderful friend, popular, funny, charming, witty, open towards and perceptive of new ideas, intellectual, squandering of your natural talents, reluctant to face the darker aspects of life, too busy to deal with feelings, and ruled by your mind rather than your heart.

Sun/Moon Harmony Rating ✦ 8 out of 10

♋ **With the Moon in CANCER, Sun in Gemini, you are likely to be** ✦
Intellectually intuitive, emotionally expressive, changeable, moody, nervous, versatile, never content, imaginative, poetic, intelligently kind, helpful, companionable, emotionally lofty, idealistic, impressionable, receptive, cleverly self-expressive, shrewd, emotionally defensive, unstable, able to express insights on a personal level, self-protective, innately interested in others yet private, self-preserving, devoted to family and siblings, dedicated to neighbourhood social events and causes, clannish, perceptive, and occasionally moved to emotional evasiveness.

Sun/Moon Harmony Rating ✦ 6 out of 10

♌ **With the Moon in LEO, Sun in Gemini, you are likely to be** ✦
Proud, independent, individualistic, flighty on the surface with a great strength within, positive, a good dramatist and story-teller, improvising, fearless, sociable, generous, passionate, radiant, popular, spirited, inspirational, contagiously optimistic, youthful, enthusiastic, romantic, open, flexible, witty, a natural salesperson, demonstrative, charismatic, extroverted, honest, warm, bold, inclined to get carried away, direct, vain, frivolous, lively, friendly, expressive, ambitious, self-centred, boastful, emotionally idealistic, helpful, intelligent, a colourful conservationist, warmly convivial, and in possession of a childlike sense of fun.

Sun/Moon Harmony Rating ✦ 8 out of 10

♍ With the Moon in VIRGO, Sun in Gemini, you are likely to be ✦ Intelligent, judgemental, cool, calm and collected, critical, verbally expressive, a worrier, clever, discriminating, logical, awkward about showing feelings, analytical, technically skilled, a perfectionist, methodical, studious, innovative, mentally alert, a good communicator, efficient, aspiring, busy, mentally dextrous, efficient, undemonstrative, objectively rational, cool-headed, altruistic, bright, quick-witted, sociable yet uptight, and in possession of an overly active mind that can't switch off.

Sun/Moon Harmony Rating ✦ 6 out of 10**

♎ With the Moon in LIBRA, Sun in Gemini, you are likely to be ✦ Lively, intellectual, sociable, gregarious, friendly, easy-going, sporadically affectionate, popular, a hider of feelings, verbally expressive, charming, approachable, popular, distanced from your true emotional power, accessible, civilised, cooperative, approval-seeking, hospitable, indecisive, interested in people, romantically idealistic, flirtatious, acutely observant, quick-witted, persuasive, artistically sensitive, abstract, emotionally naïve, and conflicted between independence and needing social sustenance through partnerships.

Sun/Moon Harmony Rating ✦ 8.5 out of 10**

♏ With the Moon in SCORPIO, Sun in Gemini, you are likely to be ✦ Intensely expressive, provocative, powerfully intellectual, a great social force, magnetic, socially persuasive, multifaceted, highly charged, restless, extreme, keenly insightful, acutely perceptive, investigative, intriguingly popular, resourceful, vitally sensual, alternating between breezy and intense, penetrative yet surface-skimming, sarcastic, scathing, passionate yet dispassionate, courageous, an astute observer, quick-witted, deep-hearted, colourful, independent, charismatic, communicative yet secretive, self-reliant, potentially ruthless and manipulative, and socially influential.

Sun/Moon Harmony Rating ✦ 6 out of 10

♐ **With the Moon in SAGITTARIUS, Sun in Gemini, you are likely to be ✦** Eager, curious, seeking, open to experience, emotionally immature but responsive, adventurous, friendly, independent, idealistic, a traveller of body and mind, sociable, honest, insincere, an eternal student, a traveller, rationalising, impatient with petty details and restrictions of daily life, flamboyant, generous, in possession of a voracious appetite for people and experiences, full of good ideas, intellectually insightful, indiscreet, a great talker, prone to preach, blunt, intellectual, inquisitive, an adventurer, freedom-seeking, distant from your feelings, emotionally reckless, a free spirit, non-committal, a good teacher, in possession of an intelligent sense of humour, far-sighted, intellectually speedy, optimistic, a lover of learning, inspiring, outrageous, spontaneous, aspiring, gregarious, expansive, verbose, superficially philosophical, a voyager, and guided by reason rather than emotion.

Sun/Moon Harmony Rating ✦ 9 out of 10

♑ **With the Moon in CAPRICORN, Sun in Gemini, you are likely to be ✦** Steadfast, resourceful, witty, independent, a devoted friend, striving, driven to succeed, cool, a cynical optimist, unemotional, intellectually wise, shrewd, clever, attracted to social events with an intellectual slant, impatient with the emotional realm, bright, organised, efficient, understanding of practical applications and wisdom, a realist, a clear-thinker, inventive, socially honourable, fearless, uptight, socially rigid, self-contained, aware of human character, sardonically humorous, serious yet carefree, and sociable yet solitary.

Sun/Moon Harmony Rating ✦ 7 out of 10**

♒ **With the Moon in AQUARIUS, Sun in Gemini, you are likely to be ✦** Gregarious, unconventional, witty, in possession of a unique sense of humour, prophetic, clear-thinking, restless, tolerant, independent, idealistic, alert, adaptable, neglectful of realities, emotionally detached, eccentric, 'different', paradoxical, honest, flighty, nervous, original, forward-moving, inventive, impersonal in relationships, clear-headed, highly observant, acutely aware of the human condition, progressive, scientifically oriented, objective, living an unusual lifestyle in some way, well-meaning, open to the unusual, emotionally naïve, freedom-loving, unorthodox, impractical, humanitarian, committed to your ideals and convictions, and in possession of an insatiable sociable streak.

Sun/Moon Harmony Rating ✦ 8 out of 10**

♓ With the Moon in PISCES, Sun in Gemini, you are likely to be ✦ Whimsical, childlike, versatile, changeable, imaginative, intuitive, able to blend realism with mysticism, idealistic, unable to concentrate, cheeky, lacking in boundaries, confused, good-natured, friendly, emotionally intelligent, apt to wander off and go into flights of fancy, hot and cold emotions, sentimental, independent but vulnerable, an intellectual poet, humorous, intelligently insightful, generous, receptive, creative, reverent, forgiving, superficial, adaptable, prone to drifting and wasting time in daydreams, impressionable, idealistic but easily swayed, gullible, impractical, evasive, perceptive, chameleon-like, moody, vacillating, talkative, nervous, submissive yet cunning, emotionally intelligent, able to mix and work with all types of people, and aware of the needs of others.

Sun/Moon Harmony Rating ✦ 8 out of 10

**If your Moon is in Libra or Aquarius, your Sun and Moon will form what is known in astrology as a trine aspect. This aspect is the easiest, most flowing and harmonious astrological aspect, ensuring that your Sun and Moon, or spirit and soul, are well integrated. With both luminaries in Air signs, this gives them the best possible degree of complementary energy - a blending of the elements suggests a balanced expression of personality. One drawback of the trine aspect lies in the fact that its easy flow can be too harmonious; if our path is too smooth and difficulties don't arise to challenge us from time to time, we can often become lazy and complacent, stunting our growth and spiritual evolution. As Air signs, you share the art of sociability, are highly idealistic, affable, romantic, possess a good intellect, have a love of truth and beauty, are reasonable, broad-minded, independent but devoted to your ideals, have an artistic sensitivity, are tolerant, understanding, civilised and dignified, and have avant-garde tastes, but may be detached, cool, head over heart-oriented, and restless.*

CANCER SUN & MOON COMBINATIONS

♈ **With the Moon in ARIES, Sun in Cancer, you are likely to be** ✦
Sociable, devoted, moody, loyal, sensitive, restless, emotionally expressive, enthusiastic, loyal, temperamental, hot-tempered, sulky, childish, sensitive, ego-based, emotionally bold, a tenacious warrior, shrewd, strong, insightful, vulnerable but brave, active imagination, loving, protective, demonstrative, affectionate, creative, gentle but spirited, dependent yet independent, defensive but forthright, receptive, self-assertive, and torn between security and risk.

Sun/Moon Harmony Rating ✦ 6 out of 10

♉ **With the Moon in TAURUS, Sun in Cancer, you are likely to be** ✦
Gentle, easy-going but moody, pragmatically emotional, traditional, possessive, a homebody, clingy, stubborn, materialistic, security-seeking, patient, loving of home comforts, slow, steady-paced, afraid of change, supportive, comfort-seeking, tenacious, determined, emotionally placid, clannish, domestic, devoted, logical but intuitive, mothering and smothering, imaginative yet grounded, faithful, soft-hearted, tender, resourceful, dependable, modest, peace-loving, considerate, thoughtful, sensible, persistent, and dedicated to your family.

Sun/Moon Harmony Rating ✦ 7.5 out of 10

♊ **With the Moon in GEMINI, Sun in Cancer, you are likely to be** ✦
Changeable, friendly, sharing, hospitable, emotionally versatile, self-reflective, a sympathetic conversationalist, whimsically charming, quick-witted and poetically adept, emotionally perceptive and expressive, clever, able to listen to others' needs, quietly sociable, emotionally intelligent, scatterbrained, socially nervous and timid, moody, restless, creative, in possession of a good memory for personal detail, giving, supportive, helpful, understanding, accommodating, responsive, shrewdly perceptive, aware of others' needs, and an effervescent and welcoming host or hostess.

Sun/Moon Harmony Rating ✦ 9 out of 10

♋ With the Moon in CANCER, Sun in Cancer, you are likely to be ✦ Retentive, passive, sensitive, intuitive, emotional, compassionate, kind, tender, sympathetic, security-seeking, mothering, shy, reticent, hidden, private, eccentric, peaceful, imaginative, poetic, devoted, helpful, companionable, self-protective, romantic, secretive, clannish, instinctive, habitual, defensive, home-loving, artistic, attached to the past, nourishing, moody, affectionate, nurturing, tenacious, psychic, easily hurt, evasive, elusive, a worrier, sulky, dependent, and attached to people and possessions.

Sun/Moon Harmony Rating ✦ 7 out of 10

♌ With the Moon in LEO, Sun in Cancer, you are likely to be ✦ Individualistic, aristocratic, shrewd, gentle on the surface with a great strength within, friendly, subtly dramatic, artistic, dramatic, generous in helping others, inspirational, quietly passionate, radiantly loving, affectionate, adoring, caring, romantically imaginative, proud of family, warmly hospitable, charismatic, gently charming, bold, dependent on others, approval-seeking, glamorising of others and failing to see their true colours, modestly ambitious, creative, emotionally radiating warmth, big-hearted, hearty, comfort-loving, loving of creature comforts, helpful, demonstrative, and creatively imaginative. Richard D. Bach's, "It was morning, and the new Sun sparkled gold across the ripples of a gentle sea," perhaps best sums you up.

Sun/Moon Harmony Rating ✦ 8 out of 10

♍ With the Moon in VIRGO, Sun in Cancer, you are likely to be ✦ Imaginatively analysing, dutiful, reflective, attentive, caring, helpful, concerned, sympathetic, loyal, timid, shrewd, fussy, intelligent, solemn, calm and collected, clever, discriminating, an emotional perfectionist, a devoted researcher, serious, kind-hearted, efficient, reserved, emotional yet rational, doubtful, balanced between the feelings and the intellect, altruistic, devoted to others, a good domestic organiser, retiring, introverted, self-controlled, self-contained, introverted, sympathetic but practical, self-doubting, pure, conscientious, prude, private, socially adaptable, able to combine imagination with efficiency, articulate, morally proper, and able to combine compassion and common sense.

Sun/Moon Harmony Rating ✦ 7.5 out of 10

♎ With the Moon in LIBRA, Sun in Cancer, you are likely to be ✦ Intelligent, sociable, refined, adaptable, generally well-balanced and moderate, easy-going, gentle, affectionate, nervous, people-pleasing, loving, clingy, dependent, graceful, subtly charming, sharing, gracious, cooperative, hospitable, romantically idealistic, endearing, delightful, polite, artistically sensitive, elegant, socially aware, tentative yet eager for attention, sensitive, tender, defensive yet devoted, articulate, peace-loving, concerned for the welfare of others, and dependent on family and close relationships for emotional nourishment.

Sun/Moon Harmony Rating ✦ 8 out of 10

♏ With the Moon in SCORPIO, Sun in Cancer, you are likely to be ✦ Magnetic, compelling, intensely emotional, formidable, dramatic, defensive, suspicious, powerfully protective of self and others, subtle yet forceful, possessive, vindictive, moody, insightful, probing, committed, strong-willed, initiating, daring, single-minded, cautious, transformative, intensely dedicated, resilient, strong, passionate, unyielding, resourceful, tenacious, investigative, controlling, persevering, tenacious, devoted to loved ones, penetrative, secretive, hidden, unwaveringly loyal, mysterious, unshakable, courageous, exacting, manipulative, intriguing, acutely perceptive, emotionally powerful, and in possession of deep healing capabilities.

Sun/Moon Harmony Rating ✦ 7.5 out of 10**

♐ With the Moon in SAGITTARIUS, Sun in Cancer, you are likely to be ✦ Warmly loving, colourful, restless, eager, cautious yet adventurous, friendly, idealistic, torn between freedom and security, big-hearted, honest, subtle yet larger-than-life, dramatic, morally certain, inquisitive, an adventurer, hearty, conflicted between your need for privacy and your yearnings for adventure, sarcastic to hide your vulnerabilities, traditional yet progressive, kind, intuitive, visionary, reserved yet talkative, a romantic traveller, able to see the 'bigger picture', idealistic, philosophical, imaginative, emotionally reckless, sensitive yet open, in possession of a zany or dry sense of humour, optimistic, a lover of learning, inspiring, aspiring, all-embracing, playful, affectionate, gregarious, socially concerned, good-humoured, expressive yet shy, broad-minded, expansive, and guided by reason and emotion.

Sun/Moon Harmony Rating ✦ 7 out of 10

♑ With the Moon in CAPRICORN, Sun in Cancer, you are likely to be ✦ Dependable, tenacious, strong-minded, patient, determined, a gentle disciplinarian, steadfast, authoritative, resourceful, committed, driven to succeed, ambitious, responsible, dedicated, considerate, critical, reserved, withdrawn, cool, organised, down-to-Earth, efficient, reliable, serious, sensual, a good leader, hard-headed but soft-hearted, sensible, reflective, materialistic, security-seeking, introverted, in possession of a good business sense, a firm but tender parent, closed off from others when hurt, understanding of practical applications and wisdom, economical, personally honourable, overly-strict on self and others, fearless, uptight, socially rigid, self-contained, capable, caring, dutiful, devoted to family, pragmatic yet sensitive, perceptive, intensely loyal, purposeful, a natural counsellor, diplomatic, compassionate, wise, helpful, concerned, and intuitively shrewd.

Sun/Moon Harmony Rating ✦ 8 out of 10

♒ With the Moon in AQUARIUS, Sun in Cancer, you are likely to be ✦ Torn between independence and co-dependence, friendly, idealistic, emotionally detached, compassionate, nurturing of your 'brothers', protective of the underdog, whole-hearted, visionary, unconventional, paradoxical, feeling and thinking, imaginative, sympathetic to the human condition, honest, loyal, shrewd, faithful, original, progressive yet nostalgic, encouraging, attracted to eccentric characters, acutely aware of human need, thoughtful, living an unusual family lifestyle in some way, nurturing to many, emotionally naïve, over-identifying with causes, dedicated to group causes, attached to friends, unorthodox, impractical, humanitarian, committed to your ideals, emotionally intelligent, and ruled by your mind and your heart.

Sun/Moon Harmony Rating ✦ 7.5 out of 10

♓ With the Moon in PISCES, Sun in Cancer, you are likely to be ✦ Sensitive, wallowing, adaptable, elusive, highly imaginative, intuitive, mystical, dreamy, a chaser of spiritual rainbows, good-natured, shy, easily hurt, kind-hearted, emotional, sentimental, gentle, accepting, understanding, vulnerable, gullible, trusting, private, hidden, poetic, impressionable, insightful, nurturing, receptive, creative, forgiving, retiring, withdrawn, self-sacrificing, empathetic, prone to drifting and wasting time in daydreams, easily swayed, impractical, evasive, psychic, perceptive, romantic, whimsical, charitable, blowing with the wind, reflective, and aware of the needs of others.

Sun/Moon Harmony Rating ✦ 7.5 out of 10**

**If your Moon is in Scorpio or Pisces, your Sun and Moon will form what is known in astrology as a trine aspect. This aspect is the easiest, most flowing and harmonious astrological aspect, ensuring that your Sun and Moon, or spirit and soul, are well integrated. With both luminaries in Water signs, this gives them the best possible degree of complementary energy - a blending of the elements suggests a balanced expression of personality. One drawback of the trine aspect lies in the fact that its easy flow can be too harmonious; if our path is too smooth and difficulties don't arise to challenge us from time to time, we can often become lazy and complacent, stunting our growth and spiritual evolution. As Water signs, you share the art of sensitivity, creativity, intrigue, compassion, a nurturing instinct, poetry, understanding, spirituality, a deep need for connection and merging with others, but may be overly sensitive, illogical, clingy, impractical, too emotional, irrational, dependent, manipulative, and elusive.

LEO SUN & MOON COMBINATIONS

♈ With the Moon in ARIES, Sun in Leo, you are likely to be ✦
Confident, brave, passionate, adventurous, self-interested, vain, active, rash, honourable, dramatic, proud, boastful, overbearing, pompous, enthusiastic, generous, domineering, affectionate, all-embracing, impressive, extroverted, independent, egocentric, approval-seeking, honest, inspirational, whole-hearted, loyal, adventurous, hot-tempered, dazzling, a show-off, charismatic, a leader, courageous, assertive, temperamental, insensitive, playful, ambitious, theatrical, self-reliant, energetic, emotionally bold and reckless, restless, speak before thinking, pioneering, original, forward-looking, lively, fun, bright, an individualist, one who has moral integrity, flamboyant, and prone to grandiosity.

Sun/Moon Harmony Rating ✦ 8 out of 10**

♉ With the Moon in TAURUS, Sun in Leo, you are likely to be ✦
Level-headed, pragmatic, dictatorial, productive, bossy, strong, brave, a leader, proud, determined, possessive, stubborn, generous, materialistic, patient, regal, luxury-loving, subjective, steady-paced, opinionated, tenacious, devoted, stoic, faithful, magnetic, seeking of power, artistic, self-seeking, loyal, friendly, robust, capable, resourceful, extravagant, dependable, demanding, unflappable, entrepreneurial, ambitious, peace-loving but strong-willed, philanthropic, realistic, sensible, persistent, commanding, dedicated and loving of grandeur.

Sun/Moon Harmony Rating ✦ 6.5 out of 10

♊ With the Moon in GEMINI, Sun in Leo, you are likely to be ✦
Changeable, friendly, bright, lively, zestful, effervescent, sociable, versatile, quick-witted, flippant, charismatic, an opportunist, perceptive, clever, a perennial student of life, approachable, charming, inspiring, honourable but light-hearted, playful, stimulating, warm-hearted, optimistic, resilient, occasionally unruly and fickle, flexible yet stubborn, iconoclastic, popular, curious, emotionally impulsive, restless, inconsistently creative, a people person, warmly spontaneous, aspiring, youthfully spirited, communicative, socially aware, childish, gifted, intellectual, theatrical, a wonderful friend, funny, fun, impressionable, flirtatious, adaptable, open to new ideas, adventurous, bold, reluctant to face the darker aspects of life, too busy to deal with feelings, and ruled equally by your head and your heart.

Sun/Moon Harmony Rating ✦ 8.5 out of 10

♋ With the Moon in CANCER, Sun in Leo, you are likely to be ✦ Proud of family, sensitive, intuitive, emotionally expressive, jealous, ardent, dramatic, loving of home and family, temperamental, torn between introversion and extroversion, affectionate, understanding, vulnerable, in possession of a vast inner strength, aesthetically sensitive, ardent, passionately tender, distorted, anxious, self-absorbed, tenacious, devoted, compassionate, sulky, clingy, reflective, possessive, kind-hearted, dedicated, imaginative, creative, gentle-spirited, optimistic, hopeful, faithful, colourful, moody, clannish, dependable, receptive, loyal, conflicted between personal privacy and outer involvement with others, a sensitive individualist, protective of self and others, and occasionally moved to emotional tantrums.

Sun/Moon Harmony Rating ✦ 6.5 out of 10

♌ With the Moon in LEO, Sun in Leo, you are likely to be ✦ Generous, proud, vain, pompous, extraverted, individualistic, strong, courageous, visionary, brave, fearless, bold, artistic, playful, affectionate, arrogant, generous, passionate, impetuous, radiant, enthusiastic, a good leader, romantic, inspirational, charismatic, commanding, warm, demanding, open, regal, powerful, charming, extroverted, honest, single-minded, magnanimous, inclined to get carried away by romance and drama, direct, expressive, ambitious, creative, artistic, flamboyant, prone to sulking, uplifting, attention-seeking, dignified, emotionally radiating warmth, idealistic, luxury-loving, extravagant, demonstrative, inflexible, gullible and authoritative.

Sun/Moon Harmony Rating ✦ 8 out of 10

♍ **With the Moon in VIRGO, Sun in Leo, you are likely to be** ✦
Intelligent, judgemental, cool, calm and collected, charming, down-to-Earth yet dramatic, purposeful, discerning, discriminating, a commanding perfectionist, methodical, studious, highly moral, prudish, high-minded, helpful, a striver for excellence, pushy, defiant, articulate, aspiring, dogged, thorough, self-critical, fussy, serious but warm, kind-hearted, dutiful, self-contained, considerate, respectful, mentally alert, efficient, a good organiser, mentally dextrous, pedantic, genuine, choosy, caring, stubborn, wild-at-heart yet conventional, obsessive compulsive, spirited yet grounded, objectively rational, cool-headed, conflicted between being the king or the king's servant, willing to help and do what needs to be done, altruistic, bright, devoted, dry-witted, in possession of high standards, and feisty yet uptight.

Sun/Moon Harmony Rating ✦ 5.5 out of 10

♎ **With the Moon in LIBRA, Sun in Leo, you are likely to be** ✦
Sociable, people-loving, glamorous, artistic, aesthetically aware, luxury-seeking, attractive, refined, easy-going, affectionate, loving, charismatic, indecisive, charming, popular, graceful, pleasure-seeking, regally friendly, eager to engage, reasonable, smooth, fair, diplomatic, stylish, idealistic, vain, unconsciously snobbish, prone to laziness, procrastinating, approachable, tolerant, distanced from your true emotional power, civilised, sharing, gracious, cooperative, approval-seeking, outgoing, hospitable, hedonistic, indecisive, interested in people, romantically idealistic, endearing, delightful, colourfully persuasive, artistically sensitive, emotionally naïve, and conflicted between self-reliance and needing others.

Sun/Moon Harmony Rating ✦ 9 out of 10

♏ **With the Moon in SCORPIO, Sun in Leo, you are likely to be** ✦
Dramatic, defiant, powerfully instinctive, theatrical, intense, powerful, forceful, commanding, magnetic, complex, dangerous, feisty, highly charged, extreme, possessive, keenly insightful, loyal, investigative, charismatic, imperious, unbending, fanatical, shrewd, strong-willed, dominating, intensely dedicated, passionate, unyielding, resourceful, resilient, controlling, ambitious, proud, insatiable, sceptical, a survivor, stubborn, influential, persevering, thorough, devoted, courageous, emotionally expressive, an astute observer, perceptive, self-reliant, dogmatic, exacting, potentially ruthless and dictatorial, manipulative, and emotionally powerful.

Sun/Moon Harmony Rating ✦ 7.5 out of 10

♐ With the Moon in SAGITTARIUS, Sun in Leo, you are likely to be ✦ Eager, adventurous, impractical, gregarious, independent, idealistic, zestful, inspiring, big-hearted, honest, insensitive, impatient, prone to preach, arrogant, unaware of the subtleties of social interaction, outspoken, generous, sincere, a visionary, boastful, philosophical, able to see the 'big picture', emotionally reckless, pompous, bold, a free spirit, non-committal, a good leader, confident, enthusiastic, positive, sarcastic, direct, in possession of a crazy sense of humour, far-sighted, extraverted, optimistic, a lover of learning, outrageous, aspiring, gregarious, ambitious, sociable, warm, thoughtless, broad-minded, expansive, verbose, theatrical, dramatic, freedom-seeking, and guided by reason rather than emotion.

Sun/Moon Harmony Rating ✦ 8.5 out of 10**

♑ With the Moon in CAPRICORN, Sun in Leo, you are likely to be ✦ Dependable, practical, steadfast, resourceful, committed, independent, driven to succeed, ambitious, purposeful, stubborn, wilful, persevering, guarded, self-protective, critical, cool-headed, wise, determined, harsh, direct, diligent, shrewd, organised, down-to-Earth, an excellent leader, efficient, authoritative, serious, highly moral, courageous, impatient with imperfection, sensible, materialistic, understanding of practical applications and wisdom, tense, self-controlled, personally honourable, highly principled, fearless, uptight, socially rigid, self-contained, sardonically humorous, a workaholic, a practical visionary, self-demanding, sprightly yet sombre, and domineering.

Sun/Moon Harmony Rating ✦ 6 out of 10

♒ With the Moon in AQUARIUS, Sun in Leo, you are likely to be ✦
Warm yet cool, friendly, tolerant, frank, independent, freedom-seeking, idealistic, emotionally detached yet romantic, eccentrically theatrical, vain yet vulnerable, unconventional, paradoxical, imaginative, opinionated, honest, loyal, original, forward-moving, inventive, impersonal in relationships, highly observant, strongly social, loving of friendship and groups, individualistic, in possession of deep convictions, flamboyant or bohemian, an objective and visionary leader, optimistic, vividly imaginative, aristocratic, truthful, proud, endearing, idiosyncratic, perceptive, broad-minded, acutely aware of the human condition, progressive, scientifically oriented, objective, living an unusual lifestyle in some way, well-intentioned, open to the unusual, emotionally naïve, over-identifying with causes, blunt and insensitive when comparing people with your ideals, unorthodox, impractical, humanitarian, globally aware, courageous and committed to your ideals, and in possession of an eternal sense of hope and belief in human potential.

Sun/Moon Harmony Rating ✦ 7.5 out of 10

♓ With the Moon in PISCES, Sun in Leo, you are likely to be ✦
Intuitive, generous, highly imaginative, gregarious, able to blend objectivity with mysticism, devoted, self-indulgent, escapist, aware of beauty and tragedy, prone to dejection, emotionally unsettled, caring, open, overly idealistic, a chaser of spiritual rainbows, hearty, good-natured, intriguing, kind, modest yet proud, charismatic, endearing, charming, able to be introverted or extraverted as called for, emotionally expressive, warmly sentimental, understanding, self-assured yet vulnerable, a dramatist, a poet, altruistic, humorous, receptive, artistic, creative, pleasure-seeking, mysterious, empathetic, people-pleasing, impressionable, easily swayed, gullible, impractical, evasive, perceptive, emotionally charged, and aware of the needs of others.

Sun/Moon Harmony Rating ✦ 8 out of 10

*If your Moon is in Aries or Sagittarius, your Sun and Moon will form what is known in astrology as a trine aspect. This aspect is the easiest, most flowing and harmonious astrological aspect, ensuring that your Sun and Moon, or spirit and soul, are well integrated. With both luminaries in Fire signs, this gives them the best possible degree of complementary energy - a blending of the elements suggests a balanced expression of

personality. One drawback of the trine aspect lies in the fact that its easy flow can be too harmonious; if our path is too smooth and difficulties don't arise to challenge us from time to time, we can often become lazy and complacent, stunting our growth and spiritual evolution. As Fire signs, you share the art of vitality, zest, enthusiasm, broad-mindedness, affability, idealism, independence, drive, ambition, force, affection, warm-heartedness, generosity, sociability, and have extravagant tastes, but may be temperamental, dramatic, overbearing, egocentric, restless, bossy, insensitive, careless, arrogant, and self-centred.

VIRGO SUN & MOON COMBINATIONS

♈ With the Moon in ARIES, Sun in Virgo, you are likely to be ✦ Devoted, dutiful, persistent, self-contained, emotionally cool, impatient with others' shortcomings, pragmatic, self-motivated, adaptable, fussy, resourceful, meticulous, professional, mentally quick, sensual, analytical, choosy, pragmatic, a workaholic, bossy, detached, critical of others, competitive, aloof, precise, skilful, picky, overly cerebral with emotions, demanding, self-controlled, caustically witty, dedicated to work, critical, a good delegator, self-sufficient, verbose, diligent, forthright, a perfectionist, impatient, irritable, steady, rational yet feisty, and in possession of an indefatigable resilience and an unwavering belief in yourself and your abilities.
Sun/Moon Harmony Rating ✦ 6 out of 10

♉ With the Moon in TAURUS, Sun in Virgo, you are likely to be ✦ Stable, modest, dependable, cool, calm and collected, deliberate, sensual, greedy, consistent, level-headed, pragmatically intellectual, dedicated, critical, stubborn, dutiful, supportive, self-sacrificing, domestic, routined, unimaginative, staid, materialistic, nature-loving, certainty-seeking, fruitful, loving, self-restrained, Earthy, a craftsperson, diligent, financially savvy, organised, reserved, black-and-white in your thinking, kind, affectionate, in possession of a shrewd business sense, infinitely patient, slow and steady-paced, persevering, enduring, loyal, emotionally placid, nervous yet grounded, flighty yet rooted, devoted, dry-humoured, logical, stoic, faithful, peaceful, capable, resourceful, peace-loving but strong-willed, reliable, realistic, sensible, persistent, and dedicated to working hard for an income and thereby gaining security.
Sun/Moon Harmony Rating ✦ 8 out of 10**

♊ With the Moon in GEMINI, Sun in Virgo, you are likely to be ✦ Changeable, hot and cold, skilful, critical, dissatisfied, fitful, adaptable, intellectually bright, discerning, debonair, cerebral, emotionally versatile, shallow, a jack-of-all-trades, effective, unsympathetic, efficient, perceptive, discriminating, analytical, narrow-minded, observant, applied, prone to worry and over-thinking, clever, rational, inquisitive, an eternal learner, clear-thinking, precise, practically intelligent, pragmatic, objective, able to apply your mind, in possession of mental ingenuity, refined in taste, persuasive, unemotional, mobile, logical, anxious, nervous, self-critical, torn between solitude and social activity, communicative, able to work alone and with others, concise, articulate, alert, unsentimental, and a good reasoner.

Sun/Moon Harmony Rating ✦ 6.5 out of 10

♋ With the Moon in CANCER, Sun in Virgo, you are likely to be ✦ Gentle, sensitive, caring, nourishing to others, tenacious, retiring, emotionally articulate but moody, kind-hearted, dutiful, sentimental, sympathetic, fertile, self-repressed, conscientious, defensive, nervous, tense, principled but flexible, doting, self-reflective, shy, a complainer and whinger, self-critical and self-pitying, easily depleted, easily stuck, reticent, private, logical yet imaginative, poetic, considerate, concerned for the welfare of others, devoted to family, helpful, companionable, protective, giving, withdrawn, a good counsellor, easily hurt, sensual, enduringly loyal, dependable, supportive, reliable, and able to analyse and process your emotions.

Sun/Moon Harmony Rating ✦ 8 out of 10

♌ With the Moon in LEO, Sun in Virgo, you are likely to be ✦ Proud, individualistic, hard-working, artistically refined, aesthetic, honourable, discreet but radiant, emotionally articulate, expressive, verbose, hospitable, dutiful, calm on the surface with a great strength within, self-controlled, gently artistic, quietly generous, warm-hearted, capable, trustworthy, sensually romantic, affectionate, snobbish, gently passionate, conflicted between vanity and modesty, controlling, devoted, patient, comfort-seeking, helpful, encouraging, supportive, skilful, an elitist, noble-minded, and masterful.

Sun/Moon Harmony Rating ✦ 7.5 out of 10

♍ With the Moon in VIRGO, Sun in Virgo, you are likely to be ✦ Judgemental, nervous, hard-working, a thinker and a doer, cool, calm and collected, aloof, critical, studious, a perfectionist, discriminating, methodical, studious, devoted, dedicated, practical, modest, reserved, helpful, focused on health, analytical, discriminating, thoughtful, productive, consistent, supportive, kind, unassuming, caring, rigid, conventional, down-to-Earth, attentive, industrious, constructive, resourceful, efficient, objective, rational, cool-headed, logical, neglectful or unaware of your deeper potential, dutiful, self-critical, scathing, willing to help and do what needs to be done, pragmatic, skilful, reliable, persevering, stable, altruistic, humble, modestly wise, lucid, responsible, poised, and in possession of a good deal of common sense.

Sun/Moon Harmony Rating ✦ 7.5 out of 10

♎ With the Moon in LIBRA, Sun in Virgo, you are likely to be ✦ Harmonious, peace-loving, introverted, aesthetically aware, orderly, aesthetic, pleasant, courteous, polite, elegant, ethereal, sentimental, attractive, artistic, sensual, able to work with principles easily, quietly sociable, refined, graceful, well-balanced, moderate, easy-going, loving of simplicity, charming, a hider of feelings, distanced from your true emotional power, gracious, hospitable, detached, pleasure-seeking, romantic, modest, endearing, delightful, gently persuasive, artistically sensitive, charitable, helpful, cooperative, reasonable, tolerant, a practical idealist, and conflicted between self-reliance and needing others.

Sun/Moon Harmony Rating ✦ 8 out of 10

♏ With the Moon in SCORPIO, Sun in Virgo, you are likely to be ✦ Intense, discriminating, meticulous, substantial, an extreme worker, deeply anxious, single-minded, robust, highly resilient, subjectively responsive, acutely intelligent, tight, pious, scrutinising, passionately dedicated, persistent, committed, repressed emotionally, self-sufficient, charged, astute, concentrated, tightly controlled, serious, unable to relax, resourceful, alternating between being extreme and being modest, highly critical and judgemental, strong-willed, ruthless, sensually passionate, obsessive compulsive, unyielding, sustaining, controlling, shrewd, persevering, thorough, hard-working, penetrative, analytical, secretive, probing, intensely loyal, emotionally stoic, tense, strategic, perceptive, self-reliant, exacting, manipulative, and in possession of a difficult, cool temperament.

Sun/Moon Harmony Rating ✦ 6 out of 10

♐ With the Moon in SAGITTARIUS, Sun in Virgo, you are likely to be ✦ Giving, gregarious, helpful, dutiful, rational but idealistic, versatile, intellectually enthusiastic, restless but controlled, interested in philosophy, spirituality and religion, articulate, philosophical yet logical, broad-minded, moralistic, grounded yet seeking, perceptive, adventurous yet conventional, quick-witted, urbane, a dedicated student and thinker, embracing of novel ideas, honest, reasonable, frank, studious, intelligent, mentally dextrous, prone to preach and boss, a good guide or mentor, distant from your feelings, emotionally nervous, mentally agile, gently optimistic, ardently sensual, gently exuberant, a lover of learning, aspiring, objective, ambitious, broad-minded yet rigid, adaptable, and guided by reason and logic rather than emotion.

Sun/Moon Harmony Rating ✦ 7 out of 10

♑ With the Moon in CAPRICORN, Sun in Virgo, you are likely to be ✦ Dedicated, staunch, disciplined, conscientious, devoted, refined, shrewd, rational, dependable, cynical, down-to-Earth, steadfast, pragmatic, modest, a workaholic, controlled, emotionally repressed, cool, aloof, dictatorial, resourceful, committed, driven to succeed, conventional, ambitious, reserved, pessimistic, withdrawn, polished, methodical, frugal, quietly dignified, realistic, logical, industrious, self-restrained, helpful, organised, productive, efficient, reliable, organised, serious, critical, a perfectionist, tight-fisted, timid, sensible, introverted, understanding of practical applications and wisdom, economical, practical, honourable, uptight, socially rigid, self-contained, and willing to work long and hard to achieve your goals.

Sun/Moon Harmony Rating ✦ 7 out of 10**

♒ With the Moon in AQUARIUS, Sun in Virgo, you are likely to be ✦ Tolerant, objective, contrary, nervous, detached, cool, aloof, discontent, living an unusual lifestyle in some way, paradoxical, attracted to health fads, socially timid, a progressive thinker, dispassionately critical, acutely aware of the human condition, kind, pragmatically helpful, contradictory, quirky, an intellectual, untouched by passions, rational, thoughtful, cool-headed, observant, applied but scattered, a naïve eccentric, philanthropic, dedicated to worthy ideals and causes, well-meaning, open to the unusual, unemotional, helpful, sensible yet rebellious, changeable, dissatisfied, unique, a humanitarian, uncertain, respectful, sceptical, shrewd, conflicted between solitude and social stimulation, realistic, committed to principles, embracing of abstract concepts, analytical, scientific, independent, and devoted to social causes.

Sun/Moon Harmony Rating ✦ 7.5 out of 10

♓ With the Moon in PISCES, Sun in Virgo, you are likely to be ✦ Loving, sympathetic, sensual, caring, able to mix realism with mysticism, insightful, idealistic yet grounded, compassionate, wholesome, a natural counsellor, inspiring, refined, discreetly generous, self-critical, good-natured, gentle, kind, impressionable, affable, inconsistent, pessimistic, unstable, unsure, prone to depression, self-doubting, sentimental, modest, downplaying of own abilities, supportive, a pragmatic poet, able to bring dreams into reality, needy, introverted, withdrawn, despondent, easily discouraged, self-sacrificing, diffident, torn between being impractical and practical, procrastinating, evasive, melancholic, self-pitying, an escapist, sensitive, cleverly intuitive, perceptive, and in possession of an innate love of beauty, art and peace.

Sun/Moon Harmony Rating ✦ 7.5 out of 10

"If your Moon is in Taurus or Capricorn, your Sun and Moon will form what is known in astrology as a trine aspect. This aspect is the easiest, most flowing and harmonious astrological aspect, ensuring that your Sun and Moon, or spirit and soul, are well integrated. With both luminaries in Earth signs, this gives them the best possible degree of complementary energy - a blending of the elements suggests a balanced expression of personality. One drawback of the trine aspect lies in the fact that its easy flow can be too harmonious; if our path is too smooth and difficulties

don't arise to challenge us from time to time, we can often become lazy and complacent, stunting our growth and spiritual evolution. As Earth signs, you share the art of practical application, devotion, rational thinking, logic, a love of beauty and peace, determination, pragmatism, sensibility, conservatism, realism, sensuality, fruitfulness, and a gentle, caring approach to all your relationships and endeavors, but may be staid, rigid, unimaginative, materialistic, slow, lazy, narrow-minded, and lacking in enthusiasm and zest.

LIBRA SUN & MOON COMBINATIONS

♈ With the Moon in ARIES, Sun in Libra, you are likely to be ✦ Conflicted between independence and needing others, diplomatic, sociable, gracefully bold, a rash judge, hospitable, entertaining, influential, convivial, convincing, cheeky, fun-loving, romantic, emotionally naïve, a peace-making crusader, gentle yet impulsive, intriguing, able to make sound judgements, gregarious, the ability to win others over, assertive, temperamental, insensitive, ambitious, considered, polite, charming, avidly intellectual, persuasive, aesthetic, attractive, athletically elegant, respectful of others' opinions, pioneering, original, lively, witty, bright, breezy, an intelligent individualist, and one who has moral integrity.

Sun/Moon Harmony Rating ✦ 8 out of 10

♉ With the Moon in TAURUS, Sun in Libra, you are likely to be ✦ Calm, level-headed, pragmatically intellectual, easy-going, possessive, hedonistic, artistic, creative, aesthetically aware, stylish, affectionate, nurturing, emotionally generous, cooperative, lacking in depth, loving, gullible, considerate, thoughtful, gentle, infinitely patient, slow and steady-paced, tasteful, loving of music and art, indulgent, sociable, emotionally placid, pleasant, faithful, friendly, manipulative, philanthropic, thoughtful, comfort- and pleasure-seeking, impartial, effortlessly charming, a connoisseur, realistic, sensible, prudish, and dedicated to grounding your inspiration and idealism.

Sun/Moon Harmony Rating ✦ 8.5 out of 10

♊ With the Moon in GEMINI, Sun in Libra, you are likely to be ✦ Intellectual, a free spirit and social butterfly, friendly, bright, breezy, conciliatory, emotionally versatile, quick-witted, perceptive, clever, childlike, inspiring, inconsistent, unreliable, stimulating, youthful, questioning, carefree, flirtatious, versatile, articulate, casual, sociable, funny, detached, curious, impulsive, restless, easily bored, flighty, uncommitted, communicative, socially aware, emotionally naïve, entertaining, good with words and ideas, socially gifted, reasonable, clear-minded, emotionally immature, lazy, a wonderful friend, popular, easily swept away, open, likeable, idealistic, squandering of your natural talents, reluctant to face the darker aspects of life, shallow, cunning, a trickster, and ruled almost exclusively by your intellect.

Sun/Moon Harmony Rating ✦ 7.5 out of 10**

♋ With the Moon in CANCER, Sun in Libra, you are likely to be ✦ Harmonious, tactful, sensitive, diplomatic, graceful, loving, poised, nurturing, emotional, able to blend emotions with intellect, intuitive, aesthetic, tasteful, elegant, affectionate, compassionate, quietly charming, caring, tender, focused on domestic harmony, refined, exquisitely composed, intimate, devoted, a peacemaker, attached, dependent, sharing, sympathetic, understanding, artistically imaginative, peaceful, finicky, ethereal, vulnerable, intelligently kind, helpful, companionable, manipulative, subjective, clingy, socially timid but sociable, courteous, understatedly stylish, affable, pleasant, over-romanticising, easily unbalanced, supportive of others, and concerned for others.

Sun/Moon Harmony Rating ✦ 8 out of 10

♌ With the Moon in LEO, Sun in Libra, you are likely to be ✦
Popular, gracious, vacillating, chivalrous, vain, relationship-seeking, likable, companionable, artistically inspired, desiring to uplift and encourage others, diplomatic, glamorous, elegant, pleasure-seeking, commanding, leisurely, individualistic but sociable, optimistic, indecisive, dependent on others for your wellbeing and self-confidence, gracefully dramatic, artistic, generous, subtly passionate, radiant, enthusiastic, romantic, open, easily flattered, charismatic, charming, self-indulgent, hedonistic, inclined to get carried away by romance and idealism, eager for praise, friendly, expressive, reliant on others' admiration, self-centred, intelligently creative, addicted to love, warm, engaging, playful, tasteful, refined, luxury-loving, demonstrative, creatively imaginative, vivacious, big-hearted, aesthetically aware, civilised, a visionary, trusting, ardent, affectionate, a gentle wit, noble, and appealing to others.

Sun/Moon Harmony Rating ✦ 8 out of 10

♍ With the Moon in VIRGO, Sun in Libra, you are likely to be ✦
Intelligent, judgemental, courteous, devoted to helping others, detached, focused on justice and fairness, aloof, calm and collected, refined, loving of purity and simplicity, finicky, eminently civilised, self-critical, clever, indecisive yet discerning, cooperative, discriminating, independent, understatedly witty, rational, reasonable, trying to achieve emotional balance, civilised, sensual, fussy, tasteful, prudish, scathing (of) crudeness, methodical, nit-picking, studious, gentle, kind, helpful, mentally alert, unassuming, efficient but often procrastinating, caring, understated, quality-seeking, coolly reserved, socially conventional, polite, objectively rational, cool-headed, altruistic, genuinely kind, bright, and devoted to both ideas and ideals.

Sun/Moon Harmony Rating ✦ 6 out of 10

♎ With the Moon in LIBRA, Sun in Libra, you are likely to be ✦
Sociable, idealistic, co-dependent, elegant, indecisive, charming, flirtatious, refined, well-balanced, easy-going, moderate, easy-going, sharing, loving, manipulative, affectionate, popular, inspired, graceful, approachable, accessible, civilised, sharing, gracious, cooperative, hospitable, hedonistic, romantic, observant, loving of people, delightful, persuasive, artistically sensitive, naïve, and conflicted between independence and needing others.

Sun/Moon Harmony Rating ✦ 8 out of 10

♏ With the Moon in SCORPIO, Sun in Libra, you are likely to be ✦ Sociable, intense, intriguing, self-possessed, astutely minded, artistically charged, lustful, sensitive, promiscuous, highly charged, magnetic, possessive of others, moody, emotionally intelligent, intuitive, easily unbalanced, keenly insightful, investigative, strongly focused on justice, ethereally mysterious, socially regenerative, in possession of strong desires, prone to temptation, conflicted between extreme and moderate behaviours, strong-willed, self-judging, appealing, socially passionate, broody, suspicious, paranoid, resourceful, resilient, secretive, manipulative, passionate yet dispassionate, emotionally influential and charismatic, courageous, incisive, a good observer, and acutely perceptive.

Sun/Moon Harmony Rating ✦ 7 out of 10

♐ With the Moon in SAGITTARIUS, Sun in Libra, you are likely to be ✦ Persuasive, eager to please others, hopeful, expressive, loving of life, joyful, generous, adventurous, well-received, calm yet restless, ardent but flighty, enthusiastic, independent, open, idealistic, an intellectual philosophiser, objective, spirited, a believer, romantic, impatient with restrictions of daily life, wise, indecisive, socially charged, intellectual, interested, engaged, one who brings out the best in others, engaging, sociable, inquisitive, easy-going, inspiring, a traveller, an avid student of life, clever, witty, charming, warm, distant from your feelings, emotionally reckless, a free spirit, far-sighted, positive, knowledgeable, good-humoured, self-promoting, emotionally naïve, optimistic, inspiring, aspiring, gregarious, socially caring, direct but courteous, broad-minded, expansive, trusting, verbose, emotionally philosophical, and guided by reason rather than emotion.

Sun/Moon Harmony Rating ✦ 8.5 out of 10

♑ With the Moon in CAPRICORN, Sun in Libra, you are likely to be ✦
An introverted people-liker, purposeful, dependable, persuasive, Earthy yet ethereal, fair, rational, courteous, sophisticated, ambitious, graceful, sensual, resourceful, committed, aloof, distant from your feelings, dutiful, self-interested yet cooperative, tidy, pragmatic, tasteful, orderly, tactful, well-mannered, reserved, cool, gentle, wise, kind-hearted, strategic, skilful at managing people, sensitive to social nuances, responsible, dedicated to those you love, shrewd, efficient and effortless, opportunistic, manipulative, controlling, reliable, socially serious, sensible, materialistic, hedonistic, reliant on the physical senses for pleasure, understanding of practical applications and wisdom, personally honourable, adhering to morals, torn between solitude and sociability, uptight, self-contained, aware of human relationships, and sardonically humorous.

Sun/Moon Harmony Rating ✦ 7 out of 10

♒ With the Moon in AQUARIUS, Sun in Libra, you are likely to be ✦
Frank, easy-going, original, tolerant, friendly, independent yet dependent, torn between freedom and needing others, sociable, idealistic, emotionally detached, gracefully eccentric, one with unconventional tastes, glamorously aloof, cool, mysterious, paradoxical, intriguing, imaginative, thoughtful, humane, sympathetic, honest, unassuming, forward-moving, inventive, impersonal in relationships, objective, clear-headed, observant, aware of the human condition, progressive, scientifically and intellectually oriented, living an unusual lifestyle in some way, well-meaning, open to the unusual, emotionally naïve, trusting, rational, outgoing, communicative, gracefully anarchistic, truth-seeking, receptive, artistically refined, principled, just, fair, romanticising of others, socially conscious, open to new ideas, approachable, beauty-focused, over-identifying with causes and people, torn between freedom and commitment in relationships, a people-lover, unorthodox, impractical, scatterbrained, loyal, a humanitarian, committed to your ideals, focused on both Universal and the personal realms of experience, lazy, naïve, ineffectual, a dreamer, blind to your dependence on others, and potentially a genius.

Sun/Moon Harmony Rating ✦ 8 out of 10**

♓ With the Moon in PISCES, Sun in Libra, you are likely to be ✦ Intuitive, socially graceful, quietly charming, highly imaginative, able to blend rationality and mysticism, confused, ethereal, gullible, impractical, spiritual, deeply idealistic, co-dependent, a chaser of spiritual rainbows, idolising of others, relationship-oriented, cooperative, helpful, adaptable, kind-hearted, good-natured, intriguing, mysterious, too trusting, friendly, accessible, approachable, emotional, apt to go into flights of fancy, sentimental, accepting, forgiving, understanding, vulnerable, a thinker and a poet, insightful, generous, idle, lazy, reflective, manipulative, receptive, creative, reverent, empathetic, compassionate, a humanitarian, prone to drifting and wasting time in daydreams, impressionable, idealistic but easily swayed, evasive, sensitive, psychic, perceptive, emotionally intelligent, ruled by your feelings, able to mix and work with all types of people, aware of the needs of others, artistic, wistful, inconstant, changeable, a dreamy romantic, loving, moody, involved, wishy-washy, helpful, and lacking in conviction.

Sun/Moon Harmony Rating ✦ 8 out of 10

If your Moon is in Gemini or Aquarius, your Sun and Moon will form what is known in astrology as a trine aspect. This aspect is the easiest, most flowing and harmonious astrological aspect, ensuring that your Sun and Moon, or spirit and soul, are well integrated. With both luminaries in Air signs, this gives them the best possible degree of complementary energy - a blending of the elements suggests a balanced expression of personality. One drawback of the trine aspect lies in the fact that its easy flow can be too harmonious; if our path is too smooth and difficulties don't arise to challenge us from time to time, we can often become lazy and complacent, stunting our growth and spiritual evolution. As Air signs, you share the art of sociability, are highly idealistic, affable, romantic, possess a good intellect, have a love of truth and beauty, are reasonable, broad-minded, independent but devoted to your ideals, have an artistic sensitivity, are tolerant, understanding, civilised and dignified, and have avant-garde tastes, but may be detached, cool, head over heart-oriented, and restless.

SCORPIO SUN & MOON COMBINATIONS

♈ With the Moon in ARIES, Sun in Scorpio, you are likely to be ✦ Astute, robust, intense, self-preserving, proud, incisive, persuasive, arrogant, sharp, alert, penetrative, unable to relax, resilient, a formidable enemy, acutely aware, brash, intensely purposeful, unwilling to compromise, suspicious, motivated, powerful, sarcastic, self-protective, charismatic, torn between being light-hearted and dark, volatile, enthusiastic, eager, extreme, loyal, dedicated, adventurous, hot-tempered, courageous, magnetic, moody, intolerant, a self-starter, impatient yet circumspect, passionate, highly-sexed, assertive, unyielding, temperamental, insensitive, reckless, destructive, a powerful leader, tenacious, wilful, ambitious, self-reliant, energetic, emotionally bold, self-confident, acid-tongued, opinionated, bossy, pioneering, witty, bright, passive-aggressive, impulsive, compulsive, charismatic, charming, strategic, and a strong individualist.

Sun/Moon Harmony Rating ✦ 6.5 out of 10

♉ With the Moon in TAURUS, Sun in Scorpio, you are likely to be ✦ Possessive, firm, stubborn, fixed, unyielding, solid, consistent, materialistic, gentle yet volatile, jealous, persevering, loyal, motivated, steady-paced but intense, tenacious, broody, deeply sensual, controlling, contained, inflexible, unmovable, vindictive, emotionally powerful, explosive, inward, devoted, stoic, faithful, capable, insightful, determined, unforgiving, in possession of a smouldering passion, shrewd, proud, committed, all-or-nothing, resourceful, dependable, peace-loving but strong-willed, persistent, and unwaveringly dedicated.

Sun/Moon Harmony Rating ✦ 7.5 out of 10

♊ With the Moon in GEMINI, Sun in Scorpio, you are likely to be ✦ Torn between freedom and containment, cunning, changeable, an intense social presence, intensely friendly but broody, lucid, fascinating, spirited, curious, psychologically understanding, satirical, clever, socially mysterious, articulate, paradoxical, profound, sharp-witted, perceptive, clever, manipulative, likely to suffer from foot in mouth syndrome, self-serving, stimulating, able to interpret others' motives, anxious, flexible yet stubborn, curious, contradictory, emotionally destructive, experimental, vivid, passionate yet detached, insightful, penetrative, probing, gossipy, rumour-spreading, restless, nervous, creative, strongly aware, gifted, loyal, idealistic, emotionally intellectual, and always on a deep inner quest.

Sun/Moon Harmony Rating ✦ 6.5 out of 10

♋ With the Moon in CANCER, Sun in Scorpio, you are likely to be ✦ Deeply sensitive, easily hurt, shrewd, intuitive, security- and survival-oriented, sentimental, emotional, deep, strong, compassionate, intense, hidden, tough yet tender, nurturing, demanding, imaginative, feelings-based, loyal, possessive, unable to let go of the past, satirical, dependent, secretive, nostalgic, perceptive, vengeful, insightful, passionately committed, resilient, manipulative, probing, determined, clingy, instinctive, resourceful, fanatical, sincere, supportive, attentive, intensely guarded, poetic, moody and broody, devoted to family, self-protective, needy, suspicious, past-dwelling, jealous, smothering, occasionally moved to emotional volatility

Sun/Moon Harmony Rating ✦ 7 out of 10**

♌ With the Moon in LEO, Sun in Scorpio, you are likely to ✦
Fearless, courageous, all-or-nothing, vain, intolerant, broody, ambitious, prone to tantrums, sulky, whole-hearted, forthright, proud, egocentric, individualistic, feisty on the surface with a great strength within, prone to emotional outbursts, ardent, wilful, ruthless, dramatic, driven by sex, money and power, a prima donna, flamboyant, extreme, charismatic, passionate, magnetic, pompous, enthusiastic, inflated, uncompromising, determined, pursuing of excellence, dictatorial, powerful, romantic, highly-charged, intense, bossy, powerful, extroverted, bold, driven, fiercely loyal, anarchistic, direct, vain, stubborn, strong, upfront yet secretive, tense, inspiring, purposeful, controlling, emotionally expressive, theatrical, deeply aware of social nuances, ambitious, despotic, self-centred, self-reliant, deeply creative, affectionate and demonstrative.

Sun/Moon Harmony Rating ✦ 7.5 out of 10

♍ With the Moon in VIRGO, Sun in Scorpio, you are likely to be ✦
Robust, fussy, discriminating, efficient, puritanical, intelligent, judgemental, highly critical, shrewd, an emotional extremist, methodical, calculating, a devoted researcher, helpful, cool, serious, intense, brooding, prone to self-criticism, intense, agile, mentally alert, rigid, compulsive, a worrier, reserved, conventional, uptight, tense, fearful, motivated, hard-working, clear-thinking, quietly dedicated, conscientious, pedantic, difficult, organised, a relentless perfectionist, analytical, witty, forceful yet modest, self-effacing, anxious, logical, cautious, cutting, accurate, healing, 'entitled', narrow-minded, strategic, principled, productive, obsessive, self-controlled and in possession of an excellent intellect.

Sun/Moon Harmony Rating ✦ 6.5 out of 10

♎ With the Moon in LIBRA, Sun in Scorpio, you are likely to be ✦
Introverted but sociable, instinctively compromising, vivid, expressive, keen, refined, paradoxical, affectionate, perceptive, charming, sensual, a commanding presence, powerful, a hider of feelings, charming, magnetically sociable, innately just, distanced from your true emotional power, hedonistic, incisive, romantic, passionate, cooperative yet demanding, acutely observant, naughty but nice, eloquent, co-dependent, honourable, engaging, suave, able to perceive feelings, probing of others, relationship-oriented, witty, humorous, able to see the darker side of human nature, intense and delightful at the same time, persuasive, artistically sensitive, abstract, conflicted, and in possession of expensive tastes.

Sun/Moon Harmony Rating ✦ 8.5 out of 10

♏ With the Moon in SCORPIO, Sun in Scorpio, you are likely to be ✦
Intense, compelling, loyal, emotional, powerful, self-possessed, devoted, enduring, wary, driven, self-motivated, deep, black and white, shrewd, forceful, highly charged, obsessive, sarcastic, relentless, introspective, controlled, focused, channelled, dictatorial, extreme, possessive, cynical, keenly insightful, investigative, unbending, strong-willed, passionate, unyielding, resourceful, vengeful, resilient, controlling, stubborn, persevering, unapologetic, thorough, psychologically penetrative, secretive, courageous, perceptive, self-reliant, dogmatic, stern, exacting, ruthless, compulsive, manipulative, and emotionally powerful.

Sun/Moon Harmony Rating ✦ 6 out of 10

♐ With the Moon in SAGITTARIUS, Sun in Scorpio, you are likely to be ✦
Passionate, keen, a stern judge, uncompromising, emotionally reckless, eager, adventurous, fascinating, self-sufficient, intuitive, impatient, restless, dictatorial and preaching, forceful, dramatic, focused, unshakable, persuasive, investigative, generous, commanding, intellectually discerning, ardent, outspoken, unaware of the subtleties of social interaction, intensely inquisitive, feisty, extreme, compulsive, unbreakable, expansive, a passionate crusader, fixated, vital, excessive, spirited, probing, questing, powerful, witty, far-sighted, deeply philosophical, brooding yet optimistic, self-preserving, a voracious student, inspiring, outrageous, aspiring, socially intense, articulate, sharp, in possession of strong moral integrity, and often torn between reason and emotion.

Sun/Moon Harmony Rating ✦ 7.5 out of 10

♑ With the Moon in CAPRICORN, Sun in Scorpio, you are likely to be ✦ Cautious, mistrustful, dependable, steadfast, resourceful, effective, tough, tenacious, self-demanding, judgemental, enigmatic, cynical, quietly powerful, calculating, painstaking, committed, unbending, ambitious, robust, critical, driven to succeed, self-righteous, persevering, defensive, unyielding, determined, withdrawn, all-or-nothing, broody, cool, resilient, courageous, efficient, tight-fisted, deeply wise, dry-witted, harsh, bitter, resentful, disciplined, earnest, sombre, authoritative, aware, shrewd, organised, loyal, darkly intense, direct, strong-willed, down-to-Earth, satirical, penetrative, complex, serious, introverted, personally honourable, ruthless, overly-strict on self and others, hard-working, inflexible, fearless, uptight, socially rigid, self-contained.

Sun/Moon Harmony Rating ✦ 7.5 out of 10

♒ With the Moon in AQUARIUS, Sun in Scorpio, you are likely to be ✦ Stubborn, independent, complex, intense, eccentric, passionately dispassionate, exacting, powerfully intellectual, broody, contrary, unruly, frustrated, extreme, difficult, proud, unconventional, tenacious, cool, sharp, aloof, paradoxical, imaginative, scrutinising, original, hard to reach, rebellious, hot and cold, indifferent yet interested, controlled, insistent on the truth, articulate, fussy, discerning, clear-headed, focused, highly observant, radical, wilful, principled but intolerant, self-reflecting, magnetic, acutely aware of the human experience, progressive, scientifically investigative, living an unusual lifestyle in some way, open to the unusual and darker aspects of life, interested in occult matters, enigmatic, isolated, emotionally intense, over-identifying with causes, unorthodox, idealistic, loyal, strongly humanitarian, courageous and committed to your ideals, a law unto yourself, and in possession of a deep sense of belief in human potential.

Sun/Moon Harmony Rating ✦ 6 out of 10

♓ With the Moon in PISCES, Sun in Scorpio, you are likely to be ✦ Highly imaginative, mystical, interested in occult subjects, intuitive, reflective, secretive, lacking boundaries, complex yet naïve, intriguing, a natural healer, emotionally intense, lurid, self-indulgent, insightful, telepathic, lacking in objectivity, sensitive, psychic, sharply perceptive, conflicted between trust and mistrust, prone to addictions or self-destruction, emotional, ruled by your feelings, prone to despair, deeply sentimental, an escapist, yearning, understanding, elusive, acutely aware of others' suffering, vulnerable, a poet, altruistic, psychologically insightful, receptive, creative, devoted to loved ones, mysterious, empathetic, impressionable yet strong, impractical, evasive, and acutely aware of the needs of others.

Sun/Moon Harmony Rating ✦ 8 out of 10**

*If your Moon is in Cancer or Pisces, your Sun and Moon will form what is known in astrology as a trine aspect. This aspect is the easiest, most flowing and harmonious astrological aspect, ensuring that your Sun and Moon, or spirit and soul, are well integrated. With both luminaries in Water signs, this gives them the best possible degree of complementary energy - a blending of the elements suggests a balanced expression of personality. One drawback of the trine aspect lies in the fact that its easy flow can be too harmonious; if our path is too smooth and difficulties don't arise to challenge us from time to time, we can often become lazy and complacent, stunting our growth and spiritual evolution. As Water signs, you share the art of sensitivity, creativity, intrigue, compassion, a nurturing instinct, poetry, understanding, spirituality, a deep need for connection and merging with others, but may be overly sensitive, illogical, clingy, impractical, too emotional, irrational, dependent, manipulative, and elusive.

SAGITTARIUS SUN & MOON COMBINATIONS

♈ With the Moon in ARIES, Sun in Sagittarius, you are likely to ✦ Heroic, passionate, outspoken, pioneering, original, arrogant, extroverted, optimistic, egocentric, showy, forthright, a big talker, expressive, fearless, self-assured, courageous, bold, restless, impatient, on the go, adventurous, direct, active, blunt but sincere, emotionally naïve, self-interested, impulsive, impractical, progressive, alert, childish, impetuous, enthusiastic, independent, genuine, innocently charming, hopeful, emotionally demanding, warm, generous, exaggerating, competitive, expansive, sociable, infectiously enthusiastic, unsubtle, honest, explorative, assertive, confident, insensitive, buoyant, energetic, driven to succeed, bossy, popular, domineering, emotionally reckless, forward-looking, lively, witty, frank, bright, an individualist, and possess a touchy ego and moral integrity, as well as being a maverick with a crusading temperament.

Sun/Moon Harmony Rating ✦ 7.5 out of 10**

♉ With the Moon in TAURUS, Sun in Sagittarius, you are likely to ✦ Conflicted between freedom and foundation, driven, a down-to-Earth dreamer, restrainedly idealistic, argumentative, materialistic, extravagant, luxury-loving, expansive, pleasure-seeking, a connoisseur, easy-going, romantic, a modestly passionate learner, big-hearted, appreciative, seductive, seeking of the good life, calm but expansive, approachable, affable, a slave to your expensive tastes, in possession of entrenched beliefs, unshakable, measuredly optimistic, sensitive to beauty and philosophy, artistic, creative, sexy, sensual, steadily aspiring, tenacious, physically and mentally robust, devoted yet flighty, restless yet grounded, gently charming, faithful, bossy, friendly, warm-hearted, generous, productive, a practical philosopher, enthusiastic about making money, an entrepreneur, ambitious, strong-willed, philanthropic, in possession of a strong sense of self, and dedicated to activating your inspired ideas in the real, material world.

Sun/Moon Harmony Rating ✦ 6.5 out of 10

♊ With the Moon in GEMINI, Sun in Sagittarius, you are likely to be ✦ Persuasive, charming, sociable, witty, inquisitive, blunt, mentally dextrous, emotionally agile, flexible, deft, cheeky, a free spirit, changeable, non-committal, philosophical yet superficial, friendly, bright, breezy, versatile, adaptable, quick, careless, stimulating, flippant, vital, perceptive, clever, inspiring, curious, childlike, full of wonder and awe, emotionally impulsive, vivacious, zany, inconsistent, expressive, restless, easily bored, active, inspired, a live wire, unsubtle, direct, humorous, funny, communicative, socially aware, unsentimental, naïve, immature, irresponsible, intellectually capable, unreliable, zestful, an opportunist, cunning, funny, easily swept away by ideas and concepts, open towards and perceptive of new ideas, idealistic, intellectual, fun-loving, squandering of your natural talents, too busy to deal with feelings, scattered, with too many irons in the fire, and in possession of the gift of the gab and a sunny, breezy and light-hearted disposition.

Sun/Moon Harmony Rating ✦ 8 out of 10

♋ With the Moon in CANCER, Sun in Sagittarius, you are likely to be ✦ Sensitive, affable, temperamental, friendly but private, uplifting, an enthusiastic supporter of others, clannish, devoted, romantic, a prophetic visionary, over-extended, understatedly brilliant, in possession of pizzazz and a sense of theatrics, charming, affectionate, sensual, demonstrative, inspired to help others, changeable, inconsistent, moody, adaptable, torn between security and freedom, deeply feeling, emotionally charged, richly imaginative, genuinely caring, boundlessly hopeful, indirectly self-assertive, intuitive, idealistic, emotionally expressive, dramatic, passionate about family, subtly persuasive, tuned into others, insightful, helpful, giving, compassionate, kind-hearted, generous, creative, kind, gentle-spirited, helpful, companionable, a sensitive individualist, emotionally nurturing, defensive, ruled equally by your mind and your heart, and occasionally moved to dramatic outbursts which may undermine your greatest talents and achievements.

Sun/Moon Harmony Rating ✦ 8 out of 10

♌ With the Moon in LEO, Sun in Sagittarius, you are likely to be ✦ Pompous, radiant, vain, noble, a gambler, involved, overbearing, pure-of-heart, inflated, gregarious, flamboyant, egotistical, proud, independent, warm-hearted, individualistic, chivalrous, autocratic, impatient, sociable, playful, dramatic, fearless, bold, artistic, generous to a fault, extravagant, charismatic, in love with love, passionate, an effective leader, zestful, vital, uplifting, immediate, sulky, childish, demanding, bossy, enthusiastic, active, adventurous, friendly, a good leader, enthusiastically romantic, explorative, open, powerful, extroverted, self-interested, honest, inclined to get carried away by drama and fun, idealistic, direct, controlling, expressive, ambitious, grandiose, theatrical, emotionally warm, luxury-loving, demonstrative, expressive, stylish, creatively imaginative, optimistic, larger than life, honourable, and able to inspire and uplift others with your vitality and radiance.

Sun/Moon Harmony Rating ✦ 7.5 out of 10**

♍ With the Moon in VIRGO, Sun in Sagittarius, you are likely to be ✦ A curious mixture of devotion to obligations and to freedom, intelligent, reasonable, just, hot and cold, rapport-seeking, restless yet dutiful, socially concerned, judgemental, bold but cautious, clever, sharp-witted, logical, intellectually precise and discerning, able to convey ideas easily, objective, discriminating, genuine, an intellectual perfectionist, snobby, cavalier yet careful, able to categorise knowledge, quietly charming, uncomfortable with emotions, pedantic, boldly dogmatic, morally sound, humorously tactful, academic, nervous, highly strung, striving, a pragmatic philosophiser, studious, an avid learner, outspoken yet reserved, bossy yet diffident, helpful, generous, serious, academic, kind-hearted, genuinely caring, mentally alert, efficient, mentally dextrous, straightforward, adaptable, quietly passionate, motivated, intolerant of others' weaknesses, analytical, critical, altruistic, conscientious, effective, self-disciplined, bright, devoted to ideals, dry-witted, zestful yet uptight, and able to dedicate all your efforts into something worthwhile.

Sun/Moon Harmony Rating ✦ 6 out of 10

♎ With the Moon in LIBRA, Sun in Sagittarius, you are likely to be ✦ Stylish, charming, sociable, refined, easy-going, likeable, clever, effervescent, lively, classy, extravagant, intellectually precocious, gregarious, able to see life from endlessly new vantage points, affectionate, confident but indecisive, convivial, amorous, gracious, warmly sincere, positive, observant, socially aware, popular, approachable, ethereal and spirited, courteous, eager for life, tolerant, ingenious, chivalrous, accessible, civilised, hospitable, hedonistic, interested in others, romantically idealistic, endearing, loving of people, colourfully persuasive, procrastinating, outgoing, a generous spirit, prophetic, artistic, creative, gracefully enthusiastic, flirtatious, inspiring, hopeful, vain, entertaining, emotionally naïve, a philosopher, a maverick but a seeker of justice, and conflicted between independence and needing others.

Sun/Moon Harmony Rating ✦ 8.5 out of 10

♏ With the Moon in SCORPIO, Sun in Sagittarius, you are likely to ✦ Confident, intense, sociable, judicial and exacting, vivid, feisty, satirical, keenly instinctive, keen to acquire self-knowledge, volatile, magnetic, highly motivated, self-dramatising, socially powerful, forceful, blunt, intelligent, scrutinising, questioning, ambitious, highly charged, extreme, active, aggressively optimistic, over-zealous, undeterred, morally intense, pushy, keenly insightful, philosophical, investigative, narcissistic, fanatical, self-destructive, a troublemaker when bored, insatiable, strong-willed, dominating, passionate, unyielding, purposeful, sharp, over-indulgent, highly sexed, seductive, overbearing, extremely resilient, persuasive, charismatic, devoted to truth at any cost, fiercely independent, penetrative, emotionally expressive, courageously dedicated, compulsive, perceptive, self-reliant, exacting, manipulative, possess an unshakeable belief in yourself and others' individual worth, and in possession of a strong sense of self and personal integrity.

Sun/Moon Harmony Rating ✦ 7 out of 10

♐ With the Moon in SAGITTARIUS, Sun in Sagittarius, you are likely to be ✦ Big-hearted, warm, all-embracing, entertaining, wise-cracking, restless, a perennial student of life, noble, a wanderer, frank, tolerant, talkative, eager, impatient, gregarious, feisty, broad-minded, fiercely independent, sincere, dazzling, outdoorsy, idealistic, explorative, an avid traveller, honest, adventurous, impatient with petty details and restrictions, principled, moralistic, full of faith, benevolent, adverse to limitations, sloppy, irresponsible, a visionary, self-confident, outspoken, prone to preach, loving of a challenge, far-sighted, insensitive, blunt, a daredevil, rash, inquisitive, self-assured, zestful, emotionally reckless, a free spirit, in possession of a keen sense of humour, extravagant, careless, contagiously optimistic, inspiring, outrageous, aspiring, trusting, naïve, expansive, verbose, philosophical, freedom-seeking, and have an intense moral certainty, residing in the realm of limitless possibilities and being guided by reason rather than emotion.

Sun/Moon Harmony Rating ✦ 7 out of 10

♑ With the Moon in CAPRICORN, Sun in Sagittarius, you are likely to be ✦ Facile yet profound, verbose, independent, steadfast, broad-minded, ambitious, dogmatically blunt, opportunistic, power-grabbing, driven, reasonable, moralistic, rational, logical, articulated, detached, realistic, pragmatically philosophical, a practical dreamer, tough-minded, forceful, aggressive, assertive, delightfully witty, sensual, ardent, enterprising, astute, blunt, overpowering, committed to worthy causes, driven to succeed, unstoppable, unemotional, ruled by reason and logic, charged, intense, dressed for success, profoundly wise, efficient, personally honourable, bold, fearless, socially uptight, sardonically humorous, and in possession of an overall attitude of 'shoot for the stars' - while remaining firmly planted in the Earth at the same time.

Sun/Moon Harmony Rating ✦ 7.5 out of 10

♒ With the Moon in AQUARIUS, Sun in Sagittarius, you are likely to be ✦ Sharp-witted, a nutty professor, a mad scientist, mentally agile, independent, freedom-seeking, philanthropic, eccentric, a broad-minded humanitarian, intellectual, restless, a people person, globally socially aware, incisive, unrealistic, gregarious, a high-minded genius, full of bright ideas, congenial, sociable, friendly, tolerant, extroverted, academic, shocking, highly idealistic, emotionally detached, unconventional, a revolutionary, loquacious, a social activist, unpredictable, evasive, paradoxical, unconventional, honest, original, forward-moving, inventive, impersonal in relationships, clear-headed, charismatic, a social visionary, a truth-seeker, impatient with practical details, irresponsible, absent-minded, highly observant, acutely aware of the human condition, progressive, scientifically oriented, prophetic, objective, living an unusual lifestyle in some way, out of touch, abstract, open to the unusual, emotionally naïve, blunt and insensitive when comparing people with your ideals, freedom-loving, unorthodox, idealistic, impractical, loyal, exceptionally individual, socially conscious, committed to your ideals, a law unto yourself, in possession of an eternal sense of hope and belief in others, and interested in making friends right across the fascinating broad spectrum of human viewpoints.

Sun/Moon Harmony Rating ✦ 9 out of 10

♓ With the Moon in PISCES, Sun in Sagittarius, you are likely to be ✦ Deeply idealistic, creative, unassuming, imaginative, easily swept away, giving, warm, intuitive, romantic, emotionally expressive, prophetic, insightful, perceptive, enthusiastically mystical, enriching to others, wistful, lacking in focus and discrimination, trusting, naïve, a chaser of spiritual rainbows, philosophical, elusive, receptive, sociable yet withdrawn, procrastinating, good-natured, hearty, intriguing, friendly, emotional, full of faith, fervent, sentimental, far-sighted but dreamy, impulsive, careless, tolerant, accepting, irresponsible, understanding, independent but vulnerable, a keen poet, altruistic, a visionary, generous, receptive, artistic, reverent, empathetic, impressionable, innocent, easily swayed, gullible, impractical, evasive, emotionally intelligent, adaptable, adverse to limitations and boundaries, dramatic, hopeful, able to mix and work with all types of people, aware of the needs of others, and in possession of a refreshing philosophy of life.

Sun/Moon Harmony Rating ✦ 9 out of 10

**If your Moon is in Aries or Leo, your Sun and Moon will form what is known in astrology as a trine aspect. This aspect is the easiest, most flowing and harmonious astrological aspect, ensuring that your Sun and Moon, or spirit and soul, are well integrated. With both luminaries in Fire signs, this gives them the best possible degree of complementary energy - a blending of the elements suggests a balanced expression of personality. One drawback of the trine aspect lies in the fact that its easy flow can be too harmonious; if our path is too smooth and difficulties don't arise to challenge us from time to time, we can often become lazy and complacent, stunting our growth and spiritual evolution. As Fire signs, you share the art of vitality, zest, enthusiasm, broad-mindedness, affability, idealism, independence, drive, ambition, force, affection, warm-heartedness, generosity, sociability, and have extravagant tastes, but may be temperamental, dramatic, overbearing, egocentric, restless, bossy, insensitive, careless, arrogant, and self-centred.

CAPRICORN SUN & MOON COMBINATIONS

♈ With the Moon in ARIES, Sun in Capricorn, you are likely to be ◆ Dutiful, persistent, a sore loser, wilful, ambitious, self-interested, purposeful, quick-thinking and acting, enterprising, shrewd, self-motivated, pioneering, adventurous yet grounded, impatient with others' shortcomings, moody and temperamental, a realist, eager to get ahead, action-oriented, successful, powerful, vital, robust, zealous, strong, entitled, competitive, able to combine fun with wisdom to good effect, pragmatic, resourceful, meticulous, commanding, an astute thinker, honest, able to blend realism with idealism, dictatorial, professional, impressive, a workaholic, bossy, authoritarian, detached, entrepreneurial, self-disciplined, recognition-seeking, precise, inspired, skilful, demanding, self-controlled, caustically witty, dedicated to winning at all costs, self-important, a great leader, a good delegator, easily enthused, self-sufficient, diligent, forthright, a perfectionist, impatient, irritable, steady, rational yet feisty, in possession of an indefatigable resilience, and able to ground your idealism.

Sun/Moon Harmony Rating ◆ 7 out of 10

♉ With the Moon in TAURUS, Sun in Capricorn, you are likely to be ✦ Solid, possessive, stable, caring, dependable, cool, calm and collected, careful, deliberate, deeply sensual, greedy, consistent, dedicated, cynical, ambitious, stubborn, conscientious, dutiful, supportive, self-sacrificing, a staunch supporter of the status quo, dignified, graceful, cautious, domestic, routined, unimaginative, staid, materialistic, nature-loving, security-seeking, fruitful, self-restrained, down-to-Earth, diligent, financially savvy, organised, reserved, affectionate, in possession of a shrewd business sense, infinitely patient, slow and steady-paced, persevering, enduring, loyal, devoted, logical, stoic, faithful, peaceful, capable, resourceful, realistic, sensible, persistent, and dedicated to working hard for a substantial income to ensure security.

Sun/Moon Harmony Rating ✦ 8 out of 10**

♊ With the Moon in GEMINI, Sun in Capricorn, you are likely to be ✦ Intelligent, clever, cunning, manipulative, a craftsperson, skilful, critical, analytical, astute, adaptable, independent, resourceful, bright, discerning, articulate, debonair, cerebral, emotionally conventional, detached, cool, conflicted between conservatism and having fun, a jack-of-all-trades and master-of-all, shrewd, polished, decisive, organised yet scattered, talented, quick, efficient, perceptive, communicative, discriminating, observant, applied, able to balance work and play, rational, nimble, clear-thinking, precise, practically intelligent, pragmatic and straightforward, objective, able to apply your mind to anything, nervous, in possession of mental ingenuity, refined in taste, persuasive, unemotional, upwardly mobile, logical, concise, alert, unsentimental, and able to reason.

Sun/Moon Harmony Rating ✦ 8 out of 10

♋ With the Moon in CANCER, Sun in Capricorn, you are likely to be ✦ Tough but tender, gentle, devoted, caring, retiring, emotionally repressed, cynical, anxious, sacrificing, moody, dependable, sensitive, nourishing, timid yet tenacious, over-sensitivity, practical yet emotional, dutiful, sentimental, compassionate, private, conscientious, defensive, courteous, deeply sensual, enduringly loyal, tense, reliable, virtuous, prudish, doting, self-reflective, a complainer and whinger, pessimistic, prone to depression, self-critical and self-pitying, reticent, withdrawn, discerning, considerate, concerned for the welfare of others, helpful, protective, a good wise counsellor, supportive, and able to analyse and process your emotions.

Sun/Moon Harmony Rating ✦ 7.5 out of 10

♌ With the Moon in LEO, Sun in Capricorn, you are likely to be ✦ Artistically refined, able to balance work and play, aesthetic, helpful, grounded but buoyant, understatedly charming, honourable, honest, proud yet humble, individualistic, wilful, discreet but radiant, expressive, vibrant, forceful, hospitable, a good host, self-centred, calm on the surface with a great strength within, self-controlled, gently artistic, dignified, bossy, in possession of a down-to-Earth zest, romantic but sceptical, quietly generous, gentle and warm-hearted, capable, trustworthy, sensually romantic, quality-seeking, affectionate, accomplished, recognition-seeking, snobbish, gently passionate, conflicted between vanity and modesty, praise-seeking, driven, a good leader and organiser, dedicated to excellent, controlling, dedicated, patient, pleasure-seeking, sensually indulgent, encouraging, supportive, skilful, an elitist, noble-minded, masterful, and high standards-oriented.

Sun/Moon Harmony Rating ✦ 7.5 out of 10

♍ With the Moon in VIRGO, Sun in Capricorn, you are likely to be ✦ Critical, aloof, studious, focused, dignified, virtuous, cynical, discriminating, humble, modestly wise, lucid, responsible, sensual, cautious, controlled, methodical, precise, prudish, a perfectionist, stable, logical, respectful, judgemental, hard-working, cool, calm and collected, trustworthy, methodical, devoted, dedicated, practical, modest, reserved, helpful, analytical, thoughtful, productive, consistent, supportive, kind, scrupulous, efficient, caring, rigid, conventional, down-to-Earth, attentive, industrious, constructive, resourceful, objective, rational, cool-headed, dutiful, scathing, willing to help and do what needs to be done, pragmatic, skilful, reliable, persevering, stable, poised, and in possession of a good deal of common sense.

Sun/Moon Harmony Rating ✦ 7.5 out of 10**

♎ With the Moon in LIBRA, Sun in Capricorn, you are likely to be ✦ Introverted, graceful, stylish, aesthetically aware, noble, orderly, emotionally elusive, high-minded, moderate, sophisticated, intelligent, peace-seeking, astute in business, tasteful, pleasant, romantic, modest, classy, liberal yet conservative, endearing, courteous, polite, elegant, patient, inclined to be opportunistic, ethereally sensual, attractive, artistic, quietly sociable, articulate, clear-headed, a friendly loner, refined, well-balanced, loving of simplicity, understatedly charming, a hider of feelings, gracious, shrewd, socially aware, chic, hospitable, pleasure-seeking, delightful, gently persuasive, artistically sensitive, charitable, helpful, rational, a practical idealist, and conflicted between lofty ambitions and relationships.

Sun/Moon Harmony Rating ✦ 8.5 out of 10

♏ With the Moon in SCORPIO, Sun in Capricorn, you are likely to be ✦ Intense, powerful, tireless, steadfast, unshakable, rigid, austere, persevering, all-or-nothing, narrow-minded, complex, cynical, strongly disciplined, manipulative, self-mastering, deeply aware of the self, tense, serious, strategic, perceptive, self-reliant, strongly principled, suspicious, concentrated, tightly controlled, serious, meticulous, substantial, ambitious, enduring, obsessive, deeply anxious, harsh, tight, pious, strong-willed, ruthless, sensually passionate, unable to tolerate fools, broody, aloof, fearless, scrutinising, ruthless, passionately dedicated, undiluted, single-minded, robust, highly resilient, discriminating, subjectively responsive, acutely intelligent, persistent, committed, repressed emotionally, self-sufficient, charged, astute, focused, unable to relax, heavy, resourceful, critical and judgemental, obsessive compulsive, unyielding, sustaining, controlling, shrewd, thorough, hard-working, penetrative, compulsive, secretive, intensely loyal, emotionally stoic, exacting, manipulative, and in possession of a difficult but strong temperament.

Sun/Moon Harmony Rating ✦ 6.5 out of 10

♐ With the Moon in SAGITTARIUS, Sun in Capricorn, you are likely to be ✦ Helpful, dutiful, rational but idealistic, ambitious, witty, sarcastic, zealous, authoritative, earnest, morally strong, faithful, restless but controlled, cautiously adventurous, verbose, articulate, philosophical yet logical, broad-minded, able to see the big picture, ethical, responsible, moralistic, grounded yet seeking, cleverly perceptive, strong, charismatic, dry-humoured, adventurous yet conventional, urbane, a dedicated student and thinker, embracing of novel ideas, honest, reasonable, frank, studious, intelligent, mentally dextrous, prone to preach and boss, a good guide or mentor, distant from your feelings, emotionally nervous, mentally agile, gently optimistic, ardently sensual, gently exuberant, a lover of learning, aspiring, objective, ambitious, broad-minded yet rigid, and guided by reason and logic rather than emotion.

Sun/Moon Harmony Rating ✦ 7.5 out of 10

♑ With the Moon in CAPRICORN, Sun in Capricorn, you are likely to be ✦ Self-controlled, persevering, emotionally repressed, cool, aloof, dedicated, emotionally isolated, staunch, disciplined, conscientious, devoted, refined, shrewd, rational, trustworthy, dependable, defensive, cynical, down-to-Earth, steadfast, pragmatic, humble, a workaholic, dictatorial, resourceful, committed, driven to succeed, conventional, ambitious, reserved, pessimistic, able to overcome most obstacles, withdrawn, methodical, frugal, dignified, realistic, logical, industrious, self-restrained, helpful, organised, productive, efficient, reliable, organised, serious, critical, tight-fisted, timid, sensible, introverted, understanding of practical applications and wisdom, economical, practical, honourable, uptight, socially rigid, professional, fearful, sophisticated, autocratic, self-contained, materialistic, protective, and willing to work long and hard to achieve your goals.

Sun/Moon Harmony Rating ✦ 7 out of 10

♒ With the Moon in AQUARIUS, Sun in Capricorn, you are likely to be ✦ Objective, humane, impersonal, rational, thoughtful, cool-headed, observant, applied but scattered, solitary, concise, slightly eccentric, contrary, lucid, paradoxical, diligent, nervous, detached, cool, aloof, quirky yet practical, discontent, living an unusual lifestyle in some way, paradoxical, socially timid, dedicated to worthy ideals and causes, self-contained, attracted to academia, well-meaning, open to the unusual, emotionally repressed, helpful, sensible yet rebellious, a progressive thinker, dispassionately critical, standoffish, acutely aware of the human condition, kind, pragmatically helpful, contradictory, an intellectual, untouched by passions, philanthropic, changeable, dissatisfied, unique, a pragmatic humanitarian, inconsistent, respectful, unstable, sceptical, conflicted between solitude and being around groups, realistic yet idealistic, committed to principles and ideals, embracing of abstract concepts, and devoted to social causes.

Sun/Moon Harmony Rating ✦ 7 out of 10

♓ With the Moon in PISCES, Sun in Capricorn, you are likely to be ✦ Compassionate, helpful, caring, able to mix realism with mysticism, ethereally sensual, insightful, idealistic yet grounded, artistic, wholesome, a natural counsellor, refined, gentle, kind, pessimistic, cynical, romantic, unstable, unsure, prone to depression, a martyr, sentimental, modest, downplaying of own abilities, supportive, a pragmatic poet, able to bring dreams into reality, needy, introverted, withdrawn, whimsical, despondent, easily discouraged, self-sacrificing, diffident, torn between being impractical and practical, evasive, melancholic, an escapist, sensitive, cleverly intuitive, perceptive, tough but tender, and torn between responsibilities and escapism.

Sun/Moon Harmony Rating ✦ 7.5 out of 10

*"If your Moon is in Taurus or Virgo, your Sun and Moon will form what is known in astrology as a trine aspect. This aspect is the easiest, most flowing and harmonious astrological aspect, ensuring that your Sun and Moon, or spirit and soul, are well integrated. With both luminaries in Earth signs, this gives them the best possible degree of complementary energy - a blending of the elements suggests a balanced expression of personality. One drawback of the trine aspect lies in the fact that its easy flow can be too harmonious; if our path is too smooth and difficulties

don't arise to challenge us from time to time, we can often become lazy and complacent, stunting our growth and spiritual evolution. As Earth signs, you share the art of practical application, devotion, rational thinking, logic, a love of beauty and peace, determination, pragmatism, sensibility, conservatism, realism, sensuality, fruitfulness and a gentle, caring approach to all your relationships and endeavours, but may be staid, rigid, unimaginative, materialistic, slow, lazy, narrow-minded and lacking in enthusiasm and zest.

AQUARIUS SUN & MOON COMBINATIONS

♈ With the Moon in ARIES, Sun in Aquarius, you are likely to be ✦ Observant, astute, self-interested, alert, emotionally detached, enthusiastic, independent, honest, devoted to truth, loyal, adventurous, hot-tempered, independent, courageous, prophetic, overly assertive, temperamental, insensitive, ambitious, self-reliant, energetic, emotionally bold and reckless, restless, speak before thinking, a fast communicator, soundly intellectual, acid-tongued, respectful of others' opinions, pioneering, original, forward-looking, lively, witty, frank, bright, off-the-wall, rebellious, an intelligent individualist, one who has moral integrity, and a maverick truth-seeker.

Sun/Moon Harmony Rating ✦ 8 out of 10

♉ With the Moon in TAURUS, Sun in Aquarius, you are likely to be ✦ Calm, level-headed, pragmatically intellectual, easy-going, possessive, stubborn, materialistic, gentle, infinitely patient, slow and steady-paced, conflicted between security and freedom, tenacious, emotionally placid, devoted to causes, reluctant to listen to others' views if convinced your own are correct, logical and detached in emotional matters, stoic, faithful, friendly, capable, determined, resourceful, dependable, an eccentric entrepreneur, ambitious, peace-loving but strong-willed, reliable, philanthropic, thoughtful, realistic, sensible, persistent, and dedicated to grounding your inspiration and idealism.

Sun/Moon Harmony Rating ✦ 5 out of 10

♊ **With the Moon in GEMINI, Sun in Aquarius, you are likely to be** ✦
A free spirit, changeable, friendly, bright, breezy, emotionally versatile, quick-witted, philosophical but flippant, perceptive, clever, inspiring, stimulating, sociable, detached, flexible yet stubborn, iconoclastic, curious, emotionally impulsive, restless, easily bored, logical, creative, progressive, communicative, strongly socially aware, unsentimental, emotionally naïve, gifted, a wonderful friend, original, popular, funny, easily swept away by ideas and concepts, open towards and perceptive of new ideas, idealistic, intellectual, squandering of your natural talents, reluctant to face the darker aspects of life, too busy to deal with feelings, and ruled by your mind rather than your gut instincts.

Sun/Moon Harmony Rating ✦ 9 out of 10**

♋ **With the Moon in CANCER, Sun in Aquarius, you are likely to be** ✦
Passive, sensitive, intuitive, emotionally expressive, strongly socially conscious, compassionate, a kind-hearted rebel, sympathetic, shy, emotionally reticent, hidden, private, eccentric, peaceful, imaginative, poetic, intelligently kind, devoted to truth and the triumph of the human spirit, helpful, companionable, emotionally lofty, progressive but old-fashioned values, able to express Universal insights through personal projection, a sensitive individualist, self-protective, unconsciously prejudiced, likely to become absorbed with abstract causes which cuts you off from your feelings, and occasionally moved to emotional outbursts.

Sun/Moon Harmony Rating ✦ 5 out of 10

♌ **With the Moon in LEO, Sun in Aquarius, you are likely to be** ✦
Proud, independent, individualistic, gentle on the surface with a great strength within, dramatic, a fearless defender of principles and causes, artistic, wise and generous in helping others, visionary, passionate, radiantly humanitarian, enthusiastic for new and original ideas, trustworthy, a good leader of groups, romantically imaginative, open, charismatic, powerful, extroverted, honest, passionate, warm, bold, inclined to get carried away by romance and idealism and forget to return to Earth, direct, vain, glamorising of others and failing to see their true colours, friendly, stubbornly controlling, generous, expressive, ambitious, despotic, self-centred, self-reliant, creative, emotionally radiating warmth, emotionally idealistic, luxury-loving, helpful, demonstrative, and creatively imaginative.

Sun/Moon Harmony Rating ✦ 7 out of 10

♍ With the Moon in VIRGO, Sun in Aquarius, you are likely to be ✦ Puritanical, intelligent, judgemental, cool, calm and collected, aloof, critical, clever, discriminating, an emotional perfectionist, methodical, studious, a devoted researcher, helpful, a truth-seeker, serious, kind-hearted, innovative, mentally alert, unassuming, mentally dextrous, efficient, undemonstrative, caring, rigid, reserved, rebellious yet conventional, objectively rational, cool-headed, willing to help and do what needs to be done, altruistic, genuinely kind, bright, devoted to ideals, dry-witted, and radical yet uptight.

Sun/Moon Harmony Rating ✦ 6 out of 10

♎ With the Moon in LIBRA, Sun in Aquarius, you are likely to be ✦ Lively, intellectual, able to work with principles easily, see life from endlessly new vantage points, sociable, refined, paradoxical, generally well-balanced and moderate, easy-going, sporadically affectionate, popular, a hider of feelings, graceful, charming, approachable, tolerant, distanced from your true emotional power, accessible, civilised, sharing, gracious, cooperative, approval-seeking, hospitable, hedonistic, indecisive, interested in people, places and purposes globally, romantically idealistic, endearing, acutely observant, loving of people, quick witted, honest, shocking and delightful at the same time, colourfully persuasive, artistically sensitive, abstract, emotionally naïve, and conflicted between independence and needing others.

Sun/Moon Harmony Rating ✦ 9 out of 10**

♏ With the Moon in SCORPIO, Sun in Aquarius, you are likely to be ✦ Intense, powerfully intellectual, forceful, highly charged, extreme and radical, possessive, keenly insightful, investigative, unbending, strong-willed, self-judging, a reformer, dominating, intensely dedicated to ideals, passionate, unyielding, resourceful, resilient, controlling, stubborn, persevering and thorough, devoted to truth at any cost, fiercely principled, psychologically penetrative, secretive, passionate yet dispassionate, loyal, emotional, courageously dedicated to reform and improvement for the welfare of others, an astute observer, perceptive, self-reliant, dogmatic, stern, exacting, potentially ruthless and manipulative, and emotionally powerful.

Sun/Moon Harmony Rating ✦ 6 out of 10

♐ With the Moon in SAGITTARIUS, Sun in Aquarius, you are likely to be ✦ Eager, friendly, independent, idealistic, a traveller of body and mind, big-hearted, honest, adventurous, rationalising, impatient with petty details and restrictions of daily life, prone to preach when advancing causes, unaware of the subtleties of social interaction, intellectual, inquisitive, an adventurer, able to see the 'big picture', distant from your feelings, emotionally reckless, a free spirit, non-committal, a good teacher, in possession of a zany sense of humour, far-sighted, intellectually speedy, optimistic, a lover of learning, inspiring, outrageous, aspiring, gregarious, socially concerned, broad-minded, rebellious, expansive, verbose

Sun/Moon Harmony Rating ✦ 9 out of 10

♑ With the Moon in CAPRICORN, Sun in Aquarius, you are likely to be ✦ Dependable, steadfast, resourceful, committed to causes, independent, driven to succeed, ambitious to make the world a better place, critical, reserved, withdrawn, cool, unemotional, wise, shrewd, organised, down-to-Earth, efficient, reliable, serious, sensible, materialistic, introverted, understanding of practical applications and wisdom, economical, brotherly, a practical reformer, 'a rebel with a cause', inventive, personally honourable, overly-strict when adhering to principles, fearless, uptight, socially rigid, self-contained, aware of human character, sardonically humorous, and willing to work in the present for the future good.

Sun/Moon Harmony Rating ✦ 6.5 out of 10

♒ With the Moon in AQUARIUS, Sun in Aquarius, you are likely to be ✦ Friendly and tolerant, independent, idealistic, emotionally detached, eccentric, 'different', unconventional, aloof, paradoxical, imaginative, sympathetic, honest, original, forward-moving, inventive, impersonal in relationships, clear-headed, highly observant, acutely aware of the human condition, progressive, scientifically oriented, objective, living an unusual lifestyle in some way, well-meaning, open to the unusual, emotionally naïve, over-identifying with causes, blunt and insensitive when comparing people with your ideals, freedom-loving, unorthodox, impractical, loyal, humanitarian, globally aware, courageous and committed to your ideals, a law unto yourself, and in possession of an eternal sense of hope and belief in human potential.

Sun/Moon Harmony Rating ✦ 8 out of 10

♓ With the Moon in PISCES, Sun in Aquarius, you are likely to be ✦ Highly imaginative, intuitive, with the ability to blend common sense and mysticism, over-idealistic, a chaser of spiritual rainbows, heart in the right place, good-natured, intriguing, kindly, friendly, emotionally intelligent, apt to wander off on your own and go into flights of fancy, hot and cold emotions, sentimental, gentle, accepting, understanding, independent but vulnerable, a thinker and a poet, altruistic, in possession of a Universal outlook, humorous, psychologically insightful, generous, receptive, creative, reverent, forgiving, devoutly committed to social causes, mysterious, empathetic, humanitarian, prone to drifting and wasting time in daydreams, impressionable, idealistic but easily swayed, gullible, impractical, evasive, sensitive, psychic, perceptive, able to mix and work with all types of people, and aware of the needs of others.

Sun/Moon Harmony Rating ✦ 8 out of 10

**If your Moon is in Gemini or Libra, your Sun and Moon will form what is known in astrology as a trine aspect. This aspect is the easiest, most flowing and harmonious astrological aspect, ensuring that your Sun and Moon, or spirit and soul, are well integrated. With both luminaries in Air signs, this gives them the best possible degree of complementary energy - a blending of the elements suggests a balanced expression of personality. One drawback of the trine aspect lies in the fact that its easy flow can be too harmonious; if our path is too smooth and difficulties don't arise to challenge us from time to time, we can often become lazy and complacent, stunting our growth and spiritual evolution. As Air signs, you share the art of sociability, are highly idealistic, affable, romantic, possess a good intellect, have a love of truth and beauty, are reasonable, broad-minded, independent but devoted to your ideals, have an artistic sensitivity, are tolerant, understanding, civilised and dignified, and have avant-garde tastes, but may be detached, cool, head over heart-oriented, and restless.*

PISCES SUN & MOON COMBINATIONS

♈ **With the Moon in ARIES, Sun in Pisces, you are likely to be** ✦ Devoted to truth, understanding, romantic, quarrelsome, innocently childlike, independent, loyal, prophetic, affectionate, robustly sensual, emotionally edgy and reckless, frustrated, respectful of others' feelings, humble but self-centred, artistic, touchy, pioneering, original, impetuous, emotionally fluctuating, forward-looking, sensitive, off-the-wall, adventurous, vividly imaginative, wilful, moody, a quick thinker, a saviour, nervous, quietly charismatic, warmth and optimistic, spirited, fun-loving, resilient, adaptable, big-hearted, and always battling the paradox between romantic vulnerability and forthright assertiveness.

Sun/Moon Harmony Rating ✦ 6 out of 10

♉ **With the Moon in TAURUS, Sun in Pisces, you are likely to be** ✦ Calm, sensitive to beauty, level-headed, harmonious, charming, easy-going, gentle, infinitely patient, able to transform your imaginative ideas in tangible outcomes, feminine, fair-minded, a practical romantic, slow-paced, able to manifest dreams on the material plane, practically idealistic, subjective and emotional, able to manoeuvre situations to suit your security and lifestyle needs, helpful, emotionally placid, devoted to people, animals and causes, emotionally demonstrative, loving of simple pleasures and delights, sensual, manipulative, artistic, musical, faithful, friendly, resourceful, peace-loving but strong-willed, able to bring your romantic nature down to Earth, old-fashioned, strongly seductive, shrewd and philanthropic with money, caring, idealistic but down-to-Earth, thoughtful, compassionate, moody, sociable, warm, needy, security-striving, both a dreamer and a realist, and dedicated to grounding your inspiration, spirituality and idealism.

Sun/Moon Harmony Rating ✦ 7.5 out of 10

♊ With the Moon in GEMINI, Sun in Pisces, you are likely to be ✦ Fanciful, a free spirit, childlike, humorous, imaginative, changeable, friendly, breezy, emotionally versatile, lacking in confidence, open, alternating between timidity and sociability, philosophical but flippant, perceptive, inspiring, charming and stimulating, like a leaf blowing in the wind, sociable, impressionable, flexible, curious, emotionally restless, fickle, non-committal, creative, aware of others' feelings, careless, easily influenced by others, sentimental, temperamental, emotionally naïve, forgiving, gifted, a sparkling friend, whimsical, popular, poetic, good with words, funny, sometimes reticent and sometimes talkative, intuitive, easily swept away by ideas and concepts, open towards and perceptive of new ideas, self-doubting, self-pitying, idealistic, eternally youthful, wordy and expressive, dependent on others, able to mimic with sharp precision, intelligently creative, emotionally and socially intelligent, squandering of your natural talents, diplomatic, appreciative of a wide variety of people, fluent and originally self-expressive, fun-loving, reluctant to face the darker aspects of life, too busy and dreamy to deal with feelings, and ruled by both your head and your heart.

Sun/Moon Harmony Rating ✦ 6.5 out of 10

♋ With the Moon in CANCER, Sun in Pisces, you are likely to be ✦ Ultra-sensitive, intuitive, romantic, emotional, kind-hearted, sympathetic, shy, emotionally reticent, retiring, ruled by matters of the heart, hidden, private, thoughtful and caring, a bit of a hermit, peaceful, imaginative, poetic, creative, deeply kind, devoted to feelings and easing others' pain, a deep sense of the human spirit, helpful, companionable, old-fashioned, nurturing, introspective, colourfully imaginative, timid, a healer, good-humoured, able to express personal insights with close loved ones, self-protective, likely to take in 'lame ducks', involved, defensive, devious, fearful, overly sensitive, offended at the slightest provocation, easily overcome by more extroverted and 'powerful' personalities, moody, unreasonable, quiet, genuinely compassionate, and instinctively understanding of the human heart and psyche.

Sun/Moon Harmony Rating ✦ 8.5 out of 10**

♌ With the Moon in LEO, Sun in Pisces, you are likely to be ✦ Proud, individualistic, charming on the surface with a gentle strength within, dramatic, sensitive, prone to dramatise your weaknesses in order to manipulate others' sympathy, in possession of a rich inner world, apparently sure of self but insecure inside, artistic, wise and generous in helping others, visionary, passionate, sociable, radiantly caring, receptive, enthusiastic, innocent, trusting, a dynamic healer, richly spiritual, romantically imaginative and creative, open, a tragic romantic, charismatic, quietly passionate, unstable, warm, inclined to get carried away by romance and idealism, theatrical, intuitively insightful, fluctuating in inspiration, huffy, emotionally volatile, sometimes mysterious, vain, glamorising of others and failing to see their true colours, friendly, generous and giving, emotionally demonstrative and expressive, creative, emotionally radiating warmth, emotionally idealistic, luxury-loving, helpful, affectionate, seductive, attractive, moody, and unwaveringly loyal and devoted to loved ones.

Sun/Moon Harmony Rating ✦ 7 out of 10

♍ With the Moon in VIRGO, Sun in Pisces, you are likely to be ✦ Emotionally intelligent, perceptive, intellectually intuitive, both head and heart-oriented, an emotional perfectionist, well-liked, broad in mind and outlook, willing to look at things from all angles, divided between logic and intuition, a devoted spiritualist, a good healer, helpful, considerate, kind-hearted, unassuming, modest, caring, adaptable, reserved, altruistic, genuinely kind, a quiet thinker, dry-witted, self-sacrificing, nervous and fretful, polite, discerning but forgiving, an artist-scientist, interested in holistic health and healing, appreciative, a logical metaphysician, courteous, self-pitying, dedicated to ideals, understated, respectful of others, refined in tastes, and a devoted servant.

Sun/Moon Harmony Rating ✦ 6 out of 10

♎ With the Moon in LIBRA, Sun in Pisces, you are likely to be ✦ Emotionally intelligent, cultured, sensitive, whimsical, gifted with insights, gullible, eloquent, intuitive, diplomatic, emotionally refined, graceful, gentle, peaceable, romantic, generally well-balanced and moderate, easy-going, a hider of feelings, artistic, charming, approachable, tolerant, sharing, gracious, blessed with the ability to inspire others through your graceful self-expression, unrealistic, sociable, imaginative, cooperative, gregarious, cagey, approval-seeking, compliant, agreeable, hedonistic, indecisive, romantically idealistic, endearing, delightful company, artistically sensitive, trusting, tasteful, inspiring, creative, attracted to beautiful things, emotionally naïve, and conflicted between rational and emotional thought.

Sun/Moon Harmony Rating ✦ 9 out of 10

♏ With the Moon in SCORPIO, Sun in Pisces, you are likely to be ✦ Intense, powerfully sensitive, insightful, investigative, self-protective, complex, feelings-based, richly imaginative, strong in adversity, resourceful, helpful, manipulative, sometimes extreme and sometimes gentle, understanding of the human spirit, compassionate to others' crises and tragedies, courageous and timid at the same time, drawn to sensationalism, resilient, irrationally suspicious of others' motives, devoted to ideals, embracing of the comic and the tragic together, psychologically penetrative, self-pitying, evasive, secretive, hidden, loyal, emotional, perceptive, emotionally powerful, torn between self-sacrifice versus self-reliance and control, and constantly experiencing pulls towards agony or ecstasy.

Sun/Moon Harmony Rating ✦ 8.5 out of 10**

♐ With the Moon in SAGITTARIUS, Sun in Pisces, you are likely to be
✦ Eager, endearingly naïve, adventurous, friendly, a traveller of body and mind, big-hearted, trusting, believing, generous, warm, impatient with petty details and restrictions of daily life, prone to exaggeration, inquisitive, one who sees the best in everyone, an adventurer, affectionate, charismatic, able to see the 'big picture', idealistic, widely imaginative, lacking in focus, wanting to be all things to all people, exuberant, deeply spiritual and/or religious, emotionalising of moral issues, emotionally reckless and careless, a free spirit, faithful to social causes, devious, non-committal, a good teacher, in possession of a zany sense of humour, far-sighted, optimistic, a lover of learning, inspiring, able to make others laugh, procrastinating, morally confused, self-deceiving, aspiring, enlightening, a seeker of truth, gregarious, socially concerned, broad-minded, expansive, emotionally philosophical, freedom-seeking, and guided by both reason and emotion.

Sun/Moon Harmony Rating ✦ 7.5 out of 10

♑ With the Moon in CAPRICORN, Sun in Pisces, you are likely to be
✦ Committed to causes, driven to help others, ambitious to make others' lives better in some way, perceptive, cautious, reserved, withdrawn, cool, wise, pragmatic and resourceful in the use of your imagination, unassuming, introverted, understanding of the practical applications of wisdom, prone to pessimism and worry, secretive and defensive, moralistic and judgemental in human relations, discreetly ambitious, a practical dreamer, a realist and an idealist at the same time, personally honourable, uptight, creatively down-to-Earth, a pillar of strength, aware of human character, sardonically humorous, charitable, serious and self-reflective, devoted, quietly adaptable, abiding, circumspect, a reserved romantic, strategic, dutiful, dependable, and able to pin down the elusive.

Sun/Moon Harmony Rating ✦ 6 out of 10

♒ With the Moon in AQUARIUS, Sun in Pisces, you are likely to be ✦ Friendly and tolerant, idealistic, eccentric, 'different', unconventional, aloof, paradoxical, interested in science fiction and fantasy, imaginative, sympathetic, original, forward-flowing, highly observant, acutely aware of the human condition, living an unusual lifestyle in some way, well-meaning, a missionary, a servant of Universal concerns, open to the unusual, emotionally naïve, drawn to unusual art and beauty, over-identifying with causes, sociable, freedom-loving, unorthodox, impractical, loyal, humanitarian, easily influenced, globally aware, easy-going, aware of the human condition, able to use both the left and right sides of the brain, accepting of the whole gamut of society, morally trustworthy, genuinely desiring to make the world a better place, charitable, emotionally gullible, easily overwhelmed by the woes and causes of the world, devoted to your ideals, and in possession of an eternal sense of hope and belief in the triumph of the human spirit.

Sun/Moon Harmony Rating ✦ 7.5 out of 10

♓ With the Moon in PISCES, Sun in Pisces, you are likely to be ✦ Highly imaginative, overly sensitive, intuitive, mystical, over-idealistic, a chaser of spiritual rainbows, good-natured, unworldly, shy, gentle, intriguing, kindly, friendly, emotional, easily moved, intensely subjective, passive, self-sabotaging, apt to go into flights of fancy and fantasy, an escapist, deeply sentimental, accepting, impressionable, adrift at sea, understanding, vulnerable, an artist and a poet, altruistic, self-sacrificing, unsure, able to identify with the whole spectrum of human joys and sorrows, hopelessly romantic, in possession of a Universal outlook, generous, receptive, creative, forgiving, mysterious, selfless, concerned with the welfare of others, empathetic, prone to drifting and wasting time in daydreams, easily swayed, gullible, impractical, evasive, psychic, adaptable, and aware of the feelings of others.

Sun/Moon Harmony Rating ✦ 8 out of 10

"If your Moon is in Cancer or Scorpio, your Sun and Moon will form what is known in astrology as a trine aspect. This aspect is the easiest, most flowing and harmonious astrological aspect, ensuring that your Sun and Moon, or spirit and soul, are well integrated. With both luminaries in Water signs, this gives them the best possible degree of complementary

energy - a blending of the elements suggests a balanced expression of personality. One drawback of the trine aspect lies in the fact that its easy flow can be too harmonious; if our path is too smooth and difficulties don't arise to challenge us from time to time, we can often become lazy and complacent, stunting our growth and spiritual evolution. As Water signs, you share the art of sensitivity, creativity, intrigue, compassion, a nurturing instinct, poetry, understanding, spirituality, a deep need for connection and merging with others, but may be overly sensitive, illogical, clingy, impractical, too emotional, irrational, dependent, manipulative and elusive.

BODY & HEALTH

Health is not just the absence of disease but a state of vitality, of energy, of creativity - a higher state of consciousness. Health is that state of awareness in which your intelligence, and all the elements and forces that structure your body, are in complete harmony with the elements and the forces that structure the body of the Universe.

Deepak Chopra

Hear how each sign the body's portion sways,
How every part its proper lord obeys
And what the members of the human frame
Wherein to rule, their several forces claim
First to the Ram, the Head hath been assigned;
Lord of the sinews, Neck, the Bull we find;
The arms and shoulders joined in union fair
Possess the Twins, each one an equal share.
The Crab, as sovereign o'er the Breast presides;
The Lion, the shoulder blades and sides.
Down to the flank, the Virgin's lot descends,
And with the buttock Libra's influence ends;
The fiery Scorpion in the groin delights,
The Centaur in the thighs exerts its rights,
While either knee doth Capricornus rule,
The legs the province of Aquarius cool;
Last, the twain Fishes as their region meet,
Hold jurisdiction on the pairs of feet.

C.W. King

> A physician without a knowledge of astrology
> has no right to call himself a physician.
>
> **Hippocrates**

In ancient times, and still even today, the movement of the stars and planets was believed to affect bodily functions, and to both cause ailments and cure them. Hippocrates, the fifth century BC Greek physician, 'father of medicine' and supposed author of the Hippocratic Oath, maintained that no one should be allowed to practise medicine who had not first studied astrology. Another Greek physician, Claudius Galen, brought together a vast array of knowledge and ideas in the second century AD which dominated medical practice until the seventeenth century. Among his teachings was a diagnostic technique which assumed that illnesses and their treatments were affected by and governed by the phases of the Moon. Indeed, for centuries, astrology was a compulsory component of medical training, albeit only one aspect of diagnosis and treatment.

Medical or health astrology concerns particular ways of determining and interpreting an individual's horoscope with particular reference to health issues - diagnosis of current dis-eases, identification of areas of bodily weaknesses, and the prescription of natural cures and remedies in alignment with the individual's natal placements.

During the Middle Ages, many drawings of the 'zodiac man' were etched, showing which zodiac signs corresponded to different areas of the body, and providing information as to the best times of the year to undertake cures for ailments affecting the corresponding body parts.

Health astrology persists today in many forms and among astrologers themselves, from whom clients seek counsel on health-related issues, and while it certainly cannot and should not be used as a substitute for appropriate medical attention, one's Sun sign, along with other natal chart factors, can indicate areas of potential problems or afflictions. Indeed, this branch of astrology has been found to be surprisingly accurate in a great many cases. Despite this, the following information should not be viewed or utilised as a substitute for professional medical advice should you be personally concerned about any of the areas listed for your Sun sign.

BACH FLOWER ESSENCES

In the 1930s, British bacteriologist, medical doctor, homeopath and spiritual writer Dr Edward Bach developed a special system of alternative medicines known as the Bach Flower Remedies or Essences, inspired by classical homeopathic principles and traditions, and his own intuitive leanings. He associated plants of 'the 12 Healers' with personality types, which relate to our innate, essential natures. Still in use today by many natural therapists, the original 38 remedies appear to be effective emotional-healing agents, widely applied and revered by countless individuals for almost a century.

Among many other benefits, the following have been reported after using the Bach remedies: feeling uplifted, calm, relaxed, happier; a state of relief and wellbeing; increased awareness, joy and fulfilment; improved health and vigour; transcending limitations and actualising latent potential; deeper feelings of emotional expression; and greater love and acceptance of self.

Because these ethereal remedies are considered an 'energy' medicine that work deeply on the vibrational, spiritual, emotional, even subconscious levels, certain essences align with each zodiac sign and their respective cosmic influences.

The following flower remedies are intuitively attuned to a sign each, appearing to work psychically and spiritually to facilitate healing on deep emotional and ethereal levels that suit that sign's specific energy needs.

FLOWER ESSENCE FOR EACH SIGN

Aries ✦ Impatiens

Taurus ✦ Cerato

Gemini ✦ Gentian

Cancer ✦ Clematis

Leo ✦ Vervain

Virgo ✦ Centaury

Libra ✦ Scleranthus

Scorpio ✦ Chicory

Sagittarius ✦ Agrimony

Capricorn ✦ Mimulus

Aquarius ✦ Water Violet

Pisces ✦ Rock Rose

ORIENTAL PHYSIOLOGY

Yin and *Yang*, the most universally recognised complementary polarity of the masculine and feminine concepts, form the basis in Eastern physiology of what is known as the Eight Principles. This is a way of understanding and describing the state and condition of the chi (energy, life force) according to eight parameters. There are four pairs of opposites - yin/yang, deficiency/excess, interior/exterior, and cold/hot. For instance, a person may have an internal 'chi' condition that could be described as *yin*, deficient, interior and cold, or *yang*, excessive, exterior and hot, pointing to *yin* and *yang* imbalances, respectively. The union of feminine and masculine energies within the individual is the basis for all creation: female receptivity plus male action equals (pro)creativity. An intricate balance is of course needed between the two complementary opposites, but it is generally believed that more *yang* than *yin* energy confers greater benefit than more *yin* than *yang*.

VITAMINS & MINERALS

Just as the planets and zodiac signs govern various physiological processes in our bodies, so too do they 'rule' the vitamins, minerals and other nutrients necessary for our survival, growth and harmony. Each zodiac sign has energies and functions that indicate a higher or lesser need for some nutrients over others. The lack of certain elements or planetary prominence in the horoscope may suggest the need for certain vitamins and minerals; for example, one who lacks the Fire element or has a weak Sun, Mars, or Jupiter placement, may benefit from vitamin D, iron, chromium, or silica.

TISSUE SALTS

Homeopathy and astrology have colluded to provide a wonderful list of astrological tonics, one particularly suited to each of the twelve signs. These are called 'homeopathic cell salts', 'tissue salts' or 'biochemic cell salts', and are inexpensive, easy to take, and available in most health food stores. They are considered to be gentle, effective and safe, even for children, people in fragile health states, and the elderly. Although the full picture, drawn from a full natal horoscope, gives a fuller, more accurate idea of an individual's unique constitutional make-up, even simply working with one's date of birth can be enough for the medical astrologer to suggest the use of a particular cell salt based upon the correlation with that individual's Sun sign. As well as the cell salts having a significant effect upon physical ailments, they can also profoundly influence the body's subtle energy systems, including the mental, emotional and spiritual bodies.

HUMORS

Greek physician Hippocrates (460 - 370 BC) theorised that certain human behaviours were caused by body fluids, called 'humors'. Later, Greek physician Galen developed the first typology of temperaments to encompass many facets of the human psyche and physiology. These also related to the classical elements of Fire, Earth, Air and Water - as choleric, melancholic, sanguine and phlegmatic, respectively. The Greeks sought equilibrium in the four qualities of hot, cold, wet (moist), and dry, the elements of Earth, Air, Fire and Water, and the four humors of choler or yellow bile, melancholer or black bile, blood and phlegm. If balance was achieved, the person was said to be well- or even-tempered, and the importance of determining the temperament allowed for imbalances to be treated.

ARIES ✦ HEALTH

Aries is associated with the Head (particularly the cerebrum, where the upper brain lies), Skull, Face, Brain, Sinuses, Pituitary Gland, the Muscular System, the Adrenals, Blood Pressure, and the Left Cerebellum and the Frontal Lobe areas of the brain. Fevers and accidents are typical of all Fire signs, especially the highly-strung and risk-taking Aries, but recovery is usually rapid and achieved through willpower and an inherent physical fortitude.

Burns, injuries from sharp objects, and head injuries are common, Aries being the most vulnerable of the zodiac to these, so care is needed to curb any tendencies which may place Aries natives at risk of these.

Every Arien, at some stage in his life, will indulge in rash or reckless behaviour that brings an injury to the head or face. The root cause of most head conditions such as headaches and migraines, can usually be attributed to alcohol consumption, liver dysfunction, and/or emotions like anger, stress, frustration and impatience, which are frequently expressed by the Ram.

Some other ailments Aries may suffer from are epilepsy, neuralgia, brain inflammations, hay fever, dizziness, nose bleeds, high blood pressure, acne, sinuses, upper jaw conditions, toothaches, and ear and eye complaints. They may also encounter difficulties with the cerebrum and carotid arteries, as these too are Aries-ruled areas.

Generally, Aries boasts robust health, good energy reserves and impressive recuperative powers, but they can burn themselves out to a temporary standstill more easily than most too.

Ariens seldom suffer from drawn-out chronic illness, especially in their younger years; should they acquire a dis-ease, their decline or demise is likely to be just as rapid as its onset, although swift recoveries are usually guaranteed.

Ariens need abundant exercise to keep their systems in good working order. Exercise is important for everyone of course, but for Ariens it is vital to their wellbeing and effective functioning. They may well be so enthusiastic that they overdo physical regimes or sporting pursuits, and moderation may be needed if excessive strain or injury is to be avoided. Learning to avoid overdoing things in general, both mentally and physically, will keep Ariens healthy, as will slowing down and resting regularly.

Aries's ruling planet Mars is traditionally associated with the Left Ear, Kidneys, Veins, Blood, Iron and Motor Nerves, and rules the Gonads (sex glands) and the Genitals. As well, it governs the Forehead, Bile, Nose, Gall Bladder, Penis, Left Hemisphere of the Brain, and the Muscular System. Other Mars-influenced health concerns may involve the muscles, head, adrenal glands, inflammations, red blood corpuscles, and energy levels.

Overall, the Ram represents energy activation, its nature hot, dry, fast and inflammatory.

ARIES ✦ ORIENTAL PHYSIOLOGY

Being a masculine sign, Aries tends more towards conditions of *Yang* theme and nature, and when these are actively engaged and embraced, this sign will physically function better with more optimal health outcomes. Regardless of this, balance of both polarities is always desirable. Examples of *Yang* concepts are male, Sun, daylight, warmth, brightness, outer, activity, outdoors, above, speed, movement, dryness and expansion.

ARIES ✦ VITAMINS & MINERALS

Arian natives would benefit from the main mineral that is ruled by their ruling planet Mars: Iron.

ARIES ✦ TISSUE SALT: KALI PHOS.

The cell salt corresponding with Aries is *Kali Phos.*, which helps to repair nerves, muscles, and the brain's grey matter. It is considered a nerve nutrient, with a significant effect upon nerve cells, especially those of the brain. Used for all forms of mental fatigue and its offshoots, *Kali Phos.* is beneficial for insomnia, dizziness, depression, neuralgia, irritability, hysteria, headaches, and all other types of nervous disorders.

ARIES ✦ HUMOR: CHOLERIC

The Fire element corresponds with the humor choleric, which is characterised by a short response time-delay, but response sustained for a relatively long time. Driven by their goals, for which they will use others as tools to achieve them, a choleric disposition represents touchiness, restlessness, aggression, spirit, excitement, changeability, impulsiveness, activity and optimism.

A person with a choleric temperament is one who is strong, wilful, and even aggressive if necessary. Impatience and anxiety are features, and physically these traits can elicit a response from the liver - stronger than usual biliary secretions.

The choleric character is associated with Fire, which is the ruling element of summer, the season with which the person under this influence has the greatest affinity. The Martian and Sun types, referring to Mars in Aries and the Sun in Leo, are the most common types amongst the cholerics.

Choleric is associated with the ego level of self. Its taste is salty and sour, its nature acidic, its indication yellow bile. The choleric humor is associated with the astral body˚*, and with hot and dry conditions.

˚*A couple of thousand years ago, the Mesopotamians, Chinese and Egyptians, and more recently the Arabs, practised a medicine called 'of three bodies'. According to the doctors of the ancient world (who often practised as astrologers as well), a human being had three bodies: the physical body, the ethereal (or vital) body and the astral body, imparting a holistic approach to health. In modern medicine, usually only the physical body is focused upon fully. According to tradition, this physical body comprises three principles or states corresponding to three primordial elements: solid (Earth), liquid (Water) and gas (Air). This is the material body, the physical outer cover of muscles, nerves and organs held together by the skeleton. The Fire element corresponds with the astral body, which sits outside the physical body in one's auric field.*

*The primordial element linked to the astral body is Fire, and it includes seven points, or doors, of perception which correspond exactly with the chakras. The astral body has a degree of vibration and radiance which is far higher than that of the ethereal body, an area which sits just beyond the physical body in one's auric field. Ancient physicians believed that this radiance covered an area varying from 40 centimetres to three metres around the physical body, and that this area varied greatly depending on the psychic energy of the individual. (The higher the levels, the larger the area of the radiance). The astral body is described as a diffused outer layer with whirls and flashing swirls of colour which move constantly. The intensity of its colour and movement varies according to the pattern of thoughts, feelings, emotions, moods and desires of the individual.

TAURUS ✦ HEALTH

Taurus is associated with the Throat, Tonsils, Neck, Thyroid, Metabolism, the Five Senses, Gums, Middle Ear, Cheeks, Cervical Vertebra, Shoulders, Hypothalamus and Base of the Brain, Thymus, the Cerebellum or Lower Brain, Ears, Lips, Chin, Cheeks, Tongue, Lower Jaw, and Vocal Cords. Parts of the body or health concerned with illness or vulnerability are the Thyroid Gland, Carotid Arteries, Sense of Taste, Tonsils, Occipital Area, Jugular Vein, Larynx, Pharynx, and the Back of the Head. As a result, Taureans are particularly prone to throat infections, obesity, goitre, laryngitis and tonsillitis.

As a rule, the most vulnerable part of the Taurus body is the throat. Infections or a breakdown in general health will usually appear here first. The neck and shoulders are also weak spots for Taureans.

The typical Taurean is, like its prototype the Bull, endowed with a vigorous constitution and strong health. Arising from characteristic excesses and indiscretions of diet, accompanied by a sluggish (albeit strong) constitution, constipation may also be a problem for Taurus. When sick or involved in an accident (unusual), the Bull is very robust and can normally withstand high amounts of discomfort or pain. Taurus's stubbornness can lead to a determined resilience and refusal to let anything get the better of them, but if it does, music and refined surroundings have a profound effect on Taurus, and assist greatly in recovering from illness.

Taureans love their food and have a reputation for overeating, so can put on weight very easily, creating health concerns if weight gets out of control. A moderate diet is essential but not always easy for this native. Thyroid issues, especially hypothyroid, weight gain, blood pressure, sore throats, glandular swellings in the neck, sluggish bowels, constipation and haemorrhoids, gout, and tight muscles in the neck or shoulders are very real manifestations of Taurus's inordinate fondness for comfort and the good things in life.

As Taurus governs the neck, throat and ears, it also affects the voice (many Taureans have beautiful singing voices), throat area and the lower parts of the head including the chin and tongue. Dis-eases that afflict this area of the body, including sore throats and stiff necks, are Taurus-ruled, as are any injuries or wounds which occur in these locations.

Taurus rules the five senses and is a keen user of them. Being a creature of habit and this means that extremes and sudden changes should be avoided. If the body is subjected to sudden switches in diet, climate, or physical activity, for example, they are likely to become ill. Therefore, Taureans should make all changes gradually, working up to them so that the body has plenty of time to adjust and adapt. If Taureans abide by this rule, they should remain healthy and stable.

Since Taurus is an Earth sign with great natural affinity for the physical body, she usually possesses above-average strength. Her constitution is remarkable for its stamina and endurance, and the burdens of work she can carry are extraordinary. Because of this, she is reluctant to surrender or admit to illness. When Taurus does get sick or injured, it tends to take longer than average to get back to par again.

Taureans should also guard against any Venus-ruled conditions or afflictions, such as those affecting the following body areas, which Venus rules (sharing many with Taurus): Thymus and Thyroid Glands, Venous Circulation, Saliva Ducts, Hormones, Kidneys, Sugar Balance, Hair Shafts and Production, Skin, Neck and the Throat, the Inner Ear, Balance and the Centre of Gravity. Venus is also associated with the Chin, Complexion, Cheeks, Viral Infections, and complaints caused by excesses or pleasures. The veins, venous system and ovaries may also be particularly weak spots for Taurean and Venusian natives.

Overall, Taurus's nature is cool, dry and enduring.

TAURUS ✦ ORIENTAL PHYSIOLOGY

Being a feminine sign, Taurus tends more towards conditions of a *Yin* theme and nature, and when these are actively engaged and embraced, this sign will physically function better with more optimal health outcomes. Regardless of this, balance of both polarities is always desirable. Examples of *Yin* concepts are female, Moon, night, cold, dark, inner, contracting, passive, decreasing, inside, below, damp and slow.

TAURUS ✦ VITAMINS & MINERALS

Taurean natives would benefit from vitamins and minerals that are ruled by their ruling planet Venus: iodine, copper, sodium/potassium balance, and the bioflavonoids (or vitamin P).

TAURUS ✦ TISSUE SALT: NAT SULPH.

The cell salt corresponding with Taurus is *Nat Sulph.*, whose main function is to control and regulate the supply of water in the body, and remove excess fluids from the body. This cell salt is one of the most important salts affecting the digestive organs and functions, including the pancreatic juices, bile of the liver and the secretions of the kidneys; all are regulated by *Nat Sulph*.

TAURUS ✦ HUMOR: MELANCHOLIC

The Earth element corresponds with the humor melancholic, which is characterised by long response time delay, and response sustained at length, if not seemingly permanently. Driven by the fear of rejection and the unknown, they tend to be rigid, moody, anxious, sober, pessimistic, unsociable, responsible and quiet.

The melancholic temperament is analogous with the Earth, which is the main element in autumn (or fall), the season with which Earth signs have many points in common. The nervous system and physical and mental powers reign supreme in melancholic types, although they may often behave in nervous, worried, or unstable ways, too. The Mercurial (Virgo) melancholic is distinguishable from the Saturnian (Capricorn) melancholic through the former's obviously more eccentric and less withdrawn mannerisms.

A melancholic disposition represents anxiety, peace and inflexibility. Its taste is sweet and astringent, its nature alkaline, its indication black bile. The melancholic humor is associated with the physical and solid body´, and with cold and dry conditions.

Additionally, the ethereal (or vital) body, comprises four ethers or subtle fluids, which are governed by the four Fixed signs of the zodiac: Taurus, Leo, Scorpio and Aquarius. Taurus corresponds to the chemical ether, which rules the basic functions of the physical body - assimilation, elimination, absorption and expulsion.

*See under **ARIES** ✦ HUMOR: CHOLERIC.

GEMINI ✦ HEALTH

Gemini is associated with the Hands, Shoulders, Arms, Fingers, Clavicle, Sternum, Windpipe and Bronchial Tubes, Lungs, Trachea, Capillaries, Breath, Thoracic Vertebrae, Body Tubing, Nervous System, Upper Ribs, and the Parietal Lobe, Thymus Gland and Pons areas of the Brain, and its natives may suffer from disorders, conditions or accidents to these parts. But the most common ailments are those affecting the nervous system and mental faculties.

Geminis are particularly liable to nervous debility and exhaustion, insomnia, neuritis, mental strain, and intense irritability; the chief remedy for these afflictions is to avoid stress, worry and overactivity. Fractures of the arms, hands and collarbones are common, as well as the allergic triad - asthma, eczema, hay fever, and most other allergies. Dairy products should be minimised due to their mucus-forming properties.

Nowhere in the zodiac are body and mind so entwined as in people born under Gemini. The Water signs Cancer, Scorpio and Pisces, are influenced by their emotions, and these in turn affect their bodies. But Gemini is an intellectual sign, and his mental processes tend to override emotions. Geminis need to rest their busy brains with much more sleep than other mere mortals, but since he is naturally vulnerable to insomnia, he rarely gets enough slumber.

Interestingly but perhaps not surprisingly, Gemini will likely suffer emotional breakdowns more easily from boredom and confinement than from overactivity. These natives need the freedom to move, speak and do as they please, and their living space should be as airy, uncluttered and light as possible. Geminis don't like to be down for long and cannot tolerate being confined to bed or anywhere else, although they usually recover quickly, taking flight as soon as they can – and often well before.

Because this sign governs the lungs and respiratory system, issues concerning oxygenation of the blood, coughs, colds, influenza, bronchitis, speech problems and other chest or lung complaints are likely causes of ill-health.

Afflictions, injuries and conditions affecting the arms, shoulders, hands and body tubing are also a possibility, as these too are vulnerable areas.

Although not necessarily strong, Geminis are almost certainly wiry and are known as being perpetually young, so generally don't suffer too much with their health. Any difficulties that arise are usually psychologically based and can be attributed to the vast amounts of nervous energy which may not be burned off properly. Geminis must also guard the health of their lungs as this is one of the susceptible areas, and although smoking is hazardous for everybody, Gemini natives are particularly prone to the side effects of smoking. This, combined with his lack of thought nor care for tomorrow (it never comes, right?), means that a lung dis-ease which may accumulate over many years, is ignored or unknown until it is too late. Geminis should therefore be particularly careful not to smoke or be exposed to cigarette smoke, even though it may indeed be a fidgety and sociable habit that proves extremely difficult to give up.

Gemini's ruling planet Mercury governs the Nervous System, Sensory Nerves, Nerve Fluid, Right Cerebral Hemisphere, Tongue, Bile, Buttocks, Hearing, Speech, Hands and Body Tubing. Mercury is believed to control the whole nervous system, and there is an emphasis on the mental processes, which are usually bright and quick in those under its influence, but also makes him vulnerable to nervousness and unspent restless energy. Mercury is also associated with respiration and the mental faculties, such as memory, and nervous or mental disorders may manifest if the Gemini does not take care to nurture the health of his mind. Mercury rules the brain and mind; it is changeable in nature. As a Mercurial child, he may be afflicted with headaches, speech impediments, all manner of respiratory ailments, poor dietary assimilation, intestinal gas, lung and breathing disorders, asthma, and tinnitus or hearing loss.

Overall, Gemini represents the energy of connection and communication, its nature hot, moist, quick and nervous.

GEMINI ✦ ORIENTAL PHYSIOLOGY

Being a masculine sign, Gemini tends more towards conditions of a *Yang* theme and nature, and when these are actively engaged and embraced, this sign will physically function better with more optimal health outcomes. Regardless of this, balance of both polarities is always desirable. Examples of *Yang* concepts are male, Sun, daylight, warmth, brightness, outer, activity, outdoors, above, speed, movement, dryness and expansion.

GEMINI ✦ VITAMINS & MINERALS

Gemini natives would benefit from vitamins and minerals that are ruled by their ruling planet Mercury: the B complex vitamins and magnesium, which assist with proper functioning of the nervous system.

GEMINI ✦ TISSUE SALT: KALI MUR.

The cell salt corresponding with Gemini is *Kali Mur.*, which is an essential component of muscles, blood, mucous membranes, nerve cells and brain cells. It serves to regulate the fibrin of the blood and help rapid-thinking Geminis to maintain clarity and focus without burning out.

GEMINI ✦ HUMOR: SANGUINE

The Air element corresponds with the humor sanguine, which is characterised by quick, impulsive, and relatively short-lived reactions. Sanguine types are analogous with Air, which is the main element in spring, the season with which this temperament has an affinity. Sanguine characters are ruled by Venus and Jupiter, hence the labels Venusian and Jupiterian Sanguines.

Sanguine types are driven by the need for attention and acceptance, social contact, relating, relationships, and trying to impress others. A sanguine disposition represents positivity, optimism, extroversion, expressiveness, talkativeness and light-heartedness. They are generally responsive, carefree, easy-going and lively.

Overall, a sanguine disposition represents sociability and openness. Its taste is bitter, its nature acidic, its indication blood. The sanguine humor is associated with the *gas*˟ body, and with hot and moist conditions.

˟*See under* **ARIES** ✦ *HUMOR: CHOLERIC.*

CANCER ♦ HEALTH

Firstly, it must be noted that the sign Cancer has nothing to do with the dis-ease of the same name. However, because Cancer rules the breasts, women of this sign should ensure they regularly examine them and have periodic medical check-ups regarding this area.

The sign Cancer is associated with the Stomach, Breasts, Lacteal Ducts, Fluidic and Lymphatic Systems, Membranes, Pancreas, Diaphragm, Womb, Chest, Elbows, Thoracic Duct, Blood Serum, and the Alimentary Canal. It also governs the higher organs of digestion.

Principal rulerships, some mentioned previously, include hollow and round organs (e.g. stomach, uterus), pericardium, synovial capsules of joints, vertebral discs, upper lobes of the liver, gall bladder, salivary glands, and the chest cavity. The lymphatic and sympathetic nervous system are particular areas that may prove vulnerable.

The most common accidents to which Cancerians are liable are chest injuries and broken ribs, while their most frequent ailments are ulcers, rheumatism, all complaints involving excess fluids and mucous congestion (such as pneumonia and bronchitis), and all diseases of the stomach and female uterine system. As well, these natives are naturally inclined to over-indulge in food, with consequent indigestion.

Worry can cause Cancerian ailments - emotional stress is an ever-present enemy - and will usually manifest in mental health issues such as melancholia and depression, or physical complaints to do with the abdomen, breast area, or uterus. Sunshine is extremely therapeutic for this sign, as it lifts despondency as well as helps to dry up mucous-related conditions.

Typical illnesses often arise from the upper digestive tract, such as catarrh, anaemia, low energy levels, coughs and indigestion. Flatulence, obesity, contraction of the diaphragm due to panic attacks, and liver complaints are also conditions to watch for. Cancerians may also be vulnerable to eating disorders.

Menstrual issues and disorders in females, such as endometriosis, troublesome periods, fluid retention and premenstrual syndromes, may be a problem, and they may also suffer from hypochondria or psychosomatic illnesses, which are brought on purely by their tendency to be overly emotionally sensitive. In fact, of all the zodiac signs Cancerians are the most susceptible to psychosomatic conditions, as stress and tension can have a most deleterious physical effect on them. This tendency can either put them off food and make them irritable, or it can generate an insatiable appetite that can lead to emotional or comfort-eating, digestive problems and/or weight gain.

Keeping the sensitive Cancerian system in good order requires regular, cyclical exercise. Swimming from as early an age as possible, as well as dancing, are recommended. The vitality of Cancerian people is naturally quite low, but can be encouraged through regular physical activity and a robust, healthy diet.

Disorders affecting the liver and pancreas are prevalent amongst those born under the sign of the Crab, and because both their ruler the Moon and the zodiac sign itself governs over mucous membranes, these are areas commonly prone to illness or adverse conditions.

Cancer rules the Solar Plexus chakra, that highly sensitive nervous 'centre' in the abdomen commonly referred to as 'the pit of the stomach'. It is here - not always the brain - that one first registers what is going on around them, and as a result, the digestion can be frequently upset.

Cancer people are not usually robust in youth and seem to catch more than their share of childhood illnesses. Her recuperative powers may also be somewhat weak, and chronic ailments prevalent. Once she reaches adulthood, her delicate constitution may gather more physical strength and she is then likely to live to a fine old age.

Cancer's ruler the Moon bears a powerful influence on the Crab's health. Sharing many body areas with the sign over which it rules, the Moon governs Body Fluids, Mucous Membranes, Blood, the Lymphatic System, Stomach, Breasts, Womb, Ovaries, Bladder, Oesophagus, Synovial Fluid, the whole Alimentary System, the Senses of Taste and Sight (left eye in males, right eye in females), and the left-hand side of the body.

The Moon has always been considered a fruitful celestial body, encouraging reproduction and the nurturing care of children through the flow of maternal cycles and instinct. The Moon tends to rule over functional ailments rather than organic ones. It has been said that overall health is best when the natal Moon is in a negative/feminine sign like Cancer.

Overall, Cancer represents the energy of enfolding and containment, its nature cold, moist and nourishing.

CANCER ✦ ORIENTAL PHYSIOLOGY

Being a feminine sign, Cancer tends more towards conditions of a *Yin* theme and nature, and when these are actively engaged and embraced, this sign will physically function better with more optimal health outcomes. Regardless of this, balance of both polarities is always desirable. Examples of *Yin* concepts are female, Moon, night, cold, dark, inner, contracting, passive, decreasing, inside, below, damp and slow.

CANCER ✦ VITAMINS & MINERALS

Cancer natives would benefit from vitamins and minerals that are ruled by their ruling planet the Moon, which are those that help to regulate the body's delicate fluid balance, and those that support the nervous system, to reduce worry and excessive emotions: sodium, chloride, potassium, magnesium, and the B complex vitamins.

CANCER ✦ TISSUE SALT: CALC FLUOR.

The cell salt corresponding with Cancer is *Calc Fluor*. Found mainly in the bones, teeth, nerves and muscles, *Calc Fluor.* is especially needed in a potent form in the brain, heart, lungs, kidneys, eyelid, bone covers, muscles and ligaments, as it is necessary where elasticity of the tissue is required for proper functioning. This tissue salt enables the fibres to stretch and then return to their original form.

CANCER ✦ HUMOR: PHLEGMATIC

The Water element corresponds with the phlegmatic humor, characterised by a longer response-delay, but short-lived response. Generally low in drive and motivation, phlegmatic natives seek to preserve low energy stores. Phlegmatic types usually give the impression of being calm, naïve and simple, longing for peace in the soul.

Generally inward, people with this temperament tend to be private, reasonable, patient, caring, thoughtful, passive, sluggish, content, tolerant, have a rich inner life, and seek quiet, peaceful environments. Being impressionable, phlegmatic types are often 'awakened' by others' interests in a subject. Steadfast, placid, controlled, reliable, even-tempered, consistent in their habits, they make steady and loyal friends. Their speech may be slow or hesitant, and they may appear clumsy or ponderous. On a physical level, the home of this humor is in the veins and lymphatics, and this humor nourishes the body on a deep and fundamental level.

A phlegmatic disposition represents a slow, even temperament. Its taste is sweet, its nature alkaline, its indication phlegm. The phlegmatic humor is connected with the *liquid* body, and is traditionally associated with cold and wet conditions.

˚See under **ARIES** ✦ HUMOR: CHOLERIC.

LEO ✦ HEALTH

Leo is associated with the Heart˚, Back, Spine, Upper Back, Forearms, Dorsal Vertebrae, Aorta and Wrists. The Superior and Inferior Vena Cava, Spleen and the Blood is also a domain of Leo's, and the blood, coupled with the heart, are essentially the providers and the sustainers of life.

The vitality of Leo is usually boundless, and they have the ability to absorb the vivifying power of the Sun to the fullest extent; sunshine, coupled with fresh air, is their finest tonic and restorative.

Being of the Fire element, Leos are prone to high fevers, sudden illnesses and accidents. Moreover, perhaps due to their extravagant, indulgent and active lifestyle, prone to heart conditions, cardiovascular events, back injury and pain, and even spinal injuries. They should be wary of overindulging in strenuous physical activity, as this can put a strain on the heart.

Essentially, the heart, spine, back and eyes are the parts of the body most liable to afflictions or injury. Curvature of the spine, angina, irregular heartbeat, palpitations, hypertension, heart dis-ease and back problems in general frequently afflict the Lion. Circulatory problems, meningitis and eye diseases are other common complaints.

The typical Leo is never down for long, seeing incapacitation as a sign of weakness. And although they are normally vital, they can burn themselves out every now and again through over-exertion. Conversely though, because they are naturally energetic, they should guard against being idle or under-occupied as this can weaken the heart and the Leo native may become morose and gloomy, which further affects health and energy levels. In fact, health difficulties may well centre around those parts of the body that control the vitality of it.

Possessing the most robust constitution of the zodiac, Leos are theoretically and arguably the healthiest of all the signs. Their nerves, muscles and vital organs are usually arranged in fine functional balance, and a fiery, outgoing temperament gives them the will to survive - and thrive - in the most challenging of situations.

They can throw off illnesses very rapidly, such are their extraordinary powers of recuperation. Furthermore, fortunately the Leo temperament is largely sanguine and positive, so they are generally able to snap out of depression or despondency relatively quickly.

Leos seldom suffer from chronic or lingering conditions, although periodic eye trouble can be an issue. When illness strikes, it is usually sudden and swift. As a patient, they are inclined to require a lot of attention and, being naturally melodramatic, frequently convince themselves they are in worse shape than they actually are. Initially, they may find it wonderful to be given the opportunity to rest, but this rapidly turns into boredom and restlessness.

A distinct danger period for Leo-born people occurs in middle age. At this stage of life, the superb nervous system that served them so well in their youth becomes easily upset, so they must guard against becoming emotional over trivial things and small provocations.

Diet-wise, they have a natural liking for rich and extravagant foods, but the heart being one of their most vulnerable areas, Leos should watch what they eat and ensure it is heart-enriching and sustaining. Indeed, their great fondness for pleasure can be a health hazard in itself, as they are also an inveterate partygoer, exposing themselves to the dangers of drinking or eating to excess more than they should.

Leo's ruling body the Sun affects the Brain, Heart, Spleen, Sinews, Circulatory System, Cells, the Back, Spinal Cord and the right-hand side of the body, and Lions may experience issues, conditions, afflictions, or injuries in any or all of these parts of the body. The Sun shows vitality, the 'life force', and natural strength of constitution. Solar-ruled weak spots, where dis-ease is most like to occur, are related to the circulation, the blood, the spine, the heart and the eyes.

Overall, Leo represents the energy of dynamism and indulgence, its nature hot, dry and excessive.

The heart is arguably our most vital organ. The ancient Egyptians took the connection between the physical and the spiritual heart very seriously, which is why the heart was the only organ they left in the body at the time of embalming, for they believed that the heart contained one's soul.

The Spiritual Heart ✦ "The heart is a common organ, and rather humble, too. It works unceasingly throughout our lives, never speaking in words or equations, yet carrying the spark of the Divine within. The brain thinks, but the heart knows. The brain analyses, disassembles and reassembles the patterns found in the past, while the heart feels into the future. The heart trusts, carrying us forward into what can be. This is the essence (of the heart), carrying the spiritual pattern of human destiny, our highest future." - **Robert Simmons**

LEO ✦ ORIENTAL PHYSIOLOGY

Being a masculine sign, Leo tends more towards conditions of a *Yang* theme and nature, and when these are actively engaged and embraced, this sign will physically function better with more optimal health outcomes. Regardless of this, balance of both polarities is always desirable. Examples of *Yang* concepts are male, Sun, daylight, warmth, brightness, outer, activity, outdoors, above, speed, movement, dryness and expansion.

LEO ✦ VITAMINS & MINERALS

Leo natives would benefit from the main vitamin that is governed by their ruler the Sun: vitamin D.

LEO ✦ TISSUE SALT: MAG PHOS.

The cell salt corresponding with Leo is *Mag Phos.*, which helps restore nervous force and muscular vigour. Along with *Kali Phos.*, this tissue salt is a principal nerve tonic and remedy. Physiologically *Mag Phos.* has a longstanding tradition of use in conditions involving cramps, nerves, convulsions or spasms, and can help prevent heart attacks and epileptic crises. It can be used as a pain-reliever and is even regarded as a natural aspirin without the side effects.

LEO ✦ HUMOR: CHOLERIC

The Fire element corresponds with the humor choleric, which is characterised by a short response time-delay, but response sustained for a relatively long time. Driven by their goals, for which they will use others as tools to achieve them, a choleric disposition represents touchiness, restlessness, aggression, spirit, excitement, changeability, impulsiveness, activity and optimism.

A person with a choleric temperament is one who is strong, wilful, and even aggressive if necessary. Impatience and anxiety are features, and physically these traits can elicit a response from the liver - stronger than usual biliary secretions.

The choleric character is associated with Fire, which is the ruling element of summer, the season with which the person under this influence has the greatest affinity. The Martian and Sun types, referring to Mars in Aries and the Sun in Leo, are the most common types amongst the cholerics.

Choleric is associated with the ego level of self. Its taste is salty and sour, its nature acidic, its indication yellow bile. The choleric humor is associated with the astral body[**], and with hot and dry conditions.

[**]*See under* **ARIES** ✦ *HUMOR: CHOLERIC.*

VIRGO ✦ HEALTH

Virgo is associated with the Intestines, Digestive System, Lymphatic System, Duodenum, Gall Bladder, Pancreas, Spleen, Nervous System, Abdomen, Colon, Hands, the Liver's Enzyme Production, and Fingernails and Toenails. As Virgo governs the abdomen and intestines, it makes Virgoans susceptible to a wide range of digestive complaints. Peptic ulcers are a notable threat to Virgos, as her delicate nervous system, coupled with food sensitivities and precarious digestive functioning, may result in such flare-ups. Other digestive conditions such as indigestion, constipation, colic, malabsorption, bloating, malnutrition, hernias and diarrhoea, may also present regularly.

Virgo fares best in a cool, crisp climate with natural surroundings, and fresh, unpolluted air. Principal rulerships include the absorption and assimilation of nutrients, the abdomen and Solar Plexus, affinities with hygiene, sanitation and diet, and the autonomic nervous system through its control of the digestive system.

As a general rule, Virgoan health is good, though they are prone to incessant worry and fussing, and to resort to all kinds of different remedies.

Perhaps ironically, given their normally health-conscious propensity, a morbid craving for alcohol or other drugs may be present, especially in Virgos who find themselves unable to cope with reality. Hypochondria is also an ever-present danger for the normally health-conscious Virgoan, particularly those who are inclined to take far too many pills, potions, tonics and vitamin shots to supplement an often highly selective and specialised diet. Moreover, this sign is the most pedantic when it comes to label-checking, analysing and even verifying. Many Virgos are food faddists, even bordering on radical, with many adopting a lifestyle that involves veganism, organic foods, or fad diets.

Generally, quite strong in constitution, Virgos may feel compelled to have frequent health and medical check-ups, if for nothing else but her peace of mind. She certainly doesn't allow any symptom to go on too long without reporting it. Because of this, an illness seldom develops to the stage where it is difficult or impossible to treat.

Nervous system conditions are common in this sign, so Virgo natives would benefit considerably from relaxation techniques such as breathwork, yoga and meditation, to calm their overactive minds and frayed spirits. Additionally, as a result of stress and woes, they are often vulnerable to migraines, stomach aches, depression, headaches, and even various psychosomatic complaints.

Virgos tend towards being workaholics, consequently neglecting other areas of life, for example working through a lunch break or failing to get adequate fresh air or exercise due to workplace duties and responsibilities, or working for long hours.

As a child of nature, it is essential that Virgos spend as much time as possible in clean air and natural surroundings. Naturally drawn to health, nutrition and lifestyle and alternative medicines, medically administered drugs don't suit many Virgoans; holistic and energetic remedies seem to agree with her mental and physical constitution and are often favoured, with excellent results. Balance and moderation are always the best answer to any health issues, and Virgo is a sound advocate of the benefits of these virtues.

The typical Virgoan will usually live to a ripe old age, but, due to her tendency to worry about her health, she can often teeter on the border of obsessive/compulsive behaviours, especially those concerning health.

Virgo's ruling planet Mercury governs the Nervous System, Sensory Nerves, Nerve Fluid, Right Cerebral Hemisphere, Tongue, Bile, Buttocks, Hearing, Speech, Hands and Body Tubing. Mercury is said to control the entire nervous system, particularly the brain and the mind, with an emphasis on the mental processes, which are usually bright and quick in those born under its influence, but also makes its natives vulnerable to nervousness and unspent restless energy. Mercury is also associated with respiration. As a Mercurial child, Virgos may be afflicted with headaches, speech impediments, all manner of respiratory ailments, poor dietary assimilation, intestinal gas, hearing loss and respiratory disorders.

Overall, Virgoan nature is cold, dry and adaptable.

VIRGO ✦ ORIENTAL PHYSIOLOGY

Being a feminine sign, Virgo tends more towards conditions of a *Yin* theme and nature, and when these are actively engaged and embraced, this sign will physically function better with more optimal health outcomes. Regardless of this, balance of both polarities is always desirable. Examples of *Yin* concepts are female, Moon, night, cold, dark, inner, contracting, passive, decreasing, inside, below, damp and slow.

VIRGO ✦ VITAMINS & MINERALS

Virgoan natives would benefit from vitamins and minerals that are ruled by their ruling planet Mercury: the B complex vitamins and magnesium, which assist with proper functioning of the nervous system.

VIRGO ✦ TISSUE SALT: KALI SULPH.

The cell salt corresponding with Virgo is *Kali Sulph*. Found in the epidermal and epithelial cells, it carries oxygen to the cells and acts as a lubricant. Virgo diets need to tend to the processes of elimination through the skin and the liver, and this cell salt helps to facilitate this, thereby cleansing the body. It also improves nutritional absorption, which can particularly benefit Virgo considering this sign rules the digestive system.

VIRGO ✦ HUMOR: MELANCHOLIC

The Earth element corresponds with the humor melancholic, which is characterised by long response time delay, and response sustained at length, if not seemingly permanently. Driven by the fear of rejection and the unknown, they tend to be rigid, moody, anxious, sober, pessimistic, unsociable, responsible and quiet.

The melancholic temperament is analogous with the Earth, which is the main element in autumn (or fall), the season with which Earth signs have many points in common. The nervous system and physical and mental powers reign supreme in melancholic types, although they may often behave in nervous, worried, or unstable ways, too. The Mercurial (Virgo) melancholic is distinguish able from the Saturnian (Capricorn) melancholic through the former's obviously more eccentric and less withdrawn mannerisms.

A melancholic disposition represents anxiety, peace and inflexibility. Its taste is sweet and astringent, its nature alkaline, its indication black bile. The melancholic humor is associated with the physical and solid body*, and with cold and dry conditions.

*See under **ARIES** ✦ HUMOR: CHOLERIC.

LIBRA ✦ HEALTH

Libra is associated with the Kidneys, Skin, Glands, Fallopian Tubes, Urethra, Loins, Vasomotor System, Lumbar Region (Lower Back), Lumbar Vertebrae, Adrenals (with Aries), Acid/Alkaline, Sugar and Temperature Balance, Ears, Blood Vessels, and Blood Cell Membranes.

The kidneys, lumbar regions and skin are particular areas of focus, and its subjects are liable to experience disorders affecting these parts, such as stones, lumbago, nephritis, eczema and other eruptive skin conditions, as well as urinary troubles and diabetic conditions. Liquid processes are also associated with Libra.

Principal rulerships include all endocrine glands, ureters, bladder, physical balance and Eustachian tube*, regulation of acid/alkaline balance in the body, homeostasis-regulating systems, metabolism/thyroid balance, hormones and ovaries.

As a result of any imbalance, Librans may experience urological ailments, chronic back ache, skin troubles, fluid retention, thyroid/metabolic problems, hormonal issues, lower back pain and hypertension due to kidney dysfunction. Sensitivity in the renal system means that Librans more than most need to ensure an adequate fluid intake, including ample purified water and herbal teas. This will maintain and keep Libra's sensitive equilibrium in balance, help clear up any skin disorders, and to keep the kidneys functioning optimally.

Librans fare well on an alkaline-style diet with an abundance of fresh fruits, vegetables and juices. Seafoods and other foods rich in zinc, selenium and iodine are also important to support metabolic and thyroid functions.

As an Air sign, Libra's nerves are prone to overstrain, and he should avoid over-worry, depression and stress. Living or working alone for prolonged periods can be detrimental to Libran health, which may manifest as the typical illnesses attributed to this sign.

Although Libran people usually enjoy good health, they are not as robust as they may appear. Their constitution is very delicate and easily upset by minor ailments and psychological disharmonies; indeed, they have an inherent distaste for discordant conditions, having a natural revulsion for excessive noise, loud people, disharmonious surroundings, vulgarity, coarseness - and just about every other antisocial vibration.

Librans should also guard against any Venus-ruled conditions or afflictions, such as those affecting the following parts of the body or bodily systems, over which Venus rules (and some of which it shares with Libra): Thymus and Thyroid Glands, Venous Circulation, Saliva Ducts, Hormones, Kidneys, Sugar Balance, Hair Shafts and Production, Skin, Neck and the Throat, the Inner Ear, Balance and the Centre of Gravity. Venus is also associated with the Chin, Complexion, Cheeks, Viral Infections, and complaints caused by excesses or pleasures.

Overall, Libra represents the energy of balance, its nature warm, moist and balancing. The basic health rule for Librans is "moderation in all things."

The Eustachian tube is a narrow passage leading from the pharynx to the cavity of the middle ear, permitting the equalisation of pressure on each side of the eardrums.

LIBRA ✦ ORIENTAL PHYSIOLOGY

Being a masculine sign, Libra tends more towards conditions of a *Yang* theme and nature, and when these are actively engaged and embraced, this sign will physically function better with more optimal health outcomes. Regardless of this, balance of both polarities is always desirable. Examples of *Yang* concepts are male, Sun, daylight, warmth, brightness, outer, activity, outdoors, above, speed, movement, dryness and expansion.

LIBRA ✦ VITAMINS & MINERALS

Libran natives would benefit from vitamins and minerals that are ruled by their ruling planet Venus: iodine, copper, sodium/potassium balance, and the bioflavonoids (or Vitamin P).

LIBRA ✦ TISSUE SALT: NAT PHOS.

The cell salt corresponding with Libra is *Nat Phos.*, which is found in blood, muscles, nerve and brain cells and intracellular fluid. It regulates the body's acid/alkaline balance, preventing an excess of either, especially in the bloodstream, and catalyses lactic acid and fat emulsion. Being a sign whose balance and equilibrium is easily upset, Librans need this cell salt to harmonise the balance between acids and alkalis. This is the biochemic acid stabiliser, so is useful in the prevention or treatment of such conditions as gout, digestive upsets, heartburn, stomach acidity, stones and ulcers; in fact, all complaints arising from over-acidity respond well to this salt.

LIBRA ✦ HUMOR: SANGUINE

The Air element corresponds with the humor sanguine, which is characterised by quick, impulsive, and relatively short-lived reactions. Sanguine types are analogous with Air, which is the main element in spring, the season with which this temperament has an affinity. Sanguine characters are ruled by Venus and Jupiter, hence the labels Venusian and Jupiterian Sanguines.

Sanguine types are driven by the need for attention and acceptance, social contact, relating, relationships, and trying to impress others. A sanguine disposition represents positivity, optimism, extroversion, expressiveness, talkativeness and light-heartedness. They are generally responsive, carefree, easy-going and lively.

Overall, a sanguine disposition represents sociability and openness. Its taste is bitter, its nature acidic, its indication blood. The sanguine humor is associated with the gas˚ body, and with hot and moist conditions.

˚See under **ARIES** ✦ *HUMOR: CHOLERIC.*

SCORPIO ✦ HEALTH

Scorpio is associated with the Reproductive System, Pelvis, Orifices, Colon, Rectum, Bladder, other Organs of Elimination, Immune System, Prostate Gland, the Nose, and Hormones. It also governs the Pubic and Nasal Bones, Sigmoid Flexure, Sweat Glands, the Sphenoid Area of the Brain, and Haemoglobin.

Just as Scorpio energy must be evenly spent and controlled, so the physical system needs a regular, controlled diet. This may not be easy, as Scorpio being a sign of extremes, has a tendency towards self-indulgence in food and drink (although on the other side of the coin is her extraordinary self-control, which she uses to great effect when necessary), which often provokes stomach upsets and eliminatory complaints, such as constipation.

Moderation doesn't come easily to Scorpio, but she must cultivate it, both in diet and exercise. The martial arts may interest her, not just for the physical aspect, but for their spiritual and esoteric qualities; the mind- and spirit-discipline these call for are appealing to Scorpio.

Principal rulerships include functions and organs necessary for the species survival, for example reproduction, genetic coding, hormones, ovaries and testes, as well as the purification and eliminatory systems of the body.

Whatever ails Scorpio, their extraordinary willpower and resilience will see them bounce back quickly. The phoenix symbolises Scorpio, and this sign's amazing dynamism and fortitude will usually see her rise from the metaphoric ashes and fly again with transformed wings after bouts of ill-health.

Many Scorpios, due to their passion, simmering emotions, intensity and never doing things by halves (largely fuelled by their Mars-ruled influence), are prone to accidents. Hernias, haemorrhoids, poor toxin elimination, hormone problems, and prostate, bladder, and reproductive system complaints, are the most common ailments to afflict Scorpios. Additionally, uro-genital problems and blockages may manifest.

Pluto, being the modern ruler of Scorpio, is linked, like Mars its traditional ruler, with the gonads. Pluto is connected with all Excretory Functions,

Genitalia, Anus, Rectum, Bladder, Urethra, Sweat Glands, Sinus Cavities, Pituitary Gland, Reproductive System, Mastoid Cavity, and the Immune System. Plutonian ailments may afflict the Scorpio native - conditions associated with the immune system, transformative and genetic functions, and the endocrine system. Other complaints may include sexually transmitted infections, other genital problems, libido issues, obsessions, compulsions, mucous and sinus congestion, hernias, uterine and prostate ailments, and infections and epidemics of all natures.

Excessive drinking can be a problem for Scorpio souls. However, it should be noted they can generally 'hold' their alcohol better than most, and tend to outdistance most of their associates in the liquor stakes. There is a strong self-destructive streak to this character, and although she doesn't deliberately set out to destroy herself, she refuses to acknowledge any limits as she wishes ardently to experience all life has to offer - which includes the good, the bad, the ugly, and the downright perilous. Often this search for sensation and knowledge leads to dangerous experimentation with drugs, substances Scorpios have a strong leaning towards.

Occult phenomena, with their self-charging emotional energies and intricate rites of invocation, are likely to draw Scorpios in too. The changes in perception that psychic stimuli and narcotics induce can be fascinating - but occasionally hazardous - to a psyche of this nature. And sexual excess is another area Scorpio may find difficult to resist. But she can just as easily exercise her tremendous self-control and give up a bad habit if she deems it detrimental to her health. Indeed, her inner resources are stronger and more pronounced than any other zodiac sign, standing her in good stead in any health crisis.

One of her most vulnerable areas is the stomach. Various disturbances are likely in the digestive system, especially as a result of the excesses and extremes previously mentioned. This is why it is so important that she prevent the build-up of emotional and dietary corrosives that weaken the organs and attack the stomach, causing ulcers and the like. Brooding, worry and depression should always be watched by Scorpions.

The Scorpio constitution is generally robust, rugged and healthy. No other Sun sign has at its disposal such a great reserve of sheer tenacious energy. But there is always a danger that she may push herself beyond physical endurance once she's resolved to accomplish something, ignoring the normal limitations that frequently culminates in a breakdown of some kind. Therefore, she should remain ever conscious of the fact that her will is often stronger than her body. Ultimately, she has a strong constitution provided she keeps her elimination channels clear and open and takes care not to push her body beyond its capacity.

A most important health reminder for Scorpio is that so pernicious is her power to resent, seethe and hate, she can literally poison herself with her own emotions. When unwell, Scorpios need a secluded, even hidden environment, in order to process and rebalance their minds, bodies and spirits.

Scorpio represents the energy of survival and purification, her nature watery, cold and magnetic.

SCORPIO ✦ ORIENTAL PHYSIOLOGY

Being a feminine sign, Scorpio tends more towards conditions of a *Yin* theme and nature, and when these are actively engaged and embraced, this sign will physically function better with more optimal health outcomes. Regardless of this, balance of both polarities is always desirable. Examples of *Yin* concepts are female, Moon, night, cold, dark, inner, contracting, passive, decreasing, inside, below, damp and slow.

SCORPIO ✦ VITAMINS & MINERALS

Scorpio natives would benefit from vitamins and minerals that are ruled by their ruling planet Pluto: vitamin E, zinc and selenium, which all assist to balance the hormonal and reproductive systems.

SCORPIO ✦ TISSUE SALT: CALC SULPH.

The cell salt corresponding with Scorpio is *Calc Sulph.*, which is found in bile, mucous membranes and tissues, and promotes continual blood cleansing. An excellent blood purifier, it also has a potent detoxifying effect on the liver. It can be used for cellular regeneration, and as a purifying agent is essential to all healing processes. Along with the cell salt Silica, this is the salt most commonly used for wound-healing. *Calc Sulph.* provides a coating to all the bodily areas associated with Scorpio, such as the colon, internal sexual organs, large intestine, prostate gland, and eliminative channels and outlets. When a deficiency occurs, toxic build-up can result; other manifestations of *Calc Sulph.* lack are impotence and infertility, as it renders the body incapable of providing an adequate protective coating for egg and sperm. Overall, this tissue salt is effective in preventing general ill health and infections of all kinds.

SCORPIO ✦ HUMOR: PHLEGMATIC

The Water element corresponds with the phlegmatic humor, characterised by a longer response-delay, but short-lived response. Generally low in drive and motivation, phlegmatic natives seek to preserve low energy stores. Phlegmatic types usually give the impression of being calm, naïve and simple, longing for peace in the soul.

Generally inward, people with this temperament tend to be private, reasonable, patient, caring, thoughtful, passive, sluggish, content, tolerant, have a rich inner life and seek quiet, peaceful environments. Being impressionable, phlegmatic types are often 'awakened' by others' interests in a subject. Steadfast, placid, controlled, reliable, even-tempered, consistent in their habits, they make steady and loyal friends. Their speech may be slow or hesitant, and they may appear clumsy or ponderous. On a physical level, the home of this humor is in the veins and lymphatics, and this humor nourishes the body on a deep and fundamental level.

A phlegmatic disposition represents a slow, even temperament. Its taste is sweet, its nature alkaline, its indication phlegm. The phlegmatic humor is connected with the *liquid* body, and is traditionally associated with cold and wet conditions.

*See under ARIES ✦ HUMOR: CHOLERIC.

SAGITTARIUS ✦ HEALTH

Jupiter natures rebel against confinement, and too much of it can bring on serious illness. If the Sagittarian can survive that, and the wear and tear of scattering his energies, he'll live to be as old as Methuselah. Most Archers retain their faculties, razor sharp and refined by age, to the end. Senility is almost never a problem.

Linda Goodman

Many blessings do the advancing years bring with them.

Horace, Sagittarius

Sagittarius is associated with the Hips, Thighs, Liver, Sciatic Nerves, Pelvis, Blood, Loins, Femur, Femoral Artery, Blood Vessels, Iliac Nerves, Coccyx Vertebrae, Ischium, Occipital Lobe, Sacral Region, and Gluteus Muscles.

Typical Sagittarians are usually healthy and energetic, and their optimistic outlook ensures they usually recover quickly from any illness, as well as keeping them strong in mind if sickness strikes. The hips, thighs, nerves and arteries are under the rule of Sagittarius, and its subjects may suffer rheumatism in the lower legs, as well as sciatica, pelvic disorders, jaundice, gout, and nervous disorders. The lungs and throat may also be delicate, and Sagittarians can be prone to bronchitis and lung troubles. Sagittarians often suffer from hips and leg conditions or accidents - the commonest accidents suffered by Sagittarians are those affecting the lower limbs, dislocation of the hip and thigh (femur) fractures - the whole range of arthritic and rheumatic problems, and injuries arising from sports and outdoor adventures.

The typical Sagittarian needs constant contact with a wide variety of people and experiences to keep himself in good health. His nervous system is keenly adapted to respond to the joys and freedoms of outdoor activities and he must keep on the go - visiting, participating, discussing, exchanging. Any prolonged curtailment or restraint is likely to be damaging to his spirit, and in turn, his health, even leading to breakdowns.

Sagittarians have above average resistance to most dis-eases and he is rarely incapacitated with serious afflictions; on the rare occasion he is confined to bed, he soon becomes restless, bored and distressed.

His longevity is one of the best in the zodiac, provided he doesn't burn himself out with speedy, reckless pursuits or careless, thrill-seeking activities. He needs to temper his use of energy reserves and take care not to over-extend himself to the point of exhaustion. He often doesn't make the best of his vitality, as he has a habit of scattering his energies in ways that produce very little that is worthwhile, purposeful, substantial, or productive.

A great believer in tomorrow, he is helped by an extremely optimistic attitude toward life. Being so good-natured and cheerful helps to keep him fit on all levels.

Sagittarius's ruling planet Jupiter is associated with the Blood, Arterial System, Pleura, Right Ear, Liver, Hips, Thighs, Arteries, Semen, Lungs, Varicose Veins, Nerve Sheaths, Glycogen, Suprarenals, Blood Fibrin, Upper Forehead, and the Disposal and Dispersal of Body Fats. It is also connected with the Pituitary Gland, which regulates hormone production and bodily growth. Jovial Jupiter's influence upon Sagittarius is also likely to indicate health problems arising from over-indulgence in food and alcohol. Biliousness is highly likely if his diet is not watched carefully. Jupiterian conditions may arise if he indulges in a careless or extravagant lifestyle, such as high cholesterol, liver ailments, obesity, diabetes, stroke, hypertension and gout.

Overall, Sagittarius represents the energy of movement and freedom, its nature dry, hot and expansive.

SAGITTARIUS ✦ ORIENTAL PHYSIOLOGY

Being a masculine sign, Sagittarius tends more towards conditions of a *Yang* theme and nature, and when these are actively engaged and embraced, this sign will physically function better with more optimal health outcomes. Regardless of this, balance of both polarities is always desirable. Examples of *Yang* concepts are male, Sun, daylight, warmth, brightness, outer, activity, outdoors, above, speed, movement, dryness and expansion.

SAGITTARIUS ✦ VITAMINS & MINERALS

Sagittarian natives would benefit from the minerals that are ruled by their ruling planet Jupiter: silica and chromium.

SAGITTARIUS ✦ TISSUE SALT: SILICA

The cell salt corresponding with Sagittarius is *Silica*. Present in the body in only trace amounts, *Silica* is vital to bone development, dental health, cartilage flexibility, and the health of connective tissues. Found mainly in connective tissues, the epidermis and the brain, it is a basic nutrient for the hair, skin, teeth and nails, used to cleanse and eliminate wastes, with a slow but deep and long-lasting effect on the body. *Silica* is referred to as the 'homeopathic surgeon' due to its ability to assist the body to throw off non-functional organic matter. As Sagittarius rules the liver, sciatic nerve, hips, thighs, and the autonomic nervous system, Sagittarians who are under stress tend to use up their *Silica*, leaving them more susceptible to chronic problems involving liver function or hip degeneration as they age.

SAGITTARIUS ✦ HUMOR: CHOLERIC

The Fire element corresponds with the humor choleric, which is characterised by a short response time-delay, but response sustained for a relatively long time. Driven by their goals, for which they will use others as tools to achieve them, a choleric disposition represents touchiness, restlessness, aggression, spirit, excitement, changeability, impulsiveness, activity and optimism.

A person with a choleric temperament is one who is strong, wilful, and even aggressive if necessary. Impatience and anxiety are features, and physically these traits can elicit a response from the liver - stronger than usual biliary secretions.

The choleric character is associated with Fire, which is the ruling element of summer, the season with which the person under this influence has the greatest affinity. The Martian and Sun types, referring to Mars in Aries and the Sun in Leo, are the most common types amongst the cholerics.

Choleric is associated with the ego level of self. Its taste is salty and sour, its nature acidic, its indication yellow bile. The choleric humor is associated with the astral body**, and with hot and dry conditions.

***See under ARIES ✦ HUMOR: CHOLERIC.*

CAPRICORN ✦ HEALTH

Generally speaking, if they avoid lingering illnesses caused by lingering depressions, the Capricorn tenacity for life is remarkable. But it's no fun to be the last leaf on the tree if you're suffering from arthritis and rheumatism. The Goat must seek the sunlight and laugh at the rain to stay healthy.

Linda Goodman

Capricorn is associated with the Knees, Joints, Ligaments, Bones, Skin, Hair, Nails, Teeth, Corpus Callosum, Synovial Fluid, Parathyroid Glands, Mastoid Bone, and Gallbladder. Most Capricorns are less than robust when they are young, but their resistance to diseases seems to increase as they age. Being sober, sensible and temperate, they are the most likely of the signs to live to a substantial age. One of the natural survivors of the zodiac, there is not much in the way of sickness that they can't shake off or come to terms with. It has been said that Capricorns are 'born old and grow young', therefore the older they are, the younger and more active they seem to be for their age.

Capricorns usually encounter three main health problems. The first occurs in childhood, when they are likely to be either sickly or weaker than most of their peers, catching every minor complaint going around. The second problem is they are more liable to psychosomatic illnesses than most other signs; they are great worriers and can literally worry themselves sick. Thirdly, they are subject to vague aches and pains, the most pernicious of which are rheumatism and arthritis. However, the health troubles that afflict Capricorn natives are not the kind that will shorten life; they are much more inclined to cause discomfort and irritations that, unfortunately, may persist over long periods of time.

Capricorn rules the muscles and the bones, particularly the knees. Everything that hardens and protects in the body is under its influence. It gives a tough, wiry constitution that is capable of undergoing extreme hardship. The symbol for Capricorn, the Goat, is a very hardy animal with qualities of endurance and the ability to survive in austere conditions. When struck by illness, Capricorns are usually slow but steady to recover, and persevere to overcome what ails them at all costs.

Anxiety, over-responsibility, over-work, gloominess and general pessimism tend to take their toll on Capricornian health however, so they need to learn to relax, lighten up and have fun. Psychologically, they need to guard against fear, worry, withdrawal and depression, for their physical health suffers due to these introspective emotions. Capricorn's worst health hazard is indeed their angst; this not only affects their appetite, but also impairs the entire constitution.

Chronic fatigue can be a manifestation of the Capricornian tendency to be melancholic. It is in their later years, when negativity and morbidity have become habitual, that the worst effects may be felt. With Capricorn people, excessive drinking is more likely to be a self-medication for depression or the like, than an addiction or extreme behaviour.

Being the great organiser and leader, Capricorns seem to thrive on clearing away obstacles and sorting out tangles in everyday affairs, and it is important to her health and spirit that she be busily involved in some sort of work or project, as she has a strong distaste for being idle or lazy.

On a more positive note, the Capricornian nervous system is highly developed and they are not easily unbalanced. Robust and strong-willed in times of crisis, this sign is the best equipped of anyone to take charge. But their problem will always lie in coming to terms with their own internal pressures and sorrows.

The commonest physical ills of Capricorns are knee problems, joint inflammations, cartilage issues, skin disorders, constipation, toothache and earache. They should ensure they get enough calcium, for they are susceptible to bone and joint dis-eases such as osteoporosis, osteoarthritis, dental problems and knee joint issues, and calcium and other co-nutrients like vitamin D will attenuate this risk.

As Capricorn is linked with the strong, consistent energy of Saturn, illnesses will be steadily overcome through determination, practicality and health wisdom. Saturn governs the Teeth, Spleen, Gall Bladder, Phlegm, Bones and Stones, Skin, Vagus Nerve, Joints, Ligaments, Sigmoid Colon, Mastoid Bone, Hearing and Sluggishness. It is also associated with the anterior lobe of the Pituitary Gland, which regulates hormonal activity.

Capricorn represents the energy of structure and form, its nature cool, dry and structured.

CAPRICORN ✦ ORIENTAL PHYSIOLOGY

Being a feminine sign, Capricorn tends more towards conditions of a *Yin* theme and nature, and when these are actively engaged and embraced, this sign will physically function better with more optimal health outcomes. Regardless of this, balance of both polarities is always desirable. Examples of *Yin* concepts are female, Moon, night, cold, dark, inner, contracting, passive, decreasing, inside, below, damp and slow.

CAPRICORN ✦ VITAMINS & MINERALS

Capricornian natives would benefit from vitamins and minerals that are ruled by their ruling planet Saturn: sulphur, calcium and phosphorus.

CAPRICORN ✦ TISSUE SALT: CALC PHOS.

The cell salt corresponding with Capricorn is *Calc Phos.*, which is an important constituent of bones and is found in abundance in all tissues, fertile soil, blood plasma and corpuscles, saliva, bone, gastric juices, epidermal fibres, new blood cells, and the dentin of teeth. Regarded as a 'life-sustaining mineral', it has numerous crucial functions. It is essential for the proper growth and nutrition of the body, strengthens bones, helps to builds new blood cells, and improves gastric digestive function so all ingested vitamins and minerals are better assimilated. Its sedative properties also make it a useful remedy for sleeplessness. Since it often intensifies the action of other cell salts, it is a good companion remedy. Capricorn rules the skeletal system, and especially the teeth, joints and knees, so could benefit from this cell salt.

CAPRICORN ✦ HUMOR: MELANCHOLIC

The Earth element corresponds with the humor melancholic, which is characterised by long response time delay, and response sustained at length, if not seemingly permanently. Driven by the fear of rejection and the unknown, they tend to be rigid, moody, anxious, sober, pessimistic, unsociable, responsible and quiet.

The melancholic temperament is analogous with the Earth, which is the main element in autumn (or fall), the season with which Earth signs have many points in common. The nervous system and physical and mental powers reign supreme in melancholic types, although they may often behave in nervous, worried, or unstable ways, too. The Mercurial (Virgo) melancholic is distinguishable from the Saturnian (Capricorn) melancholic through the former's obviously more eccentric and less withdrawn mannerisms.

A melancholic disposition represents anxiety, peace and inflexibility. Its taste is sweet and astringent, its nature alkaline, its indication black bile. The melancholic humor is associated with the physical and *solid* body˚, and with cold and dry conditions.

˚See under **ARIES** ✦ HUMOR: CHOLERIC.

AQUARIUS ✦ HEALTH

The fact that the mind rules the body is, in spite of its neglect by biology and medicine, the most fundamental fact which we know about the process of life.

Franz Alexander, M.D., Aquarius

Aquarius is associated with the Lower Legs (Calves, Ankles, Fibula, Tibia, Heels), Blood Circulatory System, Heart Valves, Oxidation Processes of the Body, the Pituitary Gland, Sympathetic Nervous System, Motor Nerves, and Spinal Cord. Varicose veins, circulatory problems, nervous conditions, hypertension, weakness of limbs, ankle troubles, anaemia, cramps, blood pressure issues, anxiety, cold hands and feet, eye problems and haemorrhoids may be conditions which ail him.

Principal rulerships, some mentioned previously, include the blood and circulation, nerve impulses and energy, lower leg, hypothalamus, and the cellular mitochondria in which energy is generated. Aquarius also has affinities with the meridian systems, auras, chakras and biorhythms, and therefore respond well to alternative therapies and energetic forms of treatment.

Aquarians more than most, need an abundance of fresh air, sleep and regular exercise to stay healthy. They tend to eat unusual combinations of foods and large amounts of a single food, which can create health imbalances. They also need to take extra care with their usage of salt, as they tend to have a 'savoury tooth' and this can lead to excesses.

Aquarians are among the longest-lived types of the zodiac. Their constitution is wiry rather than strong and although they are quite willing to engage in physical toil if needed, they're not essentially built for stamina or prolonged exertion.

They have tremendous reserves of nervous energy, and it is this rather than physical vitality that keeps them going at such a rate. When they have an idea or an ideal to work towards, they have the capacity for intense effort for lengthy periods - but their mental interest must be engaged.

Aquarians also need their friends around them; companionship is like a therapy for these souls whenever they feel jaded or depleted, and denied this connection with a wide variety of people, they may feel under par. Yet they also require very definite periods of seclusion, to relax in solitude or wander off alone into a forest to restore the mind, body and spirit. Their dynamism will rapidly return if they take this necessary time out when needed.

Often an Aquarian's manic mental activity manifests as nervous complaints and stress-related conditions, which usually sort themselves out without much fuss, but the Water Bearer does have a distinct propensity to act like an antenna to abounding energies and vibrations, and if these are discordant, his nervous system may suffer.

Aquarius seems to be vulnerable to prevailing weather conditions - which are always too hot, too cold, too humid, or too dry. Perhaps more than other signs who are not so sensitive to the surrounding environment and its energy waves, these souls need to live in the climate and location that suits their constitution and needs.

Circulatory problems and diseases of the blood and nervous system are common in Aquarians, and they are prone to varicose veins, and calf and ankle accidents or afflictions.

As Aquarius is linked with the sudden and unexpected energy of the planet Uranus, they may suffer from unpredictable, inexplicable illnesses that can then clear up again just as mysteriously. Uranus governs the Overall Brain, Cerebral and Nervous Functions, Rhythmic Systems, Spasms, Electricity, Nerves, Ankles, and the Circulation. Uranus is also associated with fractures, and if these occur, they usually strike below the knee.

Uranus is linked with the 'pineal body', the curious 'Third Eye', and believed to rule those parts of the physical eye which, when developed, can see the human aura.

Overall, Aquarius represents patterns of energy flow, its nature hot, moist and electric.

AQUARIUS ✦ ORIENTAL PHYSIOLOGY

Being a masculine sign, Aquarius tends more towards conditions of a *Yang* theme and nature, and when these are actively engaged and embraced, this sign will physically function better with more optimal health outcomes. Regardless of this, balance of both polarities is always desirable. Examples of *Yang* concepts are male, Sun, daylight, warmth, brightness, outer, activity, outdoors, above, speed, movement, dryness and expansion.

AQUARIUS ✦ VITAMINS & MINERALS

Aquarian natives would benefit from vitamins and minerals that are ruled by their ruling planet Uranus: vitamin B12, magnesium, calcium and manganese are some vitamins and minerals that assist with proper functioning of the nervous and electrical conduction systems of the body.

AQUARIUS ✦ TISSUE SALT: NAT MUR.

The cell salt corresponding with Aquarius is *Nat Mur.*, which is simply salt, a substance present in the natural world in greater quantities than any other except water. It is essential to life and health. Any condition involving too much dryness or too much moisture indicates the use of this salt, which has a fluid-regulating effect by attracting or drawing away water from affected parts of the body, to redistribute it wherever it is needed. Aquarius rules the circulation and blood, the ankles, the spinal cord and the electrical impulses of the nerves, and *Nat Mur.* may help in supporting the smooth and even flow of electricity through and across the nerves.

AQUARIUS ✦ HUMOR: SANGUINE

The Air element corresponds with the humor sanguine, which is characterised by quick, impulsive and relatively short-lived reactions.

Sanguine types are analogous with Air, which is the main element in spring, the season with which this temperament has an affinity. Sanguine characters are ruled by Venus and Jupiter, hence the labels Venusian and Jupiterian Sanguines.

Sanguine types are driven by the need for attention and acceptance, social contact, relating, relationships, and trying to impress others. A sanguine disposition represents positivity, optimism, extroversion, expressiveness, talkativeness and light-heartedness. They are generally responsive, carefree, easy-going and lively.

Overall, a sanguine disposition represents sociability and openness. Its taste is bitter, its nature acidic, its indication blood. The sanguine humor is associated with the *gas˚* body, and with hot and moist conditions.

˚*See under* **ARIES** ✦ *HUMOR: CHOLERIC.*

PISCES ✦ HEALTH

Pisces is associated with the Feet, Toes, Lymphatic System, Immune System, Clotting Mechanisms, Blood Circulation, Veins, Body Fluids, Synovia, Nervous Digestion, Liver, Pineal Gland, Peritoneum, Appendix, Allergies, and the Gastro-Abdominal System. Pisceans are healthy people as long as they feel loved and have an outlet for their dreamy natures. Unhappy or despondent Pisceans are prone to problems arising from their escapist tendencies, such as indulging in alcohol, drugs or even developing eating disorders as a way of coping with emotions that may feel unbearable. Having such a delicate and impressionable constitution, intoxicants and narcotics should be avoided. Pisces are more susceptible than most to addiction-related physical and mental health problems should they choose that path. Indeed, being easily led and rather weak-willed, an addiction or a compulsion of some kind will likely be an issue for Pisceans at some stage in their life. Pisceans are also vulnerable to depression and distress, a manifestation of constantly having to struggle to swim against the current to avoid being pulled under or overwhelmed.

Principal rulerships, as well as those already mentioned, include diffusion/movement of fluids and gases, immune and lymphatic functions, and cerebral spinal fluid.

Finding comfortable shoes can be a problem for Pisceans, as this sign rules the feet. Also, troubles with or deformities of the feet and toes, hands, or hips, may afflict Pisceans, and they may suffer such conditions such as bunions, chilblains, gout, corns, boils and foot deformities which make finding proper-fitting shoes even harder to find. Vein and circulation problems, the lymphatic system and the spleen in its lymphatic role, and inexplicable conditions that are difficult to diagnose or treat can also affect the Fish. Flus, colds and pneumonia are common ailments too, which the Fish may find hard to shake off. Curiously, a typical Pisces may become more forgetful than usual when an illness is about to strike.

The sensitive psyche of the Piscean can suffer greatly in times of stress, and has little to draw on in terms of physical resources. Although they have a hidden inner resistance to many ills, one of her greatest challenges is to discover her latent strengths and call upon them. As well, she has an uncanny ability to hypnotise herself into or out of anything she chooses, therefore choosing her thoughts with care is paramount to her health - both physical and mental.

Overall Pisces's health prospects are generally good, if she can avoid becoming too receptive to surrounding people and conditions, as she is prone to attracting similar conditions to those in her immediate environment, such is her receptivity, and as such are more vulnerable than most to infectious diseases. Easily picking up vibrations in the atmosphere, she can be physically affected by such things as an unkind word, an argument or even depressing weather. This sensitivity can disturb the Piscean constitution and afflict her greatly with emotionally based health conditions.

Pisces should also beware of overindulgence in food, of which they are very fond. Poor eating habits can bring troubles with intestinal functions and digestive issues; sluggishness of the liver may also be a problem. Her metabolism is weaker and less dynamic than that of the other signs, often possessing a slow metabolism, which is why she may often wake up sleepy-eyed and listless. She can also run out of energy quite quickly.

Pisces are the most suggestible sign of the zodiac, so respond very well to optimistic and encouraging doctors; if they are assured they're making progress by someone in authority or one whose opinion they respect, they invariably show immediate improvement.

Pisces's ruling planet Neptune is connected with weakness, suggestibility, psychosomatic illnesses, delusions, obsessions, tendency to allergies, viruses and infections, sleep disorders, habits, poisons, hypochondria, alcoholism and drug abuse, parasites, food sensitivities and misdiagnoses. Neptune governs the Lymphatic System, Spleen, Pineal Gland, Immune System, White Blood Cells, Seminal Fluid, Fallopian Tubes, Intrauterine Fluid, Fluid in Flesh, and those parts of the nervous system which are receptive to psychic impressions. It is also influential in the functioning of the chakras (the psychic centres of bodily energy) and the human aura. Its governance extends to the Thalamus, a brain structure which affects the transmission of stimuli between the sensory organs.

Pisces's dreamy nature can lead her to forget to eat or drink. She needs to pay particular attention to her nutrition, hydration and sleeping regime, or her immune system will suffer. When unwell, this soul needs quiet, peaceful surroundings as near as possible to water, be it the ocean, a lake, or a spa health retreat. Music, fresh air, sunshine and regular grounding activities will also help restore balance to a frayed spirit.

Pisces represents the energy of nebulousness and diffusion, its nature cold, watery and receptive.

PISCES ✦ ORIENTAL PHYSIOLOGY

Being a feminine sign, Pisces tends more towards conditions of a *Yin* theme and nature, and when these are actively engaged and embraced, this sign will physically function better with more optimal health outcomes. Regardless of this, balance of both polarities is always desirable. Examples of *Yin* concepts are female, Moon, night, cold, dark, inner, contracting, passive, decreasing, inside, below, damp and slow.

PISCES ✦ VITAMINS & MINERALS

Piscean natives would benefit from vitamins and minerals that are ruled by their ruling planet Neptune: vitamins A and C, zinc and potassium.

PISCES ✦ TISSUE SALT: FERR PHOS.

The cell salt corresponding with Pisces is *Ferr Phos.*, which is a mineral compound of iron and phosphorous. Both these substances occur in the body independently; phosphorous contributes to bone and muscle health, and iron aids the exchange of oxygen in the blood. *Ferr Phos.* is the only common metal salt among the twelve cell salts, and is vital in its function of making all of the other salts more effective. Pisces rules the lymphatic system and the feet. Just as the feet are the foundation of the whole body, iron is the foundation of the blood. *Ferr Phos.* delivers oxygen to all organs and tissues, and enables the blood and the lymphatic system to carry waste and toxins away from affected tissues. Iron is known as a magnetic compound and on a spiritual level, this magnetism is made possible by a deep intuitive knowledge, of both the interlocking bodily cycles and the rotations of cosmic activity.

PISCES ✦ HUMOR: PHELGMATIC

The Water element corresponds with the phlegmatic humor, characterised by a longer response-delay, but short-lived response. Generally low in drive and motivation, phlegmatic natives seek to preserve low energy stores. Phlegmatic types usually give the impression of being calm, naïve and simple, longing for peace in the soul.

Generally inward, people with this temperament tend to be private, reasonable, patient, caring, thoughtful, passive, sluggish, content, tolerant, have a rich inner life, and seek quiet, peaceful environments. Being impressionable, phlegmatic types are often 'awakened' by others' interests in a subject. Steadfast, placid, controlled, reliable, even-tempered, consistent in their habits, they make steady and loyal friends. Their speech may be slow or hesitant, and they may appear clumsy or ponderous. On a physical level, the home of this humor is in the veins and lymphatics, and this humor nourishes the body on a deep and fundamental level.

A phlegmatic disposition represents a slow, even temperament. Its taste is sweet, its nature alkaline, its indication phlegm. The phlegmatic humor is connected with the *liquid* body, and is traditionally associated with cold and wet conditions.

˙*See under* **ARIES** ✦ *HUMOR: CHOLERIC.*

MONEY ATTRIBUTES OF EACH SIGN

Striving for financial gain and abundance with a healthy inner moral compass is a noble intention. When we have more money, we are better placed to help ourselves and of course help others; after all, as Abraham Maslow's Hierarchy of model (1943) attests, once our primary and base survival needs have been satisfied, we can then advance higher towards loftier achievements, such as self-confidence, creativity and self-actualisation. Prosperity allows us to turn our attention to these more transcendental matters - to reach for lives not just of material comfort and luxuries, but of meaning, generosity, balance, harmony, fulfilment and joy. Our Sun sign can offer clues as to how we go about acquiring, earning, saving, maintaining, and allowing the overall flow of giving and receiving money. What's your money style and your lucky colour for increased earning or cash-magnetising potential, according to *your* zodiac sign?

WHO SHOULD YOU GO INTO BUSINESS WITH?

Each zodiac sign belongs to a certain mode - Cardinal, Fixed or Mutable. As previously outlined elsewhere in the text, these astrological quadruplicities represent the three basic qualities inherent in all life: creation (Cardinal), preservation (Fixed) and destruction (Mutable).
In essence, the Cardinal signs are adept at using their enthusiasm and enterprise to initiate the beginnings of a project or business, the Fixed signs are masters of endurance, determination, stability, tenacity, focus and fixity of purpose to last the distance and see things through to completion, and the Mutable signs are skilled at maintaining flexibility, adaptability, movement, freshness, and the flow of ideas throughout. This being the case, two Cardinal signs working together may both burn out before a project can lift itself off the ground, two Fixed signs may both be too rigid and obstinate rendering undertakings stuck and immovable, and two Mutable signs may not be able to sustain their interest due to scattered energies, lack of focus, over-flexibility, and too many pots on the boil at once. It is therefore not recommended that two signs of the same mode work together when it comes to serious business partnerships; rather you should choose someone who is from a different mode to yourself, so that they may complement your own style for a greater chance of success.

ARIES ✦ MONEY STYLE

Colour for Increased Earning Power ✦ Red

It doesn't seem to break the Mars spirit that cash doesn't always cling to him, perhaps because what he seeks is not necessarily in the bank.

Linda Goodman

Aries is essentially an idealist when it comes to money and what it can buy. "Give him a choice of money or glory, and he'll take glory any time," Linda Goodman remarked on the Aries spirit when it comes to financial matters. Conquering and striving is what the Ram is all about, and whether he has one dollar in the bank or one million, he will feel rich just for having run - and won - the race to attain it.

Aries are likely to make money from entrepreneurial enterprises but need to watch out for impulsive decisions and the need for instant gratification and quick returns. They spend freely and on a whim, with a penchant for risk-taking, and often neglect to put in safeguards like insurance and savings plans.

Aries enjoys the thrill of gambling, and any speculative spending is usually done so only if there is opportunity to make money swiftly and easily.

Money is important to Aries, mainly because of the things it can buy, and being impetuous and rather childlike, he tends to spend lavishly and thoughtlessly. Usually willing to save up for certain things, he is lucky that money comes to him so freely. Moreover, he has a knack for keeping the money flowing in, but it can sometimes flow right out again just as easily! On top of this, he is incredibly generous, but needs to keep this in check as he is inclined to give too freely on a regular basis, his intrinsic generosity sometimes opening the gateway for others to take advantage of him.

Aries is forever trying to widen his financial horizons by whatever means possible. Being an independent spirit and a bit of a freedom-seeker, he loves that money can indeed buy him the lifestyle he so desires - and that, to the fun-loving, adventure-seeking Ram, is the ultimate freedom.

ARIES ✦ DOING BUSINESS

Ideal business partners ✦ Gemini & Aquarius

Aries, being a Cardinal sign, would benefit greatly from going into business with Gemini, a sign of Mutable charge and flexibility, or Aquarius, a Fixed sign whose originality and fixity of vision will help carry his plans through to completion. With either of these two complementary signs, business is likely to reach great heights. If he seeks them out, he's likely to be pleasantly surprised that the partnership allows his wildest dreams to unfold.

TAURUS ✦ MONEY STYLE

Colour for Increased Earning Power ✦ Green

The Bull and his money are seldom parted. Not every Taurean is a millionaire, but you won't find many of them standing in line for free soup. Taurus likes to build empires slowly and surely. Oddly, Taurus likes to accumulate power, along with cash, but simply for the sensual enjoyment of possessing it.

Linda Goodman

Taurus and money are like a hand and glove. "Sooner or later, money will come to Taurus, and it usually sticks like glue when it does," observed astrologer Linda Goodman.

Taureans are very competent financially, know the value of money, and tend to seek secure investments. Rarely fooled by get-rich-quick schemes, Taurus only invests after careful and thorough research.

Handling money with care, wisdom and caution is instinctive and comes as second nature to this native. However, having a knack for amassing money in the bank and also spending on good-quality and luxury items, she may be prone to greed and over-accumulation.

Taurus, more than any other sign, has an innate and robust sense of money. She puts money into bricks and mortar and insures everything. Relating to the Second House of the horoscope, which is connected to the material realm, possessions, income and security, a substantial and regular income is vital to Taureans.

Although she is possessive about most things in life, with money she often has a generous heart and open pockets, liking to help friends and family out if they are needing help.

Taurus can be protective of her resources and seldom wastes money. Careful, controlled, cautious and patient, she's the least likely of the zodiac to be wildly extravagant or to make frivolous purchases. She does, however, have an insatiable appetite for luxury, beauty and comfort, and those things that only money can buy; she is ruled by the opulent Venus, after all.

Perhaps Taurus's biggest potential downfall lies in being unable to distinguish between need and greed, and although generous at times, at other times she may withhold or hoard money stubbornly.

Taurus can make money by almost any venture, as she has a natural flair for sniffing things out that will increase her stores of cash, investments, or savings. Farms, land, real estate, art, and general finance are all areas that she could benefit from investing in, as she is instinctively drawn to and possesses knowledge around each. Conversely, she can also be insecure with regards to finances, as she feels she has to work harder and longer than most to achieve financial stability.

Taurus enjoys giving the impression of wealth and is capable of making money work for herself extremely efficiently, through putting it into different schemes, and manipulating it shrewdly and successfully.

Usually, her money prospects are good and wealth, or at least a steady stream of prosperity, tends to flow to Venusian subjects, whether through their career, investments in luxuries, legacy, or a fortunate marriage.

Finally, it's no coincidence that Taurus has superior mastery over money and the things it can buy; her special phrase after all, is "I possess." And this Venusian goddess takes that responsibility very, very seriously.

TAURUS ✦ DOING BUSINESS

Ideal business partners ✦ Cancer & Pisces

Taurus, being a Fixed sign, would benefit greatly from going into business with Cancer, a sign of enterprising Cardinality, or Pisces, a sign of Mutable imagination and adaptability. With either of these two complementary signs, her business is likely to reach great heights. If she seeks them out, she's likely to be pleasantly surprised that the partnership allows her wildest dreams to unfold.

GEMINI ✦ MONEY STYLE

Colour for Increased Earning Power ✦ Yellow

Gemini finances will flow best where turnover is quick or work is done on a commission-basis or piecework, rather than a settled salary. His clever ideas often make him money too. Although Gemini is adaptable to nearly any financial situation, he must guard against being fickle and becoming bored with ventures that require time, patience and endurance, to ensure money does not slip through his fingers.

Being gregarious and generous, he shares his money with others but can be somewhat careless in holding onto it for extended periods of time. With little foresight or thought for tomorrow, he often lives for the moment and spends whatever is in his pocket at the time.

Banks can be a foreign concept to the Gemini native, as saving money for a rainy day or unexpected misfortune is alien to him. Money in the bank is not important to Gemini, who is resourceful and always able to raise cash when required, even if by questionable means (remember that Gemini is the smooth-talking conman of the zodiac); in fact, a Gemini probably invented scams and the get-rich-scheme concept. Although quick-witted and acutely intelligent, it would do him well to remember the saying "a fool and his money are soon parted", because it especially applies to the Gemini and his relationship with his wallet.

Bright, clever, and imaginative as he is, he is impractical with money. He has a happy-go-lucky streak which sees money fall into his lap through sheer chance, but needs to make sure that he doesn't forget to pay debts. Forgetting to pay his dues can be for two reasons: firstly, he tends to have far too many things on his mind to remember such pesky details, and secondly, he is the trickster of the zodiac, ever hoping that the creditor may conveniently forget what is owed.

Calculations, budgets and spreadsheets are not Gemini's idea of fun, particularly if he has to concentrate or sit still for a period of time, but they are imperative for the scatterbrained Gemini, the type to forget why he entered the supermarket in the first place, and then ends up with a basket-full of unnecessary things which were not on his list (if he made one in the first place).

To counter boredom and receive through a variety of sources, many Geminis may spread their money over a number of different types of investments and hobbies.

He shows no hesitation in borrowing money and lending in return, and never worries about running up enormous debts on credit cards. A natural gambler and shrewd, clever investor, Gemini indulges in a regular flutter - and very frequently wins on the gamble.

GEMINI ✦ DOING BUSINESS

Ideal business partners ✦ Aries & Leo

Gemini, being a Mutable sign, would benefit greatly from going into business with Aries, a sign of enterprising Cardinality, or Leo, a Fixed sign whose willpower and fixity of focus will help carry his plans through to completion. With either of these two complementary signs, business is likely to reach great heights. If he seeks them out, he might be well surprised that the partnership allows his wildest dreams to unfold.

CANCER ✦ MONEY STYLE

Colour for Increased Earning Power ✦ Silver

No one is a more capable manager of funds than the Crab. He's an expert at accumulating cash and making it grow... it will seldom dwindle in his tenacious hands or run through his shrewd fingers, and you won't catch him tossing bundles of it out the window for the sheer joy of it.

Linda Goodman

Being ruled by the changeable and fluctuating Moon, Cancerians may experience many ups and downs with income. Also, being comprised of primal female energy, any legacies, or inheritances this native receives are likely to come from a mother or female relatives.

Cancerians are good at keeping hold of money and are careful in their investments and purchases, being shrewd in all financial decisions; moreover, they have a natural aversion to taking risks.

Being security-oriented, the Cancerian likes to build a solid nest egg. Although being a Cardinal sign she has a natural flair for business, she rarely trusts others, so financial affairs are usually self-managed.

Cancer is instinctively cautious and loves the security that money can provide her. However, she is prone to cling to it too tightly, and this may come across as mean or greedy. Accused though she may be of meanness, she is wildly generous with loved ones, as she naturally strives to provide nurturance, protection and security for those she holds dear.

There is one word that describes Cancer perfectly - dependable. One of the reasons for this is again that pressing desire for security. However, it is important to remember that Cancerians are leaders and quite the genius at achieving not only stability in themselves, but in their financial situations as well. Essentially, she is gifted with the enviable knack of making money, and the even more fortunate facility of hanging onto it.

Because she is a Cardinal sign, she is full of enterprise, and even though she may be content to sit back in comfort while learning her trade of choice, it won't be long before her amazing memory and ability to adapt to her surroundings enable her to make considerable progress - and cash!

Cancer's financial situation will usually be fairly secure, albeit mildly fluctuating, as extravagance is not in her make-up. She understands the value of money and hates to see it wasted, especially if it has taken hard work or familial sacrifices to earn it. Her need for a solid, stable domestic situation sees her saving with gusto towards a home to call her very own, for she also likes to possess in every sense of the word. And to the Cancerian, there is no possession more important, more potent, more meaningful, than the home.

This basic underlying need for security tends to attract money, because quite simply, it buys those things that bring her peace of mind.

Overall, Cancer has an instinctive understanding of money matters, and using her shrewd, intuitive and imaginative powers, she can come up with ingenious ways of making it - and perhaps more importantly, keeping it!

CANCER ✦ DOING BUSINESS

Ideal business partners ✦ Taurus & Virgo

Cancer, being a Cardinal sign, would benefit greatly from going into business with Virgo, a sign of Mutable charge and flexibility, or Taurus, a Fixed sign whose dedication and monetary acumen will help carry Cancer's plans through to completion. With either of these two complementary signs, business is likely to reach great heights. If she seeks them out, she's likely to be pleasantly surprised that the partnership allows her wildest dreams to unfold.

LEO ✦ MONEY STYLE

Colour for Increased Earning Power ✦ Gold

Leos are naturally big spenders and often live well above their means, with money simply falling through their buttery gold fingers. The Lion can be extravagant with finances and occasionally indulges in excessive spending, especially if to impress others with status symbols. However, this apparent recklessness can be reined in through their typically fixed, controlled nature.

The Leo's financial standing is usually good and steady, with financial flow often coming by favour of superiors, by legacy from a 'father', or through wise investments.

They tend to spend more money than they should on decorating their 'palace' and thrones, as this sign is notorious for its pride and sense of style. However, they have a generous heart and an innate ability to generate more than enough money for themselves and others.

If a typical Leo were asked whether fame or fortune appealed to them more, most Lions would say fame. Many Leos desire both simultaneously of course, but praise and recognition for their personal and financial prowess is of vital importance to them also. Even if they do feel that fame is more important than fortune, deep down they seem to expect the fortune to follow naturally, as fame's natural complementary partner.

The typical Lion's resources are usually used to benefit others, and this includes money. Although they spend lavishly when they have the money, it is not a matter of serious concern to them. If, however, it can buy him power, authority, or status among his peers, he will set his sights on achieving his financial goals with gusto. He may be 'penny wise and pound foolish', so the saying goes, but is willing to undertake almost any kind of work or enterprise to obtain the funds required to fuel his expensive tastes and propensity for surrounding himself with luxury.

Being more concerned than most with his image, he vainly prefers designer labels and brand names over generic ones which may be more suited to his budget and future financial goals. However, he is usually willing to save up for certain things, and is fortunate enough for money to tend to flow in freely.

The Lion is ever seeking to widen his financial horizons by whatever means possible. Overall, being a luxury-seeker, he loves that money can indeed buy him the lifestyle he so craves and desires - and that, to the showy and dignified Lion, is the ultimate luxury.

LEO ✦ DOING BUSINESS

Ideal business partners ✦ Gemini & Libra

Leo, being a Fixed sign, would benefit greatly from going into business with Libra, a sign of smooth Cardinality, or Gemini, a sign of Mutable acuity, liveliness and adaptability. With either of these two complementary signs, business is likely to reach great heights. If he seeks them out, he's likely to be pleasantly surprised that the partnership allows his wildest dreams to unfold.

VIRGO ✦ MONEY STYLE

Colour for Increased Earning Power ✦ Yellow

Virgos are hardworking and meticulous in their acquisition of money. Cautious and even 'mean' in the financial department, she analyses all monetary decisions before taking calculated risks and is innately financially literate and intelligent.

Virgo is thrifty, budgets carefully and painstakingly, and rarely spends money on frivolous purchases, preferring to shop around, compare prices and seek out bargains. By living modestly and spending below their income, Virgo always seems to have money in the bank and knows where any money goes. Financial planning and analysis ensure investments that grow slowly but steadily in value are a distinct preference for the vigilant Virgo.

Virgos are good at balancing money and take great care to save. Sensible to a fault, she pays her bills on time and likes to save her pennies for a rainy day, always with some left over to give - but only if the recipient is deserving, otherwise she can be decidedly stingy and tight with her money.

She tends to spend her funds on things of quality, preferring to wait until she has the finances needed to make her purchase - debt makes her uncomfortable and nervous. In fact, the ever-self-critical Virgo views being indebted as a weakness and aims to avoid it at all costs.

Anything she finds worthwhile enough to save money for is usually of the highest possible standard and she rarely indulges in impulsive or ill-considered spending sprees; indeed, it is a rare Virgo who wastes money or makes a purchase they regret later. Retail therapy is not her style, unless of course it is 'investing' in a state-of-the-art juice extractor or the like, that she has carefully researched. In fact, she views such purchases as a kind of health insurance so deems it money well spent.

Sincere, dependable and honest, Virgo is not one to flash her money or status symbols around for others to see, for the modest and prudent Virgo has usually accumulated a tidy mass of wealth or at least some kind of financial stability underneath her cool, controlled façade without need nor thought for accolades or praise – even from herself.

VIRGO ✦ DOING BUSINESS

Ideal business partners ✦ Cancer & Scorpio

Virgo, being a Mutable sign, would benefit greatly from going into business with Cancer, a sign of imagination-rich Cardinality, or Scorpio, a Fixed sign whose passion and fixity of purpose will help carry her plans through to completion. With either of these two complementary signs, business is likely to reach great heights. If she seeks them out, she's likely to be pleasantly surprised that the partnership allows her wildest dreams to unfold.

LIBRA ✦ MONEY STYLE

Colour for Increased Earning Power ✦ Green

Libran New Age author Stuart Wilde once said, "The key to success is to raise your own energy; when you do, people will naturally be attracted to you. And when they show up, bill 'em!" This quip reveals much about the Scales' financial nature, in that being of the Air element, these natives are naturally quite gifted when it comes to charming cash right out of people's wallets.

Libra is interested in making money in partnership with another person, but often needs to seek the advice of a professional financial advisor to diversify his finances.

He may be indecisive and lazy when it comes to handling money, preferring to allow others to make things happen for him through delegating the tedious details; money seems to fall into Libra's lap without too much effort because of this.

He may also be meticulous about financial planning, but frequently finds himself in debt due to his innate leaning towards the 'good life'. Fortunately, he always seems to earn enough to pay off any debt. Libran investments are carefully researched and designed to achieve long-term security, but only when he can be bothered. Always generous and willing to spend on luxury and quality, Libra loves to window shop and can never resist a bargain.

Vague and indecisive as he is, he knows one thing for sure: he likes to look his best, wear stylish clothes, and have lovely things around him. Because of this, he needs a steady stream of money.

Librans seem to have no trouble finding a partner to support their extravagant tastes and lifestyles too, so may find themselves in the fortunate position of not having to necessarily work more than they absolutely have to, which frees them up for more pleasurable or intellectual pursuits.

If he is not careful, his outgoings may frequently exceed his income, mainly because he adores giving gifts, buying luxuries, and exercising his generosity. Although he may appear quite open, he seldom reveals the whole truth of his financial situation to others, especially when it is dire. And despite his easy-going approach to personal money, he has excellent business acumen.

Libra's money prospects are usually good and wealth, or at least a sense of prosperity, tends to flow naturally to Venusian subjects, whether through their careers, commodity or luxury investments, legacy, or a fortunate marriage.

LIBRA ✦ DOING BUSINESS

Ideal business partners ✦ Leo & Sagittarius

Libra, being a Cardinal sign, would benefit greatly from going into business with Sagittarius, a sign of Mutable enthusiasm and flexibility, or Leo, a Fixed sign whose leadership and determination will carry his plans through to completion. With either of these two complementary signs, business is likely to reach great heights. If he seeks them out, he's likely to be pleasantly surprised that the partnership allows his wildest dreams to unfold.

SCORPIO ✦ MONEY STYLE

Colour for Increased Earning Power ✦ Dark red

Love, sex, birth and life, as well as death, are nature's most potent transformative mediums, and Scorpios are interested in all of these. Money carries a transforming energy too, and Scorpio is interested in money for that reason if nothing else. To Scorpio, money is power, money generates change, and perhaps most importantly, money can control. Even the word 'plutocrat' comes from Pluto, Scorpio's ruling planet, and refers in large part to a wealthy group of individuals who join forces to form a reigning financial superpower.

Scorpios are competent in making money shrewdly and creatively with a great deal of acumen. Being mistrustful of others and secretive in all their affairs, Scorpio rarely loses money, but when she does lose money, it is usually due to a betrayal of some kind. She is financially passionate and can use it to control others. Money comes and goes for her, but sometimes stays fixed for long periods of time. In essence, it often goes through many births and deaths in the Scorpionic experience and exerts a regenerative influence over her life.

Scorpio strives patiently and passionately to achieve long-term financial prospects, thinking and planning ahead. Like everything else in life, she applies herself to her finances intensely. She possesses an innately resilient quality that sees her always bouncing back from financial setbacks, no matter how dire, time and time again.

Her main source of income usually comes from - or should come from - investments, legacies and inheritances.

The observant and intuitive Scorpio is often in the right place at the right time for opportunities and to make opportunistic contacts. Always in control of her finances, she has an attitude of 'what's mine is mine', although she is not necessarily mean or greedy, unlike her opposite counterpart Taurus.

She has an instinct for self-preservation and secrecy, which shows itself in well-ordered finances aimed primarily at conserving wealth and frequently, keeping it private and hidden. Scorpio can also be a lavish spender and enjoys making risky investments, intuitively knowing that the outcomes will always be to her advantage.

SCORPIO ✦ DOING BUSINESS

Ideal business partners ✦ Virgo & Capricorn

Scorpio, being a Fixed sign, would benefit greatly from going into business with Capricorn, a sign of dedicated, enterprising Cardinality, or Virgo, a sign of Mutable flexibility and service. With either of these two complementary signs, business is likely to reach great heights. If she seeks them out, she's likely to be pleasantly surprised that the partnership allows her wildest dreams to unfold.

SAGITTARIUS ✦ MONEY STYLE

Colour for Increased Earning Power ✦ Royal blue

The Archer aims to acquire wealth, and often succeeds. He is interested in financial security but often tries to hide this in the offhand, careless and impulsive manner in which he treats money. More than most, Sagittarius is attracted to gambling, get-rich-quick schemes and grandiose ideas, but will be luckier in all things monetary if he follows a single course of action to the end – not always easy for a Mutable sign - and avoids speculative risks (even if he is the luckiest sign of the zodiac when it comes to spinning the dice).

He should definitely not allow himself to become overly optimistic or idealistic in money matters, as although his ruling planet Jupiter endows him with the blessings of spontaneous luck, he tends to drift along thinking (and hoping) his luck will change without actually doing much to change it. This only serves to make him directionless and lacking in true purpose and meaning, which is a waste of his intelligence and natural charm. Perhaps his luck will change, but he should never assume that it will. And as saving is not one of his virtues, he will have nothing to fall back on should he fall from his cloud.

Sagittarius loves money mostly for the adventure and freedom it can buy, but it slips through his fingers easily as he becomes easily bored with mundane financial matters and rarely bothers to educate himself on the nitty gritty, 'tedious' dynamics of money.

Naturally extravagant, Sagittarius enjoys money when he has some and tends to run up huge debts when he doesn't. A born gambler, he also tends to leave financial planning to chance, rarely looking at nor caring about bank statements.

Being innately trusting, Sagittarius is easily drawn in to get-rich-schemes. He is, however, naturally lucky at attracting money and wealth through his innately optimistic outlook and thoughtless attitude towards finances, which seems to paradoxically draw money to him. Usually willing to save up for certain things, he is fortunate indeed that money is drawn in so easily.

Sagittarius is forever trying to widen his financial horizons in whatever means possible. Being an independent, free spirit and quintessential freedom-seeker, he loves that money can indeed buy him the lifestyle he desires - and that, to the Archer, is the ultimate freedom.

SAGITTARIUS ✦ DOING BUSINESS

Ideal business partners ✦ Libra & Aquarius

Sagittarius, being a Mutable sign, would benefit greatly from going into business with Libra, a sign of graceful, enterprising Cardinality, or Aquarius, a Fixed sign whose ingenuity and futuristic visions will help carry his plans through to completion. With either of these two complementary signs, business is likely to reach great heights. If he seeks them out, he's likely to be pleasantly surprised that the partnership allows his wildest dreams to unfold.

CAPRICORN ✦ MONEY STYLE

Colour for Increased Earning Power ✦ Deep green

Capricorn is the financial guru of the zodiac. Capricorns have an innate respect for and inner knowing around money and rarely if ever spend frivolously or impulsively. Purchases are typically of excellent quality and designed to last. Her cautious and shrewd nature means that she plans her financial future carefully, and savings, insurance and pension plans are drawn up meticulously. She rarely, if ever, takes a risk with her money, however if she does, it is very calculated and well thought out, and almost always has a beneficial outcome.

Capricorn is cautious in financial matters, possessing an uncanny ability to create wealth through a natural shrewdness, ambition, determination and wise, carefully planned investments.

It could be said that Capricorn is the sign of the business man or woman, and although that is a generalisation, it is true that she is often the hardest-working and highest-striving sign of the zodiac. Material success, prestige and status are important goals for the Goat, and she'll stop at nothing to achieve them. She strives for financial independence as she is loath to rely on anyone for much at all; in fact, she might even save towards her own nursing home so her dear loved ones don't have to bear the burden and part with their own pennies.

In essence, she is serious, conscientious and responsible with her finances, however much or little she has at any time.

Capricorn seems to have an inborn, inbuilt sense of financial and business acumen, and knows instinctively how to race ahead of the pack. She uses her own efforts to achieve wealth; with money itself she can be extremely detached, but does enjoy spending her earnings on exceptional quality possessions and investments that increase in value over time.

The Goat is an excellent saver and always has a stash, however small, put away in case of unexpected misfortunes (which, by the way, rarely seem to befall her as she tends to have a robust resistance to such things).

Capricorns more than the other signs, must guard against being mean, possessive, or stingy with their money, as they are prone to being tight-fisted when it comes to sharing with others and to overall generosity.

Although she is a bit of a hoarder who likes to conserve money, she is also an efficient trader. After all, her key phrase is "I Utilise," and use she does - money, power, status, people, *anything* which will propel her further along the path towards prosperity. In fact, she uses everything that comes her way in life; indeed, everything and anything that will enable her to climb her way, little by little, to the very top.

CAPRICORN ✦ DOING BUSINESS

Ideal business partners ✦ Scorpio & Pisces

Capricorn, being a Cardinal sign, would benefit greatly from going into business with Pisces, a sign of Mutable adaptability and intuition, or Scorpio, a Fixed sign whose perceptiveness, insight and tenacity will help carry her plans through to completion. With either of these two complementary signs, business is likely to reach great heights. If she seeks them out, she's likely to be pleasantly surprised that the partnership allows her wildest dreams to unfold.

AQUARIUS ✦ MONEY STYLE

Colour for Increased Earning Power ✦ Aqua or electric blue

Aquarian writer W. Somerset Maugham once said, "Money is like a sixth sense without which you cannot make complete use of the other five; it is the string with which a sardonic destiny directs the motions of its puppets." These statements reveal much about the Water Bearer's financial nature. It is a rare Aquarian who pursues money for its own sake. He may be shrewd, clever, successful, and even have expensive tastes, but the Water Bearer is not avaricious. To him, money is indeed the sixth sense. He tends to take financial gain for granted, as it always seems to be there when he needs it, and it flows naturally when he is doing the right thing, trusting his instincts, following his truest callings, and acting on inspired ideas and hunches.

Aquarians are either frugal or impulsive in their spending habits, depending on which planetary ruler is strongest. If Saturn is strong, the Water Bearer is tight-fisted, prudent and careful, knowing to the cent how much money he has. If Uranus is strong, his financial world is usually chaotic, fuelled by mounting debts, unexpected expenses, and unusual business schemes.

Aquarians are generally not spendthrifts however, caring more for ideals than for material possessions, and he is intelligent enough to discern what is a wise investment and what is not.

His innate futuristic thinking and foresight can make him have almost prophetic visions about his future financial standing, which he should really tap into as it can be used to great advantage. His instincts are usually excellent, scrupulous even, as is his potential for money-making - and both will work best when he's not even trying. Just like he doesn't make a conscious effort to be intuitive, money will similarly arrive as a side-effect of trying to accomplish another aim altogether.

Therefore, it would do the Aquarian well to explore the possibility of doing professionally an aspect of what he is already doing voluntarily. Aquarians have a natural sense of compassion and generosity, which can occasionally get the better of him. Many Aquarians are charitable and philanthropic, due to their aim to achieve a better lot for all, but these laudable qualities can also place an enormous burden on his resources and monetary status.

Security is of less concern to the Water Bearer than freedom; and indeed, money buys him freedom and independence, which enables him to live the life he pleases; this freedom, to live as he chooses, is his loftiest ideal and one he will go to great lengths to achieve.

He may create money through inventions, unique talents, or genius ideas that no one else has thought of. A brilliant invention, remarkable innovation, or quirky concept, borne out of his innate desire to improve humankind, could well make the Aquarian his fortune.

Aquarians, more so than any other Sun sign, have fine talents and often incipient genius lying latent and undeveloped in their subconscious, but unfortunately it may only be on rare occasions that these are ever called into play.

Many Aquarians, apparently quite ordinary and undistinguished, might rise to a high place in the world if they would but apply themselves to developing these hidden powers. Self-confidence, overcoming their inclination for fixed obstinacy, recognition of worthwhile ideas, and the ability to share, develop and generate those ideas, are needed to pull it off.

AQUARIUS ✦ DOING BUSINESS

Ideal business partners ✦ Aries & Sagittarius

Aquarius, being a Fixed sign, would benefit greatly from going into business with Aries, a sign of inspired, initiating Cardinality, or Sagittarius, a sign of Mutable flexibility and opportune social networks. With either of these two complementary signs, business is likely to reach great heights. If he seeks them out, he's likely to be pleasantly surprised that the partnership allows his wildest dreams to unfold.

PISCES ✦ MONEY STYLE

Colour for Increased Earning Power ✦ Purple

"If someone's dumb enough to offer me a million dollars to make a picture, I'm certainly not dumb enough to turn it down," quipped actress Elizabeth Taylor, encapsulating the Piscean attitude to money: that is, that Pisceans may not seek money out necessarily, but will definitely take it should it be offered to them, and the less hard they need to work for it, the better; this leaves them with ample time to pursue the more spiritual endeavours they are naturally drawn to. Feeling good, peace of mind and spirit, and helping others are the things that matter most to Pisceans.

Money is generally not important to the Fish. Of course, they need it as much as anyone else, and many of them attain great wealth, but financial gain is not generally her primary objective.

Being impractical and not particularly future-oriented, money tends to flow in and then out for the typical Fish. She overlooks details, rarely checks bank statements, and is not inclined to budget, which can mean financial disaster potentially looms around every corner.

She tends to be rather careless and thoughtless with money, therefore it would be wise for her to enlist the professional counsel of a financial advisor to stop her spending her money on meaningless investments or purchases. She is receptive to financial advice and assistance, being impressionable and pliable. Deep down, the Fish seems to know she is out of her depth when big monetary decisions beckon her.

Although she has the enviable ability to marry into or inherit money, or to have it fall into her lap in inexplicable ways by the hand of nebulous Neptune's influence, she's more aware than most of its temporal qualities.

The typical Piscean heart is free from greed. She seems to possess a refreshing lack of intensity, a kind of wispy carelessness, about tomorrow, coupled with a gentle acceptance of yesterday and an intuitive knowing of today, an attitude that spills over into the realm of her finances too. She cares little for where her next dollar may come from, as long as her basic needs are met, because her spiritual journey is of far greater urgency and concern for her soul.

Pisces tends to earn money intuitively and instinctively, and she follows her hunches rather than applying logic, shrewd tactics, or practicality. She tends to be overly generous and charitable at times, with almost any kind of misfortune being enough to move her to give. Although her giving nature is one of her many endearing virtues, she can be easily taken advantage of because of it, so needs to be wary of who she gives or lends money to, as she is far from scrupulous in assessing who is genuinely worthy of her open purse.

As a naturally generous and trusting sign, she falls easily for woeful tales and despairs to think of anyone going hungry or cold, frequently finding herself prey to financial deception, frauds and scams, sometimes getting tricked out of large amounts of money.

Pisceans care the least about money of all the signs, preferring to live their own brand of fantasy in their minds; as long as their job pays the bills and puts food on the table, Pisces is generally content. She may cry poor sometimes, but is often too lazy or complacent to raise herself up to higher places.

Her biggest stumbling block is her passivity, her tendency to go with the flow rather than making things happen proactively to create her own healthy financial circumstances. Developing greater tenacity and focus will help the dreamy Fish achieve her wildest dreams and fantasies, and will guard against missing out on money-making opportunities, which she is often too head-in-clouds to notice.

PISCES ✦ DOING BUSINESS

Ideal business partners ✦ Taurus & Capricorn

Pisces, being a Mutable sign, would benefit greatly from going into business with Taurus, a Fixed sign whose dedication and steadfastness will help carry her plans through to completion, or Capricorn, a sign of enterprising, astute and shrewd Cardinality. With either of these two complementary signs, business is likely to reach great heights. If she seeks them out, she's likely to be pleasantly surprised that the partnership allows her wildest dreams to unfold.

COLOUR LUCK & MAGIC

Colour was first isolated by Sir Isaac Newton, who confirmed the presence of seven basic colours in the spectrum by projecting sunlight through a prism. Each of the seven colours has its own wavelength, and it is these variations of the wavelengths that are the distinguishing characteristic of each colour. When the wavelengths become very short, they become invisible to the human eye's perception, but the colour may still exist (ultraviolet); similarly for wavelengths longer than red (infrared).

Chromatomancy, or divination by colour, is a form of energy therapy that has been used for thousands of years by many different cultures. It works on the principle that we make both instinctive and rational choices or preferences based on circumstances which are already present in ourselves; colour also has an effect on the energy in an environment, and we in turn respond consciously or subconsciously to our surroundings. If we look at the causes, and try to understand the reasons, as to why we are so receptive to one particular colour over another, we will see that there is a subtle link between certain hues and our emotional and instinctive individual reactions. The colour which we give to things results from a combination of three elements: 1. The light or the vibration of a body; 2. The context in which it is found and the interaction between its own light and that of its environment; 3. The sensitivity of the eye's retina which sees the body in question. Because of this, a colour can vary, depending on the individual's perceptions, namely, his sensitivity, his mood, and his view of reality.

People have long understood that their vision of reality depends a lot on their moods, feelings and emotions. Chromotherapy*, or colour healing, stems from this body of evidence, and its main application is the use of colours for healing purposes. Colours are generally associated with characteristics, feelings, stones, metals, plants and flowers, planets and even the zodiac signs. In varying cultures, they play a significant role in ceremonies and regalia.

We vibrate to the frequency of colour, shown through its continual movement and change in our aura^.

One of the most beautiful examples of colour is the rainbow. This architect of colour is caused by the refraction and internal reflection of light in raindrops. Colour can be perceived as either a pigment, or as illumination. The colour spectrum can be divided into eight main colours: red, orange, yellow, green, turquoise, blue, violet and magenta. Each colour has a wavelength and frequency that carry different therapeutic qualities which have indirect effects upon our health and bodily systems, and because of this, coupled with the fact that we as living energy centres emanate colour, colour can be a great medium in healing, calming, energising and attracting.

Aristotle, in the fourth century BCE, considered blue and yellow to be the true primary colours and related them to life's polarities: Sun and Moon, male and female, stimulation and sedation, in and out, expansion and contraction. He also associated colours with the four elements of Fire, Earth, Air and Water.

Hippocrates, the father of medicine, used colour extensively in medicinal healing and recognised that the therapeutic effects of a white violet differed from those of a purple one.

In the fifteenth century, Paracelsus placed particular importance on the role of colour in healing.

Each Sun sign and planetary body has a specific colour or colours which when used in combination with wishing rituals, can enhance their power immensely. Coloured candles can be used to good effect, as the fire energy of the flame/s increases the power of any wish, and flames are also a useful aid to meditating on, focusing upon, or clarifying what you want. Coloured candles help to focus the energy for whatever purpose the colour is in sympathy with (e.g. green for money, pink for romance, orange for joy, etc.).

As well, each of the eight colours of the rainbow spectrum also has a complementary colour to which it is matched. Red is complementary to turquoise, orange to blue, yellow to violet, and green to magenta. If these colour pairs enhance each other's most spellbinding qualities and energies, perhaps you could try wearing your Sun sign's lucky colour with its matching complementary colour in order to produce extra magical results!

With all this in mind, wearing or using your Sun sign or ruling planet's magical colour/s on a regular basis will undoubtedly bring great benefits.

The aura is defined as an energy field, which interpenetrates with, and radiates beyond, the physical body. Clairvoyantly seen, the aura is full of light, colour and shade. The trained healer or seer sees or senses indications within the aura as to the spiritual, physical and emotional state of the individual. Much of the auric colour and energy emanates from the chakras.

One of the best methods of colour healing is through 'colour-breathing'. Since air contains radiations from the Sun, stars and planetary bodies, it effectively contains all the colours of the spectrum. A chromotherapist therefore, can practice deep rhythmic breathing while visualising the rays. The first three rays - red, orange and yellow - are magnetic and should be visualised as flowing up from the Earth towards the Solar Plexus (or near centre of the physical body). The last three - blue, indigo and violet - are electrical and are thus breathed in from the ether and through the Crown, then downwards. The green ray - the middle of the colour spectrum - flows into the system horizontally.

ARIES ✦ LUCKY COLOURS

For Aries ✦ Red, Orange and Yellow - the brighter, the better! Autumnal colours and white are also fortuitous, but should be worn accompanied by other colours.

For Mars ✦ Red.

Ruled by Mars, the dynamic and headstrong personality of this Fire-inspired sign takes ownership of the colour red. Wearing this colour emphasises Aries' outgoing and commanding nature.

Red and orange, and their respective complementary rainbow spectrum complementary colours, turquoise and blue, are Aries's special lucky colours! These shades can be worn or otherwise used together to dazzling and mesmerising effect.

TAURUS ✦ LUCKY COLOURS

For Taurus ✦ All Shades of Blue, Green and Brown, Pink and Indigo - and like a real Bull, avoid Red (except soft shades of Rose). All colours should be subdued and not too bright. Emerald Green is a Taurean colour, and can be balanced with Rose Pink.

For Venus ✦ Blue, Pink, Yellow, Green.

Ruled by Venus, the first Earth sign of the zodiac has affinity with colours that reflect the principles of spring, new shoots of life, and harmony - green being the most common. Pink, pale blue and all pastel shades are also colours for Taurus.

Blue and green, and their respective complementary rainbow spectrum colours orange and magenta, are Taurus's special lucky colours! These can be worn or otherwise used together to dazzling and mesmerising effect.

GEMINI ✦ LUCKY COLOURS

For Gemini ✦ Silver, White, Dove-Grey, Light Green, Yellow, Pale Yellow (balance with a Light Mauve), White with Red Spots.

For Mercury ✦ Yellow, Jade Green.

The sign of the Twins likes to circulate and communicate. His colour is the yellow of summer sunshine, energy, and Mercury, which bursts forth like this effervescent character in a social setting.

Yellow and violet, its complementary rainbow spectrum complementary colour, as well as silver, are Gemini's special lucky colours! These can be worn or otherwise used together to dazzling and mesmerising effect.

CANCER ✦ LUCKY COLOURS

For Cancer ✦ White, Silver, Emerald Green, Smoky Grey, Silvery Grey, Pastel Shades, Glistening Whites, Opalescent and Iridescent Hues.

For The Moon ✦ Silver, Dark Blue, Violet, White, Cream, Nondescript Colours

The shy but determined Cancerian feels happiest in silvery blues, silvers, shimmery whites and smoky greys.

Violet and its complementary rainbow spectrum colour yellow, and white and silver, are Cancer's special lucky colours! These can be worn or otherwise used together to dazzling and mesmerising effect.

LEO ✦ LUCKY COLOURS

These children of the Sun are born with a joyous sense of power and vitality, and as the Sun encompasses within itself all the colours of the spectrum, so this soul can have an instinctive noesis for harmonising with each of the seven rays of progress.

Patricia Crowther

For Leo ✦ Gold, Scarlet, Orange, Deep Yellows, Royal Purple, Light Green, White.

For the Sun ✦ Yellow, Gold, Orange.

Leo is a sign that loves glamour and strives to be bright, bold and beautiful. Appearance is therefore very important to Leos - he always dresses for impact and attention. He appreciates - and looks magnificent in - all bright colours!

Gold and orange, and their respective rainbow spectrum complementary colours indigo and blue, are Leo's special lucky colours! These colours can be mixed and matched to dazzling and mesmerising effect.

VIRGO ✦ LUCKY COLOURS

For Virgo ✦ Mixed Hues, Grey, Navy, Pale Gold, Pale Blue, Brown, Beige, Green, Blue-Greens, Black, Yellow, anything spotted or speckled.

For Mercury ✦ Yellow, Jade Green.

Ruled by Mercury, the planet of the communication and the intellect, yellow is Virgo's primary colour, followed closely by more conservative, smart and Earthy colours such as green and dark brown.

Green and yellow and their respective complementary rainbow spectrum colours magenta and violet, are Virgo's special lucky colours! These can be worn or otherwise used together to dazzling and mesmerising effect.

LIBRA ✦ LUCKY COLOURS

For Libra ✦ Blue, Violet, Dark Crimson, Amber, Lemon Yellow, Light Blue, Green, Pink, All Pastel Shades, particularly Rose, Aqua, Light Green (balance with Indigo Blue).

For Venus ✦ Blue, Pink, Yellow, Green.

Ruled by Venus, Librans are naturally drawn to pink and blue. Because they are more ambitious and dynamic than their fellow Venusian-ruled Taurus, they tend to favour the stronger sapphire blue.

Blue and orange, its rainbow spectrum complementary colour, as well as pink, are Libra's special lucky colours! The three can be worn or otherwise used together to dazzling and mesmerising effect.

SCORPIO ✦ LUCKY COLOURS

For Scorpio ✦ Black, Burgundy, Russet Brown, Maroon, all deep shades of Red and Red-Brown.

For Mars and Pluto ✦ Red, Cerise, Burgundy, Beetroot, Plum, Brown, Black, Grey, Infra-red, Dark Purple.

Scorpios have a strong presence and great sexual magnetism, hence the dark, blood red associated with this sign. She also instinctively gravitates towards black and likes to accessorise with red.

Red and turquoise, its complementary rainbow spectrum colour, as well as black, are Scorpio's special lucky colours! These can be worn or otherwise used together to dazzling and mesmerising effect.

SAGITTARIUS ✦ LUCKY COLOURS

For Sagittarius ✦ Purple, Deep Royal Blue, Indigo, Orange, Yellow, Green, Rich Purple, Mauve.

For Jupiter ✦ Azure*, Purple, Turquoise, Blue, Indigo, Gold, Yellow

Being the most sophisticated of the Fire signs and ruled by Jupiter, Sagittarians reflect this by being drawn to the colours purple and dark royal blue.

Turquoise and blue, and their respective complementary rainbow spectrum colours red and orange, as well as purple, are Sagittarius's special lucky colours! These can be worn or otherwise used together to dazzling and mesmerising effect.

*'Azure' is from the Arabic for Lapiz Lazuli, the amazingly brilliant blue gemstone. It is used to describe the colour blue, particularly when it symbolises royalty. This was particularly so with heraldry, where blue is also represented by the planet Jupiter, the Archer's ruler. In alchemy, azure is the colour ascribed to the mercurial water and quintessence. Alchemist and Hermetic philosopher Thomas Vaughan likened the colour azure to 'the body of heaven on a clear day'.

CAPRICORN ✦ LUCKY COLOURS

For Capricorn ✦ Black, Grey, Brown, Dark Blue, Violet, Forest Green, Navy, all dark shades.

For Saturn ✦ Green.

As an Earth sign with a tendency to be sombre and reserved, Capricorns usually prefer classic, stylish, simple and conservative colours such as black, browns and dark greens.

Green and magenta, its complementary rainbow spectrum complementary colour, as well as black, are Capricorn's special lucky colours! The three can be worn or otherwise used together to dazzling and mesmerising effect.

AQUARIUS ✦ LUCKY COLOURS

For Aquarius ✦ Electric Blue, Ultramarine Blue, Turquoise, Sky Blue, Electric Green, Violet, Purple, Grey, Deep Amethyst.

For Uranus ✦ Light blue, Silvery White, Cobalt Blue, Shocking Pink*, electric and glaring hues, fluorescent colours, and stripes and swirls of many colours.

Aquarius's zany style is usually years ahead of everyone else's, and he reflects this by wearing bold colours which usually make an impact, are eye-catching or add shock value: such as electric blue, turquoise and aquamarine.

Blue (particularly in shades of turquoise and electric blue) and its complementary rainbow spectrum colour red, as well as purple, are Aquarius's special lucky colours! These can be worn or otherwise used together to dazzling and mesmerising effect.

A trend-setting pink, which was an attention-grabbing magenta, was named 'shocking pink' in the thirties, 'hot pink' in the fifties, and 'kinky pink' in the sixties, and was a fashion leader and bold statement in each of these eras. The colour pink came into vogue through its proliferated use in the cosmetics industry during the sixties - a most defining and memorable decade - when no stylish woman would leave the house without her trusty pink lipstick. At other times, it took a back seat and was dismissed as vulgar, sensational, ostentatious and showy.

PISCES ✦ LUCKY COLOURS

For Pisces ✦ Sea Green, Purple, Violet, Silver, Deep Blue, Magenta, Pure White, Aqua, Indigo, Mauve.

For Neptune ✦ Azure blue*, Jacaranda, Lilac, Lavender, Violet, Mauve, and opalescent, iridescent and translucent colours. Also, any colours which have a quality of being faint, indefinite, ethereal, misty, shadowy, or 'ghostly'.

Pisces, being a chameleon, carries in it traits of all the other signs. She is the original dreamer and is comfortable in most colours, but tends towards serene hues like sea green and pale, shimmery shades.

Sea green and magenta, complementing each other in the rainbow spectrum, as well as silver and purple, are Pisces's special lucky colours! These can be worn or otherwise used together to dazzling and mesmerising effect.

'Azure' is from the Arabic for Lapis Lazuli, the brilliant blue gold-speckled gemstone. It is used to describe the colour blue, particularly when it symbolises royalty. This was particularly so with heraldry, where blue is also represented by the planet Jupiter, Pisces's traditional, secondary ruler.

CHAKRA CORRESPONDENCES FOR EACH SIGN

The word 'chakra' comes from the Sanskrit and means 'wheel', disc' or 'circle'. The chakras are funnel-shaped spinning or swirling energy vortexes of multicoloured light, that absorb and distribute life-force, the subtle energy known as *prana*.

Although chakras cannot be tangibly palpated or seen, are vitally important to one's physical health, emotional wellbeing and spiritual growth, and are regarded as making up a complete integrated system that works holistically.

The seven master chakras - Root, Sacral, Solar Plexus, Heart, Throat, Third Eye and Crown - lie in the centre line of the body, with the first five embedded within the spinal column. Each chakra vibrates at a different vibrational frequency and on a different note, and responds to specific life issues or 'thought forms'.

The lower body chakras deal with physical issues. As we move up the body, the chakras correspond to increasingly spiritual concerns. As a consequence, each chakra's energy vibrates at a different rate, depending on whether it governs earthbound or ethereal issues. The lower chakras have slower and denser vibrations, while the higher chakras spin at faster speeds with higher vibrations.

Because the chakras have no physical manifestation and cannot be located using any scientific instrument, they have tended to be viewed with scepticism by many Western medical professionals, a distinction they share with energy points in acupuncture and the notion of meridians. Instead, they are believed to have been sensed intuitively by many people over numerous centuries, and indeed people in yoga positions and in deep meditation have reported experiencing the sensation of a surge of energy rising from the base of the spine and emerging through the top of the head. Some people have even said they have seen points of blue light when their *kundalini** energy has risen from the lowest chakra to the highest, as well as experiencing a profound sense of happiness, peace and ecstasy.

In summary, the Universal Life Force enters the body through the Crown chakra at the top of the head. As it works its way through the body, it flows through the other centres. As it spreads to the Base chakra, it is said to arouse the kundalini energy, which yogis believe sleeps in a coiled serpentine form.

SANSKRIT NAMES & MEANINGS FOR THE 7 CHAKRAS

"Om mani padme hum"
(Hail to the jewel in the lotus)

Base - Muladhara - "Root Support"
Sacral - Svadisthana - "Creative Feminine Abode"
Solar Plexus - Manipura - "City of the Shining Jewel"
Heart - Anahata - "Not Stuck"
Throat - Vishuddha - "Purified"
Third Eye - Ajna - "Command"
Crown - Sahasrara - "Thousand-petaled Lotus"

Kundalini is a primary energy found at the base of our spine. It is said to resemble a coiled snake. In most of us, this 'serpent power' is lying dormant, awaiting our spiritual actualisation. The Tantras, which are spiritual texts on some Hindu, Buddhist and Jain practices, teach that when we begin to work with our spiritual and soul energy systems, this force will begin to uncoil and move up through our being, allowing for our primal and most sacred power to unfold, helping one to attain a deep state of enlightenment. Kundalini shakti – the transformative power or creative force inside an individual. It is this individual manifestation of the larger Shakti, which is the creative force of the Universe (counterpart to the cosmic consciousness identified with Shiva).

✦ On *kundalini* ✦ "She is beautiful like a chain of lightning and fine like a lotus fibre, and shines in the minds of the sages. She is extremely subtle; the awakener of pure knowledge; the embodiment of all bliss, whose true nature is pure consciousness. Shining in her mouth is the *Brahmadvara*. This place… is sprinkled by ambrosia." - **Sat Cakra Nirupana**

ARIES & LEO ✦ SOLAR PLEXUS CHAKRA

Personal Power

Location ✦ Behind the Navel

Colour ✦ Yellow

Concerned with ✦ Personal Power, Confidence & Control

Gland ✦ Adrenals

Crystals ✦ Citrine, Amber, Ametrine, Yellow Jasper, Golden Beryl, Sunstone, Yellow Sapphire, Tiger's Eye, Yellow Tourmaline

Essential Oils ✦ Chamomile, Neroli, Bergamot, Benzoin, Clary Sage, Dill, Palmarosa, Cypress, Fennel, Lemon, Hyssop, Juniper, Marjoram, Sage, Black Pepper

Animal ✦ Ram

Shape ✦ Downward Triangle

Element ✦ Fire

Planets ✦ Mars, Sun

Zodiac Signs ✦ Aries, Leo

Flower ✦ 10-petalled Lotus

Energy State ✦ Plasma

Mantra ✦ RAM

Positive Expression (Flow) ✦ Intelligent, optimistic, forgiving, thoughtful, perceptive

Negative Expression (Blockage) ✦ Impractical, daydreaming, imbalance between head and heart, lack of confidence, difficulty manifesting desires, low self-esteem, misuse of power, over-reliance on will, dominance, shame

The Solar Plexus chakra is located at the diaphragm. Its Sanskrit name is *manipura*, and its symbol is a ten-petal yellow lotus flower whose centre contains a red downward-pointing triangle. This is the home of one's inner power, a golden, bright sphere of light and pure being. One's force and strength can be accessed through this centre. Balance in this chakra is expressed as self-confidence, a feeling of personal empowerment, logical thought processes, and goal manifestation. It corresponds to the pancreas and the solar nerve plexus. Crystals that can be used to cleanse and balance this chakra are mostly gold and yellow-hued stones. If the Solar Plexus chakra is weak, yellow can be worn to promote personal power and the confidence and ability to manifest one's desires.

TAURUS & LIBRA ✦ HEART CHAKRA

Unconditional Love

Location ✦ Heart Region
Colour ✦ Green
Concerned with ✦ Love & Compassion
Gland ✦ Thymus
Crystals ✦ Rose Quartz, Jade, Green Aventurine, Rhodonite, Pink Opal, Serpentine, Watermelon Tourmaline, Emerald, Morganite, Pink Calcite, Malachite, Rhodochrosite
Essential Oils ✦ Clove, Lavender, Lime, Bergamot, Benzoin, Cinnamon, Geranium, Grapefruit, Linden Blossom, Rose, Neroli, Mandarin, Sandalwood, Palmarosa
Animal ✦ Antelope, Dove
Shape ✦ Hexagram
Element ✦ Air
Planets ✦ Venus
Zodiac Signs ✦ Libra, Taurus
Flower ✦ 12-petalled Lotus
Energy State ✦ Gas
Mantra ✦ YAM

Positive Expression (Flow) ✦ Loving, accepts self and others, innate healer, generous, compassionate

Negative Expression (Blockage) ✦ Selfish, envious, jealous, possessive, egotistical, melodramatic, loneliness, lack of emotional fulfilment, difficulty giving or receiving love, lack of compassion, unhealthy relationships, loving too much, unresolved sorrow

The Heart chakra is located in the region of the physical heart. Its Sanskrit name is *anahata*, and its symbol is a twelve-petal green/grey lotus flower whose centre contains a green circle and two intersecting triangles making up a six-pointed star representing balance (six is also the number of Venus, the planetary energy with which the Heart chakra resonates). A blockage in this chakra is especially significant because it is in the middle, uniting the upper and lower chakras. Among other things, a blockage can manifest as a lack of overall emotional fulfilment and difficulty receiving love or being in a state of love. Balance in this chakra is expressed as unconditional positive regard for ourselves and others, as well as openness to give, accept and receive compassion. This centre is the generator of all human emotions: kindness, jealousy, empathy, hatred, anger, etc. It can be considered the most powerful of all the chakras because it has complete authority to create or destroy; as such, living from a place of *pure heart energy* may also be the most challenging to master. The spiritual lessons of this chakra are to learn compassion, practice forgiveness, and the meaning of conscious love, often referred to as 'unconditional love', which makes the heart a potential universal instrument of goodness. It corresponds to the thymus and the cardiac nerve plexus. Crystals that can be used to cleanse and balance this chakra are mostly green and pink stones. If the Heart chakra is weak, light green or rose pink can be worn to promote love and emotional nourishment.

GEMINI & VIRGO ✦ THROAT CHAKRA

Communication & Expression

Location ✦ Throat Region

Colour ✦ Blue

Concerned with ✦ Communication, Speech & Self-Expression

Gland ✦ Thyroid

Crystals ✦ Blue Lace Agate, Amazonite, Blue Fluorite, Chrysocolla, Blue Chalcedony, Angelite, Aquamarine, Azeztulite, Azurite, Blue Calcite, Larimar, Lapiz Lazuli, Aqua Aura Quartz, Malachite, Blue Sapphire, Turquoise, Blue Tourmaline

Essential Oils ✦ Cajeput, Blue Chamomile, Elemi, Cypress, Myrrh, Eucalyptus, Palmarosa, Black Pepper, Rosemary, Yarrow, Sage

Animal ✦ Bull, Elephant, Lion

Shape ✦ Downward Triangle

Element ✦ Spirit/Ether

Planets ✦ Mercury

Zodiac Signs ✦ Gemini, Virgo

Flower ✦ 16-petalled Lotus

Energy State ✦ Vibration

Mantra ✦ HAM

Positive Expression (Flow) ✦ Spiritual, self-expressive, willing to work with the Divine, articulate, cooperative, effective communication

Negative Expression (Blockage) ✦ Indecisive or wilful, idealistic versus realistic, arrogant, deceptive to self or others, judgemental, problems with self-expression (expression of own truths), inability to communicate ideas or uncontrolled, low-value or inconsistent communication, problems with creativity, manipulative

The Throat chakra is located at the base of the throat. Its Sanskrit name is *vishuddha*, and its symbol is a sixteen-petal blue lotus flower whose centre contains a downward-pointing triangle within which is a circle representing the full Moon. The purpose of this chakra is to help one express energy by verbalising emotions, desires and thoughts with clarity and integrity.

It is possible to listen to and speak angelic wisdom through this centre, a process also referred to as channelling. Balance in this chakra is expressed as easy, flowing communication with oneself and others on all levels. It corresponds to the thyroid and parathyroid glands and the pharyngeal nerve plexus. Crystals that can be used to cleanse and balance this chakra are mostly blue or blue-green stones; amber also helps cleanse and balance this area. If the Throat chakra is weak, blue, aqua, or turquoise can be worn to assist with communication, expression and clarity.

CANCER & SCORPIO ✦ SACRAL CHAKRA

Creativity

Location ✦ Below the Navel

Colour ✦ Orange

Concerned with ✦ Physical, Sexual, Creative & Material Desires

Gland ✦ Cells of Leydig*

Crystals ✦ Carnelian, Amber, Orange Calcite, Citrine, Golden Labradorite (Orange Sunstone), Topaz, Tangerine Quartz, Thulite, Red Jasper

Essential Oils ✦ Carrot Seed, Dill, Geranium, Jasmine, Hyssop, Neroli, Marjoram, Sandalwood, Rose

Animal ✦ Sea Creatures

Shape ✦ Light Blue Crescent

Element ✦ Water

Planets ✦ Moon, Pluto

Zodiac Signs ✦ Cancer, Scorpio

Flower ✦ 6-petalled Lotus

Energy State ✦ Liquid

Mantra ✦ VAM

*The Sacral chakra regulates what are called the 'cells of Leydig', which are testicular or ovarian cells that produce and secrete testosterone.

Positive Expression (Flow) ✦ Balanced, creative, personally vital, sensually & sexually expressive & responsive

Negative Expression (Blockage) ✦ Imbalanced, over- or undersexed, inflexible, emotionally cold, low energy, low libido, inhibiting, difficulty changing, difficulty experiencing joy, hyper-emotional, overly focused on physical pleasures

The Sacral chakra is located around the sexual organ and reproductive region. Its Sanskrit name is *svadhisthana*, and its symbol is a six-petalled orange lotus flower containing a second lotus flower and an upward-pointing crescent Moon in a white circle. This is the 'home' of one's pleasure. The purpose of this chakra is to express one's identity, personal power, personality and sexuality through utilising creative drives. Balance in this region is expressed as originality, creative flow and vitality. It corresponds to the reproductive sex glands and the sacral nerve plexus. Crystals that can be used to cleanse and balance this chakra are mostly orange and deep-dark yellow stones. If the Sacral chakra is weak, orange can be worn to enhance creativity, libido, or procreation.

SAGITTARIUS & PISCES ✦ THIRD EYE CHAKRA

Intuition

Location ✦ Between the Physical Eyes
Colour ✦ Dark Blue/Indigo
Concerned with ✦ Clairvoyance, Wisdom, Intuition & Vision
Gland ✦ Pineal
Crystals ✦ Lapis Lazuli, Amethyst, Azurite, Charoite, Lepidolite, Sugilite, Azeztulite, Turquoise, Iolite, Larimar, Blue Calcite, Moldavite, Angelite, Phenacite, Tanzanite, Purple Fluorite
Essential Oils ✦ Basil, Angelica Seed, Carrot Seed, Clove Bud, Clary Sage, Ginger, Melissa, Peppermint, Black Pepper
Animal ✦ Owl
Shape ✦ Downward Triangle
Element ✦ Light, Avyakta
Planets ✦ Jupiter, Neptune
Zodiac Signs ✦ Sagittarius, Pisces
Flower ✦ 2-petalled Lotus
Energy State ✦ Imagery
Mantra ✦ OM

Every high thought of beauty and love looks far ahead, as through a wizard's telescope, up to the sixth world, the realm of pure insight.
Robert Ellwood

Positive Expression (Flow) ✦ Spiritually wise, intuitive, personal awareness of the Divine

Negative Expression (Blockage) ✦ Too self-sufficient, lack of imagination, vision or concentration, clouded intuition, inability to see the bigger picture, delusional, distorted imagination or intuition, over-reliance on logic and intellect

Ajna is like the Moon, beautifully white. It shines with the glory of meditation. Within this lotus dwells the subtle mind. When the yogi... becomes dissolved in this place, which is the abode of uninterrupted bliss, he then sees sparks of fire distinctly shining.
Sat Cakra Nirupana

The Third Eye chakra is located between and just above the physical eyes. Its Sanskrit name is *ajna*, and its symbol is two large white lotus petals on each side of a white circle, within which is a downward-pointing triangle. This is the home of one's intuition or sixth sense; the mind's eye. The purpose of this chakra is to help one to perceive unseen energies such as spirit guides and angels, using innate clairvoyant or other psychic skills. Through this centre, one is able to recognise and process spiritual information and wisdom, as it is also connected to the conscious mind. The seat of the soul is said to lie at this point, between and behind the two eyebrows, in a place known as the third or single eye. Also referred to as the tenth door, *daswan dwar, tisra til*, and mount of transfiguration, by concentrating on this point, one can gain access to his soul, as this point is a doorway through which the soul can enter into the spiritual realms within. These are inner dimensions that exist concurrently with our physical Universe. Balance in this chakra is expressed as developed and sound senses of intuition, clairvoyance, clairaudience and clairsentience. It corresponds to the pituitary gland and the carotid nerve plexus. Crystals that can be used to cleanse and balance this chakra are mostly indigo, deep blue and purple stones.

CAPRICORN ✦ ROOT CHAKRA

Security

Location ✦ Base of Spine
Colour ✦ Red
Concerned with ✦ Security & Survival
Gland ✦ Gonads
Crystals ✦ Garnet, Fire Agate, Bloodstone, Boji Stone, Red Calcite, Carnelian, Cuprite, Hematite, Brecciated Jasper, Brown Jasper, Red Jasper, Obsidian, Smoky Quartz, Ruby, Black Sapphire, Zircon, Black Tourmaline
Essential Oils ✦ Benzoin, Vetiver, Patchouli, Sandalwood
Animal ✦ Bull, Elephant, Ox
Shape ✦ Yellow Square
Element ✦ Earth
Planets ✦ Saturn, Earth
Zodiac Signs ✦ Capricorn
Flower ✦ 4-petalled Lotus
Energy State ✦ Solid
Mantra ✦ LAM

Positive Expression (Flow) ✦ Energetic, productive, grounded, stable, serves others, committed

Negative Expression (Blockage) ✦ Angry, self-indulgent, aggressive, plodding, habitual, tied down, prone to anxiety, ungrounded, fearful about security and survival, flighty, difficulty letting go, lack of sense of belonging, weak constitution, overly practical, lacking dreams and imagination

The Base chakra, otherwise known as the Root chakra, is located at the base of the spine. Its Sanskrit name is *muladhara*, and its symbol is a four-petalled crimson lotus flower around a yellow square containing a downward-pointing white triangle. This is the home of one's physical reality. The purpose of this chakra is to ground the body and awareness of one's life on Earth. Healing of and balancing these areas enables one to heighten consciousness and feel empowered to transform from merely having to survive to wanting to strive towards and achieve greater things. Harmony in this chakra is expressed as groundedness, stability and reliability. When this chakra is balanced one is caring, focused, self-confident, secure, strong and happy, but out of balance it can make one sexually predatory or frigid, manipulative, or guilt-ridden. It corresponds to the adrenal glands and the coccygeal nerve plexus. Crystals that can be used to cleanse and balance this chakra are mostly red, black, deep grey and brown stones.

AQUARIUS ✦ CROWN CHAKRA

Wisdom

Location ✦ Top of Head

Colour ✦ Purple, Violet, White

Concerned with ✦ Spiritual Wisdom & Enlightenment

Gland ✦ Pineal

Crystals ✦ Diamond, Amethyst, Clear Quartz, Herkimer Diamond, Angelite, Danburite, Ametrine, Charoite, Azeztulite, Lepidolite, Phenacite, Selenite, Tanzanite, Sugilite, Purple Fluorite

Essential Oils ✦ Neroli, Cedarwood, Frankincense, Linden Blossom, Jasmine, Rose, Rosewood

Animal ✦ No Animals

Shape ✦ Upward Triangle

Element ✦ Consciousness/Knowing/Cosmic

Planets ✦ Uranus

Zodiac Signs ✦ Aquarius

Flower ✦ 1,000-petalled Lotus

Energy State ✦ Information, Enlightenment

Mantra ✦ Any, All

Positive Expression (Flow) ✦ Spiritual, At Oneness, Connectedness, Divine Love

Negative Expression (Blockage) ◆ Self-Righteous, spacey, ungrounded, impractical, alienated, indecisive, lack of common sense, difficulty with finishing things, depressed, confused, plagued by a sense of meaninglessness, delusional

The lotus of the thousand petals, lustrous and whiter than the full Moon, has its head turned downward. It charms. It sheds its rays in profusion and is moist and cool like nectar. The most excellent of men who has controlled his mind and known this place is never again born the Wandering, as there is nothing in the three worlds which binds him.

Sat Cakra Nirupana

The Crown chakra is located just above the crown of the head and does not, therefore have a 'physical' position. Its Sanskrit name is *sahasrara*, and its symbol is the thousand-petal white lotus flower. This is the level of super-consciousness or *samadhi*, a plane beyond time, space and consciousness. Balance in this chakra is expressed as cosmic connection and awareness. Its primary purpose is to keep the soul connected to the angelic body and All That One Is. One is able to access Divine, Angelic and Spiritual wisdom through this chakra, as it is connected to the higher, astral* and subconscious mind realms. It corresponds to the pineal gland and the cerebral cortex nerve plexus. Crystals that can be used to cleanse and balance this chakra are clear or violet stones.

The astral body is the third body or level of consciousness, also called the desire or emotional body. The astral body is the Lower Self of emotion, imagination, memory, thinking and will - all the mind functions in response to sensory perception. In the process of incarnation, the astral body is composed of the planetary bodies in their aspects to one another to form a matrix for the physical body. This matrix is, in a sense, the true horoscope guiding the structure of the body and defining karmic factors. It is the field of dreams and the subconscious mind, and is the vehicle for most psychic activities. It is a doorway to the superconscious mind and the Collective Unconscious. The Akasha or Akashic Records can be accessed via this portal, along with activating the Third Eye simultaneously for extra potency.

LUCKY CAREER TIPS & PATHS THAT WILL MAKE YOUR BANK BALANCE & SPIRITUAL SELF SOAR

The world is always ready to receive talent with open arms.
Oliver Wendell Holmes

The branch of astrology known as 'vocational astrology' encompasses the areas of one's calling, career path, or ideal profession. Careers, jobs and occupations can all mean different things to different people, but to simplify the definition, here a vocation refers to one's true calling, one's authentic path, and a dynamic way of life which rewards one with a monetary income in some form, and/or leads to the deep fulfillment of personal and spiritual needs.

An ideal vocation will provide self-fulfillment, ego satisfaction, and feed one's inner drive to accomplish what they ultimately wish to achieve, whether that be to gain recognition, prestige, wealth or approval, to travel, to learn and fulfill an inner need for knowledge, an urge to serve others in some way, or a yearning to improve community, societal or global conditions.

A purpose in life is important if we are to attain fulfillment and self-realisation. Many people gain this through their work, providing the job or career they choose suits their temperament, needs, desires, talents and aspirations. If our professional life is unsatisfactory or disharmonious in any way, frustration, unhappiness, and even despair can result.

Although one's whole horoscope would need to be drawn up and interpreted in order to gain more substantial, deeper insights into that person's ideal career, vocation and professional purpose – with a particular focus on the Tenth house or Midheaven point - one can begin by being guided by their Sun sign, which can provide many pointers to a suitable, and therefore successful and fulfilling, career path.

ARIES CAREERS

Aries likes to be active, either mentally or physically, and will quickly tire of a routine or dreary role. Monotony and small details are the Ram's biggest enemies, and because he has an abundance of enthusiasm, he should avoid any occupations that are slow-paced, tedious or require patience, precision, or perfection. Aries has a great need to forge ahead and dislikes limits or restrictions placed on his boundless vitality.

Ariens are particularly suited to owning and operating their own business, for three reasons: they can lead rather than follow; being their own boss means they are in control; and it provides a challenge which will bring out the best of him.

His ruler is Mars, the god of war, and coupled with his love of danger, innovations, discovery and novelty, occupations that involve adventure, crime, emergencies, surgery, pioneering, exploration, action, medical experiments, firearms, mining, competition, destruction and construction, machinery, metals, motivation, leadership, physical effort, sport and stamina, will more than likely hold appeal for him.

Energetic, enterprising, initiating and motivated, Aries is a born leader whose needs are best met by occupations that allow a large degree of autonomy, freedom, independence and leading opportunities.

As the Ram has ample self-confidence and the ability to uplift others, he would ultimately make a great coach who teaches, guides, motivates, or trains others. Advertising, public relations, broadcasting and television (especially adventure, lifestyle or reality programs) may also appeal to his spirit of adventure.

The following fields or occupations may attract Aries's attention: Engineering, Extreme Adventure Tour Operator, Mechanical Work, Politics, the Armed Forces, Butcher, Metal Worker, Explorer, Firefighting, Police Force/Law Enforcement, Arms Manufacturer, Soldier, Dentist, Professional Athlete/Sportsperson, Rally Driver, Motivational/Inspirational Speaker, and any work requiring enterprise, efficiency, leadership and initiative.

TAURUS CAREERS

Taurus Sun natives are methodical, patient, persistent, appreciative of beauty and seekers of peace, security and material gain.

With the gentle sensuality and appreciation of aesthetics that typifies this sign, the world of art, hospitality and physical therapies may hold appeal. Being one of the most physical and sensual signs of the zodiac, her interests and concerns lie mainly in the realm of the physical senses.

Taurus is rarely afraid of hard work and does not shy away from getting her hands dirty, or literally, 'into the dirt,' making her an ideal candidate for the landscaping, gardening, plumbing and drainage professions.

Many Taureans, especially males, are physically strong, robust and muscular, making them well-suited for 'hands-on' manual labour such as nursery, garden and crop work. Indeed, the typical Bull tends to love nature, the outdoors, the simple things in life, and plenty of good, nutritious, natural food. Being so connected to the Earth, many derive great satisfaction from building, mining (especially for precious gems, resources and materials) and bricklaying.

Having a natural 'green thumb' and an appreciation for finances and structure, the following fields may also hold appeal: Building, Finance, Architecture, Surveying, Farming, Banking, Gardening, Horticulture, Landscaping and Real Estate.

As well as having a deep reverence for nature, Taurus, via its connection with Venus, is associated with everything that tantalises the senses, and is beautiful, aesthetically pleasing, colourful, elegant, refined, attractive, decorative, artistic, ornamental and luxurious.

As Taurus rules the throat, she may have a resonance with music you also have a resonance with music and in particularly with singing, or creating sounds and rhythms.

Fields and occupations that suit those who appreciate beauty, aesthetics and the senses, are Artist, Etiquette Specialist, Boutique and Gift Shop Worker, Photographer, Massage Therapist, Gourmet Food Worker, Cake Decorating, Hairdresser, Florist, Painting, Interior Decorating, Jeweller, Craftsperson, Model, Beautician, Confectioner, Fashion Designer, Furnishings Specialist, Milliner, Musician, Resort Worker and Singer.

Taurus seeks security and stability, so her ideal career will be one that is enduring. She prefers to work in a vocational field that offers routine and a steady, consistent income, therefore, unpredictable, pressured, deadline-based, or fast-paced work is not suitable for the gentle, unhurried Bull; she will be much happier and healthier in occupations where she can operate at her own pace.

Being very financially oriented, Taureans may also find satisfaction in careers involving money, such as Accounting, Insurance, Cashiering, Economics, Property Dealer, Financial and Investment Advice, the Mint, the Stock Market or in a Treasury position.

GEMINI CAREERS

You're sure to find a Gemini or two skimming through the halls and matching wits with people in a radio station, a public relations firm, a publishing house, a telephone answering service, an auto showroom or an advertising agency... when you've found this quicksilver person, study him carefully... the first thing you'll notice is a nervous energy that fairly snaps, crackles and pops in the air around him.

Linda Goodman

Sun in Gemini natives possess mental and physical agility, wit, versatility, swiftness and usually excellent verbal or written communicative skills. Under the influence of Mercury the trickster, Gemini is capable of bringing a humorous and breezy touch to even the tensest situation. Running on raw nerves much of the time, his ideal vocation offers variety, mental stimulation, novelty, interaction with other people, and the ability to choose his dexterity and charm.

Occupations involving travel would suit the Gemini temperament. Because 'variety is the spice of life' for him, travelling and being in new, ever-changing surroundings can bring excitement and happiness to his professional self. Geminis must travel, moving from place to place, always delighting in new scenery and new friends, colleagues, business associates and acquaintances. The epithet of butterfly is often bestowed to the Gemini's restless, changeable nature, inferring a general fickleness of character, but his is no mere wish, he simply must move as the wind blows.

He is the most likely of all the zodiac signs to have more than a few careers during his lifetime - sometimes even three at once! Indeed, being a Gemini gives him an unmatched versatility and sense of curiosity which means that at any one time he may have several fingers in several pies. With this, there is an ever-present danger that he will flit from one job to another without ever mastering or specialising in anything, like the quintessential Jack-of-all-trades, master of none.

Although Gemini is inexhaustibly adaptable, his job must offer some degree of variety and flexibility, and abundant opportunities to communicate and be in contact with others, either physically, mentally, verbally or through travel, books, magazines, email, the internet, or almost any other form of correspondence and exchange.

There are many fields which involve various types of communication and correspondence and which would suit the Geminian spirit, such as: Driver, Courier, Writer, Lecturer, Politician, Public Speaker, Sales Representative, Teacher, Tutor, Travel Consultant, Professor, Coach or Trainer.

Gemini rules the hands, and possessing good manual dexterity, they make excellent Designers, Manicurists, Craftspeople, Engravers, Tattooists, Commercial Artists, Composers, Surgeons, Osteopaths, Sculptors and Instrumentalists. These are just a few of the multitude of occupations that allow expression through the use of hands and a quick, agile mind.

For Geminis, the following fields may also hold appeal: Journalism, Communication, Travel, Transport, Agencies, Teaching, Publishing, Advertising, Printing, Secretarial or Clerical Work, Broadcasting, Commentary, Linguistics, Chauffeur, Telephone Operator, Translator, Interpreter, Postman and Navigator.

Perhaps the career best suited to Gemini is that of a salesperson. With his verbal skills, he seems to convince even the most sophisticated, hard-nosed, discerning, or cynical buyer to purchase his product or accept an offer. Gemini can literally sell ice to an eskimo. Even better, a travelling salesperson position would suit his love of travel, movement, 'mind food', mobility and need for new surroundings.

Gemini's love of words and communication means that the seriously intellectual Gemini is capable of becoming an eminent scientific researcher, high-ranking professor, or inspirational teacher. Having the gift of the gab and ample character and charm, he can also be a successful politician or actor. Indeed, in politics, he'd go to any length to defeat an opponent, using gossip, scandals and exaggeration if necessary, his Mutable nature allowing him to support whatever platform seems appropriate to the audience he is addressing at the time.

In fact, despite being a jack of all trades with too many fingers in too many pies, with true focus, there is very little the Twins cannot set their mind to and master.

CANCER CAREERS

Invention is activity of mind, as fire is air in motion; sharpening of the spiritual sight,to discern hidden aptitudes.

Martin Farquhar Tupper, Cancer

Sun in Cancer natives are emotional, loving, feeling, protective and nurturing, and shrewd and clever in business. Being of the Water element and ruled by the Moon, this soul is sensitive and it is second nature to her to care deeply about others. Although she possesses a soft and tender character, she has an unshakable tenacious streak, so once a particular goal or line of work is decided upon, she will persevere until it is achieved; once she commits herself to a specific career path, she usually sticks with it and gives it her all.

In a broad sense, Cancer is the most suited to domestic work, such as housework, cleaning, caring, and running and organising the domestic, familial front. After all, Cancer and the Fourth House rule the home and family, so she has an instinctive knack of knowing how to maintain the home and hearth - both others' and her own. She may also enjoy a career that involves homes, such as real estate, property, working from home in some capacity, the building industry, interior design, or house renovations.

Cancer's natural desire to care for and nurture other people would be an invaluable asset for occupations involving the care of children or the elderly, nannying, governess work, nursing, counselling, missionary work, and many other avenues which allow opportunities to help others.

Cancer is also related to nutrition and all aspects of the food and beverage industries, so suitable professions might be in the fields of naturopathy, dietetics, restaurants, food stores, and cooking (especially from home).

Because the Crab is naturally protective, conservative and cautious, she is naturally well-equipped for any type of career which involves managing or handling money, and although reticent and quite shy, she has a surprisingly good head for business and enterprise.

Her strong sense of heritage, history, roots, origins and nostalgia would make her a great Antiques Dealer, Collector of Nostalgia, Historian, Museum Curator, or Family History Consultant.

The following fields and positions may hold appeal for this feeling, caring, determined, family-and-home-oriented spirit: Work-From-Home, Chef/Cook, Social Worker, Hotelier, Elderly or Child Welfare Officer, Family Counsellor, Commerce, Landscape Designer, Caterer, Midwife, Governess, Nanny, Laundry Work, Nursing, In-Home Care, Childcare, Family Day Care, Palliative Care and Supplying Domestic Needs.

Above all, Cancer seeks shelter, protection, comfort, peace and security, and so may stay in the same job for fear of the unknown or because it fits into her snug 'comfort zone.' This, coupled with her need for financial stability in order to provide for her loved ones and dependants, makes her a solid, caring, dependable worker in any field she chooses to undertake.

LEO CAREERS

Souls born under the influence of Leo have an inbuilt trust in life and the opportunity for being brilliantly creative. They exude confidence and affection and are frequently the life and soul of any group. The power of the Sun-soul shines on all and draws many who benefit from such a benevolent heart.
Patricia Crowther

Sun in Leo characters are natural leaders and authority figures. Leadership roles and management and executive positions are sure to be right up this cat's alley, to enable him to utilise his commanding presence and natural flair for 'being boss'. The creative and dramatic arts are also prominent vocational callings for Leo. His ideal vocation taps into his inborn creativity, and allows him to shine in some way, as well as to lead or rule over others, making the following fields appealing: Chairman, Director, Party Planner, Promotions and (as captain in) Professional Sports.

Leos are known for their dramatism and flair for theatrics, and anything which involves display and presentation. Demonstrative and expressive, the following careers will naturally attract the Leonine spirit: Entertainer, Costume Designer, Window Display Designer, Actor, Dancer, Singer, Talk Show Host, Motivational Speaker, Circus Artist/Performer, Fashion Designer, Big Animal Trainer, Teacher, and performing for an audience in any capacity.

Leos need to express their natural exuberance and enthusiasm for life in their work, and often become deeply involved in whatever their profession is, so much so that work and leisure often become one and the same - indivisible - especially if the job allows them artistic and creative freedom, input and expression. He is one of the most likely types to mix business with pleasure, and his professional life may become so demanding that there is little time left for hobbies or recreation, in which case he simply turns his career into his play and vice versa.

Glamour and luxury also play a big part in Leo's vocational calling, and any field which encompasses these, such as the fashion industry and modelling, will attract him.

Being so fixedly determined, if there is something that he sets his heart upon, he will most likely achieve it and he is highly unlikely to give up until he does.

Leos are excellent organisers and have broad vision, but cannot be bothered fussing over small details - so he needs to be in a position where he can delegate the smaller bits and pieces to other people while he remains firmly at the helm and in control; tedium and intricacies are not his forte.

Having such an authoritative presence, Leos would make effective top-ranking military officers, highly placed civil servants, diplomats, or almost any other eminent government post. Professions allied to high finance, stockbroking and banking are also suitable, as are principals of schools and universities. Any work entailing the use of gold will also undoubtedly lead to success for the Sun-ruled Lion.

Leo will never be truly happy if he has to play second fiddle or be a subordinate to others for long periods of time, and must therefore choose a professional path which offers opportunities for high levels of success, fame, accolade, recognition, or wealth - preferably all of these at once!

Leos make fantastic business owners, because they enjoy being their own boss and running the show their way, but because they have such am insatiable sense of creativity, style and showmanship, the Lion tends to shine brightest when working around others.

When asked whether fame or fortune is more important in their career path, most Leos will jump at fame. And if a talented Lion can have the bonus and pleasure of achieving both, then he will be one proud cat and with his extravagantly generous spirit, the drinks will always be on him.

VIRGO CAREERS

Service may be physical, social, or spiritual. For some, like Mother Teresa (a Virgo), it may mean going far from home to minister to the sick and dying. For others, it may mean doing much - perhaps very quietly - where one is. Some may be called mainly to work for a good cause; some may be teachers of the Way. Some may find that their calling to service can be mainly fulfilled within their vocation. (After all) to be a thoroughly dedicated, conscientious artist... is equally service.

Robert Ellwood

Sun in Virgo natives have unrivalled analytical, organisational and managerial skills. Yet this modest character also tends to be humble and introverted, so would rather avoid the limelight and is happy to let others shine.

Information, financial, medical, healing and service industries all appeal to the Virgoan spirit and suit her multitude of skills. Multitalented and smart, her ideal vocation utilises her mental and manual dexterity, problem-solving abilities, and her healing 'touch', as well as providing a healthy, clean, safe and peaceful environment.

Most Virgos are practical and methodical, with a natural ability to deal with routine work and fine details. Her concise and usually accurate judgement is more likely to be influenced by facts and logic than by fantasy or idealism, as her planetary ruler Mercury keeps her well-rooted in reason and rational thought.

Down-to-earth, she will normally tend towards vocations where the ultimate goals and tasks are realistic, measurable and achievable.

In many ways Virgo is a follower rather than a leader, and her unassuming nature often keeps her in 'safe', secure occupations where she happily and dutifully carries out any duties assigned to her.

As attention to detail is one of the prominent traits of this sign, this skill can be put to excellent use in the following fields: Accountancy, Research, Engraving, Statistics, Microscopical Analysis, Critic, Clerical and Secretarial Work, Libraries, Computer Programming, Watch-Making, Editing, Design and Drawing, Mathematics, Electronics, Languages, Switchboards, Cataloguing, Disseminating Data, Mapping, Proof-Reading, Pathology, Microsurgery - and many other activities which entail fine detail, counting, calculating or small components.

Virgo is specifically related to health, cleanliness and hygiene, and most Virgins are particularly fussy and careful about what they eat. She likes to know how food has been prepared or cooked, and reads labels with a fine-toothed comb, painstakingly examining what has been added to foodstuffs. Because of this, and her emphasis on and interest in nutrition and a healthy lifestyle, the following careers may hold appeal for her: Working in a Health Food Store, Health Resort Worker, Retreat Operator, Health Inspector, Health Researcher, or Health Supplement Manufacturer. A career as a Nurse, Chemist, Doctor, Social Worker, Osteopath, Naturopath, Chiropractor, Dietician, Nutritionist, Hygienist, Psychologist, Herbalist, Physician, Nurse, or any other type of medical, healing or health worker could prove very rewarding too.

With their Earthy, discriminating natures, urge to serve others, eye for detail, and love of health and nutrition, many Virgos can also be found in the areas of Horticulture, Personal Assistants, Teaching, Food Supplies, Nature Photography and Public Health, Safety and Hygiene.

Overall, Virgos make a valuable asset in any workplace, as they are dutiful, orderly, efficient, helpful, and everything they undertake has a distinct purpose.

Any career where she can combine her need for routine and high standards with her urge to serve and help others, is ideal. Ultimately, she is at her best and happiest when working steadily in the background, giving stability and practical assistance to all around her.

LIBRA CAREERS

Sun in Libra natives possess enviable traits - people skills, logical reasoning, style, sophistication, natural charm and an innate 'gift of the gab'. This character adores networking and mingling with others, smoothing over troubled waters, negotiating, mediating, and generally buzzing around the social circuit.

Alongside Leo, Libra is the most likely of all the signs to mix business with pleasure.

His graceful manner and sense of style wins over many, his ideal vocation giving him the chance to shine, work in a beautiful environment, and enjoy plenty of mental and social stimulation.

Any work that is carried out in pleasant, harmonious surroundings, and which is creative and encompasses art suits the Libran spirit. He is far better working in partnership than alone, and if he is ever thinking of going into business, he should always do so with a partner (who should take the lead in the partnership is another matter). In most cases responsibilities will be evenly shared, but the partner will have to learn to cope with Libra's occasional over-extravagance.

Libra is rarely suited to any vocation that involves difficult, dirty, complicated, underpaid, or unpleasant working conditions.

Because Libra is the symbol of balance and equilibrium, it is appropriate that the Libran period occurs at a time of year when day and night are almost equal. Because of this principle of harmony, there are very few extremes in the Libran's character. Therefore, balance in all aspects of a Libran's life is of paramount importance, especially in the workplace where he is likely to spend a substantial amount of his time.

Libra doesn't tend to have competitive, aggressive, strident, or assertive qualities, so any vocation in which there are high pressures, confrontation, conflict, discord, competition or 'rat race' elements will at their best irritate his sensitive equilibrium, or at their worst exhaust and burn him out.

A typical Libran is bristling with creativity, artistic tendencies and a flair for design and coordination. He would therefore make an ideal Artist, Dancer, Model, Beautician, Hairdresser, Fashion Designer, Furnisher,

Decorator, Luxury Trader, Dressmaker, Salesperson, Poet, Art Dealer, or Interior Designer.

Strangely enough, Librans are often interested in law and politics, but only as a means to social or public prominence - and only if it guarantees a source of income which will maintain his lifestyle and love of luxury and pleasures.

A born strategist, Libra usually excels at any type of arbitration. Well-known for his tact, charm, impartiality, diplomacy and urge for fairness and justice, he'd also make a great Diplomat, Mediator, Negotiator, Advisor, Marriage Counsellor, Legal Aid Worker, Air Steward/ess, Personnel Manager, Lawyer, or Advocate.

In the bluntest sense, most Librans make good promoters and con artists; game playing and clever planning are his strong points. Being an Air sign, he can choose to use his intellect to manipulate and win others over. In fact, he enjoys putting other people to work on his deals, sometimes dominating (albeit subtly) to serve his own needs. In fact, a Scorpio/Libra combination in the birth horoscope can produce a financial genius who can build a fortune by outwitting the gullible.

Overall, because of Libra's innate sense of style and connection to Venus, he can be very successful in the fields of art, beauty, symmetry, luxuries, romance, graphic design, pleasure, dancing, aesthetics and theatrical work. He could also consider working in a Boutique or Gift Shop, A Music Shop, an Art Gallery or even a Dating Agency - Librans make fantastic matchmakers!

Although he is not especially creative himself, he is a master at applying touches and attractiveness to others' original ideas - and has no issues in using this clever tactic to his advantage in any field he undertakes.

SCORPIO CAREERS

The modesty of certain ambitious persons consists in becoming great without making too much noise; it may be said that they advance in the world on tiptoe.

Voltaire, Scorpio

Sun in Scorpio characters are generally powerful, intense, controlling, disciplined, resilient and puts their heart and soul into everything they undertake. This is an "all or nothing" energy, and it was probably a Scorpio who penned the phrase, "If a job's worth doing, it's worth doing well." There are no half-hearted attempts here; a Scorpio either gives a job their all, or they give it absolutely nothing.

Of all the signs, this is the most determined and persevering; Scorpio never gives up, gives out, or gives in. She frequently puts herself to the test, pushes herself to the limits, and is always demanding as much from herself as she does of others.

With her penetrating perception she picks up things that other people miss and perceives the environment – and others - with astonishing accuracy and insight. These can be excellent business skills.

As a typical Scorpio, she is a natural sleuth and somewhat psychic, making her ideal for the investigative and detective fields. Excelling at uncovering hidden facts and secret information, this ability makes her efficient in such fields as Archaeology, Industrial Chemistry, Clairvoyance, Surveillance, Private Investigation, Astronomy, Forensics, Psychoanalysis, Undercover 'Gossip', Crime Reporting/Writing, Astrology, Botany, Geology, Government or Industrial Espionage, Psychic Mediumship, Surgery, Criminal Psychology, Psychiatry, Undercover Work, Exploration, Science and any other occupations which involve the unravelling or unveiling of concealed, secret, deep or unknown facts and mysteries. Indeed, any work demanding determined effort, a passionate temperament, or intense concentration is her ideal path.

Scorpio, being connected with the realm of sex, is suitable for work or fields that deal with the exploitation of sex, either overtly, covertly, or symbolically. She, more than anyone, knows how to capitalise on the 'sex sells' concept.

Scorpio is also connected with death, and knows instinctively that everything that has a beginning also has an end - and it is the end with which she is most concerned. Butchers, Coroners, Waste Disposal, Livestock Farmers, Undertakers, Death Doulas, Transition Aides (helping people to 'pass over'), Cemetery Workers, Mediumship, Ghost Hunting/Ghost Tours, Exorcism, Fishing Industry Workers, Coffin Makers and Funeral Directors are all occupations related to Scorpio. However, with death also comes rebirth, and Scorpios are also suited to the transformational or healing professions, such as Trance Work, Art Therapies, Meditation, Past Life Therapy, Psychiatry, Psychology and Counselling.

Being a Water sign, and a secretive one at that, any profession dealing with Plumbing, Drainage, Dam Building and Maintenance, or working underground in Mines, Caves, Lakes, Rivers, or the Ocean in any capacity are suitable career fields.

On the other side of the coin, some Scorpios dwell on the fringes, in the shadows, on the deviant side of the law, such as Drug Smugglers, Gangsters, Illegal 'Sport' Operators, Underground and Underworld Activities, and many more, the ultimate expression of Scorpio's clandestine leanings. This may stem from a simmering jealousy of people occupying positions of power, wealth, status, or privilege to which the Scorpio herself feels entitled; or it may stem from the Scorpio's single-minded need for power and control over others.

Scorpio's sense of purpose and incisive mind makes her an excellent businessperson, a successful researcher, a masterful detective, and second to none at reaching the bottom of things and solving complex puzzles. Her resourcefulness, accomplishment of the seemingly impossible, shrewdness, and ability to outwit others makes her good at sealing nearly every deal she makes.

SAGITTARIUS CAREERS

Many Sagittarians seek the stage and no one is happier giving encore after encore for an excited audience. He'll sing himself hoarse or dance his shoes off for the sheer exhilaration of performing. Show business is full of Archers.
Linda Goodman

There is no man, no woman, so small but that they cannot make their life great by high endeavour.
Thomas Carlyle, Sagittarius

Sun in Sagittarius natives are cheerful, optimistic, active, idealistic, generous, exuberant, flexible and sociable. A natural teacher and mentor, Sagittarius passes on knowledge in any way he can, and always gives it with an open, benevolent heart. Adaptable, versatile and with a great love of novelty and stimulation, boredom and repetition will repel the Archer, so it would be wise for him to choose a profession that satisfies his innate need for variety and fresh ideas and faces. Sagittarians usually cannot and will not undertake dull, monotonous or routine work, and his ideal vocations offers freedom, diversity, variation, and opportunities for mental and social invigoration and growth.

A typical Sagittarian tends to enjoy working outdoors, in nature or with animals. The Archer naturally gravitates to most sporting or outdoor professions, and for this reason he is suited to Travel, Exploration, Outdoor Adventure, Nature Sports, Skydiving or Bungee Jumping Instructor, and Hunting.

Whatever his chosen path, he needs ample opportunities to develop mentally, physically, spiritually, emotionally and financially.

Ideal careers for Sagittarius are: Freelance Anything, Professor, Lecturer, Teacher, Lawyer, Athlete, Barrister, Foreign Affairs, Philosopher, Veterinary Surgeon, Explorer, Travel Agent, Public Speaker, Animal Breeder, Horse Trainer, Sportsperson, Jockey, Priest, Faith Healer, Poet, Publisher, Bookseller, Judge, Magistrate, Writer and Librarian.

He will instinctively be drawn towards and excel in fields which expand the mind and broaden horizons or relations such as Tourism, Trekking, Voyaging, Exploring, Discovering, Foreign Correspondence, Literature, Astronomy, Metaphysics, Overseas Travel, Religion, the Shipping Industry, Seafaring, Sailing and the scientific community. The Archer also has a flair for Drama, Flamboyance, Artful Expression and Theatrics, so a career in show business could well be his calling.

An eternal student on a quest for knowledge, he may moonlight as an avid reader or university student studying for a degree. At other times, he may lack direction and drift aimlessly, but his ruler Jupiter endows him with enough wisdom, intelligence, and luck to eventually climb out of any career rut he finds himself in.

Because Sagittarians have broad vision and are far-sighted, they may be gifted with the ability of foresight and forecasting, in both mundane and psychic matters.

Also clever with words and with a natural sense of justice, he naturally understands the law and its intricacies, making a good lawyer or barrister, or perhaps even a judge or magistrate.

His love of ideas, religion and philosophies may make him a fine Priest, Minister, or Spiritual Healer.

Generally full of enthusiasm, joviality and energy, it would be fatal to this free spirit to find himself in any vocation that proves dreary, detailed, ordinary, staid, slow-moving, or uninspiring.

CAPRICORN CAREERS

Sun in Capricorn souls are natural organisers and leaders. Her practical skills of planning, building, ordering and managing resources will bring her much success in business, but her cautious and conservative nature can sometimes hold her back from her goals. More opportunities will open up if she acknowledges her own worth and power and takes calculated risks. Her ideal vocation would be something that brings advancement and leadership opportunities.

Capricorn is essentially a down-to-earth sign for whom the basic fundamentals of life are important. She likes to build her career, family, home, finances and overall lifestyle upon a solid, well-laid foundation, and feel uneasy when conditions are unstable, changeable, or insecure.

Unlikely to be attracted to any vocation based on imagination, creativity, fantasy, artistry, or vague dreams unless there are sound financial or practical reasons for doing so, she usually aims for something 'safe', realistic, sensible, measurable and achievable.

Most Goats would do well in any type of field where good management, organisational skills, executive ability and meticulous planning are prerequisites.

Being an Earth sign, making a living from the land may hold appeal for her, and careers based on such rural industries as Farming, Agriculture and Mining may be suitable.

Any type of occupation that has enduring qualities and which offers sufficient long-term prospects and opportunities for promotion will attract the Goat. She seldom rushes into anything because she likes to think things out carefully, which may influence her choice of career.

Often the most hard-working, steadfast, stoic and ambitious of all the signs, has an outstanding ability to ignore any obstacles or impediments in her path that might prevent her from achieving her goals.

Many Goats spend a great many years studying for their specialist qualification – her patience and perseverance in this area is second to none. Her tenacity, dedication and self-discipline will also be evident as she sure-footedly ascends the ladders of career, material and financial success.

Some fields of employment that specifically resonate with Capricorn are Plastering, Building, Restoration and Repair, Surveyor, Elderly Care, Excavation, Banking, Finance, Crystallography, Administration, Dentistry, Economics, Mineralogy, Government, Real Estate, Chiropractic, Politics, Osteopathy, Public or Civil Service, Bricklaying, Architecture, Civil Engineering, Pottery, Quarrying, Sculpture and Stone Masonry.

Capricorn is not outwardly showy, socially gregarious, or overtly charming, instead preferring to work alone quietly and seriously behind the scenes.

Dutiful, traditional and with ample integrity, Capricorn is usually an admired and respected member of any company. She loves to lead, making an excellent and efficient authoritative figure, although at times she can be heavy-handed, critical, or harsh on her subordinates.

Overall, the business world is a natural place for the Capricorn spirit, and whatever she chooses to do she will undoubtedly apply herself diligently, responsibly, seriously, consistently and conscientiously, minus the fanfare and noise.

AQUARIUS CAREERS

*The best kind of heroism is to be found
in the relentless practice of one's profession.*
Richard Schnickel, Aquarius

Sun in Aquarius subjects are inventive, original, futuristic, innovative and objective. Computers, modern technology, and anything new or cutting edge and mentally challenging will attract this brilliant mind.

Being a humanitarian, rebellious and revolutionary at heart, alternative healing paths (especially within groups or communities) and social groups and issues will also appeal, for he loves to effect societal change.

In no way could the Aquarian be described as conventional, so it is natural that many of this sign choose a career which is different, unorthodox, unexpected, or embraces the unusual or alternative. This is the sign of inventors, scientists, social workers, great thinkers, humanists, occultists, political reformers and revolutionaries. Alternative therapies, gadgets, coming up with new and innovative ideas, or working for political reform, are all hobbies that often develop into careers for the Water Bearer.

His ideal vocation allows him freedom, independence, autonomy, occasionally working within groups, and to invent new systems and ideas which benefit society.

For the more Saturnian or conventional Aquarians, Aviation, Counselling, Electrics and Electronics, Radar, Sonar or Television, Photography, Research, Selling Unusual Antiques or Books, Specialist Hobbies or Social Clubs, may hold appeal.

Ideal careers for Aquarius overall are: Scientist, Astrologer, Inventor, Radiologist, Art Dealer, Television Broadcaster, Ecologist, Human Rights Advocator, Protestor, Radical Healer, Magician, Laser Technician, Recording Studio Engineer, Telecommunications Worker, Social Worker, New Age Healer or Teacher, Aid Worker, Politician, Laboratory Technician, Sociologist, Aeronautic Worker, Broadcaster, Faith Healer, Nuclear Physicist, Science and Space Technologist, Alternative Health Worker or Self-Development Guru. Many of these professions reflect the fact that Aquarians are ahead of their time and have impeccable futuristic vision.

The Aquarian mind is scientific and abstract with finely balanced powers of reasoning. Being also kind, tolerant and diplomatic in his worldview, he would do well to share his ideas and ideals through writing, journalism, research and even acting, as he also possesses an accessible imaginative quality.

Those Water Bearers strongly influenced by their ruler Uranus, are blessed with an element of the 'Avant Garde' in their natures and don't fit the standard, conventional mould, which can be refreshing or shocking, depending on how they choose to express it. Essentially, Uranus rules astrologers, anything to do with electricity, natural and social scientists, aviators, inventors, and those delving into the more obscure occult realms in general.

Its influence is most pronounced in all aspects of computer programming and technology, space science and concepts in futuristic and/or technological advancement. Some purely Uranian types will be fiercely self-sufficient and radical nonconformists who prefer to blaze new trails, challenge the status quo, alter the world for the better, and experiment with new progressive ideas or methods, carving for themselves a deeply life-changing and original career as they go - and might even reinvent themselves into eccentric millionaires in the meantime!

PISCES CAREERS

> For the advanced soul working through this sign, there is an immense rapport with those less fortunate in the fame of life. We find Pisceans in hospitals, charitable institutions, and wherever they can lighten the suffering of others.
>
> **Patricia Crowther**

It's a rare Piscean who is found behind a teller's desk or in a mundane office job; she is far more frequently found in more spiritual or creative realms of occupation and pastime, fields that suit her imaginative and artistic nature and yearnings. And if she is found in a conventional, orthodox, structured job, she is likely to feel disenchanted and even trapped. A nine to five structure is as foreign and fatal to her as being, well, a fish out of water.

The streams of life she likes to swim in are those of esoterism and fantasy. Having such a deep imagination and a highly evolved affinity with psychism, the Fish will likely excel in most types of careers that involve idealism, mysteries, impressionism, creativity and romanticism. Her inherent talents will also flourish in the fields of clothing, dance, fabrics, furnishings, the film industry, oceanic art, gifts, jewellery, literature, painting, perfumes and oils, cosmetics, anaesthetics, drugs and alcohol (including the smuggling of illicit substances across bodies of water), pets, puzzles, souvenirs, stage and costume design, and anything to do with the sea, such as the shipping, sailing, oil and fishing industries.

She has very little worldly ambitions and if she does happen to accumulate money or status, it is usually through inheritance or the company she keeps.

With the Sun in Pisces, she is spiritually gifted and best suited to professions in which she can help, counsel or care for others in some way. Her impeccable empathy, perceptiveness and intuition endows her with exceptional healing capacities, giving her potential to make a great spiritual healer.

While many Pisceans aspire to spiritual or healing quests or vocations, the majority have adapted themselves to and even wish to be a part of the material plane. In this respect, the multifaceted imagination and creative power of the Fish may prompt her to embrace the world of theatre, dance, film and the arts in general. In these fields, the real and the unreal, the actual and the imaginary, the literal and the fantastical, can merge and intermingle, and she will feel at home.

Astrologers, including this writer, have long noted that most people working within the spiritual or New Age realms have either the Sun, Moon, Tenth House or Ascendant in Pisces, or an otherwise prominent Pisces in their birth chart.

The Piscean can also do well in the business and political world, often making a powerful, albeit idealistic, executive and administrator. However, because the Fish yearns so strongly to be living and working by her intuitive faculties, others who are more materially, technically, or scientifically inclined may find her methods and style difficult to understand.

Most Fishy types prefers to work clandestinely, as she does not seek praise or recognition.

Her natural urge to explore emotions, provide a listening ear or warm shoulder, and heal, is strong. And as this is the sign of Universal love and compassion, she will often be found working with, or at least drawn in some way to, the underprivileged, marginalised, disadvantaged and emotionally disturbed. Generally, Pisceans are very altruistic and usually ready to take on the burdens of those around it, but there is another type of Fish who wishes to have no responsibilities whatsoever.

Pisces may also be drawn to working in secluded or hidden places dealing with confinement, like mental health facilities, detention centres, or prisons, but no matter her individual style and tastes, all Pisceans will feel occasionally compelled to seek out their own seclusion and solitude from others - and their profession must allow them this liberty, or they will end up dissatisfied, disillusioned or burnt out. Pisceans are so susceptible to taking on the feelings of others, and absorbing the vibrations around them, that they need regular periods of alone time to rebuild their strength and restore their spirit. Without regular 'cleansings', her waters easily become polluted by others' negativity; Pisces is a psychic sponge, and for this reason she should exercise careful discrimination in her choice of profession, career path, colleagues and working environment.

Piscean confidence can easily evaporate, leaving her unable to cope or rendering her helpless and vulnerable to danger, bullying and deceit, circumstances in which she needs a practical, supportive, motivating and encouraging partner at work (as well as in her private life) if she is to overcome these obstacles.

To most typical Pisceans, the following fields and professions are ideal and may hold appeal: Spiritual Retreat Operator, Nursing, Cinematography, Special-Effects Artist, Oil Worker, Deep Sea Fisher, Photography, Creative Arts, Counsellor, Actor, Storyteller, Designer, Magician, Poet, Illusionist, New Age Healer, Foot/Shoe Specialist, Cartoonist, Virtual-Reality Producer, Spiritual Worker, Faith Healer, Anaesthetist, Social Worker, Priest, Costume Designer, Prop Designer, Composer, Yoga or Meditation Teacher, Writer, Artist, Hypnotist, Animator, Metaphysical Speaker or Workshop Facilitator, or Religious Leader. Many of these professions reflect the fact that Pisceans work well with spiritual ways of thinking and assuming different identities.

Of course, this does not account for everyone born under the sign of the Fish, but for those who are strongly in tune with their ruler Neptune, there is certainly an element of the 'creative artist/actor' in her nature and she can slip into almost any role required.

Some purely Neptunian types will be more than happy to remain behind the scenes, and certainly do not expect accolades or recognition, but through their amazingly adaptable and highly creative work, will certainly attract much credit for their efforts anyway!

LUCKY ZODIAC PLACES

Mundane astrology charts the birth and operations of nations; countries, regions, cities and major towns come under zodiacal influence, just as individuals do. Often the Ascendant, the sign of the First House, characterises the nation as a whole, and is even more significant than the Sun sign. Various methods are used to determine which zodiac sign holds sway where. Countries with a definite and incontestable birthday - for example, 25 December 1066, the day William the Conqueror was crowned King of England - have a standard birth chart. But in places which have evolved more organically, zodiacal influences may be assessed by their broader characteristics or functions - a watery place might be ruled by a Water sign, rolling hills and grazing cattle might be governed by Taurus, areas with historical libraries or marked learning establishments might be presided over by Sagittarius, Gemini or Virgo, and locations born out of innovation, technology, government overthrow, rebellion or revolution, might logically be ruled by Aquarius.

ARIES PLACES

As the Fire element and Choleric humor corresponds with hot and dry conditions, warm, arid, and low-humidity places suit Aries's constitution, disposition and temperament.

The following nations, countries and cities are also places whose vibrations are closely allied with this sign: Israel, Iran, Luxembourg, Germany, Palestine, Marseilles, England, France (Burgundy), Poland (Krakow), Italy (Florence, Naples, Padua), Haiti and United States (Las Vegas, Brunswick).

South Africa, Lithuania, Mongolia, Sierra Leone, Morocco, Czech Republic, Japan, Syria, Bangladesh, Canada and Zimbabwe, are also in tune with the Arien energy, as are all capital cities and sporting facilities and any places where battles are fought or have been won, or empires have been built.

Any extreme adventure holiday, a road trip across Wild West America with exhilarating stops at Las Vegas and the Grand Canyon, a drive along Australia's famous Nullarbor Plain, or a desert trek on camelback (think Central Australia or Saudi Arabia) or somewhere where the climate is hot and dry (while there at least!) and that offers plenty of action and novelty, could very well be the Ram's ticket to Arien heaven!

TAURUS PLACES

As the Earth element and melancholic humor correspond with cold and dry conditions, arid but cool places suit Taurus's constitution, disposition and temperament.

The following nations, countries and cities are also places whose vibrations are closely allied with this sign: Vanuatu, Rhodes, Austria, Tasmania, Russia, Cyprus, Switzerland, Greece, Cayman Islands, Persia, Serbia, the Greek Islands, Cuba, East Timor, Iran, Surinam, Guyana, Rural and Urban Ireland (Dublin), Germany (Leipzig), Capri, Turkey, Italy (Palermo, Mantua, Parma), Iran, United States (St Louis) and Ecuador.

Guadeloupe, Israel, Jamaica, Mayotte, Sierra Leonne, Tanzania, Yemen, Paraguay and Togo are also in tune with Taurean energy, as are beautifully kept gardens, luxury hotels, upper class restaurants, and rolling, green countryside.

Visiting the rolling hills of a sprawling vineyard, anywhere where the food and wine are of excellent quality, strolling through any city's botanical gardens, being spoilt by her loved one anywhere, places that are peaceful and slow-paced far from hustle and bustle, taking a trip to Australia's Uluru where Earth powers reign and temperatures plummet at night (arid and cool), and indulging her senses in spas, massage, beauty treatments and any therapy which uses the powers of the Earth to restore or refresh the mind, body and spirit, could very well be the Bull's ticket to Taurean heaven!

GEMINI PLACES

As the Air element and sanguine humor corresponds with hot and moist conditions, warm, humid, tropical places suit Gemini's constitution, disposition and temperament.

The following nations, countries and cities are also places whose vibrations are closely allied with this sign: Canada, Morocco, the Maldives, Lower Egypt, St Lucia, Belgium, Wales, Armenia, Sardinia,

United States (New York, San Francisco), Sweden, England (London), Greece, Italy (Lombardy), Melbourne (Australia), Spain (Cordoba), Tunisia, Ecuador, Bermuda, South Africa, Tonga, Germany (Nuremberg), Angola, Eritrea, Guyana, Iceland, Gibraltar, Kuwait, St Pierre and Miquelon, Norway and Switzerland.

City centres and educational establishments are also in tune with the Geminian energy, as are libraries and disco halls.

A fun-filled tour with friends and strangers alike, visiting all the party capitals of the world such as Ibiza, Los Angeles or the Greek Islands, and all places that fulfil his insatiable curiosity, fun-loving nature, need for knowledge, and childlike sense of wonder, such as Disneyland, Bollywood or Magic Kingdom, could very well be the Twins' ticket to Geminian heaven!

CANCER PLACES

As the Water element and phlegmatic humor corresponds with cold and moist conditions, cool, damp, rainy places suit Cancer's constitution, disposition and temperament.

The following nations, countries and cities are also places whose vibrations are closely allied with this sign: Mauritius, Comoros Islands, United States (New York), Paraguay, Tokyo, New Zealand, Mexico, Stockholm, Milan, Scotland, Canada, Netherlands (Amsterdam), Turkey (Istanbul), Italy (Venice), Burundi, Cayman Islands and Rhodesia.

The Bahamas, Rwanda, Republic of Cabo Verde Islands, Malawi, Iraq, Laos, The Seychelles, Venezuela, Mozambique, Slovenia, Madagascar, Liberia, Columbia, Denmark, Algeria, Solomon Islands, the Philippines, Argentina, Somalia, the Wallis and Futuna Islands and Vietnam are other places connected with Cancerians.

Anywhere peaceful near or on water and cellars are also in tune with the Cancerian energy, as are romantic and family-oriented places.

A country-style stay at a French vineyard that is run by a long line of a generational family, a dreamy boat ride in Venice, being wined and dined on any waterfront, walking alongside the canals of Amsterdam, attending a Full Moon festival, a stroll along the River Seine, a day viewing beautiful art in a quiet gallery, climbing the Eiffel Tower with her beloved, or a holiday spent by the ocean collecting crabs and frolicking with her family, could all very well be the Crab's ticket to Cancerian heaven!

LEO PLACES

As the Fire element and Choleric humor corresponds with hot and dry conditions, warm, arid, and low-humidity places suit Leo's constitution, disposition and temperament.

The following nations, features and cities are also places whose vibrations are closely allied with this sign: Sicily, Vanuatu, Stonehenge, Bristol, Macedonia, Puerto Rico, Columbia, Singapore, Romania, Indonesia, Switzerland, Italy (Rome), France (the Riviera), Mali, Mongolia, Seychelles, Czech Republic (Prague), Ivory Coast, Southern Iraq, Bosnia, Gabon, Malaysia, Afghanistan, Liberia, Oman, Peru, Senegal, The Congo, Burkina Faso, Bahrain, Turkey, Bohemia, Maldives, North Korea, South Korea, Lebanon, India (Mumbai) and United States (Chicago, Philadelphia, Los Angeles).

Exclusive resorts, jungles, mansions, palaces and castles are also in tune with the Leonine energy, as are places whose climate is warm and dry for the most part of the year.

Any luxury adventure holiday, a road trip across Wild West America with an obligatory stop at Las Vegas and the Grand Canyon, a drive along Australia's famous Nullarbor Plain, or a desert trek on camelback (e.g. Central Australia or Saudi Arabia), or somewhere exotic, where the climate is hot and dry (while there at least!) and that offers plenty of pampering, 'brag book' photo moments, and opportunities to shop, could very well be the Lion's ticket to Leonine heaven!

VIRGO PLACES

As the Earth element and melancholic humor correspond with cold and dry conditions, arid but cool places suit Virgo's constitution, disposition and temperament.

The following nations and cities are also places whose vibrations are closely allied with this sign: Brazil, Kurdistan, The Eastern Mediterranean,

Mali, Croatia, Mexico, West Indies, Syria and Iraq*, Switzerland, Greece (Crete, Athens), France (Paris, Lyon), Turkey, Germany (Heidelberg) and United States (Boston). Silesia, Niger, New Caledonia, Armenia, Belarus, St Marino, North Korea, Saudi Arabia, Egypt, Honduras, Costa Rica, Honduras, Estonia, Guatemala, Ethiopia, Trinidad and Tobago, Malta, Gozo, Qatar, Papua New Guinea, El Salvador and Uruguay are also in tune with the Virgoan energy, as are libraries, research facilities and health farms and retreats.

Visiting the scenic countryside, anywhere something new can be learned, places of intellectual greatness, advancement or history such as famous universities, book stores, laboratories, research institutions and museums, taking self-guided tours through places that are peaceful and away from hustle and bustle, health retreats of all kinds, yoga and meditation getaways, indulging her senses in fresh country air, and undergoing a cleansing regime with healthful food and practices to restore and refresh her mind, body and spirit, could very well be the Maiden's ticket to Virgoan heaven!

*Mesopotamia is the ancient name for Iraq and Syria, and the rest of the land between the rivers Tigris and Euphrates. Formerly known as the 'fertile crescent', this was the ancient world's grain silo.

LIBRA PLACES

As the Air element and Sanguine humor corresponds with hot and moist conditions, warm, humid, tropical places suit Libra's constitution, disposition and temperament.

The following nations, countries and cities are also places whose vibrations are closely allied with this sign: Paris, Argentina, Korea, China, Tibet, Burma, St Lucia, The Bahamas, Uganda, Botswana, Copenhagen, Frankfurt, Vienna, Siberia, Indochina, Portugal (Lisbon), France (Arles), Upper Egypt, Uganda, St Pierre and Miquelon, Canada and El Salvador.

Costa Rica, Fiji, Equatorial Guinea, Iraq, Israel, Cuba, Saudi Arabia, Lesotho, Nigeria, Madagascar, Thailand, Japan and Austria (Vienna) are also in tune with Libran energy, as are cruise liners, art galleries, ballrooms and grand dining rooms.

Visiting places which boast elegant architecture, tasteful culture, beautiful art galleries, excellent food and wine, quality shopping opportunities, being pampered and spoilt on a peaceful palm-fringed tropical island, or undertaking the ultimate pilgrimage to the aesthetically stunning and love-inspired Taj Mahal, could very well be the Scales' ticket to Libran heaven!

SCORPIO PLACES

As the Water element and phlegmatic humor corresponds with cold and moist conditions, cool, damp, rainy places suit Scorpio's constitution, disposition and temperament.

The following nations, countries and cities are also places whose vibrations are closely allied with this sign: Cuba, Norway, The Seychelles, Antiqua and Barbuda, Puerto Rico, Micronesia, Lebanon, Korea, Liverpool (England), Dominican Republic, Martinique, Algeria, Morocco, Angola, Valencia, Queensland, Uruguay, Queensland, South Africa, Syria, Tibet and United States (Cincinnati, New Orleans, Washington DC).

Finland, Bavaria, the Transvaal, Wellington, Mexico, Panama, Hungary, St Vincent and the Grenadines, Zambia, Turkey and Chad are also in tune with the Scorpion energy, as are desert islands, anywhere which boasts dark cobble-stoned alleys, cities whose dwellings have basements and cellars, and places where vermin and reptiles breed.

A guided tour to any place whose history is steeped in the occult, underworld criminality, inquisitions, genocide, tragic figures, or ghosts, a visit to Scotland Yard or the American FBI Headquarters, or any other place which allows her to probe into the dark corners of its bygone past or investigate the underbelly of a city, a walk through a famous cemetery, gothic architecture-spotting, and visiting otherwise creepy and profoundly interesting places in which she can undertake her own investigative detective work and take self-guided strolls at midnight, could very well be the Scorpion's ticket to Scorpion heaven!

SAGITTARIUS PLACES

As the Fire element and Choleric humor corresponds with hot and dry conditions, warm, arid, and low-humidity places suit Sagittarius's constitution, disposition and temperament.

The following nations, countries and cities are also locations whose vibrations are closely allied with this sign: Saudi Arabia, Barbados, Chile, Madagascar, Santo Domingo, India, Prague, Australia (Sydney), Singapore, China, Kazakhstan, Spain, South Africa, Germany (Stuttgart), Avignon, Toronto, Italy (Tuscany), the Australian outback, Bangladesh, Hungary and Ireland.

Bhutan, Kenya, Lebanon, Anguilla, Mauritania, Netherlands, Central African Republic, Benin, Tanzania, Mayotte, Surinam and Yemen are also in tune with the Sagittarian energy, as are anywhere foreign, well-known universities and grand libraries, and upper rooms with fireplaces.

Any extravagant adventure holiday that feeds your need for adventure, a road trip across Wild West America with breathtaking stops at Las Vegas and the Grand Canyon, visits to some of the world's famous universities, religious temples and libraries, a drive along Australia's famous Nullarbor Plain (to appeal to his freedom and love of wide, open spaces), or a desert trek on horseback (e.g. Central Australia or Saudi Arabia) or somewhere exotic, where the climate is hot and dry (while there at least!) and that offers plenty of opportunities for him to delve into the region's history, philosophies, religions, culture and learning or legal institutions, could very well be the Archer's ticket to Sagittarian heaven!

CAPRICORN PLACES

As the Earth element and melancholic humor correspond with cold and dry conditions, arid but cool places suit Capricorn's constitution, disposition and temperament.

The following nations, countries and cities are also places whose vibrations are closely allied with this sign: Libya, Monaco, New Caledonia, Macedonia, Nicaragua, Nauru, India (Delhi), Mauritius, Mexico, Bulgaria, Great Britain and the United Kingdom, Australia, Hong Kong, Afghanistan, Haiti, Lithuania, Sudan, Burma, Slovakia, Cameroon, Brunei and the Shetlands (Orkney).

Many parts of Europe, such as Greece, Belgium (Brussels), Bosnia, Albania, Poland, Sweden and England (Oxford) are also in tune with the Capricornian energy, as are mountainous and thorny regions.

Taking a White House tour, visiting other famous parliamentary, traditional or governmental institutions, going to places of historical authoritative significance where powerful leaders have reigned or currently rule, climbing Mount Everest or taking a pilgrimage to any other mountainous region, trekking through a cool desert region, and indulging her senses and intellect in natural surroundings where the call of the Earth is strong in order to refresh her mind, body and spirit, could very well be the Goat's ticket to Capricornian heaven!

AQUARIUS PLACES

As the Air element and Sanguine humor corresponds with hot and moist conditions, warm, humid, tropical places suit Aquarius's constitution, disposition and temperament.

The following nations, countries and cities are also places whose vibrations are closely allied with this sign: Australia, Chile, St Vincent and the Grenadines, Venezuela, Finland, Sri Lanka, Ethiopia, Italy (Trent), The Vatican City, Prussia, Lithuania, Japan, Jordan, Canada, Germany (Bremen, Hamburg), Liechtenstein, Sweden (Stockholm), Austria (Salzburg), Russia (Leningrad, St Petersburg, Moscow, Siberia), Cyprus and Scandinavia.

Israel, Nepal, Gambia, Great Britain, Iran, Abyssinia, New Zealand, United States (Los Angeles) and some parts of Arabia and Poland, are also in tune with the Aquarian energy, as are hippie trails, communes, and offbeat and unusual places.

A group adventure to the ski slopes or a palm-tree fringed tropical island paradise upon which a hippie retreat or commune exists, and places which boast quirky architecture and futuristic designs, could very well be the Water Bearer's ticket to Aquarian heaven!

PISCES PLACES

As the Water element and phlegmatic humor correspond with cold and wet conditions, cool, rainy, damp or 'watery' places suit Pisces's constitution, disposition and temperament.

The following nations, countries and cities are also places whose vibrations are closely allied with this sign: the Maldives, Guadeloupe, North Africa, the Sahara and Gobi deserts, Samoa, Albania, Ivory Coast, Gambia, Ghana, French Guyana, Santo Domingo, Mediterranean Islands, St Lucia, Martinique, Scandinavia, France (Normandy), Reunion, Portugal (Lisbon), Spain (Galicia, Seville), Poland (Warsaw), Morocco, Jerusalem, Santiago de Compostela, Taiwan, Tunisia, Bulgaria, Mauritius, Upper Egypt (Nubia), United States (Vermont, Hollywood), South Surin Island (Thailand)*, Calabria, Alexandria, Ratisbon, Germany (Worms), Lancaster, Compostela, watery and aquatic places of all kinds, and old hermitages.

An organised tour through United States, and particularly a visit to the acting and movie capital of the world, Hollywood, California, or a leisurely trip through scenic and romantic Europe, with a couple of spooky ghost tours, gothic architecture-spotting, and abandoned mental asylums or old-style convent visits thrown in for good measure, could very well be the Fish's ticket to Piscean heaven!

South Surin Island (Koh Surin Tai) is home to the Moken people, who live in houseboats or in thatched huts on stilts, diving and fishing for sustenance and livelihood. The most interesting thing about the Moken people is their unique and remarkable ability to see underwater. They maintain a nomadic, sea-based culture, and believe that the sea has a spirit; in fact, they believe that all things have spirits. They have a complex series of rituals, centred around totem poles, to communicate with these spirits. They survive against all the odds their capitalist 'concrete jungle' neighbours in neighbouring Thailand are faced with, because they are prepared to follow messages delivered in ways other than totem poles. When the tide suddenly changes and rapidly recedes a long way out, they interpret this as a message to "run for the higher grounds of the hills," for since the 2004 Boxing Day Tsunami, the ocean has become a "people eating sea." Indeed, while the 2004 disaster killed over 227,000 others, even though it struck the South Surin Island, it claimed just one member of the Moken people, a weak elderly man who was too slow to flee and overlooked in the rush for safety. Today there are two to three thousand 'water people' living in the region, and Pisces might well relate to these people's close connections to spirits and the sea.

CRYSTAL MAGIC

Beautiful and strong is the material of stones, but more beautiful and much more powerful is the mystery that emanates from them.

Chinese Poet & Alchemist, Li Po, 8th Century A.D.

Each crystal and mineral of the Earth embodies different qualities, patterns and expressions of the Divine language, the ethereal fabric, the whispers of the Universe.

The human body is a sophisticated, multi-faceted 'antenna-system' comprised of a crystalline matrix that is constantly transmitting and receiving all manner of energies; therefore, it can be assumed that energy-healers who use quartz, shells and stones - also crystalline materials - in their healing practices, have the power to promote resonant interactions with the liquid 'crystal' structures found within human tissues.

All crystals work through vibrational balancing and energy-channelling. Much of the magic – and healing properties - of crystals lie in their colour, which is determined by the rate at which their atoms vibrate; these vibrations can be matched to the energy emitted by your own body's aura. And just as light can be focused and refracted through gemstones, so too can all kinds of psychic energy, from healing energies to Divine communications.

Gemstones can help us attune to higher vibrations and bring them into our own experience and being. This theory of crystal resonance suggests that the characteristic energy patterns emanated by any stone can be transferred into the 'liquid crystal medium' of our bodies through resonance.

Our bodies, being composed of these tuneable liquids, can mimic and mirror any consistent vibrational pattern with which we come into contact; we can therefore resonate with the healthful qualities of various crystals and minerals.

Crystals and precious stones have been valued throughout world cultures over many centuries for their healing virtues and capacities to imbue courage, strength, protection, clairvoyance, love, and numerous other qualities. Wearing gemstones is one of the simplest and most effective self-healing practices one can undertake, and wearing or carrying those stones whose vibrations correspond with the qualities one wishes to embody, brings their energetic currents into engagement with your body.

Over time the phenomenon of energetic integration, may be felt tangibly and one's own vibrational field may internalise the stone's currents, adjust to them and effectively 'store' them, making them, eventually, a part of one's own vibrational make-up. And we seem to know from the resonances we feel within our bodies when in contact with these gemstones, that crystals emanate tangible, if for the most part immeasurable, currents.

Crystals can also act as transmitters and amplifiers of one's will or intentions, particularly if the individual's will or intentions are in sympathy with the crystal's energy.

The mineral kingdom refers to stones, minerals and crystals and the associations and vibrations they carry. When working with stones, we are working with several different layers of spiritual energy, and although they can be regarded as inanimate 'psychic batteries', they are actually moving, vibrating masses of energy that transmit deep potential and power into our lives. Some crystals and stones even have receptive powers, which means they can absorb energy and retain it within until cleansed or re-programmed.

Crystals which align with your Sun sign or ruling planet are your most fortuitous and therefore strongest 'attractors' and 'amplifiers'. However, this does not mean that the only stones you can usefully work with are the ones astrologically matched with your Sun sign or ruling planet. All stones carry deep potential to resonate with an individual, but those in harmony with your cosmic blueprint are especially powerful.

In ancient times, people made correlations between each of the twelve precious stones of the time (mentioned in the Bible, they were sardius, topaz, carbuncle, emerald, sapphire, diamond, opal, agate, amethyst, beryl, onyx and jasper), and one of the twelve zodiac signs. Moreover, there are seven crystalline systems recognised in crystallography (or the science of the laws which influence the formation, structure and geometric, physical and chemical properties of crystallised matter) as analogous with the seven traditional ruling planets of the zodiac.

However, nobody is under the rule of one planet alone. We are all in essence a complex combination of every planet, many elements and varying aspects, depending on their positions, placements, and prominence in our birth charts.

Your lucky stones are to assist you to tune into your Sun sign's energy and planetary influences, but you are by no means limited to the ones listed for your sign alone. Above all, let your stones, whichever ones you choose, work for you, and allow them to resonate with your own unique and magical inner crystalline matrix.

✦ CLEAR QUARTZ ✦

The Master Healer ✦ For All Zodiac Signs

A common, well-known and popular gem, clear quartz (sometimes known as rock crystal) is balancing and harmonising, an all-purpose 'jack-of-all-trades' stone. It amplifies the magic of any work you do or wishes you make. It is connected with all the chakras and increases the power of all other crystals. Clear quartz is a deep soul cleanser, which unblocks and regulates energy and emotions on all levels.

In various cultures, quartz crystal is reputed to be the most powerful crystal, the 'grandfather crystal' and the 'chief of the Stone People'. Clear quartz is also considered to be the only gemstone that is modifiable to suit your needs*, as other crystals automatically contain and retain their own specific resonance or inherent signature.

In essence, clear quartz is the most easily programmable and the most overall healing and readily accessible crystals of the mineral kingdom, holding a unique significance in the Universe of gems. And because of its all-encompassing nature and wide-ranging healing abilities, it has zodiacal affinities with all the signs.

*To program your clear quartz crystal, simply hold it on your Third Eye chakra (between and just above the physical eyes) and concentrate on the purpose for which you wish to use it. Be positive and receptive while you allow your crystal to fill with this energy. If you wish, you could also state the intention of the programming out loud, for example, 'I program this crystal for love / spirit connection / meditation / abundance / protection or (insert your own word here)'. You could also run your clear quartz crystal under running water, allow it to dry naturally, then hold the stone with both hands, bring it up to your mouth and blow into it sharply three times in order to impregnate it with your own breath. Then, hold it firmly in one hand and silently invite and welcome it into your life as a friend, helper and guide.

ARIES ✦ LUCKY CRYSTALS, STONES & GEMS

ARIES BIRTH STONES ✦ Ruby, Bloodstone, Aquamarine, Diamond
MYSTICAL BIRTH STONE ✦ Jade
MARCH BIRTH STONES ✦ Jasper, Bloodstone, Aquamarine
APRIL BIRTH STONES ✦ Sapphire, Diamond, Zircon

Ruby, Bloodstone, Aquamarine, Diamond (primary birthstones), Red Coral (for Mars), Jasper, Sapphire and Zircon (March & April birthstones) are this sign's luckiest stones, and one of these gems should be worn about the person to ensure good luck and increase overall magnetism. Hematite, Pyrite, Magnetite, Aventurine, Carnelian, Fire Agate, Citrine, Amethyst, Kunzite, Apache Tear, Kyanite, Flint, Tibetan Quartz, Malachite, Rhodochrosite, Mahogany Obsidian, Lapis Lazuli, Titanium Quartz, Emerald, Tektite, Orange Spinel, Topaz, Garnet, Red Jasper and Pink Tourmaline also align with Aries' energy.

TAURUS ✦ LUCKY CRYSTALS, STONES & GEMS

TAURUS BIRTH STONES ✦ Diamond, Sapphire, Emerald
MYSTICAL BIRTH STONE ✦ Opal
APRIL BIRTH STONES ✦ Sapphire, Diamond, Zircon
MAY BIRTH STONES ✦ Agate, Emerald, Tourmaline, Chrysoprase

Diamond, Sapphire, Emerald (primary birthstones), Jade, Rose Quartz (Venusian gems), Zircon, Agate, Tourmaline and Chrysoprase (April & May birthstones) are this sign's luckiest stones, and one or more of these gems should be worn about the person to ensure good luck and increase overall magnetism. Lapis Lazuli, Coral, Moss Agate, Aquamarine, Boji Stone, Copper, Topaz, Carnelian, Azurite, Chrysocolla, Variscite, Malachite, Kyanite, Tibetan Quartz, Amazonite, Green Aventurine, Green Calcite, Olivine, Spinel, Titanium Quartz, Selenite, Rhodonite and Tiger's Eye also align with Taurean energy.

GEMINI ✦ LUCKY CRYSTALS, STONES & GEMS

GEMINI BIRTH STONES ✦ Alexandrite, Agate, Citrine
MYSTICAL BIRTH STONE ✦ Sapphire
MAY BIRTH STONES ✦ Agate, Emerald, Tourmaline, Chrysoprase
JUNE BIRTH STONES ✦ Emerald, Pearl, Moonstone

Alexandrite, Agate, Citrine (primary birthstones), Emerald (Mercury), Tourmaline, Chrysoprase, Pearl and Moonstone (May & June birthstones) are this sign's luckiest stones, and at least one of these gems should be worn about the person to ensure good luck and increase overall magnetism. Serpentine, Hematite, Aquamarine, Calcite, Tiger's Eye, Chrysocolla, Apophyllite, Noble or Iridescent Opal, Rainbow Quartz, Hyaline Quartz, Colourless Tourmaline, Apatite, Celestine, Celestite, Marble, Tibetan Quartz, Titanium Quartz, Blue Spinel, Goldstone, Green Obsidian, Zoisite, Variscite, Topaz, Ulexite, Epidote, Dendritic Agate, Sapphire, Tourmilated and Rutilated Quartz, Jade, Diamond and all gems that sparkle brilliantly are also in harmony with Geminian energy.

CANCER ✦ LUCKY CRYSTALS, STONES & GEMS

CANCER BIRTH STONES ✦ Moonstone, Pearl, Ruby
MYSTICAL BIRTH STONE ✦ Moonstone
LUNAR BIRTH STONES ✦ Aquamarine, Opal, Clear Quartz, Emerald, Diamond, Selenite, Moonstone
JUNE BIRTH STONES ✦ Emerald, Pearl, Moonstone
JULY BIRTH STONES ✦ Onyx, Ruby, Turquoise, Carnelian

Moonstone, Pearl, Ruby (primary birthstones), Emerald, Onyx, Turquoise and Carnelian (June & July birthstones) are this sign's luckiest stones, and at least one of these gems should be worn about the person to ensure good luck and increase overall magnetism. Fire Agate, Moss Agate, Dendritic Agate, Beryl, Rhodonite, Aventurine, Opal, Amber, Brown Spinel, Chrysoprase, Pink Tourmaline, Green Garnet Grossularite, Blue Agate, White Onyx, Snowflake Obsidian, Tibetan Quartz, Titanium Quartz, Tektite and Calcite (green, blue and orange), also align with Cancerian energy.

LEO ✦ LUCKY CRYSTALS, STONES & GEMS

LEO BIRTH STONES ✦ Citrine, Ruby, Peridot
MYSTICAL BIRTH STONE ✦ Ruby
JULY BIRTH STONES ✦ Onyx, Turquoise, Ruby, Carnelian
AUGUST BIRTH STONES ✦ Carnelian, Moonstone, Peridot, Sardonyx

Citrine, Ruby, Peridot (primary birthstones), Onyx, Turquoise, Carnelian, Moonstone and Sardonyx (July & August birth stones) are this sign's luckiest stones, and one or more of these gems should be worn about the person to ensure good luck and increase overall magnetism. Boji Stone, Fire Agate, Diamond, Amber, Chrysolite, Cat's Eye, Golden Beryl, Yellow Spinel, Garnet, Chrysocolla, Tiger's Eye, Kunzite, Sunstone, Emerald, Green and Pink Tourmaline, Calcite (orange and yellow), Golden Healer, Larimar, Petalite, Clear Quartz, Tibetan Quartz, Pyrite, Labradorite, Titanium Quartz, Yellow Sapphire, Aqua Aura, Red Obsidian, Golden Topaz, Heliodor, Rhodochrosite and all yellow/orange stones also align with Leonine energy. To bring about even greater luck these stones should be set in gold, since this is the metal of the Sun, ruler of Leo.

VIRGO ✦ LUCKY CRYSTALS, STONES & GEMS

VIRGO BIRTH STONES ✦ Sapphire, Carnelian, Peridot, Sardonyx
MYSTICAL BIRTH STONE ✦ Diamond
AUGUST BIRTH STONES ✦ Peridot, Sardonyx, Moonstone, Carnelian
SEPTEMBER BIRTH STONES ✦ Peridot, Sapphire, Lapis Lazuli

Sapphire, Carnelian, Peridot, Sardonyx (primary birthstones), Moonstone, Lapis Lazuli (August & September birthstones) and Emerald (Mercury) are this sign's luckiest stones, and one or more of these gems should be worn about the person to ensure good luck and increase overall magnetism. Banded Agate, Jade, Diamond, Jasper, Labradorite, Hematite, Rutilated Quartz, Amazonite, Citrine, Opal, Magnetite, Blue Topaz, Amber, Smithsonite, Moss Agate, Rubellite, Purple Obsidian, Sodalite, Sugilite, Dioptase, Chrysocolla, Amethyst, True Jasper, Snowflake Obsidian, Cat's Eye, Hawk's Eye, Grey Onyx, Grey Amber, Alexandrite and Garnet also align with Virgo's energy.

LIBRA ✦ LUCKY CRYSTALS, STONES & GEMS

LIBRA BIRTH STONES ✦ Opal, Tourmaline, Sapphire
MYSTICAL BIRTH STONE ✦ Agate
SEPTEMBER BIRTH STONES ✦ Peridot, Sapphire, Lapis Lazuli
OCTOBER BIRTH STONES ✦ Opal, Aquamarine, Tourmaline

Opal, Tourmaline, Sapphire (primary birthstones), Jade, Rose Quartz, Diamond (Venusian gems), Peridot, Sapphire, Aquamarine and Lapis Lazuli (September & October birthstones) are this sign's luckiest stones, and one or more of these gems should be worn about the person to ensure good luck and increase overall magnetism. Moonstone, Green Tourmaline, Marble, Sardonyx, Jacinth, Sunstone, Topaz, Kunzite, Mahogany Obsidian, Ametrine, Aventurine, Chrysoprase, Citrine, Moss Agate, Amazonite, Malachite, Bloodstone, Kyanite, Apophyllite, Tibetan Quartz, Titanium Quartz and Green Spinel also align with Libra's energy.

SCORPIO ✦ LUCKY CRYSTALS, STONES & GEMS

SCORPIO BIRTH STONES ✦ Topaz, Malachite, Peridot
MYSTICAL BIRTH STONE ✦ Jasper
OCTOBER BIRTH STONES ✦ Opal, Aquamarine, Tourmaline
NOVEMBER BIRTH STONES ✦ Topaz, Citrine, Pearl

Topaz, Malachite, Peridot (primary birthstones), Opal, Aquamarine, Tourmaline, Citrine, Pearl (October & November birthstones) and Red Coral (Mars) are this sign's luckiest stones, and one or more of these gems should be worn about the person to ensure good luck and increase overall magnetism. Labradorite, Hematite, Carnelian, Moonstone, Turquoise, Magnetite, Ruby, Beryl, Red Spinel, Rhodochrosite, Emerald, Apache Tear, Obsidian, Hiddenite, Stibnite, Tibetan Quartz, Titanium Quartz, Variscite, Boji Stone, Flint, Shiva Lingam, Dioptase, Green Tourmaline, True Jasper, Yellow Calcite, Iron Tiger's Eye, Red Jasper, Jacinth, Sunstone, Red Amber, Garnet, Kunzite and Herkimer Diamond also align with Scorpio's energy. Additionally, all scarlet and dark red stones are especially beneficial attractors for Scorpios.

SAGITTARIUS ✦ LUCKY CRYSTALS, STONES & GEMS

SAGITTARIUS BIRTH STONES ✦ Topaz, Turquoise, Zircon
MYSTICAL BIRTH STONE ✦ Pearl
NOVEMBER BIRTH STONES ✦ Topaz, Citrine, Pearl
DECEMBER BIRTH STONES ✦ Ruby, Turquoise, Bloodstone, Lapis Lazuli, Zircon, Tanzanite (modern)

Topaz, Turquoise, Zircon (primary birthstones), Yellow Sapphire, Amethyst (Jupiter), Ruby, Bloodstone, Citrine, Pearl, Lapis Lazuli and Tanzanite (November & December birthstones) are this sign's luckiest stones, and one or more of these gems should be worn about the person to ensure good luck and increase overall magnetism. Dark Blue Spinel, Azurite, Labradorite, Obsidian, Smoky Quartz, Lazurite, Blue Lace Agate, Dioptase, Gold Obsidian, Cyanite, Garnet, Okenite, Sodalite, Rhodochrosite, Charoite, Snowflake Obsidian, Malachite, Pink Tourmaline and Sugilite also align with Sagittarian energy.

CAPRICORN ✦ LUCKY CRYSTALS, STONES & GEMS

CAPRICORN BIRTH STONES ✦ Garnet, Turquoise, Smoky Quartz, Jet
MYSTICAL BIRTH STONE ✦ Onyx
DECEMBER BIRTH STONES ✦ Ruby, Turquoise, Bloodstone, Lapis Lazuli, Zircon, Tanzanite
JANUARY BIRTH STONES ✦ Garnet, Zircon

Garnet, Turquoise, Smoky Quartz, Jet (primary birthstones), Zircon, Ruby (December & January birthstones) and Blue Sapphire (Saturn) are this sign's luckiest stones, and at least one of these gems should be worn about the person to ensure good luck and increase overall magnetism. Black Coral, White Onyx, Banded Agate, Snowflake Obsidian, Mahogany Obsidian, Black Pearl, Amethyst, Tiger's Eye, Black Onyx, Carnelian, Tourmaline (green and black), Hematite, Tibetan Quartz, Titanium Quartz, Aragonite, Malachite, Stibnite, Chalcopyrite, Azurite, Amber, Fluorite, Galena, Labradorite, Magnetite, Clear Quartz and Peridot also align with Capricorn's energy.

AQUARIUS ✦ LUCKY CRYSTALS, STONES & GEMS

AQUARIUS BIRTH STONES ✦ Amethyst, Garnet, Aquamarine
MYSTICAL BIRTH STONE ✦ Emerald
JANUARY BIRTH STONES ✦ Zircon, Garnet
FEBRUARY BIRTH STONES ✦ Amethyst, Hyacinth

Amethyst, Garnet, Aquamarine (primary birthstones), Zircon (January birth stone), Hyacinth (February birth stone), Jacinth, Jargoon (Uranus) and Blue Sapphire (Saturn) are this sign's luckiest stones, and one or more of these gems should be worn about the person to ensure good luck and increase overall magnetism. Magnetite, Sugilite, Chrysocolla, Tourmaline, Alexandrite, Apatite, Jade, Diamond, Bixbyite, Blue Obsidian, Lapis Lazuli, Chrysoprase, Blue Celestite, Azurite, Spirit Cactus Quartz, Fuchsite, Boji Stone, Black Pearl, Hematite, Blue Quartz, Amber (Uranus), Angelite, Blue Lace Agate, Labradorite, Clear Quartz, Moonstone, Imperial Topaz, Fluorite, Antacamite, Tibetan Quartz, Titanium Quartz, Larimar and Turquoise also align with Aquarius's energy

PISCES ✦ LUCKY CRYSTALS, STONES & GEMS

PISCES BIRTH STONES ✦ Amethyst, Turquoise, Aquamarine
MYSTICAL BIRTH STONE ✦ Bloodstone
FEBRUARY BIRTH STONES ✦ Amethyst, Hyacinth
MARCH BIRTH STONES ✦ Jasper, Bloodstone, Aquamarine

Amethyst, Turquoise, Aquamarine (primary birthstones), Jasper, Hyacinth, Bloodstone (February & March birthstones) and Yellow Sapphire (Jupiter) are this sign's luckiest stones, and one or more of these gems should be worn about the person to ensure good luck and increase overall magnetism. Coral, Mother of Pearl and Emerald are also particularly auspicious gemstones for Pisces. Moonstone, Clear Quartz, Labradorite, Fire Agate, Beryl, Staurolite, Chrysoprase, Pumice, Chrysolite, Sugilite, Sand, Blue Lace Agate, Tibetan Quartz, Green Grossular Garnet, Sodalite, Citrine, Titanium Quartz, Chevron Amethyst, Diaspore, Sunstone, Calcite, Tourmaline, Smithsonite, Spessartine, Angelite, Carnelian, Bixbyite, Anglesite, Opal, Smoky Quartz, Green Fluorite, Pearl, Blue Quartz, Milky Quartz, Rose Quartz, Spirit Cactus Quartz, Imperial Topaz, Jade and Larimar also align with Piscean energy.

LUCKY SUN SIGN NUMBERS

Everything that exists has a vibration. The vibration of sound, music, colour, matter, even our words, thoughts, and names show form. All vibration is measurable. To measure we need numbers. Numbers are the basis of all. Numbers are the key to all mysteries.
Shirley Blackwell Lawrence, *Behind Numerology*

Using the principles of numerology, your Sun sign's number was added up according to the principle of corresponding a number with a letter, for example 1=A, 2=B, 3=C and so on in sequence and up to 9=I, then beginning again at number 1 for the next letter J and following this same sequence. Following this system, the sum of the letters in Aries, for example, vibrates to the number 7. The other number is the one that resonates with each sign's planet in traditional astrology systems.

ARIES ✦ 7 for Aries & 9 for Mars
TAURUS ✦ 1 for Taurus & 6 for Venus
GEMINI ✦ 3 for Gemini & 5 for Mercury
CANCER ✦ 8 for Cancer & 2 for the Moon
LEO ✦ 5 for Leo & 1 for the Sun
VIRGO ✦ 8 for Virgo & 5 for Mercury
LIBRA ✦ 6 for Libra & 6 for Venus
SCORPIO ✦ 5 for Scorpio & 9 for Mars^
SAGITTARIUS ✦ 9 for Sagittarius & 3 for Jupiter
CAPRICORN ✦ 7 for Capricorn & 8 for Saturn
AQUARIUS ✦ 5 for Aquarius & 4 for Uranus
PISCES ✦ 8 for Pisces & 7 for Neptune

^Traditional ruler.

Numerology is essentially the metaphysical* 'science' of numbers, or numerals. The use of numbers in magic is its cornerstone of power. The ancient Greek philosopher and mathematician Pythagoras, born around 590 BC, embarked on a thirty-year spiritual quest studying with important religious and esoteric teachers and healers to find the mystery of 'The Hidden Light', and came to see humankind as living in three worlds: the natural, the human and the Divine. He asserted that all things can be expressed in numerical terms, because they are ultimately reducible to numbers. Pythagoras stated that "Numbers are the first things of all of Nature" and followed the theory that "Nothing can exist without numbers."

Many believe that numbers have an arcane, mystical relationship with words, and with inanimate and animate objects; the interpretations that arose from these relationships date back to a time when the dawning intelligence of primitive man first visualised the meaning of numerals and associated it with spiritual significance. Numerology is the science of the exploration of this relationship in order to discover hidden meanings, forecast the future, or interpret the character of a person. In its more modern applications, a series of figures which correspond to an individual's name and date of birth are calculated, and practitioners believe one's prospects, fortune and nature can be deciphered from the results^.

So, what is numerology and how does one use it? Everything in the Universe has a vibrational frequency, an energy, a force, all vibrating at various rates, and we as humans are no exception; the difference between one person and another is their rate of vibration. This force or energy is constantly changing and in motion, and we can even 'tune into' and feel our vibrations if we are still for long enough.

Along with letters, sounds, colours, crystals and many other things, it is believed that numbers also have vibrations, and when we are able to familiarise ourselves with our own numerical frequencies, we can use this familiarity to add power and magic to our lives. The numerals of our birth date, the letters of our names, and the numbers of our Sun sign and ruling planets, all have a unique vibrational frequency, and herein lies the key to understanding our self and our journey through life.

Essentially, numerology refers to the knowledge contained within the numbers of our birth date and our name, which carries powerful personal magic that can help guide us through life.

Metaphysics is the study of those sciences that extend beyond the physical or tangible.

BASIC MEANINGS & KEYWORDS

Numerology recognises that numbers are vibrations, and each vibration is different to the next due to the number of cycles it oscillates at per second... Every sound, colour, fragrance and thought is a vibration, and each dances to the tune of its inherent number, each in its distinct way connected to life... Human life has an intimate connection with numbers, for they are the very essence of life's expression.

David A. Phillips

1. **Sun** ✦ Masculine influence, beginnings, independence, inventiveness, originality, leadership, exploration, innovation, ambition.
2. **Moon** ✦ Feminine influence, cooperation, partnership, tact, diplomacy, harmony, unity, emotions, imagination, adaptability.
3. **Jupiter** ✦ Communication, expression, youthfulness, self-confidence, creativity, inspiration, optimism, curiosity.
4. **Uranus** ✦ Order, form, security, stability, patience, restriction, work, values, practicality.

5 **Mercury** ✦ Freedom, inconsistency, change, variety, travel, activity, learned.
6 **Venus** ✦ Love, home, family, sense of duty, responsibility, marriage, justice, nurturing, balance, gentleness, peace, friendship.
7 **Neptune** ✦ Analysis, wisdom, mystical, spiritual, solitude, precision, research, integrity, mystery, psychic perceptions.
8 **Saturn** ✦ Money, power, success, organisation, hard work, business, health, purpose, control, authority, mastery.
9 **Mars** ✦ Completion, endings, Universal, service, humanity, philanthropy, loyalty.
10 **Fortunate** ✦ Creative, vibrant, stable, optimistic, original, successful, determined, individualistic.
11 **Master number** ✦ Prophecies, inspiration, moral courage, missionary, long-suffering, foolhardiness, enlightenment, invention.
13 **Misunderstood** ✦ Fearful, changeable, interested in the occult, fatalistic, flexible, sacred, beguiling.
22 **Master number** ✦ Powerful, successful, idealistic, attracted to the occult, creative, wise, successful, masterful, spiritually understanding.

LUCKY DAYS FOR EACH SIGN

From the most ancient times, the planets were said to rule Earthly destinies and powers, even days of the week. Days of the week were named after the seven planets which were the only ones then known: Sun Day, Moon Day (French Lundi), Mars Day (French Mardi), Mercury Day (French Mercredi), Jove Day (French Jeudi), Venus Day (French Vendredi) and Saturn Day, and as such, each day holds special powers for a particular sign or signs.

SUNDAY ✦ LUCKY DAY FOR LEO & ALL ZODIAC SIGNS

Planet ✦ The Sun
Signs ✦ Leo, all
Basic Energy ✦ Will
Basic Magic ✦ Success
Element ✦ Fire
Colours ✦ Yellow or Gold
Archangel Overseer ✦ Michael

Energy Keywords ✦ Power, Authority, Individuality, Courage, Leadership, Determination, Faith, Dignity, Willpower, Self, Optimism, Confidence, Self-reliance, Aggression, Egocentrism, Fortitude, Loyalty, Poise, Vitality

Sunday is the day of the Sun. In commonly used calendars, Sunday is the first day of the week, though in others it is the seventh. Sunday is the day of rest in most Western countries, and part of the 'weekend'. For most Christians Sunday is observed as a day of worship and rest, held as the Lord's Day, the day of Christ's resurrection. Indeed, the Russian day for Sunday is Voskresenie, meaning 'Resurrection day'; the Greek word for Sunday is Kyriake, 'the Lord's day'; and many Eastern European words for Sunday can be translated as 'without acts (no work)'". Bloody Sunday, Easter Sunday and Palm Sunday, are three well-known days with which the Sun's day is associated.

Sunday is the day for Solar magic which helps the advancement of the individual self. It is a time when you can work towards personal healing or for a new impulse to assist your life. Sunday is commonly regarded as the best day to attract and increase overall success in all endeavours and every area of life. The ancient idea of the Sabbath (coming from a Jewish word Shabbat, which means 'the seventh') asks us to use this as a day of rest, rejuvenation and relaxation. You can create your own Sabbath experience any way you wish.

In the folk rhyme 'Monday's Child', 'The child that is born on the Sabbath day, is bonny and blythe and good and gay.'

It is a day of vitality, energy, pleasure, optimism, fun, leisure, children, entertainment, pure joy and all-round success.

Yellow is the colour of the Sun, and so yellow-coloured objects such as yellow crystals and candles can be used as a magical correspondence to the Sun in spells and rituals.

The Christian Church marks Sunday as the day of rest. However, in ancient faiths, Sunday was the day on which to celebrate the gods of the Sun, such as the Greek gods Apollo and Helios.

MONDAY ✦ LUCKY DAY FOR CANCER

Planet ✦ The Moon

Signs ✦ Cancer

Basic Energy ✦ Protection, Psychism, Wishes

Element ✦ Water

Colours ✦ White, Silver or Blue

Archangel Overseer ✦ Gabriel

Energy Keywords ✦ Creativity, Intuition, Mothering, Feeling, Kindness, Protection, Domesticity, Flexibility, Sympathy, Growth, Imagination, Impressionism, Magnetism, Peace, Plasticity, Sensitivity, Psychism, Receptivity, Vision, Cycles

Monday is the day of the Moon. In commonly used calendars, Monday is the second day of the week, while in others it is the first. The English name is derived from Old English Monandaeg, and Middle English Monenday, meaning 'Moon Day'. A number of songs feature Monday, often lyrically associating it with melancholy, depression, or anxiety.

In the folk rhyme 'Monday's Child', 'Monday's child is fair of face'.

Monday is for Moon Magic. Her silvery light can be used to strengthen psychic, intuitive, imaginative, or dreaming powers, to enhance your ability to meditate, or to be inspired by your inner depths. There are many Moon goddesses if extra help is required, and even the Egyptian god Thoth is a ruler of Lunar power.

TUESDAY ✦ LUCKY DAY FOR ARIES & SCORPIO

Planet ✦ Mars
Signs ✦ Aries, Scorpio
Basic Energy ✦ Action
Basic Magic ✦ Combat, Courage, Vitality, Willpower
Element ✦ Fire
Colours ✦ Red
Archangel Overseer ✦ Camael
Energy Keywords ✦ Assertion, Force, Frankness, Will, Passion, Expression, Leadership, Construction, Courage, Strength, Defiance, Combat, Destruction, Dynamism, Audacity, Energy, Self-reliance, Fearlessness, Heroics, Impulsivity, Spontaneity

Tuesday is the day of Mars. In commonly used calendars, Tuesday is the third day of the week, though in others it is the second. The English name is derived from Old English Tiwesdaeg, and Middle English Tewesday, meaning 'Tiw's Day', the Day of Tiw or Tyr, the god of victory, war, combat, and heroic glory in Norse mythology. Tiw was equated with Mars. Shrove Tuesday, which precedes the first day of Lent in the Western Christian calendar, and Black Tuesday, referring to Tuesday 29 October 1929, part of the Great Stock Market Crash of that year, are two famous days with which Mars's day is associated.

In the folk rhyme 'Monday's Child', ' Tuesday's child is full of grace'.

Tuesday offers Mars energy to end conflicts, overcome inertia or to deal with those matters that may metaphorically need to be kick-started, or have physical energy applied to them. It can be a day of passionate feelings, strong motivations and determined efforts that bring desired results.

Tuesday is a day of enthusiasm, competition, passion, energy, courage, protection, strength, victory, anything requiring assertiveness, masculinity (Yang energy), a 'fighting spirit', determination, vitality, sexuality, virility, self-confidence, men's power, men's mysteries, drive, ambition, achievement, triumph and potency.

WEDNESDAY ✦ LUCKY DAY FOR GEMINI & VIRGO

Planet ✦ Mercury
Signs ✦ Gemini, Virgo
Basic Energy ✦ Speed
Basic Magic ✦ Communication, Study, Information
Element ✦ Air
Colours ✦ Blue, Yellow or Silver
Archangel Overseer ✦ Raphael
Energy Keywords ✦ Expression, Activity, Communication, Siblings, Dexterity, Adaptability, Intelligence, Agility, Versatility, Analysis, Verbosity, Restlessness, Neighbours, Awareness, Articulation, Brilliance, Changeability, Efficiency, Discrimination, Precision, Reason

Wednesday is the day of Mercury. In commonly used calendars, Wednesday is the fourth day of the week, though in others it is the third. The English name is derived from Old English Wodnesdaeg, and Middle English Wednesdei, meaning 'Day of Woden' or a claque of the Latin dies Mercurii, or 'Day of Mercury'. The god Woden was interpreted in the Roman era as the Germanic Mercury. Ash Wednesday, the first day of Lent in the Western Christian tradition, is perhaps the most well-known day with which Mercury's day is associated.

In the folk rhyme 'Monday's Child', 'Wednesday's child is full of woe'.

Wednesday is the time for Mercury's powers of communication, to link up with long-lost friends, to communicate with a passed over loved one, or write important correspondences. It is also an opportune day to ask for qualities such as versatility, agility, articulate expression, reason, wit, humour, adaptability, intellectuality and overall efficiency - as all are themes of Mercury. Mercury, or Hermes, is the god of thieves, so if something has been stolen from you, this day could be the time to ask for it back in some form or another.

THURSDAY ✦ LUCKY DAY FOR SAGITTARIUS & PISCES

Planet ✦ Jupiter
Signs ✦ Sagittarius, Pisces
Basic Energy ✦ Expansion
Basic Magic ✦ Luck, Money, Increase
Element ✦ Fire
Colours ✦ Purple
Archangel Overseer ✦ Sachiel
Energy Keywords ✦ Aspiration, Benevolence, Charity, Philanthropy, Generosity, Mercy, Dignity, Mind Travel, Expansion, Religion, Faith, Philosophy, Success, Understanding, Growth, Extravagance, Kindness, Humour, Optimism, Luck, Hope, Pomposity, Radiance, Reverence, Confidence, Indulgence, Opulence

Thursday is the day of Jupiter. In commonly used calendars, Thursday is the fifth day of the week, though in others it is the fourth. The English name is derived from Middle English Thuresday, meaning 'Thor's Day'. In Latin, the day was known as Iovis Dies, 'Jupiter's Day'. Thursday is known as this king of the gods' day. Thursday has its origins in the Saxon Thor's Day, and the Latin Jove (which links to the Jupiterian trait 'jovial'), from which the French Jeudi, Spanish Jueves and Italian Giovedi may derive from.

In the folk rhyme 'Monday's Child', 'Thursday's child has far to go' - you can interpret this as you please, but I don't feel it fits with Jupiter's generally optimistic, expansive nature; however, it can be taken to mean that your horizons may well open up before you on your life's journey and you therefore have far horizons that await your exploration.

Jupiter rules over business and material growth, justice, the higher mind, legal matters, ethics, publishing, luck and general increase and expansion, so if you are taking action to expand anything in your world, or seeking judgement on or clarity about your affairs, Thursday would be a powerful day on which to ask.

Thursday is a day of luck, abundance, optimism, expansion, higher learning, hope, positivity, philosophy, adventure and distant journeys, and an opportune day for making wishes or working magic involving higher education or tertiary studies, growth, idealism, philosophical endeavours, influence, worldly power, accomplishment, wisdom, overall fulfilment, games of chance, optimism and long-distance or foreign travel. Good luck, and always be careful what you wish for - because, as Ralph Waldo Emerson so eloquently noted, you will surely get it!

FRIDAY ✦ LUCKY DAY FOR TAURUS & LIBRA

Planet ✦ Venus
Signs ✦ Taurus, Libra
Basic Energy ✦ Socialising & Romance
Basic Magic ✦ Love, Friendships, Pleasure, Art, Beauty
Element ✦ Air
Colours ✦ Green
Archangel Overseer ✦ Anael
Energy Keywords ✦ Affection, Gentleness, Attraction, Diplomacy, Love, Art, Harmony, Appreciation, Sociability, Consideration, Beauty, Construction, Devotion, Cooperation, Femininity, Romance, Flirtiness

Friday is the day of Venus. In commonly used calendars, Friday is the sixth day of the week, though in others it is the fifth. The English name is derived from Old English Frigedaeg, a result of an old convention associating the goddess Frigg with the goddess Venus, with whom the day is associated. Good Friday, the day before Easter that commemorates the crucifixion of Jesus, Black Friday, referring to several historical disasters that happened on a Friday, Friday the 13th and Casual Friday, a relaxation of dress codes adopted in some corporations, are some well-known examples with which Venus's day is associated.

Venus is the goddess often associated with love, but she rules over all kinds of partnerships, and harmony, balance, beauty and aesthetics generally. If you wish to change your image or purchase a work of art for your environment, then Venus can help.

In the folk rhyme 'Monday's Child', 'Friday's child is loving and giving'. It is a day of love, relationships, business partnerships, marriage, beauty, harmony, balance, indulgence, luxury and pampering, and an opportune time for making wishes or working magic involving romance, love, relationships, beauty, social connections, art and style.

SATURDAY ✦ LUCKY DAY FOR CAPRICORN & AQUARIUS

Planet ✦ Saturn
Signs ✦ Capricorn, Aquarius
Basic Energy ✦ Restriction, Crossroads, Authority
Basic Magic ✦ Banishing, Rewards, Wisdom
Element ✦ Earth
Colours ✦ Black or Midnight Blue
Archangel Overseer ✦ Cassiel
Energy Keywords ✦ Caution, Responsibility, Rigidity, Sternness, Justice, Seriousness, Defence, Authority, Time, Fear, Humility, Law, Patience, Pessimism, Age, Respect, Sincerity, Restraint, Severity, Wisdom, Thrift

Saturday is the day of Saturn. In commonly used calendars, Saturday is the seventh day of the week, though in others it is the sixth. The Romans named Saturday Saturni dies, meaning 'Saturn's Day' no later than the 2nd century for the planet Saturn, which was believed to control the first hour of that day. Some cultures and religions observe Saturday as Shabbat or Sabbath, which stretches from sundown Friday to sundown Saturday and is the day of rest. Other religions distinguish between Saturday (Sabbath) and the Lord's Day (Sunday). Black Saturday, a day named after the beginning of tragic bushfires in Victoria Australia, Holy Saturday, the day before Easter, and Lazarus Saturday, the day before Palm Sunday which is part of the 'Holy Week', are some well-known examples with which Saturn's day is associated.

Saturday ends the week in most calendars, and is ruled by dark-browed Saturn, father of the gods and ruler of time. His help can be sought for anything to do with old age, and with establishing or breaking down boundaries, limitations and structures. His magic works slowly but although subtle it can be extremely powerful if you have the patience to allow him to work with you on whatever you are wishing for.

In the folk rhyme 'Monday's Child', 'Saturday's child works hard for a living'. It is a day of leadership, ambition, authority, hard work, perseverance, dedication, responsibility and duty, and an opportune day for making wishes or working magic involving long-term goals, careers, institutions, establishments, security, investments, karma, 'reversals', building structure, protection, solitude, privacy, determination, endings, blocking, renewing and transforming.

LUCKY CHARM & TALISMANS

When any star ascends fortunately, take a stone and herb that are under that star, make a ring of the metal that is congruous therewith, and in that fix the stone with the herb under it.

Henry Cornelius Agrippa

Many people are prepared to admit that there may be some active power in a thought made concrete in the form of a talisman or amulet which may be made for some specific purpose, or for particular wear, becoming to the wearer a continual reminder of its purpose and undoubtedly strengthening him in his aims and desires.

W. Thomas & K. Pavitt

Charms, talismans and amulets are among the oldest forms of magic. A charm or talisman is a symbol, often used to communicate a thought, prayer or wish to, or to make a connection with the Divine. It is usually in the form of an object, which has been imbued with mysterious and magical powers. A charm may be as simple as a stone, a flower or a feather, or it might be a parchment bearing writing; the meaning and significance that you attribute to the symbol is what is important. It can be created by yourself (to best effect) or by someone else, and works as a tool to activate the subconscious mind.

The exact origins of talismans, charms and amulets are lost to antiquity, but they are found across all cultures for as far back as human records can be traced.

In the writings of the philosophers and alchemists of the Middle Ages, directions are given that these talismans should be made, or commenced, under favourable aspects, so that the Work may receive the vitalising rays emanating from the planet represented.

You can use general charms such as a cross, or a lucky symbol like a horseshoe, but you will exude and therefore attract more potency and protection if you make and wear the appropriate charms with the matching gemstone, set in the right metal and created under the corresponding planetary influence.

While most people wear silver or gold, cheaper tin or copper may be more appropriate and indeed beneficial for your Sun sign. An amulet (for protection) or a talisman or charm (for intention and luck), must also be made, ordered, designed or purchased on the appropriate day of the week for its power to be most effective.

The following are three 'materials' or talismanic symbols from which to make your lucky charms, and the planetary energy under which to do it, corresponding with each Sun sign:

ARIES ✦ Diamond, Axe, Iron, Mars
TAURUS ✦ Emerald, Owl, Silver, Venus
GEMINI ✦ Agate, Caduceus, Silver, Mercury
CANCER ✦ Ruby, Anchor, Silver, the Moon
LEO ✦ Sardonyx, Heart, Gold, Sun
VIRGO ✦ Sapphire, Spider, Silver, Mercury
LIBRA ✦ Opal, Scales, Copper, Venus
SCORPIO ✦ Topaz, Tau, Iron, Mars
SAGITTARIUS ✦ Turquoise, Arrowhead, Tin, Jupiter
CAPRICORN ✦ Garnet, Cat, Lead, Saturn
AQUARIUS ✦ Amethyst, Key, Lead, Saturn
PISCES ✦ Bloodstone, Fish, Tin, Jupiter

GODS, GODDESSES, ANIMAL TOTEMS & OTHER GUIDES

Gods, goddesses, totems and guides can be summoned to help you live your life to its optimal best. Some are connected with your Sun sign, while others may be of your own personal choosing, ones you may feel particularly drawn towards. Those which align with your ruling planet and your Sun sign, give a good indication of those who will shine a guiding light along your desired path, but you can choose your own too, based upon exploration, observations, research, meditation or simple intuition - I believe choosing your own, based on your inner knowing or signpost system, is a very powerful magical tool. However, to get you started, following are some gods, goddesses and animal spirit guide ideas for your contemplation.

To invoke a god or goddess is to send an appeal or petition to a higher power (or powers) to them and bring their essence and blessings into your own energy or experience. Invocation is also a method of establishing conscious ties with those aspects of the goddess and god that dwell within us. In essence, then, we seemingly cause them to appear or make themselves known by becoming aware of them. Be aware that if you consistently call upon one particular deity power to the exclusion of all others, you will eventually begin to manifest characteristics of that energy pool within your personality. If this is done correctly in order to gain positive results, these changes will become an important part of your magical personality.

Beneficial deities and similar entities can be called in using essential oils of cinnamon, gardenia, frankincense, rose, cedarwood, jasmine and sandalwood.

GODS & GODDESSES FOR EACH SIGN

ARIES ✦ POWER DEITIES
Mars, Artemis, Bellona, Nerio, Minerva, Ares, Athena, Mercury, Ashur

TAURUS ✦ POWER DEITIES
Venus, Ceres, Lakshmi, Aphrodite, Eros, Freya, Brigid, Hymen, Vulcan, Kwan Yin (Quan Yin)

GEMINI ✦ POWER DEITIES
Mercury, Hermes, Thoth, Apollo

CANCER ✦ POWER DEITIES
Diana, Selene, Isis, Luna, Hecate, Phoebe, Artemis, Neptune

LEO ✦ POWER DEITIES
Apollo, Ra, Sol, Helios, Jove, Zeus, Jupiter

VIRGO ✦ POWER DEITIES
Mercury, Ceres, Hermes, Thoth, Demeter, Vesta, Chiron

LIBRA ✦ POWER DEITIES
Venus, Lakshmi, Aphrodite, Eros, Freya, Brigid, Hymen, Juno, Hera, Vulcan, Dionysus, Hephaestus, Pallas Athene

SCORPIO ✦ POWER DEITIES
Pluto, Hades, Persephone, Anubis, Hecate, Osiris, Mars, Ares, Vesta, Juno

SAGITTARIUS ✦ POWER DEITIES
Jupiter, Zeus, Thoth, Hermes, Lakshmi, Fortuna, Artemis, Chiron, Apollo

CAPRICORN ✦ POWER DEITIES
Saturn, Cronus, Ceres, Athene, Vesta, Hestia

AQUARIUS ✦ POWER DEITIES
Uranus, Caelus, Saturn, Cronus, Thoth, Juno, Hera, Jupiter, Pallas Athene

PISCES ✦ POWER DEITIES
Neptune, Poseidon, Jupiter, Zeus, Hypnos

ANIMAL GUIDES

Somewhere beyond the walls of our awareness... the wilderness side, the hunter side, the seeking side of ourselves is waiting to return.

Laurens van der Post

How will you know your totems? On some level, you already do... Think back to your favourite childhood animals. Which animals intrigued you, delighted you, comforted you most in childhood? Do certain animals or their images keep appearing in your life? What animals do you really love? When you go to the zoo, who do you have to visit? Conversely, which animals do you really fear or hate? (For) any extremely powerful emotion tends to indicate some sort of an alliance.

Judika Illes

Some astrological systems, such as Shamanistic* or Native American Astrology, tell us that the Sun sign we were born under has a corresponding animal totem*, which informs us about our characteristics and act as a kind of spiritual guide or mentor throughout our life's journey. These totems are described as Solar totems, because many of them share similarities with the Solar system and the sign the Sun was occupying at the time of our birth, and therefore relate to animals and animal behaviours which also correspond to environmental conditions and seasonal changes.

These animals encompass many aspects of the Solar system, from seasonal relationships, to creature instincts, to reciprocal links with the planetary vibrations, and 'clans' within nature that you are inherently closely connected with through your date of birth.

Carl Jung, an expert in dream analysis and interpretation, proposed that animals symbolise our natural instincts, operating through our dreams. He theorised that certain dream symbols, among them animals, represent core emotions and concepts, archetypes that will hold true for all of us the world over, regardless of so-called 'divisions' such as sex, customs, age, or culture. In Man and His Symbols, Jung states that primitive societies believed that each person had a bush soul and a human soul. The bush soul incarnates as a tree or animal - a totem - and when the bush soul is harmed or injured, the human soul is considered injured as well.

Some of the most important and powerful spirit guides are those belonging to the animal kingdom. Both in ancient times and in some traditional modern tribal systems, people consult with animals for their wisdom and personal power. Even though most societies today have drifted away from this connection, it has never really left us, and different creatures continue to communicate with us on both the physical and spiritual planes in an attempt to speak to our souls and spirits.

In the Native American tradition, each animal is the embodiment of a specific consciousness. To find our way through our own inner world, we as our own healers, need to be familiar with these animal allies so as to be able to access the inner space that will help in all facets of mind, body and spirit health and healing, by allowing us to enter the inner space where our consciousness is congruent with that of our special animal.

When we are plagued with limiting beliefs or negative thoughts, we need to find ways to enhance and empower ourselves, and we can achieve this by connecting with certain power animals. By reflecting or even meditating on these animals, we can work with them to harness our internal courage and strength. In her book The Complete Handbook of Quantum Healing, which lists power animals for all manner of ailments and conditions, author Deanna M. Minich tells us, "Incorporating power animals into your healing can be therapeutic, as they provide role models or even support systems, functioning much like Earth-based angels." Shamanic teachers recommend that as we begin a quest or healing journey, we begin to notice the creatures that wander, fly, or walk across our path - acknowledge them and consider what they might be saying to you. If they pause, look at you or engage you in any way, their message may be all the more personal, profound and powerful.

As part of the teaching world, animals can bring us wisdom and survival skills, while others show us how to adapt, transcend or morph. Others still can remind us of the importance of play and humour, and guide us around how to overcome life's challenges. Many are known for their loyalty and ability to love unconditionally and without judgement, while some have a grounded and healthy detachment, remaining true to themselves rather than pleasing others, an important lesson in itself. Whatever the qualities of the unique animal guides for your Sun sign, all have some enlightening soul-awakening traits that can teach us much about our own true inner selves. Ultimately, your animal spirit guides, and in particular your Solar totem animal, endow you with qualities that will enhance your life and help to activate your creativity, wisdom and intuition, helping to heal the broken or return the lost pieces of your soul and reconnect you to the natural world. The goal is the eventual absorption of something of their nature and power, so that you are able to infuse your own personal power with their essence and positive qualities.

Each sign's Solar totem animal (listed last on the lucky birds and animals list for that sign) is not the same as an animal spirit guide, which is based on metaphysical principles and is also based on one's soul's mission in this embodiment - however, one can definitely make their birth Solar totem animal their spiritual guide if they so wish, as one may find that its qualities, traits, symbolism and messages strongly resonate.

Overall, if your life is stagnant or in need of healing or an energy boost, you can request your animal spirit or spirits to come and help you change your vibration, awaken your truth, and unravel your inner forces. If you are aware of your animal spirit's presence in your life every day, you can use its particular energies to support, guide and teach you. And above all, pay attention to any signs and expressions of its lessons, and always remember to thank your chosen animal guide for its assistance with your journey.

*Shamanism is a traditional spiritual practice of the Native American culture. A shaman, one who practices this age-old art, is an intermediary between the human world and the world of the spirits. He inherits his magical powers at birth, but spends many years as an apprentice, so that he is usually much older in age before he is able to practice and call upon his skills. People ask for a shaman's help when there is a crisis on either a personal or wider spread scale, such as famine, drought, war, or illness. The shaman makes contact with the spirits by going into a trance. First, he may perform a series of rituals, which usually include drumming, singing and chanting, and when these have brought on the right conditions, he leaves his body behind to travel to the other world. There he meets with the spirits of his ancestors, who inform him what must be done to relieve the suffering of his people. If the shaman is asked to cure someone of a dis-ease, then the spirits may accompany him to find the correct medicinal herbs or treatments for his patient.

*The Algonquin word totem means a person's personal guardian.

ARIES LUCKY ANIMALS & BIRDS

Ram, Dragon, Falcon, Tiger, Leopard, Magpie, Stallion, Vulture, Robin, Hawk

ARIES FEATURE ANIMAL ✦ RED HAWK

The Hawk's Message ✦ Strike while the iron is hot.
Brings the totem gift of ✦ Initiative, courage, leadership, discernment.
Shares the power energies of ✦ Achievement, action, opportunity, wisdom, truth.
Brings forth and teaches the magic of ✦ Passion, Fire, confidence, persistence, observation.

ARIES SPIRITUAL KEEPER ✦ EAGLE

Your spiritual keeper guides your spiritual growth and brings illumination. Your spiritual keeper is determined by the season in which you were born. Regarded as the 'keepers' or 'caretakers' of the Universe, their presence is felt rather than seen.

The East Direction's totem is the Eagle. The Eagle is a symbol of freedom, victory and spirit. It flies higher than any other bird, high enough to 'touch the Sun'. The golden Eagle is a symbol of peace, and an Eagle flying overhead is a sign of Shaman power, sometimes taken as a call to that vocation. To the shaman, the Eagle is a messenger, bringing instructions from the spirit of the night. As Halifax states, "When shamans get power, it always comes from the night." The Eagle is the sacred messenger, flying high to carry our prayers to the Great Spirit and returning with gifts of illumination and clear vision. The Eagle is, above all, a potent symbol of vision and strength.

ARIES CLAN ✦ THUNDERBIRD (OR HAWK)

Your clan animal comes from a place of inner knowing and intuition, helping you to discover the essence and magic of your true self.

The Thunderbird, sometimes referred to as Hawk, is a Totem of the Fire clan, and its medicine is messenger. Thunderbird holds the Fire clan and brings thunder, lightning and rain. The greatest of all the winged creatures, the Thunderbird is closest to the Creator. His Fire and spark carry the gift of life and link the soul to the Great Mystery. His true desire is not to know what lies below, his true yearning to join with Grandfather Sky. Fly high and keep your eyes focused ever upward.

ARIES CORRESPONDING
CHINESE ASTROLOGY ANIMAL ✦ DRAGON

Each oriental animal corresponds with a Western astrology sign. For Aries, it is the Dragon.

Fixed Element Earth

✦ **Keywords** ✦

Honourable, Excitable, Healthy, Inflexible, Brave, Intelligent, Independent, Enthusiastic, Flamboyant, Vital, Energetic, Short-tempered, Proud

The Dragon is the fifth animal of the Chinese horoscope. Traditionally a yang animal, the Dragon is a mythical creature who endows qualities of self-sufficiency, wildness, sentimentality and shrewdness. They are vibrant characters, but tend to be judgemental towards others. As the noble animal symbol that represents the Chinese emperors, Dragons are born leaders and masters of ceremonies, and because of this, many Chinese parents aspire to have a Dragon child. Feisty and gifted with power and luck, many look up to the Dragon type, but the Dragon can be enthusiastic and proud to the point of impetuosity, losing their tempers easily. Dragons can be tyrannical and grab at prestige and splendour, but they are also generous, gifted, tenacious, willing and intelligent. Dragons are born monarchs, and as far as they can see, their power is indisputable and unconquerable - and for this reason they are usually successful in most endeavours they undertake.

TAURUS LUCKY ANIMALS & BIRDS

Bull, Cow, Dove, Cat, Sparrow, Goat, Swan, Rabbit, Songbirds, Beaver

TAURUS FEATURE ANIMAL ✦ BEAVER

The Beaver's Message ✦ Strength of will; persistence will pay off.

Brings the totem gift of ✦ Endurance, security through abundance, freedom from attachments.

Shares the power energies of ✦ Resourcefulness, enduring value, inner security, strategy.

Brings forth and teaches the magic of ✦ Acceptance of change, perseverance, cunning.

TAURUS SPIRITUAL KEEPER ✦ EAGLE

Your spiritual keeper guides your spiritual growth and brings illumination. Your spiritual keeper is determined by the season in which you were born. Regarded as the 'keepers' or 'caretakers' of the Universe, their presence is felt rather than seen.

The East Direction's totem is the Eagle. The Eagle is a symbol of freedom, victory and spirit. It flies higher than any other bird, high enough to 'touch the Sun'. The golden Eagle is a symbol of peace, and an Eagle flying overhead is a sign of Shaman power, sometimes taken as a call to that vocation. To the shaman, the Eagle is a messenger, bringing instructions from the spirit of the night. As Halifax states, "When shamans get power, it always comes from the night." The Eagle is the sacred messenger, flying high to carry our prayers to the Great Spirit and returning with gifts of illumination and clear vision. The Eagle is, above all, a potent symbol of vision and strength.

TAURUS CLAN ✦ TURTLE

Your clan animal comes from a place of inner knowing and intuition, helping you to discover the essence and magic of your true self.

The Turtle is the totem of the Earth clan and in mythology, during a time when there was only water and nowhere for the people and animals to go, the Turtle made a great sacrifice by letting everyone come and live on her back. In the Far East, a talisman carved in the form of a Turtle is believed to have power over all kinds of magic; the Chinese and Japanese also wear charms in the shape of Turtles to ensure a long life. In ancient times, the shape of a Turtle's shell suggested the dome of the sky and the creature became a symbol of heavenly virtue. The medicine of the Turtle is Mother Earth.

TAURUS CORRESPONDING CHINESE ASTROLOGY ANIMAL ✦ SNAKE

Each oriental animal corresponds with a Western astrology sign. For Taurus, it is the Snake.

Fixed Element Fire

✦ Keywords ✦

Quiet, wise, deep-thinking, intuitive, vain, stingy, calm exterior, intense, passionate, regulated, shrewd

The Snake is the sixth animal of the Chinese horoscope. Like Dragons, Snakes don't always have a good image in the West, but they are revered in the East and associated with wisdom. Traditionally a yin sign, Snakes are cultured, wise, sophisticated, intuitive and enjoy the finer things in life. Snakes are elegant and often beautiful, with a certain way about them that makes people look twice. Possessing sensuality and a natural talent for dressing well which adds to her allure, she is at her best when asked for advice – and here her wisdom truly shines through. An intuitive thinker, Snake types will ponder things deeply. As a connoisseur and extravagant spender, she loves luxury and style, but she has a certain naïvety that belies her worldly appearance. The Snake's charm is highly seductive, but she may be prone to indolence and possessiveness of people and 'things'.

GEMINI LUCKY ANIMALS & BIRDS

Dog, Monkey, Beetles, Small Birds, Weasel, Parrot, Squirrel, Magpie, Greyhound, Hyena, Apes, Linnet, Butterfly, Serpent, Spider, Eagle, Fox, Bee, Finch, Deer

GEMINI FEATURE ANIMAL ✦ DEER

The Deer's Message ✦ Be gentle in word, thought and touch.
Brings the totem gift of ✦ Sociability, inspiration, lively conversation, majesty, compassion.
Shares the power energies of ✦ A youthful outlook, unique humour, clear expression, gentleness.
Brings forth and teaches the magic of ✦ Grace, respectability, charm, daintiness.

GEMINI SPIRITUAL KEEPER ✦ EAGLE

Your spiritual keeper guides your spiritual growth and brings illumination. Your spiritual keeper is determined by the season in which you were born. Regarded as the 'keepers' or 'caretakers' of the Universe, their presence is felt rather than seen.

The East Direction's totem is the Eagle. The Eagle is a symbol of freedom, victory and spirit. It flies higher than any other bird, high enough to 'touch the Sun'. The golden Eagle is a symbol of peace, and an Eagle flying overhead is a sign of Shaman power, sometimes taken as a call to that vocation. To the shaman, the Eagle is a messenger, bringing instructions from the spirit of the night. As Halifax states, "When shamans get power, it always comes from the night." The Eagle is the sacred messenger, flying high to carry our prayers to the Great Spirit and returning with gifts of illumination and clear vision. The Eagle is, above all, a potent symbol of vision and strength.

GEMINI CLAN ✦ BUTTERFLY

Your clan animal comes from a place of inner knowing and intuition, helping you to discover the essence and magic of your true self.

The Butterfly, a totem of the Air clan, represents and protects all that is beautiful and holds the secrets of change and personal transformation. The Butterfly symbolises that this transformation is always available to you, and may even begin without your conscious participation. Butterfly is the power of Air, the ability to float along on a breeze, and to 'dance' from place to place. They awaken our sense of lightness and joy, and teach us to dance with life rather than take it too seriously. In the folklore of some tribes, butterflies stand for change and balance, while in others ephemeral beauty, and many tribes consider butterflies to be symbols of good luck. Butterflies symbolise metamorphosis, reawakening us to joy, and teaching us to trust in the process of change, and that life is full of surprises and to therefore live with a constant sense of passion, intensity and wonder.

GEMINI CORRESPONDING
CHINESE ASTROLOGY ANIMAL ✦ HORSE

Each oriental animal corresponds with a Western astrology sign. For Gemini, it is the Horse.

Fixed Element Fire

✦ **Keywords** ✦

Hardworking, popular, witty, vital, independent, active, sociable, intelligent, talented, perceptive, selfish, fickle, impatient

The Horse is the seventh animal of the Chinese horoscope. Traditionally a yang sign, the Horse is romantic, successful and sensual. They fall in love quickly but are fickle in romance, and are reputed to change lovers a lot more frequently than the other signs. Active and energetic, Horse types exude sex-appeal like no other. In general, the Horse is regarded as gifted, but the truth is that it is more cunning than intelligent. Rebellious and boundlessly ambitious, the Horse can be hot-headed, hot-blooded and impatient. Their characters are full of contradictions and paradoxes - they will give up everything for love, yet lose interest quickly; they are proud yet sweet-natured; envious but tolerant; arrogant yet oddly modest; conceited yet humble; they want to belong, yet crave independence; they desire love and intimacy, yet dislike being cornered. Above all, perhaps the Horse type is just like the creature itself: born to run as wild and free as the wind.

CANCER LUCKY ANIMALS & BIRDS

Crab, Otter, Seal, Eel, Seagull, Frog, Shellfish, Water-dwelling Birds, Stag, Heifer, Moth, Unicorn, White Peacock, Owl, Woodpecker

CANCER FEATURE ANIMAL ✦ WOODPECKER

The Woodpecker's Message ✦ When opportunity knocks, answer the door.
Brings the totem gift of ✦ Loyalty, protection, resourcefulness, discernment.
Shares the power energies of ✦ Progress, support, nurturance.
Brings forth and teaches the magic of ✦ Listening, sympathy, devotion.

CANCER SPIRITUAL KEEPER ✦ COYOTE

Your spiritual keeper guides your spiritual growth and brings illumination. Your spiritual keeper is determined by the season in which you were born. Regarded as the 'keepers' or 'caretakers' of the Universe, their presence is felt rather than seen.

The Direction to which your birth time belongs influences the nature of your inner senses. The South Direction's totem is the Coyote. The Coyote is a symbol of growth, fruition, emotions, productivity and fluidity. The Coyote is bold, impetuous, charming, youthful and creative, and as a spiritual keeper, can endow us with these qualities. In some native tribes, the Coyote is referred to as a trickster or joker. A clever, cunning and amazingly adaptable animal, its message is of wisdom and folly. Operating year-round, the Coyote doesn't try to trick us, but rather mirrors our own human capacity for stupidity and cleverness. Your animal keeper the Coyote is, above all, a potent symbol of the need for the balance between wisdom, trickery, skill, cleverness and cunning.

CANCER CLAN ✦ FROG

Your clan animal comes from a place of inner knowing and intuition, helping you to discover the essence and magic of your true self.

The Frog, a Totem of the Water clan, represents the song that calls the rain to Earth, and cleansing, teaching us the opportune times to purify, refresh and replenish our reserves. A charm or amulet in the shape of a frog is said to attract true friends and to help you find long-lasting love. To the Ancient Egyptians, Romans and Greeks, frogs symbolised inspiration, fertility, good luck and speedy recovery from illness, beliefs that carry over into some cultures today. People of the Frog clan have deep, easily flowing feelings, which enable them to have empathy for others and to heal. They have natural gifts for healing, sensitivity, creativity, and a deep appreciation for rain and being around water. As the Moon is so strongly associated with emotional and watery realms, Frog clan people can connect with this deep Lunar magic by studying the cycles, patterns and energies of the Moon, the ruling celestial sphere of their clan animal, the Frog.

CANCER CORRESPONDING CHINESE ASTROLOGY ANIMAL ✦ SHEEP

Each oriental animal corresponds with a Western astrology sign. For Cancer, it is the Sheep.

Fixed Element Earth

✦ **Keywords** ✦

Wise, artistic, elegant, gentle, compassionate, honest, genuine, inventive, impractical, sensitive, dependent, creative, pessimistic, materialistic

The Sheep is the eighth animal of the Chinese horoscope. Traditionally a yin sign, the Sheep is sometimes symbolised by a Goat. Typically, Sheep are timid, tasteful, altruistic, peaceful and calm. They can be easily led, however, and tend to become sulky if challenged. She needs security and harmony to be at her best. A contemplative and retiring sign, the Sheep prefers to be in her own home or within her own tribe, living peace and comfort. Creativity is one of her greatest gifts, and she can create an atmosphere of beauty, charm and fantasy with effortless ease. The catch with all these soft and fluffy characteristics is that they can frustrate or irritate more outgoing types. Her herd instinct is strong, so she can usually live with others, but frequently fails to do her share of the tasks, preferring to spend time on fun, dreamy, artistic, or impractical pursuits. Whimsical and good-natured overall, what she lacks in foresight, she makes up for in going after what she wants… and getting it.

LEO LUCKY ANIMALS & BIRDS

Lion, Wolf, Hawk, Domestic Cats, Lynx, Glow-Worm, Horse, Griffin, Peacock, Swan, Rooster, Eagle, Salmon

LEO FEATURE ANIMAL ✦ SALMON

The Salmon's Message ✦ Inspiration and motivation through example and influence.
Brings the totem gift of ✦ Focus, intuition, energy, activity, wisdom.
Shares the power energies of ✦ Motivation, purpose, noble crusades.
Brings forth and teaches the magic of ✦ Generosity, inspiration, confidence.

LEO SPIRITUAL KEEPER ✦ COYOTE

Your spiritual keeper guides your spiritual growth and brings illumination. Your spiritual keeper is determined by the season in which you were born. Regarded as the 'keepers' or 'caretakers' of the Universe, their presence is felt rather than seen.

The Direction to which your birth time belongs influences the nature of your inner senses. The South Direction's totem is the Coyote. The Coyote is a symbol of growth, fruition, emotions, productivity and fluidity. The Coyote is bold, impetuous, charming, youthful and creative, and as a spiritual keeper, can endow us with these qualities. In some native tribes, the Coyote is referred to as a trickster or joker. A clever, cunning and amazingly adaptable animal, its message is of wisdom and folly. Operating year-round, the Coyote doesn't try to trick us, but rather mirrors our own human capacity for stupidity and cleverness. Your animal keeper the Coyote is, above all, a potent symbol of the need for the balance between wisdom, trickery, skill, cleverness and cunning.

LEO CLAN ✦ THUNDERBIRD (OR HAWK)

Your clan animal comes from a place of inner knowing and intuition, helping you to discover the essence and magic of your true self.

The Thunderbird, sometimes referred to as Hawk, is a Totem of the Fire clan, and its medicine is messenger. Thunderbird holds the Fire clan and brings thunder, lightning and rain. The greatest of all the winged creatures, the Thunderbird is closest to the Creator. His Fire and spark carry the gift of life and link the soul to the Great Mystery. His true desire is not to know what lies below, his true yearning to join with Grandfather Sky. Fly high and keep your eyes focused ever upward.

LEO CORRESPONDING CHINESE ASTROLOGY ANIMAL ✦ MONKEY

Each oriental animal corresponds with a Western astrology sign. For Leo, it is the Monkey.

Fixed Element Metal

✦ Keywords ✦

Desire for Knowledge, Intelligent, Skilful, Inventive, Cunning, Dexterous, Curious, Daring, Easily Discouraged, Strong-willed, Vain, Mischievous, Improvising, Zealous

The Monkey is the ninth sign of the Chinese horoscope. Traditionally a yang sign, the Monkey's characteristics are inventiveness, vigour and wit. Adept at problem-solving, Monkeys are humorous and resourceful. Like the creature itself, Monkey types are clever tricksters with an extroverted, outgoing, and technically adept nature. Known for his humour and mischief, the Monkey can also be very conscientious and takes pride in doing any job well. A great problem-solver, his mental dexterity comes to the fore under pressure and he uses unusual methods to solve problems that can leave others stumped. On top of this, he is an excellent communicator, but may become deceitful and opportunistic when it suits his purpose.

VIRGO LUCKY ANIMALS & BIRDS

Rooster, Cat, Magpie, Parrot, Squirrel, Mouse, Insects, Fox, Monkey, Beetles, Apes, Spiders, Hyena, Weasel, Bee, Brown Bear

VIRGO FEATURE ANIMAL ✦ BEAR

The Bear's Message ✦ Embrace the power of your spirit.

Brings the totem gift of ✦ Fearlessness, leadership, inner power, protection, meditation.

Shares the power energies of ✦ Cave-dwelling (withdrawal), contemplation, protection, ferocity, strength.

Brings forth and teaches the magic of ✦ Dreamtime, vision quests, wildness, introspection.

VIRGO SPIRITUAL KEEPER ✦ COYOTE

Your spiritual keeper guides your spiritual growth and brings illumination. Your spiritual keeper is determined by the season in which you were born. Regarded as the 'keepers' or 'caretakers' of the Universe, their presence is felt rather than seen.

The Direction to which your birth time belongs influences the nature of your inner senses. The South Direction's totem is the Coyote. The Coyote is a symbol of growth, fruition, emotions, productivity and fluidity. The Coyote is bold, impetuous, charming, youthful and creative, and as a spiritual keeper, can endow us with these qualities. In some native tribes, the Coyote is referred to as a trickster or joker. A clever, cunning and amazingly adaptable animal, its message is of wisdom and folly. Operating year-round, the Coyote doesn't try to trick us, but rather mirrors our own human capacity for stupidity and cleverness. Your animal keeper the Coyote is, above all, a potent symbol of the need for the balance between wisdom, trickery, skill, cleverness and cunning.

VIRGO CLAN ✦ TURTLE

Your clan animal comes from a place of inner knowing and intuition, helping you to discover the essence and magic of your true self.

The Turtle is the totem of the Earth clan and in mythology, during a time when there was only water and nowhere for the people and animals to go, the Turtle made a great sacrifice by letting everyone come and live on her back. In the Far East, a talisman carved in the form of a Turtle is believed to have power over all kinds of magic; the Chinese and Japanese also wear charms in the shape of Turtles to ensure a long life. In ancient times, the shape of a Turtle's shell suggested the dome of the sky and the creature became a symbol of heavenly virtue. The medicine of the Turtle is Mother Earth.

VIRGO CORRESPONDING CHINESE ASTROLOGY ANIMAL ✦ ROOSTER

Each oriental animal corresponds with a Western astrology sign. For Virgo, it is the Rooster.

Fixed Element Metal

✦ Keywords ✦

Outspoken, energetic, protective, resilient, popular, stylish, bossy, competitive, clever, talkative, eccentric, always busy, opinionated, deep-thinking

The Rooster is the tenth sign of the Chinese horoscope. Although traditionally a yin sign, Roosters are associated with aggressive 'male' or 'yang' competitiveness, resilience and strength, and are typically vivacious, creative, generous and attractive. Her amusing outlook and sincere nature often make her the centre of attention. Outgoing, kind, independent and enthusiastic, the Rooster type likes to keep abreast of anything that is interesting or new, and is able to recover from any setbacks relatively quickly. Even if she is a more retiring Rooster-type, her inner extrovert will still express itself through her desire to appear chic and stylish. There tends to be an element of theatre in everything she does, and she dreads tedious or mundane tasks; this is when she delegates it to others so that she can get back to the important business of organising her next adventure, trip, project, or big plan. Energy radiates from the Rooster most of the time, and she will give almost anything a go, especially things that are artistic or creative. However, her hobbies and endeavours rarely become a career, as she doesn't like to take chances with her financial security. Despite her usual choice of unconventional forms of dress or lifestyle, she is extremely conservative deep down. She likes to be in charge and in control, and with her loved ones, is always candid, humorous and helpful.

LIBRA LUCKY ANIMALS & BIRDS

Hare, Dove, Owl, Songbirds, Swan, Sparrow, Cat, Hart, Lizard, Small Reptiles, Raven/Crow

LIBRA FEATURE ANIMAL ✦ RAVEN

The Raven's Message ✦ Bearer of magic, harbinger of messages from the cosmos.

Brings the totem gift of ✦ Easy-going nature, flow, enthusiasm.

Shares the power energies of ✦ Entrepreneurship, well-received ideas, diplomacy, sociability.

Brings forth and teaches the magic of ✦ Romance, charm, balanced give and take in relationships.

LIBRA SPIRITUAL KEEPER ✦ BEAR

Your spiritual keeper guides your spiritual growth and brings illumination. Your spiritual keeper is determined by the season in which you were born. Regarded as the 'keepers' or 'caretakers' of the Universe, their presence is felt rather than seen.

The Direction to which your birth time belongs influences the nature of your inner senses. The West Direction's totem is the Bear. The Bear is a symbol of transformation, introspection, conservation, and strength drawn from within. The Bear has played a prominent role in many Native cultures, and because of its significance, a constellation, Ursus Major, was named for it. Bears can be amazingly fast and even climb trees, and many tribal people have regarded it as too powerful a medicine, fearing that the Bear would even hunt them and kill them if it were feeling threatened or starving. Despite its ferocity and the fear it can invoke, the Bear is considered to be a highly desired ally and spiritual keeper because of its fearless and instinctively protective powers. In many ways it is the epitome of the Great Protector, the protective mother. The Bear holds the teachings and wisdom of introspection. Unlike other animals who are active during a specific time of day or night, the Bear is active both day and night, symbolising its connection with Solar energy, that of strength and power and Lunar energy, that of intuition and the inner life. It enhances and teaches those born under this totem to develop both within themselves. To the ancients, Bear symbolised resurrection; to the Japanese she is a symbol of loyalty, wisdom and strength. In the psyche, the Bear can be understood as the ability to regulate one's life, especially one's feeling life. Bear possesses a deep, intuitive connection to moving in cycles, discerning when to be still and rest, or to be fully alert. Bear medicine teaches that we can be fierce, generous and loving at the same time.

LIBRA CLAN ✦ BUTTERFLY

Your clan animal comes from a place of inner knowing and intuition, helping you to discover the essence and magic of your true self.

The Butterfly, a totem of the Air clan, represents and protects all that is beautiful and holds the secrets of change and personal transformation. The Butterfly symbolises that this transformation is always available to you, and may even begin without your conscious participation. Butterfly is the power of Air, the ability to float along on a breeze, and to 'dance' from place to place. They awaken our sense of lightness and joy, and teach us to dance with life rather than take it too seriously. In the folklore of some tribes, butterflies stand for change and balance, while in others ephemeral beauty, and many tribes consider butterflies to be symbols of good luck. Butterflies symbolise metamorphosis, teaching us to trust in the process of change, re-awaken us to joy, and teach us that life is full of surprises and to therefore live with a constant sense of passion, intensity and wonder.

LIBRA CORRESPONDING CHINESE ASTROLOGY ANIMAL ✦ DOG

Each oriental animal corresponds with a Western astrology sign. For Libra, it is the Dog.

Fixed Element Earth

✦ Keywords ✦

Loyal, honest, trustworthy, faithful, ethical, sharp-tongued, critical, stubborn, defensive, protective, noble, respectable, dutiful, intelligent

The Dog is the eleventh sign of the Chinese horoscope. Traditionally a yang animal, dogs are honest, devoted, attentive, modest and loyal. If they feel threatened, however, they can be guarded and defensive. Dogs are trustworthy and kind in their dealings with others but will react defensively if crossed. His concern for the security and protection of himself and his family can make him suspicious and critical, even self-righteous at times, but he is willing to go to great lengths to support causes, even when everyone else has given up. Dog types are well-meaning, loving, helpful, firm and devoted friends with a great noble and moral flavour to their characters. They must, however, beware of people taking advantage of their desire to save the world, by looking out for his own interests and being a little less, well, dogged.

SCORPIO LUCKY ANIMALS & BIRDS

Scorpion, Dove, Eagle, Wolf, Panther, Leopard, Owl, Wild Boar, Dragon, Scarab Beetle, Invertebrates, Tiger, Fox, Lizard, Falcon, Griffin, Phoenix, Dog, Spider, Vulture, Snake

SCORPIO FEATURE ANIMAL ✦ SNAKE

The Snake's Message ✦ Shed your old skin to make way for the new.
Brings the totem gift of ✦ Creativity, acceptance, imagination, healing.
Shares the power energies of ✦ Rebirth, transformation, ability to change, influence, power.
Brings forth and teaches the magic of ✦ Emergence of new self, expression of inner intuition.

SCORPIO SPIRITUAL KEEPER ✦ BEAR

Your spiritual keeper guides your spiritual growth and brings illumination. Your spiritual keeper is determined by the season in which you were born. Regarded as the 'keepers' or 'caretakers' of the Universe, their presence is felt rather than seen.

The Direction to which your birth time belongs influences the nature of your inner senses. The West Direction's totem is the Bear. The Bear is a symbol of transformation, introspection, conservation, and strength drawn from within. The Bear has played a prominent role in many Native cultures, and because of its significance, a constellation, Ursus Major, was named for it. Bears can be amazingly fast and even climb trees, and many tribal people have regarded it as too powerful a medicine, fearing that the Bear would even hunt them and kill them if it were feeling threatened or starving. Despite its ferocity and the fear it can invoke, the Bear is considered to be a highly desired ally and spiritual keeper because of its fearless and instinctively protective powers. In many ways it is the epitome of the Great Protector, the safeguarding mother. The Bear holds the teachings and wisdom of introspection. Unlike other animals who are active during a specific time of day or night, the Bear is active both day and night, symbolising its connection with Solar energy, that of strength and power and Lunar energy, that of intuition and the inner life. It enhances and teaches those born under this totem to develop both within themselves. To the ancients, Bear symbolised resurrection; to the Japanese she is a symbol of loyalty, wisdom and strength. In the psyche, the Bear can be understood as the ability to regulate one's life, especially one's feeling life. Bear possesses a deep, intuitive connection to moving in cycles, discerning when to be still and rest, or to be fully alert. Bear medicine teaches that we can be fierce, generous and loving at the same time.

SCORPIO CLAN ✦ FROG

Your clan animal comes from a place of inner knowing and intuition, helping you to discover the essence and magic of your true self.

The Frog, a Totem of the Water clan, represents the song that calls the rain to Earth, and cleansing, teaching us the opportune times to purify, refresh and replenish our reserves. A charm or amulet in the shape of a frog is said to attract true friends and to help you find long-lasting love. To the Ancient Egyptians, Romans and Greeks, frogs symbolised inspiration, fertility, good luck and speedy recovery from illness, beliefs that carry over into some cultures today. People of the Frog clan have deep, easily flowing feelings, which enable them to have empathy for others and to heal. They have natural gifts for healing, sensitivity, creativity, and a deep appreciation for rain and being around water. As the Moon is so strongly associated with emotional and watery realms, Frog clan people can connect with this deep Lunar magic by studying the cycles, patterns and energies of the Moon, the ruling celestial sphere of their clan animal, the Frog.

SCORPIO CORRESPONDING CHINESE ASTROLOGY ANIMAL ✦ BOAR

Each oriental animal corresponds with a Western astrology sign. For Scorpio, it is the Boar.

Fixed Element Water

✦ **Keywords** ✦

Chivalrous, gallant, loyal, reliable, intellectual, shrewd but sometimes naïve, sincere, tolerant, honest, generous, indulgent, light-hearted, lucky, easily provoked

The Boar, or Pig, is the twelfth and last sign of the Chinese zodiac. Associated with children, welfare and comfort, the Pig type has a great capacity for transforming environments, looking after those in need, and working hard to accumulate wealth, usually all at once. Traditionally a yin animal sign, Pigs are chivalrous, gallant, loyal, charming and romantic. In relationships, the Pig offers sensitivity and pure love. A powerhouse in all the caring and giving she does, she is sincere and honest in her approach; dishonesty makes her nervous. She can be a little taciturn and tends to withdraw into herself rather than socialise with other people, which makes her best suited to more natural and quiet environments, where she can build, create and improve to her heart's content.

SAGITTARIUS LUCKY ANIMALS & BIRDS

Horse, Lion, Unicorn, Eagle, Stag, Deer, All Hoofed and Hunted Animals, Elephant, Dolphin, Swan, Peacock, Bird of Paradise, Owl, Elk

SAGITTARIUS FEATURE ANIMAL ✦ ELK

The Elk's Message ✦ Application of the spiritual to the physical self to bring about healing.

Brings the totem gift of ✦ Love, heartiness, independence, strength, agility, confidence.

Shares the power energies of ✦ Optimism, happiness, spiritual evolution, stamina.

Brings forth and teaches the magic of ✦ Understanding of human nature and Spirit, trust, focus.

SAGITTARIUS SPIRITUAL KEEPER ✦ BEAR

Your spiritual keeper guides your spiritual growth and brings illumination. Your spiritual keeper is determined by the season in which you were born. Regarded as the 'keepers' or 'caretakers' of the Universe, their presence is felt rather than seen.

The Direction to which your birth time belongs influences the nature of your inner senses. The West Direction's totem is the Bear. The Bear is a symbol of transformation, introspection, conservation, and strength drawn from within. The Bear has played a prominent role in many Native cultures, and because of its significance, a constellation, Ursus Major, was named for it. Bears can be amazingly fast and even climb trees, and many tribal people have regarded it as too powerful a medicine, fearing that the Bear would even hunt them and kill them if it were feeling threatened or starving. Despite its ferocity and the fear it can invoke, the Bear is considered to be a highly desired ally and spiritual keeper because of its fearless and instinctively protective powers. In many ways it is the epitome of the Great Protector, the protective mother. The Bear holds the teachings and wisdom of introspection. Unlike other animals who are active during a specific time of day or night, the Bear is active both day and night, symbolising its connection with Solar energy, that of strength and power and Lunar energy, that of intuition and the inner life. It enhances and teaches those born under this totem to develop both within themselves. To the ancients, Bear symbolised resurrection; to the Japanese she is a symbol of loyalty, wisdom and strength. In the psyche, the Bear can be understood as the ability to regulate one's life, especially one's feeling life. Bear possesses a deep, intuitive connection to moving in cycles, discerning when to be still and rest, or to be fully alert. Bear medicine teaches that we can be fierce, generous and loving at the same time.

SAGITTARIUS CLAN ✦ THUNDERBIRD (OR HAWK)

Your clan animal comes from a place of inner knowing and intuition, helping you to discover the essence and magic of your true self.

The Thunderbird, sometimes referred to as Hawk, is a Totem of the Fire clan, and its medicine is messenger. Thunderbird holds the Fire clan and brings thunder, lightning and rain. The greatest of all the winged creatures, the Thunderbird is closest to the Creator. His Fire and spark carry the gift of life and link the soul to the Great Mystery. His true desire is not to know what lies below, his true yearning to join with Grandfather Sky. Fly high and keep your eyes focused ever upward.

SAGITTARIUS CORRESPONDING
CHINESE ASTROLOGY ANIMAL ✦ RAT

Each oriental animal corresponds with a Western astrology sign. For Sagittarius, it is the Rat.

Fixed Element Water

✦ *Keywords* ✦

Charming, short-tempered, sociable, influential, verbose, studious, enterprising, successful, imaginative, generous, clever, industrious, critical, courageous

The Rat is the first sign of the Chinese horoscope. According to legend, Buddha summoned all of the animals in the world to his side. Only twelve animals came and the Rat got there first, and so he became the first creature of the first year in the astrological cycle of twelve years. Traditionally a yang animal, the Rat is a typically likeable, hardworking, ambitious and thrifty sign. People born under this sign influence others easily with their witty charm and powers of persuasion. Rats generally work hard to achieve their goals and are usually good at saving money. They have attractive and powerful qualities, possessing both the desire and the ability to achieve success and eminence. The Rat is a mover and a pusher with leadership skills, and although devious and hungry for power over others, he knows how to use charm, clever tactics and guile to attain what he wants. He is willing to defend his loved ones at all costs.

CAPRICORN LUCKY ANIMALS & BIRDS

Dog, Elephant, Goat, Owl, Toad, Bear, Mole, Crocodile, Cloven-hoofed Animals, Bat, Serpent, Vulture, (Snow) Goose

CAPRICORN FEATURE ANIMAL ✦ GOOSE

The Goose's Message ✦ The destination at the top is more important than the climb.
Brings the totem gift of ✦ Excellence, perseverance, setting goals and achieving them.
Shares the power energies of ✦ Ambition, drive, competitiveness.
Brings forth and teaches the magic of ✦ Unique humour, sensuality, warmth.

CAPRICORN SPIRITUAL KEEPER ✦ BUFFALO

Your spiritual keeper guides your spiritual growth and brings illumination. Your spiritual keeper is determined by the season in which you were born. Regarded as the 'keepers' or 'caretakers' of the Universe, their presence is felt rather than seen.

The Direction to which your birth time belongs influences the nature of your inner senses. The North Direction's totem is the Buffalo. The Buffalo is a symbol of the mind and its sustenance - knowledge. The Buffalo (or Bison) is a revered symbol and a mighty albeit confronting animal, each beast weighing up to a tonne. It teaches us the gifts of provision, gratitude, abundance, prosperity, blessing, stability, consistency and strength. Its medicine includes manifestation, protection, Earth creativity, courage, knowledge, generosity, sharing and giving for the greater good. The Buffalo brings you the endurance and power to walk the Great Road of pure intent that leads to happiness, health and fulfilment, bringing the sustenance that offers renewal and rebirth after a long, arduous winter. The Buffalo is a reminder of the greater whole and its symbolism illustrates, in magical ways, the interconnectedness of everything in the world - and the wider Universe. Your animal keeper the Buffalo is, above all, a potent symbol of oneness, wisdom and abundance.

CAPRICORN CLAN ✦ TURTLE

Your clan animal comes from a place of inner knowing and intuition, helping you to discover the essence and magic of your true self.

The Turtle is the totem of the Earth clan and in mythology, during a time when there was only water and nowhere for the people and animals to go, the Turtle made a great sacrifice by letting everyone come and live on her back. In the Far East, a talisman carved in the form of a Turtle is believed to have power over all kinds of magic; the Chinese and Japanese also wear charms in the shape of Turtles to ensure a long life. In ancient times, the shape of a Turtle's shell suggested the dome of the sky and the creature became a symbol of heavenly virtue. The medicine of the Turtle is Mother Earth.

CAPRICORN CORRESPONDING CHINESE ASTROLOGY ANIMAL ✦ OX

Each oriental animal corresponds with a Western astrology sign. For Capricorn, it is the Ox.

Fixed Element Earth

✦ Keywords ✦

Calm, relaxed, patient, self-assured, sincere, brave, intelligent, sociable, resolute, stable, purposeful, stubborn, diligent

The Ox is the second sign of the Chinese horoscope. For centuries, this dutiful creature has pulled the plough, making it one of humanity's most helpful and useful animals, and indeed people have respected oxen since ancient times. The Ancient Greeks considered oxen sacred and in Ancient Greece, white oxen were sacrificed to their god Zeus and black oxen were sacrificed to Hades, god of the underworld. Solid and dependable, favouring routine and method, the Ox is very stubborn and through sheer perseverance is able to succeed where others might give up or fail. Traditionally a yin animal, oxen are bright, inspiring, self-sacrificing and original. A symbol of strength, calm, patience and kindness, of all the Chinese animals, the Ox is the best at parenting, as it is the most nurturing of the Chinese zodiac animals. The Ox type is very eloquent and happy to be in the public eye, and while she doesn't talk a lot, she is able to hold her audience riveted when she does. Romance for her is not an overt affair and she is essentially down-to-earth and cautious, with a mostly hidden but deep ardour and ability to contain her emotions. If her loved ones are patient, she rewards them with great loyalty and many indulgences.

AQUARIUS LUCKY ANIMALS & BIRDS

Dog, Vulture, Cuckoo, Peacock, Albatross, Phoenix, Owl, Eel, Crow, Large Birds Which Fly Afar, Otter

AQUARIUS FEATURE ANIMAL ✦ OTTER

The Otter's Message ✦ The application of spiritual knowledge, play, fun and wisdom to daily Earthly life. If you go with the natural ebbs and flows of life, you will discover joy, wonder and simple pleasures.

Brings the totem gift of ✦ Perception, inventiveness, playfulness, original thinking.

Shares the power energies of ✦ Tolerance, courage, originality, invention, exuberance.

Brings forth and teaches the magic of ✦ Creativity, the attaining of wisdom, knowledge acquisition, and the value of play, imagination, spontaneity and joy.

AQUARIUS SPIRITUAL KEEPER ✦ BUFFALO

Your spiritual keeper guides your spiritual growth and brings illumination. Your spiritual keeper is determined by the season in which you were born. Regarded as the 'keepers' or 'caretakers' of the Universe, their presence is felt rather than seen.

The Direction to which your birth time belongs influences the nature of your inner senses. The North Direction's totem is the Buffalo. The Buffalo is a symbol of the mind and its sustenance - knowledge. The Buffalo (or Bison) is a revered symbol and a mighty albeit confronting animal, each beast weighing up to a tonne. It teaches us the gifts of provision, gratitude, abundance, prosperity, blessing, stability, consistency and strength. Its medicine includes manifestation, protection, Earth creativity, courage, knowledge, generosity, sharing and giving for the greater good. The Buffalo brings you the endurance and power to walk the Great Road of pure intent that leads to happiness, health and fulfilment, bringing the sustenance that offers renewal and rebirth after a long, arduous winter. The Buffalo is a reminder of the greater whole and its symbolism illustrates, in magical ways, the interconnectedness of everything in the world - and the wider Universe. Your animal keeper the Buffalo is, above all, a potent symbol of oneness, wisdom and abundance.

AQUARIUS CLAN ✦ BUTTERFLY

Your clan animal comes from a place of inner knowing and intuition, helping you to discover the essence and magic of your true self.

The Butterfly, a totem of the Air clan, represents and protects all that is beautiful and holds the secrets of change and personal transformation. The Butterfly symbolises that this transformation is always available to you, and may even begin without your conscious participation. Butterfly is the power of Air, the ability to float along on a breeze, and to 'dance' from place to place. They awaken our sense of lightness and joy, and teach us to dance with life rather than take it too seriously. In the folklore of some tribes, butterflies stand for change and balance, while in others ephemeral beauty, and many tribes consider butterflies to be symbols of good luck. Butterflies symbolise metamorphosis, teaching us to trust in the process of change, re-awaken us to joy, and teach us that life is full of surprises and to therefore live with a constant sense of passion, intensity and wonder.

AQUARIUS CORRESPONDING CHINESE ASTROLOGY ANIMAL ✦ TIGER

Each oriental animal corresponds with a Western astrology sign. For Aquarius, it is the Tiger.

Fixed Element Wood

✦ Keywords ✦

Sensitive, short-tempered, brave, impetuous, lucky, playful, tireless, magnetic, hesitant, authoritative, indecisive, makes poor decisions, courageous, hasty, disobedient, proud

The Tiger is the third animal of the Chinese horoscope. As the name of this magnificent creature implies, there is a lot of speed, power and movement present in the Tiger type's nature. In fact, Tiger types are quite hasty and passionate, sometimes even hot-headed, and unpredictable. Traditionally a yang animal, Tigers are generous, courageous, dynamic, liberal and active. Possessing magnetic personalities, the Tiger is a masculine sign and those born during its years tend to be generous and brave. People tend to follow his lead and he has the power to influence, because his commanding personality and expansive innovative style inspire confidence. The Tiger dislikes feeling confined or bored, and can be rash, brash, proud and authoritative. He is usually competitive and likes to win; somehow luck seems to be his friend. Certainly, he is often found in positions of power, unless his desire for mobility and novelty compels him in other directions.

PISCES LUCKY ANIMALS & BIRDS

Sheep, Ox, Seahorse, Horse, Fish, Swan, Cougar, Stork, Eagle, Dolphin and All Sea Mammals, Wolf

PISCES FEATURE ANIMAL ✦ WOLF

The Wolf's Message ✦ The idea that freedom, compassion and passion can reside harmoniously together. Birth totem Wolf individuals arrive on this plane of existence to learn the gifts of the seer. Their life path is one of love and the application of spiritual knowledge.

Brings the totem gift of ✦ Compassion, Benevolence, Generosity, Sensitivity, Identity, the 'Way of the Seer'.

Shares the power energies of ✦ Liberation, Intuition, Trust, Deep Emotions, Loyalty, Balanced Duality.

Brings forth and teaches the magic of ✦ Illumination, Psychic Ability, Mysticism, Creativity, Freedom, Cooperation, Leadership, Freedom.

PISCES SPIRITUAL KEEPER ✦ BUFFALO

Your spiritual keeper guides your spiritual growth and brings illumination. Your spiritual keeper is determined by the season in which you were born. Regarded as the 'keepers' or 'caretakers' of the Universe, their presence is felt rather than seen.

The Direction to which your birth time belongs influences the nature of your inner senses. The North Direction's totem is the Buffalo. The Buffalo is a symbol of the mind and its sustenance - knowledge. The Buffalo (or Bison) is a revered symbol and a mighty albeit confronting animal, each beast weighing up to a tonne. It teaches us the gifts of provision, gratitude, abundance, prosperity, blessing, stability, consistency and strength. Its medicine includes manifestation, protection, Earth creativity, courage, knowledge, generosity, sharing and giving for the greater good. The Buffalo brings you the endurance and power to walk the Great Road of pure intent that leads to happiness, health and fulfilment, bringing the sustenance that offers renewal and rebirth after a long, arduous winter. The Buffalo is a reminder of the greater whole and its symbolism illustrates, in magical ways, the interconnectedness of everything in the world - and the wider Universe. Your animal keeper the Buffalo is, above all, a potent symbol of oneness, wisdom and abundance.

PISCES CLAN ✦ FROG

Your clan animal comes from a place of inner knowing and intuition, helping you to discover the essence and magic of your true self.

The Frog, a Totem of the Water clan, represents the song that calls the rain to Earth, and cleansing, teaching us the opportune times to purify, refresh and replenish our reserves. A charm or amulet in the shape of a frog is said to attract true friends and to help you find long-lasting love. To the Ancient Egyptians, Romans and Greeks, frogs symbolised inspiration, fertility, good luck and speedy recovery from illness, beliefs that carry over into some cultures today. People of the Frog clan have deep, easily flowing feelings, which enable them to have empathy for others and to heal. They have natural gifts for healing, sensitivity, creativity, and a deep appreciation for rain and being around water. As the Moon is so strongly associated with emotional and watery realms, Frog clan people can connect with this deep Lunar magic by studying the cycles, patterns and energies of the Moon, the ruling celestial sphere of their clan animal, the Frog.

PISCES CORRESPONDING CHINESE ASTROLOGY ANIMAL ✦ RABBIT

Each oriental animal corresponds with a Western astrology sign. For Pisces, it is the Rabbit.

Fixed Element Wood

✦ Keywords ✦

Pleasant, talented, articulate, discerning, psychic, refined, conservative, ambitious, sensitive, successful, peaceful

The Rabbit is the fourth animal of the Chinese horoscope. Traditionally a yin animal, the Rabbit is sometimes symbolised as a cat, and is one of the most fortunate of the twelve signs. The Rabbit, or Hare as she is referred to in Chinese mythology, is the emblem of longevity and is said to be endowed with his essence by the Moon. She possesses an air of refinement, and loves peace, quiet and homely comforts. Rabbit types are mysterious, talented, sensitive and artistic, and may sometimes appear to be secretive or even unfriendly because she is generally shy of strangers. Once at ease, she is friendly and helpful, willing to offer wise advice and capable assistance. The Rabbit is extremely lucky in business and monetary transactions and for all her quiet and docile nature, she possesses a strong will and a formidable self-assurance. Arguably the luckiest of all the signs, she is also believed to be the most likely to live a long and prosperous life.

POWER METALS

Although the magic power of crystals is widely recognised and applied, the influence radiating from metals is often overlooked. Metal, too, emits a powerful energy and in fact, in Chinese philosophy, metal is considered so essential and powerful that it is classified as one of the elements, alongside Wood, Fire, Earth and Water.

Throughout the writings of early philosophers and theorists, there are countless references to the unmistakable mystic connection between the seven known planets of the time, and Earthly affairs, ailments and objects. Seven metals were connected with the seven planets, to which seven colours and the seven 'transformations' were added. So, the ancient alchemist came to share the astrological doctrine that each planet ruled a mineral: the Sun ruled gold, the Moon silver, Mars iron, Venus copper, Saturn lead, Jupiter tin, and Mercury quicksilver. Consequently, in alchemical symbolism the same sign came to represent the nominated metal and its corresponding planet.

ARIES ✦ IRON & STEEL

His metal is iron, and its unbendable strength gives him nine times as many lives to live as others; nine times as many chances of winning the battle.
Linda Goodman

IRON

Iron is a chemical element with symbol Fe (from Latin *ferrum*). By mass it is the most common element on Earth, forming much of our planet's inner and outer core. The symbol for Mars, Aries's ruler, has been used since antiquity to represent the element iron.

Iron is the metal most associated with magic. Although not glistening or beautiful like silver or gold, at times in history iron's value was considered superior. Because iron is not found in its pure state except as a meteorite, it was known as the 'Metal of Heaven'. Iron's celestial origins were recognised early in human history and meteorites were perceived as supreme conduits to the spiritual realm.

Iron is known for its protective and healing capacities; iron boxes serve to safeguard their contents, keeping their powers intact, and an iron bed is thought to be psychically protective, enhance one's dreaming processes and even promoting physical healing. These protective qualities are well-known and iron amulets are said to also guard and protect children and newborns. As well, because iron is connected with virility and fertility, an iron bed and iron jewellery are considered auspicious for romance and conception. Adopted as a symbol of fertility in folklore, wearing a bracelet made of iron is said to help with conceiving a child.

The metal iron has been used since ancient times, and is relatively soft but significantly hardened and strengthened by impurities, particularly carbon (a certain proportion of present carbon will produce steel, which can be up to a thousand times harder than pure iron).

The first production of iron began in the Middle Bronze Age, but it was several centuries before iron displaced bronze. Iron of meteoric origin was highly regarded due to its origins in the heavens, and was often used to forge weapons and tools, having a distinct advantage over bronze in warfare instruments, as it is much harder and more durable than bronze (albeit more susceptible to rust).

In more modern times, steels and iron alloys are the most common metals used in industry, due to their vast range of desirable properties and Earth's widespread abundance of iron-bearing rock. It is the most widely used of all the metals, accounting for over 90 per cent of worldwide metal production. Its low cost and high strength make it invaluable in many engineering applications, such as the construction of machinery, mechanical tools, the hulls of large ships, automobiles, and the structural components of buildings. And since it is in its pure state quite soft, it is the most commonly combined with alloying metals to create steel. This industrial iron production begins with iron ores, principally hematite and magnetite, two of Aries's 'lucky stones'.

Iron also plays a vital role in biology - iron proteins are found in all living organisms - forming complexes with molecular oxygen in haemoglobin and myoglobin, and in the functioning of various enzymes, cellular respiration, and other biochemical processes in both animals and plants.

The word iron, when used metaphorically, refers to certain traits of the metal. Used as an adjective and sometimes as a noun, it can refer to something that is sturdy, unyielding, stern, unbreakable, harsh, strong, formidable and robust. The 'Iron Lady' Margaret Thatcher was so-named because of her 'iron-fisted' style of rulership.

Iron is primarily used for healing when one feels under attack, and is believed to increase physical strength, though steel is sometimes used as an alternative.

Overall, iron has a number of good and not-so-good associations. The earliest specimens of iron were found in meteorites and it was highly prized among the Aztecs who regarded it as a metal sent from the gods. However, at the beginning of the Iron Age, smelted iron had evil connotations, and it was considered inferior to the other metals such as gold, copper and bronze. Although it is a metal usually linked with brute strength and masculinity, in some countries, people would touch iron to bring them good luck. It certainly couldn't hurt to try.

TAURUS ✦ COPPER, BRASS & BRONZE

COPPER

Copper is a chemical element with symbol Cu (from Latin *cuprum*, meaning 'from Cyprus'), and carries a special cultural significance in that it was the first metal to be used by humans, its use believed to be as early as 7000 BC. Indeed, there is evidence it has been in use for at least 10,000 years.

In alchemy, the symbol for copper was also the symbol for the goddess and planet Venus. Aphrodite (Venus's Greek counterpart) and Venus represented copper in alchemy and mythology because of copper's lustrous beauty, its ancient use in producing mirrors, and its association with Cyprus, a place which had sacred links with the goddess.

Copper is a purely positive metal and when worn it is said to attract love (combining copper with emeralds makes a highly successful - and attractive - love amulet). Considered to hold sacred properties by various cultures in North America and India, copper is believed to stimulate healing and romance. Its healing reputation is well-known and widespread in the form of copper jewellery, worn to relieve certain physical ailments, and copper jewellery is also metaphysically used as a talisman to magnetise and maintain health, luck and prosperity.

Copper is prized by craftsmen for its elegance and lustre, and its ease of use in crafting things of great aesthetic appeal. Pure copper is reddish orange/gold in colour and is soft and malleable, and like aluminium, it is 100 per cent recyclable without any loss of quality. As one of only two coloured metals, its attractiveness makes it highly desirable for design.

Copper's main modern-day applications are its use in electrical wires and implements (having very high thermal and electrical conductivity, and being ductile enough to be drawn into wire or beaten into sheets without fracturing), roofing and plumbing, industrial machinery, scientific instruments, and of course coins. The high resonance of copper makes it suitable for use in stringed musical instruments, such as violins, guitars and the double bass (traditional astrological thought associates the art of music with Venus).

Copper is usually used as a pure metal, but when a greater hardness is required, it can be combined with other elements to make an alloy, such as brass or bronze. Copper's resistance to corrosion also makes it suitable for use in, or near the ocean. Brass, an alloy of zinc and copper, is used extensively in marine applications due to its non-corrosive nature.

Copper is even found in the human body in trace amounts and has various biological functions, mainly in the liver, muscle and bone. Because it is an excellent transmitter of electricity, these properties can be used on the physical body to balance electrical flow, charge and energy within the body.

Made into jewellery, it is believed that wearing a copper bracelet can relieve arthritis-related symptoms[***]. It is also used in alternative medicine to treat various other ailments, as its absorption through the skin somehow creates a magnetic field, thereby affecting or treating nearby tissues^. Copper leaves are also a good luck charm, when they are wrapped in cloth and placed in a small green bag - the colour of Venus - one for health or money, two for love, three for fertility.

Overall, copper serves many purposes and is arguably essential in keeping the world functioning, as it pervades in all facets of (comfortable) existence: it is found in your house, coin currency, transport systems, computers, cars and cruise ships - all pretty essential things for the true Venusian experience.

*However, in various studies, no difference has been found between arthritis treated with a copper bracelet, magnetic bracelet, or placebo bracelet.

^Always check with a medical professional before applying any remedy, treatment or concept outlined here.

BRONZE

The Bronze Age began around 5600 BC after someone accidentally discovered that copper and tin combined allows a new stronger material to emerge; this new material made sharper tools and weapons than pure copper did on its own, which was a huge leap forward in humankind's development.

Spiritually, bronze can be laid upon the body to provide a high frequency metal that will strengthen your aura while clearing it of blockages that may be tough to get through with other elements and stones. It acts as a spiritual protector, and will guard the entire energy field from psychic attack and drains.

GEMINI ✦ QUICKSILVER, CHROME & ZINC

QUICKSILVER

Quicksilver, also known as mercury, is a chemical element with symbol Hg, is heavy, and as its name suggests, is silvery in colour. A mysterious, much-maligned and paradoxical metal, although its surface reflects light like shiny polished steel, the fluidity of this substance does not allow it to maintain any shape.

Mercury is nearly 14 times as heavy as water, its density meaning that heavier things can easily float on top of it. But like water, it evaporates, albeit much more slowly, and in the air it is much more noxious and dangerous than in its liquid state.

Mercury is an extremely rare element in the Earth's crust, and many former mines which produced a large proportion of the world supply, have now been completely mined out. Today China is the top producer of mercury, but because of the high toxicity of this element, the mining of cinnabar (the mineral from which it is mostly extracted) and the refining of it for mercury, are hazardous and can produce serious health effects through mercury poisoning.

Quicksilver is the only metallic element that is liquid at standard conditions for temperature and pressure. It is perhaps best - and menacingly - known as a toxin - and indeed, mercury toxicity can result from water-soluble forms of quicksilver, inhalation of its vapour, or eating seafood contaminated with it. Some countries have banned the use of mercury in all products and production methods, while many others agreed in the Minamata Convention on Mercury, to prevent emissions.

Because it is liquid like water and shiny like silver, mercury's name was derived from the word hydrargyrum (where the chemical symbol Hg comes from), a Latinised form of the Greek word hydra-gyros, meaning 'water-silver'. The element itself was named after the Roman god Mercury, known for his speed, agility and mobility.

Found in Ancient Egyptian tombs that date from 1500 BC, in China and Tibet mercury use was thought to prolong life, heal fractures, and generally promote overall wellbeing and health (although it is now known that exposure to mercury vapour can lead to serious adverse health effects.)

Its use in alchemy was widespread. Alchemists thought of Mercury as the First Matter from which all metals were formed, believing that different metals could be produced by varying the quality and quantity of sulphur contained within the mercury, the purest of these being gold. Mercury was therefore summoned in attempts to transmute the base (impure) metals into gold, which was the ultimate goal of many alchemists. This quest left a lasting legacy: the Sanskrit word for alchemy is Rasavatam, which means 'the way of mercury'; and mercury is the only metal for which the alchemical planetary name became the common name.

Used in thermometers and other measuring equipment, float valves, vermilion paint pigment, fluorescent lamps, mercury switches and other devices, mercury is also used in industrial chemicals, for electrical and electronic applications, historically as an ingredient in dental amalgams, in some batteries, as a preservative in vaccines, and as a compound in some over-the-counter drugs, as well as some niche uses including skin tanner vapour lamps, 'neon lights' and some cosmetic mascaras.

Natural sources, such as volcanoes, account for approximately half of all atmospheric mercury emissions, but the human-generated half can be divided into estimated percentages, the highest of these emissions said to come from coal-fired power plants (~65 per cent) and gold production (~11 per cent) respectively.

Despite its well-known dangers and sinister reputation as a toxic heavy metal, an increasing amount of quicksilver is being used as gaseous mercury in fluorescent lamps, and it is still used in some thermometers, especially those used to measure high temperatures. However, most of its other uses and applications are being gradually phased out due to health and safety regulations and concerns, and are being replaced with less toxic but considerably more expensive alternatives.

Mercury and most of its compounds are extremely toxic and must be handled with care, if at all. Mercury can be absorbed through the skin and mucous membranes and mercury vapours can be inhaled. The most toxic forms of mercury are its organic compounds, which can cause both acute and chronic poisoning. Pregnant women should avoid this metallic element at all costs, particularly by avoiding eating large species of fish and all varieties of shellfish, as ingested mercury is considered an accumulative neurotoxin that can adversely affect the unborn foetus in numerous ways.

ZINC

Zinc is a metal that is used in a wide range of applications. In industry, it is used in fluorescent lights, paints, plastics, alloys, rubber materials, and to galvanise steel, a process of coating a material to protect it from corrosion.

Present in sunscreen as zinc oxide, this metal helps to reflect the Sun's UV rays away from the skin, protecting the skin from damage. Zinc is also present in other everyday items like batteries and vitamin/mineral supplements.

Zinc is an important mineral essential to human health, playing crucial roles in cellular growth and development, immunity, reproductive health, wound-healing, and as a cofactor in numerous enzyme systems and functions throughout the body.

CANCER ✦ SILVER & ALUMINIUM

SILVER

The chemical symbol for silver is Ag, which comes from its Latin name *argentum*, meaning 'white' or 'shining'. It is a soft, lustrous, white transition metal, possessing the highest reflectivity, and electrical and thermal conductivity of any metal.

More abundant than gold, silver has long been regarded as a precious metal, which has numerous applications beyond its use in coin currency. Silver is very ductile, durable and malleable, and apart from being suitable as a univalent coinage metal, it can be found in jewellery, ornaments, tableware, solar panels, mirrors, stained glass, batteries, medicines, water filtration systems (it prevents algae and bacteria from building up in filters), and also in investments in the form of coins and bullions. Silver compounds are also used in disinfectants, catheters, and other medical instruments.

Natural silver will never rust, however since the industrial revolution there has been sufficient sulphur in the air to tarnish it.

Silver, like copper, is considered a purely positive metal, clean and incorruptible. No ill effects can come from wearing it, nor is any quantity considered unhealthy. Among the most popular materials for amulets, it is believed to provide a spiritually protective influence on one's aura and immediate environment. Associated with the goddesses Artemis and Diana, it is thought that wearing silver jewellery aids fertility and if you wish to start a family, charms are the most potent if carved from this metal.

Silver in its pure native form (elemental silver) is actually very rare, as it usually occurs mixed in ores with other metals. Most silver is produced as a by-product of gold, copper, zinc and lead refining.

Silver has been used for thousands of years for ornaments, adornments, utensils, trade and currency, and its value as a precious metal was long considered only second to gold. Regarded as one of the 'noble metals' along with its counterpart gold, its desirable properties led to it being ascribed a variety of mystical and even supernatural powers.

Most of us associate silver with jewellery, however only a small amount of mined silver is made into coins, jewellery and utensils. Before the advent of digital technology, the most common use of this metal was in photographic film*. When a photo is taken, silver crystals are produced from the film emulsion. These crystals react to the light and capture the image.

The crescent Moon has also been used as the alchemical symbol to represent silver since ancient times, and the visual appeal of this metal is reminiscent of the silvery Lunar light it emits.

The use of silver in photography has rapidly declined since the advent of digital technology.

ALUMINIUM

Aluminium is a pure white metal with high reflectivity which means that most of the light that shines on it is returned to the viewer, a result of the light colour.

In its natural state, it is one of the hardest metals and one of the most abundant of all the elements in the Earth's crust. The crystalline state of aluminium is called corundum, known in the mineral kingdom as rubies and sapphires, and it is found in many other minerals including turquoise, lapis lazuli and sodalite. In healing, because it is an excellent conductor for electricity, aluminium can be used externally to assist severe circulatory issues by wrapping aluminium foil around the legs and feet, and arms if applicable. The conductivity of the foil assists with the electrical flow of the body.

Edgar Cayce, famous healer and mystic, believed aluminium-based gems allow the soul to move into higher spiritual realms and remember talents and spiritual abilities from past lives. Moreover, it allows one to access ascended planes of consciousness by dissolving the sound barrier between one's world and the spirit world so it is easier to hear spirit guides.

Long-term exposure to high levels of this metal may produce neurotoxicity, so caution is always advised with any applications.

LEO ✦ GOLD, PLATINUM, COPPER & BRONZE

GOLD

Gold stands for truth, consciousness and eternity... the Cosmic impulse descends from the highest, Divine level to the material earthly world, taking on form and substance as it does so. In alchemical terms, this means that the eternal essence of gold came into creation and took on denser and darker forms as it became manifest, until only the seed of gold remained buried in the primal material.

C. Gilchrist

Alchemy is defined as an art of transmutation and precipitation - the changing of base metals into gold. The work of alchemical transmutation is designated as 'the Labour of the Sun'. This 'Eye of Ra' symbolically represents the perfection with which nature is gradually unfolding in her creations. At the physical level, the Sun of Perfection is represented by gold. Alchemy is the science and art which hasten the creations of Nature to attain perfection at their own respective level. Gold is the perfection attained by metals and minerals.

Leonard Lee

Gold is a chemical element with symbol Au (from Latin aurum, meaning 'gold', but has its roots in Proto-Germanic meaning 'shine'), and in its purest form it is a malleable, ductile, soft, dense, bright, slightly reddish-yellow metal. Pure gold is yellow in colour but is often alloyed with other minerals, such as silver or copper, to make it harder. Called a master healer because it is said to help almost every condition and will amplify the strength of other metals, crystals or substances used, metaphysically and magically gold is used for overall success, abundance and positivity. It has been a valuable and highly sought after precious metal used for coinage, jewellery and other arts since long before the beginning of recorded history.

Gold has been considered the most precious metal from the most ancient of times, and has been associated in many lands and ages with the deities. Long before the appearance of alchemy, it was considered the most perfect metal and acquired symbolic meanings connecting it with light, perfection, nobility and wisdom.

Gold is most commonly associated with jewellery and currency but symbolically its most powerful association is with the Sun. It also has a connection with hermetic alchemy. It stands for purity, sagacity, power and glory, spiritual enlightenment, honour and of course, wealth.

Gold is associated with deities either physically or as a representation. The Incas sprayed their rulers with gold dust, literally turning them into a 'gold man', and the ancient Egyptians believed that the flesh of their Sun god Ra was made of gold. Other cultures believed, and many still believe, that gold was the earthly manifestation of their gods or of the Sun itself.

Gold reflects the Sun's 'colour' and brilliance. It is thought to be incorruptible and incapable of corrosion. With long-held beliefs around and links to wealth, medieval alchemists sought the 'philosophic gold', not necessarily to attain literal riches, but for its gift of immortality and eternal life.

Precious metals often occur in their pure, natural state, turning up in veins - mineral deposits that fill the cracks in Earth's crust. They can also be found mixed with sand and gravel on riverbeds. These deposits form when erosion separates the metal from rock and water washes it into a river, where it sinks to the bottom - as often happens with gold.

Although widely used in jewellery, gold has properties that make it valuable in other industries too. For example, gold does not rust, so it is often used to make vital pieces of electronic equipment. It is also very shiny and radiant, so when used as a coating on the outside of satellites and other space instruments, gold reflects cosmic radiation that would otherwise damage the equipment.

The global consumption of new gold produced is about 50 per cent in jewellery, 40 per cent in investments, and 10 per cent in industry.

Great human achievements are frequently rewarded with gold medals, golden trophies, and other such symbols. Similarly, gold is associated with perfect or Divine principles, such as the 'golden rule' and the 'golden egg'. Our most valued older years are often considered our 'golden years', and the height of a civilisation is referred to as its 'golden age'. Overall, it is a cultural symbol of abundance, enlightenment and success.

It's not all bright news, however. Gold production is associated with contributing to hazardous pollution, and cyanide spills and mercury compounds reaching waterways, causing heavy metal contamination, are considered detrimental both to the environment and to the health of living organisms. When the used ore is dumped as waste, these dumps create long-term, highly hazardous wastes second only to nuclear waste dumps. Furthermore, gold extraction is also a highly energy-intensive industry, using an enormous amount of electricity in the extraction and grinding processes.

Pure metallic (elemental) gold is non-toxic and non-irritating when ingested, and is sometimes used as a food decoration in the form of gold leaf. Metallic gold is a component of some alcoholic drinks, and is approved as a food additive in the EU. Who's up for a glass of Gold Strike?

Note ✦ As gold is expensive, bronze or brass are often used as substitutes. Brass is primarily used when the main purpose of a charm is for protection or to attract money. Pyrite, or fool's gold, is often used for prosperity charms. Gold combines well with amber for a success amulet. Gold charms are used for promoting wisdom, increasing courage and confidence, and success in general.

PLATINUM

The word 'platinum' originates from the Spanish *plata*, meaning 'silver', referring to the colour of the metal. Platinum was discovered in the early 1700s. It is so rare that two million pounds of ore may only contain about one pound of platinum metal. Its rarity makes it even more valuable than gold. Platinum nuggets are rarely larger than a pea - anything larger would qualify as a major find.

The highest quality platinum comes from the Ural Mountains in Russia.

It can be used for jewellery, but has less glamorous uses too: it is placed in anti-pollution devices in cars to trap dirt and toxic gases.

Metaphysically, platinum creates a vibrational state of transformation. It makes you feel grounded and cosmically connected at the same time. It imparts the desirable sense that nothing can stop you from living your dreams.

COPPER & BRONZE ✦ See under 'Taurus'.

VIRGO ✦ COPPER, QUICKSILVER (MERCURY) & PLATINUM

COPPER ✦ See under 'Taurus'.

QUICKSILVER ✦ See under 'Gemini'.

PLATINUM ✦ See under 'Leo'.

LIBRA ✦ COPPER & BRONZE

COPPER & BRONZE ✦ See under 'Taurus'.

SCORPIO ✦ IRON, STEEL & PLUTONIUM

IRON ✦ See under 'Aries'.

PLUTONIUM

Plutonium is a transuranic radioactive chemical element with the symbol Pu and is named after Scorpio's ruling planet Pluto, following from the two previous elements uranium and neptunium (also named after planets).

Like most metals, plutonium has a bright silvery appearance at first, but when exposed to air it tarnishes and oxidises very quickly to a dull grey. When exposed to moist air, plutonium forms oxides and hydrides that expand up to 70 per cent in volume, which in turn can flake off as a powder that can spontaneously ignite. These properties, combined with it being radioactive and accumulative in human tissue such as bones, make the handling of plutonium dangerous.

More hazardous when inhaled than ingested, it has been linked to cancer, radiation sickness, genetic damage, and death.

Mostly a by-product of nuclear reactions, plutonium was produced in useful quantities for the first time as a major part of the Manhattan Project during World War II, which developed the first atomic bombs. The Fat Man bombs used in the bombing of Nagasaki in 1945, had plutonium cores.

As well as being used in the first few atomic bombs, plutonium is still used in nuclear weapons, and is also a key material in the development of nuclear power, and as a source of energy on space missions.

There are two aspects to the harmful effects of plutonium: its radioactivity and its heavy metal toxic effects. Metallic plutonium can become pyrophoric under the right conditions, meaning that it poses an extreme fire and explosive hazard.

Overall, plutonium is a dangerous element, with the power to destruct and perhaps even worse, to self-combust.

SAGITTARIUS ✦ TIN, ANTIMONY & BRASS

TIN

Tin is planet Earth's 49th most abundant element. It is allied with the planet Jupiter because it is one of the so-called 'temperate metals', easy to forge and work with, which is a Jupiterian quality.

A white-silvery, malleable, highly crystalline and ductile 'other metal' that is not easily oxidised in air, tin is a chemical element whose symbol is Sn. It is a main group metal in group 14 of the periodic table, sharing chemical similarity to both neighbouring group 14 elements (lead and germanium).

Tin can be worn as a pendant, engraved with symbols, and is usually used for money-attracting charms and for luck in general.

The first alloy, used in large scale since 3000 BC, was bronze, an alloy of tin and copper. Pewter is another alloy, of 85 to 90 per cent tin with the remainder consisting of antimony, copper and lead. In modern times, tin is used in many alloys, one significant application being the corrosion-resistant tin-plating of steel. Due to its low toxicity, tin-plated metal is commonly used for food and beverage packaging as tin cans, which are made mostly from steel. Some alloys which contain tin to greater or lesser degrees, and which can be used as a substitute for pure tin to make magic talismans, are bronze, pewter and brittanium.

CAPRICORN ✦ LEAD, PEWTER & PLUTONIUM

LEAD

Lead is a chemical element in the carbon group with the symbol Pb (from the Latin *plumbum*), and is a malleable, soft, corrosion-resistant, ductile and heavy metal which tarnishes to a dull greyish colour when exposed to air. When melted into a liquid, it has a shiny chrome lustre, and has been commonly used for thousands of years because it is widespread, simple to extract and easy to work with. Worldwide production and consumption of lead is increasing, with Australia, China and the United States accounting for more than half of primary production. However, with current usage rates, the supply of lead is estimated to run out in around thirty years at the time of writing.

Contrary to popular belief, pencil leads in wooden pencils have never been made from lead, but rather a type of graphite called plumbago.

Lead has many applications, including in the construction industry, batteries, pigments, the ballast keel of sailboats, cable sheathing, radiation protection, scuba diving weight belts, automobile parts and car batteries, electronic soldering, stained glass windows, organ pipes, gun bullets, ceramic glazes and plumbing.

Lead, however useful for many things, has its downside. If inhaled or swallowed, it is a highly poisonous metal, affecting almost every organ, tissue and system in the human body. The main target for lead toxicity is the nervous system, but it can also cause weakness in limbs and extremities, as well as blood pressure rises. In pregnant women, high levels of exposure can cause miscarriage. Chronic, high-level exposure can also cause adverse brain and blood conditions, and has been linked to learning and other developmental disorders.

Lead is easy to work with, but it is toxic and therefore should not come into contact with bare skin. One way of using lead is to use parchment as a base and draw a circle around the symbols with a lead pin. Pewter can be and is often used as an alternative, because perhaps this power metal is best left to its more practical outer-world applications, well away from the body.

PLUTONIUM ✦ See under 'Scorpio'.

AQUARIUS ✦ URANIUM, ALUMINIUM, PLATINUM & LEAD

URANIUM

Aquarius's metal is uranium, a radioactive element that is used in research, as a fuel and perhaps as is best known, in nuclear weapons. Uranium owes its name to Uranus, the planet which was discovered a few years prior. The similarity between these two names serves as a reminder that scientific theory and thought can produce both brilliant and terrifying inventions.

Uranium is a very heavy metal containing an abundant source of concentrated energy. Discovered in the eighteenth century, it is the principal fuel for nuclear reactors and the main raw material for nuclear weapons. It is no coincidence that the element associated with atomic energy is uranium, for the enormous power of the atom is equal to the power of Uranus.

There are two ways to release this atomic power: through fission and through fusion. In fission, the heaviest atoms are split apart, and the resulting release of energy deposits radioactive waste, which is extremely difficult to deal with, and potentially lethal to all life on our planet. In fusion, however, the lightest atoms are fused together, and the resulting release of energy does not pose a risk by leaving radioactive waste. Therefore, it makes sense that we can use this latter process to benefit humankind without the sinister possibility of destroying that which we are trying to improve. Uranus usually has the best of intentions, especially when it comes to serving humanity, so utilising it for the benefit of all, rather than the potential destruction of all, is undoubtedly far more desirable.

ALUMINIUM ✦ See under 'Cancer'.

PLATINUM ✦ See under 'Leo'.

LEAD ✦ See under 'Capricorn'.

PISCES ✦ PLATINUM, TIN, LEAD, ANTIMONY, PEWTER, TITANIUM & NEPTUNIUM

PLATINUM ✦ See under 'Leo'.

TIN ✦ See under 'Sagittarius'.

LEAD ✦ See under 'Capricorn'.

NEPTUNIUM

Neptunium is a synthetic, silvery radioactive metal first 'discovered' and produced in 1940. In the periodic table, it follows uranium, which was named after the planet Uranus, and led to it being named after the planet neighbouring Uranus, Neptune.

POWER FOODS

Let food be your medicine; let medicine be your food.
Hippocrates

CAUTION ✦ Always use foods, essential oils, alcohol and/or herbs with caution and research each one prior to use, as not all are safe for use by certain people, or under certain conditions such as pregnancy, intoxication, or illness. Some herbs and oils may be hallucinogenic, toxic in high doses, or produce other undesirable effects, and may be considered potentially harmful or hazardous if used or consumed before operating machinery, driving, or combined with alcohol or other drugs. Always consult a qualified practitioner or undertake thorough research from reliable sources before use or consumption of any of the listed essential oils, herbs, or foods.

ARIES POWER FOODS

Hot, dry, pungent and spicy foods - Mustard, Chillies, Cayenne, Curry, Horseradish, Pepper, Capers - and anything strong-tasting are associated with Aries. Onions, Garlic, Leeks, Oregano, Watercress, Spinach, Hops, Red Foods, Meat, Red Fruit and Vegetables. Power beverages for the

Ram are Coffee, Moonshine (do your research first!), Soda Pops, Bloody Mary, Alco Pops, Beer and Red Wine.

TAURUS POWER FOODS

Taurean power foods are piquant, aromatic, sensual and dense. Soft Fruits, White Meats and Seafood served with fragrant marinades, Breads, Cereals, Wheat and Oat-based foods, Zucchinis, Green Capsicum, Sweet Corn, Cabbage, Artichokes, Grapes, Beans, Peas, Asparagus, Spinach, Apples, Carrots, Plantains, Beetroot, Cereals and Ginger are also appealing to the Taurean palate. Power beverages for the Bull are Rich Earthy Coffee, Expensive Wines, Rich Liqueurs, Whisky and Rum.

GEMINI POWER FOODS

Fragrant, herbaceous, green, gamey, subtle and bittersweet characterise Gemini-style foods. Bird meats such as Chicken, Goose, Duck and Turkey, Hare, Venison, Legume Vegetables, Vegetables grown above the ground, Nuts, Fennel, Asparagus, Okra, Figs, Sprouts, Mushrooms, Carrots, Non-Cereal Seeds, Mulberries and Pomegranates also appeal to the Gemini palate. Power beverages for the Twins are anything Caffeinated, Champagne, Energy Drinks, Sparkling Drinks and Alco Pops.

CANCER POWER FOODS

Succulent and fragrant foods appeal to the Cancerian palate, as do Seafoods (especially shellfish), Caviar, Seaweed and Kelp, Cheeses, Cream, Milk, Yoghurts, Figs, Chocolate, pale vegetables with a high water content (Cucumber, Cauliflower, Lettuce, Squashes, Celery, Cabbage), Papaya, Nuts and Citrus Fruits. Power beverages for the Crab are White Wine, Milk, Spring Water, Hot Chocolate and Miso Soup.

LEO POWER FOODS

Rich, spicy, hot, and dry, aromatic, sweet and sour foods suit the Lion's tastes. Yellow and orange-coloured citrus fruits (Oranges, Lemons, Grapefruit, Tangerines), Mangoes, Nectarines, Orange Vegetables (Sweet Potato, Pumpkin, Yams, Carrot), Heart, Sunflower Oil, Walnuts, Meat, Eggs, Parsley, Spinach, Kale, Watercress, Honey, Curries, Rice, Cabbage and Eggplant also appeal to the Leonine palate. Power beverages for the Lion are Cider, Lemon Squash, Tea, luxury Liqueurs, Cocktails, and fortified and expensive Wines.

VIRGO POWER FOODS

Healthy, nutritious and earthy foods are best suited to the discerning Maiden. Blackberries, Almonds, Wheat, Endive, Corn, Millet, Rice, Barley, Rye, Oats, Swedes, Plantain, Turnips, Strawberries, Fennel, subterranean vegetables (Kohlrabi, Carrots, Celeriac, Potatoes), Mushrooms, Peas, Okra, all kinds of beans, Nuts, Bird Meat, Gooseberries, Loganberries, Pomegranates, Cress, Beetroot, Figs, Mulberries, and all foods that grow under the rich, fertile soil also appeal to the Virgoan palate. Power beverages for the Maiden are sparkling drinks (Mineral Waters, Champagne, Wines), Health Drinks, Protein Shakes, Smoothies, 'Superfood' Powders, Wheatgrass Shots and organic Wine.

LIBRA POWER FOODS

Perfumed, sweet-smelling and delicately flavoured foods all appeal to the Libran palate. Venison, Veal, Beef, Goat, Chicken, Partridge, Pheasant, Lobster, Sardines and Salmon are all flesh foods ruled by Venus. Artichokes, Sorrel, Asparagus, Parsnips, Corn, Almonds, Honey, Milk, Strawberries, Watercress, Spices, Apples, Currants, Beans, Oranges, Peaches, Celery, Apricots, Figs, Cherries, Grapes, Mangoes, Dates, Gooseberries, Raspberries, Spinach, wheat products of all Kinds and confectionary are also power foods for the Scales. Power beverages are Sherry, Fancy Cocktails, Port and sweet Liqueurs.

SCORPIO POWER FOODS

Pungent, spicy, fermented, mould-based or curdled foods appeal to the Scorpio palate. Scorpio is associated with aquatic foods such as Frogs and Snails. Foods that dwell in the 'underworld' such as Truffles and aged, 'brewed' foods, from Blue Cheese to Fish Sauce, are also attractive to the Scorpion appetite, as are 'hot' Mars-ruled plants that grow in warm climates, such as Capsicums, Nettles, Onions, Garlic, Radish, Leeks, Eggplants, Goat, spiky-skinned fruits (Pineapple, Lychees, Tart Rhubarb), and all red foods in general. Cherries, Citrus Fruits,

Cabbage, Kale and Liver are also Scorpio foods. Power beverages for the Scorpion are cellared Wines, Black Tea, Stout Beer and Dark Ales, Ruby Red Grapefruit Juice, Dark Red Drinks, black Coffee, Berry Juices and fortified Wines.

SAGITTARIUS POWER FOODS

Richly fragrant, sweet and scented foods, all ethnic cuisines, all gamey Jupiter meats (Venison, Pigeons, Antelope, Boar, Grouse, Quail, Pheasant), Asparagus, Chicory, Endive, Leeks, Turnips, Parsnips, Bilberries, Figs, Limes, Chestnuts, Olives, Currants, Sultanas, Tomatoes, Mulberries, Grapefruit, Rhubarb, Celery, Onions, Red Cabbage, Oats, White Fish, Dandelion Flowers, Garlic and all bulb vegetables are Sagittarian foods. Power beverages for the Archer are Dandelion Wine, Absinthe, Anisette Liqueur, and anything sparkling.

CAPRICORN POWER FOODS

Sour, bitter, sharp, savoury tastes appeal to the Capricornian palate. Winter foods, Salted Nuts, Onions, Spinach, Silverbeet, Christmas flavours such as roast Turkey, spit roasts, rich brown Gravies, Creamed Potatoes, Puddings, Quinces, Vegetables set in Gelatine or Marrow Jelly, subterranean vegetables (Potatoes, Celeriac, Salsify, Chicory, Swedes, Radishes, Kohlrabi, Sea-kale Beetroot, Artichokes, Eggplants), Barley, Eggs, Cheese, Prunes, Almonds, Rye, Bread, Fish, Goat's Milk, Malt, starchy foods, earthy-flavoured root vegetables and fruits are all Capricorn foods. Power beverages for the Goat are pure Guarana Powder (for its Earthy taste and stamina-inducing qualities), Gin and Tonic, and aged and fortified Wines.

AQUARIUS POWER FOODS

Health foods, Peppers, Barley, Celery, Apples, Figs, all vegetables, Limes, Star Fruit, Chillies, Kiwi Fruit, forest Berries, dried Fruits, Kumquats, and any foods with sharp, distinctive, or unusual flavours all appeal to the Aquarian palate and character. Power beverages for the Water Bearer are Vodka, Fumitory Tea, Mullein Tea, and fad health drinks.

PISCES POWER FOODS

Figs, Purslane, Chutneys, Lettuce, Melons, Rosehips, Bilberries, Green Leafy Vegetables, Sweet Cicely, Lychees, Chicory, Cucumber, Onions, Soft Cheeses, Prunes, Grapes, Strawberries, Raisins, Dates, Nuts, Pumpkin, all Seafoods, Shellfish and freshwater Fish, and all Fruit and Vegetables with a high water content appeal to the Piscean palate. Power beverages for the Fish are Water, Absinthe, Spirits mixed with Soda or Mineral Water, Wine and Champagne.

PLANTS & MAGIC

We all have many guides who assist us with different tasks and parts of our journey. If you are drawn to working with plants then ask for a guide to appear to you. It may be a specific plant that calls you and acts as your way-shower, a nature spirit or tree being, goddess or ancestor. Be open to whomever comes your way.

Fay Johnstone

Plants have long been associated with magic, medicine, superstition, nutrition, and even astrology. In ancient times, some were endowed with magical properties based upon beliefs of the time, but also upon anecdotal evidence that some herbal concoctions, flowers, or essences helped alleviate and even cure uncomfortable, painful or dis-eased physical or mental states. Whether these were based upon 'old wives tales' or beliefs in supernatural forces matters little, for in modern times we can prove and indeed have proven through scientific research and controlled experiments, that plants play an important role in our health.

Some 'magical' plants have aphrodisiac or narcotic properties, while others have formidable toxic effects, but all are considered in some way to affect the human system on physical, emotional, spiritual, or psychological levels.

Plants such as cocoa, tobacco and coffee that have grown alongside humans over the course of millennia, are still, more than ever, an integral part of our daily lives. They still incite the same pleasures, fascinations and dangers, and some still carry the same taboos. It is interesting to note that more than eighty per cent of chemical medicines in existence today, and found in pharmacists' dispensaries, are derived from plants. Notable examples are aspirin, digoxin and morphine.

In modern astrology herbs are often associated with the zodiac signs and have evolved from an old system where a specific planet rules each herb. The planet that governs a herb is chosen according to its appearance, scent and where it grows; herbs are additionally categorised as hot or cold, and dry or moist. In this way one can see how the nature of the herb corresponds to the nature of the planet. If you are familiar with your ruling planets' basic associations, you will find it easy to match it to herbs.

Although you can simply buy whatever herbs you wish to use for your magic, the optimum effect will be obtained if you can gather them at a favourable astrological time. Once you are armed with astrological knowledge, you can choose a time when the planet that rules your chosen herb is in a position of strength. Keep in mind that each planet rules a substantial number of plants, so if one isn't easily obtained, it should be simple to find another one to use for the same purpose.

There sometimes seems to be a wide variance in the list of herbs associated with a specific astrological influence. This is because the different parts of the plant have different rulerships and uses. For example, whichever planet rules it, a plant that bears fruit is naturally related to Jupiter, its flowers relate to Venus, seed or bark to Mercury, leaves to the Moon, wood to Mars, and roots to Saturn. So, as well as the planet that traditionally rules the plant, it can be regarded as having a secondary ruler according to the part of the plant being used. Although you don't need to work with a highly complex system of deciding which herb will suit your purposes, you can make your magical workings more powerful by paying attention to some of these nuances.

Essentially, different scents, herbs, flowers and plants have their own specific vibrations. Their essences should be worn on your skin (you can make up your own combinations using essential oils or flower waters), burned in an oil burner, inhaled from a cloth, diffused in a bath or bowl of steam, or burned as incense sticks.

Many plants, herbs and spices, however used, contain gentle yet effective energies that will affect not only your wishing ceremonies, but also your moods, associations and emotions, which can assist in carrying your wonderful Self in the direction of your dreams. Lifted up on incense smoke, for example, your wish is carried out to the wider Universe. Try making your own, out of any or all of your power plants, woods, flowers, shrubs, trees, or herbs!

And finally, for a bit of fun, thirty-three magical, mythical plants are: Cocoa, rosemary, tobacco, thyme, wheat, coffee, sugar cane, cinnamon, hemp, tea, pumpkin, foxglove, incense, amanita (a mushroom), tarragon, pepper, rice, belladonna, reed, ginseng, clove, ginger, sage, maize, mistletoe, lily, mandrake, St John's Wort, poppy, peyote, cinchona, verbena and the vine*.

*Some plant products can be poisonous, toxic, hallucinogenic, or even fatal if consumed. Do not consume without research, guidance or supervision by a qualified herbalist or similarly suitably qualified professional.

POWER FLOWERS & FLOWER REMEDIES

The recognition of beauty was one of the most significant events in the evolution of human consciousness. Seeing beauty in a flower could awaken humans, however briefly, to the beauty that is an essential part of their own innermost being, their true nature. Flowers, more fleeting, more ethereal, and more delicate than the plants out of which they emerge, have become... an expression in form of that which is most high, most sacred, and ultimately formless within ourselves.

Eckhart Tolle

Flower essences are part of the medicine of vibrational healing, which seeks to balance the subtle bodies in an effort to prevent any discordant or latent underlying energetic conditions from manifesting on the physical plane. They contain the etheric energy of the plant from which they are made, and since these essences deal with emotional states, it is possible to correlate the various emotions with the zodiac signs and planets. The remedies listed for each sign are either tonics for the bodily areas that that sign governs, serve to increase one's awareness of one's own healing powers, and/or are otherwise aligned with that zodiac sign or its ruling planet.

ARIES

POWER FLOWER ✦ Honeysuckle.

OTHER BIRTH FLOWERS ✦ Gorse, Nasturtium, Thistle & Peppermint.

MARCH BORN ✦ **Daffodil** ✦ The spiritually uplifting daffodil bestows dignity and chivalry on those born in March, the earliest month of the northern Hemisphere's springtime during which it first blooms. The daffodil has always been considered a cheerful flower that raises the spirits.

APRIL BORN ✦ Daisy & Sweet Pea ✦ Together with grace and a sense of delicacy, the sweet pea brings with it the possibility of a varied life for the versatile April-born.

FLOWER REMEDIES ✦ Impatiens, Vine, Heather, Tiger Lily, Indian Paintbrush, Scarlet Monkeyflower, Trumpet Vine & Cayenne.

TAURUS

POWER FLOWER ✦ Honeysuckle.

OTHER BIRTH FLOWERS ✦ Foxglove, Rose, Primula, Violet, Daisy & Columbine.

APRIL BORN ✦ See under 'Aries'.

MAY BORN ✦ Lily of the Valley ✦ Lily of the Valley is a very auspicious birth flower, symbolising joy, optimism and bright, new beginnings throughout life. Lily of the Valley signals the return of happiness.

FLOWER REMEDIES ✦ Cerato, Chicory, Chestnut Bud, Bleeding Heart, Iris, Tansy, Hound's Tongue & California Wild Rose.

GEMINI

POWER FLOWER ✦ Lavender.

OTHER BIRTH FLOWERS ✦ Iris, Myrtle & Snapdragon.

JUNE BORN ✦ Rose ✦ Love is the magnificent birth gift of the popular rose, with most representing aspects of romance, affection or feeling - rosebuds signifying unawakened love, red roses deep emotions, white roses purity and innocence, yellow roses joy and friendship, pink roses gentle emotions and gratitude, orange roses passion and desire, and black roses death and farewells. The rose has always symbolised beauty, love and fertility. It was sacred to Aphrodite and Venus, the Greek and Roman goddesses of love, respectively. The Romans often planted roses on graves, as they regarded it as a symbol of rebirth. In Islam the rose is associated with paradise, and in the Christian tradition, the rose represents the Virgin Mary's purity and beauty. One ancient Christian legend says that until Adam and Eve were expelled from the Garden of

Eden roses had no thorns; God added these to remind people that they no longer lived in a perfect world.

FLOWER REMEDIES ✦ Gentian, Mimulus, Hornbeam, White Chestnut, Madia, Morning Glory, Shasta Daisy, Blackberry, Lavender, Yerba Santa & Rabbitbrush.

CANCER

POWER FLOWER ✦ Acanthus.

OTHER BIRTH FLOWERS ✦ White Rose, Convolvulus, Geranium & Water Lily.

JUNE BORN ✦ See under 'Gemini'.

JULY BORN ✦ **Water Lily & Larkspur (Delphinium)** ✦ Named for the irrepressible dolphin (from the Greek delphis), the blooming delphinium bestows health and happiness on those born in July.

FLOWER REMEDIES ✦ Clematis, Larch, Chicory, Honeysuckle, Red Chestnut, Centaury, Golden Eardrops, Chamomile, Buttercup, Pomegranate, Pink Yarrow & Mariposa Lily.

LEO

POWER FLOWER ✦ **Sunflower** ✦ The sunflower, brought to Europe from the Americas, was called girasol by Spanish explorers, which means "turn to the Sun." It was sacred to the Incas who used it extensively in carvings and jewellery. Because the sunflower turns toward the Sun, it became associated with devotion to God. In China, the sunflower symbolised immortality, and people ate sunflower seeds in the hope of living long and happy lives.

OTHER BIRTH FLOWERS ✦ Cowslip, Forsythia, Passionflower, Peony & Heliotrope.

JULY BORN ✦ See under 'Cancer'.

AUGUST BORN ✦ **Gladiolus & Poppy** ✦ Opium, used to relieve pain and induce sleep, was originally made from a variety of poppy commonly found around the Mediterranean, before its cultivation spread along the

Silk Road through Asia and finally China, where it became the catalyst for the Opium Wars of the mid-1800s. The Greeks associated it with Hypnos, the god of sleep, and Morpheus, the god of dreams (morphine is made from opium and was named after Morpheus). In Greek mythology, Persephone was picking poppies when Hades abducted her. Since World War I, the poppy has been adopted as the flower of remembrance in the British Commonwealth, and millions of artificial poppy flowers are sold each year to be worn on Remembrance Day. Because it produces a large number of seeds, the poppy is associated with fertility. The poppy's many blessings are a capacity for renewal, and an understanding that there's a time for every purpose: beauty, loss, loyalty and courage.

FLOWER REMEDIES ✦ Vervain, Vine, Borage, Sunflower, Dandelion & Nasturtium.

VIRGO

POWER FLOWER ✦ Morning Glory.

OTHER BIRTH FLOWERS ✦ Buttercup, Pansy, Cornflower, Rosemary & Madonna Lily.

AUGUST BORN ✦ See under 'Leo'.

SEPEMBER BORN ✦ **Morning Glory & Aster** ✦ Grace, modesty and a sweetness of disposition are bestowed on those with the stylish aster as their special flower, which is considered emblematic of elegance, friendship and secret love.

FLOWER REMEDIES ✦ Centaury, Pine, Beech, Crab Apple, Corn, Dill & Filaree.

LIBRA

POWER FLOWER ✦ Rose.

OTHER BIRTH FLOWERS ✦ Bluebell, Apple Blossom, Hydrangea & Love-In-A-Mist.

SEPEMBER BORN ✦ See under 'Virgo'.

OCTOBER BORN ✦ Calendula (Marigold) ✦ Those gifted with marigold, follower of the Sun, as their birth flower are spirited lovers of nature, radiating happiness to all around them. The marigold was associated with Apollo, the Greek god of the Sun. In Greek mythology, Nereid Clytie was spurned by Apollo and turned into a marigold - ever since then, marigolds have turned to face the Sun. The seeds of the marigold were often worn as an amulet to protect the wearer from theft, and they are frequently used in love charms and in wedding decorations. As a result, marigolds came to symbolise faithfulness and long-lasting unions.

FLOWER REMEDIES ✦ Scleranthus, Agrimony, Cerato, Quaking Grass, Sweet Pea, Red Clover, Penstemon & Goldenrod.

SCORPIO

POWER FLOWER ✦ Chrysanthemum.

OTHER BIRTH FLOWERS ✦ Geranium, Rhododendron, Basil & Purple Heather.

OCTOBER BORN ✦ See under 'Libra'.

NOVEMBER BORN ✦ Chrysanthemum ✦ Japan's national flower is considered a symbol of perfection of the human spirit, and is a universal symbol of Autumn. For thousands of years, it has been the emblem of the emperor; warriors in Japan would wear this flower into battle to bring courage - and these emperor's men always won the war. In this country it is on the official seal of the imperial family, thought to be because its petals look like the Sun's rays. In the East, it symbolises good fortune, happiness, longevity and wealth. In feng shui the chrysanthemum is one of the five beneficial flowers, representing joy and laughter. The chrysanthemum symbolises perfection which is often expressed as the well-balanced philosophies of life practised by those who call it their birth flower.

FLOWER REMEDIES ✦ Chicory, Rock Rose, Willow, Holly, Sticky Monkeyflower, Sagebrush, Basil, Fuchsia, Trillium, Black-Eyed Susan & Garlic.

SAGITTARIUS

POWER FLOWER ✦ Narcissus.

OTHER BIRTH FLOWERS ✦ Carnation, Sage, Dandelion, Wallflower & Thistle.

NOVEMBER BORN ✦ See under 'Scorpio'.

DECEMBER BORN ✦ **Narcissus & Holly** ✦ Although it is one of the most enduring symbols of Christmas, holly was the gift of good luck among the Romans celebrating their midwinter festivals. The northern tribes of that great nation draped holly over doorways as shelter for friendly woodland spirits who would bring good fortune into their homes. It is believed that sprigs of holly in the house at Christmas time will bring favourable luck. Holly, emblematic of physical and spiritual renewal, also bestows the gifts of foresight, strength and resilience on those born in December.

FLOWER REMEDIES ✦ Agrimony, Wild Oat, Vervain, Larkspur, Mountain Pride & Hound's Tongue.

CAPRICORN

POWER FLOWER ✦ Carnation.

OTHER BIRTH FLOWERS ✦ Ivy, Pansy, Rue, Snowdrop, Amaranthus & Nightshade.

DECEMBER BORN ✦ See under 'Sagittarius'.

JANUARY BORN ✦ **Snowdrop & Carnation** ✦ To those born in January, the much-loved carnation promises a life of variety and empowers them with the quality of courage. Carnations remove negative energy, especially in close relationships, and in the Netherlands, red carnations are associated with love, energy and optimism. The carnation is an important flower in the Christian tradition, as it is believed carnations sprung up everywhere the Virgin Mary's tears fell as she walked to her son's crucifixion. In Mexico they are known as 'the flowers of the dead', as they are strewn around the bodies of the deceased as they are prepared for burial. Carnation can offer one protection and depending on the colour, encouragement, love, or admiration.

FLOWER REMEDIES ✦ Mimulus, Elm, Oak, Mustard, Rock Water, Gorse, Sweet Chestnut, Gentian, Saguaro & Scotch Broom.

AQUARIUS

POWER FLOWER ✦ Orchid ✦ A symbol of luxury, love and refinement.

OTHER BIRTH FLOWERS ✦ Foxglove, Gentian & Snowdrop.

JANUARY BORN ✦ See under 'Capricorn'.

FEBRUARY BORN ✦ Violet ✦ As a birth flower, thanks to Christian symbolism, the violet symbolises the gentle qualities of modesty, humility and shyness (which is where the term 'shrinking violet' comes from), together with strength of character in adversity. The Greeks associated the violet with Io, who was one of many human women loved by Zeus. Napoleon loved violets, and he used them to give hope to his followers. When he was exiled to Elba, he told his supporters that he would return, just as the violets return each spring, and as a result they used the violet as their symbol. Napoleon became affectionately known as "Caporal Violet" and gave a bunch to Josephine on their wedding day. On their anniversary each year he gave her another bunch of them, and after she died, he placed a violet from her grave into a locket, and wore it around his neck until his own death.

FLOWER REMEDIES ✦ Water Violet, Star of Bethlehem, Walnut, Vervain, Dill, Self-heal & Chamomile.

PISCES

POWER FLOWER ✦ Water Lily ✦ In Greek and Roman times, the lily was associated with Venus, and symbolised purity and chastity. The early Christians adopted this symbolism and linked the white petals and sweet fragrance of the lily with the Virgin Mary. There is another, different interpretation of the lily however, associating it with virility and sensuality, for in Ancient Egypt it was connected with the goddess of fertility and creation, Ashtar. Lilies are frequently seen at weddings and funerals; at weddings they represent innocence and purity, and at funerals they symbolise the soul, free from the body and from Earthly sins. In the East, the day lily is believed to dispel grief and sorrows.

OTHER BIRTH FLOWERS ✦ Jonquil, Poppy, Heliotrope & Carnation.

FEBRUARY BORN ✦ See under 'Aquarius'.

MARCH BORN ✦ See under 'Aries'.

FLOWER REMEDIES ✦ Rock Rose, Clematis, Aspen, Star Tulip, Yarrow, Manzanita & Lotus.

TREES & LUCKY WOODS

> The tree is a metaphor for the teacher to convey multiple layers of Universal truth. Indigenous cultures understood the value of trees in ways the modern world is just beginning to awaken to. Looking at etymology, words like truth, true, and trust all arise directly from the word tree. The relationship becomes obvious upon hearing the root meaning of tree: 'standing straight and tall'.
>
> **Jeffrey Armstrong**

Native Americans referred to trees as 'Standing People' because they stand firm, obtaining strength from their connection with the Earth. They therefore teach us the importance of being grounded, while at the same time listening to, and reaching towards, our higher aspirations. In Norse mythology, Yggdrasil, the tree of life, is a cosmic map that represents all life. The tree is connected with the Underworld through its roots, the Earth through its trunk, and the Otherworld of spirit through its branches extending into the sky.

The dryad, or tree's spirit, needs to be respected and asked when 'taking' from a tree for the purposes of magic.

The essence of tree magic lies in understanding the qualities of each type. These can be drawn on for such things as healing and spellcasting. For example, the rowan tree grows high up the sides of mountains, often in hard-to-reach places, so if you need to develop tenacity or access to difficult spiritual spaces, you can call on this tree; the oak tree is durable and strong, so if you are needing fortification or firmness, you can gain power from this sturdy plant.

When respected as living, breathing beings, trees can provide insights into the workings of Nature, cycles, and our own inner essence. Each zodiac phase is associated with a particular kind of tree, the basic qualities of which complement the nature of those born during that time. Appreciate the beauty of your affinity tree and study its nature carefully, for it has a connection with your own nature and lessons to impart.

ARIES LUCKY WOOD ✦ MAHOGANY

Mahogany is a commercially important lumber prized for its colour, beauty and durability. Its reddish-brown colour darkens over time, and displays a reddish sheen when polished. Popular as a body wood for electric guitars, mahogany's primary magical functions are spiritual growth and guidance, and fertility. While most woods have a range of differing uses and applications, mahogany is very specialised, focusing mainly on these areas, but it also possesses a powerful bond with the Earth element; it is particularly useful for channelling Earth energy.

Aside from fertility and growth, this wood does have some other uses: those of enhancing intuition, strengthening kinship bonds, and exploring and clarifying goals. An excellent wood for emotional and spiritual healing, mahogany can be used to provide guidance in these areas.

TAURUS LUCKY WOOD ✦ SYCAMORE

Bestowing gifts of divination, prosperity, strength, love and harmony, sycamores are one of the oldest tree species on Earth. Symbolising growth, versatility, persistence and endurance, the sycamore is water-resistant and often grows where other trees cannot. In magic, it is useful for askings involving growth, and, possessing regenerative properties, can be used for restorative purposes. Sycamore symbolises development, vitality and perseverance and is good to use for any magic involving prosperity, love and longevity. Believed to bring success and abundance, it can also teach humility.

GEMINI LUCKY WOODS ✦ ELDER & BEECH

ELDER ✦ The elder is considered a magical and holy tree by various cultures of western and northern Europe. Truly ancient, remnants of its existence have been found at Stone Age sites. It was believed that elder could not be struck by lightning, and so was planted nearby houses for protection.

If struck down, the resilient elder can grow from the smallest stump, and on battlefields it is among the first of the trees to spring back and return life to the destroyed land. The stems of the elder branches, their pith removed, were worn as magical amulets to protect the wearer from harm and also to bring health and good luck. One old magical chant hails elder as a bringer of prosperity: "Elder over the doorway, fortune over the threshold."

Elder carries properties of exorcism, healing, purification and protection. Elderberries, blossoms or leaves hung over doorways of houses, are said to drive away spirits, serpents and burglars. But it can be used by the druids, or tree spirits, for both good and bad magic. As a sacred tree of the Celtic calendar, it can be used to bless and heal, but as ruler of the thirteenth tree month, the elder also has unlucky associations and, in the past, would have been used in dark magic in curses. Elder is the guardian of this thirteenth month of the Celtic tree calendar, a 'month' that is three days long and contains both the end of the year (Halloween) and the beginning of the New Year (All Soul's Day).

In Irish folklore, it is said that the sidhe- or elf-arrows were fashioned of elder and that the most potent witches' wand was one formed from an elder bough.

Celtic tree lore regards the elder as the tree of transformation and regeneration, representing 'death in life and life in death'. If it is allowed, this tree can imprint into one's consciousness the sensation of harmony which arises from following one's inner prompting and experiencing the new life that rises out of death.

BEECH ✦ Beech is traditionally known as 'Queen of the Forest', because this tree is seen as the female counterpart to the oak, the 'King of the Forest'. The words for 'book' and 'beech' are of the same origin due to the historical use of the tree - closely grained and easily smoothed, beech wood was made for writing tablets. Therefore, it is also connected with ancient wisdom.

CANCER LUCKY WOOD ✦ BIRCH

The word birch comes from the Sanskrit root *bharg'*, which means 'shining', for the areas in which it grows contain snow which melts and sends cascades of water down its trunk, the birch bark taking on an appearance of liquid glitter. When it rains, the bark becomes so wet and dark, it is named the black birch. Birch carries properties of protection, exorcism, healing and purification.

The medicine of the cherry birch lies in its inner bark, which contains a rich, fragrant oil known commercially as wintergreen. The name wintergreen hints at the birch's effectiveness as a transitional plant between winter and spring. Spiritually, the black birch assists us in locating within our own bodies the signs of spring which have been buried under winter's cold, barren landscape and its oil assists us in shedding our protective winter layer to make way for our fresh 'green' selves to sprout.

The cherry birch thrives when it grows near water, giving us a signature of its gift as a tonic to the Watery elements and needs of the human body.

In Russian tradition, birch trees were deeply revered through song and story. But while eastern European folklore focuses on the protective powers of birches, the Nordic countries consider it the symbol of the Earth Mother, embodying the female, cyclical powers of growth and healing. Traditionally, witches' brooms are made of birch twigs, twine and wood, so if you feel drawn to witchcraft and the feminine aspects of magic and spirit, then birch wood might be a wise choice for you.

The immense durability of birch bark has been put to many uses; from Native American canoes and ropes to writing parchment. Using birch bark as a medium for the written word strengthens your connection to the tree's claim of being a 'tree of knowledge' and a gateway to new ideas and worlds. The tough substance of this bark indeed survives long after the original tree has died. Although strong, it is easy to work with.

In western Europe, the beautiful and graceful birch is referred to as the 'Lady of the Woods', belonging to the element of Water and under the dominion of the planet Venus. It is believed that if one wishes to communicate with the goddess, one should sit silently in a grove of birches and listen for her whispers, which travel on the gentle wisps of wind.

Throughout its life cycle, the birch continues to be both a useful and versatile resource. As a pioneer tree, it gives way to other larger trees, sacrificing itself to make way for new life. It is therefore associated with the circle of life, endings and beginnings, and new growth.

The birch tree is the Celtic tree of beginnings, an association springing from the fact that it is the first tree to grow back after a forest fire. The birch also sheds its bark, which suggests further links with renewal, as the old and worn-out is released to make way for the new. Creating and carrying a staff or wand made out of white birch wood is an ancient, wise way of allying oneself with qualities of communication, truth, perception and clearer vision. Wands can be fashioned and used to point the way to clear intent and fresh beginnings in life, or a kind of rebirthing of the soul.

The silver birch tree has special associations with the Moon as, interestingly, its bark reflects the moonlight, making the tree appear to glow in the light of a Full Moon.

LEO LUCKY WOOD ✦ WALNUT

Walnut wood teaches us clarity and focus, and how to use our intelligence and other mind gifts wisely. Holding the powers of teleportation, inspiration, the breath and astral travel, walnut is symbolic of mental wisdom.

VIRGO LUCKY WOODS ✦ BEECH & HAZEL

BEECH ✦ See under 'Gemini Lucky Wood'.

HAZEL ✦ Hazel, which was mentioned in ancient Chaldean and Egyptian records, has been one of the main sources of wood for magic for thousands of years. Apollo gave Mercury a hazel wand, which he used to instil good virtues in humankind. In Scandinavia, the hazel was sacred to the god Thor and was used for protection against lightning. Its connection with Thor also associates it with Fire, virility, childbirth, and matters of the heart. The nuts, used as charms and love tokens, signified the hazel tree's blessing of fertility, birth, and successful child-rearing.

Hazel is said to bring luck, fertility, protection, wisdom and wishes. An old legend has it that all one's wishes will come true if they carry a twig of hazel as an amulet or charm.

Celebrated in Celtic folklore as a tree of knowledge, poetry and learning, the hazel tree is reputed to have 'nine hazelnuts of wisdom', which in Celtic legend, fell into a sacred pool or well and were eaten by salmon. According to the story, the fish, called Fintan, imbibed the nine hazelnuts of wisdom and each one consumed became a spot on its scales. Whoever ate the salmon would then receive infinite wisdom.

Hazel wood is pliant and has traditionally been used for divining underground water (Pliny [23 - 79 CE] wrote about the use of hazel rods in water divining); a hazelnut on a string makes a good dowsing pendulum. Its flexibility also made it a valuable wood for making walking sticks, fishing rods, whip handles and baskets.

LIBRA LUCKY WOOD ✦ SYCAMORE

See under 'Taurus Lucky Wood'.

SCORPIO LUCKY WOOD ✦ MAHOGANY

See under 'Aries Lucky Wood'.

SAGITTARIUS LUCKY WOOD ✦ OAK

Oak wood corresponds to the Water element and the planets Jupiter and Mars, and is a symbol of strength, sovereignty, courage, wisdom, wealth, honesty, toughness, endurance, rulership, nobility, generosity, justice, protection, bravery and power. With its towering height and wide girth, it also symbolises and bestows luck, vigour, love, potency, health and prosperity. Spiritually, it was believed that the oak was a portal to the spirit world and nature gods were worshipped in oak tree groves.

The mighty oak tree has a wide trunk, very deep roots, and deeply lobed leaves. Mature trees can be well over 1,000 years old, with their life span up to 2,000 years.

Held sacred in ancient times, its noble attributes have long been harnessed for use in magic, and today the oak is still valued for its great strength and durability.

Known as the 'King of Trees', Oak has a strong association with English woodlands, which has its origins in Britain's Pagan past. It is connected with the Summer Solstice, its wood being used to fuel the sacred Midsummer fires. It also has links with royalty and kingship: King Arthur's round table was fabled to have been created from a single cross section of a large oak.

In times past, front doors were usually made from oak; this was because, although the thickness of the wood helped to keep the warmth in and unsavoury guests out, its magical properties also provided strength, fertility and protection to the house or building. The word 'druid' originates from the Celtic word 'duir', meaning 'oak' or 'door'.

Acorn nuts, the oak's divine fruit, are said to increase fertility, sexual potency, longevity, 'immortality' and youthfulness, fostering virility partly through the sensuality of their creamy texture and smoky flavour, as well as the protein richness they offer. Both nut and cone have been used magically in fertility charms. Acorns are also omens of wealth, happiness, and extremely good fortune. The acorn and the tree from which it comes, is a portent which signifies successful outcomes to any venture you want to undertake, and prosperity and growth in the future.

Oak is a grounding wood, offering the gifts of stability and strength; imbued with the tree's powerful properties, it can be used to make magical tools or charms. The power and durability of the oak tree are demonstrated by the fact its root system extends as far beneath the Earth as its branches stretch above it. Its strength is further symbolised by enduring what others around it cannot; it remains strong through challenges, and is regarded as being almost immortal, as is attested by its usually long life and ability to survive fire, lightning strikes, and other similar assaults.

Oak is one of the most sacred trees, traditionally prized by the Celts and druids, the tree's commanding presence signifying true alignment of purpose, balance and fortitude, and Witches of old often danced beneath the oak tree during ritual. Carrying any part of the oak tree draws good luck to you, but remember first to ask for permission and above all, to show recognition, appreciation, and gratitude for this wood's amazing gifts.

CAPRICORN LUCKY WOOD ✦ EBONY

One of the most powerful of woods, ebony combines both masculine and feminine energies, as well as carrying the essences of the five elements of Fire, Earth, Air, Water and Spirit, with an emphasis on Water.

The power of ebony transcends boundaries; in fact, it can be used in any types of magical workings, and in conjunction with any of the elements. Such is its potency, ebony wands are said to give the magic-worker pure, unadulterated power. This wood is believed to be the most dynamic from which to make a wand, and is believed to be especially useful in the seeking of spiritual knowledge and the exploration of one's emotional and intuitive faculties.

Ebony wood is protective and so can be used in making amulets, and has the power to transform, attract positive luck, balance energies, and break down barriers.

AQUARIUS LUCKY WOOD ✦ PINE

Pine wood corresponds to the elements of Fire and Air, and is purifying and cleansing to the physical environment, and one's overall person and personal space. In a magical sense, pine represents abundance, purification, creativity, healing, fertility and protection. It is excellent for attracting prosperity and to keep one 'on course' when one's life or dreams seem to have deviated off their intended paths; its grace and stateliness serves as a reminder to always look upwards and to think positively. It also brings about inner peace, serenity, tranquillity, fertility, abundance, health, love and optimism. Excellent for use in rising above difficulties, pine is ultimately cleansing, uplifting, rejuvenating, purifying and sanctifying.

The Native Americans looked deeply into the shapes and habits of all beings that inhabited the Earth to learn of the powers embodied in their various forms. The circular shape of the pine tree and its ability to reach a substantial age were believed to teach of the endless, cyclical wheel of time and the wisdom derived from travelling around it. According to this native wisdom, pine needles, which are wrapped at their base in small packets, were said to be reminiscent of the strength and sustenance available to humans in their unity; and the gentle and pliable wood of the pine represents strength in its softness.

To the Chinese, pine was an emblem of immortality. They planted it on graves, for the green of its leaves, which were believed to be full of chi - the vital force - and could prevent the decay of the corpse while strengthening the spirit of the departed.

Branches of pine have been used in seasonal outdoor rituals, serving a role in purifying areas of outdoor worship by sweeping the forest floor before their performance.

Pine wood, cones, branches and needles all contain unique magical powers. Pine needles and boughs are especially good for bringing luck and prosperity, while pinecones are a potent symbol of fertility. Hanging pine in any form above the doorway or mantel of your house is believed to bring good fortune to those who dwell therein. The resin of pine can be burned to clear negative energies from the air, and the smoke is said to repel evil and send it back to its source.

Where pine trees have been given centuries of time and freedom to live and grow instead of being cut down by incessant human progress, their magical sentience is undeniably strong, their trunks standing solid and tall, their branches extending with the grace and complexity that growth and maturity can bring.

Their enchanting eminence, coupled with their distinctive fragrance and abundant magical properties, make pine a gentle but powerful force to work with.

PISCES LUCKY WOOD ✦ OAK

See under 'Sagittarius Lucky Wood'.

SACRED CELTIC CALENDAR TREES

The Celts and other ancient peoples had many beliefs and traditions based around the magical lore of trees. The system of Celtic tree astrology was developed out of a natural connection with the druids' knowledge of Earth's cycles and their reverence for the sacred knowledge they believed was held by trees.

The druids had a profound connection with trees and regarded them as vessels of infinite wisdom. Their calendar, being based on a Lunar year of thirteen months, contains a tree for each of these Lunar months, corresponding with (but not exactly) each of the twelve western astrology zodiac signs, which are based on the Solar calendar. Because there are some crossovers, each zodiacal birth period has two possible trees.

SACRED TREES CORREPONDING WITH BIRTH DATE

ALDER ✦ (18 March - 14 April)
WILLOW ✦ (15 April - 12 May)
HAWTHORN ✦ (13 May - 9 June)
OAK ✦ (10 June - 7 July)
HOLLY ✦ (8 July - 4 August)
HAZEL ✦ (5 August - 1 September)
VINE MOON ✦ (2 - 29 September)
IVY MOON ✦ (30 September - 27 October)
REED MOON ✦ (28 October - 24 November)
ELDER ✦ (25 November - December 23)
BIRCH ✦ (24 December - 20 January)
ROWAN ✦ (21 January - 17 February)
ASH ✦ (18 February - 17 March)

ALDER ✦ Often referred to as 'King of the Waters', alder is one of the thirteen sacred trees of Celtic and European witchcraft. In Welsh mythology, the alder fought in the front line of the 'Battle of the Trees', against the Underworld.

Associated with the period of the year surrounding the Spring Equinox, it brings a sense of healing, balance, harmony and calm. Rebirth, fertility and equilibrium are other key features.

When cut, its wood turns from white to red as though it is bleeding, and this red colouring can be used as a dye for sacred cloths, bags and ribbons. Growing near water, the tree has feminine associations, yet its links to war also indicate masculine powers. Therefore, the alder symbolises the balancing of the masculine and feminine.

The survival strategies of the alder tree make it an excellent pioneer species, which fits well with the Arien spirit, being an initiator and motivator. It spawns a vast quantity of seeds and grows rapidly. Alder thrives around water, from marshlands to rivers, and the otter often makes its home in the waterside roots of this tree.

As a hard, oily and water-resistant wood, alder was often used to build early bridges, as well as to construct buildings, churches and cities. It is also used to make woodwind instruments, pipes and whistles.

WILLOW ✦ Willow is traditionally found on riverbanks, its roots growing in the water, connecting it with the influence of the Moon. Because of its connection with the Lunar sphere, its powers are said to be most effective when used at night, under the Moon. As a water-dwelling tree, it signifies emotional balance, intuition and water-divining magic.

The willow symbolises regeneration as cut willows always resprout. It is a fast-growing, hardy and resilient tree, being able to withstand severe frosts. With more than 300 evolving variants, the willow is a powerful survivor and revered symbol of witchcraft and enchantment.

The wood of willow is tough but elastic, and so highly flexible that it has traditionally been used for the making of baskets. In fact, it was an important resource for ancient communities, providing withies for wicker baskets; indeed, 'witch', 'wicca' and 'wicked' are said to be derived from the word wicker.

Willow is the tree of emotion, love, intuition and poetic inspiration. Ruled by Cerridwen, Celtic Moon goddess worshipped by the Welsh, a deeply mysterious figure, who is the keeper of the flaming cauldron of Divine wisdom, where immortal knowledge and the Fires of inspiration are formed, the willow can gently guide us towards this illumination.

HAWTHORN ✦ With its white flowers (virginal), red berries (fertility) and sharp thorns (maturity), the hawthorn tree symbolises the three aspects of the Triple Goddess: those of maiden, mother and crone. Thus, it is suitable for use by those interested in exploring the Female Mysteries.

Throughout western Europe, the hawthorn is greatly esteemed as a magical tree bearing protective and visionary powers in addition to its renown amongst herbalists as a heart-healer. The haw in the word means 'hedge', as the thorny-branched trees, which attain a height of up to thirty feet, were planted as hedgerows to separate fields and prevent grazing animals from passing into a neighbour's meadow by virtue of the tree's inch-long thorns. In the European autumn time, the creamy hawthorn blossoms transform into clusters of ruby-red berries and the waxy leaves turn crimson.

Hawthorn has a magical reputation and association with being a portal into 'other worlds'. In Celtic tradition, it was believed that a hawthorn tree found growing with oak and ash was a sacred place in which fairies dwelled, and that if one slept under the hawthorn at Full Moon in May or on May Eve, that one would behold entrance into the land of the sprites.

The wood of the hawthorn is fine-grained and therefore suitable for carving delicate items and magical objects. Some traditions even believe hawthorn can carry our wishes into the ether. In times past, travellers hung pieces of ribbon on the thorns of this holy tree, murmuring wishes into the cloth. When moved by the wind, these strips were believed to whisper the wishes into the ears of fairies who whimsically bestowed gifts upon humans.

Like many relatives of the rose tree, hawthorn can also be used in love spells to attract one's true love. As the guardian of the doorway to fairy realms, hawthorn wisely discerns the right timing for a wounded heart to open. Hawthorn berries and blossoms can be used to ease the grief of a broken heart and also to open it up to new love.

OAK ✦ See under 'Sagittarius Lucky Wood'.

HOLLY ✦ Holly carries a regal status in Celtic tree astrology, and is traditionally associated with Christmas in many parts of the world, used to decorate homes at Winter Solstice. Its red berries and green leaves in the dead of northern hemisphere's winter symbolise everlasting life. Holly carries properties of exorcism, healing and purification. With its protective qualities, a holly tree grown near the home is thought to provide protection from thunder, lightning and demons.

A masculine tree, the prickly leaves of the holly match its formidable associations as a tree of protection and warfare, and its wood was used to make spears and chariot wheels in ancient times.

The holly is a sacred tree of the Sun and is associated with the Sun god in Wiccan beliefs. The roots of this belief lie in the tree's hardy, evergreen qualities and its connection to the Winter Solstice, as the shortest day of the year symbolises the rebirth of the Sun, and the Wheel of the Year now turns towards the summer. Evergreens have a special significance with the Winter Solstice: they represent the undying light of the Solar influence as they retain their leaves all year.

The fine, hard wood of this tree is especially good for carving and inlay work, and its wood, berries, leaves and flowers, can be used in many spells, magical tools and charms. Its best-known use is the tradition originating from the medieval practice of hanging a 'Holy Bough' made from holly and other evergreens, in the entrance of homes at Christmas, to welcome guests. This gesture also symbolised goodwill and longevity.

HAZEL ✦ See under 'Virgo Lucky Wood'.

VINE MOON ✦ Three of the 13 Celtic Moon months are governed by plants other than trees. Birthdays that fall between 2 September and 29 September have the Vine as their special plant. The Vine Moon signifies a time to harvest the rewards of all efforts throughout the year to date.

Vine brings strength, durability and prosperity, and is associated with the fruition of plans as well as symbolising 'bacchanalian' pleasures and joy.

In Celtic astrology, the vine is often linked with grapes, although this fruit is not native to the British Isles. Because of this, it is thought that the druids used the native blackberry or bramble vines in their symbolic mythology instead, connecting the twining of vine plants to their beliefs in the spiralling growth of life energy. Indeed, both plants represent forces of vitality and life; and like the grapevine, bramble vines are associated with joy, livelihood, wellbeing and exhilaration, both types providing wine and food. Certainly in colder European climates, the grapevine was reluctant to grow, and its place was taken, spiritually and practically, by the bramble or blackberry; therefore, it is thought by Celtic scholars that the druids used the blackberry vine rather than the grape one for their Celtic Moon month calendar.

The Vine Moon occurs at the Autumnal Equinox, a time of harmony when days and nights are of equal length, symbolising balance and equilibrium. The Vine Moon is traditionally a time for plans to move into a period of fruition or harvest before the northern hemisphere's winter sets in.

Overall, it represents revelry, a time of plenty when life's cup is full and the fruits of labour are to be savoured and enjoyed.

IVY MOON ✦ Three of the 13 Celtic Moon months are governed by plants other than trees. Birthdays that fall between 30 September and 27 October have the Ivy as their special plant. The Ivy Moon is an opportune time to cast a little magic to boost health.

A spiralling symbol of immortality and magic, the ivy provides the key to the Otherworlds and kingdom of the fairies. In the Celtic lore, fairy folk, the Sidhe, were said to have once walked the Earth in the realm of mortals. Since their retreat to the Fae Kingdom in the Otherworld, they are now only seen as butterflies. This insect was assigned to the ivy by the druids because the climbing plant was thought to provide an entrance to the world of the Sidhe. The short lifespan of the butterfly (about one month) also associates this elegant creature - and fairies - with the phases of the Moon.

Ironically, although ivy was chosen as a ruler of one of the Celtic Moon months, this plant actually destroys the health of trees by growing all over them, effectively choking them and stealing their nourishment from surrounding soil. In effect, it is a parasite that clings to trees and walls by tiny 'adhesive' aerial roots that grow out from its stem, and its tenacious nature means that it is difficult to eradicate or discourage. It is a persistent, hardy and long-lived evergreen plant that can adapt to a huge range of environments. Due to its strength and longevity, it has become associated with the enduring immortality of the Spirit. Growing in a spiral formation towards the sky, it can be found just as easily across fancy landscapes, derelict buildings and dying trees - it is indeed a symbol of resurrection.

REED MOON ✦ Three of the 13 Celtic Moon months are governed by plants other than trees. Birthdays that fall between 28 October and 24 November have the Reed as their special plant. The Reed Moon signifies a time to stay inside, hibernate, reflect and recuperate. The haunting sound of reeds in the wind has inspired much of this plant's legend and folklore, closely associating it with the spirit realm.

The family of reed organ instruments includes the harmonica, clarinet, panpipes and accordion, which work upon the principle of a thin strip of metal, or reed, held in a slit, which vibrates and produces an enchanting sound as air blows past it. Early reed organs actually used real reed stalks held in pipes.

Reed is a name given to a family of hardy, large grasses that occur globally and can be found along lakes, riversides, marshes and other shallow bodies of water; the strong, fibrous roots need moisture to survive. It is a resilient, fast-growing and integral part of many habitats and landscapes, earning it the reverence and respect of Celts. The dense roots push through and bind the saturated Earth, which is thought to link the reed with the Underworld, the realm of the dead and the hidden. The druids celebrated Samhain during the Reed Moon, a time when the doors between worlds opened, reinforcing this plant's link to the world of spirit, afterlife and enchantment.

ELDER ✦ See under 'Gemini Lucky Woods'.

BIRCH ✦ See under 'Cancer Lucky Wood'.

ROWAN ✦ Rowan is the magical tree of protection, healing and success, believed to be endowed with powerful magic and healing properties. Due to the conditions in which it grows, the rowan tree symbolises tenacity. It is found growing high up on the sides of mountains, often sprouting from tiny crevices in inaccessible spots.

The rowan tree is chiefly grown for its beauty, its seasonally rich red berries adding to its appeal.

It is a very magical tree, used for wands and amulets. A forked rowan branch can help find water; wands of the wood are used for knowledge, locating metal and general divination; this is the wood to use for making any magical tool that has anything to do with divining, invocation, and communication with the spirit realms. Perhaps more than any other tree, rowan has the ability to help increase one's psychic abilities, imparting a benevolent energy that enhances receptivity to visions and insights.

In mythology, the rowan is sacred to Brigid, or Bride, the Celtic fire goddess often depicted carrying a flaming torch of inspiration, and who is remembered in the first fire festival of the Celtic calendar, Imbolc. During this celebration, the druids would build towers of rowan and lie within them, entering into a meditative trance-like state. These rituals added to the tree's reputation for bestowing prophecy and spiritual insight.

Rowan berries bear the magical pentagram - an important symbol in magical traditions. The rowan berry has a tiny five-pointed star or pentagram opposite its stalk, which earned the tree its other title of 'Witch Tree'. It is thought that the rowan is a tree of enchantment, containing wood that can be used for Otherworldly magic. The druids burned its wood before a battle, in order to contact the fairies in the Otherworld to ask for their aid. This protective property perhaps also explains why it was worn, hung in doorways, or planted near houses to offer protection against evil forces.

ASH ✦ The ash tree is the immortal 'Tree of Life' and its winged seeds, called keys, represent the keys to Universal understanding and knowledge. One of the most significant trees in Celtic and Nordic traditions, ash is associated with the ever-living Yggdrasil Tree.

Ash offers healing, protection from outside influences, and powers of divination. Providing the ash tree finds itself rooted in ideal soil conditions, it can grow to a height (up to 25 metres) that nearly rivals even the mighty oak (up to 30 metres).

The thick trunk and pale colour of ash can make it appear fragile, grey and withered, but the wood is extremely strong and flexible, making it ideal for sports equipment such as hockey sticks or rowing oars.

A traditional wood of boat-builders, it is a tenacious tree which symbolises the meeting of Fire and Water, lightning and rain, and represents the awesome force and turbulence that results when two opposing elements join up (the ash rules the third month in the Celtic calendar, a wild seasonal time of rains, floods and storms). It is also associated with royalty, as its wood was often used in the making of thrones.

THE POWER OF LOVE

Each Sun sign exudes their own love and romance style. This style is an energy unique to that sign, and has the power to magnetise to that person their true, soulful match. Unhappy or unsuccessful relationships are often the result of incompatible Sun signs, personal values, goals, hopes, viewpoints, or expectations.

Everyone has a perfect soul partner (or three!) who is especially for them, and just knowing that special person or persons are out there can illuminate one's romantic path. In this lifetime, one may not find that person or persons, but can still experience the joys and wonders of many other significant relationships which enrich and add tremendous meaning to one's life.

Some partnerships are only fleeting, but the feelings they give can last a lifetime, while others are more enduring, and the rewards and lessons they give can last a lifetime too. Small gestures of love on a frequent basis, consistent nurturing and communication, and making the effort to understand each other, are some of the many ways to stoke the flames of passion and romance.

An individual's whole natal chart would need to be examined to form an overall picture of that person's romantic nature, and although the Sun is a fantastic starting point, it is not the sole consideration. Regarding other planets, in Carl Jung's studies on psychological astrology, and in traditional synastry (the comparing of two people's natal charts to determine overall compatibility), the harmonious link between the Sun in one person's chart and the Moon in the other's (usually the man's Sun and the woman's Moon) is considered the best indication for a happy and enduring relationship. More specifically, the sextile aspect, an angle of 60 degrees, appeared most frequently between the Sun of one and the Moon of the other in fulfilling relationships. Other positive planetary contacts, such as one person's Moon to another's Venus, or the Mars to the Moon (again, traditional indications of attraction and harmony) also occurred frequently.

The feminine personal planets in a male's chart (Moon and Venus), and the masculine personal planets in a female's chart (Sun and Mars) reveal a lot about the inner self and how this is projected onto relationships.

However helpful chart analysis is in telling a story about an individual's relationship style and approach, it all depends not on one's chart, but on what that person does with the resources at their disposal, which the birth chart can indeed reveal much about. Relationships and marriages involving harmonious planetary and zodiacal energies between the two people tend to last longer because they are in sync and simply flow.

Expanding upon the other planetary considerations is beyond the scope of this book, but it is useful to know, particularly if one is interested in examining the dynamics of a current relationship on a deeper level, or is wishing to attract love into one's life.

So, for the purposes of this book and its focus on Sun signs, the following information goes some way to exploring the love style and essence of each sign.

GENERAL LUCKY-IN-LOVE TIPS

✦ To attract and retain love, the Heart chakra (an energy centre within the body) needs to be balanced and clear from blockages. The Heart chakra is located in the region of the physical heart. Its Sanskrit name is anahata, and its symbol is a twelve-petal green lotus flower whose centre contains a green circle and two intersecting triangles making up a six-pointed star symbolising balance (and also could be said to represent six as the number of Venus). Its element is Air and its colour is green. Balance in this chakra is expressed as unconditional love for ourselves and others. Crystals that can be used to cleanse and balance this chakra are mostly green and pink stones.

- Pink candles (two, representing a couple, or six, representing Venus, is preferable) can be used in love spells.
- Any 'love-attracting' wishing rituals should be done on a Friday (ruled by Venus) night around the time of the New Moon (signifying the principles of increase, beginnings and growth).
- Basil, otherwise known as witch's herb or St Joseph's wort, is said to be the most potent lover herb of all. Basil vibrates to the energy of Mars, which is all about lust and sexual energy, and it is used prolifically in all sorts of love potions and rituals throughout the world.
- Ginger has a reputation as a potent sexual tonic and aphrodisiac*. Arousing and warm, it can increase sensual vitality, particularly in men. Being warming and spicy, its vibration aligns with Mars. Cardamom is said to have aphrodisiac qualities, and saffron is also regarded as a potent, albeit expensive, desire-enhancer!
- Heartsease, another name for the wild pansy, Latin Viola tricolour, was one of the most popular additives to the love potions of the ancient Romans and Greeks.
- Wear red and pink (associated with Mars and Venus respectively), as these colours in all their shades are said to incite passion, lust and romance. Green is also connected with the heart by virtue of its association with the Heart chakra and the planet Venus, and its links with fertility, nature, abundance and new growth.
- Call upon some higher spiritual help. When working your 'love magic', some planetary influences, goddesses and gods that you can call upon are Aphrodite, Venus and Eros/Cupid, and other lesser-known deities such as Juno Lucina, Demeter, Freya, Ishtar, Circe and Hathor.
- The planet Venus has developed a rich culture of gods and goddesses associated with her varying levels of love and passion. These include the virgin - Brighid; the fertile woman - Aphrodite, (the Greek goddess); and of course, Venus (Aphrodite's Roman equivalent); the mother and provider - Demeter; and desirous or physical love - Eros/Cupid (Venus's son).
- The pine tree is sacred to Adonis (Venus's lover) and is said to balance the male and female energies. Pine is cleansing and protective and, as an evergreen, symbolises life. Its cones represent fertility.

✦ The three almost universally recognised symbols of love are the goddesses Venus and Aphrodite, and the Cupid. Venus is the patroness of flowers and vegetation, and represents the regenerative cycle of creation, as well as beauty and physical love. She can be called upon for general love wishes and rituals. The dove, roses, rings, copper, apples, rosemary and the ankh are some of her sacred symbols. Aphrodite is a Greek goddess who has the ability to brings lovers together. Her name means 'of the sea' as she is believed to have been born of the foam of the ocean. She can be called upon in ceremonies and spells for affection, love, marriage and partnership. Some of her associated symbols are the Flower of Aphrodite, swans, dolphins, frankincense and myrrh. Cupid is the Roman name for the cherubic winged boy poised with a bow and arrow; Eros is the Greek equivalent. The son of Venus/Aphrodite, he is an aspect that represents lustful love and desire.

✦ In centuries past, when people were arguably more in tune with nature and its cycles, ceremonies, rituals and festivals were held on certain dates or times of year. The following are some examples; on these days their powers can be awakened through craft and ceremony: February 2 is Brighid's Day, or Bride's Day, and represents the white goddess; February 14 is Valentine's Day, traditionally the greatest and most well-known love 'celebration' of the year; March 1 is one of the festival days of Juno Lucina, the light bearer and goddess of women and marriage; the month of April is especially linked to the love goddess Aphrodite; the Summer solstice which falls on or around June 21 is an important time for reconnecting with the spirit of love, fertility and marriage; August 1 is the first of three harvest festivals in the Celtic calendar: The Harvest Festival honours Demeter, the goddess of love, as bountiful mother and faithful wife; the Festival of Lights, Diwali, in October, is sacred to Lakshmi, the Hindu goddess of happiness, love and good fortune; the Winter solstice which falls on or around December 21, marks the turning point from long dark nights to lengthening days, and is the time of the wheel of love when virgin goddesses gave birth to their children - it is also fittingly symbolised by evergreens such as pine, ivy and holly; in Mexico, December 31, the last night of the year, is traditionally 'wishing night' and is an opportune time to make a wish for a lover in the coming year, using evergreen branches to enhance the request.

'The term 'aphrodisiac' is derived from Aphrodite, the Greek goddess of love, beauty, lust and sensuality.

✦ GEMSTONES ✦

When it comes to calling love into your life using crystals, the general rule is that any of the pink or green stones are closely aligned with matters of the heart and can therefore help entice love and romance. Although each Sun sign has its very own special gemstones, outlined elsewhere, the following stones can be universally used by all the signs, as their energies and qualities contain the power to attract and create love in all its forms, from self-love to deeper soulful connections with another, or to enhance states of being that open the heart, thus increasing your abilities to magnetise love.

✦ Rose Quartz is the ultimate love stone. It invites love into your life by helping to open your heart to receive it, and gently reminding you that you are worthy of love. Connected with the Heart chakra, it is the stone of unconditional love, enhancing all forms of it and opening up the heart. It is excellent for increasing self-worth and acceptance. The colour of rose quartz is pink, the colour of Venus, the amorous planet and goddess of desire and nurturance. Balancing and calming, it helps to heal emotional pain. Wear this stone, keep some beside your bed, or sleep with a piece under your pillow to remind you that love it coming your way - and that you wholeheartedly deserve it!

✦ Green Aventurine is considered the 'opportunity and luck stone'. Connected with the Heart chakra, it helps us to recognise opportunities and is said to place us exactly where we need to be for good things to transpire, as energetically it opens our minds and hearts to increased perception so we can recognise lucky elements. It also promotes new growth, optimism, and is an overall attractor of good fortune, chance (serendipity) and abundance.

✦ Jade, on a spiritual level, has an affinity with the Heart chakra. It harmonises relationships, and encourages compassion and the establishment of strong bonds.

✦ Emerald is reputedly a stone of constancy in love, and is said to have been brought to Earth from the planet Venus. Because it is green, it also holds deep associations with the Heart chakra.

- ✦ Rhodochrosite and Pink Morganite can be used to attract one's soul mate. These stones, as with all pink stones, can be used as an effective love magnet. They encourage you to appreciate yourself by teaching you that you are worthy of love, wholeness and happiness - and so opening you up to receive.
- ✦ Malachite, Citrine, Rhodonite, Moonstone, Beryl (Emerald, Aquamarine, Morganite), Ruby, Mangano Calcite, Garnet, Red and Pink Tourmaline, Tugtupite, Rutilated Quartz, Lodestone, Peridot and Lapis Lazuli are also known for their love properties, and can be used or worn to invite romance into your life, or to bring and retain enduring love.
- ✦ Clear Quartz can be used with any of these listed crystals to amplify their metaphysical properties.
- ✦ Shells: Although shells are not technically a crystal by popular definition, they are associated with love and are sacred to Aphrodite, the Greek love goddess, and are often used in magic talismans to attract romance.

ARIES LOVE STONES ✦ **Bloodstone, Diamond, Aquamarine** ✦ Red Coral and Ruby are also useful in raising the Ram's attracting powers.

TAURUS LOVE STONES ✦ **Emerald, Sapphire, Diamond** ✦ Jade and Rose Quartz are also useful in raising the Bull's attracting powers.

GEMINI LOVE STONES ✦ **Alexandrite, Agate, Citrine** ✦ Emerald, Tourmaline, Chrysoprase, Pearl and Moonstone are also useful in raising the Twins' attracting powers.

CANCER LOVE STONES ✦ **Moonstone, Pearl, Ruby** ✦ Emerald is also useful in raising the Crab's attracting powers.

LEO LOVE STONES ✦ **Citrine, Ruby, Peridot** ✦ Onyx, Carnelian and Sardonyx are also useful in raising the Lion's attracting powers.

VIRGO LOVE STONES ✦ **Sapphire, Carnelian, Peridot, Sardonyx** ✦ Emerald is also useful in raising the Maiden's attracting powers.

LIBRA LOVE STONES ✦ **Opal, Tourmaline, Sapphire** ✦ Jade, Rose Quartz and Diamond are also useful in raising the Scales' attracting powers.

SCORPIO LOVE STONES ✦ **Topaz, Malachite, Peridot** ✦ Red Coral is also useful in raising the Scorpion's attracting powers.

SAGITTARIUS LOVE STONES ✦ **Topaz, Zircon, Turquoise** ✦ Yellow Sapphire and Amethyst are also useful in raising the Archer's attracting powers.

CAPRICORN LOVE STONES ✦ **Garnet, Turquoise, Smoky Quartz, Jet** ✦ Blue Sapphire is also useful in raising the Goat's attracting powers.

AQUARIUS LOVE STONES ✦ **Amethyst, Garnet, Aquamarine** ✦ Zircon and Jacinth are also useful in raising the Water Bearer's attracting powers.

PISCES LOVE STONES ✦ **Amethyst, Turquoise, Aquamarine, Bloodstone** ✦ Emerald and Sapphire are also useful in raising the Fishes' attracting powers.

HOW TO ATTRACT EACH SIGN

ARIES ✦ To attract an Aries, wear the colours red or orange, and use or wear the crystal diamond.

TAURUS ✦ To attract a Taurus, wear the colours pink or green, and use or wear the crystal rose quartz.

GEMINI ✦ To attract a Gemini, wear the colours light blue or yellow, and use or wear the crystal citrine.

CANCER ✦ To attract a Cancerian, wear the colours silver or white, and use or wear the crystal moonstone.

LEO ✦ To attract a Leo, wear the colours gold or orange, and use or wear the crystal ruby.

VIRGO ✦ To attract a Virgo, wear the colours white or yellow, and use or wear the crystal sapphire..

LIBRA ✦ To attract a Libran, wear the colours pink and blue, and use or wear the crystal opal.

SCORPIO ✦ To attract a Scorpio, wear the colours red or burgundy, and use or wear the crystal malachite.

SAGITTARIUS ✦ To attract a Sagittarius, wear the colour deep purple or royal blue, and use or wear the crystal zircon.

CAPRICORN ✦ To attract a Capricorn, wear the colours brown or black, and use or wear the crystal garnet.

AQUARIUS ✦ To attract an Aquarian, wear the colours electric blue or turquoise, and use or wear the crystal aquamarine.

PISCES ✦ To attract a Pisces, wear the colours mauve or sea green, and use or wear the crystal amethyst.

ARIES ✦ LOVE STYLE

Like all the fiery signs, Aries is a child at heart. This sometimes means he can be childish; at other times it means he's childlike in the most spirited, warm-hearted way.

Liz Greene

In her quote, Liz Greene encapsulates the Ram's trusting approach to affairs of the heart. A perpetual youth, his dynamism, enthusiasm and wonder for all things related to love, courtship and romance are characteristics that he spreads around like glitter and stardust wherever he goes. A jaded, cynical Aries doesn't exist, especially when it comes to love. The Ram's style in love is characterised by his all-or-nothing, bold, daring approach; he'll give all of himself to the one he sets his sights upon.

The Ram is somewhat a paradox, for although he is capable of profound thought, deep feelings and surprising tenderness, he is prone to spontaneously running off to embark on another adventure he deems equally important, leaving a trail of bewildered and confused lovers in his wake. But confusion need not be felt, for the Aries is a simple, soft soul with basic needs that are easily met, and when he's finished his round of crusades, he'll be duly back in the arms of his adored one in no time.

One shouldn't expect stable security, soothing caresses, or consistent contentment with the Aries partner, as he is far too excitable and restless for such sentiments. Moreover, fidelity is sometimes a challenge for the amorous, flirty Ram. He can suddenly bound away to greener pastures, for the simple reason that he's learned all he can from the current relationship, and feels the urge to seek a new teacher, lover, adventure, or affair.

The Ram is a surprising sensitive and vulnerable creature underneath the fearless façade he presents to the world, but it does not often occur to him that others have feelings too; Aries is known as selfish, but a gentler description would be that rather, he is self-centred and as egocentric as a young child.

An idealist at heart, he often courts the quintessential storybook romance, but does little to sustain this romance should it come along because he becomes bored so easily. Although he can be infuriatingly dizzying and impetuous at times, he still loves having someone special to come home to, someone who keeps the home fires burning while he himself takes charge of the fires burning outside of the home.

The Aries heart always beats fast a little faster than all the other zodiac signs, especially when his passions are stirred by a new love interest. There is nothing more exuberant, more illuminous, than the Aries whose heart has been captured.

Aries likes to take the initiative and to conquer with blind enthusiasm; indeed, falling in love at first sight comes as naturally to him as eating and breathing.

Dynamic, confident and exciting, Aries adores the thrill of the chase and is the zodiac's Knight (or Queen) in shining armour! A loyal and ardent lover, he is passionate and untainted, uncomplicated and fun, childlike and adventurous; love is either a daring adventure to him, or nothing at all.

Refreshingly naïve and innocent, the Ram doesn't typically use manipulating or clever mind games, as he'd prefer to get straight to the point; direct is his way, pure and simple. Overall, Ariens are incurable romantics who just love to love. Love is, after all, life's grandest adventure to this all-conquering romance-addict.

TAURUS ✦ LOVE STYLE

There's nothing small about Taurus,
including her capacity for lasting love.
Linda Goodman

Taurus, ruled by the planet of love Venus, is the most in love with love of all the zodiac signs (including the diehard romance-seeking Libran).

Taureans need - and crave - security, affection and stability like no other sign. Because she is so very conscious of stability, it is a rare Taurean who has fleeting or numerous back-to-back love affairs. Sensuous and tactile, she is strongly attracted to love interests, but will never engage in aggressive pursuit of anybody, preferring to passively attract others to her using her natural, gentle charm.

Seductive and sensuous yet faithful and reliable, she is a good-natured, caring lover with a strong sense of family and the need for quiet and peace in her life.

The Taurus female particularly can unequivocally be called a lady. She has a strong feminine vibration, good taste and a pronounced sense for harmony and comfort. Effortless charm and grace are strong features of Taureans of any gender, and although she is rarely averse to flirtation, she will not give her heart or soul to another until she knows that any potential partner is genuine and in it for the long haul.

An enduring and loyal partner, the Bull never wishes to be involved in an open relationship arrangement, as this does not suit her style and inherent need for stability, consistency and security.

Easy-going but steadfast, if her partner makes her feel insecure or demands too much freedom, she may just show them the door; however, she is unlikely to attract this type of partnership in the first place.

Her feelings are strong, deep, sincere and for the most part silent; she does not conquer by storm or force, but rather romantically, tenderly and sentimentally.

Ruled by her senses, touch, cuddling, affection and physical closeness are very important to the Taurean, and an undemonstrative partner will leave her cold. Protection and economic security are also vital to her wellbeing in any partnership, so she often unconsciously seeks out a partner who can provide for and protect her, or at least a partner who she herself can provide for and protect - the nurturing instinct comes naturally to her, and being a homemaker is compatible with her domestic-loving nature.

Although stubborn and sometimes overly rooted in the one spot, her dependability, warmth and big-heartedness in relationships is second to none, as long as she has a partner who shares similar qualities and values.

GEMINI ♦ LOVE STYLE

He's truly the Mercurius of alchemy, the translator and the transformer, for he can show with the magic wand of his wit the distant mountain heights where the air is clear.

Liz Greene

It's true that when you're in love with a Gemini you won't walk alone. You most certainly won't. You'll have at least two people to walk with you - and both of them will be him. He was born under the sign of the Twins, you know. In his case, they're never identical Twins ... (for) the dual nature of Gemini combines two completely different personalities.

Linda Goodman

To the Twins, love is one big magical carpet ride through a sparkling, star-spangled galaxy. Essentially, either a daring adventure, or nothing at all. Hot and cold, up and down, in and out characterises the typical Gemini's nature in romantic endeavours, which usually drives their lovers crazy.

Life devoid of romantic fun, magical unions and grand-scale love affairs is like champagne without bubbles to the Gemini spirit, and being such a flirt who loves to bedazzle, outwit and impress others, he rarely fails to attract many and varied admirers and experiences of the heart.

The Gemini's ideal partner is likely to be younger and the match based on affection and companionship and a 'meeting of the minds' rather than deep, sentimental romantic love. He secretly prefers friendship over love, and his chosen partner should always be a friend as well as lover.

To Gemini, emotions are at best illogical and at worst downright useless, yet he often has an uncanny and inexplicable way of attracting feeling types, who both fascinate and terrify him at the same time. Emotional or not, if his partner can understand that Gemini is the flittery butterfly of the zodiac and allows for freedom of mobility accordingly, he will derive a sense of satisfaction from his partnerships. But often he will infuriate his lovers by not extending the same considerations and by being impossible to pin down; however, he easily wins them back over with his youthful wit and charm.

Gemini is never quite ready to become too deeply involved. Seeing so many choices, he hesitates to commit himself, for by fixing himself on one thing, he's afraid he might miss something better, which is why his emotional exchanges so often only skim the surface, even when he is a fully-fledged grown-up.

Romance to the Twins is one big, amusing game. Once and if he does marry, however, he has the potential to make a committed, if a little inconsistent marital partner, and if the partner accommodates him with enough freedom and space, he can settle down contentedly.

Minding his wandering ways is a helpful lifelong lesson for the Gemini to learn, to ensure he has fulfilling and not just fleeting, empty relationships. Gemini would also benefit by taking a pot or two off the boil occasionally, and not becoming so busy and scattered that he neglects to spend quality time with his beloved.

Incredibly open and friendly, he may also come across as insincere to more scrupulous love-seekers who are wanting stability and consistency.

As a lover and in relationships, Gemini is generally afraid of deep emotional involvement and may find it difficult to sustain close relationships, because this may mean toning down his lifestyle to accommodate the needs of another. But with the right amount of understanding from a tolerant partner, Gemini can truly flourish in relationships, bringing much to the table in terms of fun, ideas, friendship and social networks.

Perhaps Linda Goodman summed it up best when she stated, "Loving a Gemini is easy and fun, if you don't try to get too close. There's an inner core that belongs only to him, that he'll never share with another human being, even you. Keep things cool and light, and don't be overly passionate or dramatic." After all, for the Twins, love is indeed to be enjoyed for what he perceives its best features to be: edgy, breezy, flirty and above all, fun!

CANCER ✦ LOVE STYLE

To Cancer, one of the most romantic of the zodiac signs, love is tender, sentimental and as essential to life as breathing. In a true Cancerian, love has a lot to do with security, for this is the most sensitive and safety-seeking of the signs, especially when it comes to romance.

Self-sacrificing, devoted, faithful, intuitive and responsive to her partner's needs, she is also vulnerable and private; to truly open her heart to another, a Cancerian must trust that person above all else. Although emotional and exquisitely sensitive, the Crab rarely shows her feelings openly, so she may mask her emotions, be fearful of rejection and afraid to trust readily; but once she feels secure in a relationship, her love is deep, generous, giving and intensely loyal.

She loves to be adored, cherished and reassured; and she adores, cherishes and reassures in abundance in return. Nobody gives cuddles, affection and love like a Cancerian whose heart has been opened.

Kindness and sympathy are never in short supply when she is involved in a relationship, and although capable of intense passion, she is considerably discerning about where and with whom that passion is expressed; hers is a heart hard-won. And though she is notoriously slow to bare her soul, once exposed, it is a richly rewarding experience for the recipient.

With the ever-shifting moods of the Cancerian, some lovers may find her an enigma. But with the right, understanding partner, they will be able to accurately interpret that sulkiness means she feels rejected, clinginess means she needs assurance, possessiveness means she needs a deeper commitment, silence can signify fear, and crabbiness can mean she feels underappreciated. In fact, her moods and feelings are so all-consuming that it is difficult for even herself to know where one ends and a new one begins.

Overall, however, Cancer's loyalty is inextricably linked to her deep yearning for security, which provides the basis for all her relationships and without which she will seek it elsewhere. But in any case, no separation is ever easy on her delicate, sensitive soul, even if she secretly longs for freedom. After all, attachment and sheltered, safe love to her are as essential as her element Water is to life.

LEO ✦ LOVE STYLE

Love makes the world go round for the big-hearted, bold, amorous Lion. Profoundly romantic and generous with his affections, one of his main ways of demonstrating love is to lavish gifts on his partner. If his gifts – including those of love, affection, time - are received well and appreciated, he will be chuffed, if not, he will feel put out.

Above all, Leos need attention, praise, adoration and respect from their lovers - and indeed, everyone, regardless of relationship status. Extremely loyal and faithful once committed, he plays the role of lover perfectly. Anyone who does not reciprocate these qualities tends to put his Fire out, for detached, aloof, distant and hard-to-get types are not his style.

To Leo, love is a creative act, and something which must be constantly shown and shared with each other through the exchange of gestures, play, cuddles and of course sex: Leo is, after Scorpio, possibly the most ardent sign of the zodiac.

Leo is a supportive and encouraging, if not a little bossy and possessive, lover. He likes to play hard, love hard and work hard, so his friends and lovers must always slot into his hectic schedule. If they can handle his larger-than-life lifestyle, then his heart will be won over.

But Leo also needs to know when and how to compromise. Sharing the stage is not his forte, but when he allows others to occasionally make some of the plans and run the show at least some of the time, his romantic ride will be a lot smoother and easier. His need to dominate and take position at centre stage can be off-putting for more reticent types, but if his lover can accommodate his need to win and to shine, the Leo will be one happy pussycat.

His spontaneity and affectionate, romantic nature will invariably attract many admirers throughout his life. Showy and passionate, he makes for a stylish partner whose attitude to love is one of great artistry and skill. Deeply protective and proud of his partner, he will defend them fiercely and without reservation. But in return, he expects the loyalty and unwavering fidelity of his beloved.

And once he has found that special someone to whom he can give and take all of the above, he is both in for an exciting magical carpet ride of exquisite fun, unequalled love and grand adventure.

VIRGO ✦ LOVE STYLE

Most Virgos wear their heart firmly in their heads, not on their sleeves. Her willingness to advise, help and take on responsibilities is her way of showing love to her partner. Sometimes, in her sincere attempts to improve the life of her beloved, she may be a little critical, picky, pedantic and prone to worry, because even her love life isn't immune to her innate tendency to discern, dissect and analyse. But the rewards for the other person are immense, as she is a devoted, dedicated, considerate and deeply caring lover when her heart has found its home. Although sensual and feeling in romance, the other person has to be exactly the right fit to suit the Virgo's inherently fussy tastes and perfectionist nature.

Sometimes lacking in warmth and spontaneity, overt displays of attention and affection may unnerve Virgo; and in any case, she would much rather a meeting of the minds than anything else. Once she feels she has a mental rapport with a prospective lover, she will willingly be led to the next level - proving herself to be a beautifully skilful and sensuous giver of love behind the rather cool facade.

The Virgin may be aloof and mistrustful, and she will rarely put her emotional cards on the table or reveal her heart's longings prematurely, but once trust is won, she can unleash an unrivalled albeit discreet charm and incredible sensuality.

She will be unerringly attentive and dutiful towards her lover, and if loved properly in return, provide a stable, organised, solid foundation from which the relationship can grow and thrive.

Despite her steadfast faithfulness to her relationships, she would rather spend her life alone than opt for second best - and will choose to remain that way until she finds The One.

Although not known to be extreme, she also doesn't tend to do things by halves, and gives her full heart and soul to any relationship she deems worthy.

Virgo needs to beware of becoming overly picky and finding fault, for this will only serve to isolate her and ultimately lead to loneliness, anxiety, insecurity and even despair. In a truly contented Virgo, love will burn like a steady, slow-burning flame, spreading warmth, reliability and constancy.

Ultimately, she takes seriously and solemnly the promise "'til death do us part" - rarely, if ever, letting her partner down. It might be a tough gig to win over the Virgo's hard-cased heart, but once won, she will provide a deep, rich, sensual experience that is not easily forgotten.

LIBRA ✦ LOVE STYLE

Libra is the sign of marriage and partnership, so there is no desire to live alone. A completely harmonious love match is essential for the soul in Libra, and this is often attained to a degree rarely achieved by other signs.
Patricia Crowther

Love to Libra is like breathing is to life. To Libra love is open, harmonious and flowing, and he comes across as glamorously ethereal. As a lover and in relationships, he adores being in love and is accordingly accommodating and compromising.

Ruled by the planet of love Venus, Libra has a gift for both fine arts of living and loving. Cultured, stylish and seductive, he glides through life with effortless grace and breezy charm, attracting many admirers along the way. This is no surprise, given that he's the zodiac's biggest flirt.

Since he strives for a harmonic and peaceful coexistence with another, he uses his diplomacy and tact to get along wonderfully with all other signs. His biggest snag may be the fact he is so indecisive - one can sometimes wait a long time for Libra to offer a genuine emotional response, as he will put off making decisions or choices of any kind for as long as he can.

And so enchanted with the idea of love is Libra, that he may settle for Mr or Ms Right or Wrong because he is so easily swept away with romance. For this reason, many Librans will probably encounter at least one divorce in their lifetime, because their decisions are often based on keeping the peace and harmony-at-all-costs, and by the time they realise they've chosen the wrong partner, it may be too late when they find themselves in a marriage for the sake of being married.

More than any other sign, Libra is bound to be a sucker for nuptials and the glitz, romance and glamour of a wedding ceremony and honeymoon.

Fidelity may also be an issue for the flirty Libran, as he loves to circulate largely and widely amongst as many people as possible and often, particularly in his younger years, finds it hard to be 'tied down' in an exclusive relationship. This is due to his Airy nature, which lends him an air of endearing detachment and yearning for social connection.

Overall, Libra is capable of putting an enormous amount of energy and effort into his relationships, his need for harmony and balance so pronounced, that he may compromise to a fault. But in any case, Libra is the master of relationships and intuitively knows a lot about them, not through experience necessarily but through an inborn, natural knowing - and his partner is usually the lucky beneficiary of this skill.

The Scales may occasionally just need to be reminded that discussing love is not the same thing as demonstrating, feeling, showing and emoting it; he is, after all, an Air sign who resides largely in the mind space of intellect and logic, which holds no place for deep sentiments and emotional attachments. Hiding behind a captivatingly aloof façade, however intriguing, will only take him so far in matters of the heart; he needs to learn the all-important art of expressing a broader scope of emotions to ensure the stability he craves and ultimately, true success in love.

SCORPIO ✦ LOVE STYLE

It can be said that Scorpio is capable of the most intense and impassioned depth of feeling... The love nature expresses a profound fidelity and mirrors the truth: 'Love is strong as death. Many waters cannot quench love, neither can the floods drown it'.
Patricia Crowther

To Scorpio love is an intense journey of explosive passions and profundity.

Eroticism, kinky curiosities and tantric practices are likely to be a feature in the Scorpio's love life.

Her notorious passion may not always be expressed in the expected ways however, for sexuality to her largely revolves around emotions, and is the outer expression of her deep-running feelings.

Many Scorpios have a deep mystical sense of romance, sex and other matters of the heart and flesh, often viewing them as having to do less with the physical body and much more to do with the soul. Scorpio has the urge to merge, but in a deeper, more complex way than the preceding Libra. In any case, Plutonian types frequently enjoy strong and enduring relationships, which may be marked by power plays, secrecy, mysteries, and ultimately in its highest expression, personal transformation for both parties.

Scorpio doesn't do things by halves in life or love; she is in it with all her heart, or not in it at all. Grey simply doesn't exist to Scorpio; she paints only in stark blacks and whites.

Although essentially mistrustful and suspicious, once the Scorpio does surrender to another, she is faithful, loyal, deeply caring and emotionally involved. But she is the most complex and enigmatic of the zodiac, so may perplex her lover with her cool, secretive demeanour, turbulent undercurrents and rampant fantasies.

Cautious, probing and obsessive, it is not above the Scorpion to scan her lovers' phone records, snoop around in her partner's social media accounts, or investigate their computer history to investigate their movements, for she needs to know the why, when, how and where of everything in her union before fully entrusting her heart to another.

Her pressing desire to be the complete master of the love game can also be difficult to understand for more simple, superficial types, and her tendency to control and possess can make her partner want to wriggle free. Like her watery counterpart the Crab, Scorpio will grab on with both pincers and refuse to let go, especially if she believes the object of her affections is worth holding on to.

Whether she is the smouldering breed of Scorpio, or the more overtly explosive type, one thing is guaranteed in all her relationships - they will never be experienced superficially, and they are always experienced deeply. No one experiences a relationship with a Scorpio without changing - including the Scorpio herself - in some profound way; indeed, truly, madly, deeply.

SAGITTARIUS ✦ LOVE STYLE

To Sagittarius love is open and friendly, a wild adventure to be relished, explored and enjoyed. However ardent and enthusiastic he is, as a lover and in relationships, his freedom and independence will always come first, and need to be honoured and respected by any partner willing to undertake the bold carpet ride experience the Sagittarius promises.

The Archer is willing to contribute much to the union and provide the relationship with excitement, novelty, stimulation and refreshing honesty. The marked idealism that characterises the typical Sagittarian also flourishes in love; in matters of the heart, he is full of hope, optimism and great expectations.

Fun-loving and sociable, he usually fares best with a tolerant, self-sufficient partner who offers a large degree of space; in return, the Archer will be a committed, contented and passionate partner.

If tolerance is not present from his lover, his non-committal, flighty side will reign supreme and he will invariably seek broader horizons.

An incurable flirt and witty charmer, Sagittarius wins over all types with his noble, generous spirit, gregarious nature and inborn 'gift of the gab,' so he will rarely have trouble attracting admirers. While this is flattering, it can pose some obvious issues if the Archer in question is already in an exclusive relationship.

Of all the zodiac signs, Sagittarius is the most likely to have a wandering eye and an impulse to roam. In many ways a status of singleness, casual relationships or non-marriage suits the free-spirited Archer, as he likes to be able to wriggle free with a minimum of fuss if it no longer fits.

With a larger-than-life intellect, his endless questing for meaning and truth can sometimes send partners into a spin. Insecure, jealous, clingy types or homebodies have almost zero chance with the Archer, because of his innate love of travel and personal freedom.

Reliability is not one of his strong points, and his reckless streak may make lovers anxious, so if in a relationship it is important that the Sagittarius curbs any careless behaviour and exercises greater consideration and self-control. Although rarely selfish or tactless on purpose, his bluntness and directness in both words and actions can inadvertently hurt those he loves.

While this sounds like the Archer is a less than ideal lover, quite the opposite is true. If his partner respects his needs and wanderlust, he has the potential to be a warm, caring and attentive partner.

Ultimately, the Sagittarius prefers not to commit himself devotedly to one partner, for he is the quintessential free spirit, on par with Aquarius, whose love of travel, adventure and knowledge has him heading in all directions and extremely difficult to pin down; to be truly happy, Sagittarius must be allowed to move through life and its myriad experiences untrammelled and answerable to no one.

If his union can withstand all of the above, it can bear anything, and would be greatly enhanced if he allowed his lovers to share that wild ride across the galaxy with him.

Heavy, intense, or overly sensitive lovers also need not apply for his affections, as these drain the Archer's spirited energy, making him run for the nearest exit at lightning speed. And if he makes it to the exit and out, we all know what happens to the intrepid Archer... he'll head straight for the endless horizon, and you won't see him for dust.

CAPRICORN ✦ LOVE STYLE

Loyalty, protection, help and considered advice are facets of the Capricorn's understated way of demonstrating affection to her partner.

Careful and cautious in her selection of a mate, she prefers long-term commitments and devotion over flings and flirty dalliances, however tempting.

Conquering a Capricorn is no mean feat, seeing the Goat is a discerning and cool customer. Generally reserved, often downright sceptical, and perhaps a little shy when it comes to being wooed, Capricorn is notoriously difficult to please. But once her heart is captured, she is unflinchingly devoted, loving and giving.

If she is the pursuer, she will use every charm in the book to perfection to win over the heart of her desired - and to great effect, because her perseverance and stamina is second to none, and she will not stop until she achieves her ultimate aims.

If she is rejected, she tends to be resilient, possessing a profound and enviable inner strength that is sometimes misconceived as coldness. It is not that she is cold, but rather she is strong and stoic in the face of love-gone-wrong, picking herself up swiftly and continuing the climb.

Despite her well-known self-control and caution in romance, she can be very sentimental and warm when her heart is opened by love. A gentle, sensual lover, she usually holds high regard for family and find it important to honour her duties, obligations and commitments to her special loved one when they become family.

It is a rare Capricorn who believes in love at first sight, as all decisions of the heart need to be well thought out and she doesn't enter amorous adventures light-heartedly as most other signs do. She is solemn in life and love, and takes promises - including those of marriage - seriously.

Capricorn keeps her cards close to her chest and her heart well off her sleeve, until she can trust enough to let her inner warmth shine through. She is also surprisingly tender, given her tough-as-steel exterior, and makes a delightful and dedicated partner whose feelings run much deeper than others would know.

When Capricorn gives away her heart fully, it is usually forever. She places more value on respect, duty, loyalty and the power of the family bond than she does on wild passion, grand love and frivolous adventures.

Secretly, every Goat seeks out, whether consciously or not, a partner who is successful or ambitious in some way, one who is like-minded, and who can ultimately provide her with the security and stability she so craves in love and life. If she can unpeel her suit of armour, relinquish control, loosen up, accept sympathy, reveal vulnerabilities, receive affection readily, share her dry wit, unleash her unerring devotion, and surrender to deep trust, her relationships will become richer and more fulfilling. And seeing she is usually so 'old' and wise in spirit, if she can find someone who can help her free her inner child to romp and play more openly and freely, she may just have found her perfect complementary match!

AQUARIUS ✦ LOVE STYLE

A union with an Aquarian will be different from any other relationships one has known. This has the advantage that boredom and routine are excluded to a large degree, but simultaneously the disadvantage that the Water Bearer's long-suffering partner may never quite know what's going on.

Anyone who falls in love with this creature-like-no-other should be prepared for everything and anything, except a steady, predictable, slow-paced life! Therefore, the lover of an Aquarian needs to be extremely flexible and tolerant of his many whims, unique quirks and fanciful ideals. Living in a world of ideas rather than emotions, he tends to feel decidedly uncomfortable with feelings and to accordingly repress any feelings that might rise to the surface.

Charmingly naïve in most romantic adventures, he is often sincere to the extent that he doesn't even know when someone is attracted to him, and he is incapable of playing the Smooth Lover role unless he really means it.

Romantic escapades are not this cool character's style, for he is often awkward, lacking in confidence and unsure of himself. However, he is a truly interesting companion and utterly intriguing lover, keeping his partners on their toes at all times. Of course, given his enchanting innocence, this is never deliberate, it's just the way life is with an Aquarian partner.

To Uranian-ruled Aquarius, love is generally open, flowing and friendly, but he may come across as glamorously aloof and nonchalant, which can be confusing and exasperating to more sensitive souls.

In love, this free spirit is generally afraid of deep emotional involvement and thus may find it challenging to sustain close relationships, because this means adjusting his lifestyle to accommodate the needs of another. Extremely faithful once committed, Aquarius is a formidable force in the loyalty department, especially when his lover also doubles up as his friend. Indeed, love and friendship are one and the same to the Water Bearer, and he will delight his partners with surprises and lashings of help or advice, but he also has the tendency to suddenly disappear from life's circuit and immerse himself in his own inner world, or in a project he feels passionate about. And hell hath no fury like an Aquarian torn away from a special cause.

Notoriously cool, detached and a little zany, his unpredictable nature also means he can suddenly defrost without warning and be very fiery-passionate. Because being odd is so very normal to the Aquarius, he will thrill his lover with unusual gifts, then forget the 'normal' events like birthday presents and anniversary dates.

In any close relationship he naturally guards his independence and freedom, and would rather fly solo forever than to be with an incompatible partner for the sake of avoiding loneliness. In fact, loneliness isn't even in the Aquarian vocabulary; it's blissful solitude all the way with this proud Lone Ranger. Such is his need for ample and regular personal space, the typical Water Bearer often enjoys unconventional or living-apart relationships. Any heavy emotional demands, possessive behaviour, dramatic scenes, or overt expressions of sentimentality will have him packing his bags and climbing out the nearest window in no time. In fact, he prefers his partner to do the lion's share of domestic chores, as housework hinders his much-valued liberty.

Overall, if this relationship is based on friendship, it is more likely to endure than one that is only based on passion or lust. After all, for the Aquarian union with another to stand the test of time, lust, passion and sex need the solid base of friendship from which to grow.

PISCES ✦ LOVE STYLE

Love is life's great secret. It transcends fear and isolation, guiding you beyond the shadows of sentiment, to the shores of boundless being.
Dan Millman, Pisces

There is a quality in Pisces which is essentially untouched and unpossessable, no matter how formal the contract is, no matter how long you've known (her). Some part of Pisces will always belong to the cosmos, to (her) own inner self, but not to you.
Liz Greene

It's true to say that a long-term relationship is rarely experienced by the Piscean. The innate aura of sadness and disappointment with humanity as a whole is often present and lingers into old age. This is because the soul is finely tuned and ever conscious of its links with more perfect planes of being.
Patricia Crowther

People born under the sign of the Fish tend to have mixed fortunes in relationships. They are frequently a challenge to understand or truly know, and even harder to hold onto, such are their slippery, elusive natures. Moreover, she tends to choose difficult partners, sometimes hopeless or hapless others, whom she will try to nurture back to 'normality' or rescue in some way. However the Piscean chooses to walk her Life Path, she is usually in love, whether it be with a person, an ideal, an idea, a deity, or a pipedream - anything that makes her feel less alone - for it is almost impossible for the Piscean to conceive of a life on her own.

Pisces tends to lack common sense when feelings are involved or aroused; she is gullible, impressionable and sometimes foolish in her romantic choices. But if she can find the right partner, she'll grow immensely in character and emotional fulfilment.

Although Pisceans can be relatively difficult to pin down, once a relationship is well established, feelings are likely to run deep and be lifelong. The Fish's love is so readily poured into a romance that it can be all-engulfing and overwhelming - for all parties - at times, but if she is able to take charge of her emotions, she can bring something very special, ethereal and magical to the partnership.

She tends to wear rose-coloured glasses and to place her lovers on a high pedestal, making her particularly vulnerable to deceit or being taken advantage of should she leave her hazy specs on for too long, or worse, refuse to take them off.

Sexually, Pisces is more likely to be tender, sensual and romantic rather than passionate, lustful, or spontaneous.

Sensitive and subtly temperamental, she needs a partner who believes in the same magic as she does, who desires to share similar experiences, and is on the same fairytale page right up to the happy ending. Above all, she seeks a lover who is tolerant, calm and stable, to offset her whims, inconsistencies and dreaminess. It also helps if her partner is as creative and fanciful as she is, because someone with artistic leanings is more likely to understand her shifting moods and changeable, chameleon-like temperament.

Being born under a Pisces Sun, her actions and decisions are motivated primarily by feelings, impressions, emotions and intuitive impulses, a drawback being that this makes her vulnerable to every influence in her environment, both good and bad; her whole being is receptive to changes of atmosphere and she is easily swept off her feet or out to sea. Consequently, undesirable associations may have an adverse effect on her soul. Pisces, being the most flexible of all the signs, makes her very adaptable, and to her credit, she can adjust to relationship changes, fluctuations and cycles better than most.

Although possessing loads of sympathy and compassion for her lovers, she may flounder when it comes to taking positive action. Some of the weaknesses of Pisces are a timid, self-effacing attitude and a tendency to apologise or constantly make excuses. Indecision is also a Piscean fault, and by stalling or succumbing to confusion, she risks missing out on love opportunities altogether. Being so sensitive, she is likely to find it difficult to cope with the harsher realities of this materialistic world, with its tensions, struggles and fierce competitiveness. As a result, she may retreat into her relationships hoping to find salvation, even if and when they are less than ideal, and this is where a latent co-dependent streak may rise to the surface, to the detriment of the relationship.

A born idealist, the Fish possesses a vivid imagination, so she often has her head in the clouds, but on the plus side, has the ability to 'dream' a lover right into her life.

Despite – or perhaps because of - her overly trusting nature and unshakeable belief in love, Pisces are great romantics at heart and make exquisite and caring partners, but they do need time out just for themselves from time to time, as the tendency to become overwhelmed necessitates a retreat into solitude for the delicate Piscean.

Being the recipient of a Piscean's feelings can be the most healing and regenerative relationship one can experience; the only condition is to never trample on her dreams or ridicule her ideals; if one can do this, they will be richly rewarded with the generous and abundant romance she is so capable of giving. She may even give you her entire Universe, stars and all.

TAROT CARDS ✦ FOR LUCK, MAGIC, ENERGY, ABUNDANCE, QUESTING & MEANING

Tarot and astrology are inextricably linked. All the cards of the Major Arcana, which comprises 22 of the Tarot's 78 cards, are 'ruled by' or connected with either a planet or luminary, one of the twelve zodiac signs, and/or one of the four elements.

The Major Arcana cards contain the richest symbolism of all the cards in the Tarot deck, each carrying a myriad of messages for the reader to decipher. The symbolism contained within these images represents the archetypal aspects of one's character. It also describes the path the soul takes through each stage of life, revealing clues through which one can explore different parts of the Self.

Each card also represents an aspect of the universal human experience and has a name that either directly conveys the meaning of the card, such as Strength or Justice, or depicts individuals that represent these human archetypes, such as the Hermit or the Empress.

The illustrations on each card contain one or more figures, and tuning into a card's imagery enables one to grasp its meaning intuitively. Considerations include the demeanour of the characters, whether it is day or night, the background, any symbols, buildings, colours, vegetation, weather, and the prevailing season.

Every card has its own story to impart, and through entering that story one can gain deeper insights into the full picture of one's journey so far, as well as illuminating the path ahead.

There are three cards for each sign (except Scorpio, Capricorn & Pisces, which have four, two and four respectively), all of which have links to that zodiac sign, whether through the sign's rulership of that card (the first one listed for each sign), or connections with its ruling planet or element. For example, Aries's special cards are the Emperor, the Tower and Judgement. The Emperor is ruled by Aries in traditional tarot systems, the Tower is linked with Aries's ruler Mars, and Judgement is linked with Aries's element, Fire. The particular cards listed for each sign will have special meaning for that sign, and often carries powerful messages and resonant lessons for the individual to reflect upon.

SPECIAL TAROT CARDS FOR EACH SIGN

ARIES ✦ The Emperor, the Tower & Judgement.

TAURUS ✦ The Hierophant, the Empress & the World.

GEMINI ✦ The Lovers, the Magician & the Fool.

CANCER ✦ The Chariot, the High Priestess & the Moon.

LEO ✦ Strength, the Sun, Judgement.

VIRGO ✦ The Hermit, the Magician & the World.

LIBRA ✦ Justice, the Empress & the Fool.

SCORPIO ✦ Death, Judgement, the Tower & the High Priestess.

SAGITTARIUS ✦ Temperance, Wheel of Fortune & Judgement.

CAPRICORN ✦ The Devil & the World.

AQUARIUS ✦ The Star, the Fool & the World.

PISCES ✦ The Moon, the Hanged Man, Wheel of Fortune & the High Priestess.

✦ THE EMPEROR ✦

Keywords ✦ Discipline, Authority, Structure.

Number ✦ 4

Astrological Signs ✦ Aries & Scorpio.

Key Themes ✦ Authority, Father, Boss, Material Wealth & Status, Leadership, The Power to Influence, Organisation, Logic, Structure, Certainty, Discipline, Temporal Power, Action, Energy, Assertiveness, Material & Moral Power, Strength of Character, Concrete Realism, Objectivity, Willpower, Stoicism.

✦ HOW THIS CARD RELATES TO ARIES ✦

The Emperor, master and commander, is assigned to Aries, the sign of leadership. Look for the images of the Aries Ram on your Emperor card.

Corrine Kenner

The leader of the pack, the Emperor typifies the Aries personality: bold, courageous, decisive, confident, fearless, masculine and in firm control. A master and commander, a no-nonsense visionary and an aspiring as well as accomplished conqueror, the Emperor is strong, direct, forceful and pioneering in his governance.

Like Aries, the Emperor rules with his head, not his heart. He never questions or doubts himself, is hot-headed and brash, and he forges ahead into new territories with all the vigour of a youthful warrior. An initiator and self-starter, the motivated Emperor and Aries both share the qualities of passion, status and power.

The Emperor is authoritative, bossy, wilful, self-assured and doesn't indulge in petty emotions - much like the spirit of the Ram himself. And although idealistic, arduous and adventurous, the typical Arien is, like the Tarot's Emperor, ultimately ruled by reason over emotions, and logic over intuition. Aries is, after all, the born ruler who is always - and desires to be - in steely control, admired, respected and above all, an effective, headstrong, unrivalled and unconquerable leader. Considering this, the Emperor and the Aries could well be one and the same.

Ariens are recommended to carry one of these cards with them to illumine their paths, to magnetise that for which they are asking, and to help claim the magic that is their birth gift, using the symbolism of the Emperor as a guide.

✦ THE HIEROPHANT ✦

Keywords ✦ Advice, Wisdom, Counsel, Enlightenment.

Number ✦ 5

Astrological Signs ✦ Taurus.

Key Themes ✦ Search for Meaning in Life, Leaning towards Spiritual Enlightenment, Mentors & Guides, Traditional Viewpoints or Methods, Schools, Spiritual Institutions & Organisations, Spiritual Wisdom & Development, Questing, Learning, Benevolence, Stability, Rigidity, An Experienced, Older Man, Sense of Right & Wrong.

✦ HOW THIS CARD RELATES TO TAURUS ✦

The Hierophant, the keeper of tradition, is assigned to Taurus, the sign of stability, luxury and pleasure.

Corrine Kenner

Much like Taurus in the zodiacal context, the Hierophant is the quiet but all-powerful force of the Tarot experience. Deeply rooted in tradition, he adheres to imposed, structured, consistent rules.

Like the Bull, the Hierophant is unmoveable and unaffected, like a solid mountain or rock, and his consistency and sound counsel are both comforting and enlightening to the recipient.

A guardian of time-honoured and long-standing values, beliefs, rituals and practices, the Hierophant holds true and faithful to his spiritual principles, providing a stellar example of stability and convention. Loyal, dedicated and enduring, both Taurus and the Hierophant can be rocks of solidarity, assurance and comfort during difficult or uncertain times.

Taurus is seldom a rebel, and will rarely seek to overthrow what is already established, or even something with which she does not agree, just like the Hierophant, for their Path is one of peace, reliability, balance, harmony and security.

Her - like the Hierophant's - advice is simple: Live life peacefully, stay on your rightful Path, give guidance when asked, do the right thing at all times, practice kindness, acceptance and compassion, and always practice proven traditional methods, which will keep you grounded, stable and loving towards all. And indeed, on some deep primal and spiritual level, we all need the safety, shelter and sanctity both Taurus and the Hierophant can provide.

Taureans are recommended to carry one of these cards with them to illumine their paths, to magnetise that for which they are asking, and to help claim the magic that is their birth gift, using the symbolism of the Hierophant as a guide.

✦ THE LOVERS ✦

Keywords ✦ Choices, Options, Opposites.

Number ✦ 6

Astrological Signs ✦ Gemini.

Key Themes ✦ Choice, Desire, Decision, Temptations, Union, Reconciliation, Harmony, Sacrifice, Indecision, Trials & Options Linked to Relationships, Relationship Decisions Resulting in Stability, A Return to Good Health, Carefully Weighing Options, Need for Balance, Marriage & Weddings, Complementary Opposites.

✦ HOW THIS CARD RELATES TO GEMINI ✦

The Lovers, who think and speak as one, are assigned to Gemini, the sign of thought and communication. The Lovers themselves are twin souls, with their arms and hearts entwined. The sign (Gemini) represents the duality of two separate individuals working in tandem... Both the Gemini Twins and the two Lovers in the Tarot card represent a diversity of thoughts and experiences, and the versatility and expanded point of view that a partnership can bring to any situation.

Corrine Kenner

Geminis are insatiably curious, flirtatious and playful, and the same thing could be said about the essence of the Lovers. Together, the combination of Gemini and the Lovers suggests that two heads are better than one, and that two intersecting points of view can indeed coexist harmoniously.

The Lovers usually represents a choice, and any choice usually presents us with a dilemma or a duality of sorts. Gemini's dualistic nature resonates with the Lovers card, and the decisions that this card implies, are something that the Gemini soul grapples with on an almost constant basis.

The Lovers also signifies a temptation that may be present in our experience, and asks us to choose between things like clinging to our youth or ageing gracefully, taking a bite out of the forbidden apple or being resolutely disciplined, and the pervading allurements of vice or virtue.

Gemini, being the sign of the youthful, charming Twins, will usually choose to remain the Peter Pan by clinging to his innocence and carefree freedom, and will take the fateful bite of the prohibited fruit rather than exercise self-restraint. He is, after all, the cunning trickster of the zodiac and will push his luck, boundaries and limits at every opportunity possible. But Gemini would do well to grasp this card's symbolism, particularly when it relates to the all-important choices we are confronted with on our life's Path at some point or another - for the outcome of these significant decisions will have a profound impact on his future Path and a ripple effect on those around him. Knowing all this, the Lovers represents a person's deep motivations, desires, wishes and ability to select one path - something that doesn't come naturally and is therefore an acquired skill and taste for most Geminis. It may be a bitter pill to swallow when the Twins yearn to be given free rein, but the Lovers tells Gemini that he will be forgiven if that pill is balanced out with a little virtue from time to time. Hard, but certainly not impossible.

Geminis are recommended to carry one of these cards with them to illumine their paths, to magnetise that for which they are asking, and to help claim the magic that is their birth gift, using the symbolism of the Lovers as a guide.

✦ THE CHARIOT ✦

Keywords ✦ Victory, Willpower, Control.

Number ✦ 7

Astrological Signs ✦ Cancer & Sagittarius.

Key Themes ✦ Triumph Over Difficulties, Struggles & Battles, Arrival of Help at the Hour of Need, Positive & Fruitful Efforts, A Journey, Good News, Expansion, Control Regained, Progress, Success, Audacity, Faith, Fighting Spirit, Positive Outcome, Beneficial Change, An Important Achievement, Self Discipline, A Great Leap Forward, Positive Challenges, Willpower, Public Recognition, Perseverance, A Promotion or Award, Travel, Modes of Transportation, Willpower.

✦ HOW THIS CARD RELATES TO CANCER ✦

The Chariot, the protected home on wheels, is assigned to Cancer, the sign of motherhood, home, and family life. Cancer's Crab carries his home on his back.

Corrine Kenner

At first consideration, Cancer doesn't seem to have much in common with the victorious, adventurous, even boisterous, spirit of the Chariot card. If we search a little deeper however, we will find that the charioteer never leaves his family or home for too long, and only for necessary expeditions, that benefit both his domestic life and his community. Additionally, both are unquestionably resourceful, tenacious, intuitive and protective - just as a Cancerian and a seeking traveller in one might be. In any case, charioteers are usually on a quest for the betterment of their business, trade, communities, or family life, concerns they do have in common with Cancer. The Chariot carriage itself also offers a home away from home for the Cancerian chariot-steerer wishing to bring a little piece of home and familiarity along for the ride.

The Chariot ultimately suggests an inner conflict, and the fact that the charioteer is clearly having trouble keeping his horses in control is an indication that his feelings are in opposition; he knows he needs to steer the middle course, but that's no easy task. This may translate into something simple, for instance one part of you wants to remain idle while the other half wants to undertake and complete a task, leading to an internal battle which sometimes has the outcome that neither side achieves a satisfactory result. Cancer lives out every day the internal battle that the Chariot represents.

A great paradox inherent in the Crab's character is that although she is tenacious and persevering, she is also easily defeated and withdrawing if the stakes become too high (or, in a metaphorical sense, if the horses' strength overwhelms her); far from weak, but deeply vulnerable, this is Cancer's troubling conflict - to control the horses using her innate might, or let them win and take her where she doesn't particularly wish to go, because she has surrendered to outside forces. Indeed, the Chariot carries a tough lesson for the Cancerian soul to learn, for she wavers and she flinches at even slight conflicts or obstacles. But the inner war she is fighting needs to be resolved, or the horses will surely and completely throw her off balance. If she fails to restore her sense of control over that or those which seek to steer her, instead of the other way around, she will fall off and has every chance of staying there until she is ready to re-emerge from the safety of her shell - which we all know can sometimes take a very long time.

Overall, the Chariot relates to Cancer in sharing with her the eternal paradox of fragile vulnerability which leads to defeat, versus careful, calculated control which leads to personal triumph. She needs to learn that ultimately, the horses can be aligned and ride harmoniously parallel if she can draw upon her inner discipline and will to steer them in the right direction.

Cancerians are recommended to carry one of these cards with them to illumine their paths, to magnetise that for which they are asking, and to help claim the magic that is their birth gift, using the symbolism of the Chariot as a guide.

✦ STRENGTH ✦

Keywords ✦ Gentle Force, Courage, Power.

Number ✦ 8 (11 in some decks).

Astrological Signs ✦ Leo.

Key Themes ✦ Courage, Fortitude, Moral Fibre, Firmness, Power, Confidence, Great Inner Strength, Forgiveness, Compassion, Patience, Willpower, Courage of Convictions, Belief in Own Strength, Gentle Force, Determination, Domination of Instincts, Tranquil Strength, Dauntlessness, Triumph, Control of a Situation, Victory Achieved Through a Gentle, Measured Approach.

✦ HOW THIS CARD RELATES TO LEO ✦

Strength, the master of gentle force and control, is assigned to Leo, the sign of lionesque courage and heart.

Corrine Kenner

The fact that there is a lion in the Strength card suggests strong links to the sign of Leo, whose symbol is this majestic, mighty beast. 'Gentle force' is a term to describe the essence of this card, and provides another connection with Leo, who himself uses an all-powerful, wilful and confident manner to achieve his desired ends.

Leo, although prone to being overbearing, pompous, boastful and boisterous, also has a subtle streak, a side that he will bring out when the situation or need calls for it. He has the uncanny ability to discern the amount of Strength something requires, and will apply his energy accordingly, wilfully and with a self-assured air of authority.

Somehow, the fearless Lion always seems to strike just the right balance to obtain his goals. Unyielding, fixed and sturdy, he instinctively knows when to lay down and surrender, and when to stand up and fight - and does both with an unmatched nobility, valour, daring, self-confidence and unflinching determination. The Lion, like the character in the Strength card, rightly deserves his birth-given place on centre stage, to show it all off after he has successfully conquered the beast.

Leos are recommended to carry one of these cards with them to illumine their paths, to magnetise that for which they are asking, and to help claim the magic that is their birth gift, using the symbolism of Strength as a guide.

✦ THE HERMIT ✦

Keywords ✦ Withdrawal, Retreat, Solitude.

Number ✦ 9

Astrological Signs ✦ Virgo.

Key Themes ✦ Introspection, Awareness, Quiet Contemplation, Reflection, Solitude, Withdrawa, Spiritual Learning, Self-discovery, Soul-searching, Good Advice, Wisdom, Embarking on a Spiritual Quest, Re-evaluation of Plans, Slow & Profound Evolution, Search, Discovery, Knowledge, Discernment, Patience.

✦ HOW THIS CARD RELATES TO VIRGO ✦

The Hermit, the quiet leader, is assigned to Virgo, the sign of responsibility and dedicated service to others... At their core, Virgos are somewhat isolated... They are also extremely helpful, (so) once you seek them out, they are more than willing to share the wisdom they have accumulated on their own journeys... The combination of the wise old Hermit and the brash young Magician (Mercury) relates directly to Virgo's desire to teach and help other people.

Corrine Kenner

Virgo and the Hermit have much in common. Both are wise beyond measure, years and even themselves; both need regular time out to replenish their stores; both carry with them an inner wealth of knowledge, sometimes shared, at other times kept to themselves; both are on an eternal quest of self-knowledge and self-improvement; and both are essentially content to keep their own counsel and their own company.

The Hermit possesses a gentle wisdom that lights his pathway, and he uses this lantern of insight to illuminate the road ahead for other travellers of the Path.

Virgo contains the same brand of inner knowing, and ruled by the intellectual planet of Mercury, imparts her sagacity to others through her sound advice, inborn intellect, analytical understandings and sharp perceptions - but only after much contemplative and sometimes confrontative introspection.

Virgoans are recommended to carry one of these cards with them to illumine their paths, to magnetise that for which they are asking, and to help claim the magic that is their birth gift, using the symbolism of the Hermit as a guide.

✦ JUSTICE ✦

Keywords ✦ Fairness, Morality, Balance, Karma.
Number ✦ 11 (8 in some decks).
Astrological Signs ✦ Libra.
Key Themes ✦ Karma, Rational Thought, Impartial Judgement, Fairness, Equilibrium of Mind, Fair & Just Outcomes, Standing up for Beliefs, Doing What is Right, Resisting Injustice, Issuing or Accepting an Apology, Righteousness, Morality, Legal Decision or Intervention, Resolution, Balance.

✦ HOW THIS CARD RELATES TO LIBRA ✦

Justice, the model of fairness and equanimity, is assigned to Libra, the sign of equality and social grace.

Corrine Kenner

Since perception (in Libra) is razor-sharp, this sign of justice will bring equity and balance to all areas of human relationships. And with the harmonious vibrations from Venus, the high ideals of cosmic reciprocity incorporated here will find a perfect channel for expression... As diplomat and arbitrator, it is poised, like the Ape of Thoth, in the centre of the scales. It follows the middle way, holds the balance between all opposites, and upholds the light of spiritual truth and justice.

Patricia Crowther

Libra is the sign of the Scales, an instrument that keeps its harmony and equilibrium only when in balance. The Tarot Justice card depicts the scales of balance, Libra's notable emblem, and its iconographic imagery connects the card to the Libran concepts of equanimity, compromise, order, fairness, honesty, truth, and just rewards and penalties.

The symbol of the Scales further emphasises that the main function of this sign - as is the function of the Tarot's Justice - is to establish equilibrium and to maintain a balance between the conflicting forces of good and evil.

The higher nature of Libra is primarily influenced by the higher powers of the intellect and an objective state of mind, which is impartial and not attached to form or matter, but is solely interested in the flow of ideas and unbiased fairness. Symbolically, Libra's scales - like the lady in the Justice card - are constantly weighing and measuring the quality, impartiality, or justice of his social interactions and all-important relationships. The Libran scales are constantly used to weigh up whether or not a situation or person is being fair, and to decide if justice is being served. If not, Librans see it as their noble duty to rectify any imbalance, and that is why, far from being compliant and indecisive, they can sometimes be outspoken and strident. Determined to put right injustices and restore balance and harmony, Libra and Justice alike, will somehow always make exactly the just and proper decisions for all involved.

Librans are recommended to carry one of these cards with them to illumine their paths, to magnetise that for which they are asking, and to help claim the magic that is their birth gift, using the symbolism of Justice as a guide.

✦ DEATH ✦

Keywords ✦ Change, Renewal, Transformation, Endings, New Beginnings.
Number ✦ 13
Astrological Signs ✦ Scorpio.
Key Themes ✦ Endings, Transitions, New Beginnings, Death of That Which has Outlived its Usefulness, Rebirth & Regeneration, Severance, Change, A New Outlook on Life, Crossroads, Necessary Conclusion, Beneficial Turning Point, Inevitability, Transformation, Completion.

✦ HOW THIS CARD RELATES TO SCORPIO ✦
Death, the ruler of the Underworld, is assigned to Scorpio, the sign of sex, death, (and) transformation.
Corrine Kenner

The essence of Scorpio is self-mastery, which involves the deep understanding of her own transformative powers. This profound perception embraces the idea that without death, there is no life.

Scorpio contains things on a deep level, is psychologically penetrative, and usually awakens to consciousness through endings - essentially, they must go through the 'death' of something to re-emerge transformed. Indeed, the rites of passage of death and rebirth are what bring out Scorpio's best. Scorpio acknowledges this concept on a deep-seated level and indeed at all levels - physically, mentally, emotionally, psychically and spiritually - and as such most true Scorpios experience many deaths in many forms every single day - for this is the zodiac sign that instinctively knows that to die is to be reborn anew, converted into a different state, another life, a higher stage, or an entirely new plane of existence.

Scorpios, more than most, also know that matter and energy is never essentially created or destroyed, but merely transformed. This is the essence of the Death card, and is what links it so strongly with the sign of the Scorpion - as well as to the sign's other potent symbol, the legendary Phoenix, who is born anew, revived, improved and brilliant, from its own ashes.

Scorpios are recommended to carry one of these cards with them to illumine their paths, to magnetise that for which they are asking, and to help claim the magic that is their birth gift, using the symbolism of Death as a guide.

✦ TEMPERANCE ✦

Keywords ✦ Moderation, Balance, Blending, Right Timing.
Number ✦ 14
Astrological Signs ✦ Cancer & Sagittarius.
Key Themes ✦ Moderation, Successful Blend, Balance, Union of Opposites, Successful Partnerships, Blended Ideas, Pleasant Relationships, Cooperation, Revelation, Self-restraint, Waiting for Perfect

Timing, Regeneration, Advantageous Transactions & Negotiations, Mutual Understanding, Opportunities.

✦ HOW THIS CARD RELATES TO SAGITTARIUS ✦

Temperance, who straddles the divide between two worlds, is assigned to Sagittarius, the sign of long-distance travel, philosophy, and higher education. The Sagittarian archer - half horse, half man - also combines two widely different experiences, while his arrow soars across long distances on its way to new horizons.

Corrine Kenner

Although extravagant, anything but subtle, and adventurous rather than moderate, Temperance is linked to the sign of the Archer through its ability to tame the wild beast and rein in the rampant stallion. Indeed, the wayward Sagittarian spirit has much to gain from listening to the counsel of Temperance. His extroverted cheerfulness and attraction to abstract ideas and philosophies are the basis of his strengths and his weaknesses.

At his highest level of self-mastery, the Sagittarian seamlessly walks and talks his truth - confidently, generously, humanely and philosophically - and this level is experienced when the Angel of Temperance has blended her liquids in the proper combinations. Living enthusiastically and loving life tend to bring the Archer success and the fruition of his dreams and ambitions as a natural by-product of this successful blending.

However, the Sagittarius knows too well that that same expansive idealism can lead to an excess of abstraction and carelessness. Wastefulness, over-indulgence, aimlessness, meaningless chatter, wandering attention, and endlessly doing things without apparent direction or purpose, can all result and render his character lazy and recklessly carefree.

Used positively, his agile mind can uplift the entire world - and this is Temperance's loftiest and noblest aim. A wise Archer takes heed, and consequently lives through his true Spirit - with inspiration, leadership, mentorship, self-respect, integrity and courage. As Temperance embodies, successful blending, moderation and lack of excess are key.

The Temperance card also resonates with Sagittarius through its religious connotations and symbolism. On the angel's chest are the

Hebrew letters for Yahweh, the God of Israel, and a triangle, symbolic of the three persons of the Godhead: Father, Son and Spirit.

Overall, the angel exudes a deep spiritual strength and an adherence to a virtuous way of living, and essentially imparts the wisdom to be found in principle of moderation and well-judged restraint.

Sagittarians are recommended to carry one of these cards with them to illumine their paths, to magnetise that for which they are asking, and to help claim the magic that is their birth gift, using the symbolism of Temperance as a guide.

✦ THE DEVIL ✦

Keywords ✦ Temptation, Excesses, Entrapment, Bondage.

Number ✦ 15

Astrological Signs ✦ Capricorn & Cancer.

Key Themes ✦ Temptations, Bondage, Compulsion, False Sense of Entrapment, Dependency, Bad Influence, Overly Focused on Material Things, Negative or Fear-Based Thoughts, Guilt, Refusal to Face the Truth or Take Responsibility For a Situation, Addictions, Off-Balance, Excess, Irrepressible Urges, Instincts, Power Expressed in the Physical & Material World, A Passionate, Creative Person, Either Productive or Destructive, Ready to Use Any Possible Means To Reach Desired Ends, Firm Willpower, Strong Psyche, Financial & Material Aims & Achievements, Selfish Desire.

✦ HOW THIS CARD RELATES TO CAPRICORN ✦

If anyone could beat the Devil at a game of cards, it would be a Capricorn. Both understand all too well the trials and temptations of the material world. He knows that wealth and material success can liberate - or enslave - us... The mountain-climbing goat associated with the sign bears a striking resemblance to some depictions of the Devil himself.

Corrine Kenner

The Devil archetype can be found in such forms as the horned goat (Capricorn's animal) and in most cards he shares many features of a goat. The Devil is linked to the sign of Capricorn through his tendency to be seduced by the temptation of materialism and greed. Of all the signs, with the exception of perhaps Scorpio, Capricorn is the most power-hungry and controlling, and these very traits can lead to her downfall - as they can the Devil's. Indeed, this is the very essence of the Devil card's meaning - one's undoing through an excess, obsession, materialism or addiction, all concepts that this card embodies.

Like the Devil, Capricorn can be ruthless, spiritually oppressive (of the self and of others), cunning and unaffected by others' plight, and will often overlook these in her quest to reach the top or achieve purely self-serving desired ends. The more evolved Capricorn will understand that keeping people as slaves to her needs by symbolically linking them to her by chains to keep them submissive and compliant, under her orders and satisfying her needs, however subtle or secretive her tactics, can only be a lose-lose situation. And she holds the key to set her captives - and certainly herself - free if she chooses to do so, by not succumbing to the avarice, selfishness, manipulation, force and compulsions that the Devil card represents.

Capricorns are recommended to carry one of these cards with them to illumine their paths, to magnetise that for which they are asking, and to help claim the magic that is their birth gift, using the symbolism of the Devil as a guide.

✦ THE STAR ✦

Keywords ✦ Renewed Hope, Inspiration, Dreams, Optimism.

Number ✦ 17

Astrological Signs ✦ Aquarius.

Key Themes ✦ Hope, Inspiration, Creativity, Happiness, Good Luck, Rebirth, Renewal, Light After Darkness, Calm After the Storm, Restored Hope, Faith, Inspiration & Promise, A Bright Future, Imagination, Creation, Idealism, Good Prospects.

✦ HOW THIS CARD RELATES TO AQUARIUS ✦

The Star guides the glistening ecstasy within our shadow into the stardust of our potential.

Paul Hougham

The Star, a glimmering light of hope and inspiration, is assigned to Aquarius, the airy sign of social groups and futuristic thinking.

Corrine Kenner

The Water Bearer pours the aqua nostra or Waters of Life and Renewal, down upon the Earth at the beginning of the new year. In occultism, the twin streams are seen as blood and water and represent the magico-mystical energies - the magnetic fluids of new life.

Patricia Crowther

"We are all in the gutter, but some of us are looking at the stars," quipped fellow Air sign Oscar Wilde. An eternal and idealistic optimist, the Aquarian soul is a most likely star-gazing candidate. For Aquarius doesn't just believe like Pisces does, he knows. He knows that things will always get better, that there are no rainbows without the rain, and that when nothing else is available, there is always hope.

The Star's concepts share many characteristics with the socially conscious, future-oriented Water Bearer. Aquarians are naturally altruistic visionaries, revolutionaries and reformists who dream of - and act on building - a brighter tomorrow.

The lady depicted in the Star card could very well be Nut, the Egyptian goddess of the night sky, her name meaning 'night'. Arching protectively over the Earth, covered in stars, she served as a barrier between chaos and the orderly workings of the cosmos. Each evening she would swallow the Sun so she could give birth to the morning, a myth which has enchanting links with the meaning of the Star card, and the hopeful outlook of its ruler Aquarius.

Aquarians are dedicated and humane champions of their many causes, with strong ideals and convictions, and above all, are forever chasing rainbows, hopes and dreams - which always reside in the future - where the Star firmly dwells and shines at her very brightest, lighting the way for those in the present to see the Path ahead.

Aquarians are recommended to carry one of these cards with them to illumine their paths, to magnetise that for which they are asking, and to help claim the magic that is their birth gift, using the symbolism of the Star as a guide.

✦ THE MOON ✦

Keywords ✦ Hidden Depths, Illusions, Subconscious, Betrayal, Awakenings.

Number ✦ 18

Astrological Signs ✦ Cancer & Pisces.

Key Themes ✦ Dreams, Illusions and Disillusions, Subconscious Mind, Betrayal, Bad Influence of Friends or Family Circle, Private Life and Thoughts, Self-deception, Uncertainty & Confusion, Unforeseen perils, Intuition, Lack of Clarity, Psychic Awakenings, The Primitive Subconscious, Premonitions.

✦ HOW THIS CARD RELATES TO PISCES ✦

The Moon, which rules the night, is assigned to Pisces, the sign of the mystical and the subconscious. The Pisces fish swim in the reflecting pond that's pictured in most versions of the card.

Corrine Kenner

The positive aspect of the Moon card is that we are reminded of the presence of our deep inner selves that Jung labelled the 'shadow'. To be genuinely integrated and in touch with our pure Life Force, we must acknowledge and confront this darker self.

Pisces possesses the most self-deluding and arguably hidden character of all the zodiac. Her penchant for escapism, especially when faced with her own dark emotions, as portrayed by the crayfish emerging from the water in the Moon card, are well-known. If Pisceans are able to summon the courage to face the rampant watery demons of the murky depths that this card represents, she can live a life of greater integrity, truth, enlightenment and strength. But all too often, Pisces plays the victim, buries her feelings in favour of escapist behaviours, self-delusion, denial and addictions, and consequently becomes engulfed by 'woe is me' thought patterns, which only further reinforce the negative and vicious cycles inherent in her oft unexamined and self-deprecating experience.

The Tarot's Moon card conveys its messages to Pisces in a firm voice, and people of her personality type need to be cautious, for if she fails to hear its message or heed its warnings, it will be to her detriment. To address this propensity for denial, Pisces should bring her shadow Self to the water's surface and introduce it to her enlightened Self who sits in the reflection of the Sun, as the Moon does, for both have much to teach each other.

Pisceans are recommended to carry one of these cards with them to illumine their paths, to magnetise that for which they are asking, and to help claim the magic that is their birth gift, using the symbolism of the Moon as a guide.

LUCKY 13 TIPS FOR INCREASED MAGIC, LUCK & MAGNETISM

✦ ARIES ✦

1. Incorporate Arien symbols into your daily life to remind yourself of your soul's mission. Some of your symbols are the planet Mars, sporting competitions, winning, trailblazing, honeysuckle flowers, the colour red, iron, diamonds, the number 9, the head and face, spicy foods, mahogany wood, and the places England, Germany, France, Naples, Florence and Marseilles.

2. Use the precious gem Diamond in any form in your daily life - wear it, meditate with it, hold it and carry it with you everywhere! Diamond is the stone of love and endurance. It also brings fortitude, clarity, enlightenment and spiritual evolution. As a universal symbol of wealth, it might even attract material riches if that is what you are seeking. Above all, it is a solidified tonic which helps to strengthen bonds of all kinds, and attract wonderful things to you.

3. Wear or surround yourself with the colours red, orange and other bright autumnal shades.

4. Learn the way of the Scales, your opposite sign, by learning the arts of balance, moderation, tact, calmness, grace, diplomacy and consideration of others. Libra has much to teach the Aries soul. Come gently into your centre... Learn the ways of elegance and subtlety... Focus on others rather than the self... Feel the joy of give-and-take relationships... Consider all choices before acting... Celebrate your relationships and what you contribute to them... it's all within you!

5. Use your lucky numbers 7 and 9 whenever you are needing an extra stroke of luck.

6 Magnify and celebrate your sense of self, your innate confidence, your ability to inspire and uplift, your childlike sense of wonder and enthusiasm, your inborn joy, your inherent generosity of spirit, and your loyalty to those you love.

7 Remind yourself of your quest constantly, that is by speaking, breathing and truly living your personal dreams and insights - and share them with others who can help make them come true!

8 Focus your energies on developing more balance and self-reflection in your life. Connect with what you can give to relationships rather than simply what you can take. Tap into your ability to share and receive through any means possible - yes, it is in there!

9 Use your innate powers of boldness, courage, boundless energy, awareness, pure belief and eager metaphysical attunement to visualise and draw that which you desire towards you. If you can develop simple faith in the positive outcome of events, you can easily use your inexhaustible enthusiasm to great creative effect.

10 Tap into and utilise your ability to lead, inspire, guide and transform others through sharing your emotions, spirit and soul. But to do that, you'll need to temper your impetuosity and headstrong need to always win. Sometimes coming second or third can be just as glorious. Allow someone else to step up to the podium from time to time.

11 View your vast stores of energy and vitality as strengths and call forth the powers of your robust sense of self. Be who you really are, without reservation or apology, and the rest will fall into place.

12 Become the 'Leading Enlightener' of others - and yourself - that you were born to be! Selfishness has no place in the true race to the top - there's room enough for others up there too!

13 Once you have mastered grace, diplomacy and tact, as well as a greater focus on others, learn to share the resulting abundance, insights and knowledge with other people so they too can walk the Higher Path!

✦ TAURUS ✦

1. Incorporate Taurean symbols into your daily life to remind yourself of your soul's mission. Some of your symbols are the planet Venus, comfort foods, poppy flowers, daisies, gardens, countryside, the throat and thyroid, the number 6, emeralds, rose quartz crystal, the colours pink and green, beauty, massage, art, romance, cows and bulls, copper, sycamore trees, and the places Iran, Ireland, St Louis and Switzerland.

2. Use the crystal Diamond in any form in your daily life - wear it, meditate with it, hold it and carry it with you everywhere! Diamond is the precious stone of Taurus and Venus, and symbolises love and endurance. It also brings fortitude, clarity, enlightenment and spiritual evolution. As a Universal symbol of wealth, it might even attract the material riches that Taureans instinctively desire to manifest. Above all, it is a solidified tonic which helps to strengthen bonds of all kinds, and attract wonderful things to you.

3. Wear or surround yourself with the colours blue, green and rose pink.

4. Learn the way of the Scorpion, by learning greater depth of thought, spirituality, transformation and renewal. Scorpio has much to teach the Taurean spirit. Swim down to the depths of the soul... Experience death and renewal in some form on a daily basis... Delve into what makes others tick... Cultivate more passion and intensity... Be moved... Enjoy the sensual feasts and fruits of your journey with gusto... Plunge into your inner self and feel the wonder of its vastness... it's all within you!

5. Use your lucky numbers 1 and 6, whenever you are needing an extra stroke of luck.

6. Magnify and celebrate your deep sensuality, your giving nature, your riches, your patience, your steadfastness, your dedication, your loyalty and your strong sense of self.

7. Remind yourself of your quest constantly, that is by speaking, breathing and truly living your dreams and goals - give them form, something of which you are very capable!

8. Focus your energies on exploring your inner depths and transforming yourself through your higher spirit. Connect with your deep love of beauty, comfort, art and luxury, and inborn creativity through any means possible.

9   Use your innate powers of aesthetic awareness and visualisation to draw that which you desire towards you. Remember that you don't always need to see something before you can believe it. If you can develop simple faith in the positive outcome of events, you can easily use your largely untapped intuition to great creative effect.

10 Tap into and utilise your ability to provide for others, through sharing your material things, emotions, spirit and soul. But to do that, you'll need to abandon your fears, ease yourself gently off the ground and float into the soft, fluffy atmosphere - a wishing balloon might help! Release your inhibitions and fly.

11 View your practical, down-to-Earth nature as a strength and call forth the powers of your pragmatic, productive and loving self. Be who you really are, without reservation or apology, and the rest will fall into place.

12 Become the 'Dependable Provider' for others - and yourself - that you were born to be!

13 Once you have mastered a greater spiritual focus and have dived a little deeper than you may feel comfortable with, learn to share the resulting abundance, insights and knowledge with others so they too can walk the Higher Path!

✦ GEMINI ✦

1   Incorporate Geminian symbols into your daily life to remind yourself of your soul's mission. Some of your symbols are the planet Mercury, the colours light blue and yellow, computers, telephones, pairs of anything, books, newspapers, lily-of-the-valley, lavender, the nervous system, hands and arms, the number 5, agate, nuts, butterflies, birds, elder wood, and the places Wales, Belgium, Egypt, London, San Francisco and Melbourne.

2   Use the crystal Agate in any form in your daily life - wear it, meditate with it, hold it and carry it with you everywhere! Agate tunes and strengthens the body and mind and imparts a sense of strength and courage. Its power comes from its ability to promote circulation of energy around the body. Agates come in a vast array of colours and patterns, but all agates are protective and nurture natural talents and relationships, acting as shields to protect you on your spiritual journey. Grounding yet energetic, agate is a powerful healer, encouraging emotions or states of being that assist in attracting wonderful things to you.

3 Wear or surround yourself with the colours yellow, silver and jade green.
4 Learn the way of the Archer by learning to engage in deeper thought, greater spiritual awareness, and broader vision. Sagittarius has much to teach the Geminian soul. Allow your mind to soar to greater heights... Take a course in or read a book on philosophy... Widen your horizons, mentally and physically... Engage in international travel, meet foreign people... Throw an extravagant dinner party and instigate deep and meaningful conversations... Ask everyone you meet what the meaning of life is... Cultivate wisdom... Enrol in higher education - no matter your age!... Attend cultural festivals and events... Study a religious or spiritual way of life... Talk less about people and more about ideas... Gaze at the stars and feel the awe at the unimaginable depth and dimensions of the Universe... it's all within you!
5 Use your lucky numbers 3 and 5, whenever you are needing an extra stroke of luck.
6 Magnify and celebrate your agile mind, your flexibility, your youthful exuberance and your childlike wonder and curiosity.
7 Remind yourself of your mission constantly, that is by speaking, breathing and truly living your dreams and insights - try to see any goals or projects that are important to you through to the end!
8 Focus your energies on expanding your brilliant intellect and transforming yourself through your higher mind - which are strongly accessible to the clever, intelligent and peppy Geminian psyche. Connect with your powerful brainpower and inborn love of gathering information and knowledge through any means possible. Knock yourself out!
9 Use your innate powers of sociability, your gift of the gab and your natural charm to draw that which you desire towards you. If you can develop simple faith in the positive outcome of events, you can easily use your inborn charisma and mind power to great creative effect.
10 Tap into and utilise your ability to connect, link, gather, disseminate and disperse information and transform others through communicating your inspiring and uplifting thoughts and ideas. But to do that, you'll need to concentrate and focus on just one important thing at a time! Even though you are a terrific jack-of-all-trades multi-tasker, directing your energies in one direction at a time will work wonders.

11 View your restless nature as a strength and call forth the powers of your entertaining, fun-loving, humorous, gifted, unique self. Be who you really are, without reservation or apology, and the rest will fall into place.

12 Become the 'Light-hearted Enlightener' of others - and yourself - that you were born to be! The world needs more cheeky, mischievous, audacious elves!

13 Once you have mastered purer focus and direction upon one or two special projects, goals, or dreams, learn to share the resulting abundance, insights and knowledge with others so they too can walk the Higher Path!

✦ CANCER ✦

1 Incorporate all manner of Cancerian symbols into your daily life to remind yourself of your soul's mission. Some of your symbols are the Moon, the ocean, pearls, crabs, turtles, motherhood, pregnancy, the home, milk, antiques, the chest and breasts, family trees, acanthus flowers, birch wood, roses, lilies, the colours silver, cream and pearlescent, the number 2, and the places Scotland, Holland, the USA, North Africa, New York, Tokyo, Stockholm, Milan, Venice and Amsterdam.

2 Use the crystal Moonstone in any form in your daily life - wear it, meditate with it, hold it and carry it with you everywhere! Moonstone has a gentle nature, promotes kindness and peace, and is calming, balancing, soothing, healing, protective and uplifting, particularly to Lunar-inspired Crabs. This crystal opens the mind to hoping and wishing, inspiration and impulse, magic and enchantment, synchronicity and serendipity, and grants intuitive recognition and flashes of insight, allowing one to absorb what is needed from the Universe. It can assist to raise those emotions or states of being that assist in attracting wonderful things to you.

3 Wear or surround yourself with the colours white, silver and pastel shades.

4 Learn the way of the Goat by learning practical application, focus, determination, self-improvement and ambition. Capricorn has much to teach the Cancerian soul. Come gently down to Earth... Climb a little higher than you feel comfortable with... Work harder... Cultivate experience and wisdom... Become better with age... Feel the wonders of the Earth under your feet... Enjoy the sensual feasts and fruits of

your journey... Celebrate your professional achievements... Sit on top of the mountain and look out over the horizon; feel the wonder of the land below's vastness... it's all within you!

5 Use your lucky numbers 2 and 8, whenever you are needing an extra stroke of luck.

6 Magnify and celebrate your compassionate and caring nature, your empathy with others, your amazing home- and family-building skills, your imagination, inherent spirituality and your intuitively in-touch psyche.

7 Remind yourself of your mission constantly, that is by speaking, breathing and truly living your dreams and insights - give them form beyond your often hidden imagination!

8 Focus your energies on exploring your inner depths and transforming yourself through your higher psychic faculties - which are strongly accessible to the acutely feeling, receptive and sensitive Cancerian mind. Connect with your deep yearnings and inborn creativity through any means possible.

9 Use your innate powers of emotional awareness, pure belief and metaphysical attunement to visualise and draw that which you desire towards you. If you can develop simple faith in the positive outcome of events, you can easily use your in-built intuition to great creative effect.

10 Tap into and utilise your ability to guide, heal, empathise with and transform others through sharing your emotions, spirit and soul. But to do that, you'll need to ease yourself gently out of your shell and onto the plane of existence where the rest of us reside! We need you out here with us at least some of the time!

11 View your gentle, sympathetic nature as a strength and call forth the powers of your gifted, unique self. Be who you really are, without reservation or apology, and the rest will fall into place.

12 Become the 'Nourishing Enlightener' of others - and yourself - that you were born to be!

13 Once you have mastered greater self-confidence and allowed your soft inner self to come out and shine, learn to share the resulting abundance, insights and knowledge with others so they too can walk the Higher Path!

✦ LEO ✦

1. Incorporate Leonine symbols into your daily life to remind yourself of your soul's mission. Some of your symbols are the Sun, sunflowers, marigolds, walnuts, gold, rubies, the feline family, performance arts, theatres, costumes, honey, saffron, the heart and spine, palm trees, the colours gold and orange, the number 1, and the places Romania, Italy, the Czech Republic, Iraq, Rome, Los Angeles, Philadelphia, Chicago and Mumbai.

2. Use the crystal Citrine in any form in your daily life - wear it, meditate with it, hold it and carry it with you everywhere! Citrine is known in crystal healing circles as the success, prosperity, abundance and happiness stone. Citrine carries the power of your ruler the Sun, and is associated with good fortune, luck, joy and manifestation. An exceedingly beneficial stone, Citrine increases personal power and energy. A powerful cleanser and regenerator, warming, energising and highly creative, Citrine enhances all states of being and positive emotion that may assist in attracting wonderful things to you.

3. Wear or surround yourself with the colours gold, orange and deep yellows.

4. Learn the way of the Water Bearer by taking a humbler approach, a broader humanitarian application and a more global outlook. Aquarius has much to teach the Leonine soul. Help humankind... Put your hands in the melting pot of humanity and develop solidarity with others... Cultivate humility, modesty and tolerance... Embrace the brotherhood and sisterhood... Join a group... Let the spotlight shine on others... Cooperate... Be part of a collective movement... Make new friends!... Celebrate your own achievements alongside other people... it's all within you!

5. Use your lucky numbers 1 and 5, whenever you are needing an extra stroke of luck.

6. Magnify and celebrate your self-confidence, your ability to inspire and lead others, your generosity, and your enthusiastic zest for life and drama.

7. Remind yourself of your mission constantly, that is by speaking, breathing and truly living your dreams and insights - give them form beyond simply daydreaming about them!

8. Focus your energies on exploring your uncanny flair for theatrics, and transforming yourself on life's stage in order to uplift others and make

them happy. Connect with your gift for bringing out others' talents and tap into your inborn creativity through any means possible.

9. Use your innate powers of leadership, organisation, authority and childlike belief in that which is unseen, to visualise and draw that which you desire towards you. If you can develop simple faith in the positive outcome of events, you can easily use your Kingly intuition to great magnetic effect.

10. Tap into and utilise your ability to make your own and others' dreams come true! But to do that, you will need to abandon your ego and self-serving interests. You may even need to step down from the stage and work behind the scenes as you learn to cultivate a more humble, albeit inherently powerful, approach.

11. View your commanding/demanding nature as a strength and call forth the powers of your highly talented, gifted, unique self. Be who you really are, without reservation or apology, and the rest will fall into place.

12. Become the 'Bright Illuminator' of others - and yourself - that you were born to be!

13. Once you have mastered purer focus on others, a more Universal outlook and a less self-serving approach to life, learn to share the resulting abundance, insights and knowledge with others so they too can walk the Higher Path!

✦ VIRGO ✦

1. Incorporate Virgoan symbols into your daily life to remind yourself of your soul's mission. Some of your symbols are the planet Mercury, the number 5, morning glory flowers, buttercups, forget-me-nots, elder wood, the colour yellow, root vegetables, quicksilver, nickel, sardonyx, sapphires, the digestive and nervous systems, detailed patterns, nutrition, health, and the places Greece, Athens, Brazil, Turkey and Paris.

2. Use the crystal Sapphire in any form in your daily life - wear it, meditate with it, hold it and carry it with you everywhere! Sapphire encourages communication, improves mental focus and clarity, and has a calming and balancing effect on emotions. As it connects mind, body and spirit, it can be used to connect to your spirit guides and teachers, as well as for interdimensional communication. Overall, sapphire encourages you to reach for the stars, speak your truth, stay on your rightful spiritual path, and enhances states of being that will assist in attracting wonderful things to you.

3. Wear or surround yourself with the colours jade green, yellow and brown.
4. Learn the way of the Fish by learning - and practising - the art of daydreaming, spirituality and acceptance. Pisces has much to teach the Virgoan soul. Rise gently above the Earth... Reach for the stars and lose your footing... Abandon Earthly concerns and drift where the wind or tide may take you... Work easier... Develop your spiritual side... Swim with dolphins... Cultivate greater faith in the unseen and intangible... Bathe in the ocean... Dress up as a mermaid and attend a fantasy-dress party... Indulge in daydreams... Sit in a rock pool and blow bubbles... Stop worrying so much, everything is taken care of... it's all within you!
5. Use your lucky numbers 5 and 8, whenever you are needing an extra stroke of luck.
6. Magnify and celebrate your selflessness, diligence, servitude, dignity, humbleness, compassion, inherent sensuality and delightfully practical, helpful nature.
7. Remind yourself of your mission constantly, that is by speaking, breathing and truly living your thoughts, ideas and insights - give them form beyond simply analysing them to death! Put the pieces together to form a whole. See? It wasn't that hard!
8. Focus your energies on exploring your inner depths and transforming yourself through your higher thinking faculties - which are strongly accessible to the acutely intelligent, clever and discerning Virgoan mind. Connect with your deep brainpower and shrewd business sense through any means possible.
9. Use your innate powers of dexterity, discrimination, perceptiveness and pure devotion to a cause, goal, or belief, to attune yourself metaphysically and visualise that which you desire, drawing it towards you. If you can develop simple faith in the positive outcome of events, you can easily use your largely untapped intuition to great creative effect.
10. Tap into and utilise your ability to mentor, advise, heal, empathise with and transform others through sharing your emotions, spirit and soul. But to do that, you'll need to ease yourself gently off the ground and take a leap of faith into the ether! Your talents could be put to great effect in this other realm.
11. View your discriminatory and perfectionist qualities as strengths and call forth the powers of your dedicated, gifted, unique self. Be who you really are, without reservation or apology, and the rest will fall into place.

12 Become the 'Healing Server' of others - and yourself - that you were born to be!

13 Once you have mastered greater spiritual focus and surrendered to the flow of life, learn to share the resulting abundance, insights and knowledge with others so they too can walk the Higher Path!

✦ LIBRA ✦

1 Incorporate Libran symbols into your daily life to remind yourself of your soul's mission. Some of your symbols are the planet Venus, the number 6, the colours pink and blue, jade, sapphires, roses, sycamore wood, copper, scales, relationships, the kidneys, strawberries, apples, pears, and the places Australia, Canada, Japan, Tibet, Argentina, Vienna, Copenhagen and Frankfurt.

2 Use the crystal Opal in any form in your daily life - wear it, meditate with it, hold it and carry it with you everywhere! Opal is said to improve vitality by magnifying energy, enhance one's self-image, improve one's fortune or luck, have protective powers, and stimulate cosmic consciousness. Absorbent and reflective, on a spiritual level it picks up thoughts and feelings, amplifies them, and returns them to source. A protective and karmic stone, it teaches that what you put out comes back. An excellent aid for transformation, opal promotes self-worth and helps you understand your full potential, inducing states of emotion and well-being which can assist in attracting wonderful things to you.

3 Wear or surround yourself with the colours rose pink, light blue and green.

4 Learn the way of the Ram by learning to cultivate greater independence, a heightened self-awareness, decisiveness, and more initiative. Aries has much to teach the Libran soul. Rise to the challenge... Be brave and bold and plunge right in... Focus on building your self-confidence... Care less what others think of you... Get off the fence and make that decision... Fight for what you believe in... Feel the wonders of the flames lapping at your feet - or better still, develop the strength of mind to walk over hot coals... Take a risk... Speak your mind and become more assertive... Be raw, spontaneous and edgy - beauty is deeper than the skin - be courageous enough to go deeper!... Dance as if no one's watching... Jump from the frying pan into the Fire... it's all within you!

5. Use your lucky number 6 whenever you are needing an extra stroke of luck.
6. Magnify and celebrate your relating and affectionate nature, your sense of beauty and balance, your ethereal spirituality, and your dignity, grace and elegance.
7. Remind yourself of your quest constantly, that is by speaking, breathing and truly living your dreams and insights - give them form beyond simply sitting on the fence and daydreaming about them!
8. Focus your energies on exploring your ego-self, and transforming yourself through developing a stronger sense of you, that doesn't rely on others for validation or to get by. Connect with your natural charm and eloquence to get what you want through any means possible.
9. Use your innate powers of balance, justice, fairness and love to attune yourself to the metaphysical realm, and to draw that which you desire towards you. If you can develop simple faith in the positive outcome of events, you can easily use your Airy intuition to great creative effect.
10. Tap into and utilise your ability to relate, understand, empathise with and transform others through sharing your emotions, spirit and soul. But to do that, you'll need to ease yourself gently out of your warm and fuzzy comfort zone and into a clearer reality.
11. View your fair and impartial nature as a strength and call forth the powers of your delightful, gifted, unique self. Be who you really are, without reservation or apology, and the rest will fall into place.
12. Become the 'Gracious Social Equaliser' of others - and yourself - that you were born to be!
13. Once you have mastered purer focus, decisiveness, assertiveness and a stronger sense of your individual self, learn to share the resulting abundance, insights and knowledge with others so they too can walk the Higher Path!

✦ SCORPIO ✦

1. Incorporate Scorpion symbols into your daily life to remind yourself of your soul's mission. Some of your symbols are the planets Pluto and Mars, the number 9, the colours red and burgundy, opals, malachite, chrysanthemums, rhododendrons, geraniums, mahogany wood, iron, scorpions, the reproductive system, phoenixes, eagles, doves, nocturnal creatures, lizards, birth and death as one and the same, espionage, steel, and the places Syria, Morocco, Norway, New Orleans, Washington DC, Valencia and Wellington.

2. Use the crystal Malachite in any form in your daily life - wear it, meditate with it, hold it and carry it with you everywhere! Malachite is a stone of alignment and can be used for self-exploration journeys, its protective properties and its ability to absorb pollutants and negative energies. Working with malachite ultimately helps you confront whatever it is that is blocking your spiritual unfolding and wellbeing. It is regarded as "the mirror of the soul" and so some crystal experts may warn against wearing malachite as it may prove too powerful and confronting for some - but never for Scorpio. Essentially, it is a true power crystal, which helps you reclaim your dynamism and potential, helping those who are brave enough to work with it, to step into their true power. As a stone of transformation and change, it will enhance spiritual rebirth and growth, facilitating deep emotional healing, allowing one's deepest self to shift in a new, positive direction. However you use it, malachite will bring about a shift of energy, enhancing emotions and states of being that will assist in attracting wonderful things to you.

3. Wear or surround yourself with the colours sea green, purple and violet.

4. Learn the way of The Eagle… Fly, soar, surrender yourself to the ether and feel the vastness of all that is below… and within. Also, the Taurean Bull has much to offer you in terms of living life with more sensual awareness, developing more reverence for simplicity and just being. Still your mind, surrender your intensity, let go of your raging passions, learn the gentle arts of forgiveness and acceptance, trust more, come up from the depths for air once in a while, graze in the meadows of life and let down your guard.

5. Use your lucky numbers 5 and 9, whenever you are needing an extra stroke of luck.

6 Magnify and celebrate your emotions, feelings, transformative powers, your inherent spirituality and your intuitively in-touch psyche.

7 Remind yourself of your mission constantly, that is by speaking, breathing and truly living your dreams and insights - give them form beyond simply brooding, tossing and turning, or dreaming about them!

8 Focus your energies on exploring your inner depths and transforming yourself through your higher psychic faculties - which are strongly accessible to the acutely feeling, receptive and sensitive Scorpion mind. Connect with your deep imagination and inborn creativity through any means possible.

9 Use your innate powers of shadow self-awareness, regeneration and renewal, pure belief and metaphysical attunement to visualise and draw that which you desire towards you. If you can develop simple faith in the positive outcome of events, you can easily use your highly refined intuition to great creative effect.

10 Tap into and utilise your ability to connect, heal, empathise with and transform others through sharing your emotions, spirit and soul. But to do that, you'll need to soften your daunting demeanour and trust others enough to let them in! You have too much to give to keep it all to yourself.

11 View your charismatic and magnetic qualities as strengths by which you can call forth the powers of your multi-faceted, gifted, unique self. Be who you really are, without reservation or apology, and the rest will fall into place.

12 Become the 'Powerful Illuminator' of others - and yourself - that you were born to be! Focus your energies on exploring and transforming yourself so you can help and guide others to do the same.

13 Once you have mastered your true power and self-reliance, and conquered your inner demons and shadow self, learn to share the resulting abundance, insights and knowledge with others so they too can walk the Higher Path!

✦ SAGITTARIUS ✦

1. Incorporate Sagittarian symbols into your daily life to remind yourself of your soul's mission. Some of your symbols are the planet Jupiter, the number 3, the colours royal blue and purple, topaz, turquoise, archery, foreign travel, horizons, universities, philosophy, higher education, horses, deer, centaurs, Chiron, Zeus, cinnamon, carnations, oak trees, narcissus, the hips, thighs and liver, tin, and the places Australia, Spain, South Africa, Toronto, Toledo (Spain) and Avignon.

2. Use the crystal Topaz in any form in your daily life - wear it, meditate with it, hold it and carry it with you everywhere! Topaz it is an excellent stone to use for attraction and manifestation purposes, attracting people to you on friendship, love and business levels, and manifesting your desires as long as they are for the greater good. Topaz has the power to magnetise prosperity, honour, glory and recognition of your worth, and is an empathetic stone that directs energy to where it is needed most. It soothes, heals, recharges, stimulates, re-motivates, and aligns the meridians of the body, enhancing emotions and states of being that can assist in attracting wonderful things to you.

3. Wear or surround yourself with the colours purple, royal blue, azure and indigo.

4. Learn the way of the Twins. Gemini has much to teach the Sagittarian soul. Stop trying to break free from the reins and enjoy the moment... Learn simpler applications... Roam the lower planes... Gather facts and trivia for the mere enjoyment of it... Think purity and perfection... Get back in touch with your inner child... Stop trying to save the world and save yourself instead... Celebrate and appreciate the little details of life... Enjoy a fearless love affair for the fun of it... Learn some silly pieces of pointless information to share with others... Go to a party and make small talk; not everything has to be discussed in depth - the weather is a great place to start... Throw a fancy dress party and make it a children's theme... it's all within you!

5. Use your lucky numbers 3 and 9 whenever you are needing an extra stroke of luck.

6. Magnify and celebrate your independence, freedom of spirit, powerful intellect, philosophical views and idealism. You can use them to great benefit as you quest towards the ever-present but never-quite-reachable horizon!

7. Remind yourself of your mission constantly, that is by speaking, breathing and truly living your dreams and insights - give them form beyond simply idealising or philosophising about them!

8. Focus your energies on exploring your higher mind, spiritual evolution and beliefs, and transforming yourself through your intellectual faculties - which are strongly accessible to the acutely seeking, receptive, expansive and ever-evolving Sagittarian mind. Connect with your deep wisdom and inborn creative spark through any means possible.

9. Use your innate powers of global awareness, pure faith and belief in the unseen, and metaphysical attunement to visualise and draw that which you desire towards you. If you can develop simple faith in the positive outcome of events, you can easily use your keen intuition to great creative effect.

10. Tap into and utilise your ability to guide, teach, share, exchange, give to and transform others through sharing your emotions, spirit and soul. But to do that, you'll need to ease yourself off your cloud and back onto planet Earth where the rest of us reside! We need you here at least some of the time!

11. View your idealistic nature as a strength and call forth the powers of your generous, insightful gifted, unique self. Be who you really are, without reservation or apology, and the rest will fall into place.

12. Become the 'Philosophical Enlightener' of others - and yourself - that you were born to be!

13. Once you have mastered purer focus for your ideals, greater direction, and a supreme aim with your arrow, learn to share the resulting abundance, insights and knowledge with others so they too can walk the Higher Path!

✦ CAPRICORN ✦

1. Incorporate Capricornian symbols into your daily life to remind yourself of your soul's mission. Some of your symbols are the planet Saturn, the number 8, the colours black, navy blue and forest green, garnet, jet, carnation, ebony wood, lead, goats, the skin and bones, knees, teeth, institutions of power and authority, pine and poplar trees, comfreys, clock time, and the places India, Afghanistan, Mexico, Oxford and Delhi.

2. Use the crystal Garnet in any form in your daily life - wear it, meditate with it, hold it and carry it with you everywhere! Garnet is a stone of love and commitment which brings warmth, devotion, constancy, faithfulness, understanding, sincerity, trust and honesty to a relationship. It encourages you to be more creative and stimulates 'lightbulb' flashes of inspiration and thought. An energising and regenerative stone, garnet helps to dissolve unhelpful behavioural patterns and past hurts to allow you to become more self-empowered and move on. Further, if you are feeling impotent or stuck in plans that have not yet manifested, this stone assists in moving out of the stagnancy and into potent action. Garnet is a powerful attractor of abundance, drawing prosperity into your experience, and can activate other crystals, amplifying their effect. For Capricorns, garnet enhances emotions or states of being that can assist in attracting wonderful things to you.

3. Wear or surround yourself with the colours black, brown and forest green.

4. Learn the way of the Crab by learning greater compassion, deeper feelings, the value of domestic bliss, and how to show your care and affection for others more readily. Cancer has much to teach the Capricornian soul. Swim in the ocean with wild abandon... Wear a daisy chain in your hair... Get in touch with your emotions... Explore your deeper feelings, yearnings and motives... Nurture others more... Work less... Spend more time with your family... Enjoy your or others' children... Forget about practical concerns for a time... Use your imagination to climb to higher and higher places... Learn to cook... Get in touch with your maternal side... Enjoy the sensual feasts and fruits of your journey... Sit near a waterfall and feel the wonder of its vastness... it's all within you!

5. Use your lucky numbers 7 and 8 whenever you are needing an extra stroke of luck.

6. Magnify and celebrate your devotion, dedication, persistence, your caring nature, your willpower, your inherent wisdom, and your often untapped but intuitively in-touch psyche.

7. Remind yourself of your mission constantly, that is by speaking, breathing and truly living your dreams and insights - share them with others instead of keeping them to yourself!

8. Focus your energies on exploring your inner depths and transforming yourself through your high-minded ideals - which are strongly accessible to the acutely striving, aspiring and determined Capricornian mind. Connect with your deep imagination and inborn creativity through any means possible.
9. Use your innate powers of steadfastness and financial acumen to visualise and draw that which you desire towards you. If you can develop simple faith in the positive outcome of events, you can easily use your oft-neglected intuition to great creative effect.
10. Tap into and utilise your ability to guide, advise, help and elevate others through sharing your emotions, spirit and soul. But to do that, you'll need to bring your feelings closer to the surface and show a bit of vulnerability.
11. View your pragmatic, solid, structured and highly organised nature as strengths and call forth the powers of your incredibly gifted, unique self. Be who you really are, without reservation or apology, and the rest will fall into place.
12. Become the 'Mountain Path Guide Enlightener' of others - and yourself - that you were born to be!
13. Once you have mastered purer compassion for others, and become more in touch with your deeper, tender self, learn to share the resulting abundance, insights and knowledge with others so they too can walk the Higher Path!

✦ AQUARIUS ✦

1. Incorporate Aquarian symbols into your daily life to remind yourself of your soul's mission. Some of your symbols are the planet Uranus, the number 4, electrical waves, technology, long-distance flying birds, otters, fruit trees, pine trees, aluminium, amethysts, aquamarines, the shins and calves, the circulatory system, orchids, astrology, the colours electric blue and turquoise, and the places Russia, Moscow, Iran, Sweden and New Zealand.
2. Use the crystal Amethyst in any form in your daily life - wear it, meditate with it, hold it and carry it with you everywhere! Amethyst is the stone of the Third Eye, spirituality and psychic awareness. It brings calm, peace, inspiration and balance, all of which are emotions or states of being that assist in attracting wonderful things to you.

3 Wear or surround yourself with the colour electric blue and the stone or the colour turquoise. Turquoise is the stone of friendship, and so aligns with the Eleventh House, which is the astrological house ruled by Aquarius. It also brings hope, discovery, peace and balance, all of which are emotions or states of being that assist in attracting wonderful things to you.

4 Learn the way of the Lion by learning courage, boldness and confidence. Leo has much to teach the Aquarian soul. Roar... Wear the crown... Seat yourself at the head of the Table of Life... Feel the wonders of the plains under your feet... Enjoy the feasts and fruits of your journey... Lead the pride... Sit atop the Mighty Throne... it's all within you!

5 Use your lucky numbers 4, 5 and 8, whenever you are needing an extra stroke of luck.

6 Magnify and celebrate your originality, quirks, eccentricities, uniqueness and inventiveness.

7 Remind yourself of your mission constantly, that is by speaking, breathing and truly living your brilliant ideas and insights - bring them out into the sunshine!

8 Focus your energies on exploring your inner genius and transforming yourself through your higher thinking faculties - which are strongly accessible to the acutely intellectually sensitive Aquarian mind.

9 Use your innate power of magnetism and futuristic thinking to visualise and draw that which you desire towards you.

10 Tap into and utilise your ability to guide, heal and transform others through sharing your mind and thoughts. Connect with your brilliant ideas through any means possible. But to do that, you'll need to come down from that lonely mountaintop from time to time. We need you down here!

11 View your eccentric nature as a strength and call forth the powers of your unusual, gifted, unique self. Be who you really are and the rest will fall into place.

12 Become the 'Original Genius Inventor' that you were born to be!

13 Once you have mastered true self-confidence, courage and boldness, learn to share the resulting abundance, insights and knowledge with others so they too can walk the Higher Path!

✦ PISCES ✦

1. Incorporate Piscean symbols into your daily life to remind yourself of your soul's mission. Some of your symbols are the planet Neptune, the number 7, the ocean, poetry, dance, films, make-up, chameleons, fish, water mammals, alcohol, fantasy, fiction, aquamarines, amethysts, moonstones, water lilies, willows, oak trees, the colours sea green and mauve, the feet and the liver, and the places Portugal, Scandinavia, the Mediterranean, Jerusalem, Alexandria and Seville.

2. Use the crystal Amethyst in any form in your daily life - wear it, meditate with it, hold it and carry it with you everywhere! Amethyst is the stone of the Third Eye, spirituality and psychic awareness, and so aligns with the Twelfth House, which is the astrological house ruled by Pisces. It also brings calm, peace, inspiration and balance, all of which are emotions or states of being that assist in attracting wonderful things to you.

3. Wear or surround yourself with the colours sea green, purple and violet.

4. Learn the way of the Virgin by learning practical application, focus, self-improvement, purity and perfection. Virgo has much to teach the Piscean soul. Come gently down to Earth... Put your hands in the soil and sow some seeds... Wear a daisy chain in your hair... Work harder... Discriminate with wisdom... Develop discernment... Feel the wonders of the Earth under your feet... Enjoy the sensual feasts and fruits of your journey... Celebrate your achievements... Sit in the field and feel the wonder of its vastness... it's all within you!

5. Use your lucky numbers 3, 7 and 8, whenever you are needing an extra stroke of luck.

6. Magnify and celebrate your selflessness, your giving nature, your compassion, your inherent spirituality, your intuitively in-touch psyche.

7. Remind yourself of your mission constantly, that is by speaking, breathing and truly living your dreams and insights - give them form beyond simply daydreaming about them!

8. Focus your energies on exploring your inner depths and transforming yourself through your higher psychic faculties - which are strongly accessible to the acutely feeling, receptive and sensitive Piscean mind. Connect with your deep imagination and inborn creativity through any means possible.

9 Use your innate powers of other-worldly awareness, pure belief and metaphysical attunement to visualise and draw that which you desire towards you. If you can develop simple faith in the positive outcome of events, you can easily use your mystical intuition to great creative effect.

10 Tap into and utilise your ability to guide, heal, empathise with and transform others through sharing your emotions, spirit and soul. But to do that, you'll need to ease yourself gently onto planet Earth where the rest of us reside! We need you here at least some of the time!

11 View your dreamy nature as a strength and call forth the powers of your unusual, gifted, unique self. Be who you really are, without reservation or apology, and the rest will fall into place.

12 Become the 'Spiritual Enlightener' of others - and yourself - that you were born to be!

13 Once you have mastered purer focus, decisiveness and direction, learn to share the resulting abundance, insights and knowledge with others so they too can walk the Higher Path!

HAVE YOU PACKED YOUR MAGICAL BAG FOR THE JOURNEY?

If you wish to increase and draw more luck, love and abundance into your life, a power pack is essential. For each zodiac sign, it is recommended that they carry or wear the following items on their travels. Then just sit back and watch as magic pours into your experiences and realities, both inner and outer!

✦ ARIES ✦

- One of each of the following gemstones: Bloodstone, Diamond, Aquamarine, Ruby.
- Tarot cards the Emperor and The Tower (and Judgement too if you wish).
- A hawk in any form (use your imagination!).
- Something made of iron, or that symbolises it.
- A symbol of Archangel Michael, for when you are needing a bit of extra guidance or assistance from the ethereal realm.

- ✦ An axe symbol in any form.
- ✦ A postcard or image from a hot, dry place (representing your Choleric disposition). Bon Voyage!

✦ TAURUS ✦

- ✦ One of each of the following gemstones: Diamond, Emerald, Sapphire, Jade, Rose Quartz.
- ✦ Tarot cards the Hierophant & The Empress (and The World/Universe card too if you wish).
- ✦ A beaver in any form.
- ✦ Something made of silver, or that symbolises it.
- ✦ A symbol of Archangel Uriel, for when you are needing a bit of extra guidance or assistance from the ethereal realm.
- ✦ An owl symbol in any form.
- ✦ A postcard or image from a cool, dry place (representing your Melancholic disposition). Bon Voyage!

✦ GEMINI ✦

- ✦ One of each of the following gemstones: Alexandrite, Agate, Citrine, Emerald.
- ✦ Tarot Cards the Lovers and The Magician (and the Fool card too if you wish).
- ✦ A deer in any form (use your imagination!).
- ✦ Something made of silver, or that symbolises it.
- ✦ A symbol of Archangel Raphael, for when you are needing a bit of extra guidance or assistance from the ethereal realm.
- ✦ A caduceus symbol in any form.
- ✦ A postcard or image from a tropical place (representing your Sanguine disposition). Bon Voyage!

✦ CANCER ✦

- One of each of the following gemstones: Pearl, Moonstone, Ruby, Emerald.
- Tarot cards the Chariot and The High Priestess.
- A woodpecker in any form (use your imagination!).
- Something made of silver, or that symbolises it.
- A symbol of Archangel Gabriel, for when you are needing a bit of extra guidance or assistance from the ethereal realm.
- An anchor symbol in any form.
- A postcard or image from a watery, cool, rainy, or oceanic place (representing your Phlegmatic disposition). Bon Voyage!

✦ LEO ✦

- One of each of the following gemstones: Citrine, Ruby, Peridot, Turquoise, Sardonyx.
- Tarot Cards Strength and The Sun (and the Judgement card too if you wish).
- A salmon in any form (use your imagination!).
- Something made of gold, or that symbolises it.
- A symbol of Archangel Michael, for when you are needing a bit of extra guidance or assistance from the ethereal realm.
- A heart symbol in any form.
- A postcard or image from a hot, dry place (representing your Choleric disposition). Bon Voyage!

✦ VIRGO ✦

- One of each of the following gemstones: Sapphire, Carnelian, Peridot, Sardonyx, Emerald.
- Tarot cards the Hermit and The Magician (and the World/Universe card too if you wish).
- A bear in any form (use your imagination!).
- Something made of silver, or that symbolises it.
- A symbol of Archangel Uriel, for when you are needing a bit of extra guidance or assistance from the ethereal realm.

- ✦ A spider symbol in any form.
- ✦ A postcard or image from a cool, dry place (representing your Melancholic disposition). Bon Voyage!

✦ LIBRA ✦

- ✦ One of each of the following gemstones: Opal, Tourmaline, Sapphire, Jade, Rose Quartz, Diamond.
- ✦ Tarot cards Justice and The Empress (and the Fool card too if you wish).
- ✦ A raven in any form (use your imagination!).
- ✦ Something made of copper, or that symbolises it.
- ✦ A symbol of Archangel Raphael, for when you are needing a bit of extra guidance or assistance from the ethereal realm.
- ✦ A scales symbol in any form.
- ✦ A postcard or image from a tropical place (representing your Sanguine disposition). Bon Voyage!

✦ SCORPIO ✦

- ✦ One of each of the following gemstones: Topaz, Malachite, Peridot, Red Coral.
- ✦ Tarot cards Death and Judgement (and The Tower and the High Priestess cards too if you wish).
- ✦ A snake in any form (use your imagination!).
- ✦ Something made of iron, or that symbolises it.
- ✦ A symbol of Archangel Gabriel, for when you are needing a bit of extra guidance or assistance from the ethereal realm.
- ✦ A Tau symbol in any form.
- ✦ A postcard or image from a watery, cool, rainy, or oceanic place (representing your Phlegmatic disposition). Bon Voyage!

✦ SAGITTARIUS ✦

- ✦ One of each of the following gemstones: Topaz, Turquoise, Zircon, Yellow Sapphire, Amethyst.
- ✦ Tarot cards Temperance and Wheel of Fortune (and the Judgement card too if you wish).
- ✦ An elk in any form (use your imagination!).
- ✦ Something made of tin, or that symbolises it.
- ✦ A symbol of Archangel Michael, for when you are needing a bit of extra guidance or assistance from the ethereal realm.
- ✦ An arrowhead symbol in any form.
- ✦ A postcard or image from a hot, dry place (representing your Choleric disposition). Bon Voyage!

✦ CAPRICORN ✦

- ✦ One of each of the following gemstones: Garnet, Turquoise, Smoky Quartz, Jet, Blue Sapphire.
- ✦ Tarot cards the Devil and The World.
- ✦ A goose in any form (use your imagination!).
- ✦ Something made of lead, or that symbolises it.
- ✦ A symbol of Archangel Uriel, for when you are needing a bit of extra guidance or assistance from the ethereal realm.
- ✦ A cat symbol in any form.
- ✦ A postcard or image from a cool, dry place (representing your Melancholic disposition). Bon Voyage!

✦ AQUARIUS ✦

- ✦ One of each of the following gemstones: Turquoise, Garnet, Aquamarine, Amethyst, Zircon.
- ✦ Tarot cards the Star and the Fool (and The World/Universe card too if you wish).
- ✦ An otter in any form (use your imagination!).
- ✦ Something made of lead, or that symbolises it.

- ✦ A symbol of Archangel Raphael, for when you are needing a bit of extra guidance or assistance from the ethereal realm.
- ✦ A key symbol in any form.
- ✦ A postcard or image from a tropical place (representing your Sanguine disposition). Bon Voyage!
- ✦ A postcard from the future to yourself, proclaiming, 'Wish You Were Here!'.

✦ PISCES ✦

- ✦ One of each of the following gemstones: Turquoise, Bloodstone, Aquamarine, Amethyst.
- ✦ Tarot cards the Moon and The Hanged Man (and Wheel of Fortune and The High Priestess too if you wish).
- ✦ A wolf in any form (use your imagination!).
- ✦ Something made of tin, or that symbolises it.
- ✦ A symbol of Archangel Gabriel, for when you are needing a bit of extra guidance or assistance from the ethereal realm.
- ✦ A fish symbol in any form.
- ✦ A postcard or image from a watery, cool, rainy, or oceanic place (representing your Phlegmatic disposition). Bon Voyage!

FINAL WORDS ✦ TAPPING INTO THE MAGIC

✦ ARIES ✦

There is something inherently outstanding about Aries, the hot-headed Ram. Nothing is tentative about you. The cosmos has endowed you with the precious and important gifts of decisiveness, strength of conviction, bravery, heroism, passion and a complete lack of pretension.

Blessed with an inexhaustible storehouse of optimism, get-up, hope and wonder, you truly are the uplifting star of the zodiac, affecting everyone around you with your powerful and infectious cheerfulness. Never malicious but ever self-serving and confident, the Arien soul yearns to connect with life's fun, fiery and feisty side.

To really tap into your true magic, this connection with fun is imperative to your life's spring of wellbeing. Inside anyone who has a strong Aries influence in their natal chart, is a person who appears to think that he is more interesting and important than others and better than those with whom they are in competition, but deep down the Aries seeks approval and belonging. This manifests as an almost single-minded aim to win at all costs, but even having won, the inner Aries still fears they will not be liked or valued. Most Ariens are not as confident as they appear; fears can sometimes overcome them but these will never reach the surface, for they are fiercely protective of their robust egos, and their inner warrior will always ultimately triumph over any fears or insecurities.

Whether you are fully cognisant of it or not, an exquisite, ever-flowing reservoir of energy is available to you to tap into whenever it is needed. So, to attune yourself to luck, harmony and success, Ariens should wear, eat, inhale, meditate upon, create, design and dance with any or all of the suggested luck-enhancers for your Sun sign to receive the most beneficial astral vibrations these 'boosters' can offer you. Wearing, decorating and working with the amazing powers of all your lucky guides, animals, crystals, colours, woods, cards, herbs, foods, places, talismans, planetary influences, charms, numbers and other magical tips contained within the words of these very pages, will bring you greater abundance, love, magic, energy, happiness and personal power, and attract all manner of things to you like bees to sweet flowers. This, my Arien friends, I promise you - and Aquarians never lie.

✦ TAURUS ✦

I come to learn the lessons of Taurus - the lessons of patience and endurance that the Bull displays. The attributes of strength and perseverance must also become part of my character, so that I may evolve and continue in my Quest. I come to learn the true meaning of Love and to grow in Soul until the light of Love shines from within.
Patricia Crowther

There is something inherently exquisite about Taurus, the gentle, steadfast Bull. Nothing is hurried about you. The cosmos has endowed you with the precious and enviable gifts of calmness, comforting strength, consistency, stability, loyalty and unshakable devotion.

Blessed with exquisite tastes and an eye for beauty, indulgence and luxury, you have a soothing, classy, simple air of style about you that others adore, revere and seek to emulate.

Inside anyone who has a strong Taurus influence in their natal chart, is a person who takes the long-term view and proceeds slowly but surely with an indomitable and unwavering inner confidence, because Taurus is only interested in the best of everything, and they always get it - and then possess it with a fierce but modest determination.

Strong-willed and interested in the material realm, Taureans can also be greedy and cranky underneath their warm and sensual façade, and you fear losing control of your emotions, your money or your loved ones more than anything else. If you do lose control, it can be so devastating and disturbing to your deeply placid core, that it may take you a while to regain your composure. But recover you do so well, because you are nothing if not extremely resilient and robust.

Your symbol the Bull typifies the potentially explosive inner nature of your sign - for it is an animal which is strong and mostly tranquil, but can be provoked into intense and powerful rages. Thankfully, your serene nature and charming grace win out over any undesirable states of being, and you are the quintessential tortoise who always wins the race through your moderate, steady determination.

Whether you are fully cognisant of it or not, an exquisite, ever-flowing reservoir of energy is available to you to tap into whenever it is needed. So, to attune yourself to luck, harmony and success, Taureans should wear, eat, inhale, meditate upon, create, design and dance with any or all of the suggested luck-enhancers for your Sun sign to receive the most beneficial astral vibrations these 'boosters' can offer you. Wearing, decorating and working with the amazing powers of all your lucky guides, animals, crystals, colours, woods, cards, herbs, foods, places, talismans, planetary influences, charms, numbers and other magical tips contained within the words of these very pages, will bring you greater abundance, love, magic, energy, happiness and personal power, and attract all manner of things to you like bees to sweet flowers. This, my Taurean friends, I promise you - and Aquarians never lie.

✦ GEMINI ✦

There is something inherently fabulous about Gemini the Twins. Blessed with a wonderful intellect, a vivacious manner, a brilliant mind and a bedazzling wit, you truly are the enlivening social entertainer of the zodiac, affecting everyone around you with your abundance of youthful vitality. Flexible and nimble, you love to roam, wander, hop, jump and skip, leaving a trail of invisible glitter wherever you go! A refreshing breath of fresh Air, you are the Peter Pan of the zodiacal experience, possessing an enviable sense of wonder, adventure and buoyant hope.

Inside anyone who has a strong Gemini influence in their natal chart is a person who longs to find their true soul mate, the mysterious 'other' twin who will make you feel complete.

Communication is a lifeline to you, and few would ever realise that an outwardly confident Gemini is often feeling desperately alone and lost on the inside. There is also a deep sense, albeit subconscious, that the search for the lost 'other' will never come to fruition. In fact, the Gemini soul is a lot more complex than its characteristic surface superficiality suggests. But nothing is dull or forgettable about the sparkling Twins. The cosmos has endowed you with the precious and wondrous gifts of sociability, intelligence, spirit, a good sense of humour, the ability to find and create fun, and of course that unique hallmark twinkle in your eye.

Whether you are fully cognisant of it or not, an exquisite, ever-flowing reservoir of energy is available to you to tap into whenever it is needed. So, to attune yourself to luck, harmony and success, Geminis should wear, eat, inhale, meditate upon, create, design and dance with any or all of the suggested luck-enhancers for your Sun sign to receive the most beneficial astral vibrations these 'boosters' can offer you. Wearing, decorating and working with the amazing powers of all your lucky guides, animals, crystals, colours, woods, cards, herbs, foods, places, talismans, planetary influences, charms, numbers and other magical tips contained within the words of these very pages, will bring you greater abundance, love, magic, energy, happiness and personal power, and attract all manner of things to you like bees to sweet flowers. This, my Geminian friends, I promise you - and Aquarians never lie.

✦ CANCER ✦

There is something inherently amazing about Cancer, the deeply feeling hard-shelled, soft-centred Crab. Blessed with a gentle, feeling, instinctive and changeable nature, you are the caring nurturer of the zodiac. Nothing is harsh about you. The cosmos has endowed you with the precious and important gifts of tenacity, sensitivity, absorption, empathy and a captivating vulnerability. You are highly psychic, emotional and intuitive because you are the Chosen One who is open to the influx of Universal forces that channel themselves into your mind through the filter of the Lunar experience that is so unique to the Cancerian soul.

Whether you are fully cognisant of it or not, an exquisite, ever-flowing reservoir of energy is available to you to tap into whenever it is needed. So, to attune yourself to luck, harmony and success, Cancerians should wear, eat, inhale, meditate upon, create, design and dance with any or all of the suggested luck-enhancers for your Sun sign to receive the most beneficial astral vibrations these 'boosters' can offer you. Wearing, decorating and working with the amazing powers of all your lucky guides, animals, crystals, colours, woods, cards, herbs, foods, places, talismans, planetary influences, charms, numbers and other magical tips contained within the words of these very pages, will bring you greater abundance, love, magic, energy, happiness and personal power, and attract all manner of things to you like bees to sweet flowers. This, my Cancerian friends, I promise you - and Aquarians never lie.

✦ LEO ✦

There is something inherently magnificent about Leo the Lion, the King of the zodiac jungle. Blessed with strength, courage, style, excellent taste, leadership and warmth, nothing is unnoticeable about you. The cosmos has endowed you with the precious gifts of ambition, loyalty, generosity, benevolence, creativity, charm and natural flair for all you put your hand to.

Inside anyone who has a strong Leo influence in their natal chart, is someone who craves to be on top of their game. You adore receiving compliments, but bless you, because you are so vulnerable to flattery that it's endearing. For you are less self-confident than you appear to be and you seek approval, love and admiration from others at any cost. Only when admired and appreciated do you truly shine, and sometimes your arrogance and boastfulness can put others off, but these are just a cover for your deeper insecurities, of which you have more than others realise. Under your courageous façade, you are in reality very sensitive, considerably tender and easily hurt, and have inner doubts about your true worth, leading to undervaluing yourself at times. Your pride and feelings are easily shaken, but you will always lick your wounds in private. But overall, you seek meaningful experiences and although you crave adoration and recognition for yourself, you are continually searching for and bringing out the best in others also. Whether you occupy a metaphorical or literal stage in the play of life, the stage is your natural home, and what better way to explore life than upon this wonderful platform?

Whether you are fully cognisant of it or not, an exquisite, ever-flowing reservoir of energy is available to you to tap into whenever it is needed. So, to attune yourself to luck, harmony and success, Leonines should wear, eat, inhale, meditate upon, create, design and dance with any or all of the suggested luck-enhancers for your Sun sign to receive the most beneficial astral vibrations these 'boosters' can offer you. Wearing, decorating and working with the amazing powers of all your lucky guides, animals, crystals, colours, woods, cards, herbs, foods, places, talismans, planetary influences, charms, numbers and other magical tips contained within the words of these very pages, will bring you greater abundance, love, magic, energy, happiness and personal power, and attract all manner of things to you like bees to sweet flowers. This, my Leonine friends, I promise you - and Aquarians never lie.

✦ VIRGO ✦

There is something inherently impressive about Virgo. Blessed with a humble, calm servitude, a delightful lack of ego, a sharp mind and amazing powers of discernment, you truly are the dutiful helper of the zodiac, affecting everyone around you with your personal integrity and strength of character which is completely devoid of pretension and drama.

Inside anyone who has a strong Virgo influence in their natal chart, is someone who overthinks and worries too much about imperfection. The Virgo is never satisfied with his or her own standards and this incessant unease can manifest as hidden obsessive-compulsive tendencies. Far from being the worst critic of others, Virgo is their own worst critic, and any fault-finding directed at others is simply a projection of your own insecurities and doubts about yourself. You may appear to know it all, have everything under strict control and be the hardest worker in the known Universe, but these behaviours hide the fear that you may never be quite 'good enough' - by your own standards of course! Known for your hypochondriac tendencies, you may do this to elicit attention from others, for sometimes you yourself are in need of that care and nurturing you give so freely to others.

Overall, there is something inherently magical about Virgo, the beautiful Maiden. Nothing is distasteful about you. The cosmos has endowed you with the precious and important gifts of decisiveness, orderliness, an eye for detail, responsibility, devotion, practicality, efficiency, perceptiveness, intelligence, cleverness, an enviable purity, self-discipline and impeccable manners.

Whether you are fully cognisant of it or not, an exquisite, ever-flowing reservoir of energy is available to you to tap into whenever it is needed. So, to attune yourself to luck, harmony and success, Virgoans should wear, eat, inhale, meditate upon, create, design and dance with any or all of the suggested luck-enhancers for your Sun sign to receive the most beneficial astral vibrations these 'boosters' can offer you. Wearing, decorating and working with the amazing powers of all your lucky guides, animals, crystals, colours, woods, cards, herbs, foods, places, talismans, planetary influences, charms, numbers and other magical tips contained within the words of these very pages, will bring you greater abundance, love, magic, energy, happiness and personal power, and attract all manner of things to you like bees to sweet flowers. This, my Virgoan friends, I promise you - and Aquarians never lie.

✦ LIBRA ✦

There is something inherently breathtaking about Libra, the fair, balanced Scales. Nothing is distasteful about you. You are blessed with a courteous, polished, tolerant, generous, sophisticated and thoughtful character, and use it to your advantage through your relationships. Civilised and refined, you seem to have a sixth sense about what is appropriate and not appropriate, and indeed, what is required of you, in social interactions, which adds to your considerable charm. In fact, it was probably a Libran who authored the book on etiquette, social graces and manners. In your search for truth, beauty, justice and harmony, you will keep these in the forefront of your mind when engaging with anyone or embarking upon anything.

The cosmos has endowed Librans with the precious and important gifts of elegance, charm, wit, sociability, and the ability to swim deftly through society because your people skills are so impressive.

Whether you are fully cognisant of it or not, an exquisite, ever-flowing reservoir of energy is available to you to tap into whenever it is needed. So, to attune yourself to luck, harmony and success, Librans should wear, eat, inhale, meditate upon, create, design and dance with any or all of the suggested luck-enhancers for your Sun sign to receive the most beneficial astral vibrations these 'boosters' can offer you. Wearing, decorating and working with the amazing powers of all your lucky guides, animals, crystals, colours, woods, cards, herbs, foods, places, talismans, planetary influences, charms, numbers and other magical tips contained within the words of these very pages, will bring you greater abundance, love, magic, energy, happiness and personal power, and attract all manner of things to you like bees to sweet flowers. This, my Libran friends, I promise you - and Aquarians never lie.

✦ SCORPIO ✦

There is something inherently intriguing about Scorpio, the passionate one. Blessed with an unmatched intensity, strength of will, determination and personal magnetism, you truly are the potential Shamanic healers and transformers of the zodiac, affecting everyone around you with your intuitive sense of what is hidden, mysterious and unknowable to the masses.

Nothing is meek about you. The cosmos has endowed you with the precious and important gifts of allure, concentration of purpose, intrigue, complexity, depth, emotionality, resourcefulness, strong personal integrity, loyalty, penetration into others' minds, resilience and an all-or-nothing approach to everyone and everything.

Whether you are fully cognisant of it or not, an exquisite, ever-flowing reservoir of energy is available to you to tap into whenever it is needed. So, to attune yourself to luck, harmony and success, Scorpions should wear, eat, inhale, meditate upon, create, design and dance with any or all of the suggested luck-enhancers for your Sun sign to receive the most beneficial astral vibrations these 'boosters' can offer you. Wearing, decorating and working with the amazing powers of all your lucky guides, animals, crystals, colours, woods, cards, herbs, foods, places, talismans, planetary influences, charms, numbers and other magical tips contained within the words of these very pages, will bring you greater abundance, love, magic, energy, happiness and personal power, and attract all manner of things to you like bees to sweet flowers. This, my Scorpion friends, I promise you - and Aquarians never lie.

✦ SAGITTARIUS ✦

There is something inherently exceptional about Sagittarius, the enchanting Archer. Blessed with an unrivalled faith in the spiritual forces, a brilliant mind and a dazzling philosophical outlook, you truly are the Magical Adventurer of the zodiac, affecting everyone around you with your free-spirited charm and easy-going wit. Rarely malicious but ever tactless and direct, the Sagittarius seeks to broaden the mind through travel in all its forms: mind, body, soul and spirit. To really tap into your true magic, this connection with your higher purpose is imperative to your life's spring of wellbeing. You also need to honour your personal freedom and never allow yourself to be stifled or held back from your dreams. You are the sign of the idealist. Connect! Exchange! Expand! Embrace! Philosophise! Be free! Teach! Preach! Shine!

Nothing is subtle or pessimistic about you. The cosmos has endowed you with the precious and important gifts of generosity, optimism, curiosity, wanderlust, vision, far-sightedness, enthusiasm, benevolence, and a wholehearted sense of wonder and hope.

Whether you are fully cognisant of it or not, an exquisite, ever-flowing reservoir of energy is available to you to tap into whenever it is needed. So, to attune yourself to luck, harmony and success, Sagittarians should wear, eat, inhale, meditate upon, create, design and dance with any or all of the suggested luck-enhancers for your Sun sign to receive the most beneficial astral vibrations these 'boosters' can offer you. Wearing, decorating and working with the amazing powers of all your lucky guides, animals, crystals, colours, woods, cards, herbs, foods, places, talismans, planetary influences, charms, numbers and other magical tips contained within the words of these very pages, will bring you greater abundance, love, magic, energy, happiness and personal power, and attract all manner of things to you like bees to sweet flowers. This, my Sagittarian friends, I promise you - and Aquarians never lie.

✦ CAPRICORN ✦

There is something inherently monumental about Capricorn, the steady-footed Sea-Goat. Blessed with an unwavering ambition, unrivalled determination and unequalled self-discipline, they truly are the Magical Mountain-Climbers of the zodiac, affecting everyone around them with their power and sense of duty, responsibility, sensuality and calm efficiency.

Nothing is wishy-washy about you. The cosmos has endowed you with the precious gifts of strength, authority, leadership, resilience, resourcefulness, perseverance and an enviable quality of endurance that outlasts all around you. You are the wise old soul of the zodiacal experience, and have much to teach and share with others – that's if you let down your cool façade and let other people in. Accomplished, pragmatic and prudent, you are likely to be successful in any endeavour upon which you set your heart, head, or capable hooves. Overall, you are the stoic tower of strength that others can rely upon at all times and under any circumstances. Your stability and steadiness in times of crisis and calamity are among your finest qualities.

Whether you are fully cognisant of it or not, an exquisite, ever-flowing reservoir of energy is available to you to tap into whenever it is needed. So, to attune yourself to luck, harmony and success, Capricornians should wear, eat, inhale, meditate upon, create, design and dance with any or all of the suggested luck-enhancers for your Sun sign to receive the most beneficial astral vibrations these 'boosters' can offer you. Wearing, decorating and working with the amazing powers of all your lucky guides, animals, crystals, colours, woods, cards, herbs, foods, places, talismans, planetary influences, charms, numbers and other magical tips contained within the words of these very pages, will bring you greater abundance, love, magic, energy, happiness and personal power, and attract all manner of things to you like bees to sweet flowers. This, my Capricornian friends, I promise you - and Aquarians never lie.

✦ AQUARIUS ✦

There is something inherently magical about Aquarius, the Water Bearer. Blessed with a lack of arrogance, a brilliant mind and dazzling foresight, they truly are the Magical Future-Dwellers of the zodiac, affecting everyone around them with their power and sense of the weird and wonderful. Never malicious but ever perversely contradictory and rebellious, the Aquarian soul wants to connect with other like-minded souls. To really tap into your true magic, this mind and soul connection with kindred spirits is imperative to your life's spring of wellbeing. You are the sign of the group leader. Connect! Exchange! Brainstorm! Share! Embrace! Love! Shine!

Inside anyone who has a strong Aquarius influence in their natal chart, is someone who is deeply uncertain of their identity. The typical Aquarian possesses a powerful and magnetic intellect, but your ego is said to be the weakest and most precarious of the zodiac; you are not a proficient self-promoter and generally shy away from attention and focus. Although perversely reluctant to share your sparkling ideas, talent and futuristic prophecies, Aquarius is often under-credited and is actually the most intellectual of the signs; underneath a cool façade, you are pure genius just bursting with mind-blowing ideas that need to be brought out to air! They're no use sitting in the dusty recesses of your mind... or off wildly living it up on some other planet.

Further, like your ruling planet Uranus, you are the Divine Rebel of the zodiac, and although this can pay dividends in the form of societal change, you need to build within yourself a strong centre that you can return to in order to rest and refresh. Aquarius rules the circulatory system, and while this assists in the movement of your thoughts, you also need that strong centre to fall back on; for this, you would do well to take lessons in heart from your opposite sign, Leo, and its rulership over the heart, the life force, the core, the centre. Your mind and nervous system usually rule you, rather than the other way around. In order to master yourself, you need to put yourself in a position to manifest on the Earthly plane that which you visualise by becoming one with the source of your mind. This means you have to find a way to observe your own prodigious thinking processes and not just be your thoughts - by keeping them cooped up and creating nervous system and minor mental health disturbances in the process, which is at the root of most of your suffering.

There is tremendous creative and visionary potential inherent in Aquarius, but you are also fixed and tenacious, meaning that you may have difficulties giving up old opinions, ideas and positions that should've been left behind long ago. While you're busy living in the future, the ideas of your past may be stuck on that stick in the stream. Unpack your baggage from time to time, Aquarius, the journey is a lot lighter without it!

Ultimately, Aquarius is interested in the union of science and magic, being big believers in magic, despite everything the rational world has taught them. Not only can they get completely lost in Wonderland, but they also believe wholeheartedly in the adage, "When in Rome (or Wonderland)..." - they just do it a little differently to the Wonderlandians in order to stand out - and will live by this motto their entire lives. Which isn't a bad thing at all. The world needs more souls of your ilk, who stand apart from the herd. Great things transpire from those who dare to be different and above all, from those who not only dare to dream but act on those whims.

Whether you are fully cognisant of it or not, an exquisite, ever-flowing reservoir of energy is available to you to tap into whenever it is needed. So, to attune yourself to luck, harmony and success, Aquarians should wear, eat, inhale, meditate upon, create, design and dance with any or all of the suggested luck-enhancers for your Sun sign to receive the most beneficial astral vibrations these 'boosters' can offer you. Wearing, decorating and working with the amazing powers of all your lucky guides, animals, crystals, woods, colours, cards, herbs, foods, places, talismans, planetary influences, charms, numbers and other magical tips contained within the words of these very pages, will bring you greater abundance, love, magic, energy, happiness and personal power, and attract all manner of things to you like bees to sweet flowers. This, my fellow Aquarian friends, I promise you - and Aquarians never lie.

✦ PISCES ✦

There is something inherently enchanting about Pisces the Fish. Blessed with a captivatingly insightful and receptive mind, you need only choose to use this power. All too often you lose yourself in the pitfalls of confusion, vagueness and indirection, when you are more powerful than you ever dreamed conceivable.

As a Piscean, you truly are the Magical Water-Nymph of the zodiac, affecting everyone around you with your sense of the weird, fanciful and wonderful. You are the most all-embracing and formless of the zodiac, with a well-deserved reputation for brilliant sensitivity and strong impressions.

Never malicious but ever elusive and evasive, the Piscean soul seeks to connect with other like-minded souls on your own free-spirited terms. To really tap into your true magic, this soul connection is imperative to your life's spring of wellbeing. Indeed, these associations will help you become stronger, for as the saying goes, no man is an island - and no Fish need swim alone or against the current all the time as you are prone to do. The Piscean slipperiness has its advantages, allowing you to take on whatever character or image you like, and to be all things to everyone. This is a potentially tremendous strength, and fine if it makes you happy and shines a light on your path, but be mindful not to over-sacrifice yourself, be taken advantage of, or become weighed down by other people's problems; for floating effortlessly is always better than sinking.

Inside anyone who has a strong Pisces influence in their natal chart, is someone who is deeply emotional but who can, like a chameleon, cover it up with a watery façade and adapt to their surroundings as though nothing is brewing. To acknowledge your feeling and emotional nature is to gain easier access to the power within, for as long as you suppress it, block it, or try to escape from it, cloudiness, characteristic self-sabotage, or destruction may hinder your progress.

The typical Piscean possesses a beautifully packaged and presented persona, but your ego and self-confidence cups are precarious and usually teetering on empty. You are not a proficient self-promoter and generally shy away from attention and focus. Although dreamily reluctant to share your profound feelings, insights, talents and true emotional depths, Pisces is the most compassionate of all the signs; and underneath your Watery veil, you are pure spirit, just bubbling with love, inspiration, hope, belief, imagination, Universality, empathy and unadulterated magic. You are the dissolver of boundaries and embracer of Universal love, the force for the awakening of the collective higher spiritual consciousness.

Whether you are fully cognisant of it or not, an exquisite, ever-flowing reservoir of energy is available to you to tap into whenever it is needed.

So, to attune yourself to luck, harmony and success, Pisceans should wear, eat, inhale, meditate upon, create, design and dance with any or all of the suggested luck-enhancers for your Sun sign to receive the most beneficial astral vibrations these 'boosters' can offer you. Wearing, decorating and working with the amazing powers of all your lucky guides, animals, crystals, colours, woods, cards, herbs, foods, places, talismans, planetary influences, charms, numbers and other magical tips contained within the words of these very pages, will bring you greater abundance, love, magic, energy, happiness and personal power, and attract all manner of things to you like bees to sweet flowers. This, my Piscean friends, I promise you - and Aquarians might exaggerate from time to time, but when it comes to Pisces - and all eleven signs preceding her - no exaggeration is necessary, because she is wholly worthy of every applause, honour and accolade she receives as she makes her way through this wondrous Journey called Life.

◆

All the Signs
have touched my life,
Aries through Pisces,
lovers and friends
And from them I have learned so much...
The learning is not finished
The living is not ended
The loving is not over,
until your life is touched by
All the Signs.

Arlene Robertson

Good luck on the rest of your own unique and amazing life Path, and may luck always smile upon you!

ABOUT THE AUTHOR

Lani is a naturopath and author of 16 books, 12 of them comprising the Lucky Astrology book series. The latter 12 books have been fully updated and revised, and transformed into this special all-in-one compilation Lucky Astrology: The Definitive Volume. An astrologer with over 40 years' experience (having begun studying, stargazing & even practising at the ripening age of 7!), Lani's passions are writing, astrology, exploring nature, casting spells, natural health, and summoning magic, incorporating all manner of esoteric and energy medicines into her therapeutic healing work and practices.

Lani lives with her 12-year-old daughter, four ragdoll cats (and counting), and extensive range of herbs, crystals, books, and other magical wares. She hopes one day very soon, to become a crazy 'young' cat lady with more published books on the shelf, writing, tinkering and pottering on a beautiful sprawling property in Australia's wild far north - indeed, as far northward as she can go.

Books
- Divine Zodiac Messages
- Crystal Alchemy
- The Tarot: An Astrological Journey Through the Major Arcana
- Lucky Astrology: 12 book series
- Lucky Astrology: The Definitive Volume (Harnessing Your Cosmic Power)

www.ingramcontent.com/pod-product-compliance
Lightning Source LLC
Chambersburg PA
CBHW051414290426
44109CB00016B/1297